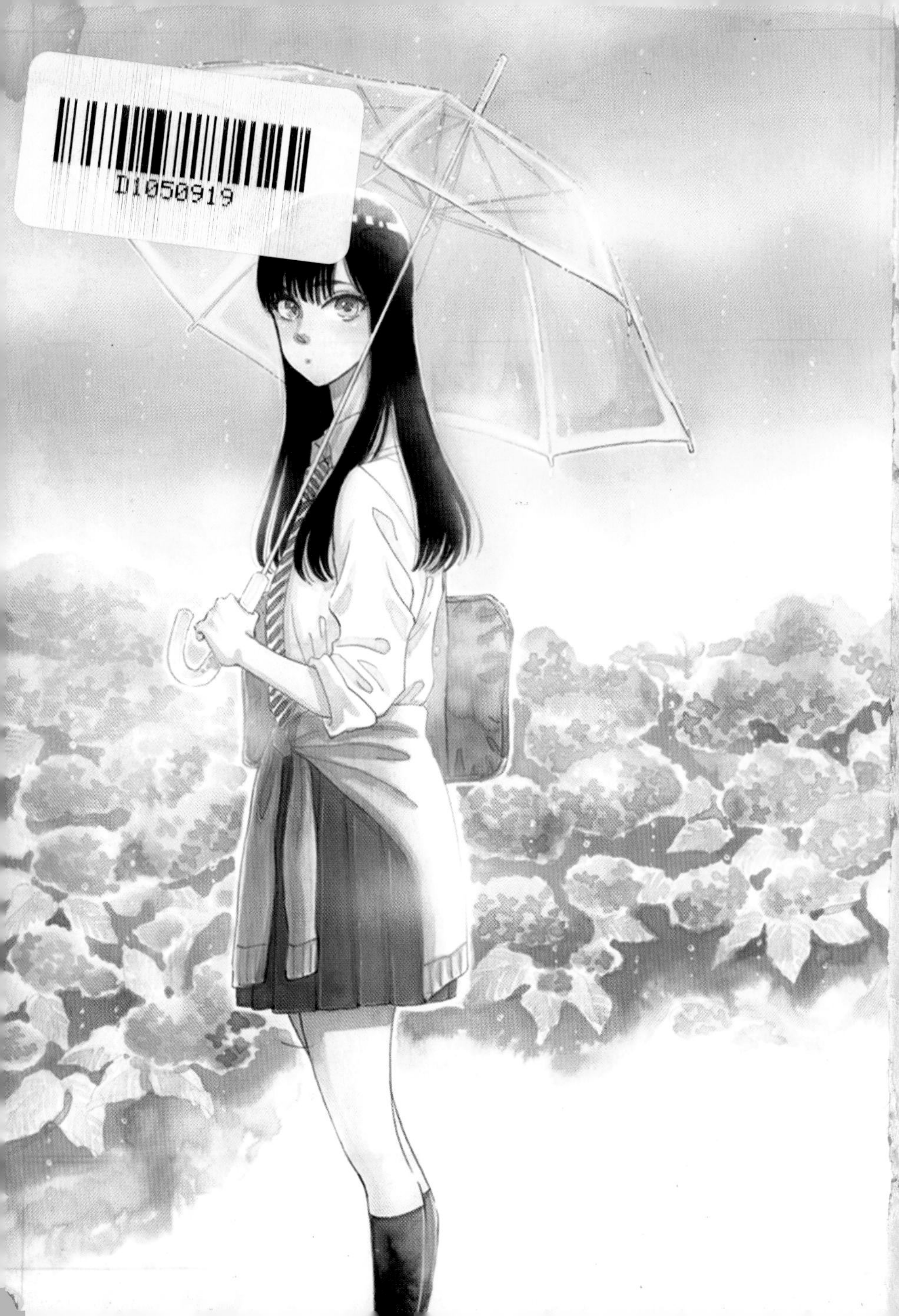

After the Rain

1

Jun Mayuzuki

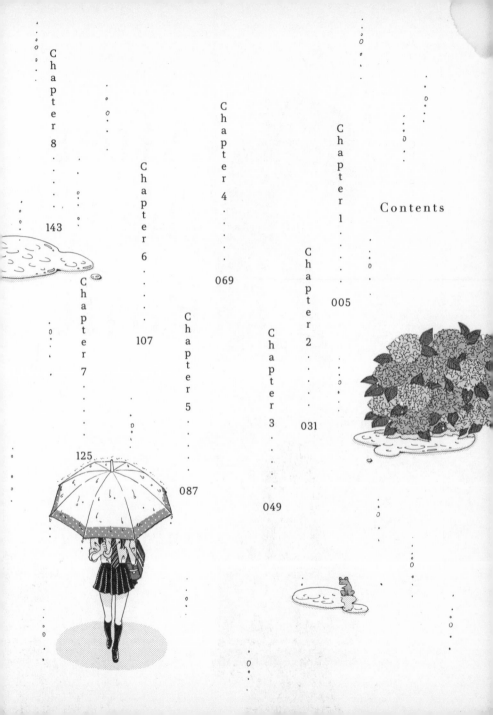

Contents

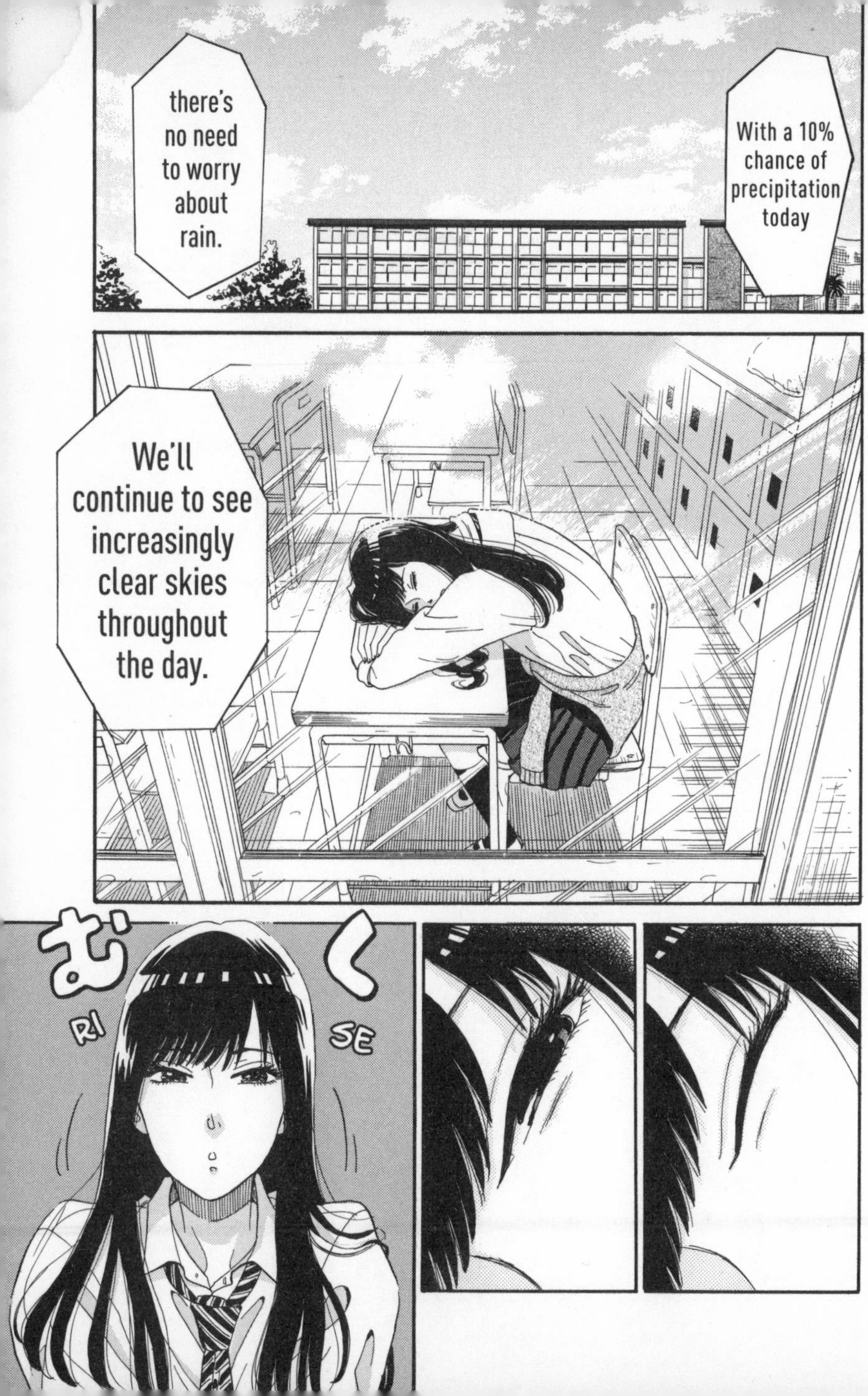
With a 10% chance of precipitation today
there's no need to worry about rain.
We'll continue to see increasingly clear skies throughout the day.
むく
RI SE

...

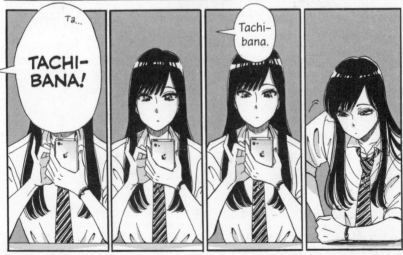

Ta...

TACHI-BANA!

Tachi-bana.

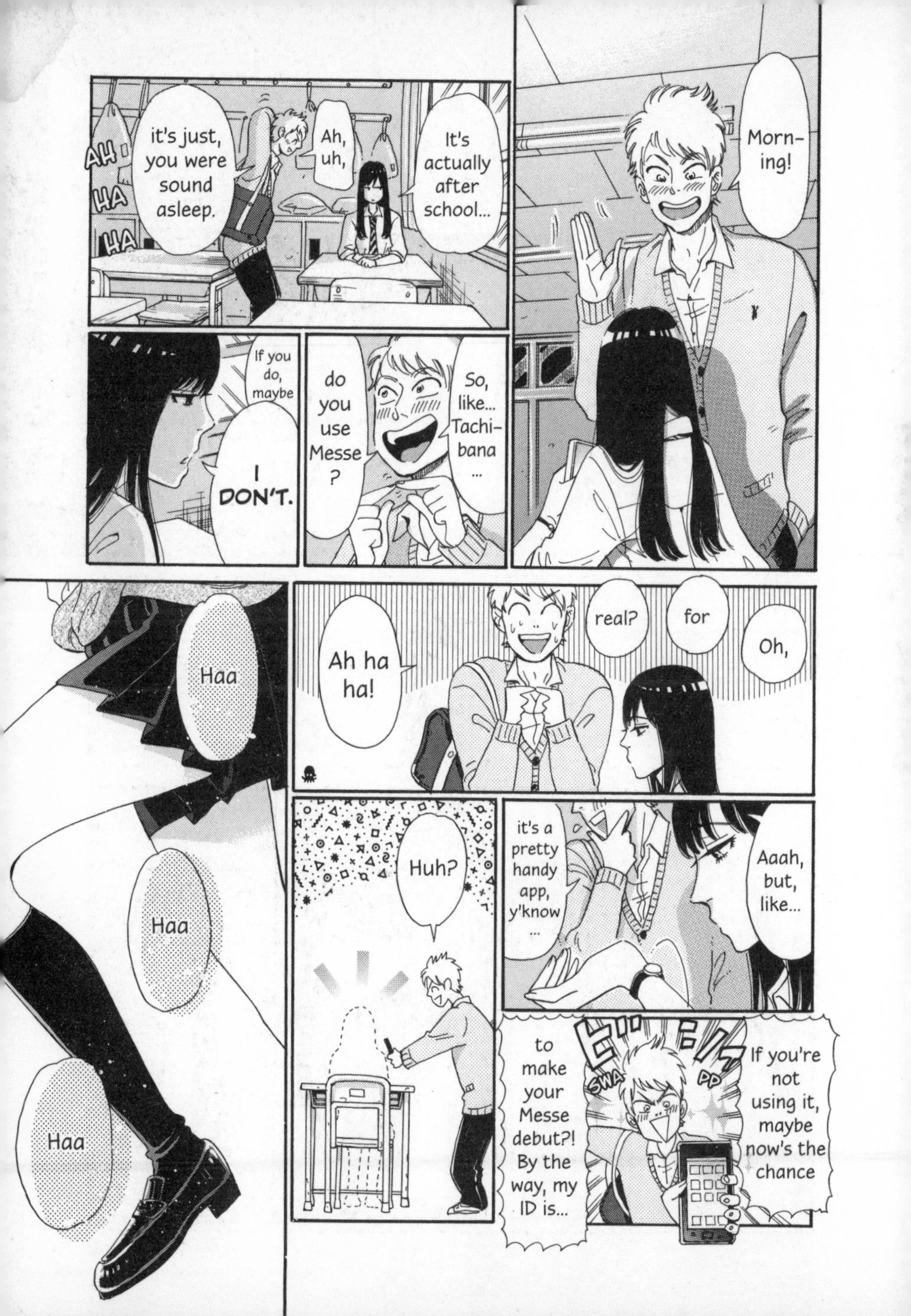
Morn-ing!
It's actually after school...
Ah, uh,
it's just, you were sound asleep.
AH HA HA
So, like... Tachi-bana...
do you use Messe?
If you do, maybe
I DON'T.
Oh,
for
real?
Ah ha ha!
Aaah, but, like...
it's a pretty handy app, y'know...
If you're not using it, maybe now's the chance
to make your Messe debut?! By the way, my ID is...
SWA
PP
Huh?
Haa
Haa
Haa

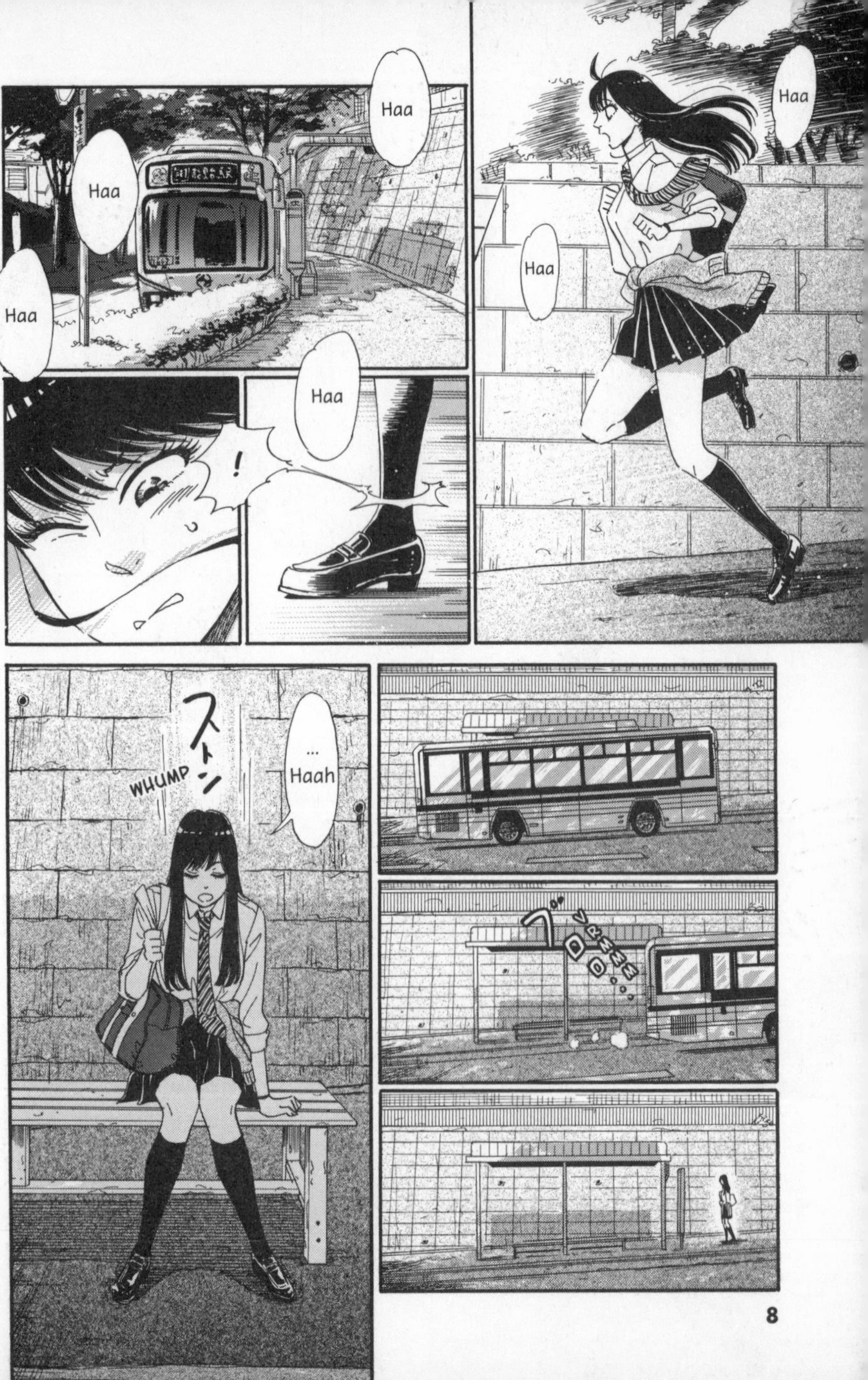
Haa
Haa
Haa
Haa
Haa
Haa
!
VRMMM
ストン
WHUMP
... Haah

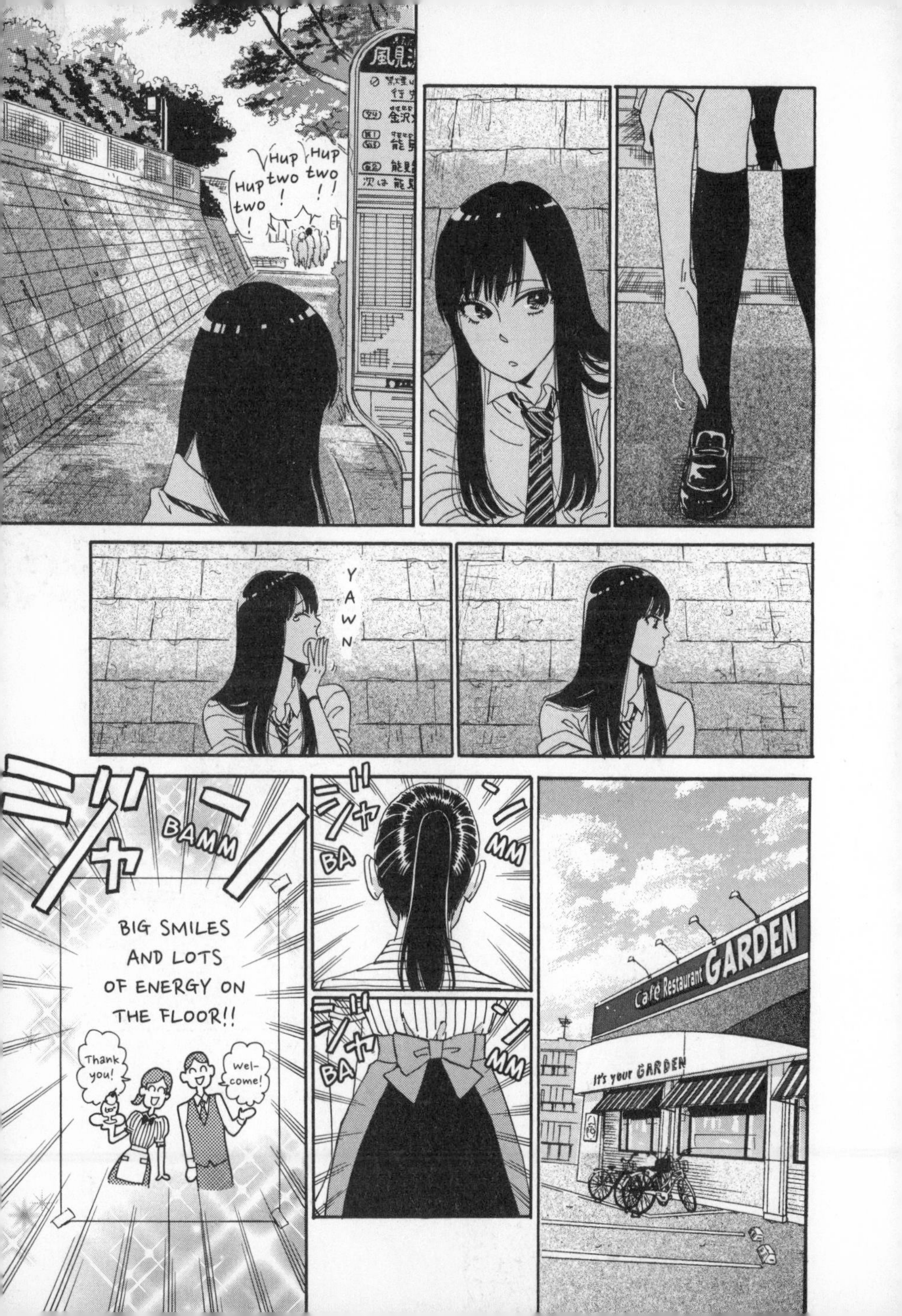
Hup two!!
Hup two!
Hup two!
YAWN
Cafe Restaurant GARDEN
It's your GARDEN
BA
MM
BA
MM
BAMM
BIG SMILES AND LOTS OF ENERGY ON THE FLOOR!!
Wel-come!
Thank you!

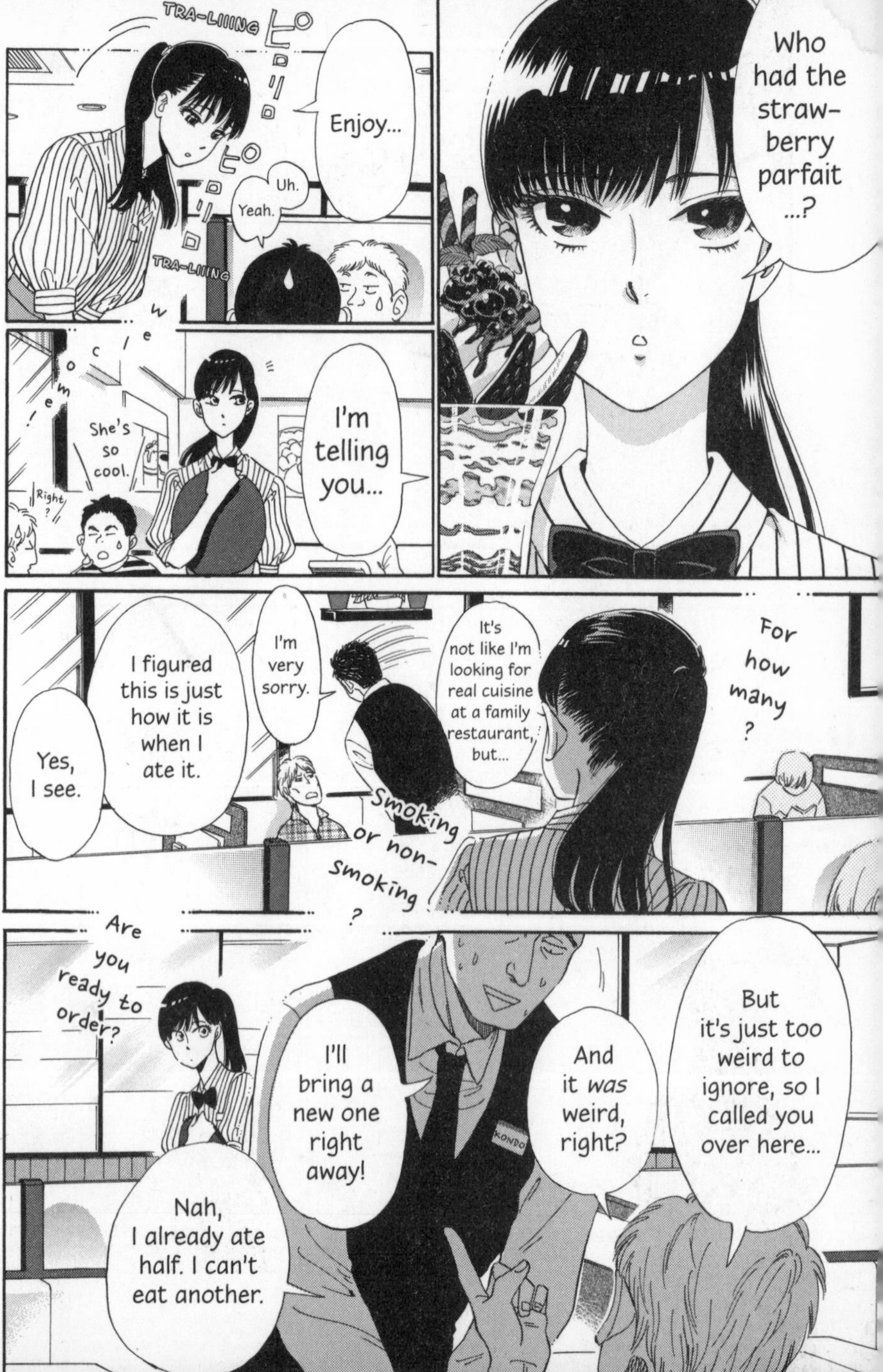
Who had the strawberry parfait ...?
TRA-LIIING
ピロリロ
Enjoy...
Uh. Yeah.
ピロリロ
TRA-LIIING
I'm telling you...
welcome!
She's so cool.
Right?
For how many?
It's not like I'm looking for real cuisine at a family restaurant, but...
Smoking or non-smoking?
I'm very sorry.
I figured this is just how it is when I ate it.
Yes, I see.
But it's just too weird to ignore, so I called you over here...
And it *was* weird, right?
I'll bring a new one right away!
Are you ready to order?
Nah, I already ate half. I can't eat another.

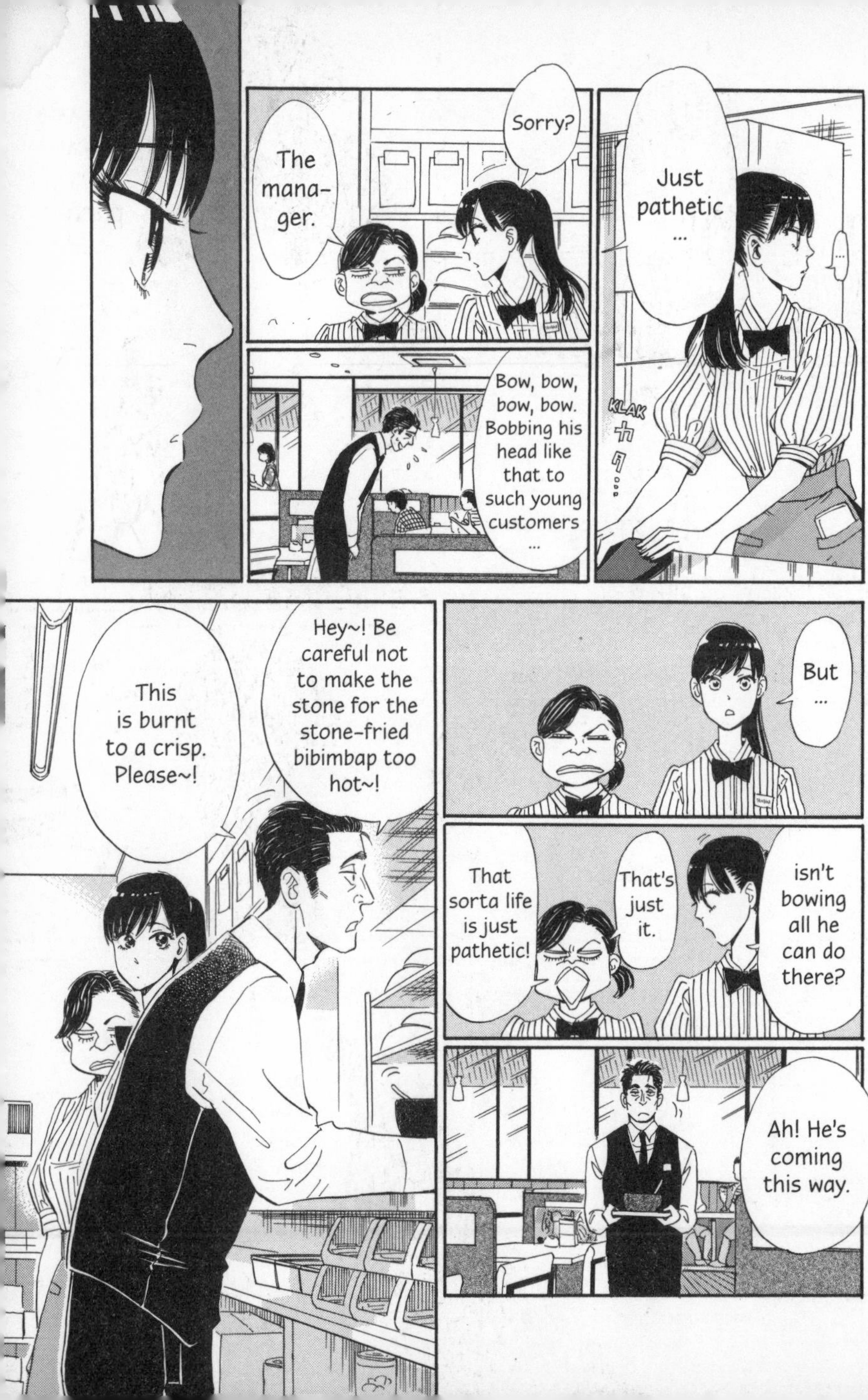
Just pathetic ...
...
KLAK
カタ...
Sorry?
The mana-ger.
Bow, bow, bow, bow. Bobbing his head like that to such young customers ...
But ...
isn't bowing all he can do there?
That's just it.
That sorta life is just pathetic!
Ah! He's coming this way.
Hey~! Be careful not to make the stone for the stone-fried bibimbap too hot~!
This is burnt to a crisp. Please~!

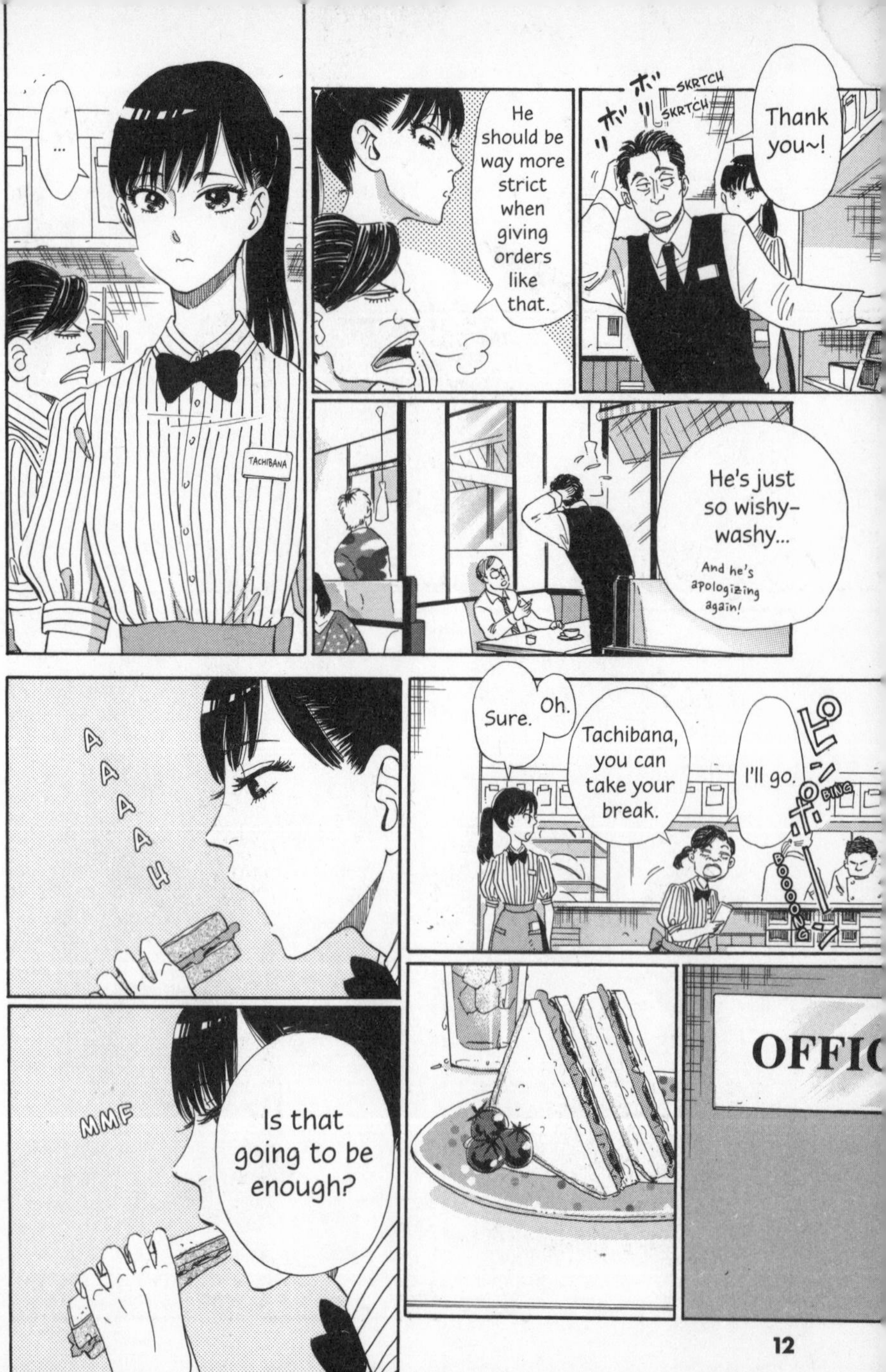
ボリ ボリ
SKRTCH SKRTCH
Thank you~!
He should be way more strict when giving orders like that.
He's just so wishy-washy...
And he's apologizing again!
...
ピンポン
BING
BOOOONG
I'll go.
Tachibana, you can take your break.
Oh.
Sure.
AAAAH
OFFIC
MMF
Is that going to be enough?

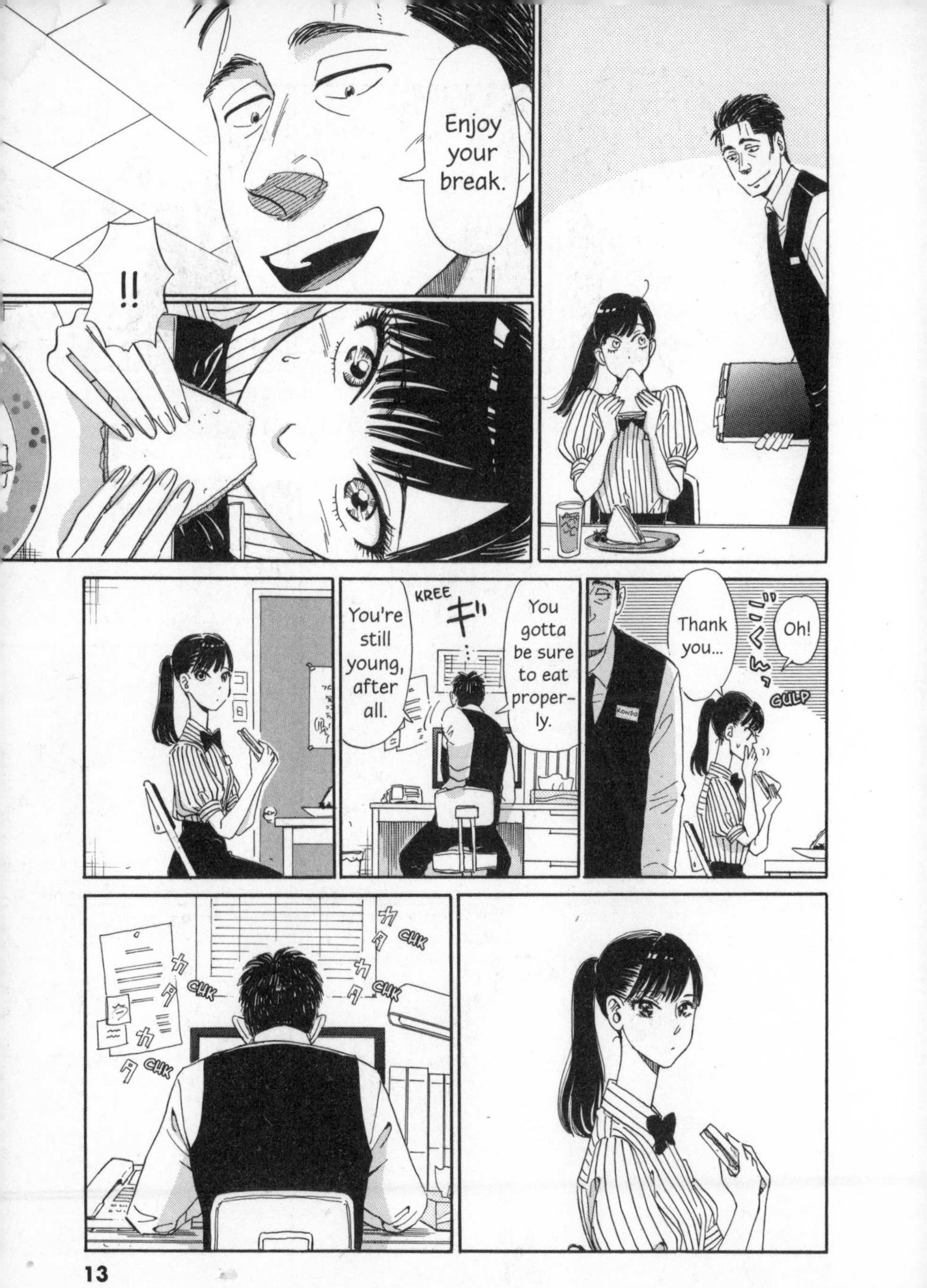
Enjoy your break.
!!
Oh!
GULP
Thank you...
You gotta be sure to eat proper-ly.
KREE
ギ
You're still young, after all.
CHK
CHK
CHK
CHK

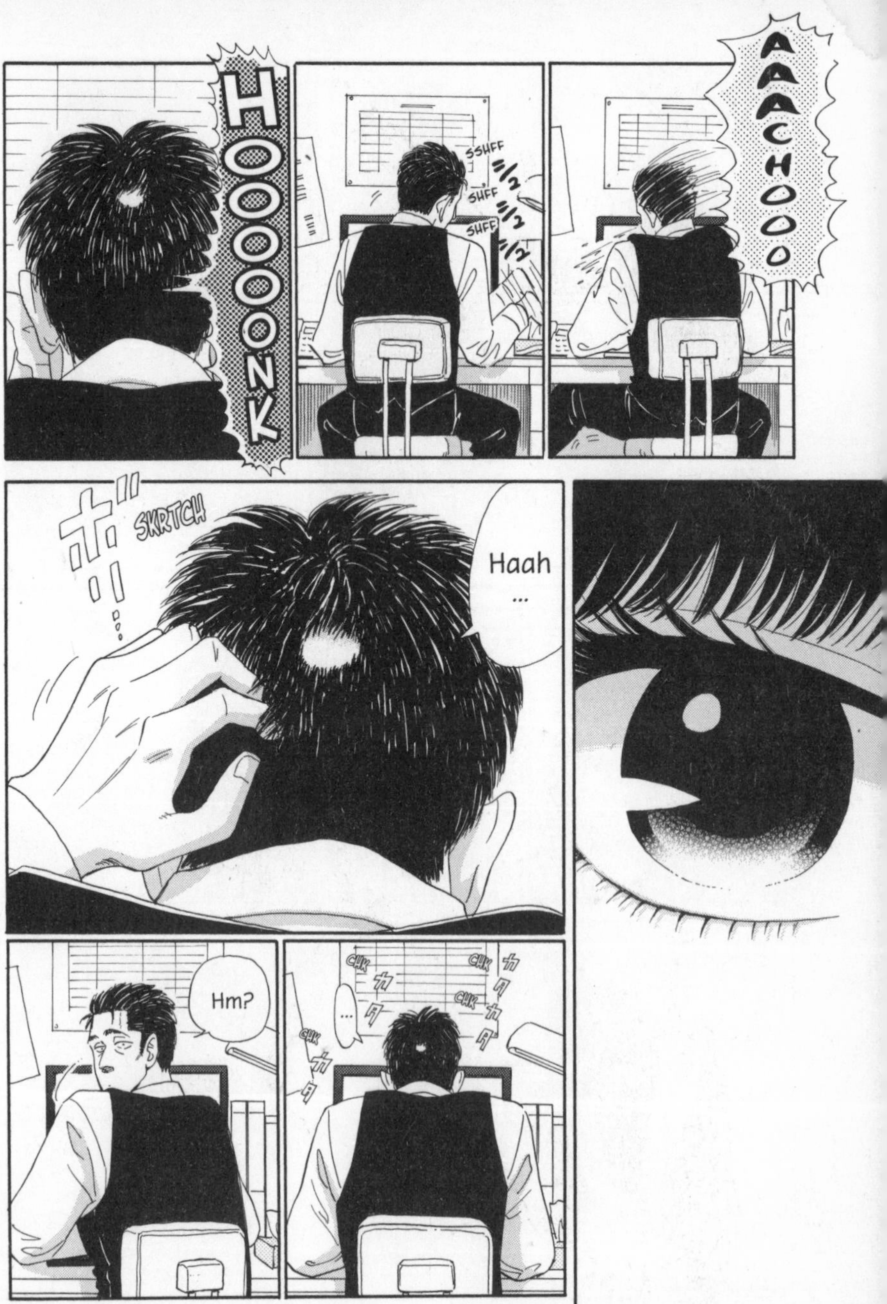
AAACHOOO
SSHFF
SHFF
SHFF
HOOOOONK
Haah ...
SKRTCH
...
CHK
CHK
CHK
CHK
Hm?

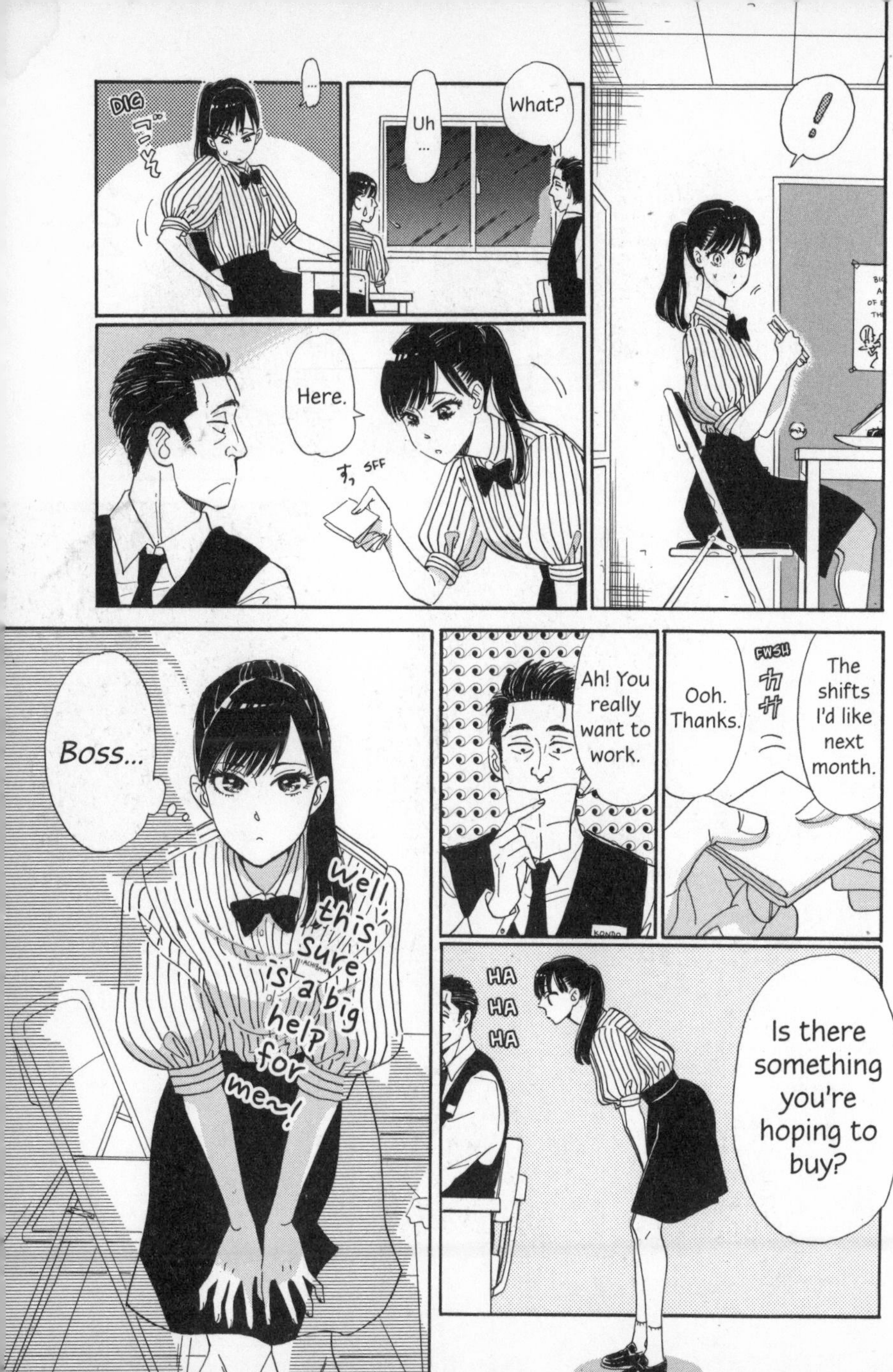
!
What?
Uh ...
...
DIG
ごそ
Here.
すっ SFF
The shifts I'd like next month.
FWSH
カサ
Ooh. Thanks.
Ah! You really want to work.
KONDO
Is there something you're hoping to buy?
HA HA HA
Boss...
Well this sure is a big help for me~!

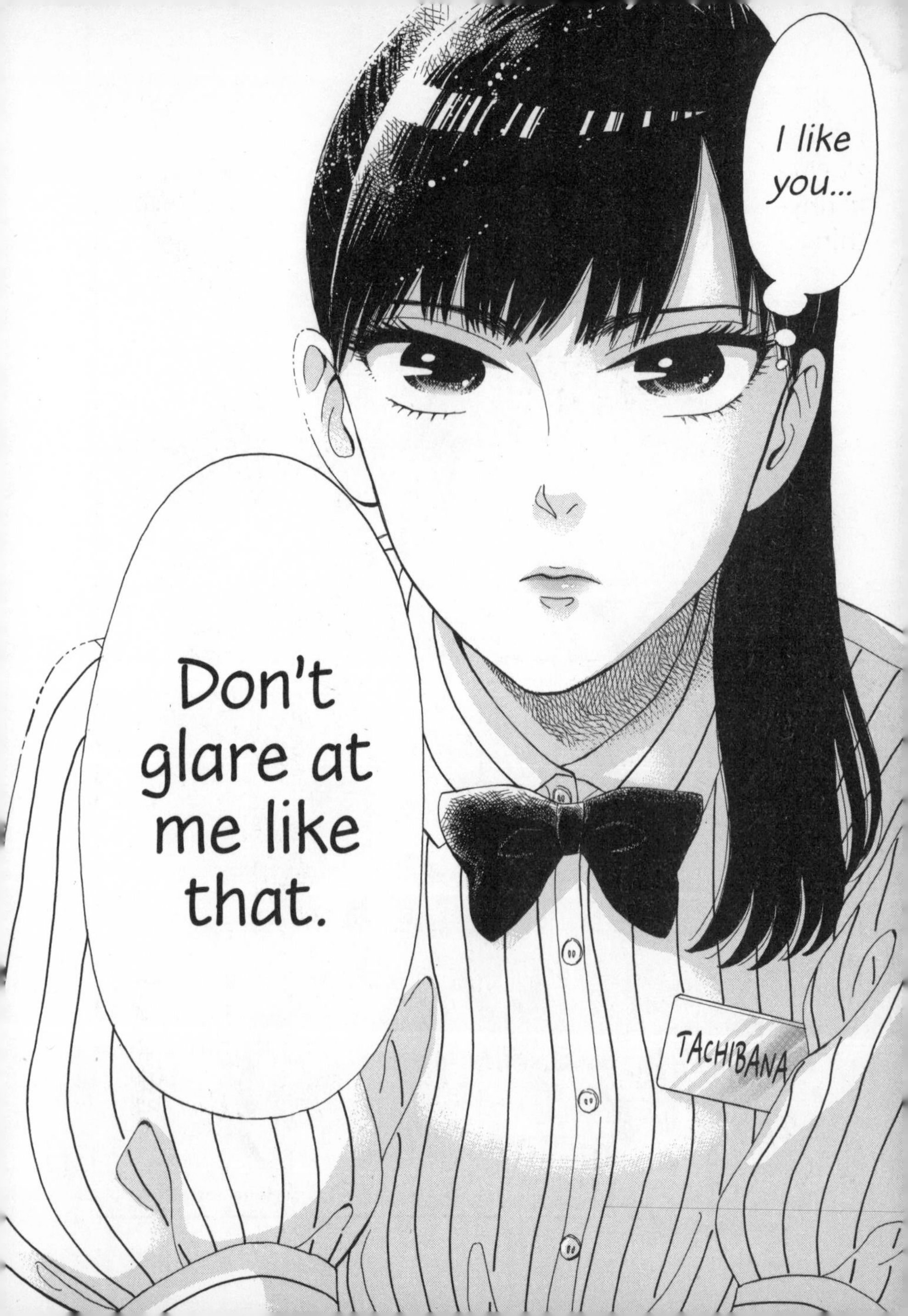
I like you...
Don't glare at me like that.
TACHIBANA

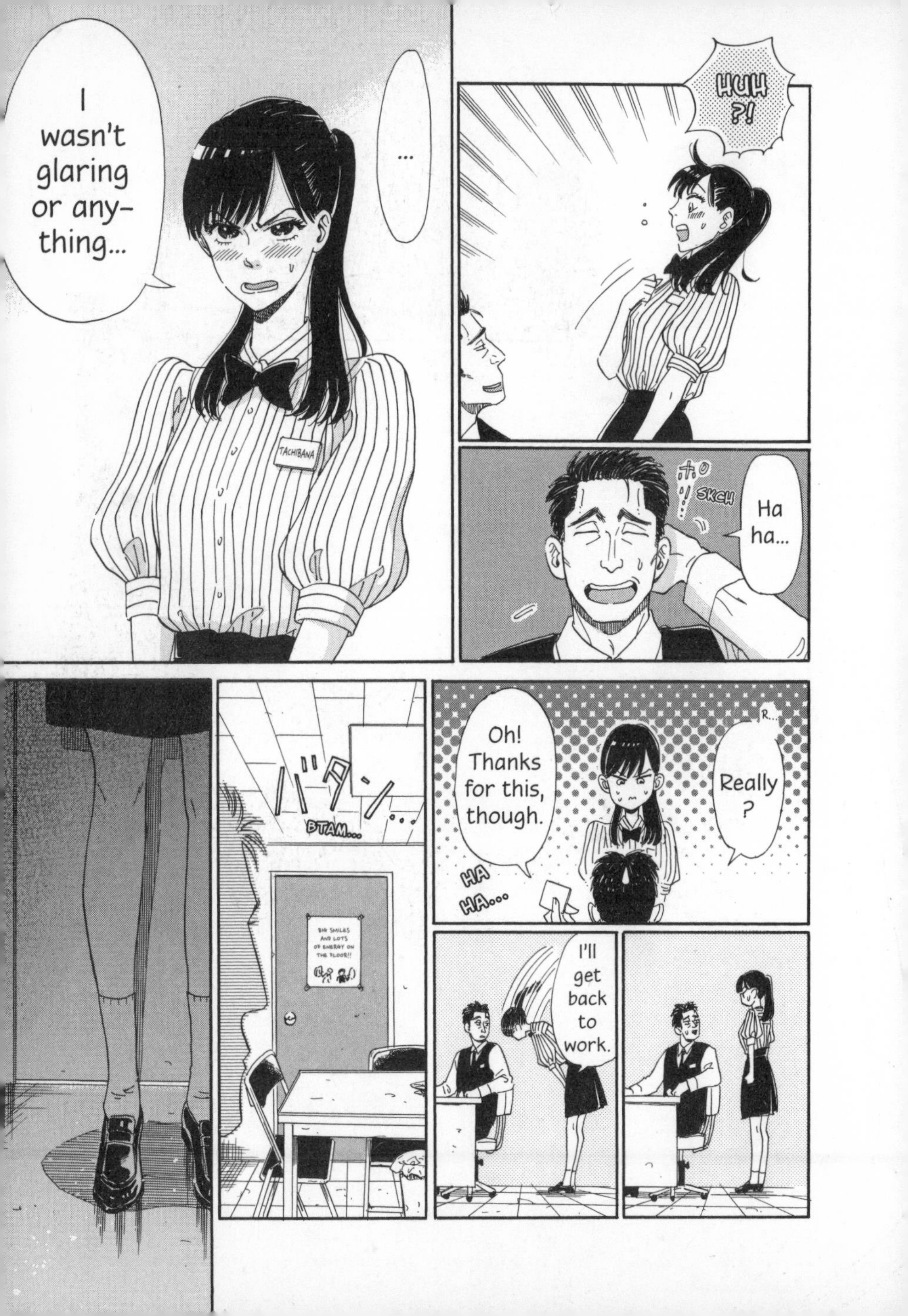
HUH ?!
SKCH
Ha ha...
...
I wasn't glaring or any-thing...
R...
Really ?
Oh! Thanks for this, though.
HA HA...
I'll get back to work.
バタン...
BTAM...
BIG SMILES AND LOTS OF ENERGY ON THE FLOOR!!

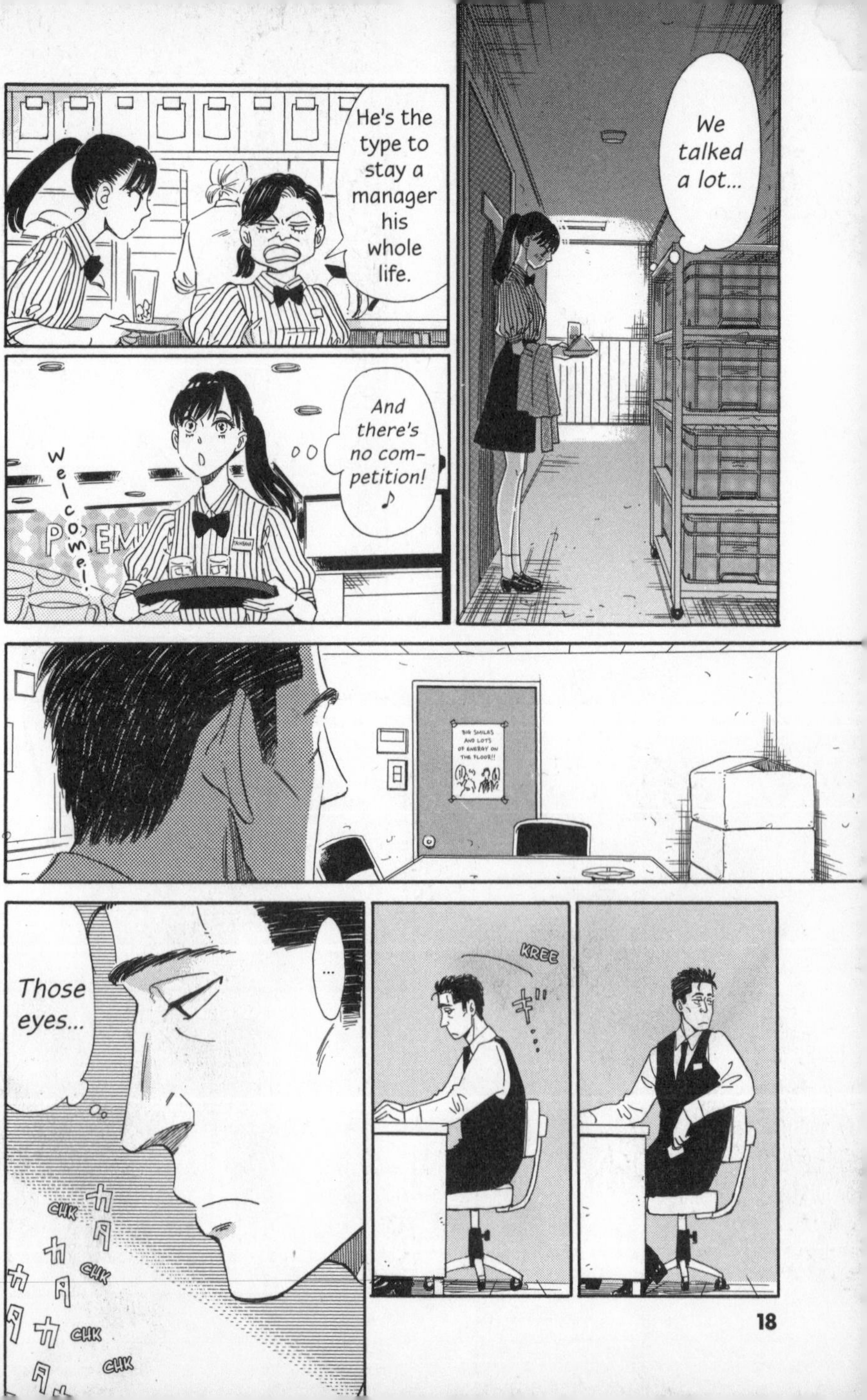
We talked a lot...
He's the type to stay a manager his whole life.
And there's no competition! ♪
Welcome!
BIG SMILES AND LOTS OF ENERGY ON THE FLOOR!!
KREE
ギ
...
Those eyes...
カタ
CHK
CHK
CHK
CHK

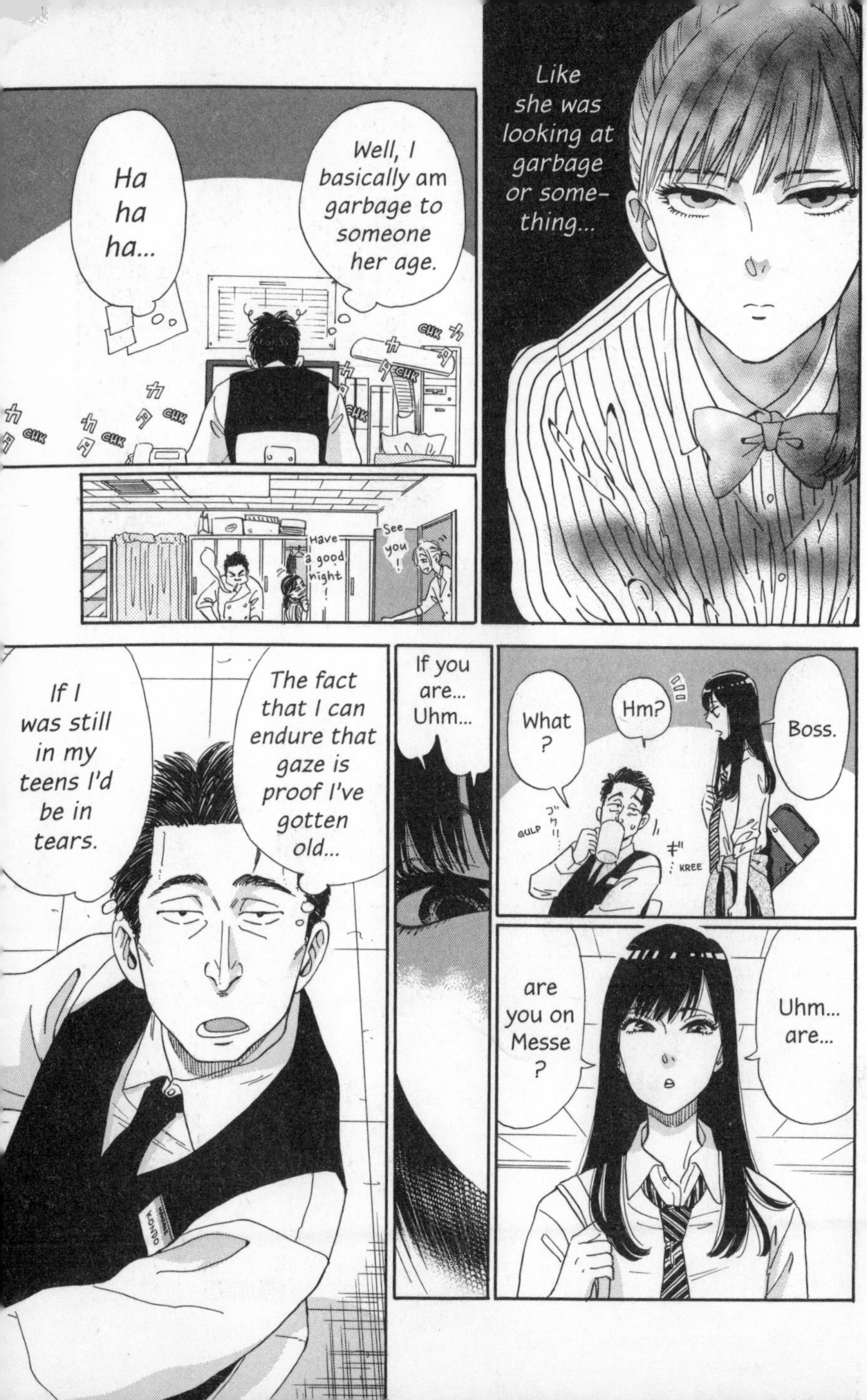
Like she was looking at garbage or some-thing...
Well, I basically am garbage to someone her age.
Ha ha ha...
CHUK
See you!
Have a good night!
Boss.
Hm?
What?
GULP
KREE
Uhm... are...
are you on Messe?
If you are... Uhm...
The fact that I can endure that gaze is proof I've gotten old...
If I was still in my teens I'd be in tears.

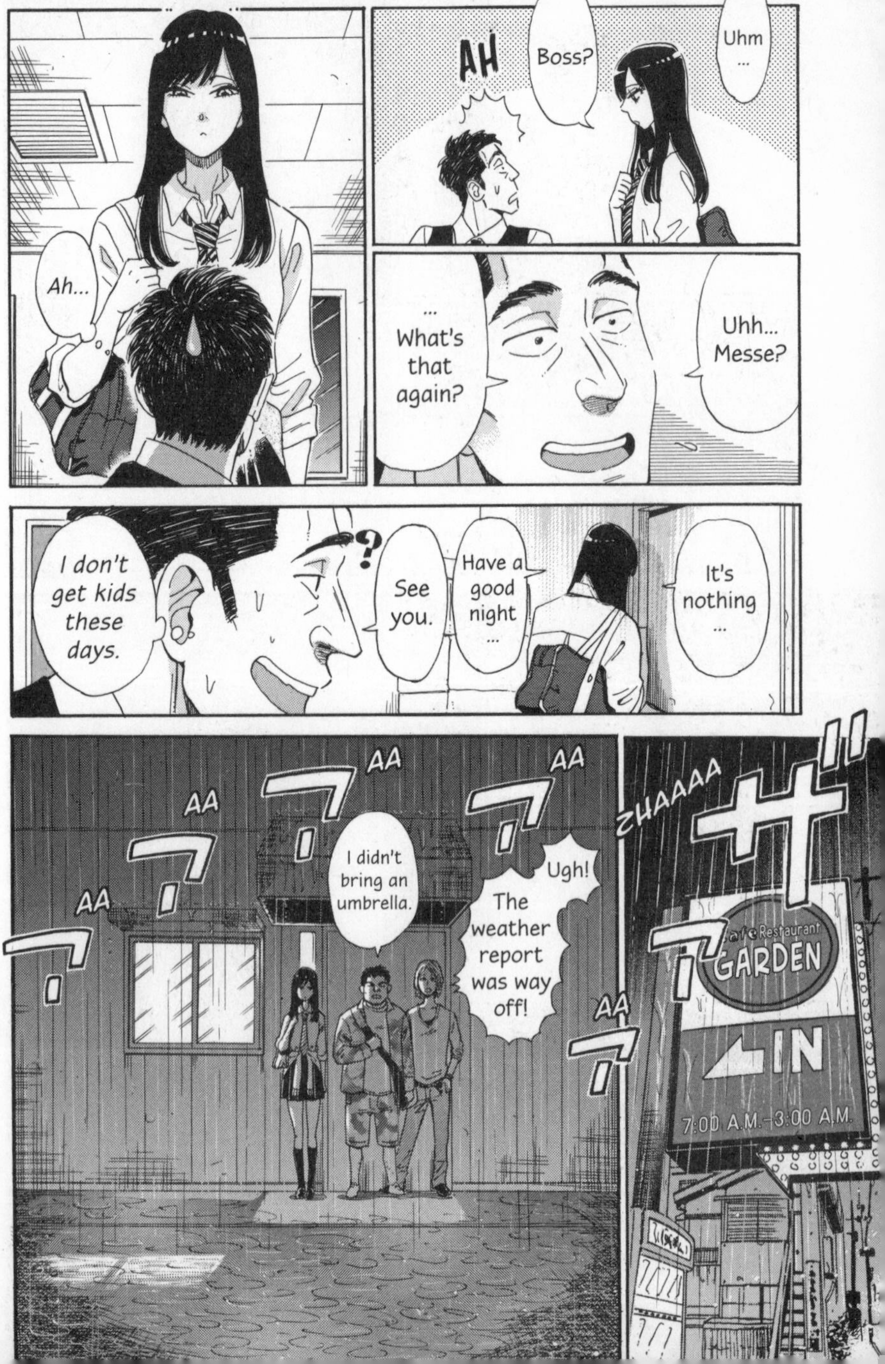
Uhm ...
Boss?
AH
Uhh... Messe?
... What's that again?
Ah...
It's nothing ...
Have a good night ...
See you.
I don't get kids these days.
ZHAAAAA
Cafe Restaurant GARDEN
IN
7:00 A.M.-3:00 A.M.
AA
AA
AA
AA
AA
Ugh! The weather report was way off!
I didn't bring an umbrella.

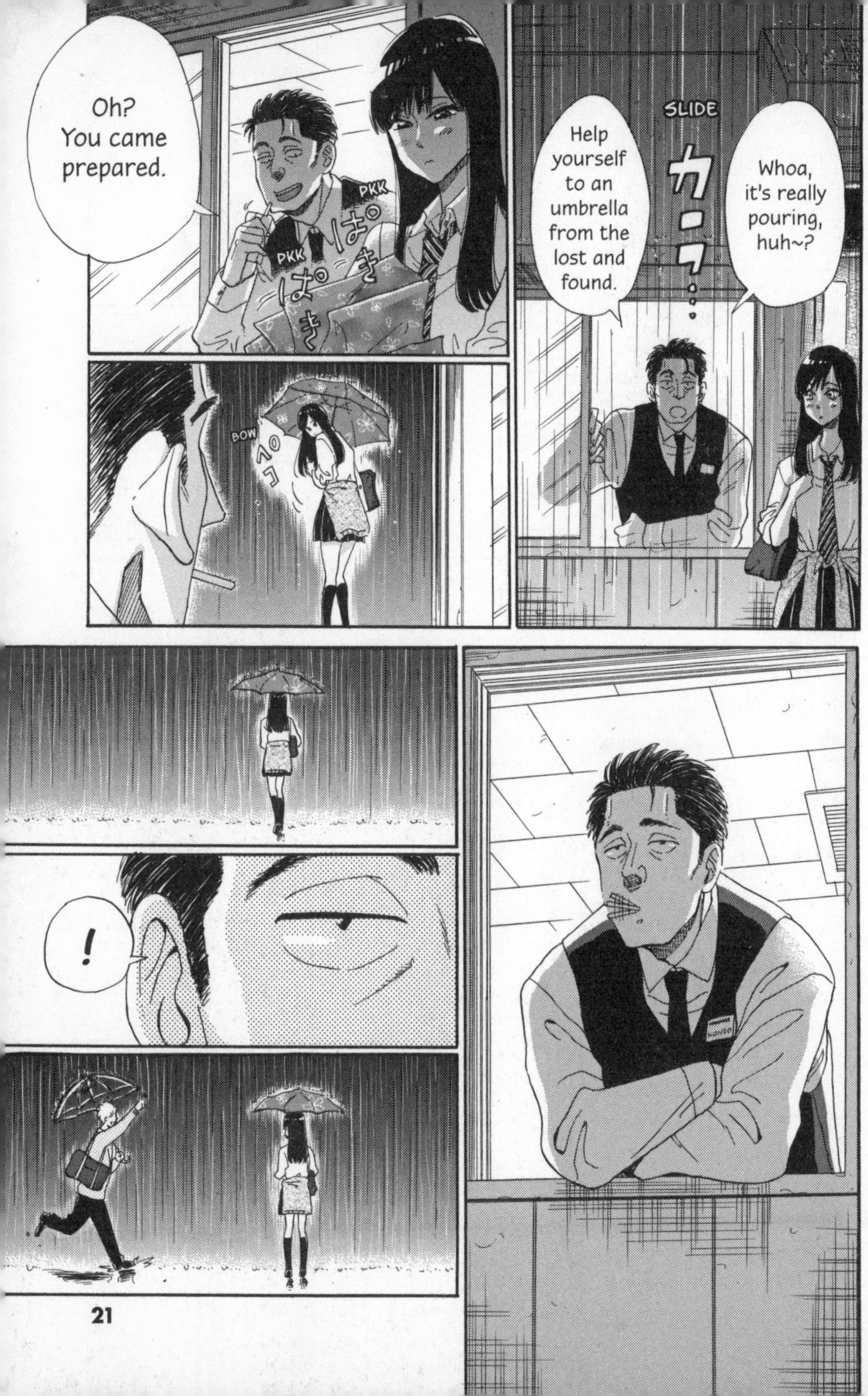
Whoa, it's really pouring, huh~?
SLIDE
Help yourself to an umbrella from the lost and found.
Oh? You came prepared.
PKK
PKK
BOW
!

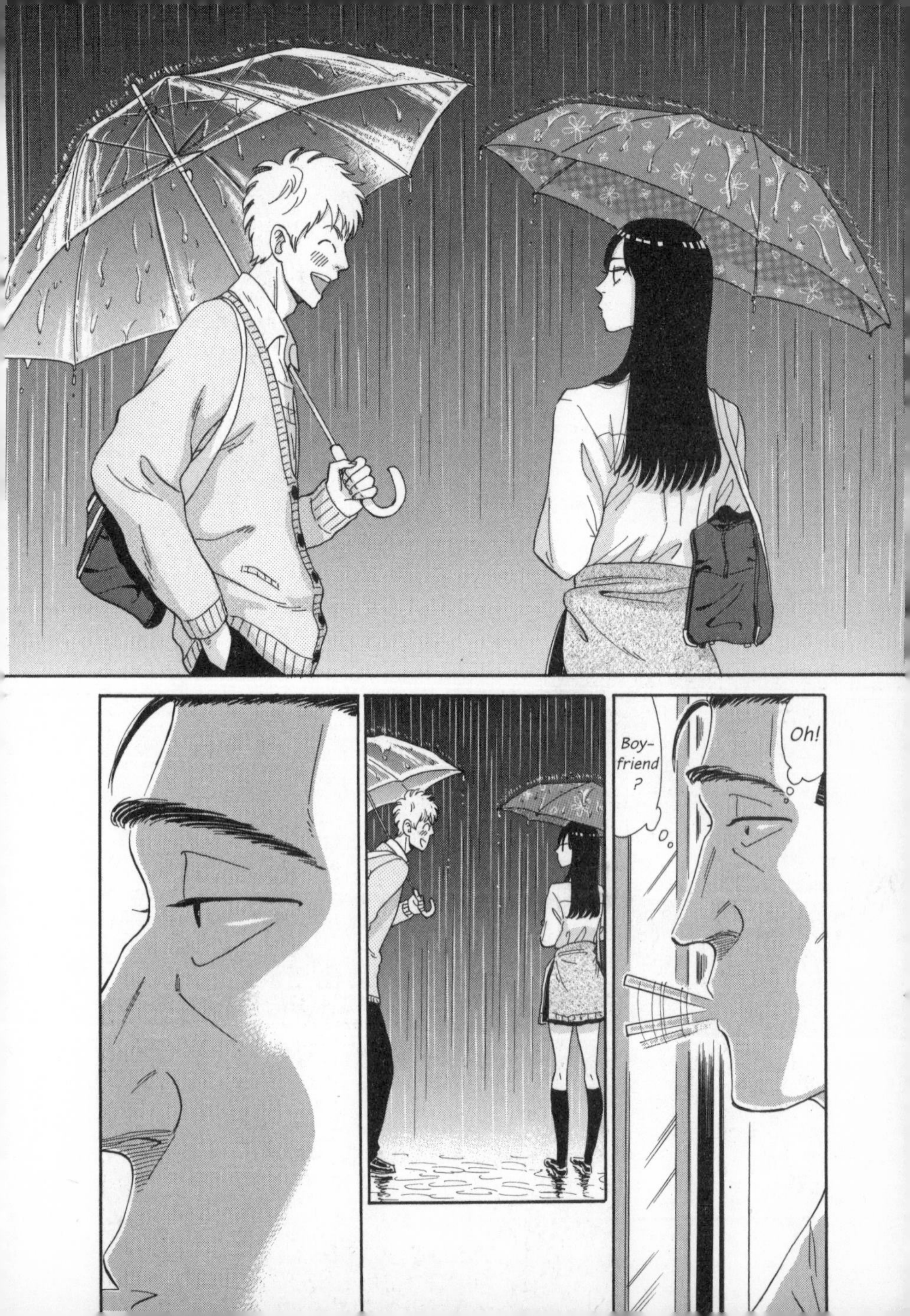
Oh!
Boy-friend?

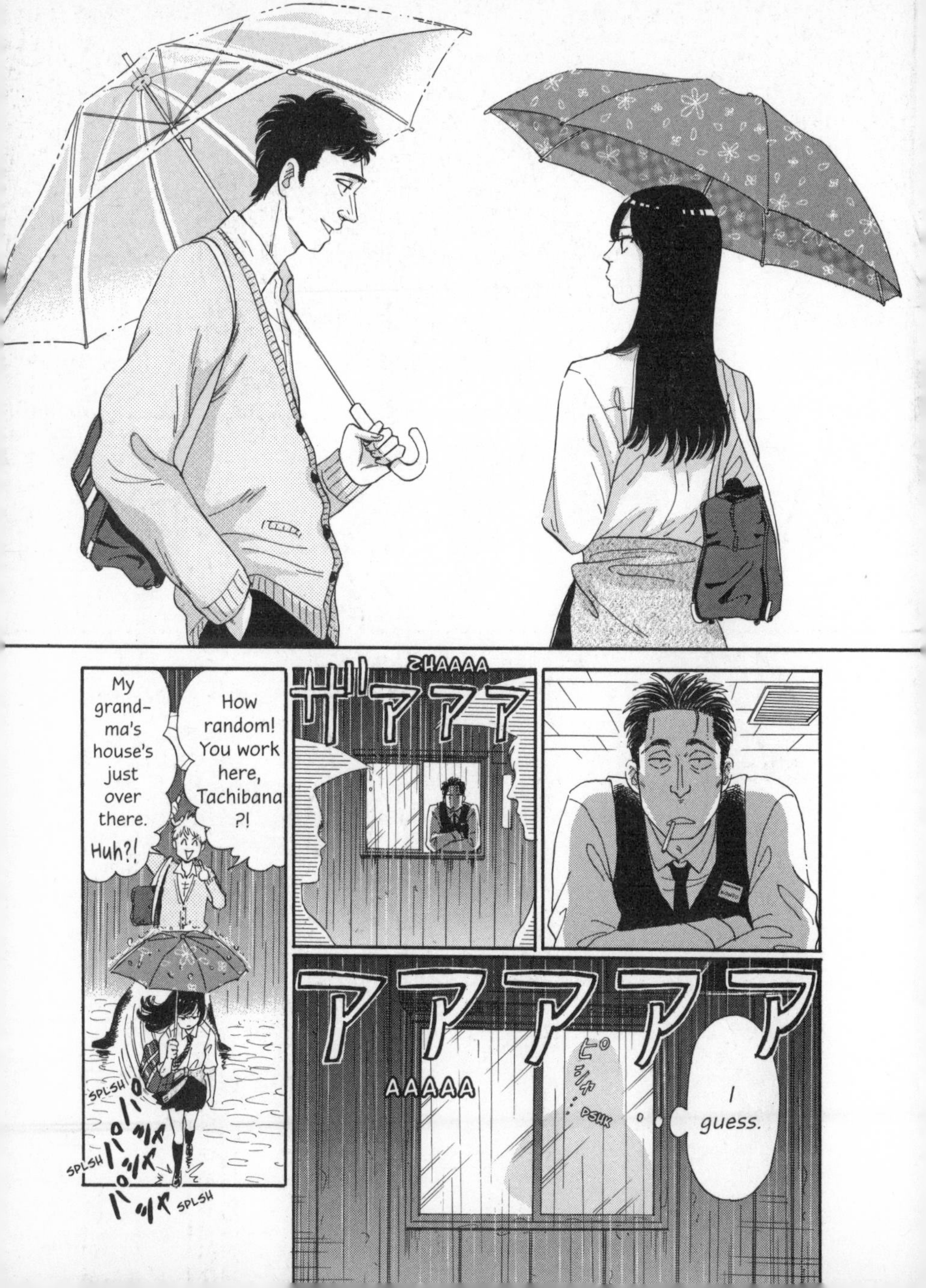
ZHAAAA
ザアアア
アアアアア
AAAAA
ピシャ
PSHK
I guess.
How random! You work here, Tachibana?!
My grandma's house's just over there.
Huh?!
SPLSH
SPLSH
SPLSH

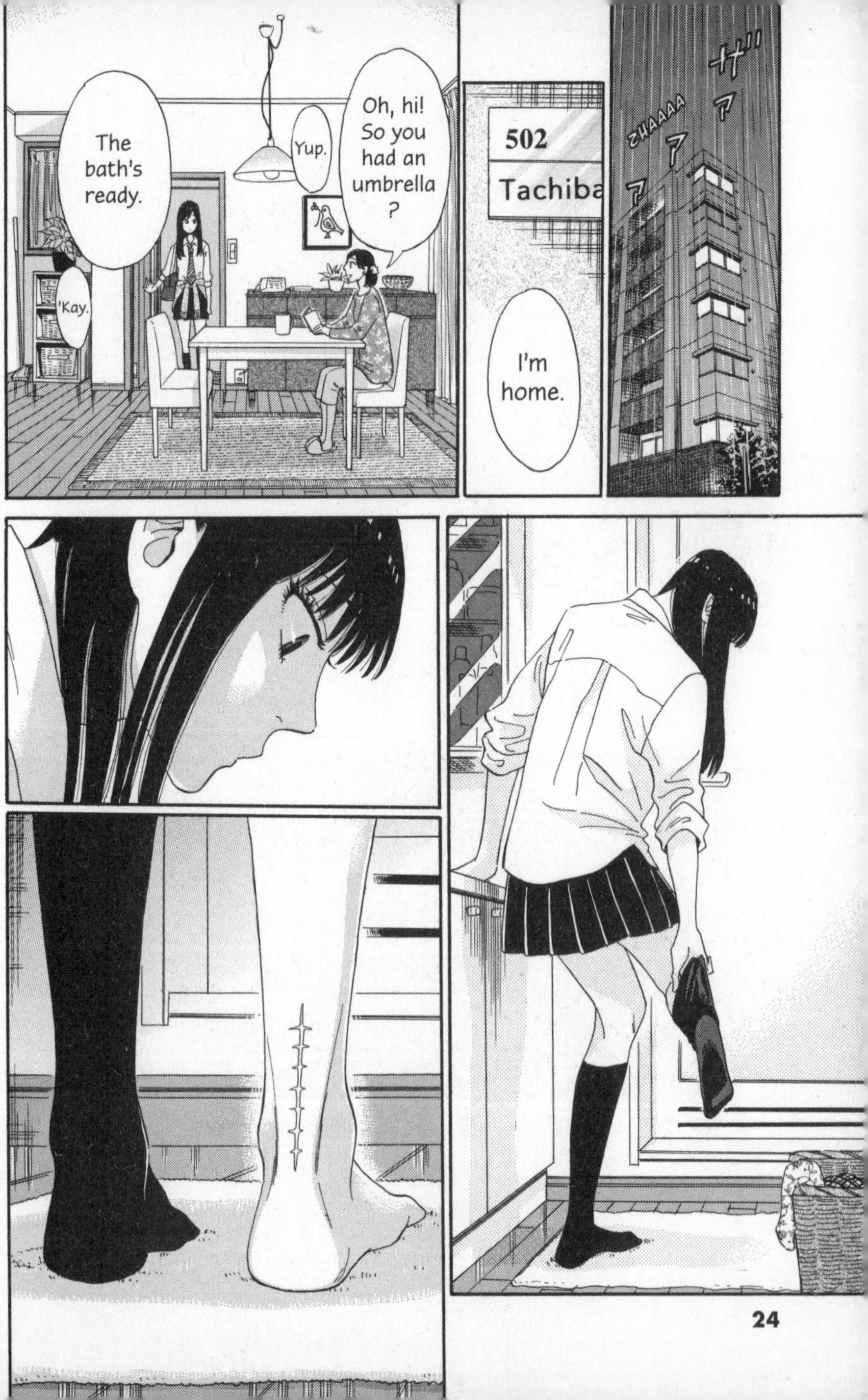
ZHAAAAA
ザアアア
502
Tachiba
I'm home.
Oh, hi! So you had an umbrella?
Yup.
The bath's ready.
'Kay.

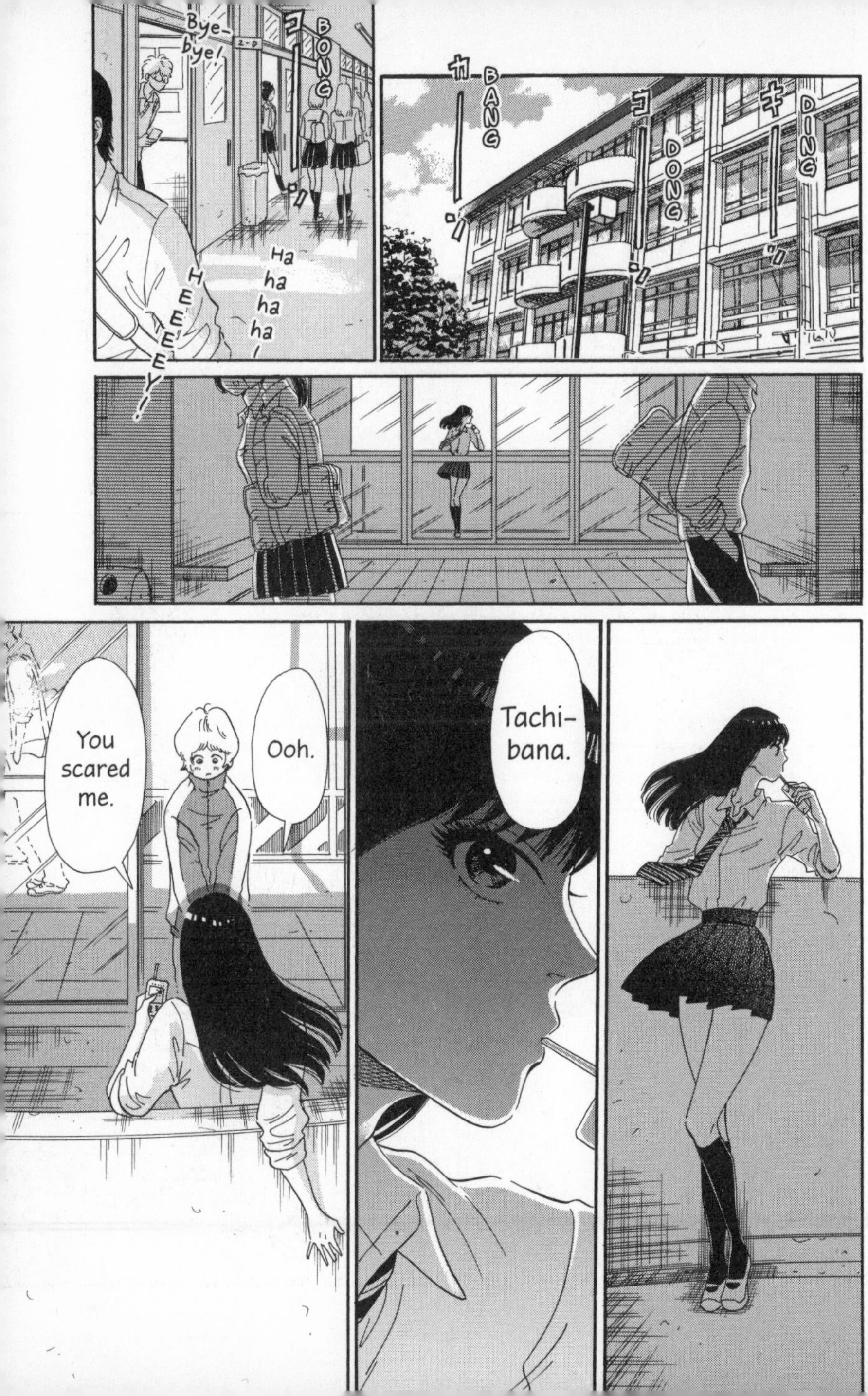
DING
DONG
BANG
BONG
Bye-bye!
Ha ha ha ha!
HEEEEEY!
Tachi-bana.
Ooh.
You scared me.

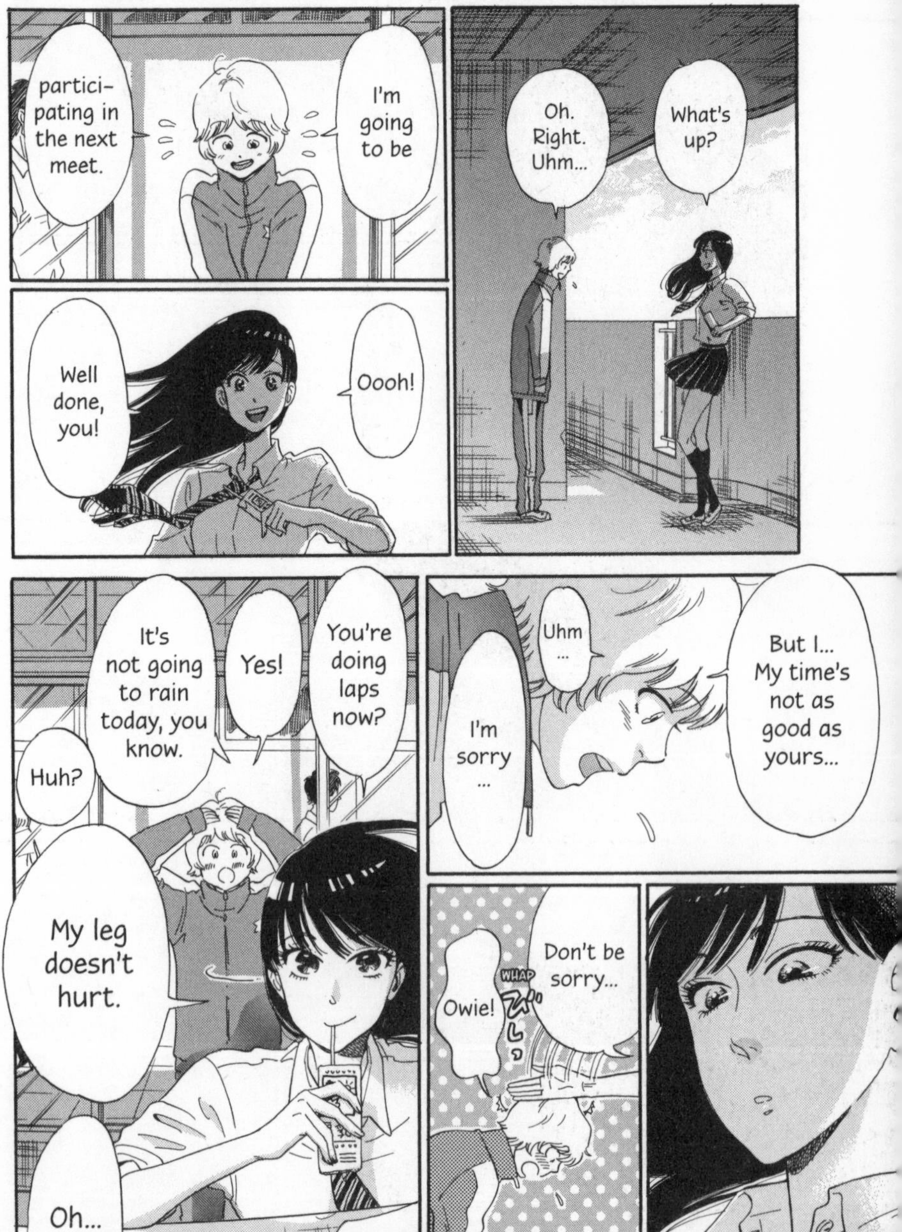
What's up?
Oh. Right. Uhm...
I'm going to be
partici-pating in the next meet.
Oooh!
Well done, you!
But I... My time's not as good as yours...
Uhm ...
I'm sorry ...
Don't be sorry...
WHAP
Owie!
You're doing laps now?
Yes!
It's not going to rain today, you know.
Huh?
My leg doesn't hurt.
Oh...

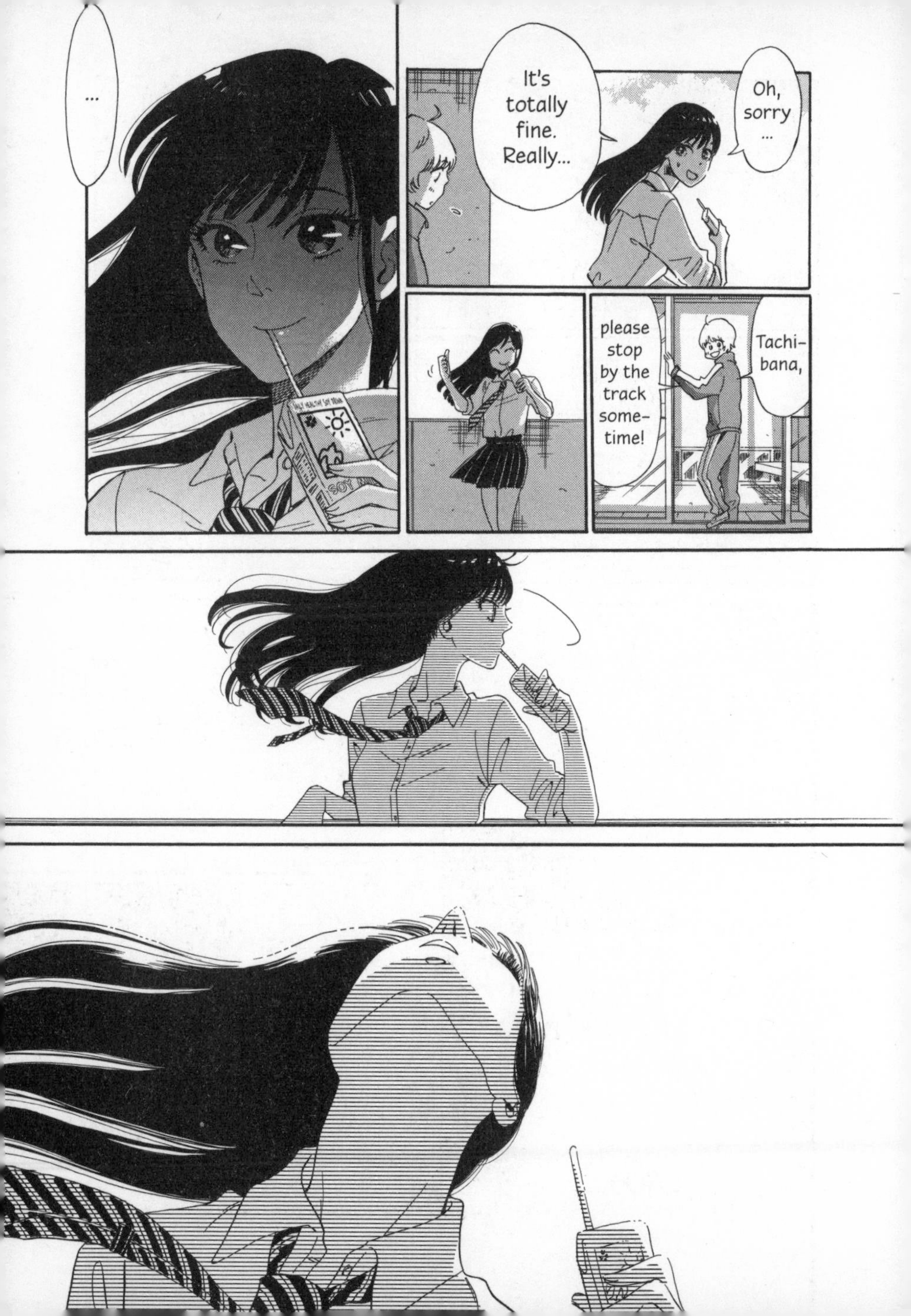
Oh, sorry ...
It's totally fine. Really...
Tachi-bana,
please stop by the track some-time!
...

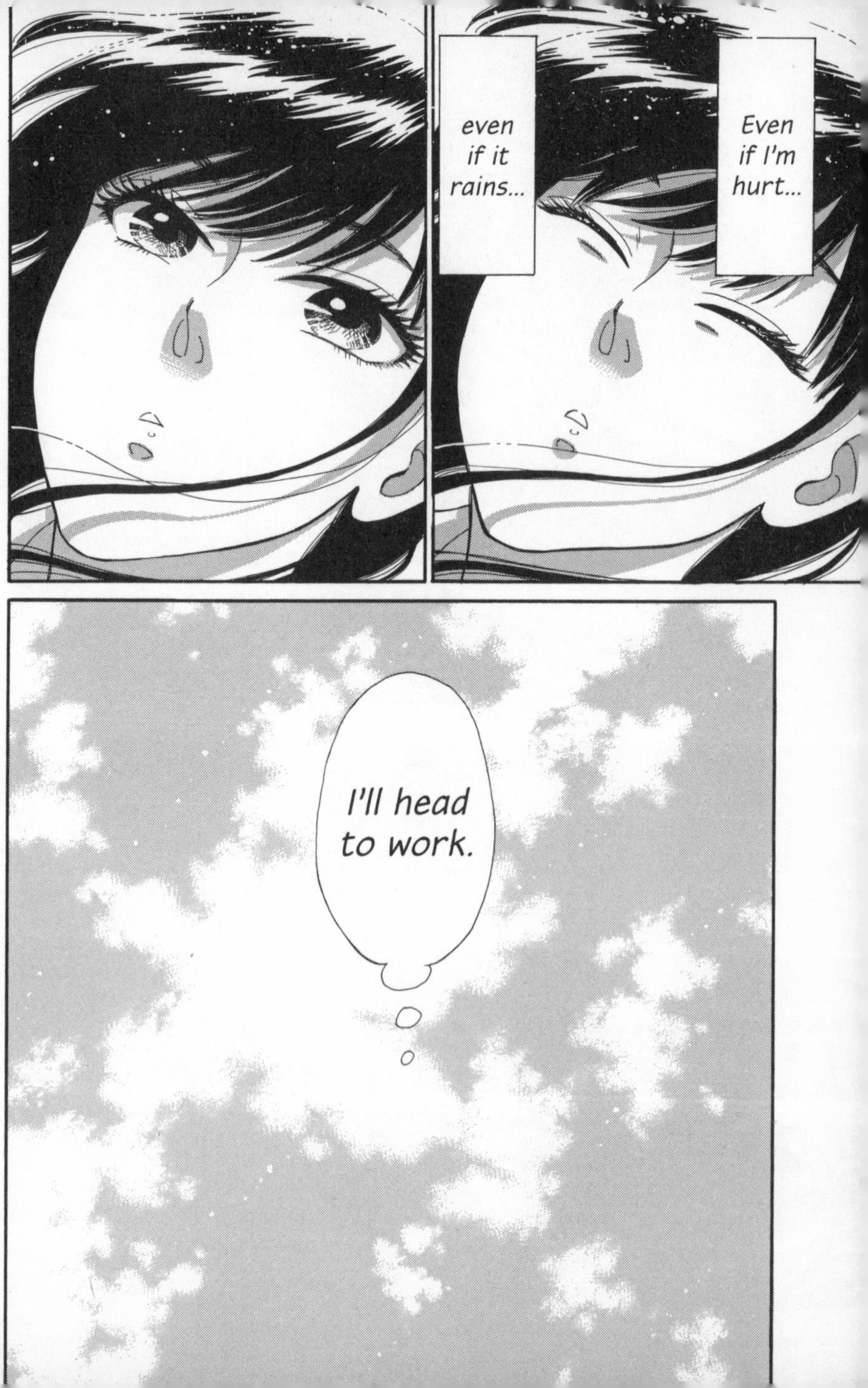
Even if I'm hurt...
even if it rains...
I'll head to work.

After
the 🌂
Rain

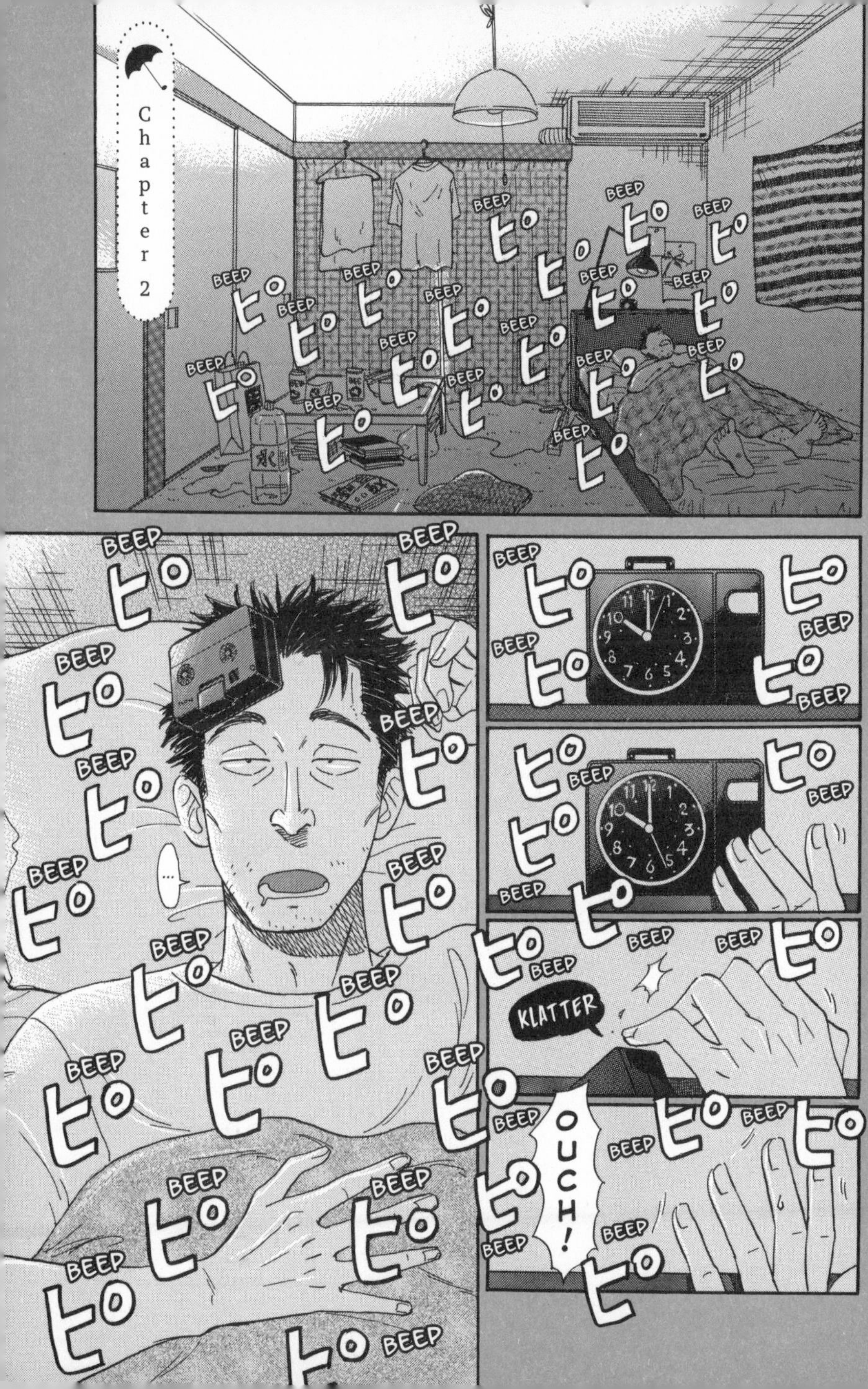
Chapter 2
BEEP
BEEP
BEEP
BEEP
KLATTER
BEEP
OUCH!
BEEP
...
BEEP

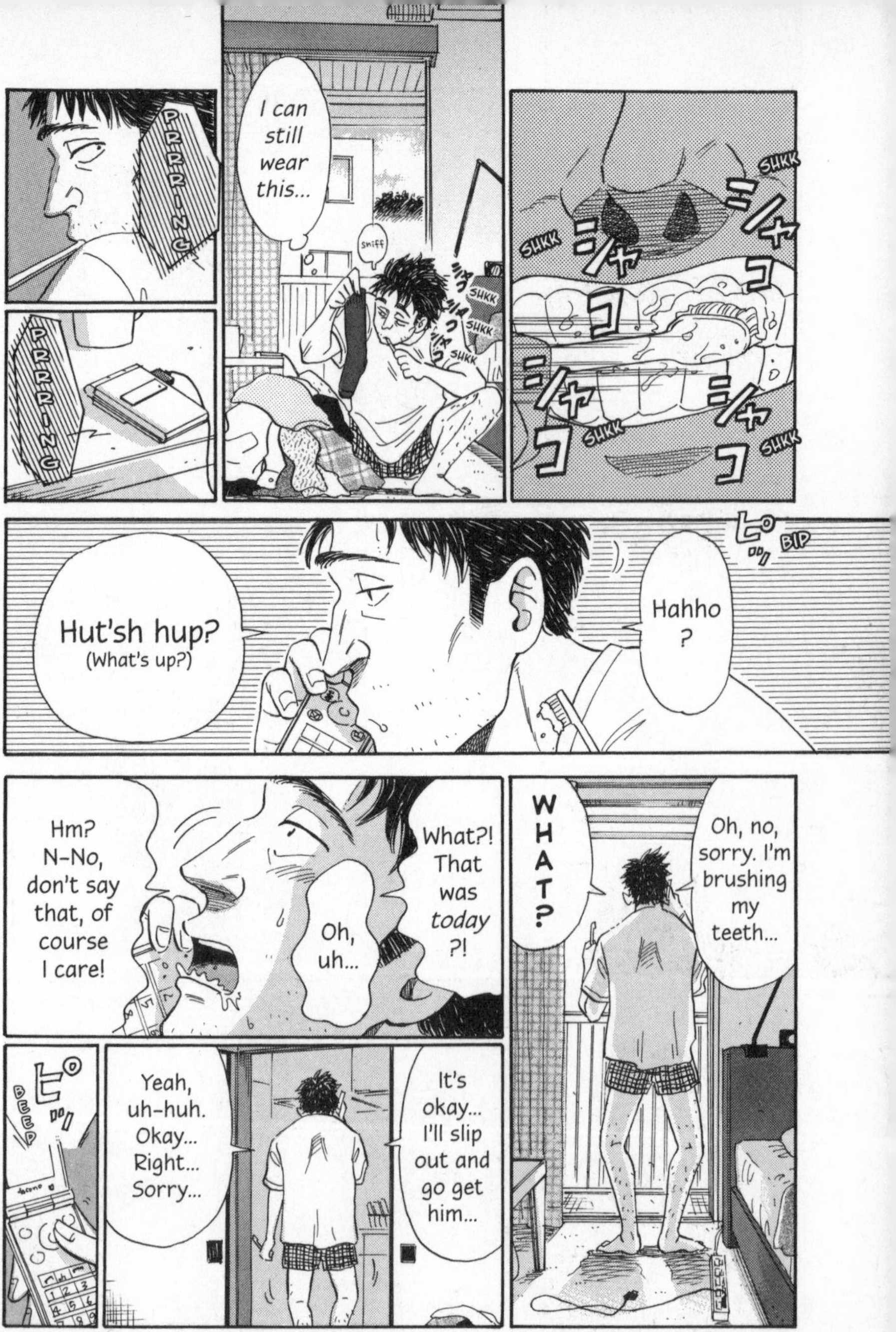
SHKK
SHKK
SHKK
SHKK
I can still wear this...
sniff
SHKK
SHKK
SHKK
PRRRING
PRRRING
BIP
Hahho ?
Hut'sh hup?
(What's up?)
Oh, no, sorry. I'm brushing my teeth...
WHAT?
What?! That was *today* ?!
Oh, uh...
Hm? N-No, don't say that, of course I care!
It's okay... I'll slip out and go get him...
Yeah, uh-huh. Okay... Right... Sorry...
BEEP

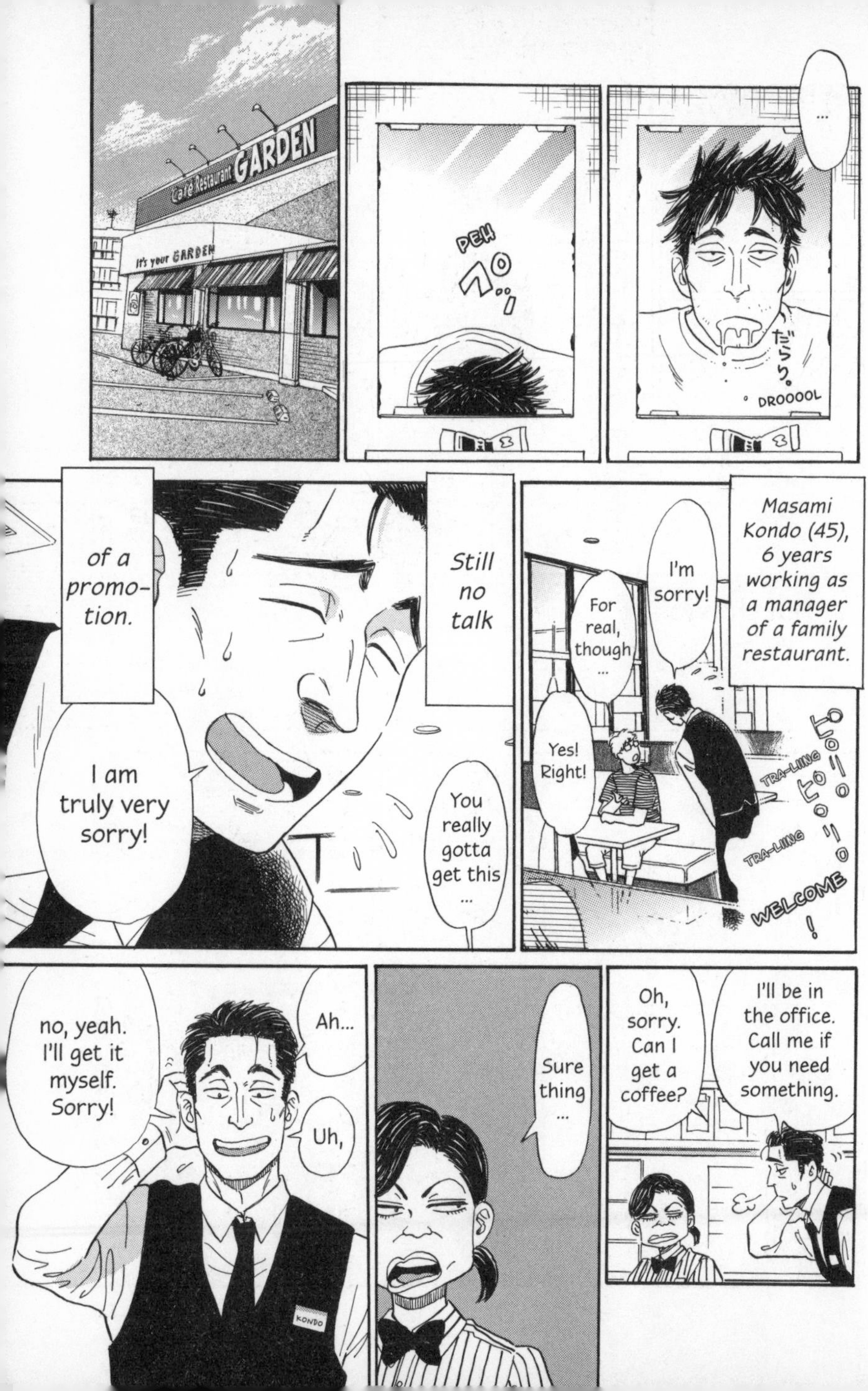
...
DROOOOL
PEH
Café Restaurant GARDEN
It's your GARDEN
Masami Kondo (45), 6 years working as a manager of a family restaurant.
I'm sorry!
For real, though ...
Yes! Right!
TRA-LIING
TRA-LIING
WELCOME!
Still no talk
of a promotion.
You really gotta get this ...
I am truly very sorry!
I'll be in the office. Call me if you need something.
Oh, sorry. Can I get a coffee?
Sure thing ...
Ah...
Uh,
no, yeah. I'll get it myself. Sorry!
KONDO

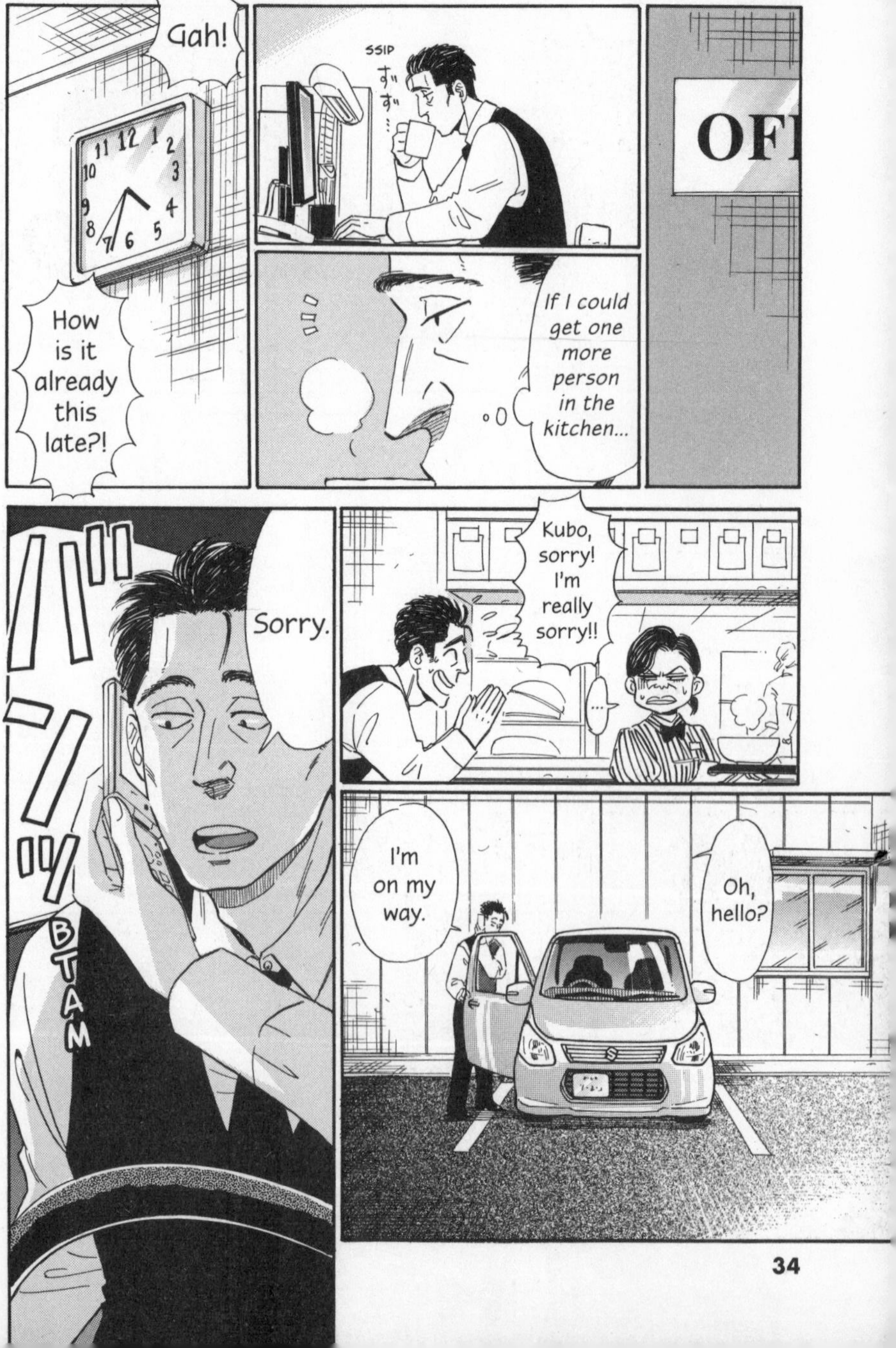
SSIP
ずず
If I could get one more person in the kitchen...
Gah!
How is it already this late?!
Kubo, sorry! I'm really sorry!!
...
Oh, hello?
I'm on my way.
Sorry.
BTAM

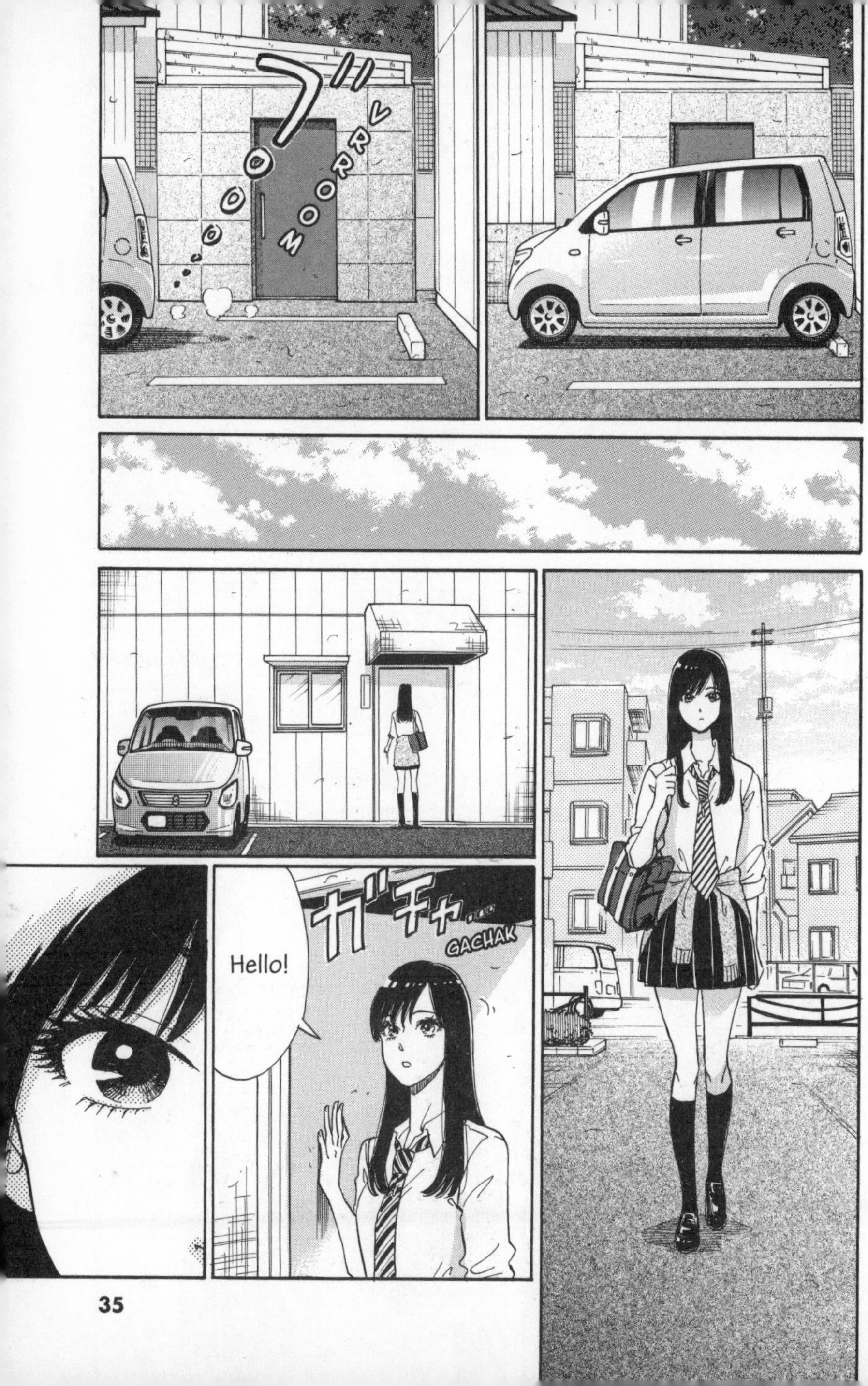

ブ
VRROOM
ガチャ...
GACHAK
Hello!

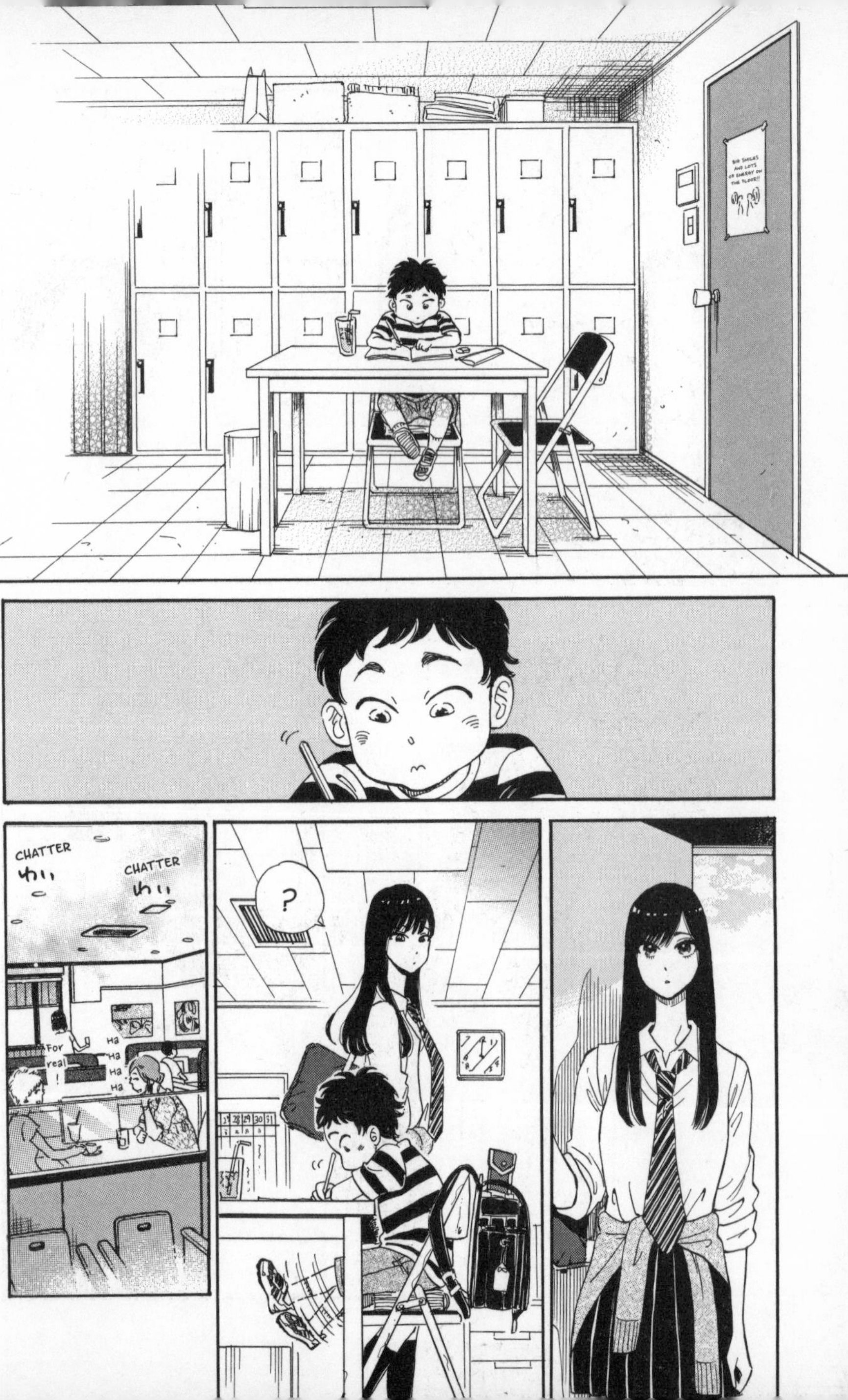
BIG SMILES AND LOTS OF ENERGY ON THE FLOOR!!
?
CHATTER
わい
CHATTER
わい
For real!
Ha Ha Ha Ha

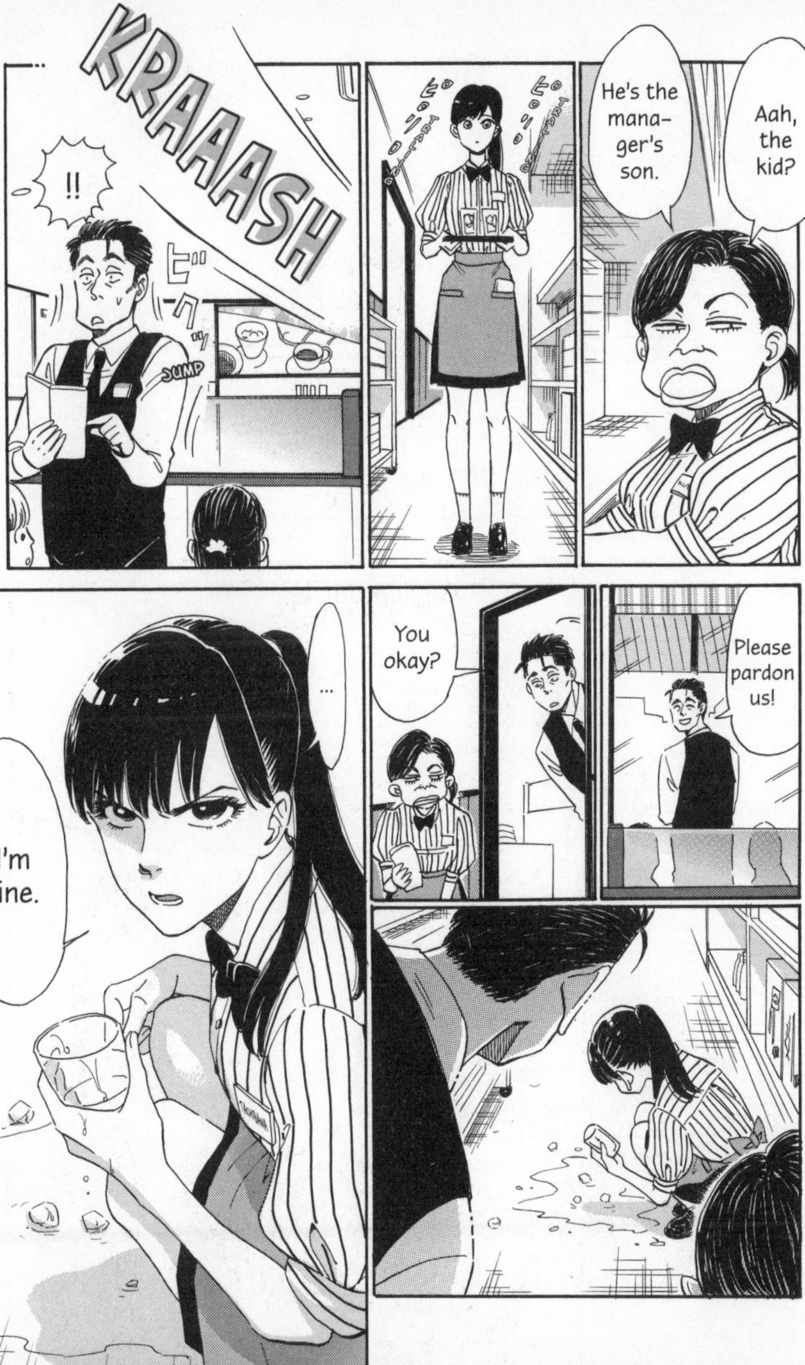
Aah, the kid?
He's the mana-ger's son.
KRAAASH
!!
ビクッ
JUMP
Please pardon us!
You okay?
...
I'm fine.

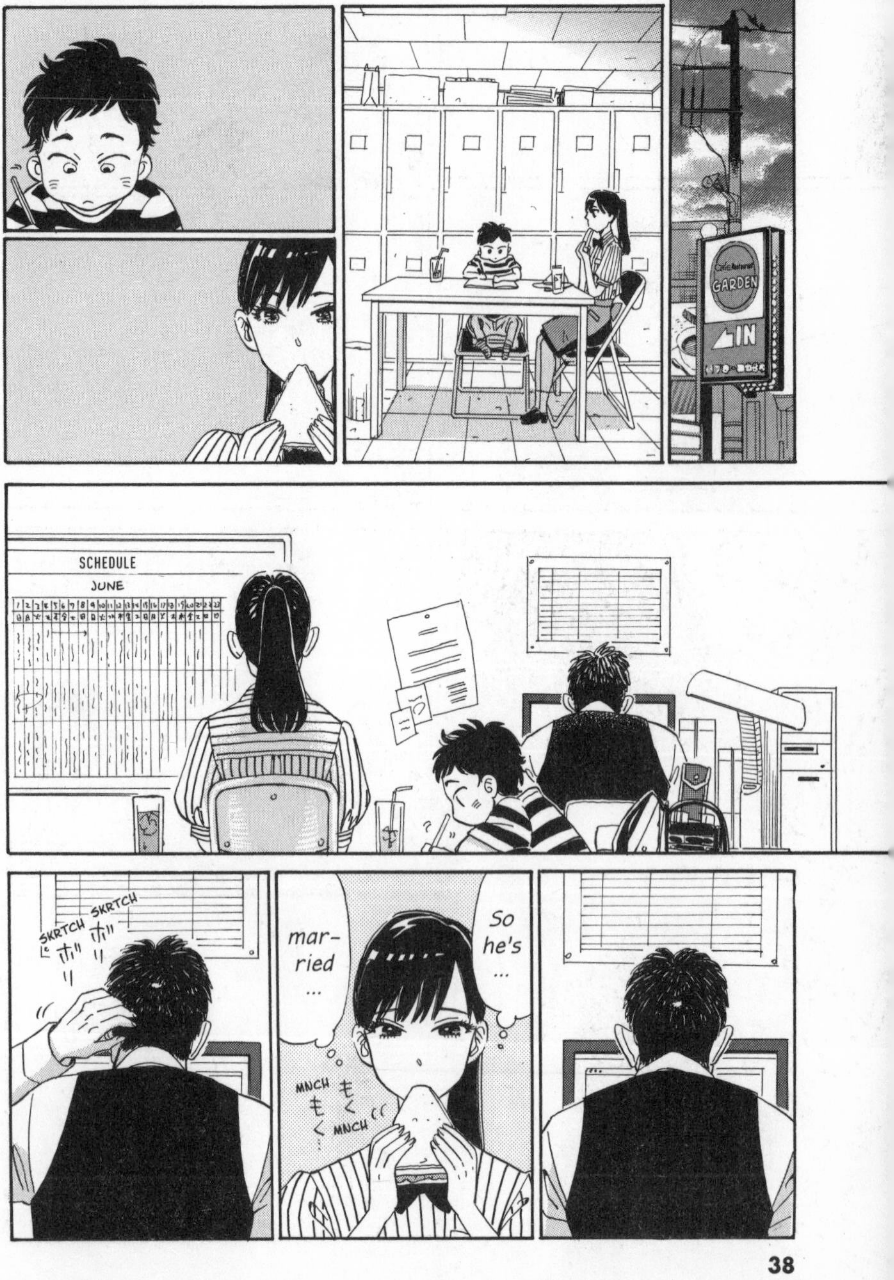
GARDEN
IN
SCHEDULE
JUNE
So he's ...
mar-ried ...
MNCH
MNCH
SKRTCH
SKRTCH

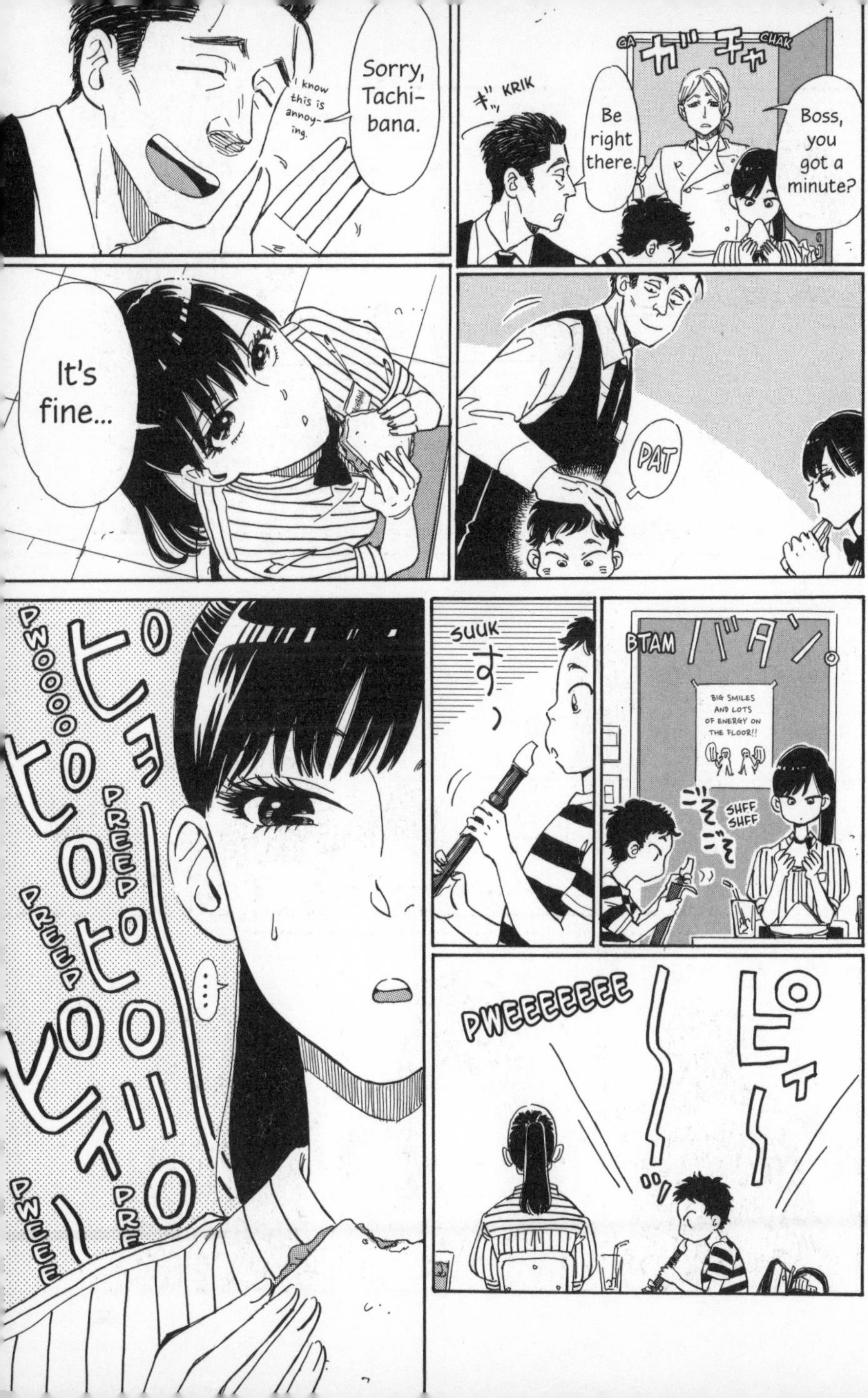

GA
CHAK
Boss, you got a minute?
KRIK
Be right there.
Sorry, Tachibana.
I know this is annoying.
PAT
It's fine...
BTAM
BIG SMILES AND LOTS OF ENERGY ON THE FLOOR!!
SHFF SHFF
SUUK
PWEEEEEEE
PWOOOOOO
PREEP
PREEP
PRE
PWEEE
....

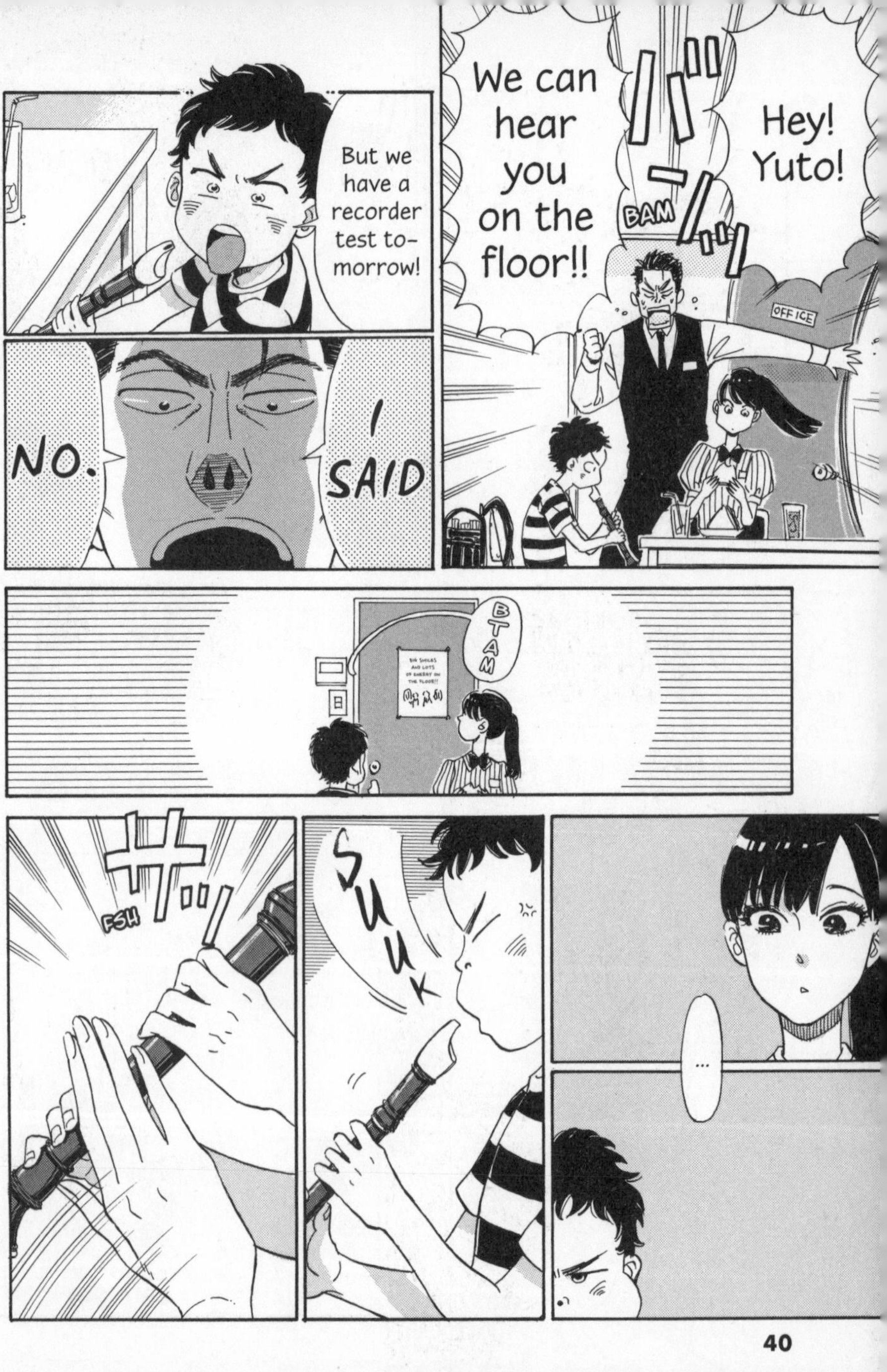
Hey! Yuto!
We can hear you on the floor!!
BAM
But we have a recorder test to-morrow!
I SAID NO.
BTAM
BIG SMILES AND LOTS OF ENERGY ON THE FLOOR!!
...
SUUK
FSH

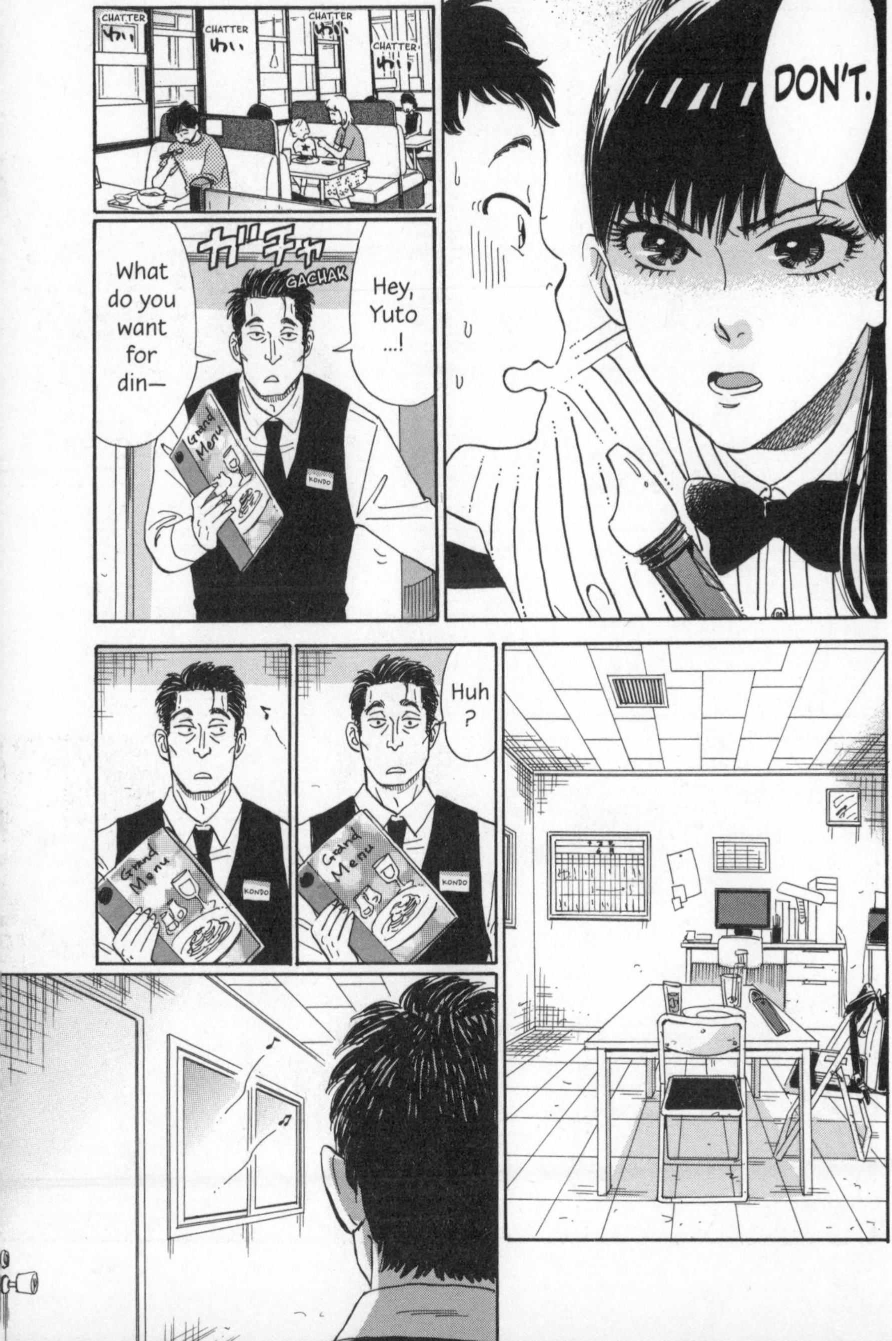
DON'T.
CHATTER
わい
CHATTER
わい
CHATTER
わい
CHATTER
わい
Hey, Yuto ...!
ガチャ
GACHAK
What do you want for din—
Huh?

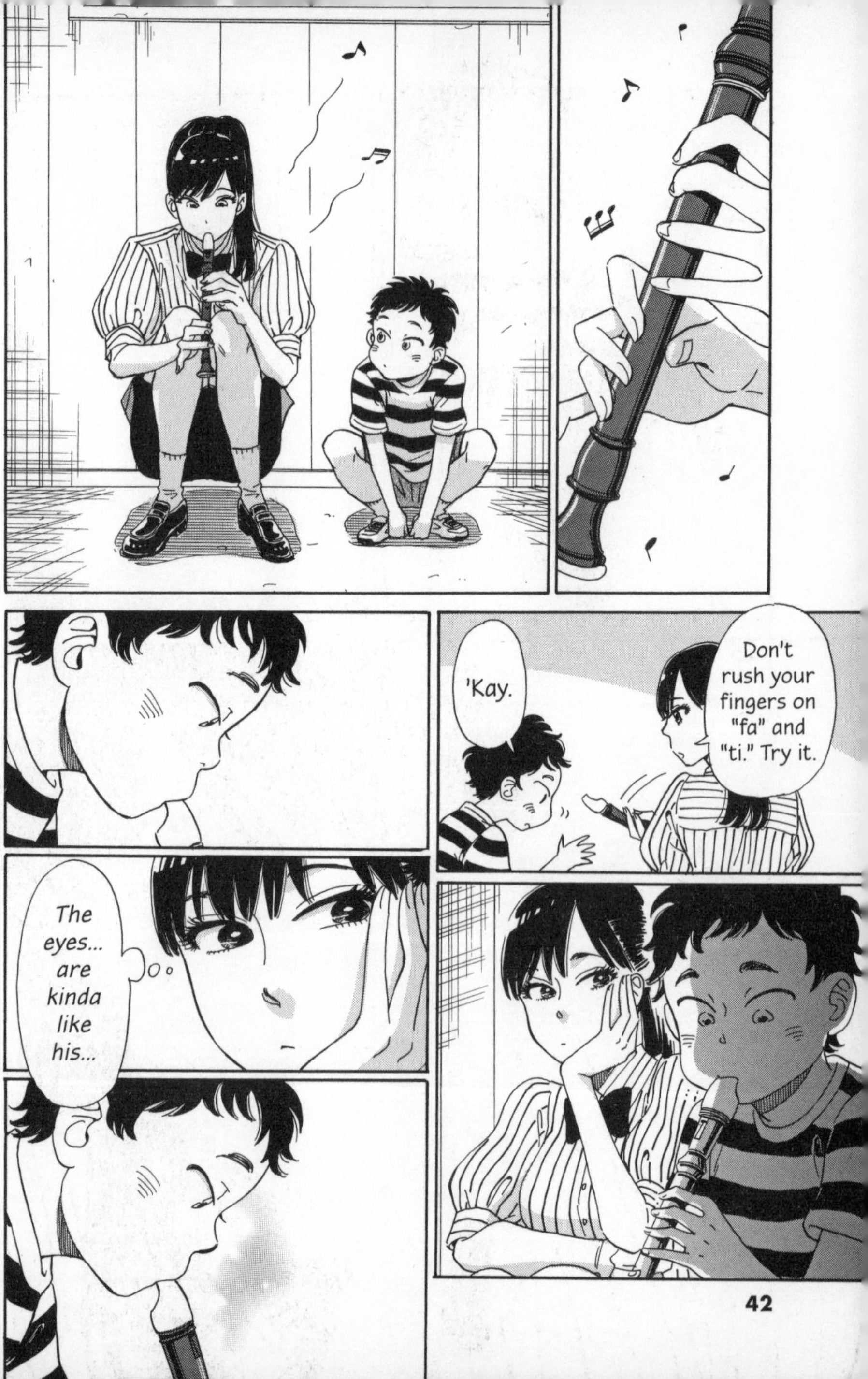
Don't rush your fingers on "fa" and "ti." Try it.
'Kay.
The eyes... are kinda like his...

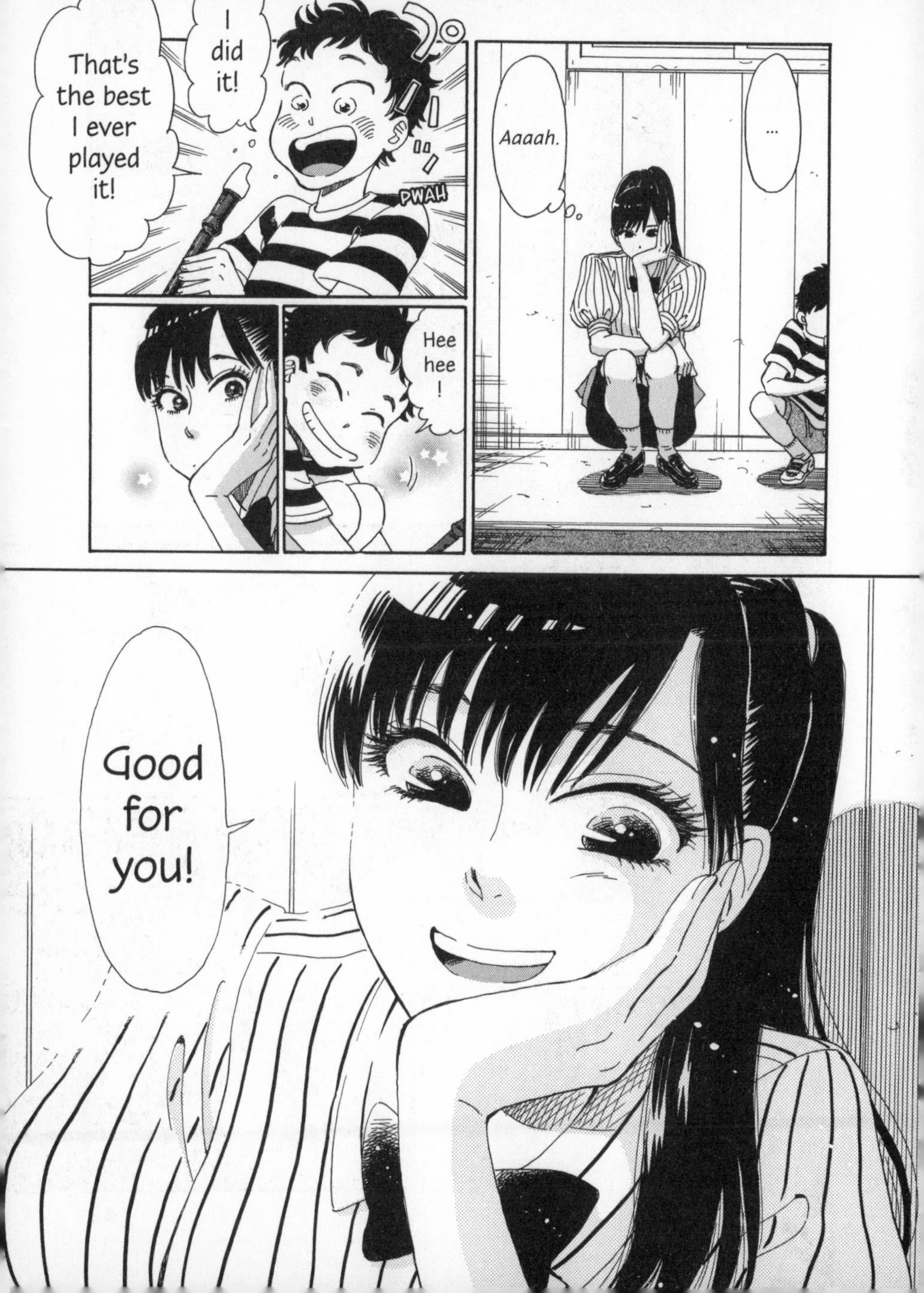
...
Aaaah.
I did it!
That's the best I ever played it!
PWAH
Hee hee!
Good for you!

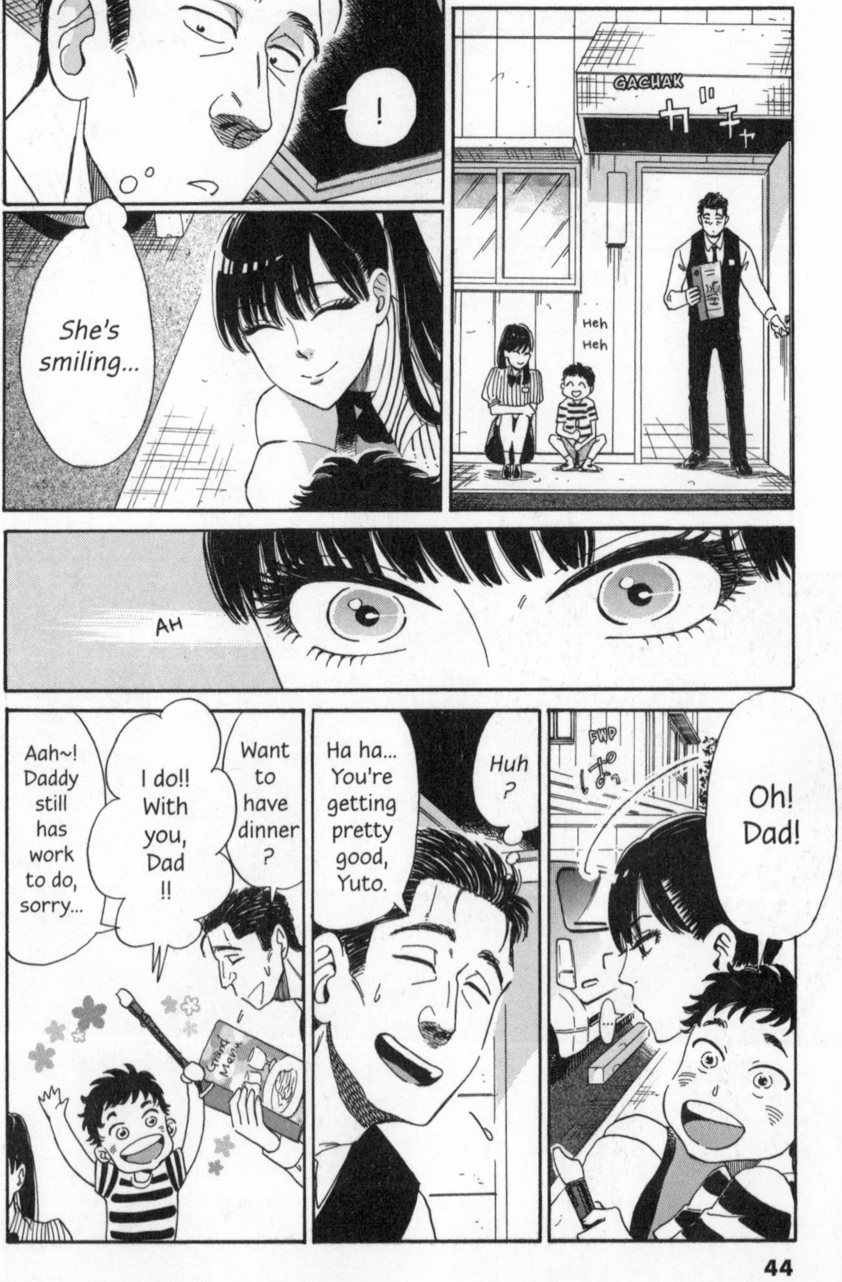
GACHAK
ガチャ
Heh
Heh
!
She's smiling...
AH
FWD
Oh! Dad!
...
Huh?
Ha ha... You're getting pretty good, Yuto.
Want to have dinner?
I do!! With you, Dad!!
Aah~! Daddy still has work to do, sorry...

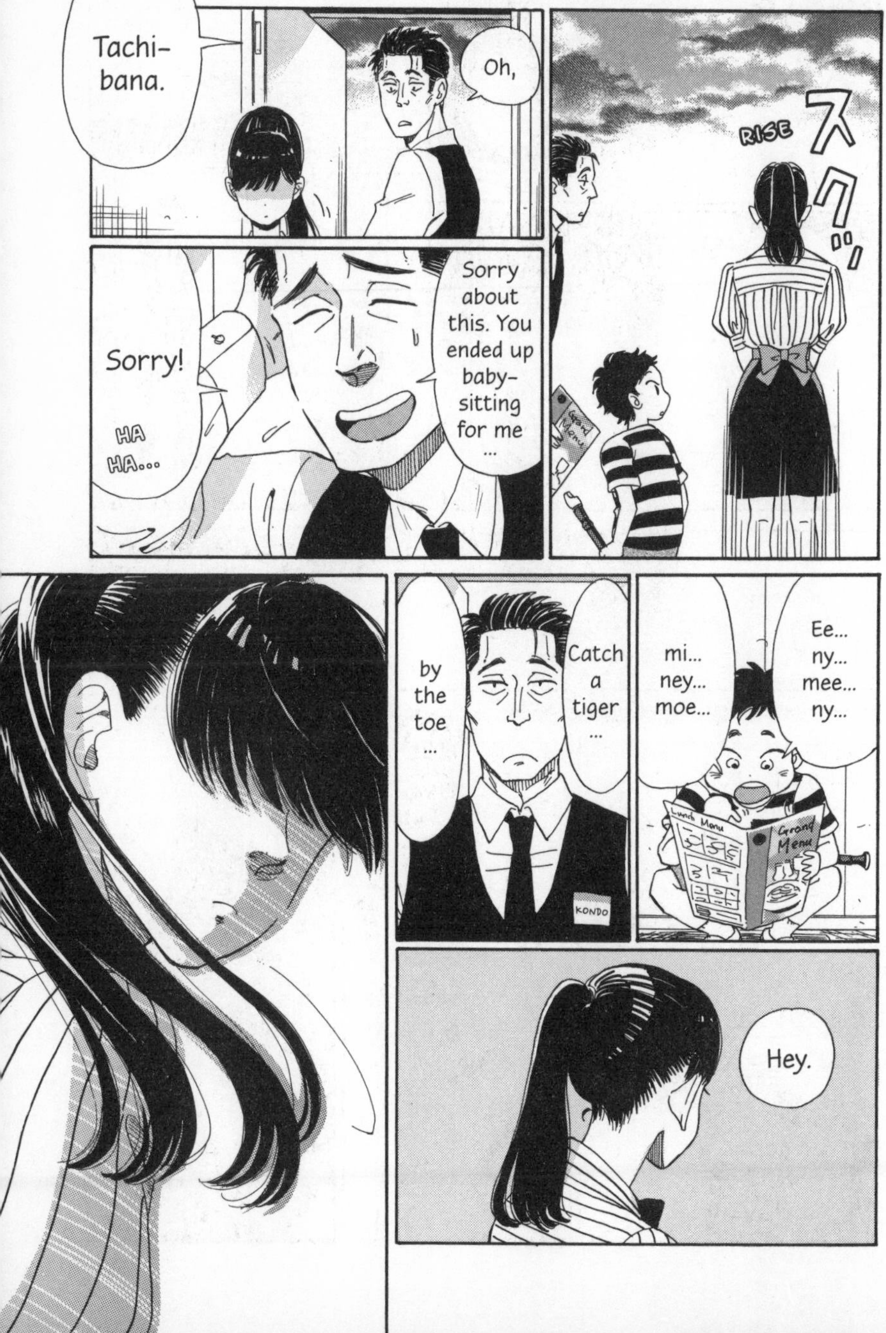
RISE
スクッ
Oh,
Tachi-bana.
Sorry about this. You ended up baby-sitting for me ...
Sorry!
HA HA...
Ee... ny... mee... ny...
mi... ney... moe...
Catch a tiger ...
by the toe ...
KONDO
Hey.

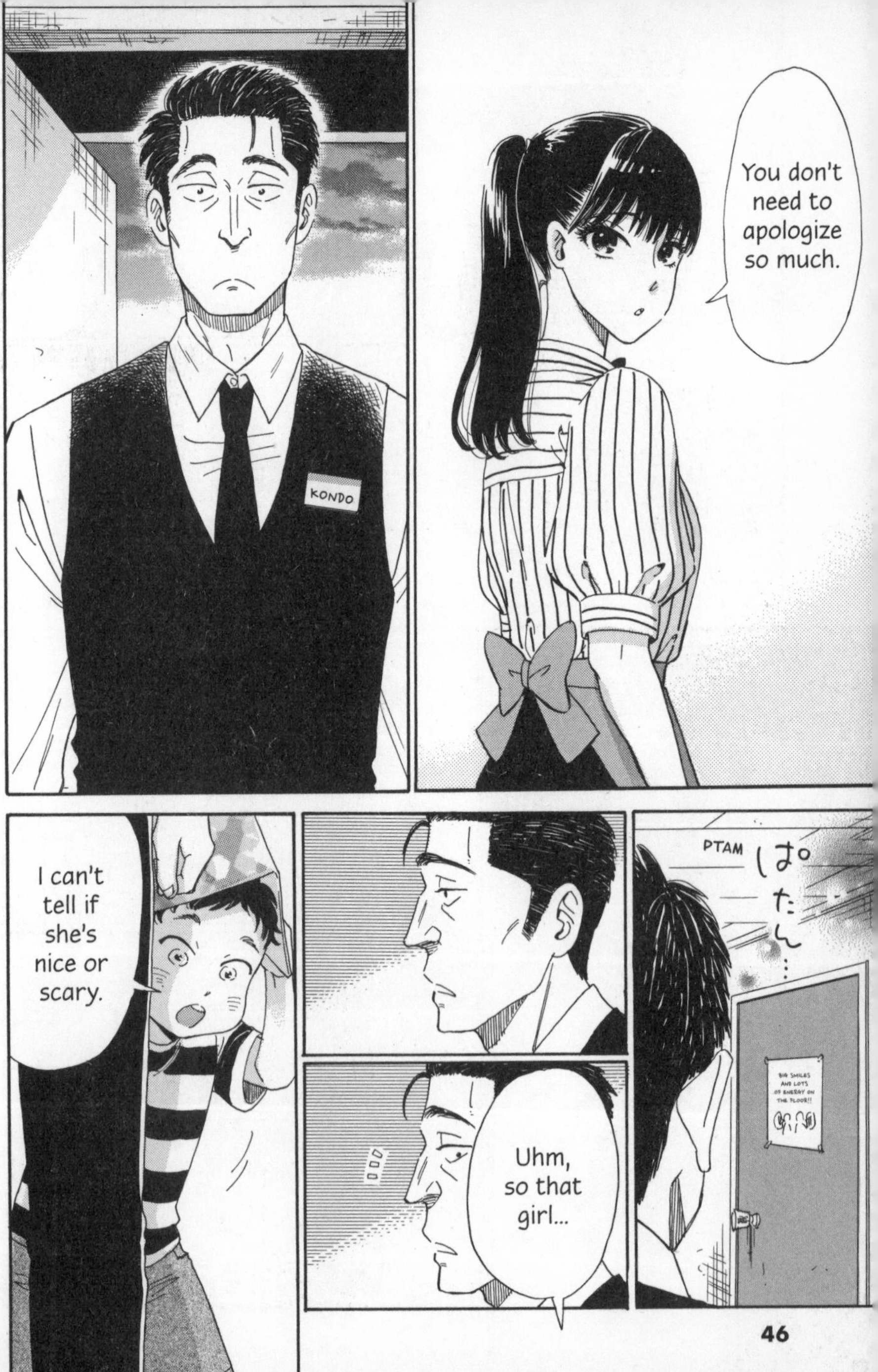
You don't need to apologize so much.
KONDO
PTAM
ぱたん…
BIG SMILES AND LOTS OF ENERGY ON THE FLOOR!!
Uhm, so that girl...
I can't tell if she's nice or scary.

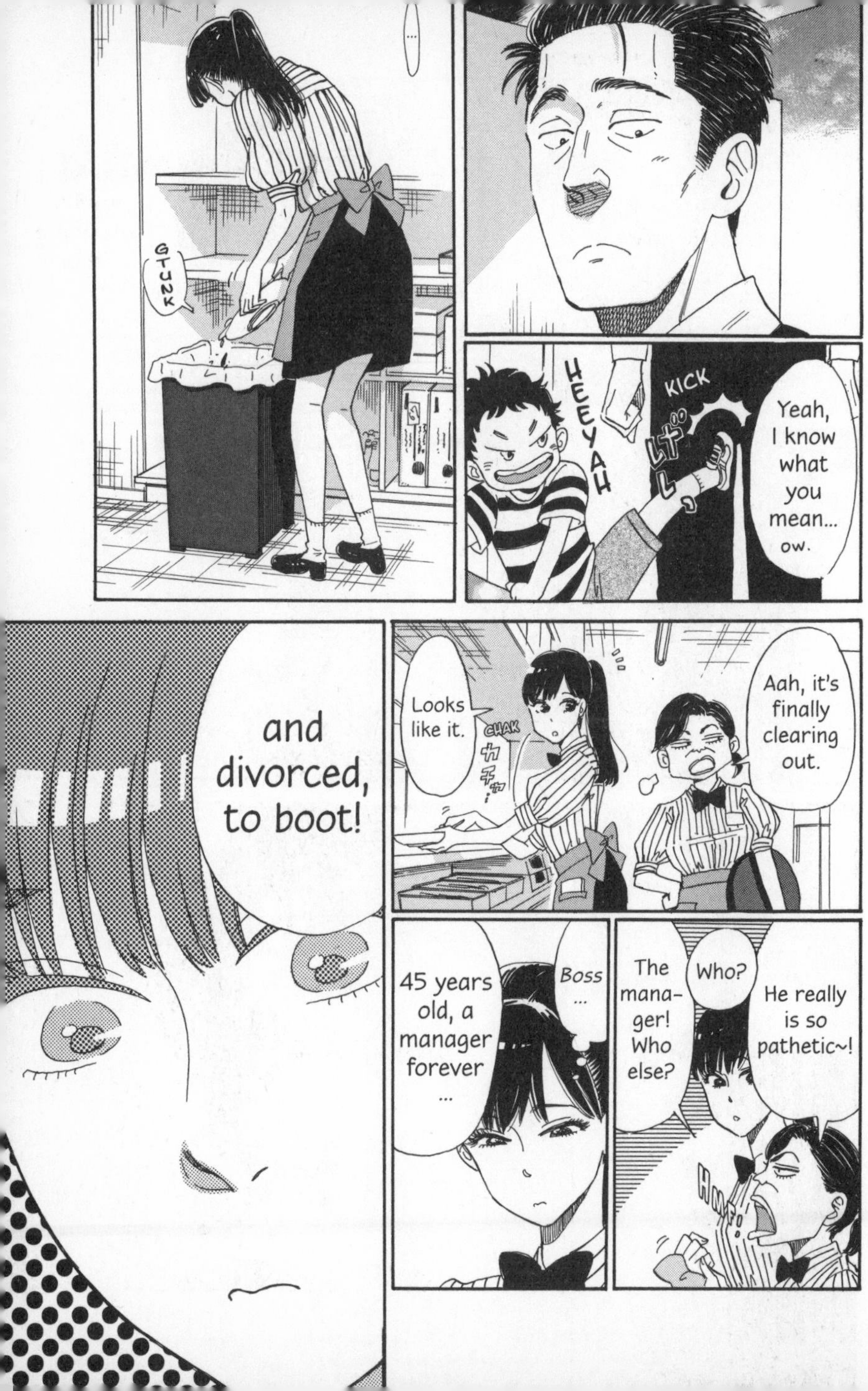
HEEYAH
KICK
Yeah, I know what you mean... ow.
...
GTUNK
Aah, it's finally clearing out.
Looks like it.
CHAK
Who?
He really is so pathetic~!
The mana-ger! Who else?
Boss ...
45 years old, a manager forever ...
and divorced, to boot!

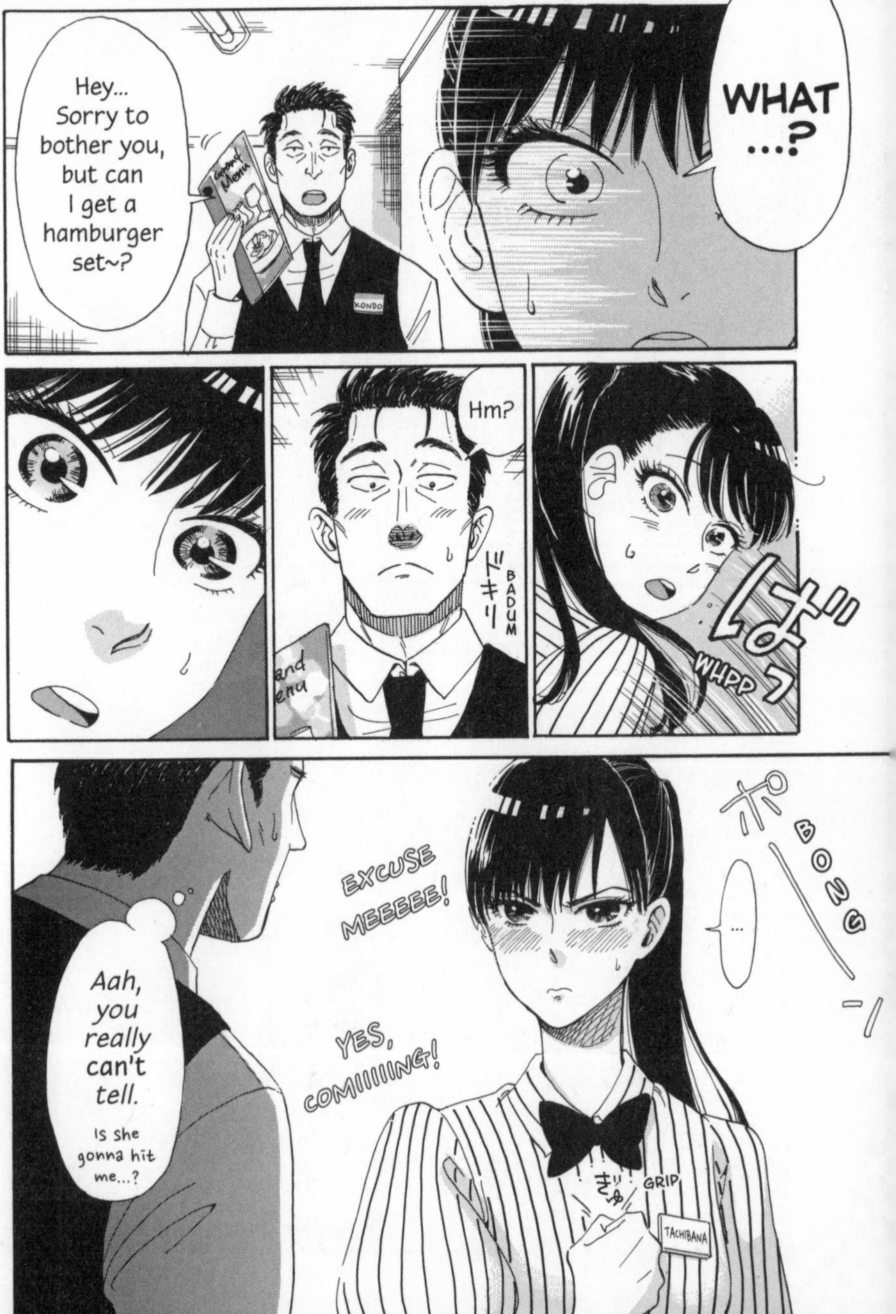
WHAT ...?
Hey... Sorry to bother you, but can I get a hamburger set~?
KONDO
ぱっ
WHPP
Hm?
ドキリ
BADUM
ポーン
BONG
...
EXCUSE MEEEEEE!
YES, COMIIIIING!
ぎゅ
GRIP
TACHIBANA
Aah, you really can't tell.
Is she gonna hit me...?

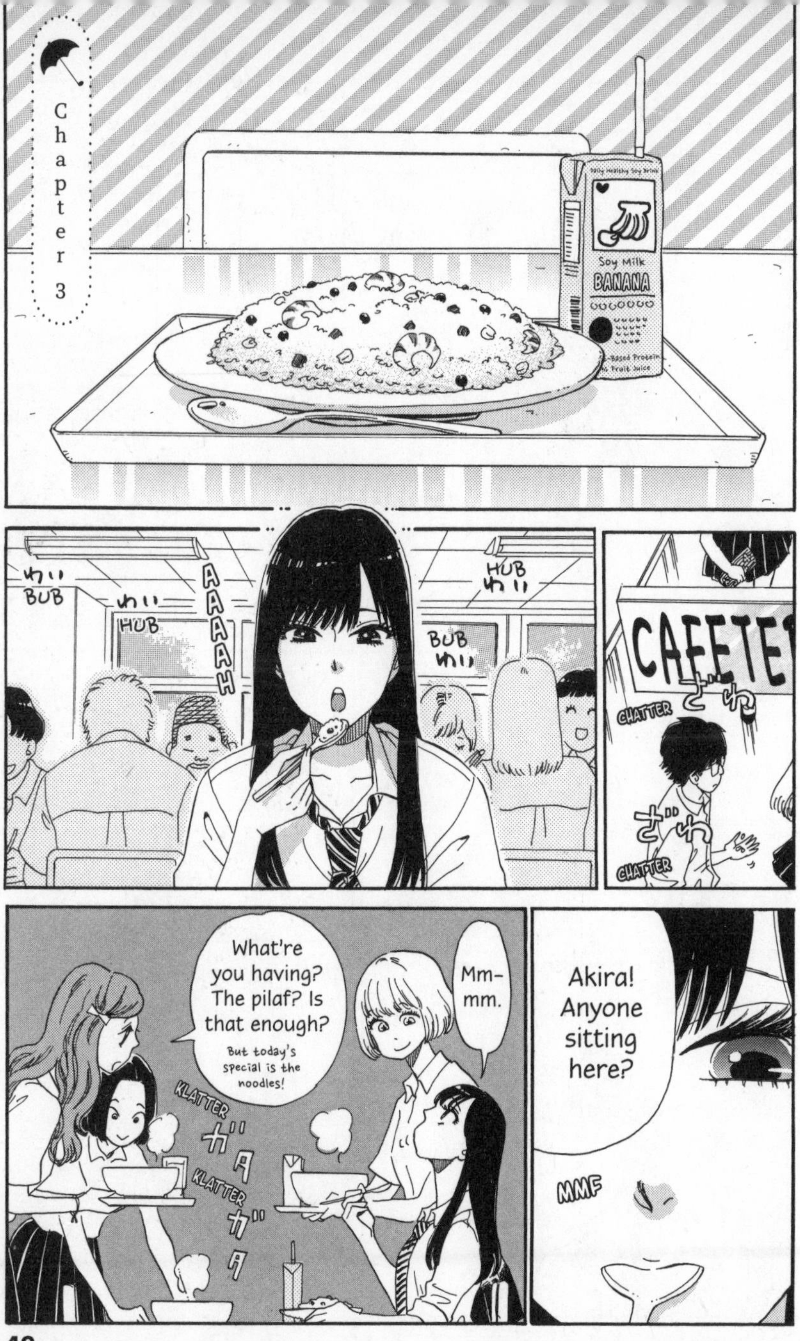
Chapter 3
Daily Healthy Soy Drink
Soy Milk
BANANA
CAFETE
CHATTER
CHATTER
AAAAAH
HUB
BUB
HUB
BUB
Akira! Anyone sitting here?
MMF
Mm-mm.
What're you having? The pilaf? Is that enough?
But today's special is the noodles!
KLATTER
KLATTER

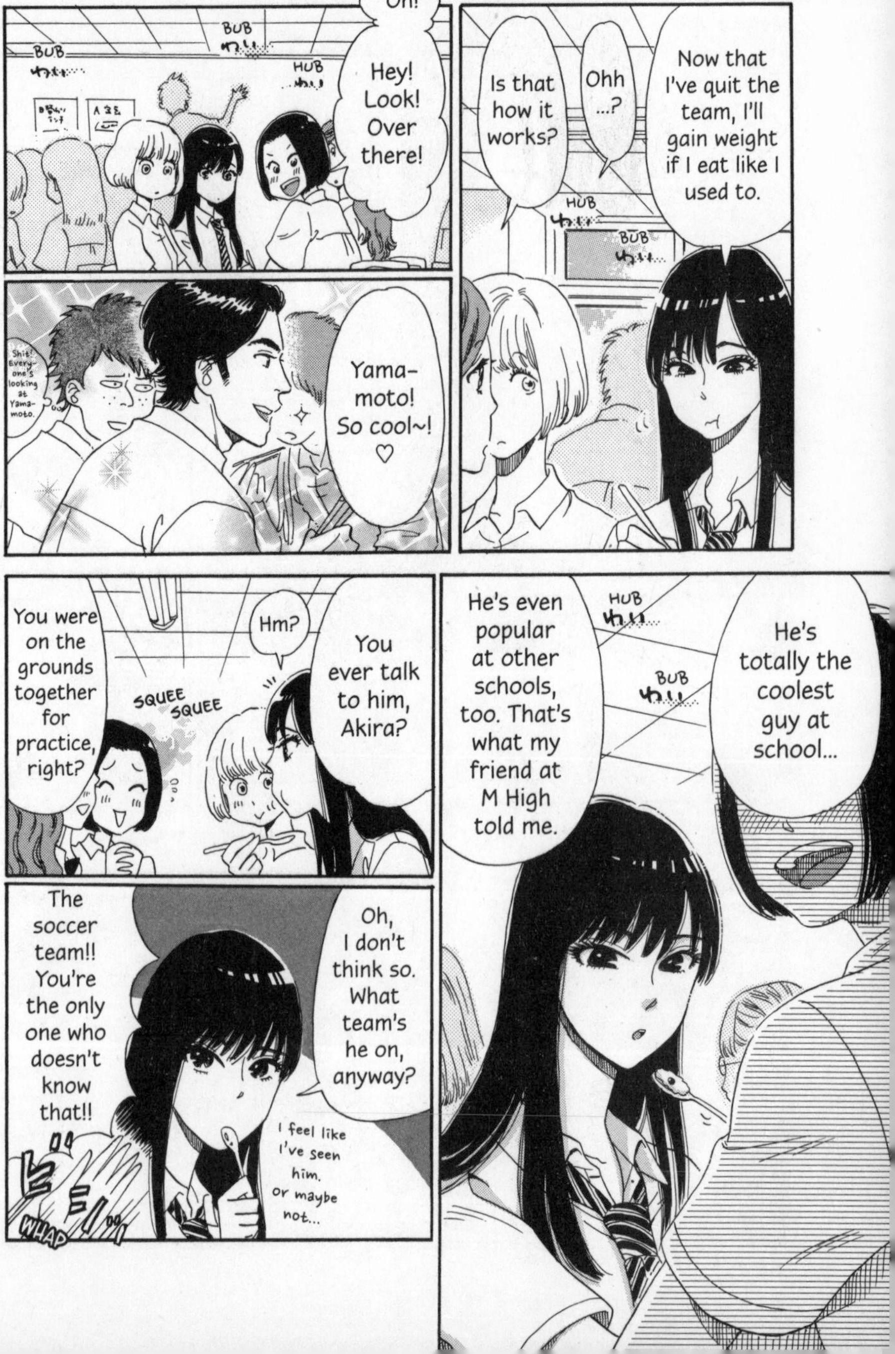
Now that I've quit the team, I'll gain weight if I eat like I used to.
Ohh ...?
Is that how it works?
HUB
BUB
Oh!
Hey! Look! Over there!
BUB
BUB
HUB
Yama-moto! So cool~! ♡
Shit! Every-one's looking at Yama-moto.
He's totally the coolest guy at school...
He's even popular at other schools, too. That's what my friend at M High told me.
HUB
BUB
You ever talk to him, Akira?
Hm?
You were on the grounds together for practice, right?
SQUEE SQUEE
Oh, I don't think so. What team's he on, anyway?
The soccer team!! You're the only one who doesn't know that!!
I feel like I've seen him. Or maybe not...
WHAP

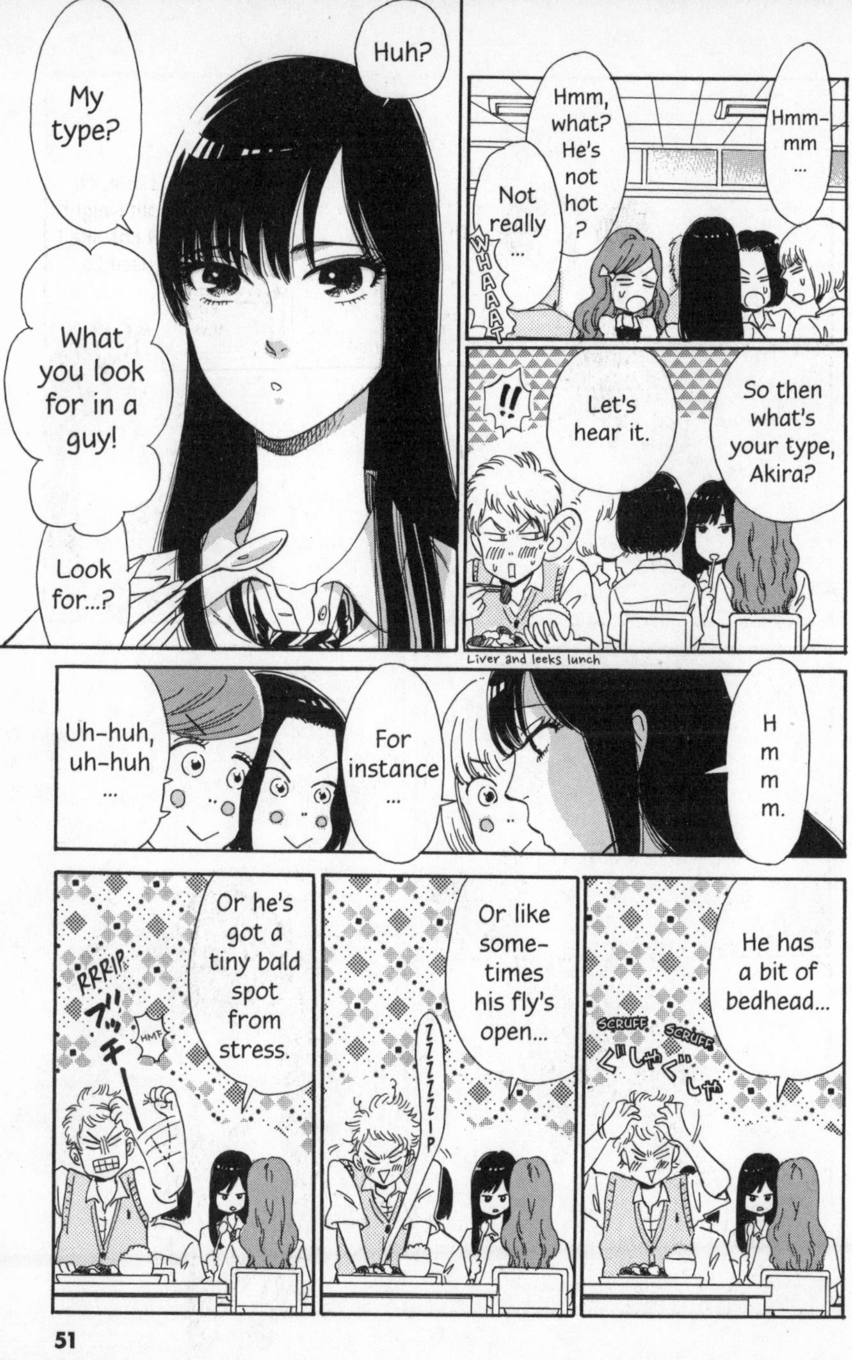
Hmmm-mm ...
Hmm, what? He's not hot?
Not really ...
WHAAAAT
So then what's your type, Akira?
Let's hear it.
!!
Liver and leeks lunch
Huh?
My type?
What you look for in a guy!
Look for...?
Hmmm.
For instance ...
Uh-huh, uh-huh ...
He has a bit of bedhead...
SCRUFF SCRUFF
ぐしゃぐしゃ
Or like sometimes his fly's open...
ZZZZZIP
Or he's got a tiny bald spot from stress.
RRRIP
ブッチー
HMF

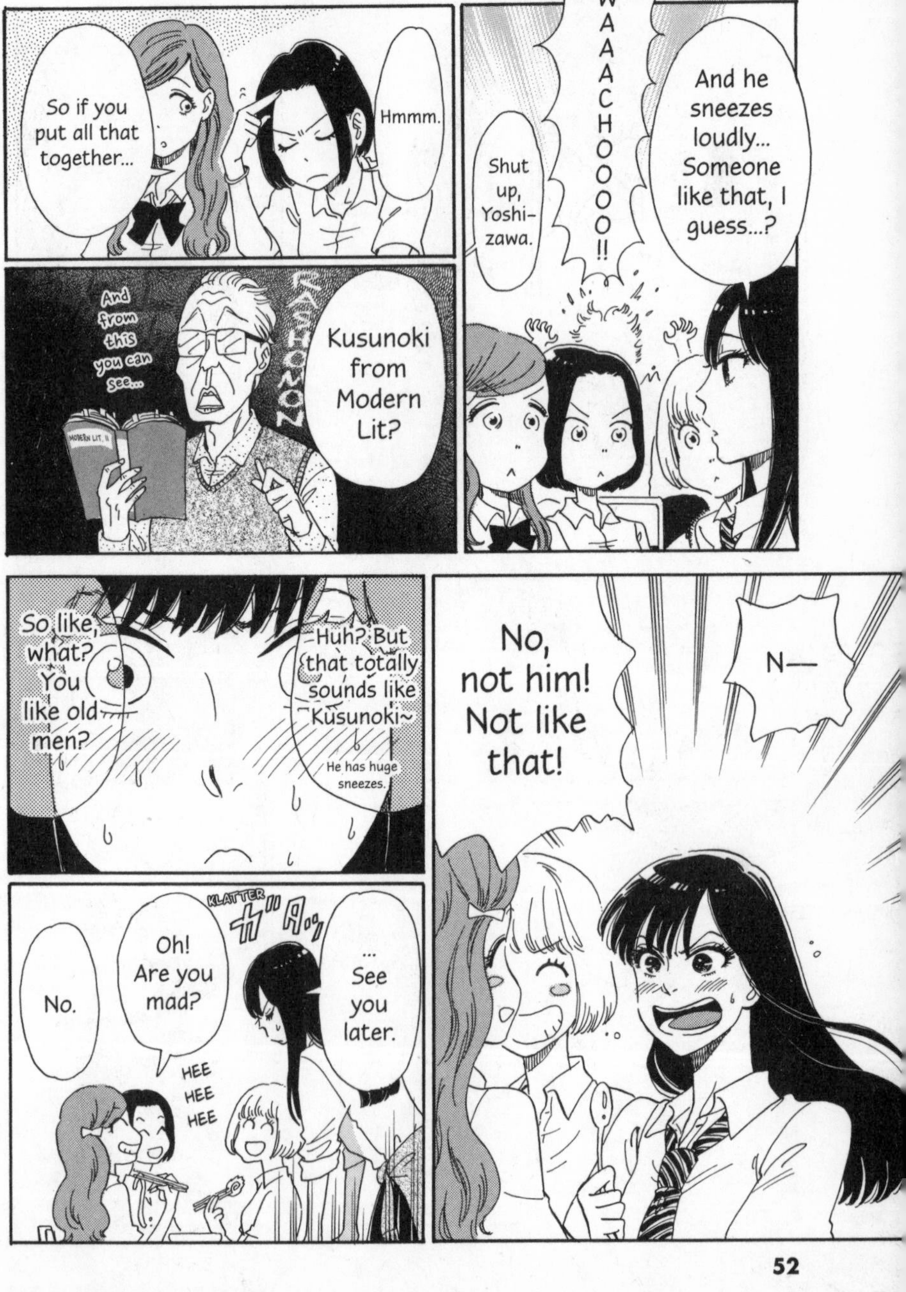

And he sneezes loudly... Someone like that, I guess...?
WAAACHOOOOO!!
Shut up, Yoshi-zawa.
Hmmm.
So if you put all that together...
Kusunoki from Modern Lit?
RASHOMON
And from this you can see...
MODERN LIT. II
N—
No, not him! Not like that!
Huh? But that totally sounds like Kusunoki~
He has huge sneezes.
So like, what? You like old men?
... See you later.
KLATTER
Oh! Are you mad?
HEE HEE HEE
No.

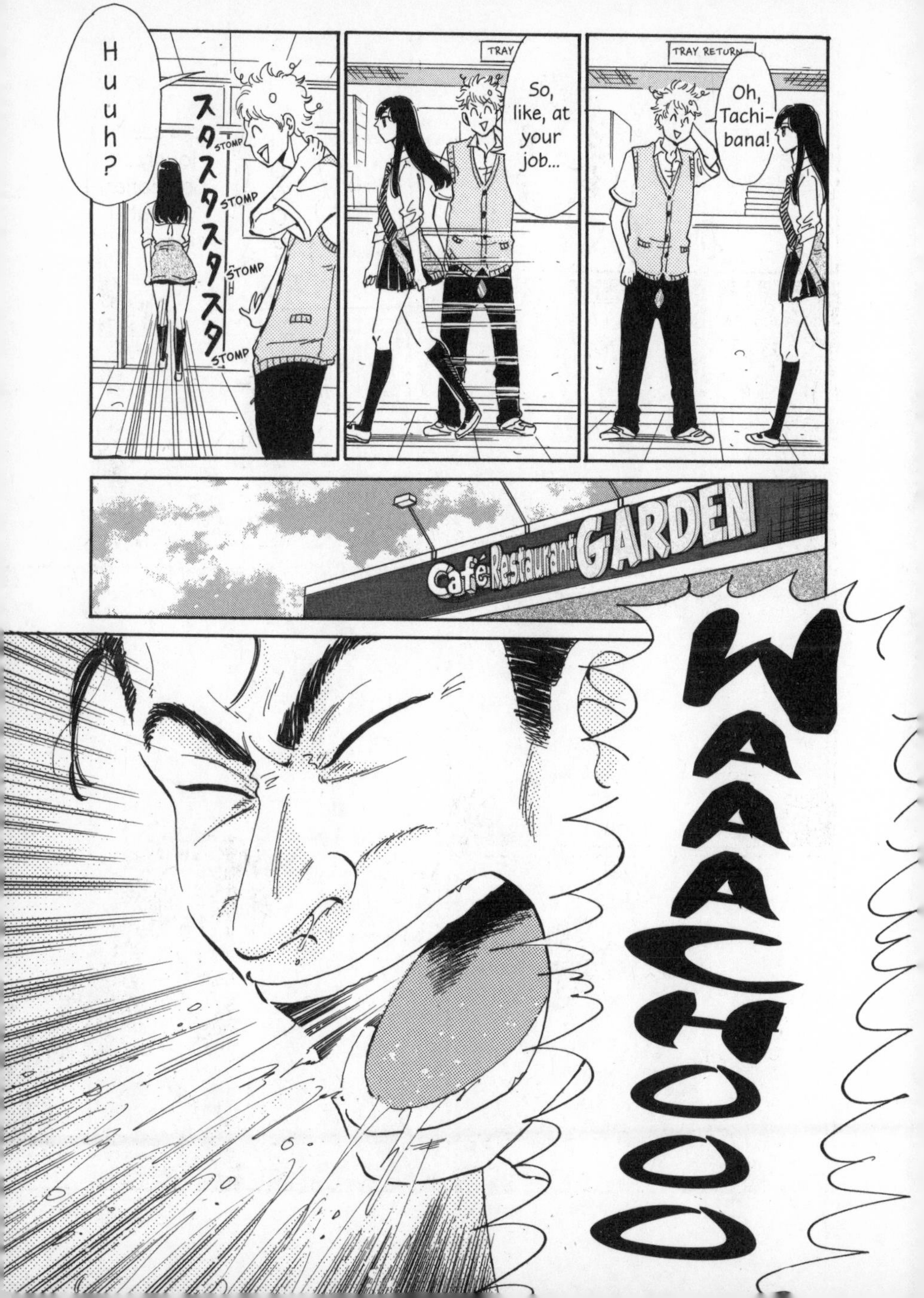
TRAY RETURN
Oh, Tachibana!
TRAY
So, like, at your job...
Huuh?
スタスタスタスタ
STOMP
STOMP
STOMP
STOMP
Café Restaurant GARDEN
WAAACHOOO

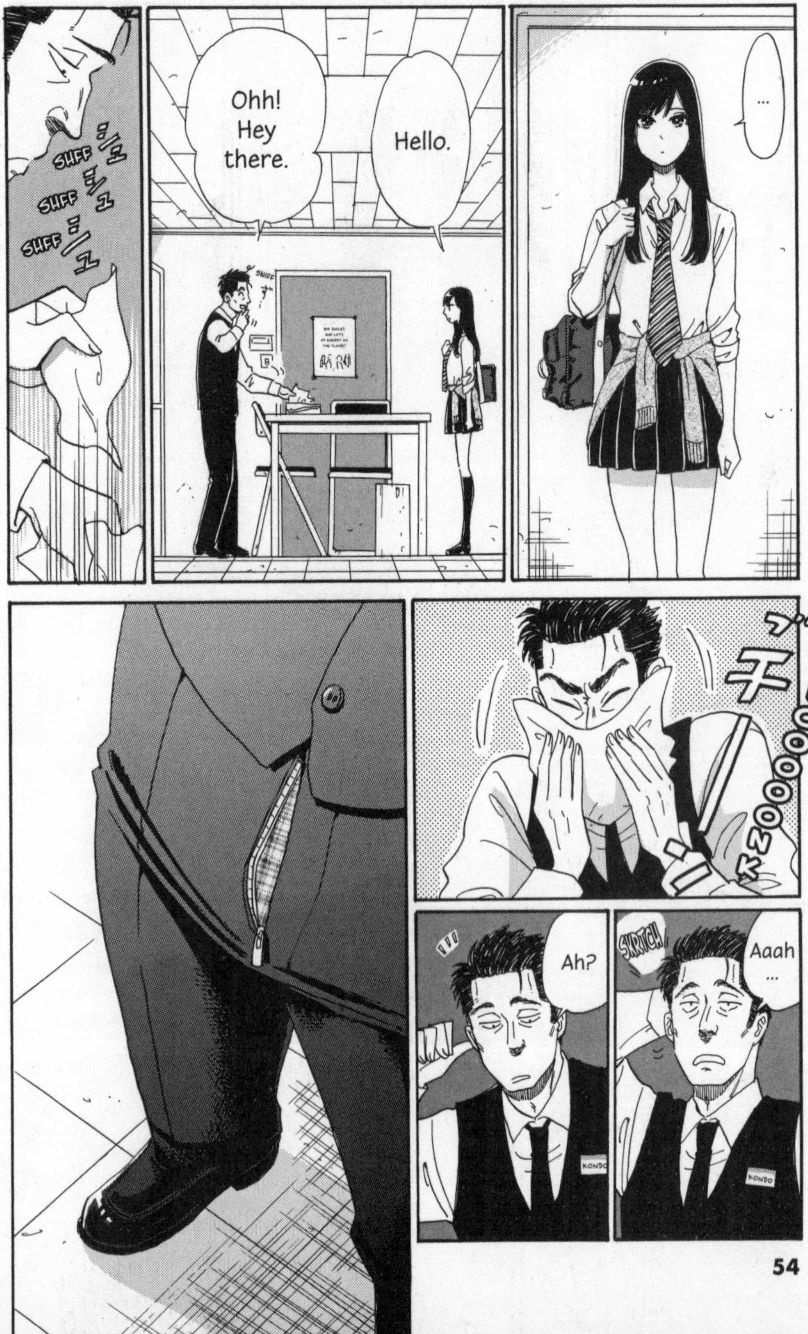
...
Hello.
Ohh! Hey there.
SNIFF
SHFF
SHFF
SHFF
HOOOOONK
SWITCH
Aaah ...
Ah?

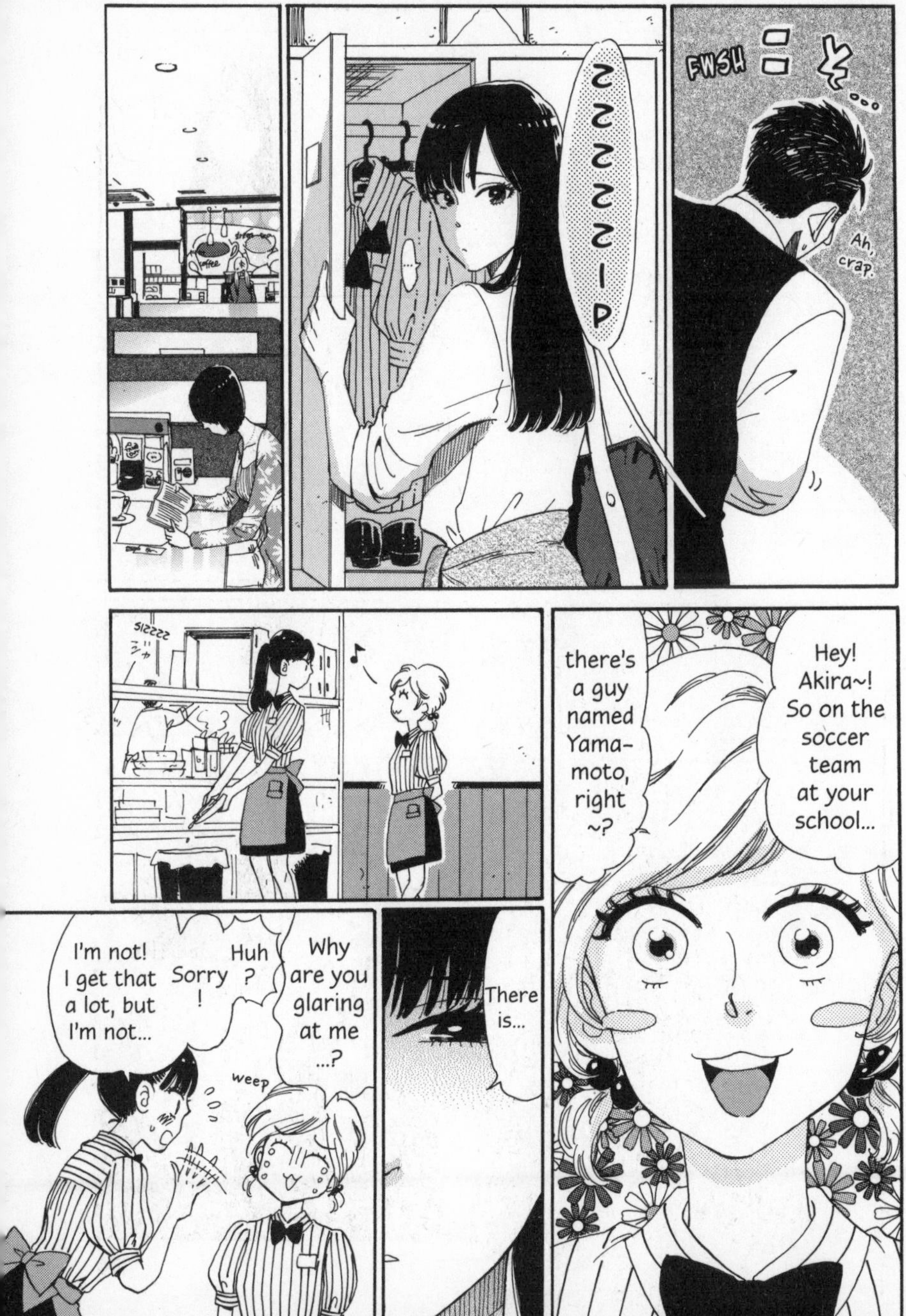
FWSH
Ah, crap.
ZZZZZIP
...
Hey! Akira~! So on the soccer team at your school...
there's a guy named Yama-moto, right ~?
SIZZZZ
There is...
Why are you glaring at me ...?
Huh ?
Sorry !
I'm not! I get that a lot, but I'm not...
weep

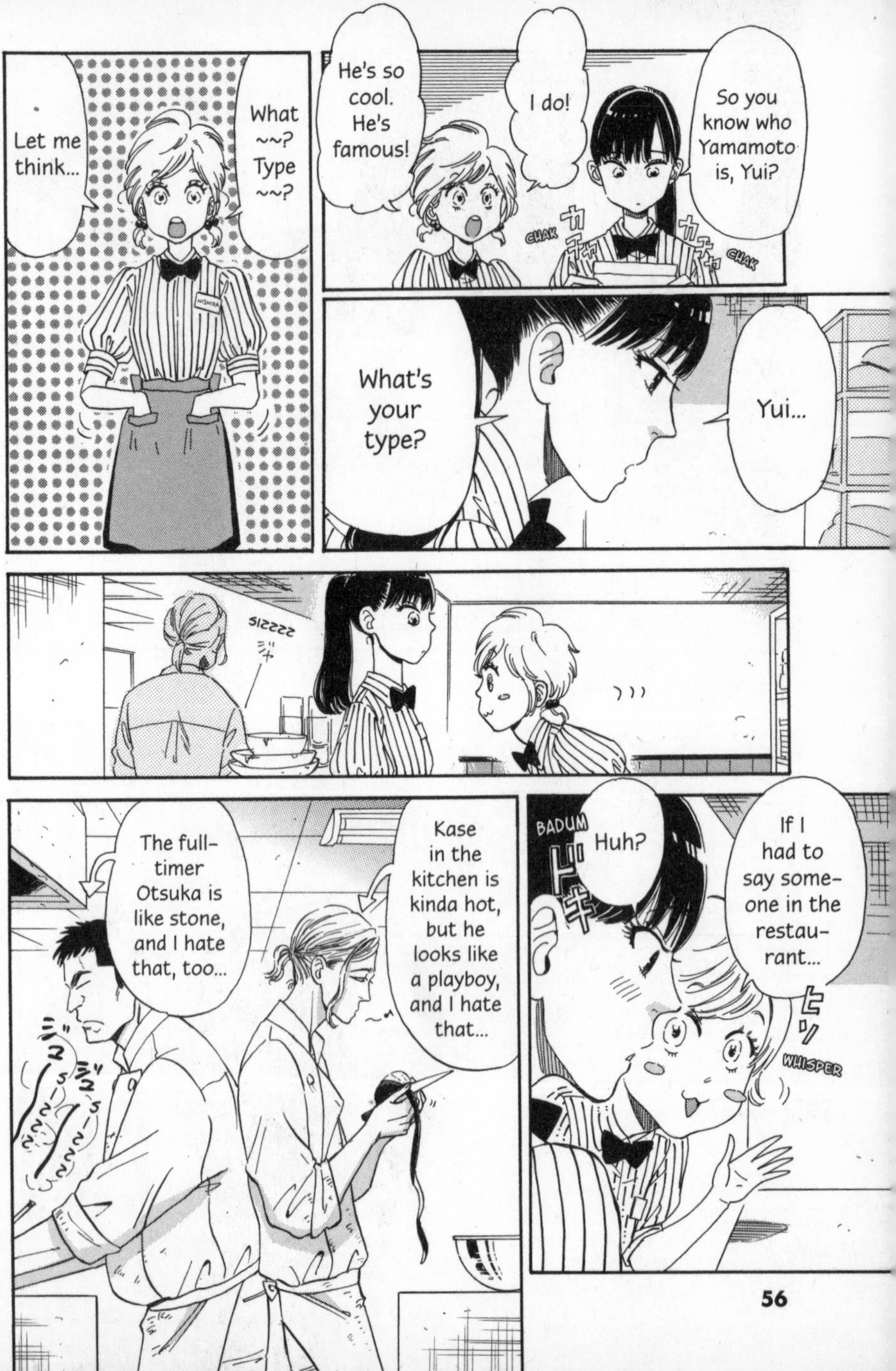
So you know who Yamamoto is, Yui?
CHAK
CHAK
I do!
He's so cool. He's famous!
Yui...
What's your type?
What ~~? Type ~~?
Let me think...
SIZZZZ
If I had to say some-one in the restau-rant...
WHISPER
Huh?
BADUM
Kase in the kitchen is kinda hot, but he looks like a playboy, and I hate that...
The full-timer Otsuka is like stone, and I hate that, too...

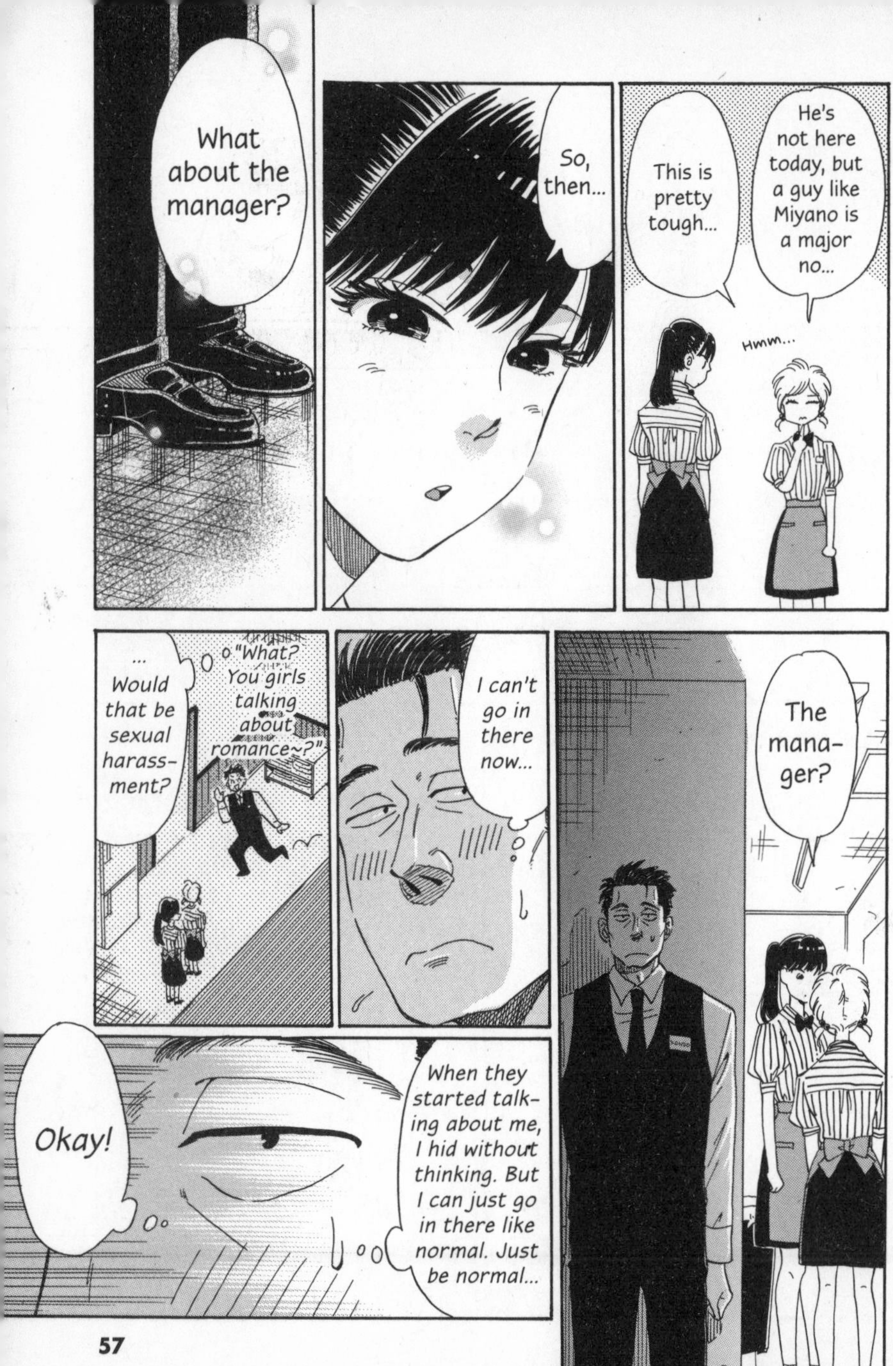

He's not here today, but a guy like Miyano is a major no...
This is pretty tough...
Hmm...
So, then...
What about the manager?
The manager?
I can't go in there now...
"What? You girls talking about romance~?"
... Would that be sexual harassment?
When they started talking about me, I hid without thinking. But I can just go in there like normal. Just be normal...
Okay!

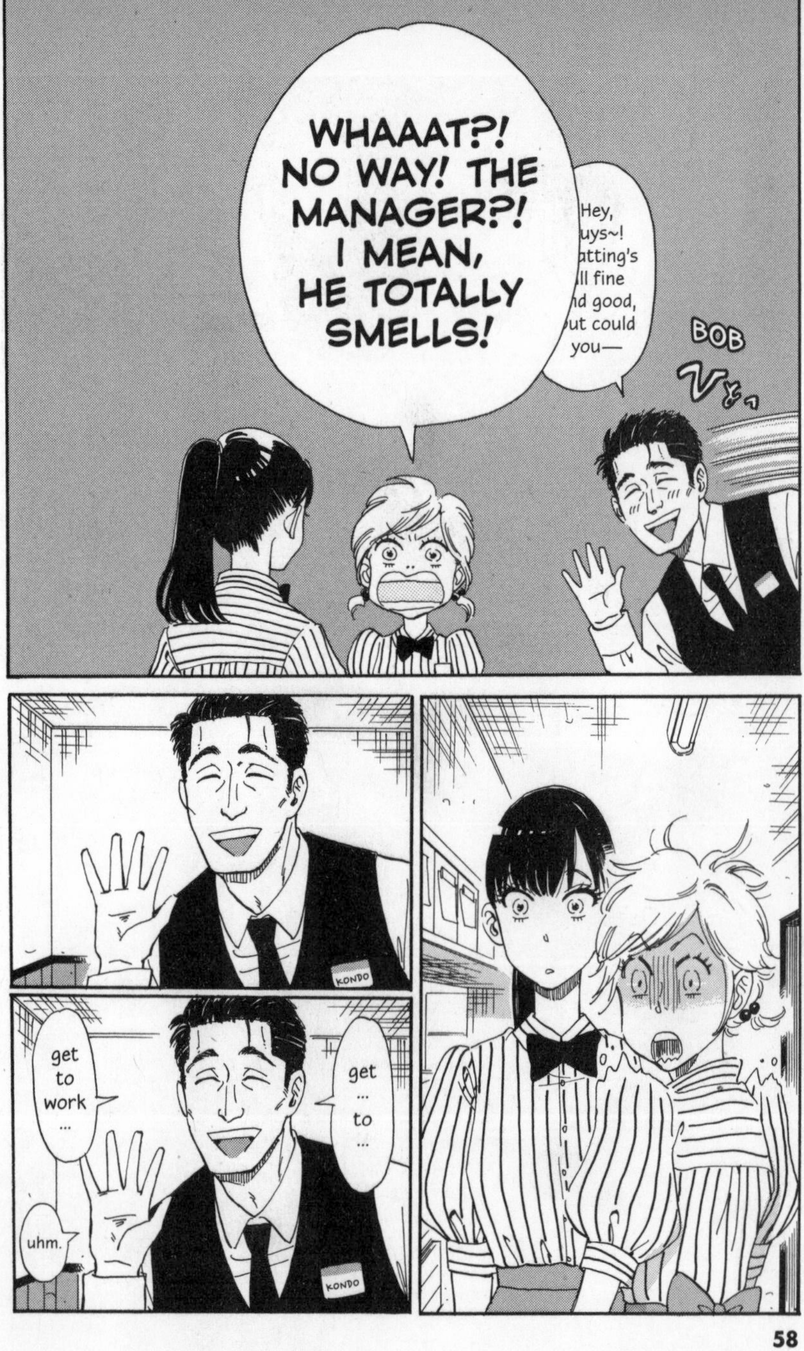
BOB
Hey, uys~! atting's ll fine nd good, ut could you—
WHAAAT?! NO WAY! THE MANAGER?! I MEAN, HE TOTALLY SMELLS!
KONDO
get ... to ...
get to work ...
uhm.
KONDO

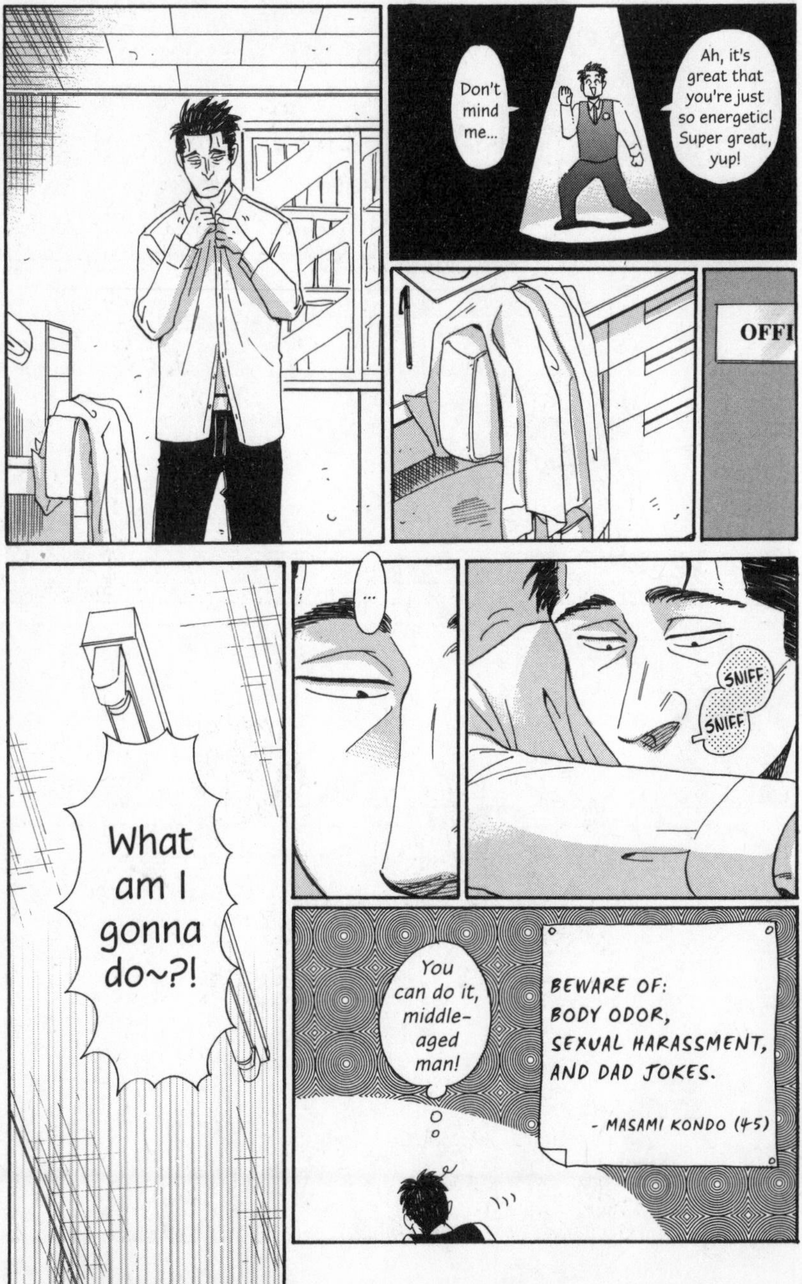
Ah, it's great that you're just so energetic! Super great, yup!
Don't mind me...
OFFI
SNIFF
SNIFF
...
BEWARE OF: BODY ODOR, SEXUAL HARASSMENT, AND DAD JOKES.
- MASAMI KONDO (45)
You can do it, middle-aged man!
What am I gonna do~?!

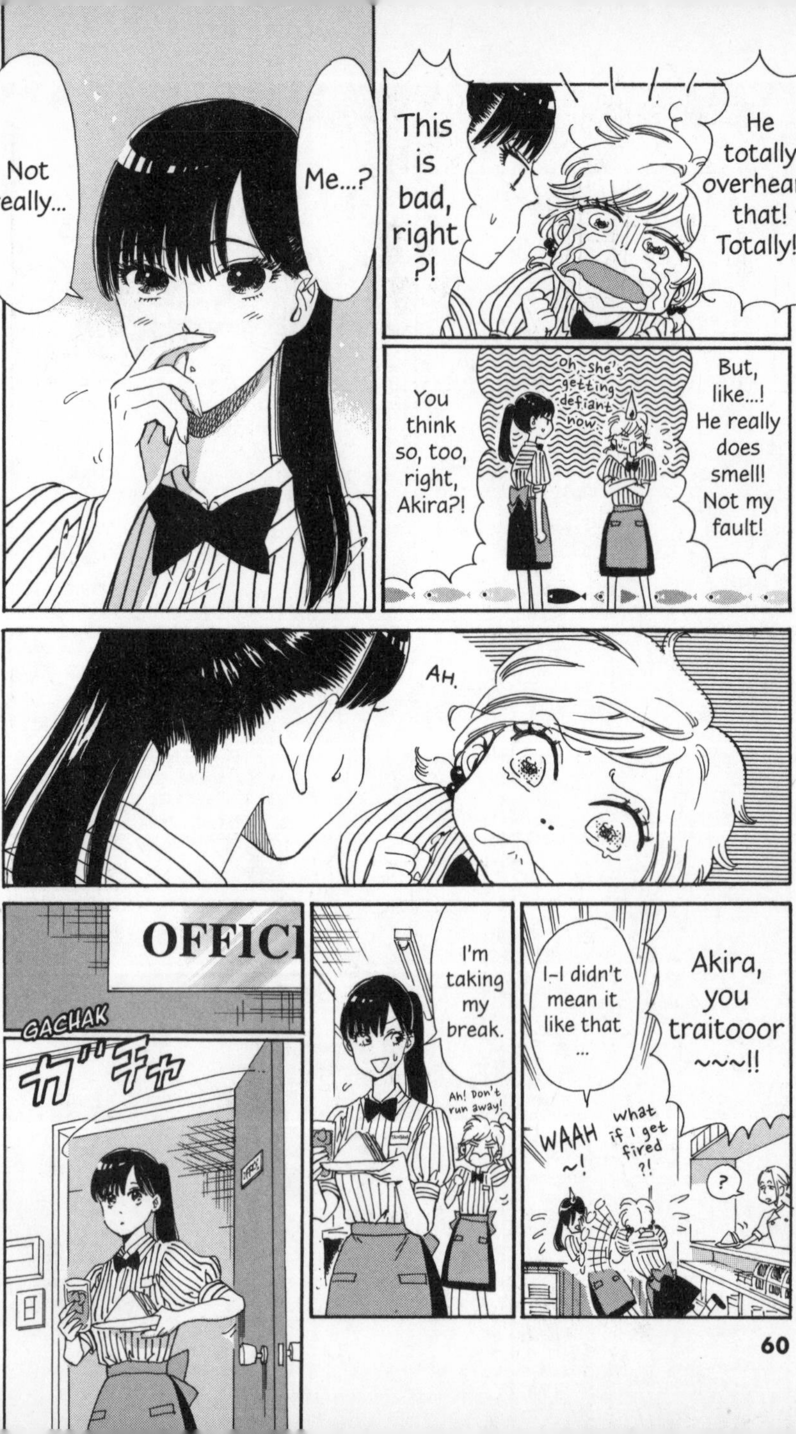
He totally overheard that! Totally!!
This is bad, right?!
But, like...! He really does smell! Not my fault!
Oh, She's getting defiant now
You think so, too, right, Akira?!
Me...?
Not really...
AH.
Akira, you traitooor ~~~!!
I-I didn't mean it like that ...
WAAH ~!
What if I get fired ?!
?
I'm taking my break.
Ah! Don't run away!
OFFIC
GACHAK
ガチャ

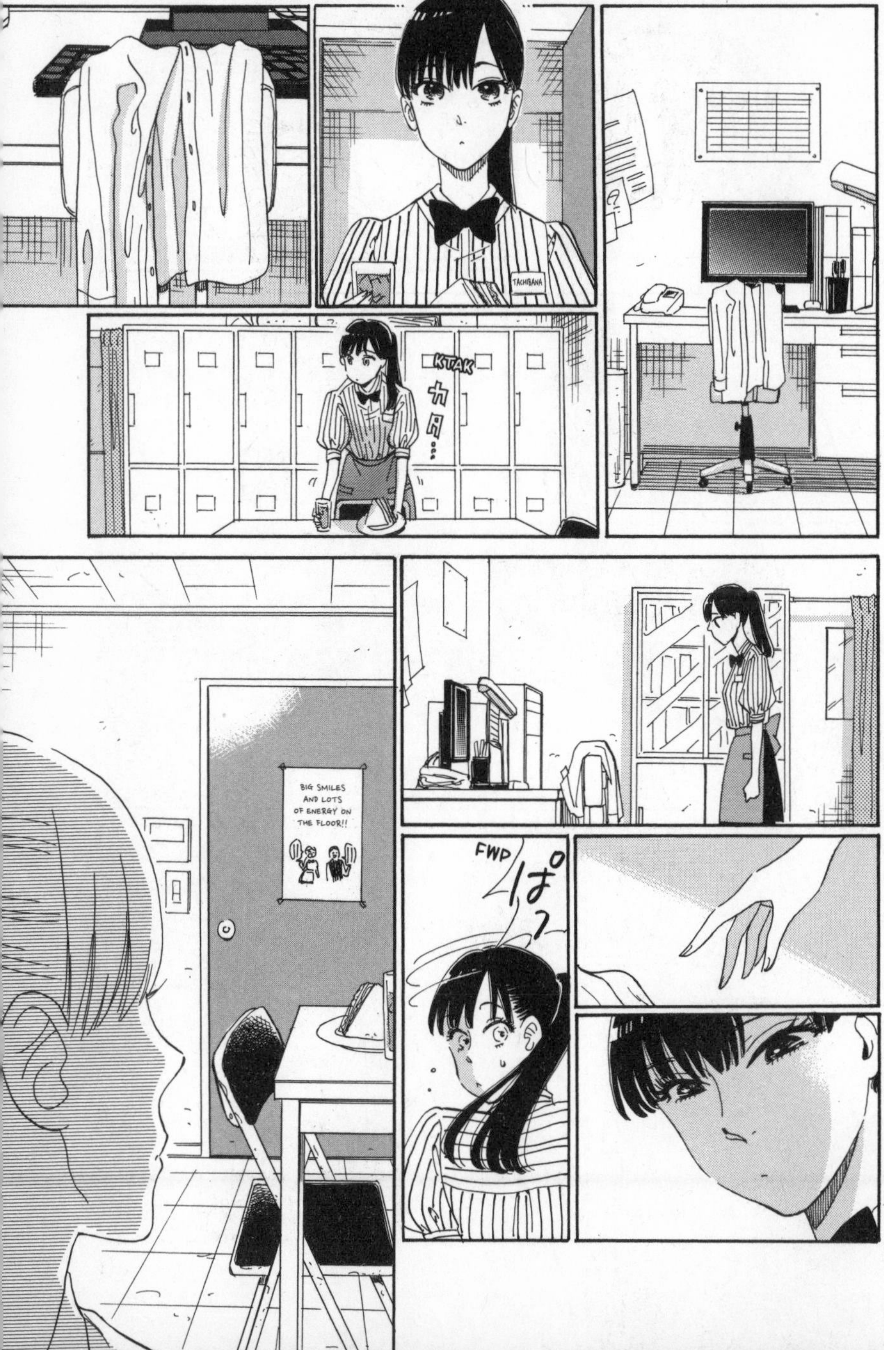
TACHIBANA
KTAK
カタ...
FWP
ぱっ
BIG SMILES AND LOTS OF ENERGY ON THE FLOOR!!

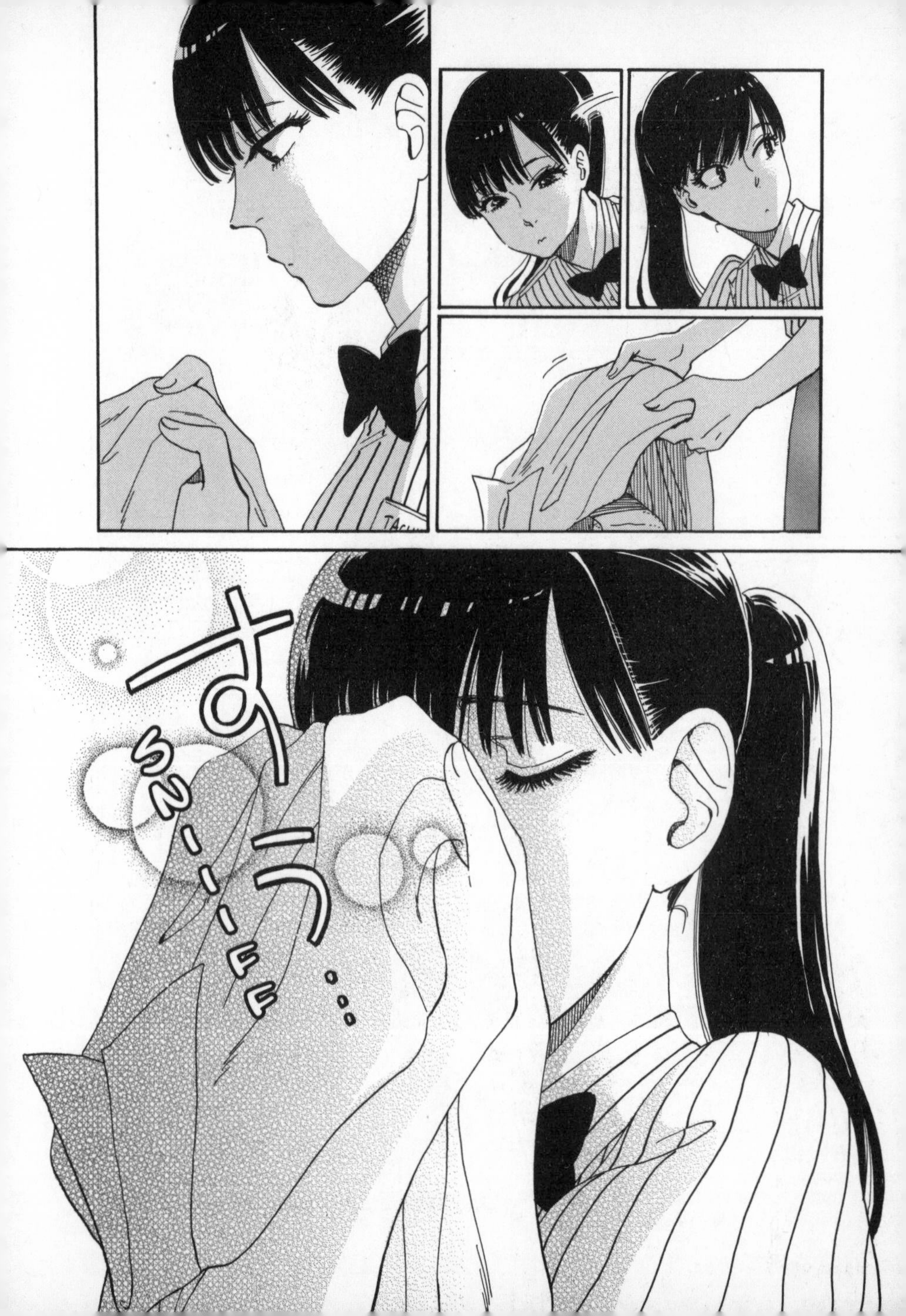
すう…
SNIIIFF

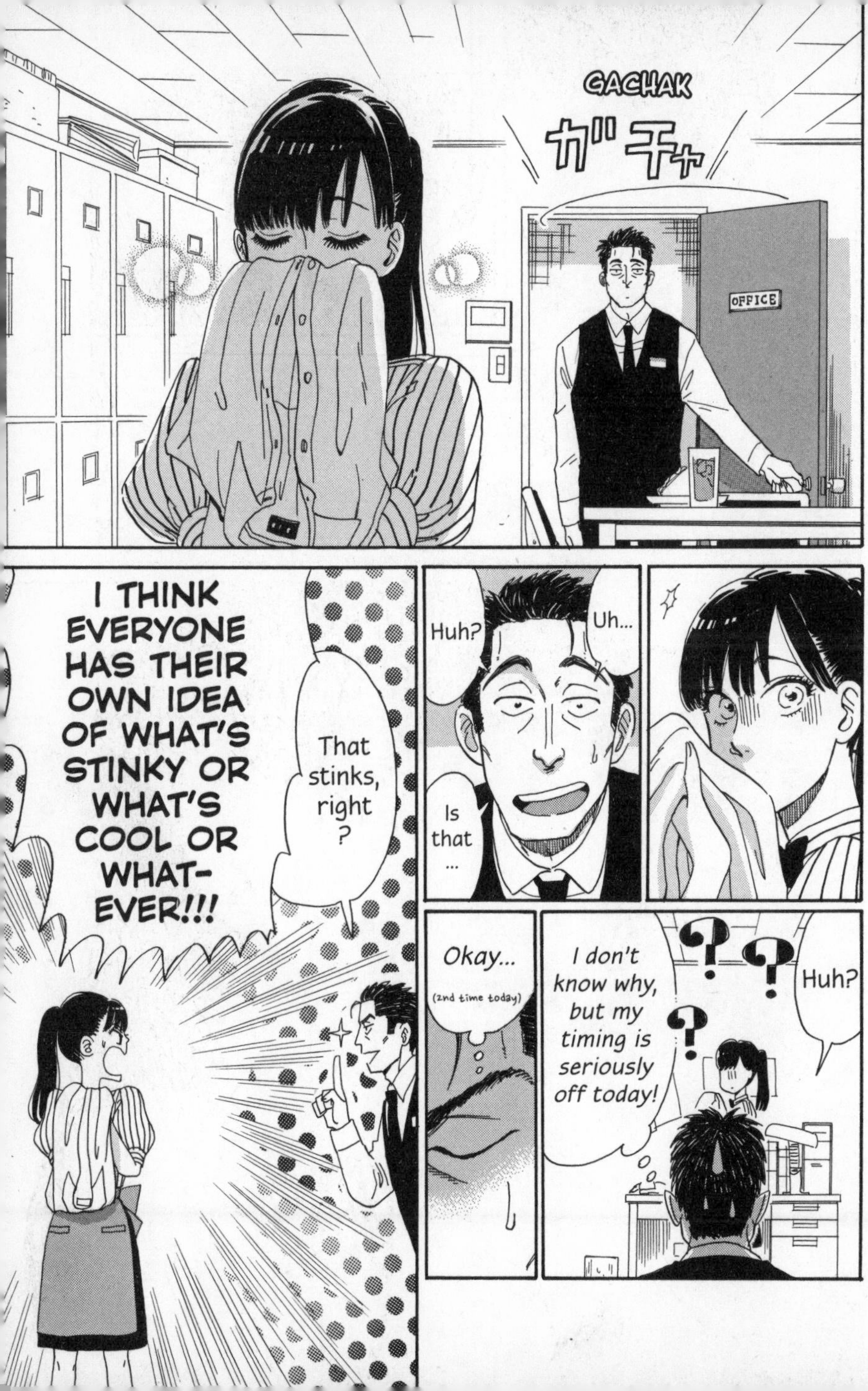
GACHAK
ガチャ
Uh...
Huh?
Is that ...
That stinks, right ?
I THINK EVERYONE HAS THEIR OWN IDEA OF WHAT'S STINKY OR WHAT'S COOL OR WHAT-EVER!!!
Huh?
I don't know why, but my timing is seriously off today!
Okay...
(2nd time today)

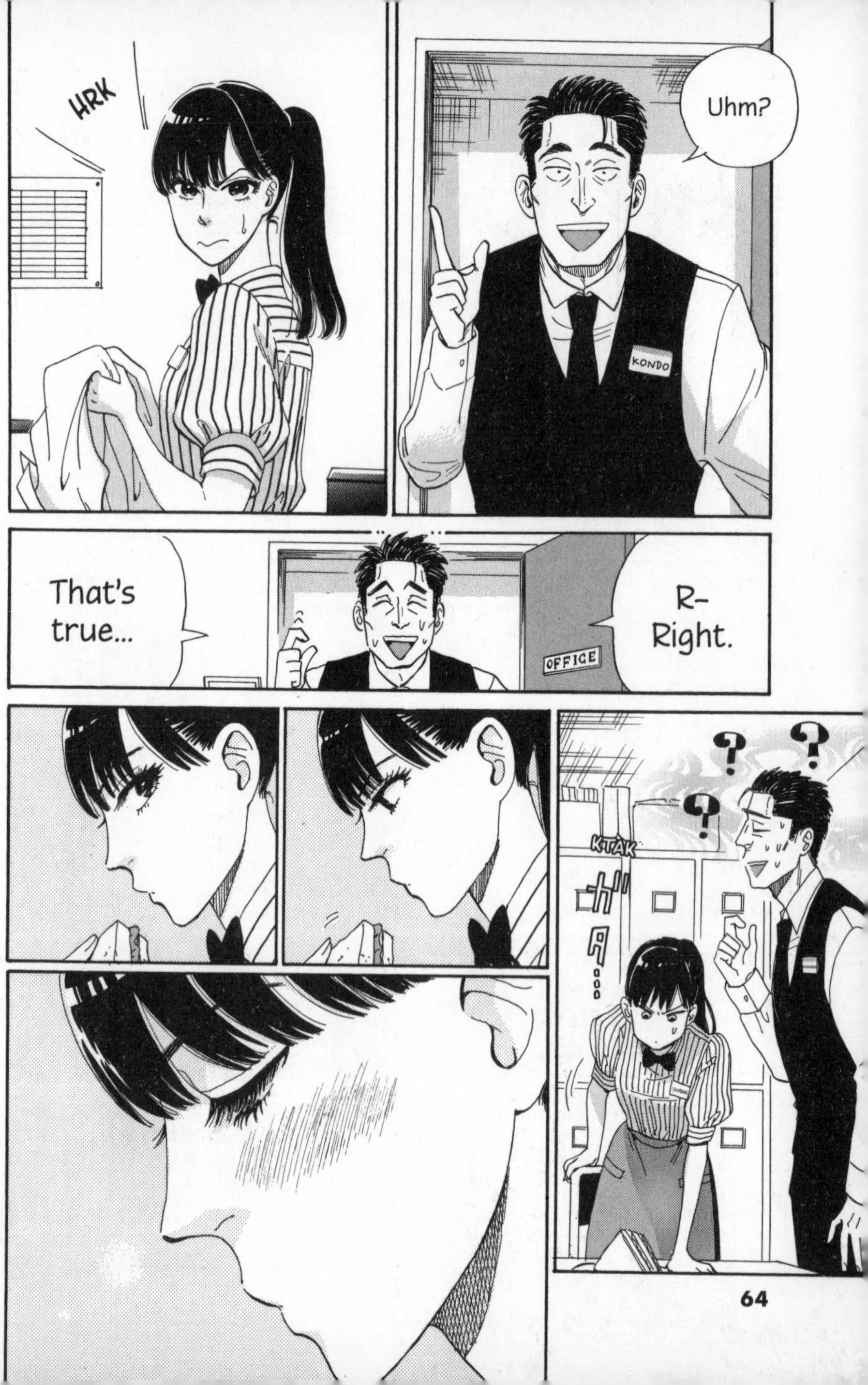

Uhm?
HRK
R-
Right.
That's true...
KTAK

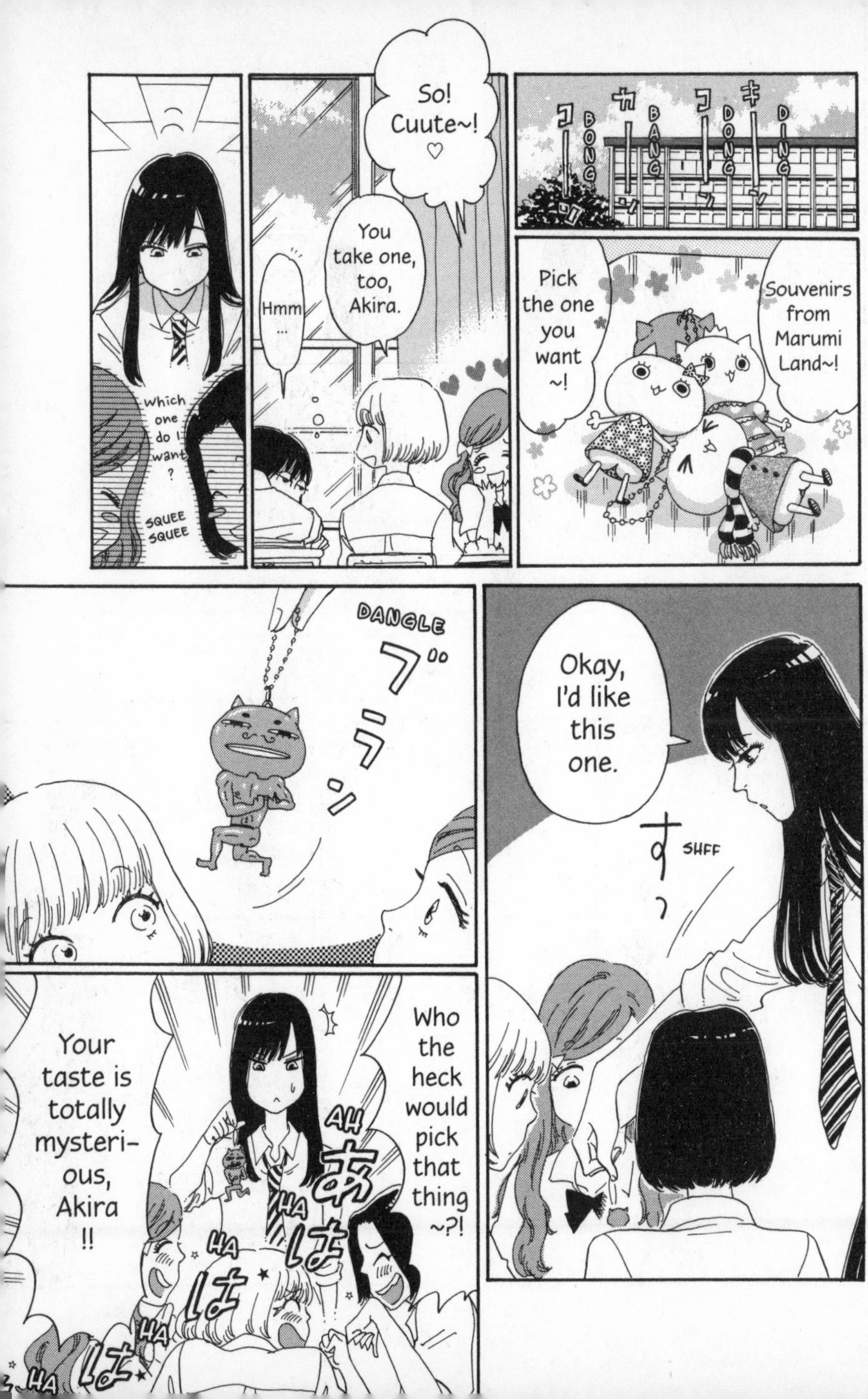
DING
DONG
BANG
BONG
Souvenirs from Marumi Land~!
Pick the one you want ~!
So! Cuute~! ♡
You take one, too, Akira.
Hmm...
Which one do I want?
SQUEE SQUEE
Okay, I'd like this one.
SHFF
DANGLE
Who the heck would pick that thing~?!
Your taste is totally mysteri-ous, Akira!!
AH
HA
HA
HA
HA

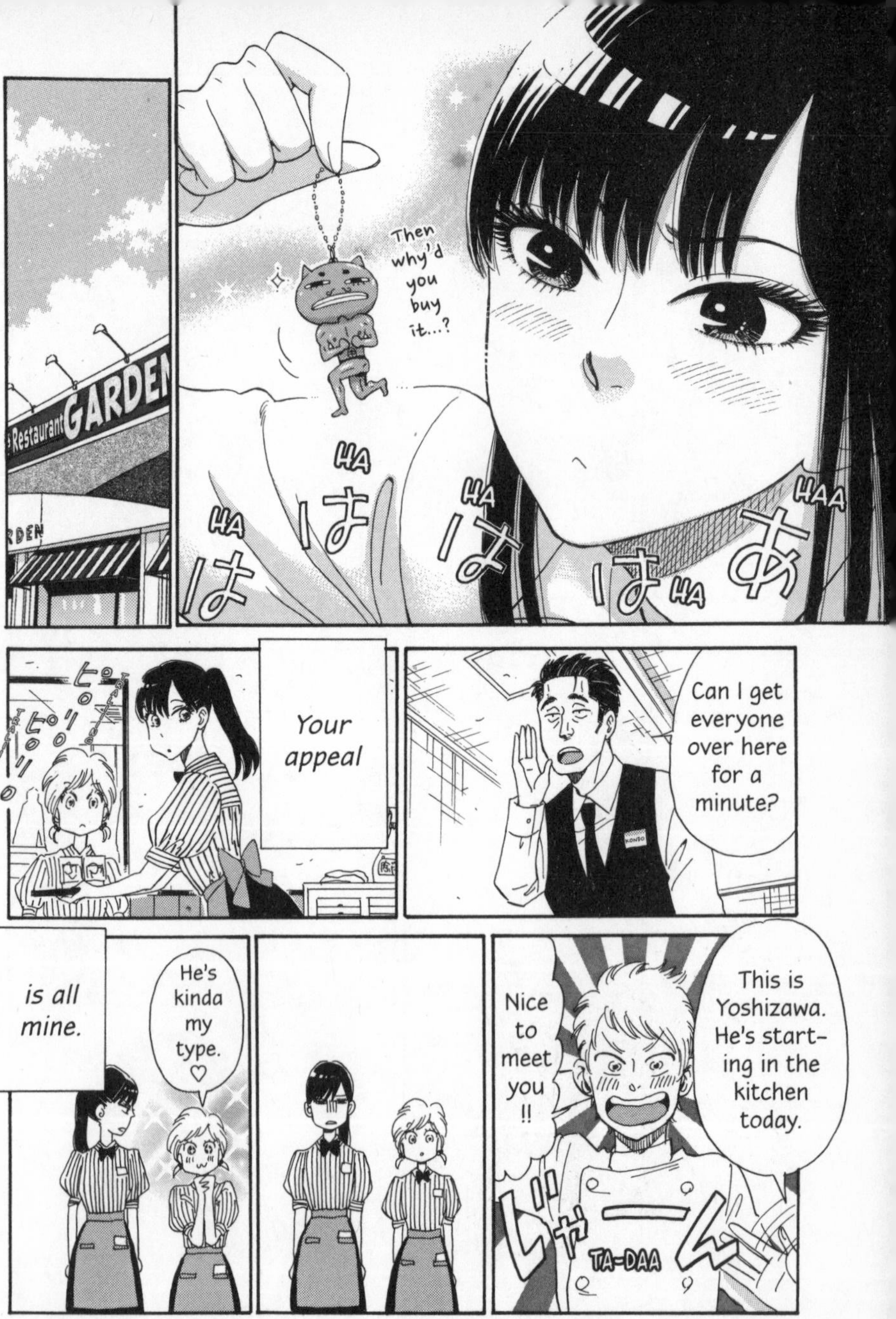
Then why'd you buy it...?
HAA
あ
HA
は
HA
は
HA
は
HA
は
Restaurant GARDEN
RDEN
Can I get everyone over here for a minute?
Your appeal
This is Yoshizawa. He's starting in the kitchen today.
Nice to meet you !!
じゃーん
TA-DAA
He's kinda my type. ♡
is all mine.

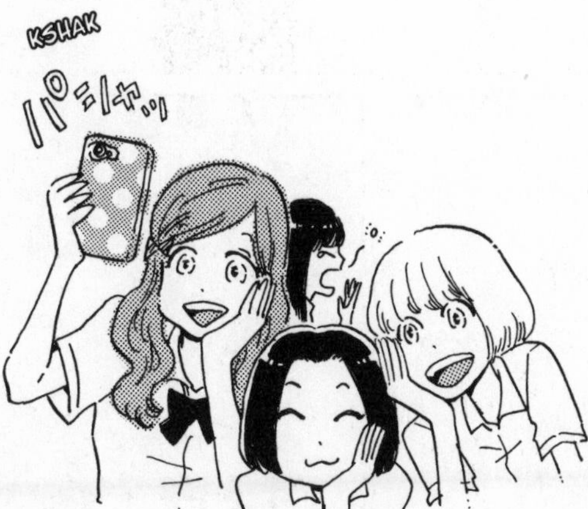
KSHAK
パシャッ

After
the ☂
Rain

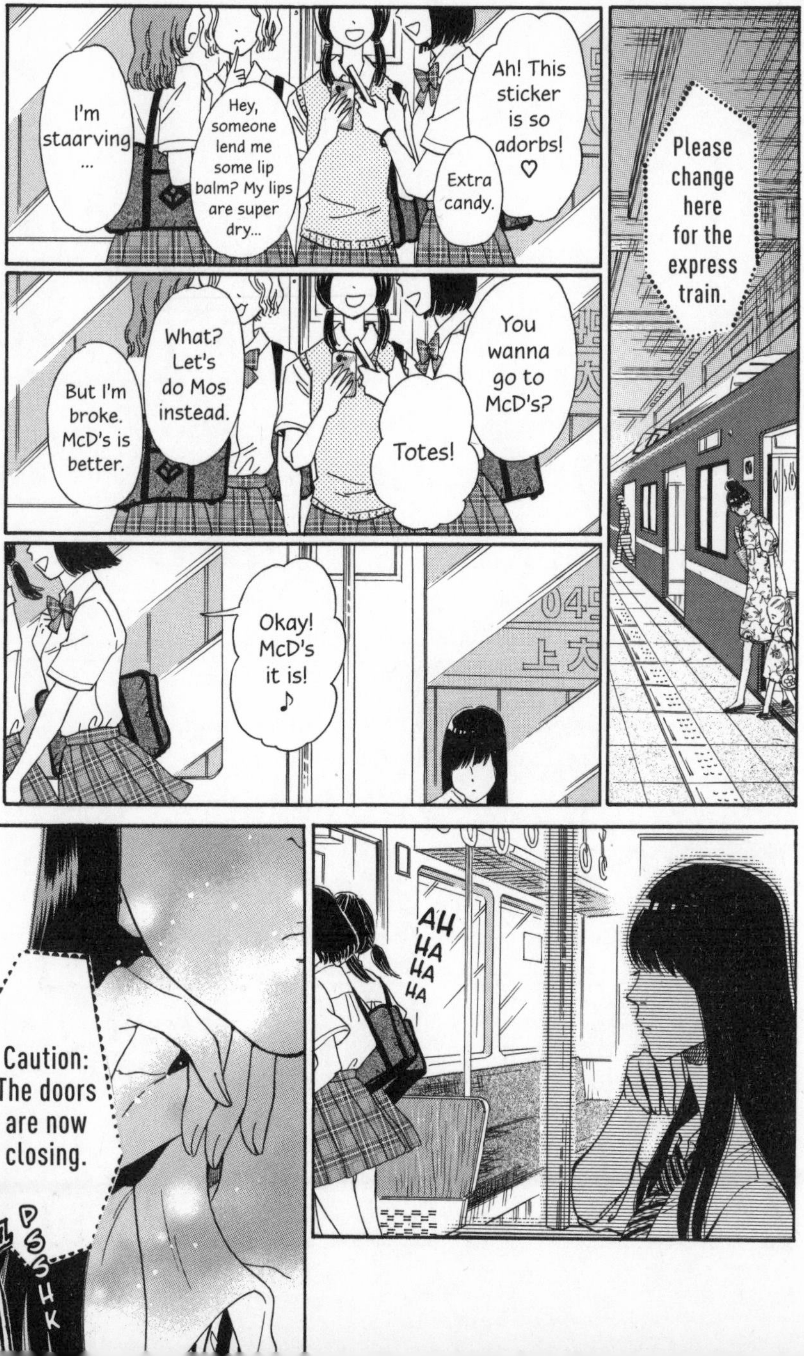
Please change here for the express train.
Ah! This sticker is so adorbs! ♡
Extra candy.
Hey, someone lend me some lip balm? My lips are super dry...
I'm staarving ...
You wanna go to McD's?
Totes!
What? Let's do Mos instead.
But I'm broke. McD's is better.
Okay! McD's it is! ♪
AH HA HA HA HA
Caution: The doors are now closing.
PSSHK
プシュー

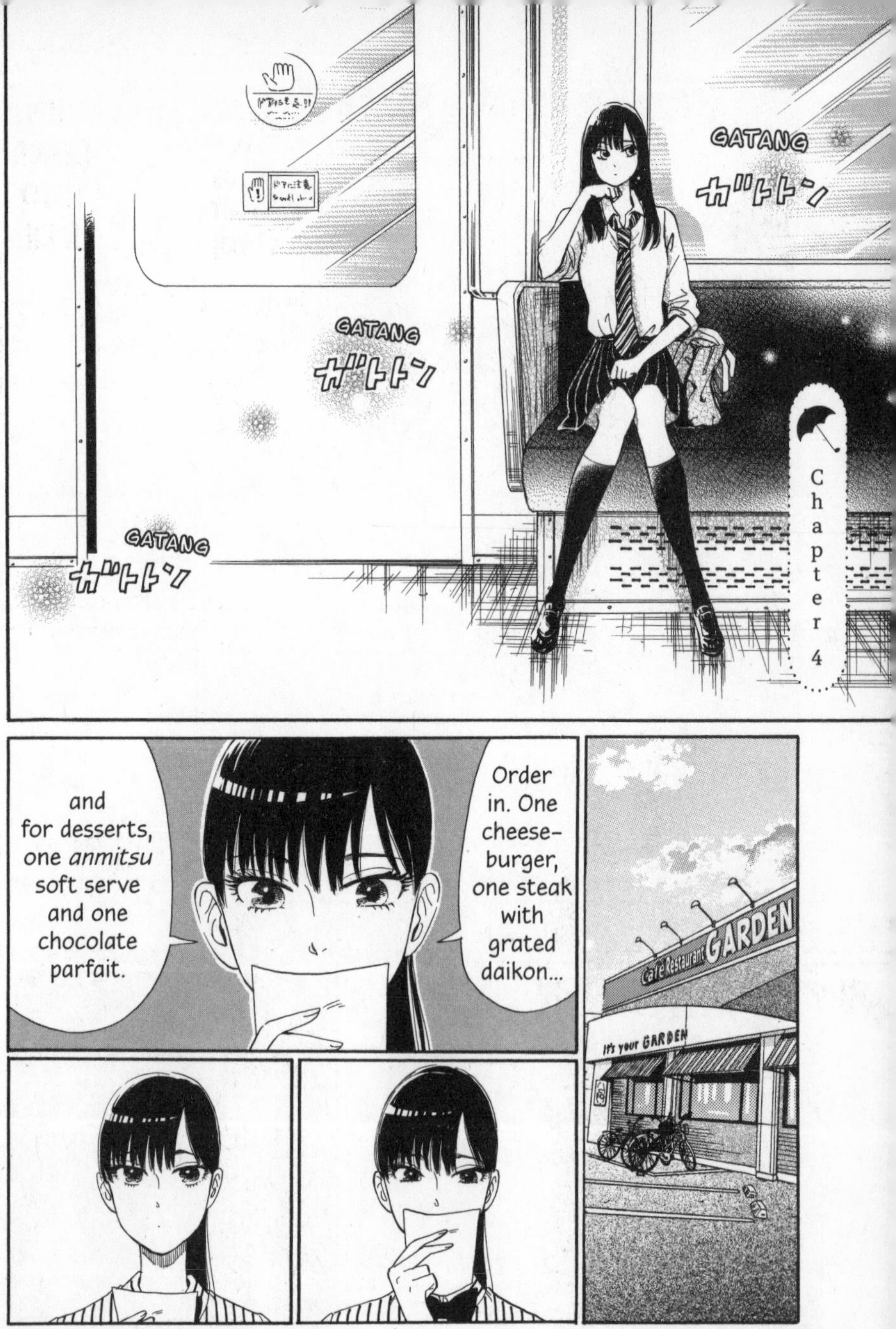
Chapter 4
GATANG
ガタトン
GATANG
ガタトン
GATANG
ガタトン
Café Restaurant GARDEN
It's your GARDEN
Order in. One cheese-burger, one steak with grated daikon...
and for desserts, one *anmitsu* soft serve and one chocolate parfait.

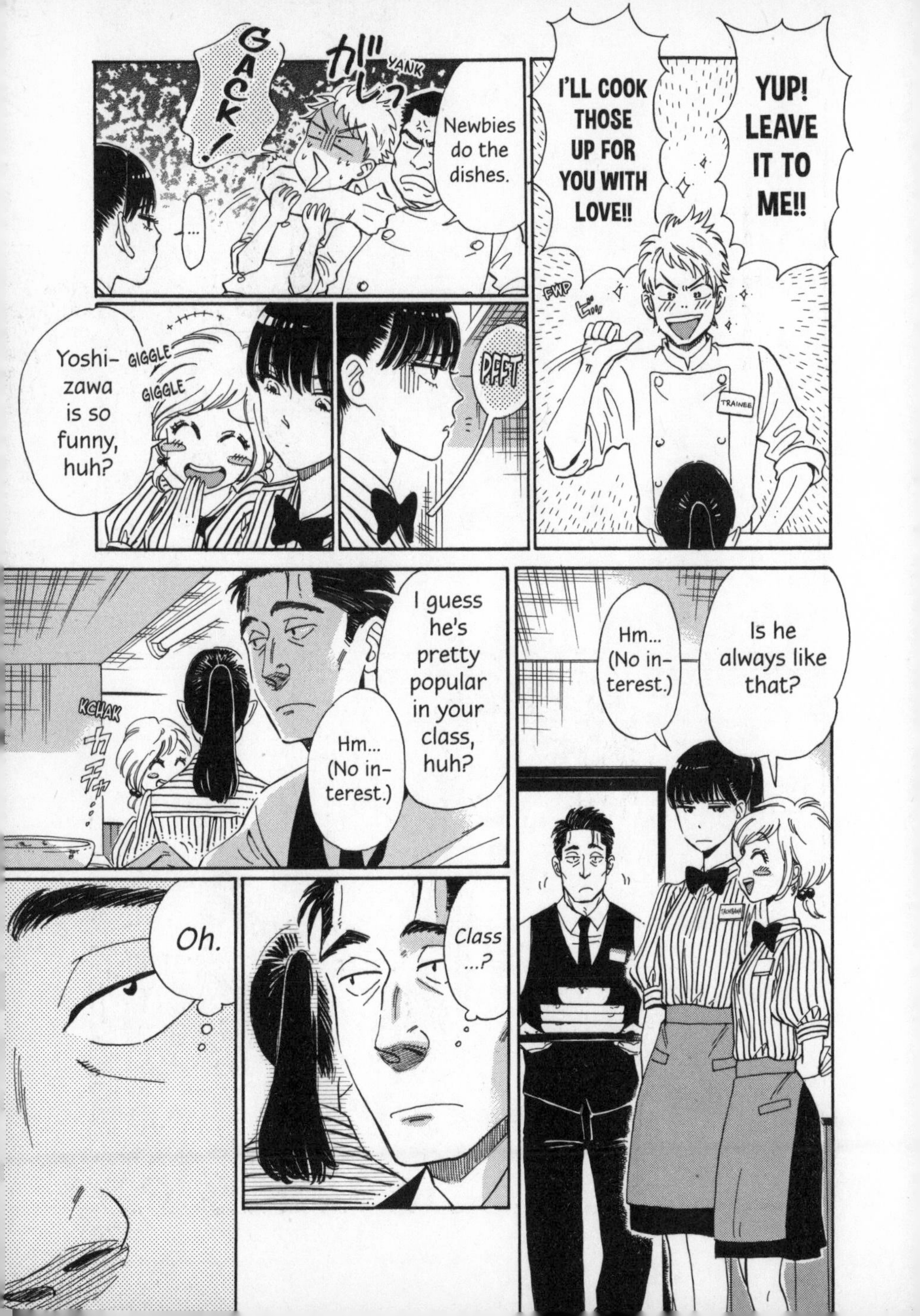
YUP! LEAVE IT TO ME!!
I'LL COOK THOSE UP FOR YOU WITH LOVE!!
FWP
TRAINEE
Newbies do the dishes.
YANK
GACK!
...
PFFT
Yoshi-zawa is so funny, huh?
GIGGLE
GIGGLE
Is he always like that?
Hm... (No in-terest.)
TACHIBANA
I guess he's pretty popular in your class, huh?
Hm... (No in-terest.)
KCHAK
Class ...?
Oh.

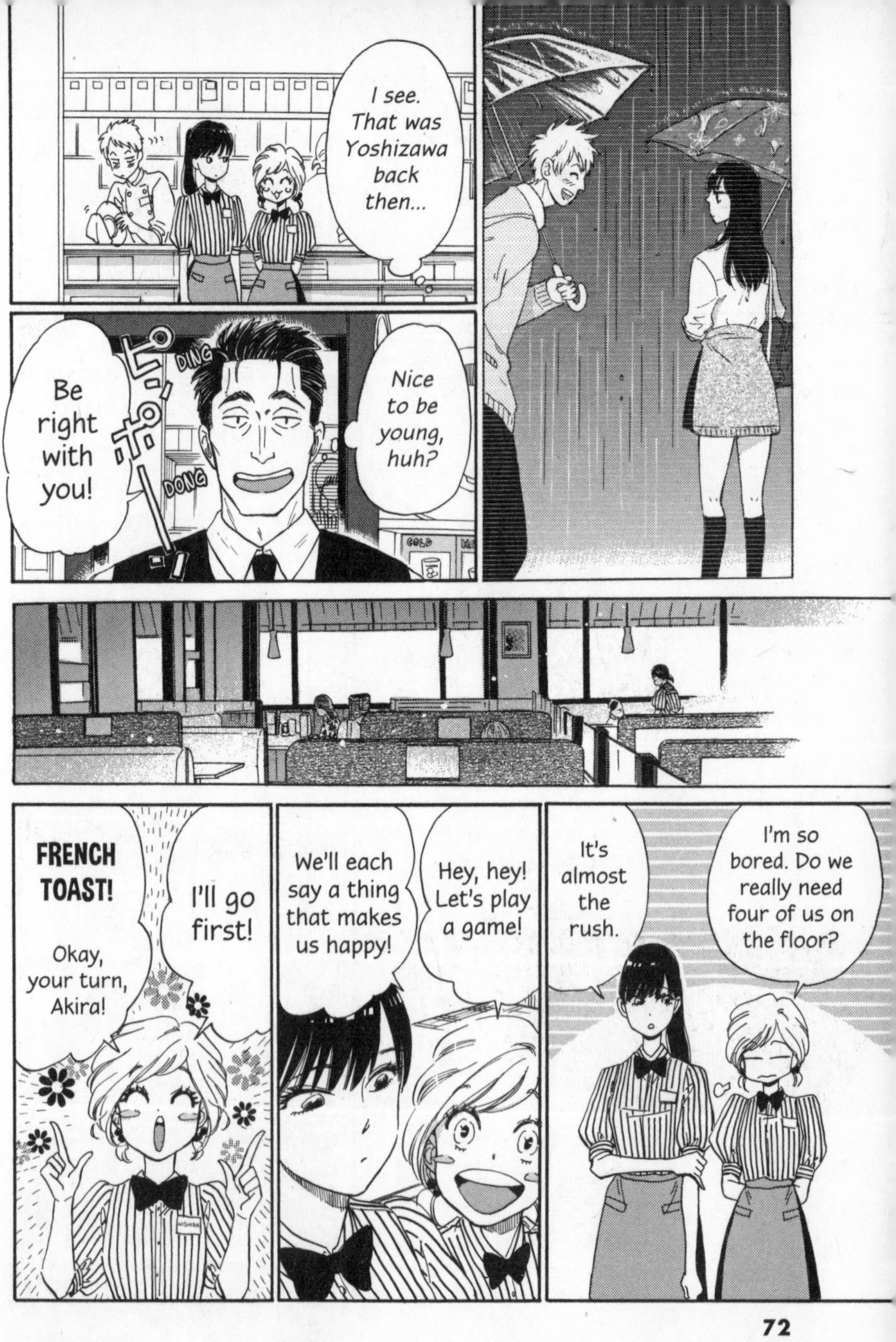
I see. That was Yoshizawa back then...
Nice to be young, huh?
DING
DONG
Be right with you!
I'm so bored. Do we really need four of us on the floor?
It's almost the rush.
Hey, hey! Let's play a game!
We'll each say a thing that makes us happy!
I'll go first!
FRENCH TOAST!
Okay, your turn, Akira!

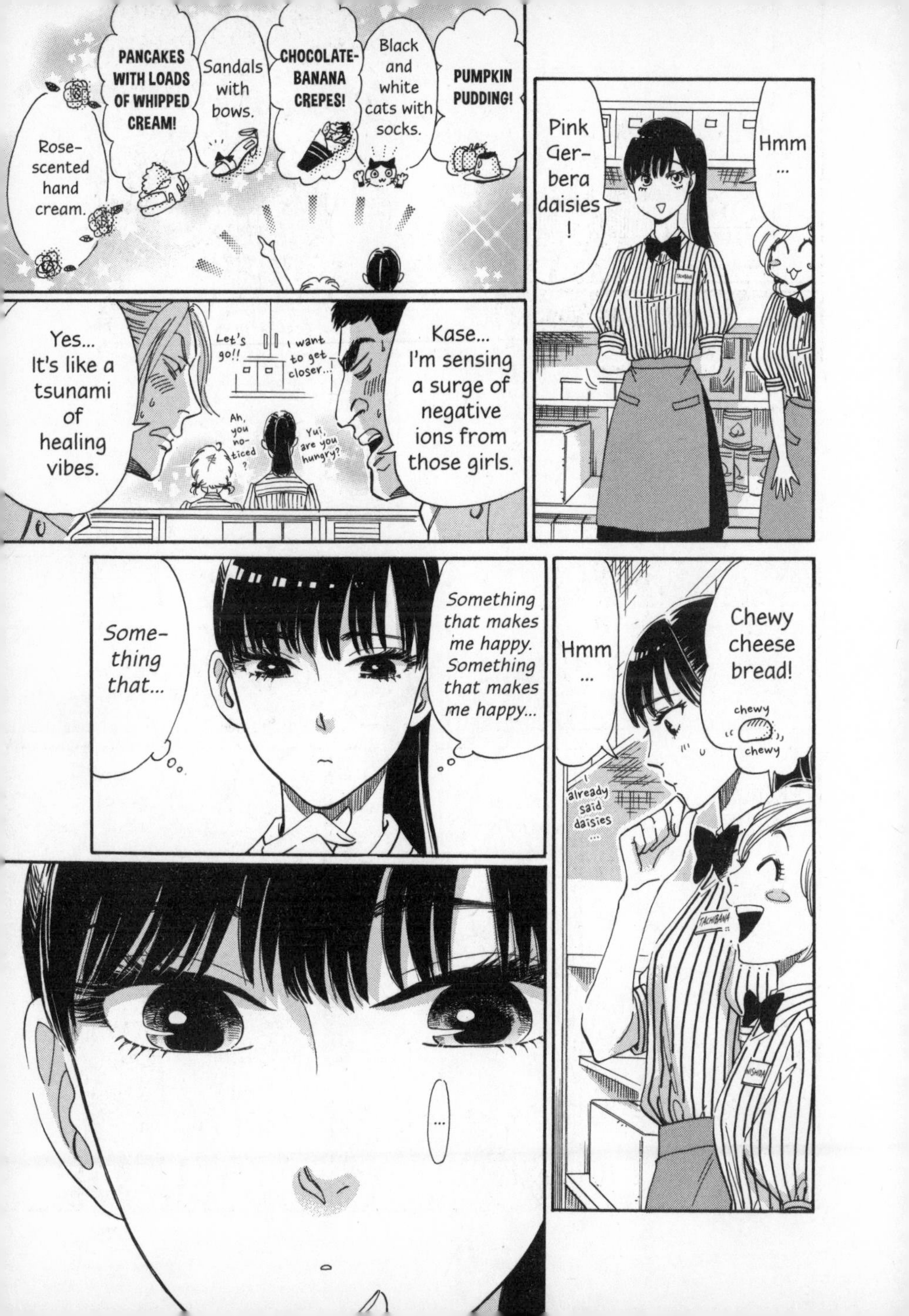
Hmm...
Pink Gerbera daisies!
PUMPKIN PUDDING!
Black and white cats with socks.
CHOCOLATE-BANANA CREPES!
Sandals with bows.
PANCAKES WITH LOADS OF WHIPPED CREAM!
Rose-scented hand cream.
Kase... I'm sensing a surge of negative ions from those girls.
I want to get closer...
Let's go!!
Yui, are you hungry?
Ah, you noticed?
Yes... It's like a tsunami of healing vibes.
Chewy cheese bread!
chewy
chewy
Hmm...
I already said daisies...
Something that makes me happy. Something that makes me happy...
Something that...
...

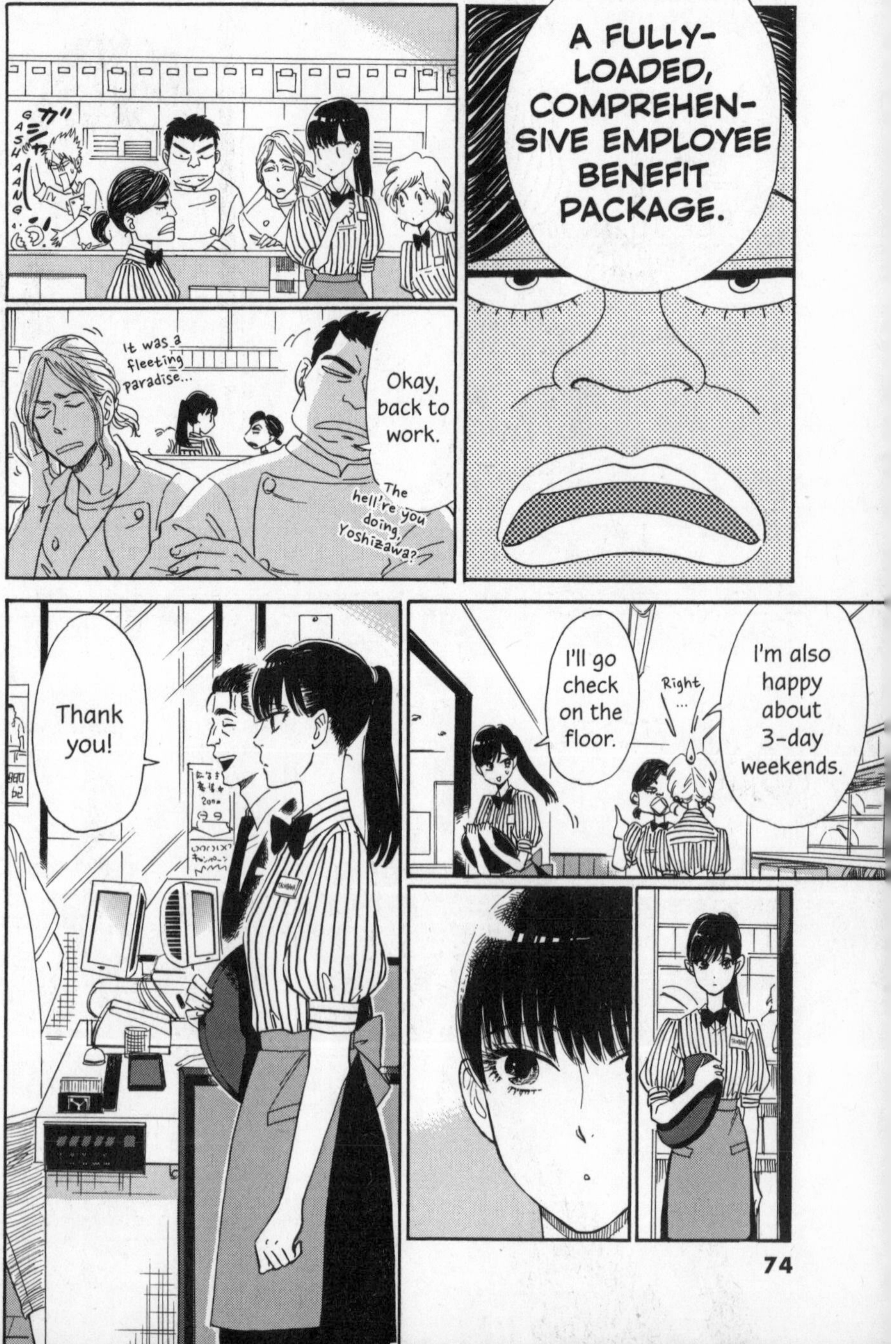
A FULLY-LOADED, COMPREHENSIVE EMPLOYEE BENEFIT PACKAGE.
GASHAANG
Okay, back to work.
It was a fleeting paradise...
The hell're you doing, Yoshizawa?
I'm also happy about 3-day weekends.
Right...
I'll go check on the floor.
Thank you!

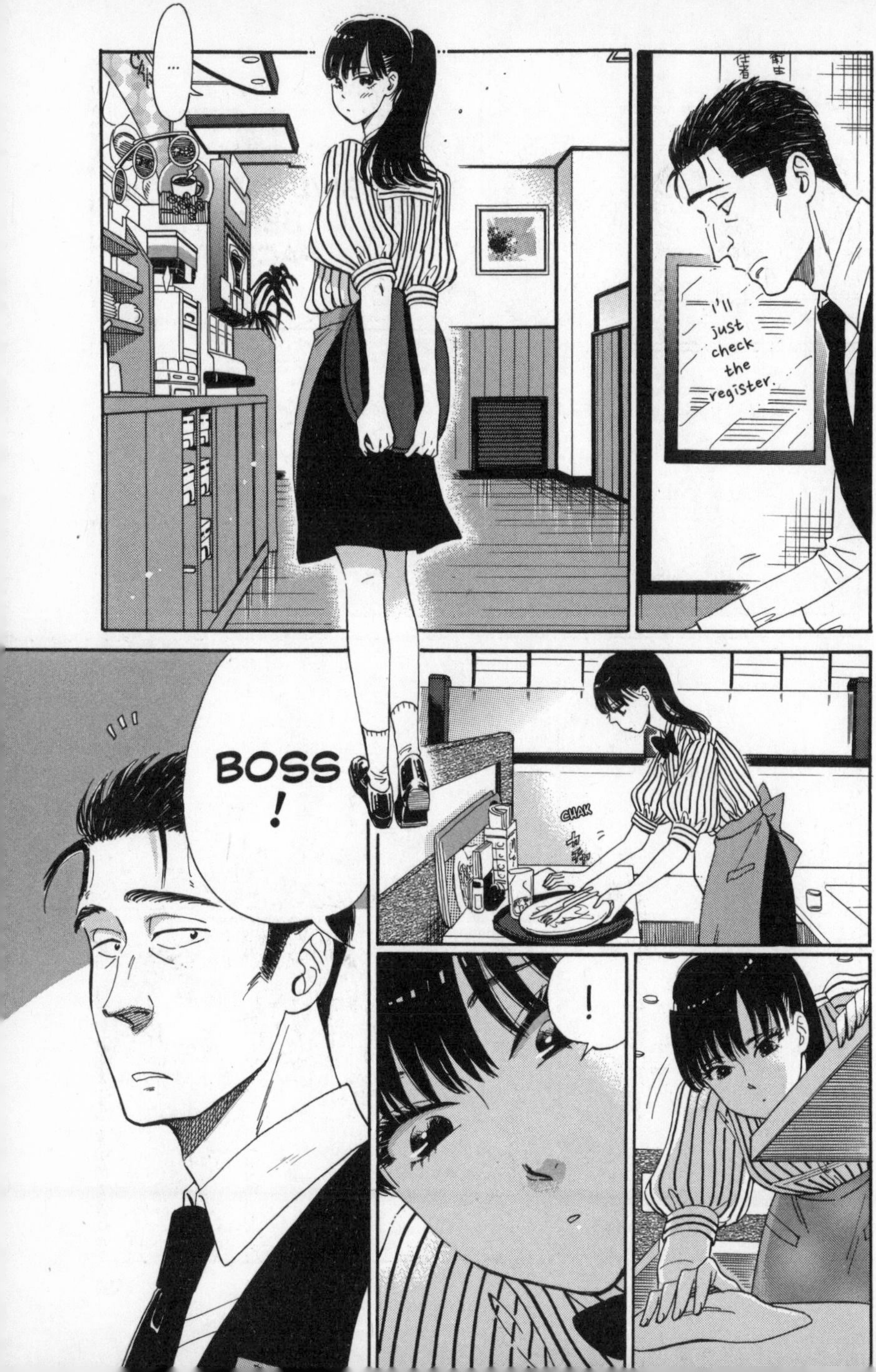

...
I'll just check the register.
BOSS!
CHAK
!

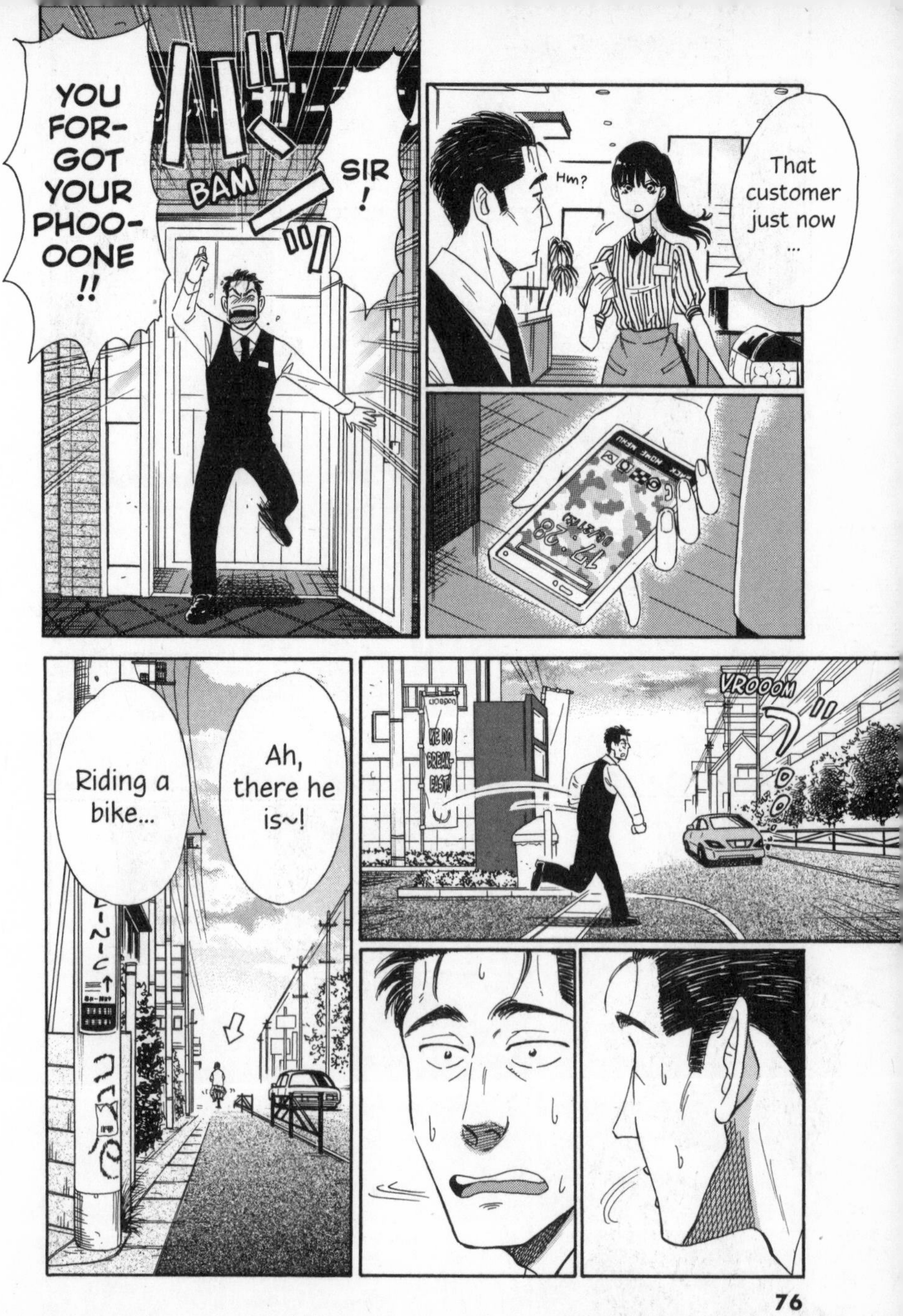

Hm?
That customer just now ...
SIR!
BAM
YOU FOR-GOT YOUR PHOOO-OONE!!
VROOOM
WE DO BREAK-FAST!
Ah, there he is~!
Riding a bike...

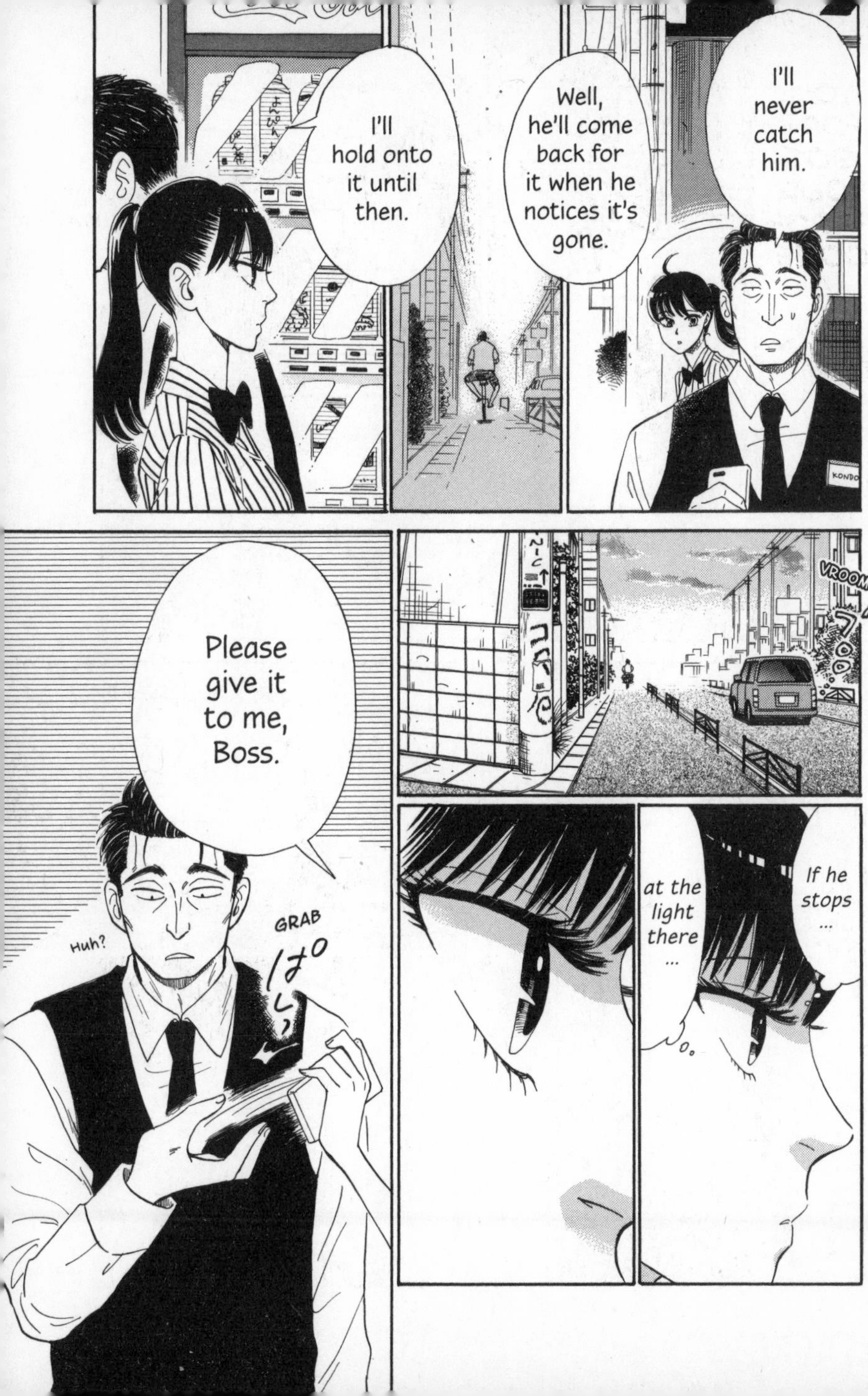
I'll never catch him.
Well, he'll come back for it when he notices it's gone.
I'll hold onto it until then.
VROOM
If he stops ...
at the light there ...
Please give it to me, Boss.
GRAB
Huh?

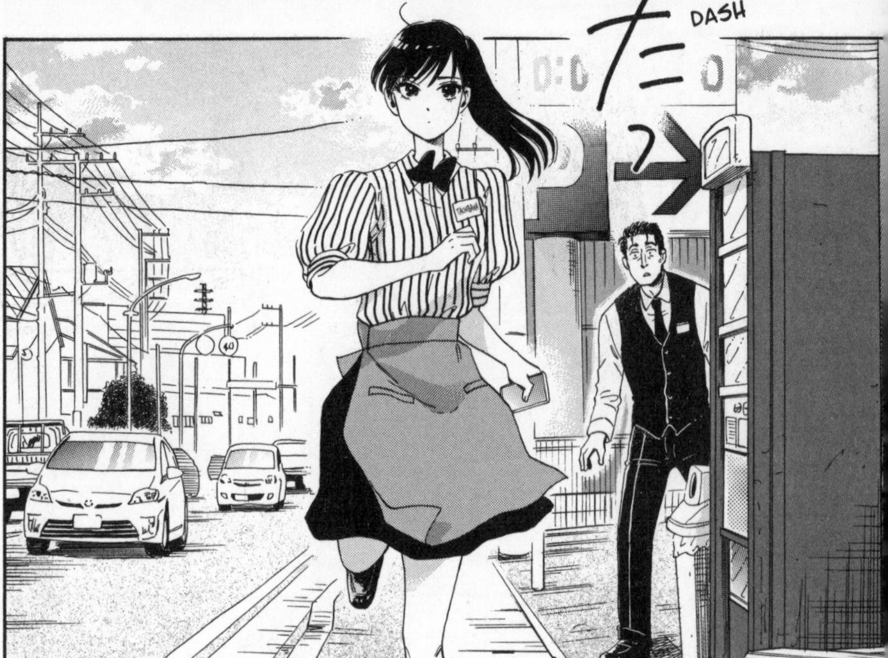
タッ
DASH

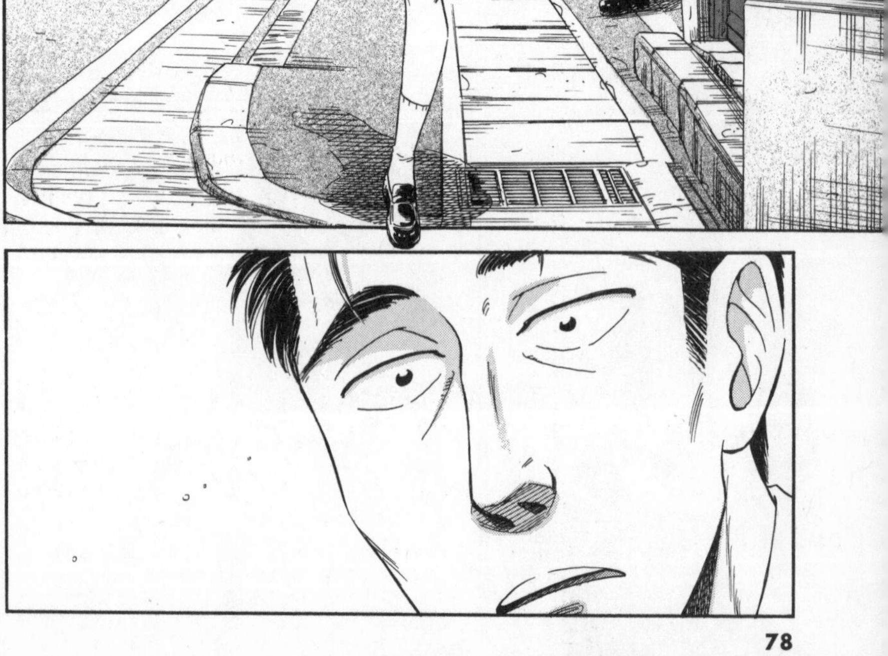

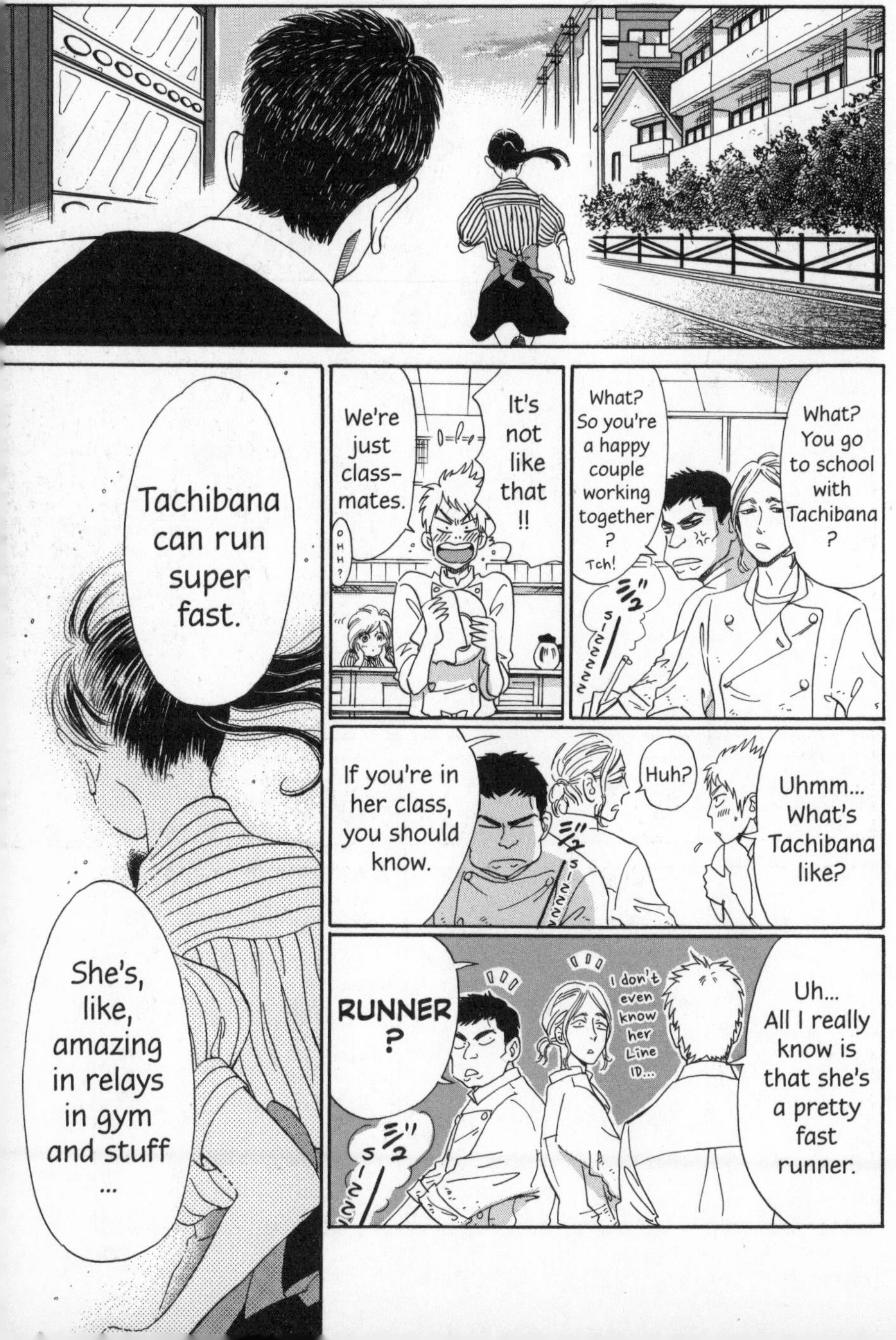
What? You go to school with Tachibana?
What? So you're a happy couple working together?
Tch!
It's not like that!!
We're just classmates.
OHH?
Uhmm... What's Tachibana like?
Huh?
If you're in her class, you should know.
Uh... All I really know is that she's a pretty fast runner.
I don't even know her Line ID...
RUNNER?
Tachibana can run super fast.
She's, like, amazing in relays in gym and stuff...

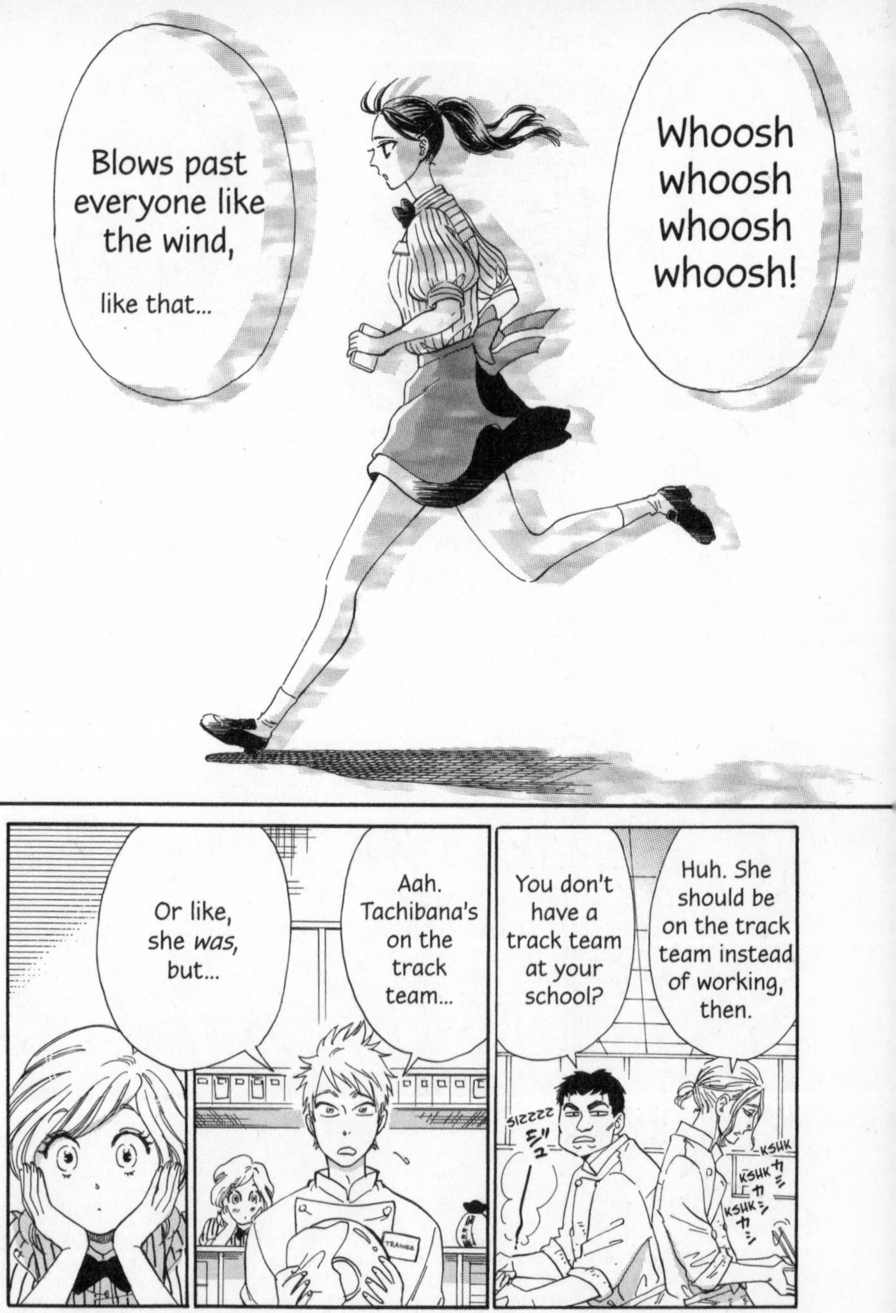
Whoosh whoosh whoosh whoosh!
Blows past everyone like the wind,
like that...
Huh. She should be on the track team instead of working, then.
KSHK
KSHK
KSHK
You don't have a track team at your school?
SIZZZZ
Aah. Tachibana's on the track team...
TRAINEE
Or like, she *was*, but...

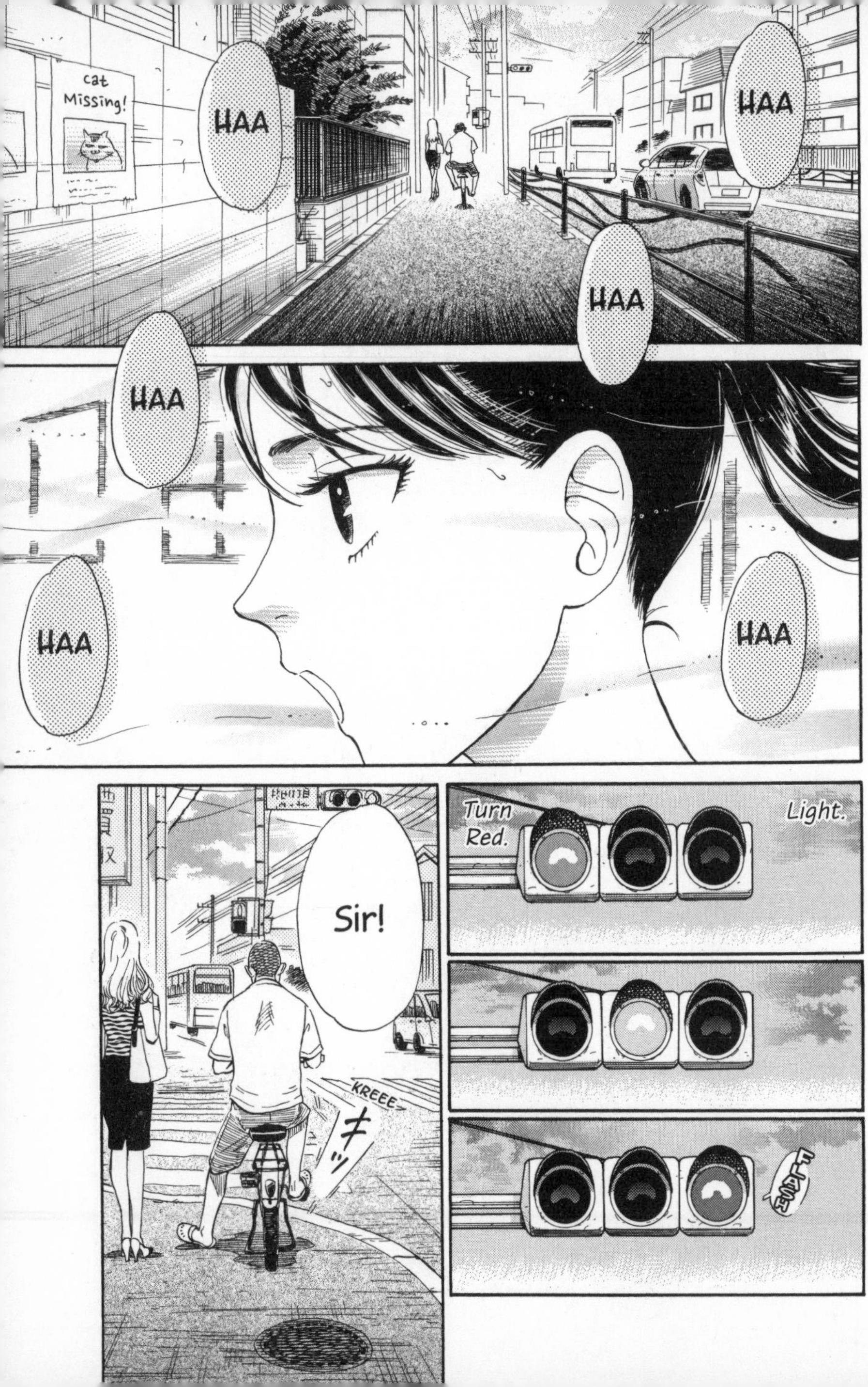
HAA
HAA
HAA
cat Missing!
HAA
HAA
HAA
Light.
Turn Red.
FLASH
Sir!
KREEE
キッ

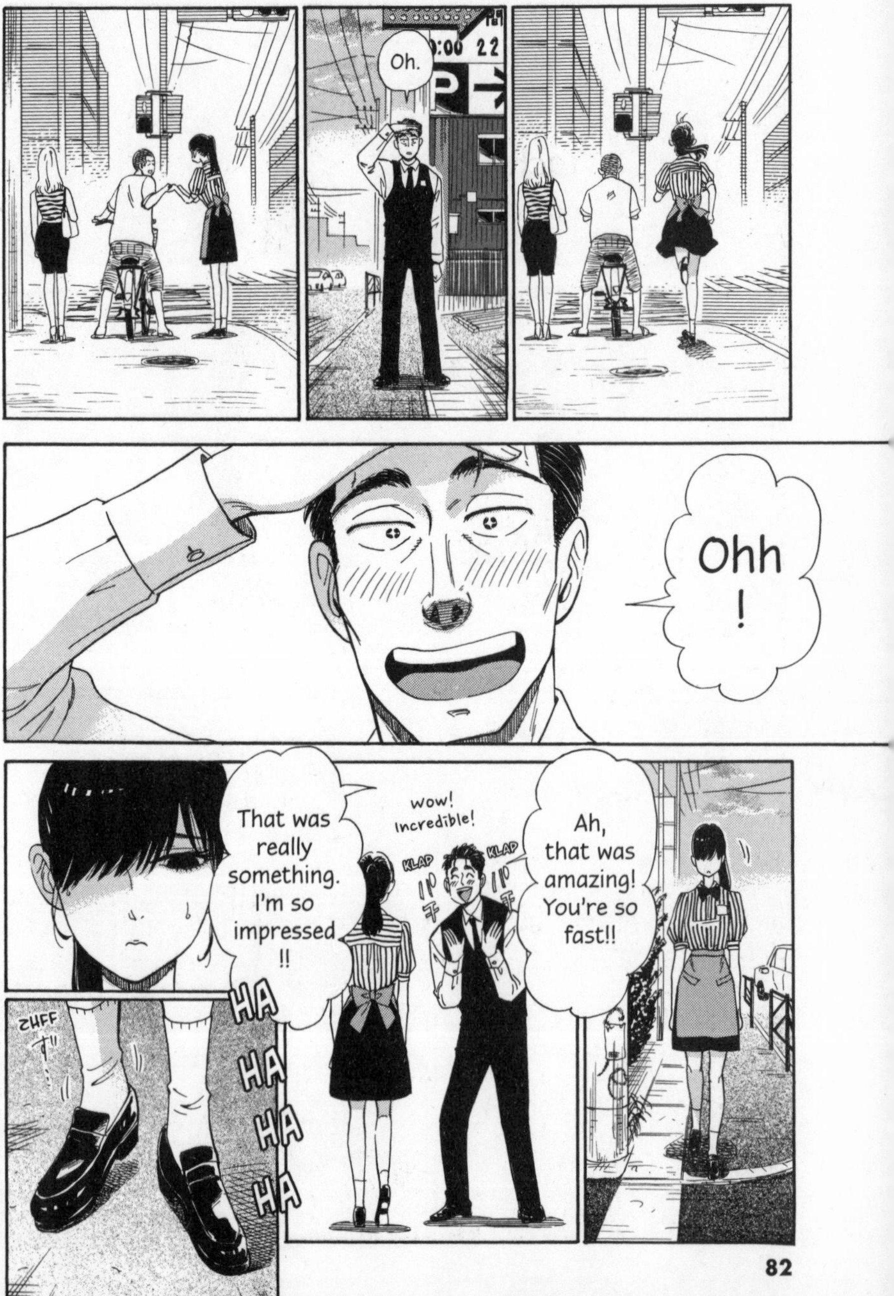
Oh.
Ohh !
Ah, that was amazing! You're so fast!!
KLAP
Wow! Incredible!
KLAP
That was really something. I'm so impressed!!
HA HA HA HA
ZHFF

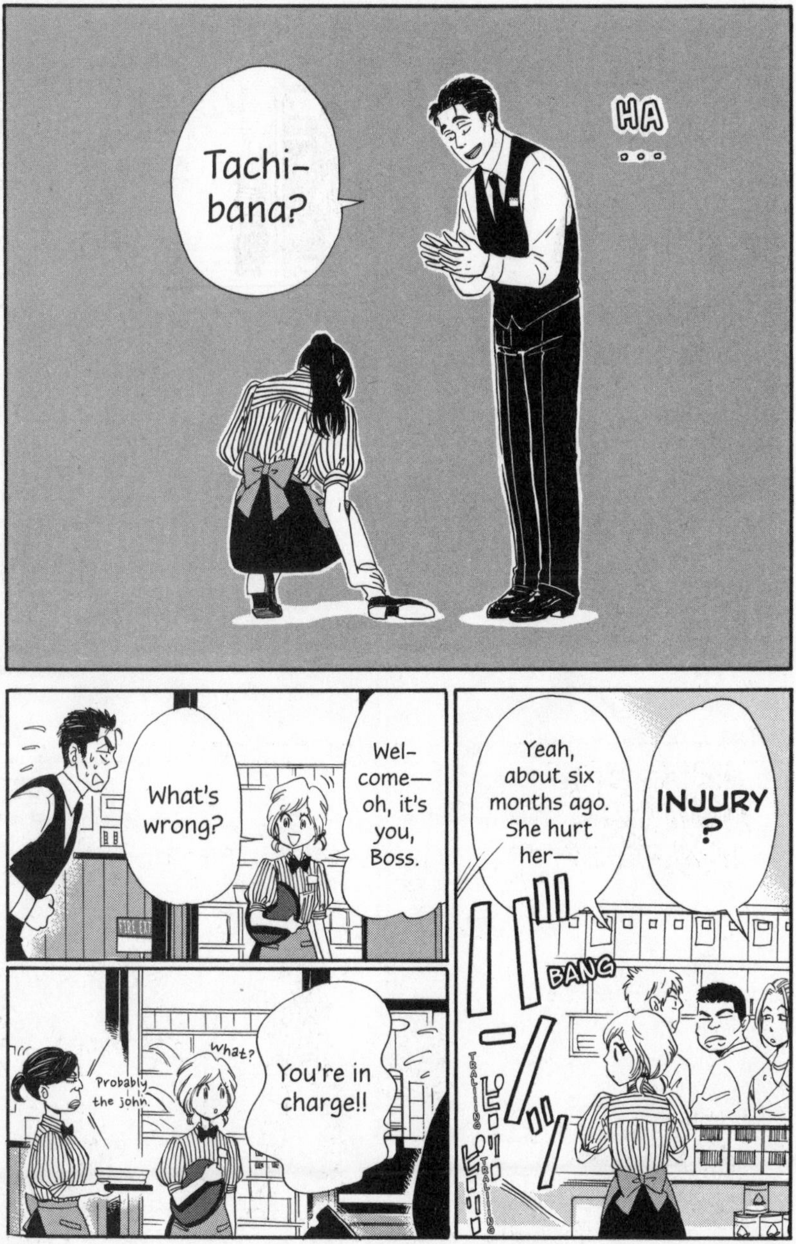
HA ...
Tachi-bana?
INJURY ?
Yeah, about six months ago. She hurt her—
BANG
TRAILING
TRAILING
Wel-come—oh, it's you, Boss.
What's wrong?
You're in charge!!
What?
Probably the john.

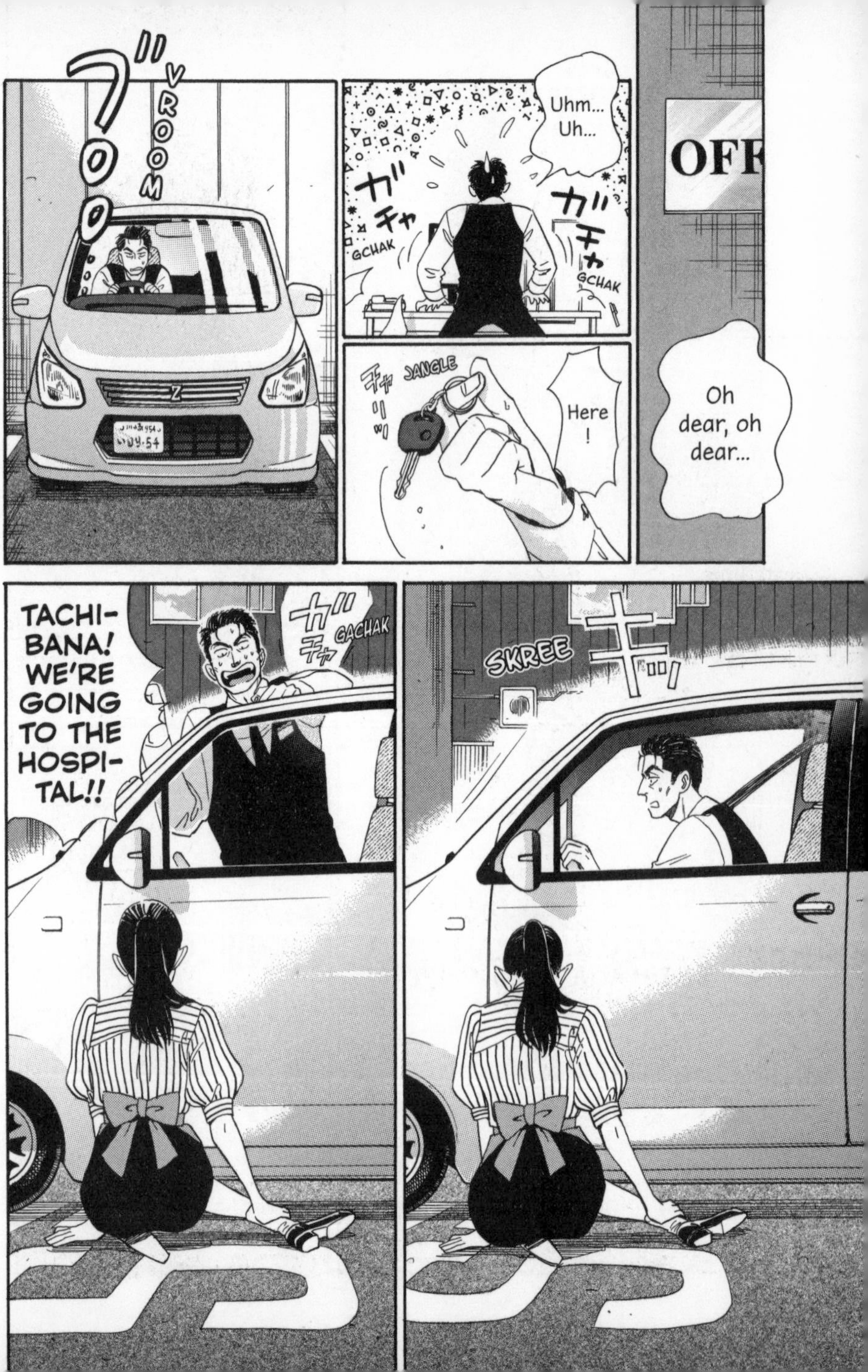
OFF
Oh dear, oh dear...
Uhm... Uh...
GCHAK
GCHAK
JANGLE
Here!
VROOM
SKREE
GACHAK
TACHIBANA! WE'RE GOING TO THE HOSPITAL!!

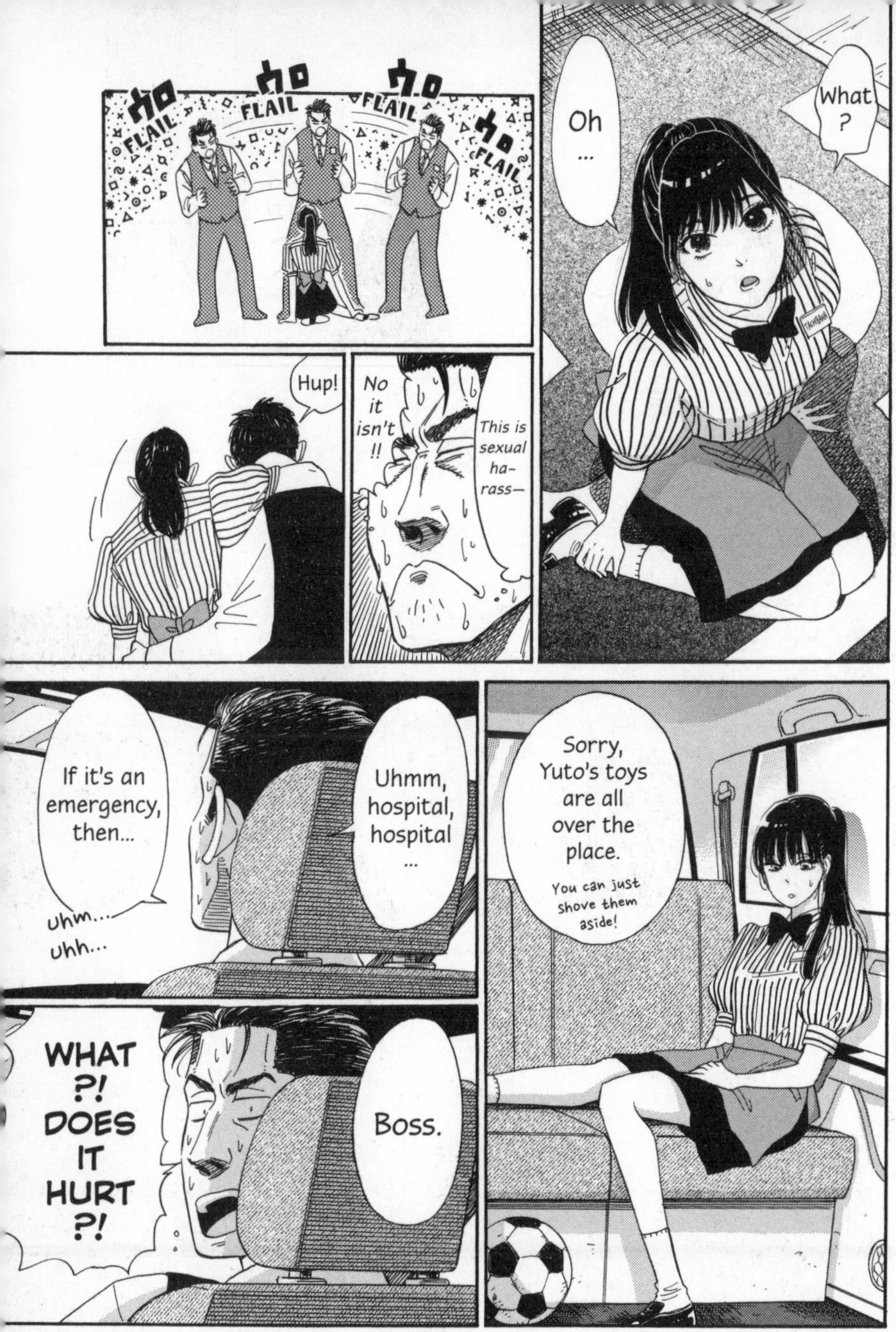
What?
Oh...
ウロ FLAIL
ウロ FLAIL
ウロ FLAIL
ウロ FLAIL
This is sexual ha-rass—
No it isn't!!
Hup!
Sorry, Yuto's toys are all over the place.
You can just shove them aside!
Uhmm, hospital, hospital...
If it's an emergency, then...
uhm... uhh...
Boss.
WHAT?! DOES IT HURT?!

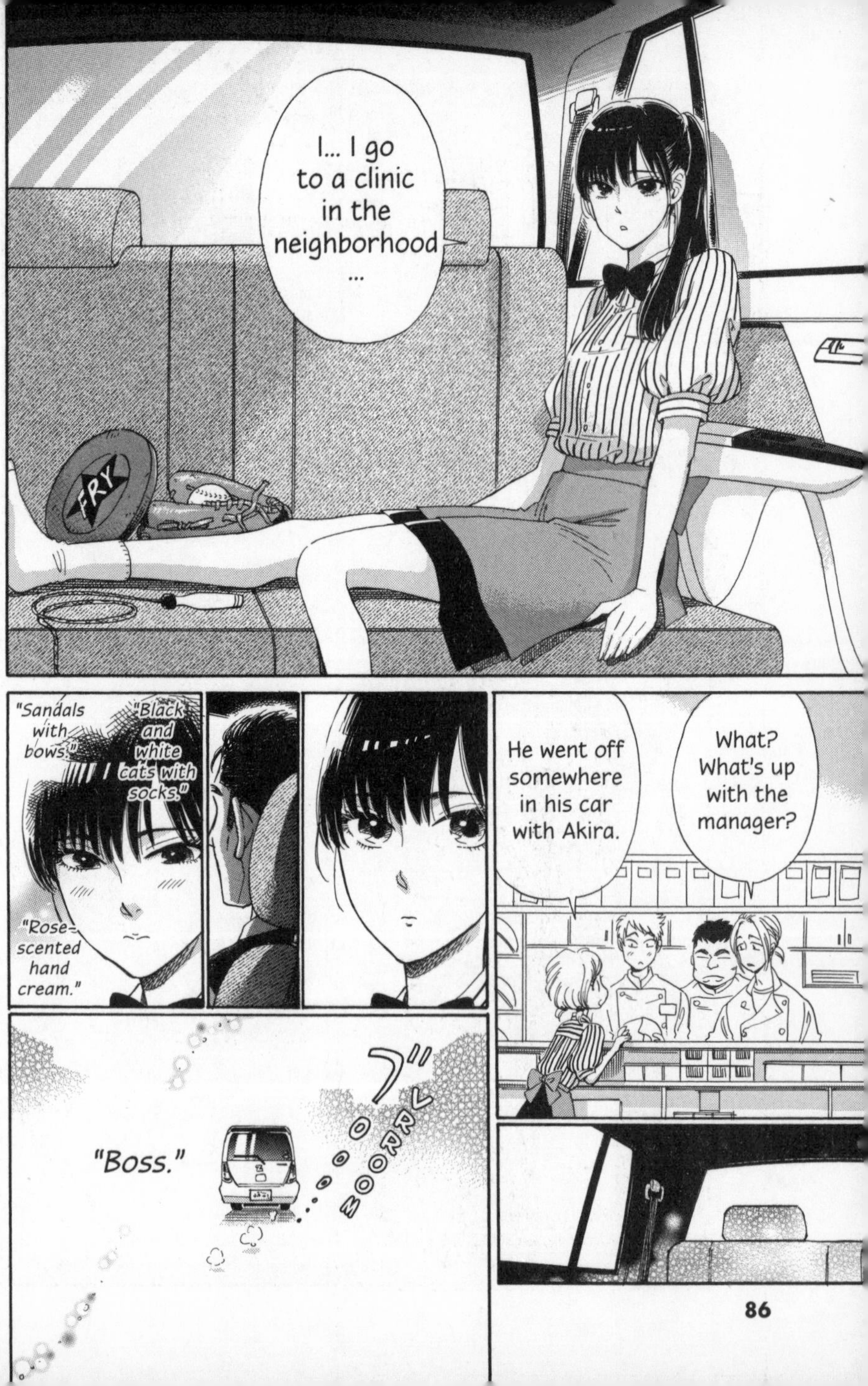
I... I go to a clinic in the neighborhood ...
What? What's up with the manager?
He went off somewhere in his car with Akira.
"Black and white cats with socks."
"Sandals with bows."
"Rose-scented hand cream."
ブ
VRROOOM
OOO...
"Boss."

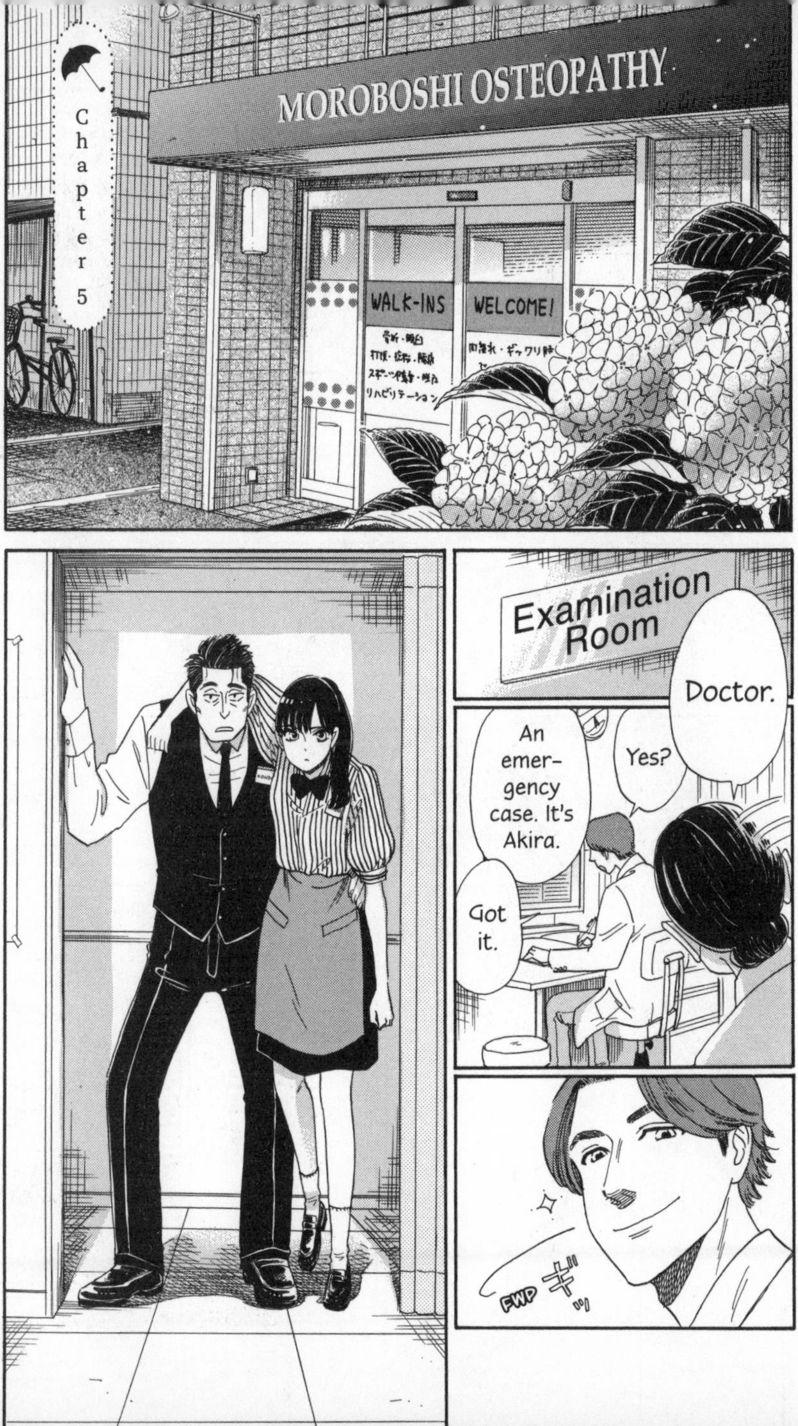
Chapter 5
MOROBOSHI OSTEOPATHY
WALK-INS
WELCOME!
リハビリテーション
Examination Room
Doctor.
Yes?
An emergency case. It's Akira.
Got it.
FWP

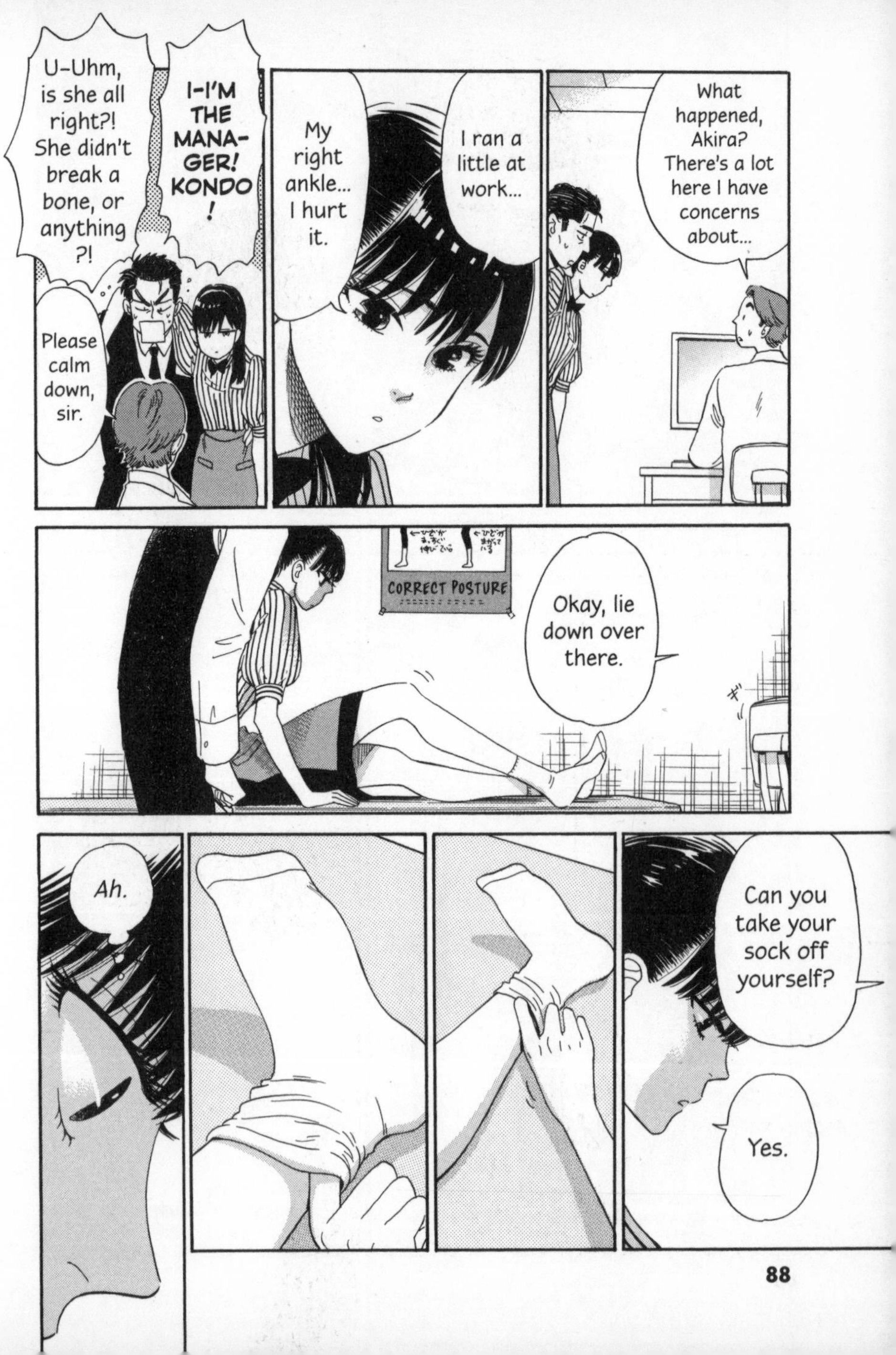
What happened, Akira? There's a lot here I have concerns about...
I ran a little at work...
My right ankle... I hurt it.
I-I'M THE MANAGER! KONDO!
U-Uhm, is she all right?! She didn't break a bone, or anything?!
Please calm down, sir.
CORRECT POSTURE
Okay, lie down over there.
Can you take your sock off yourself?
Yes.
Ah.

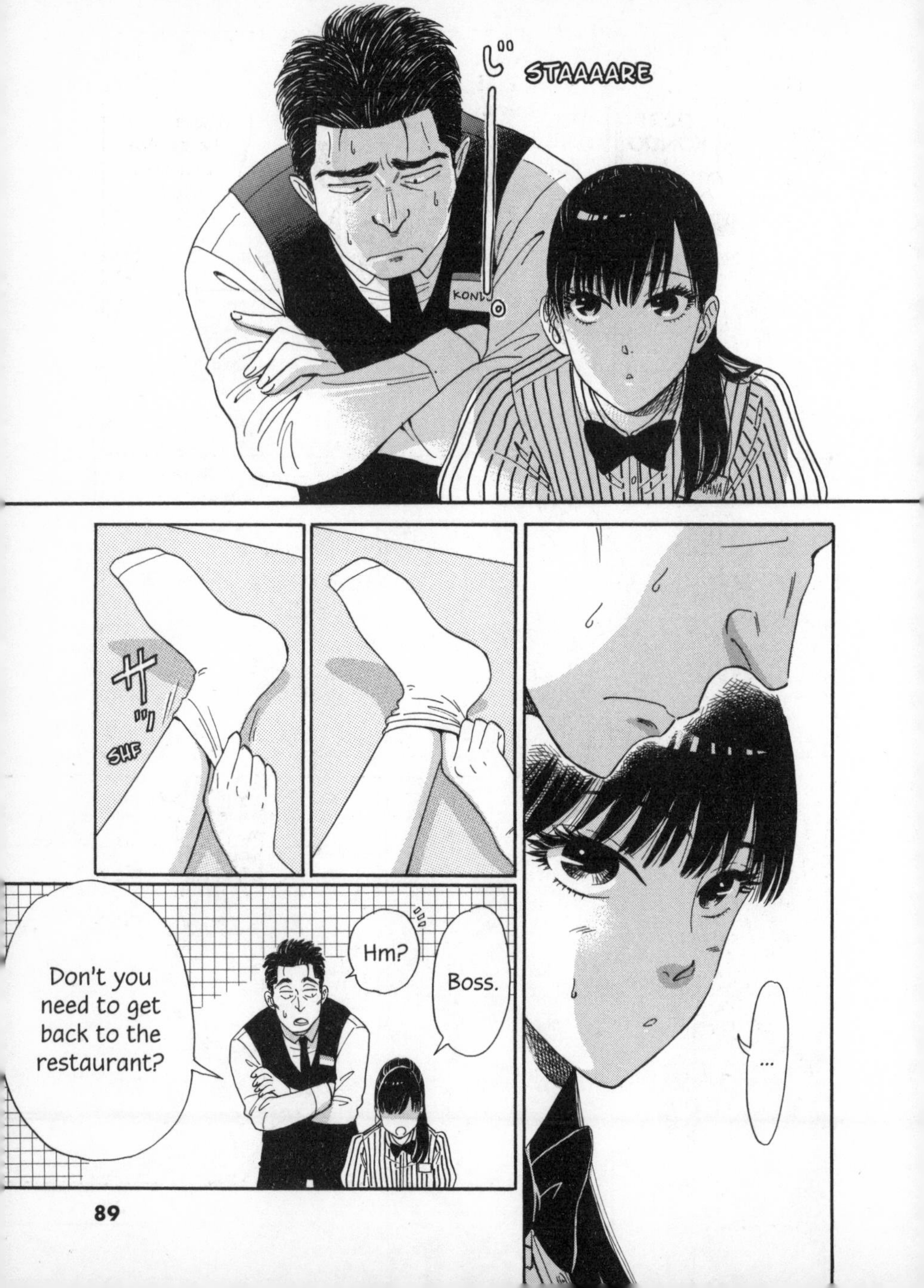
STAAAARE
...
SHF
Boss.
Hm?
Don't you need to get back to the restaurant?

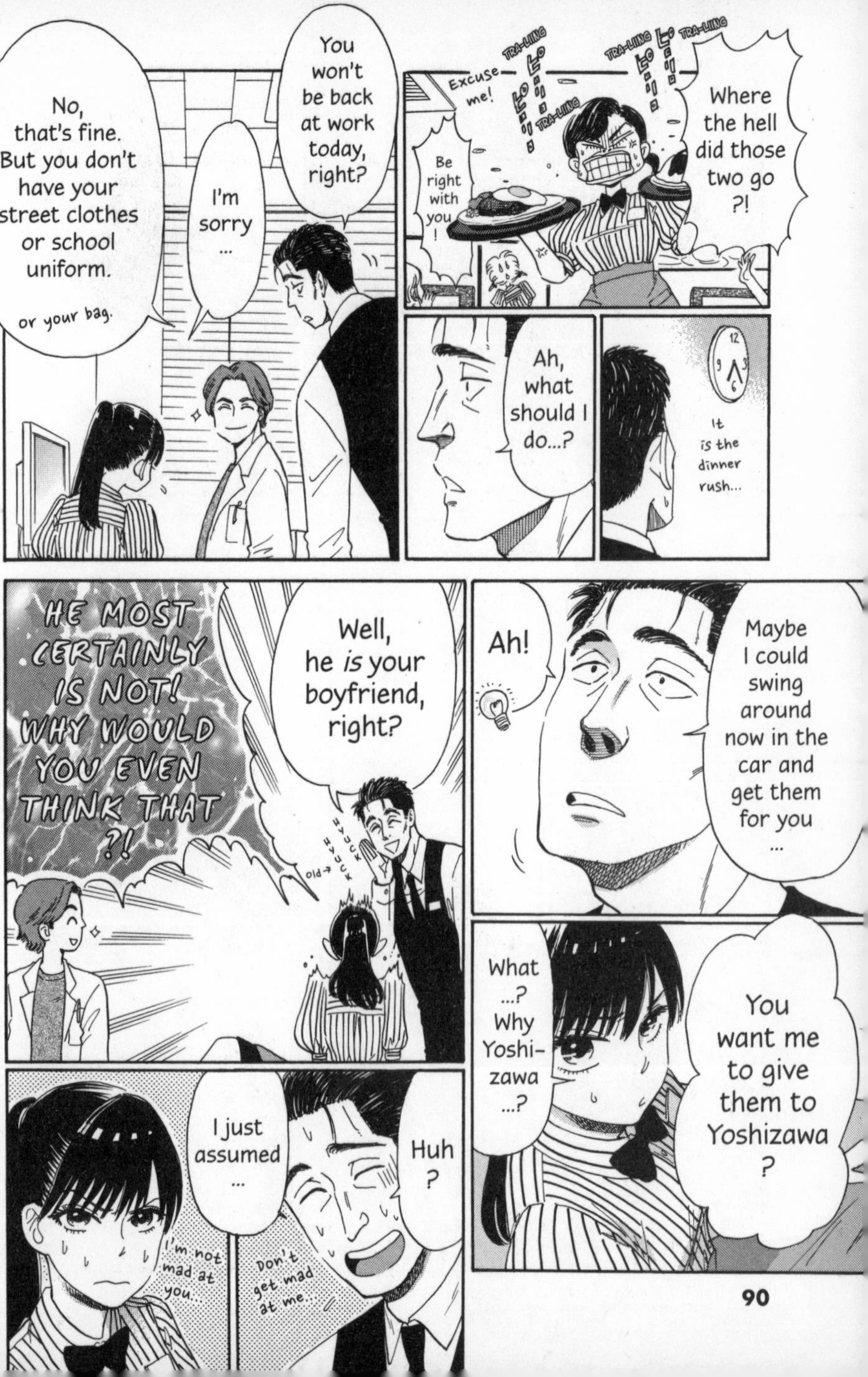
Where the hell did those two go ?!
TRA-LIING TRA-LIING
Excuse me!
TRA-LIING TRA-LIING
Be right with you !
It is the dinner rush...
Ah, what should I do...?
You won't be back at work today, right?
I'm sorry ...
No, that's fine. But you don't have your street clothes or school uniform.
or your bag.
Maybe I could swing around now in the car and get them for you ...
Ah!
Well, he *is* your boyfriend, right?
HYUCK HYUCK
old →
HE MOST CERTAINLY IS NOT! WHY WOULD YOU EVEN THINK THAT ?!
You want me to give them to Yoshizawa ?
What ...? Why Yoshi-zawa ...?
Huh ?
I just assumed ...
Don't get mad at me.
I'm not mad at you..

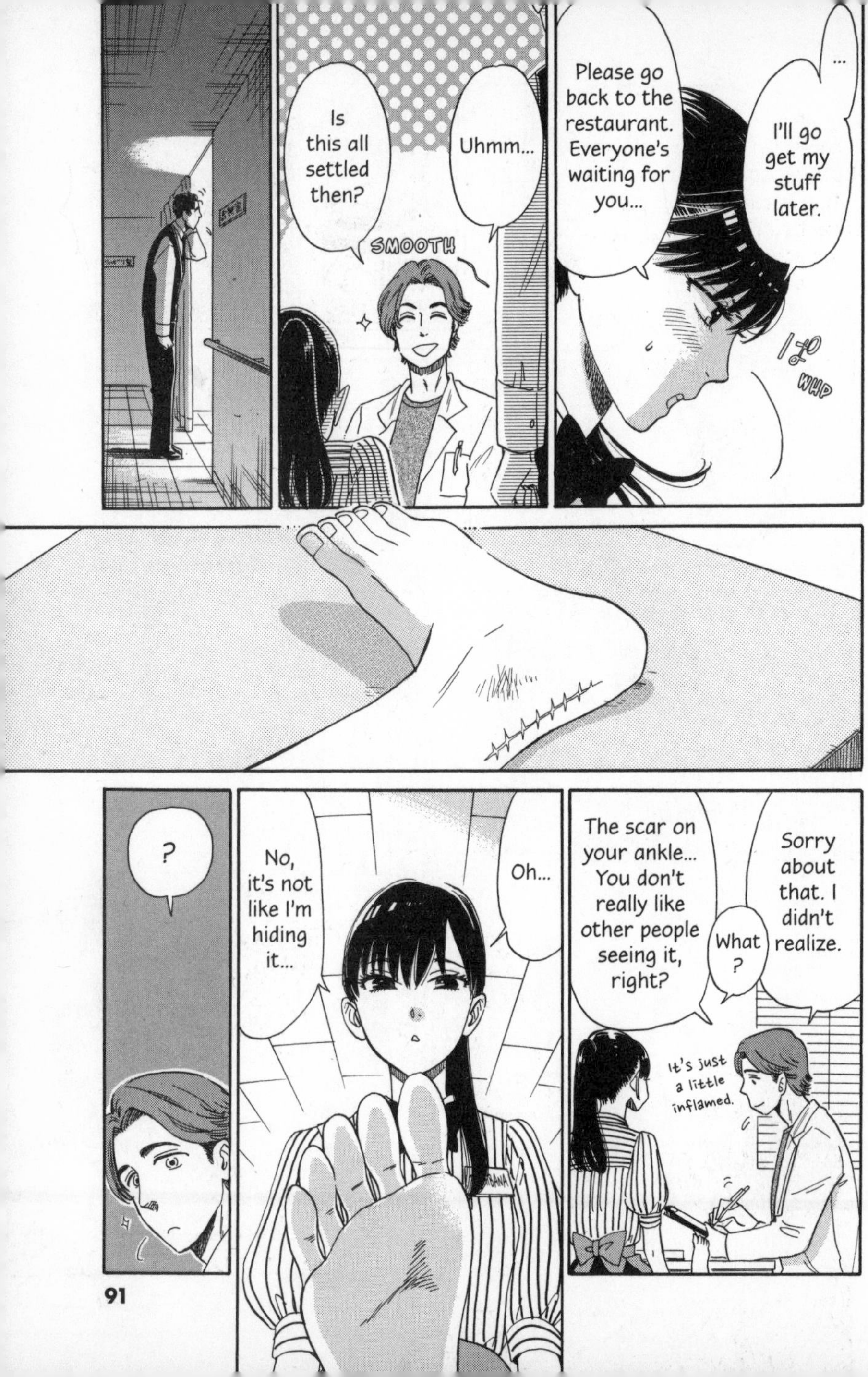
...
I'll go get my stuff later.
Please go back to the restaurant. Everyone's waiting for you...
WHP
Uhmm...
Is this all settled then?
SMOOTH
Sorry about that. I didn't realize.
What?
The scar on your ankle... You don't really like other people seeing it, right?
It's just a little inflamed.
Oh...
No, it's not like I'm hiding it...
?

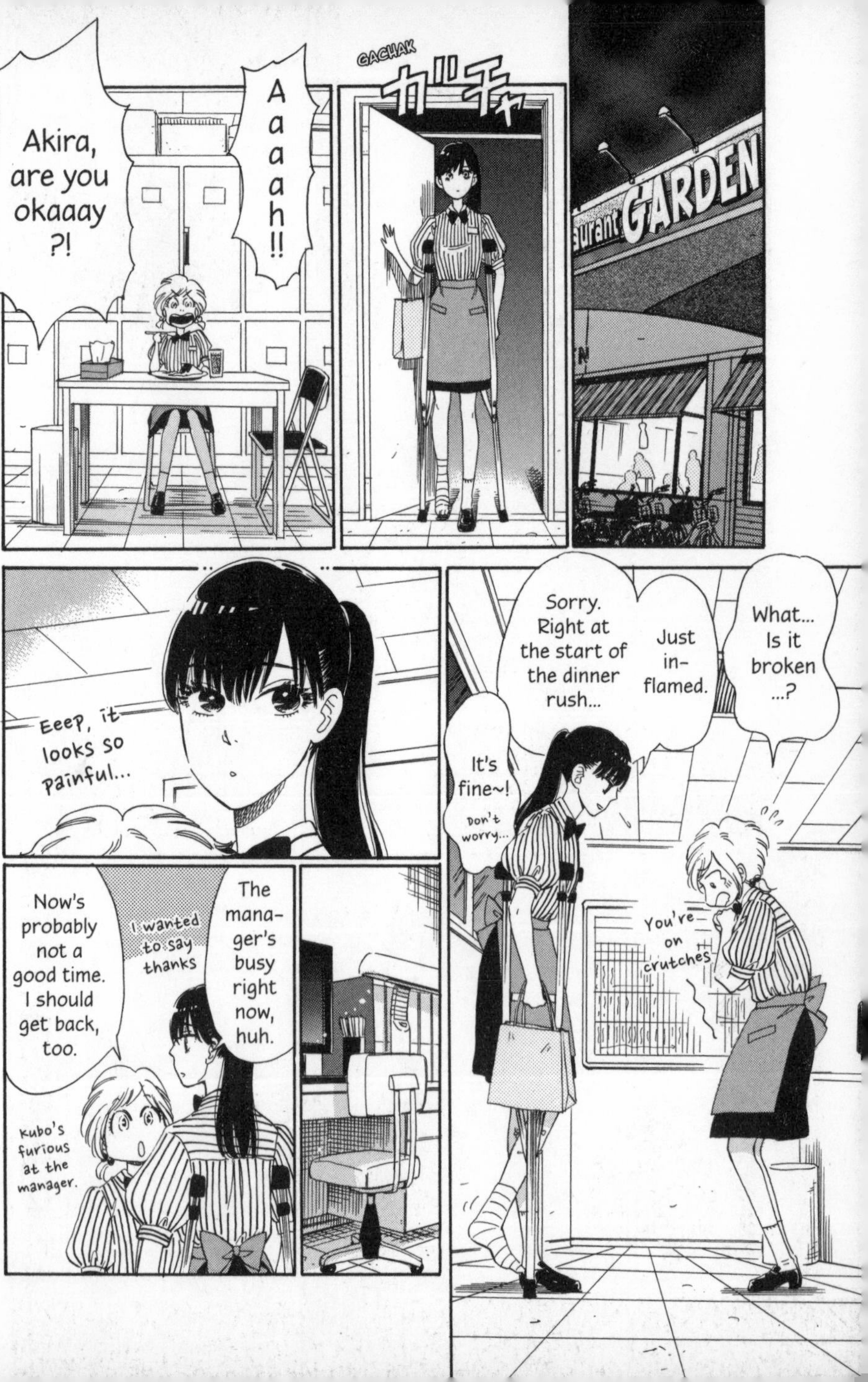

aurant GARDEN
GACHAK
カチャ
Aaaah!!
Akira, are you okaaay?!
What... Is it broken...?
Just in-flamed.
Sorry. Right at the start of the dinner rush...
It's fine~!
Don't worry...
You're on crutches
Eeep, it looks so painful...
The mana-ger's busy right now, huh.
I wanted to say thanks
Now's probably not a good time. I should get back, too.
Kubo's furious at the manager.

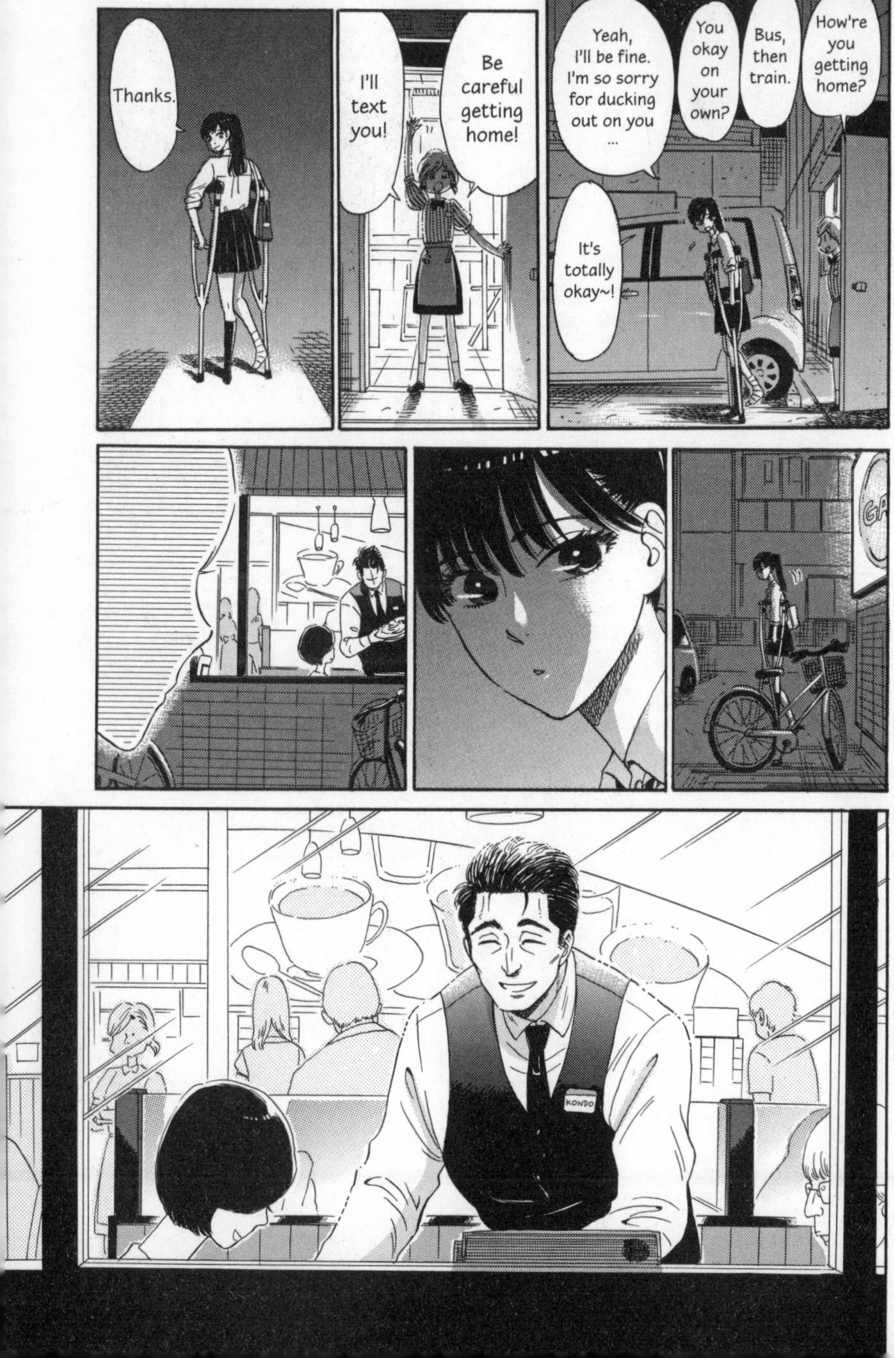
How're you getting home?
Bus, then train.
You okay on your own?
Yeah, I'll be fine. I'm so sorry for ducking out on you ...
It's totally okay~!
Be careful getting home!
I'll text you!
Thanks.
KONDO

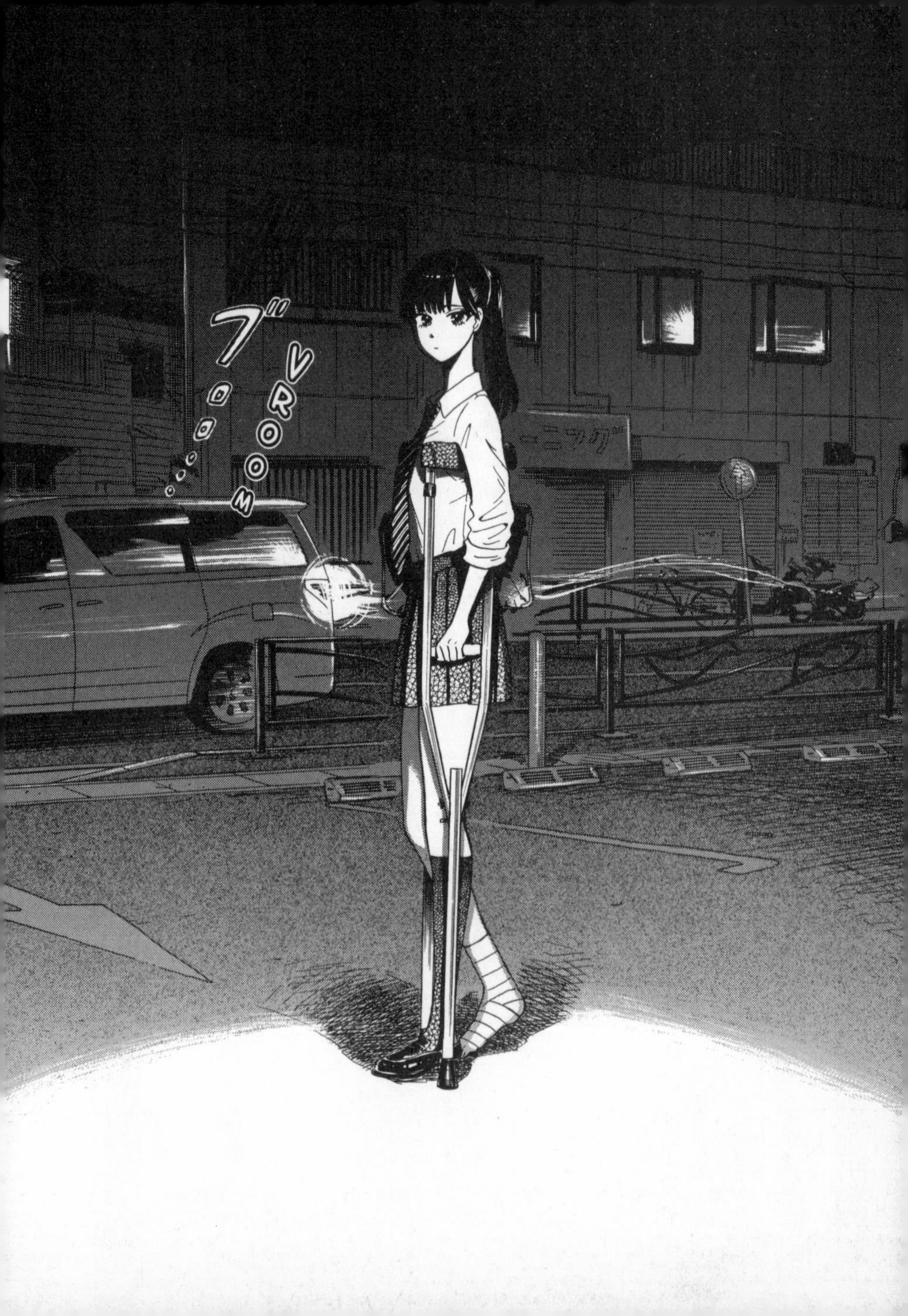
ブロロロロロ
VROOM

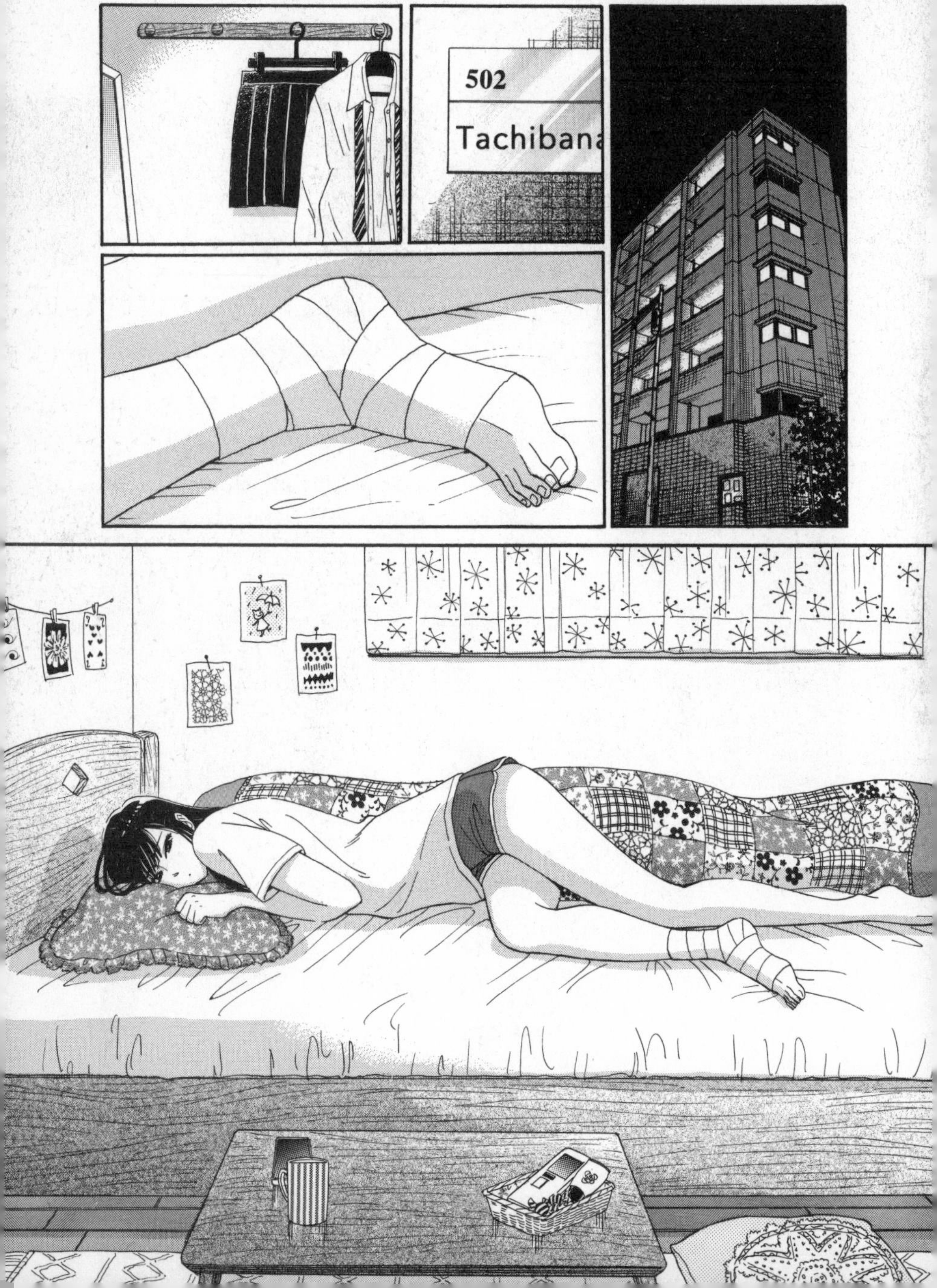
502
Tachibana

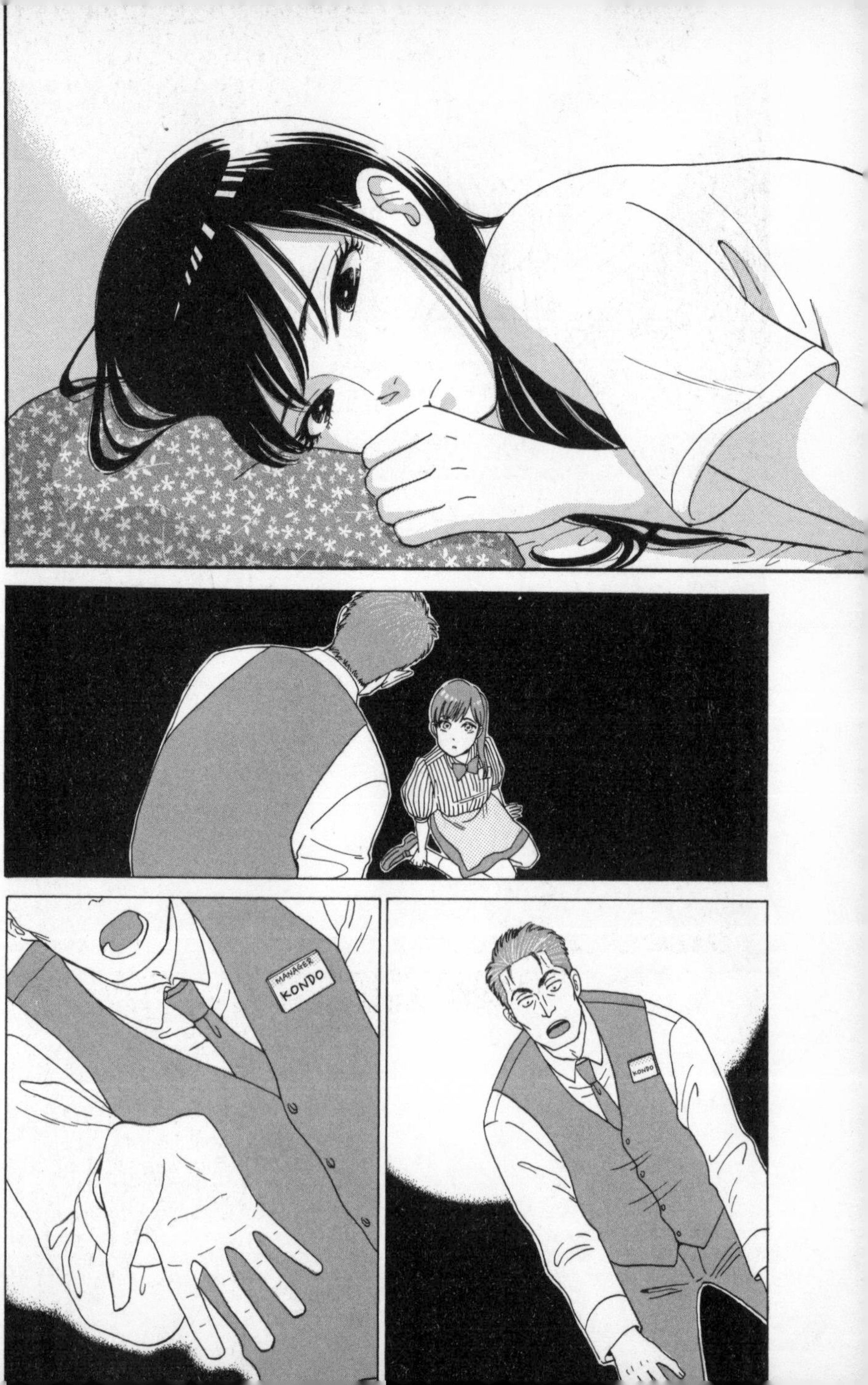
KONDO
MANAGER
KONDO

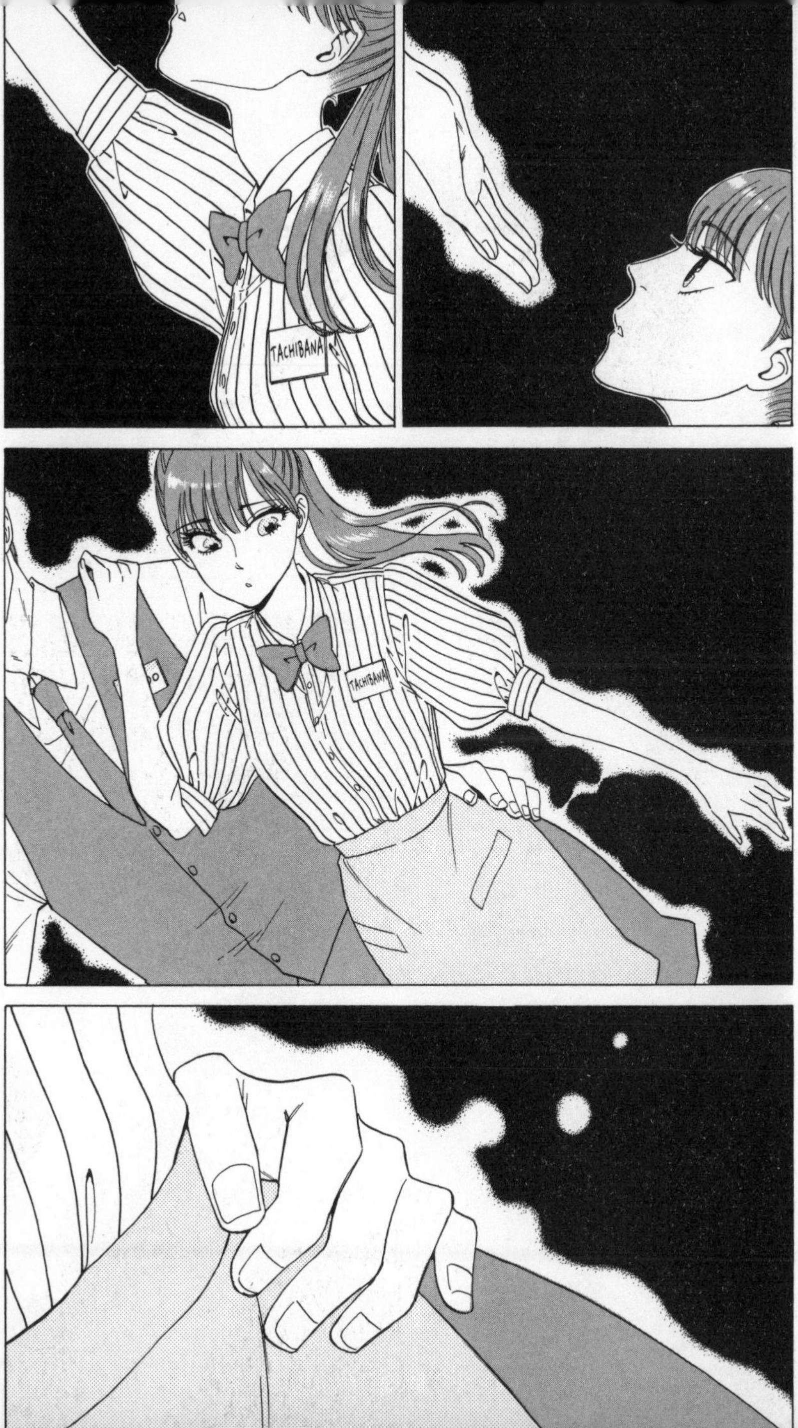
TACHIBANA
TACHIBANA

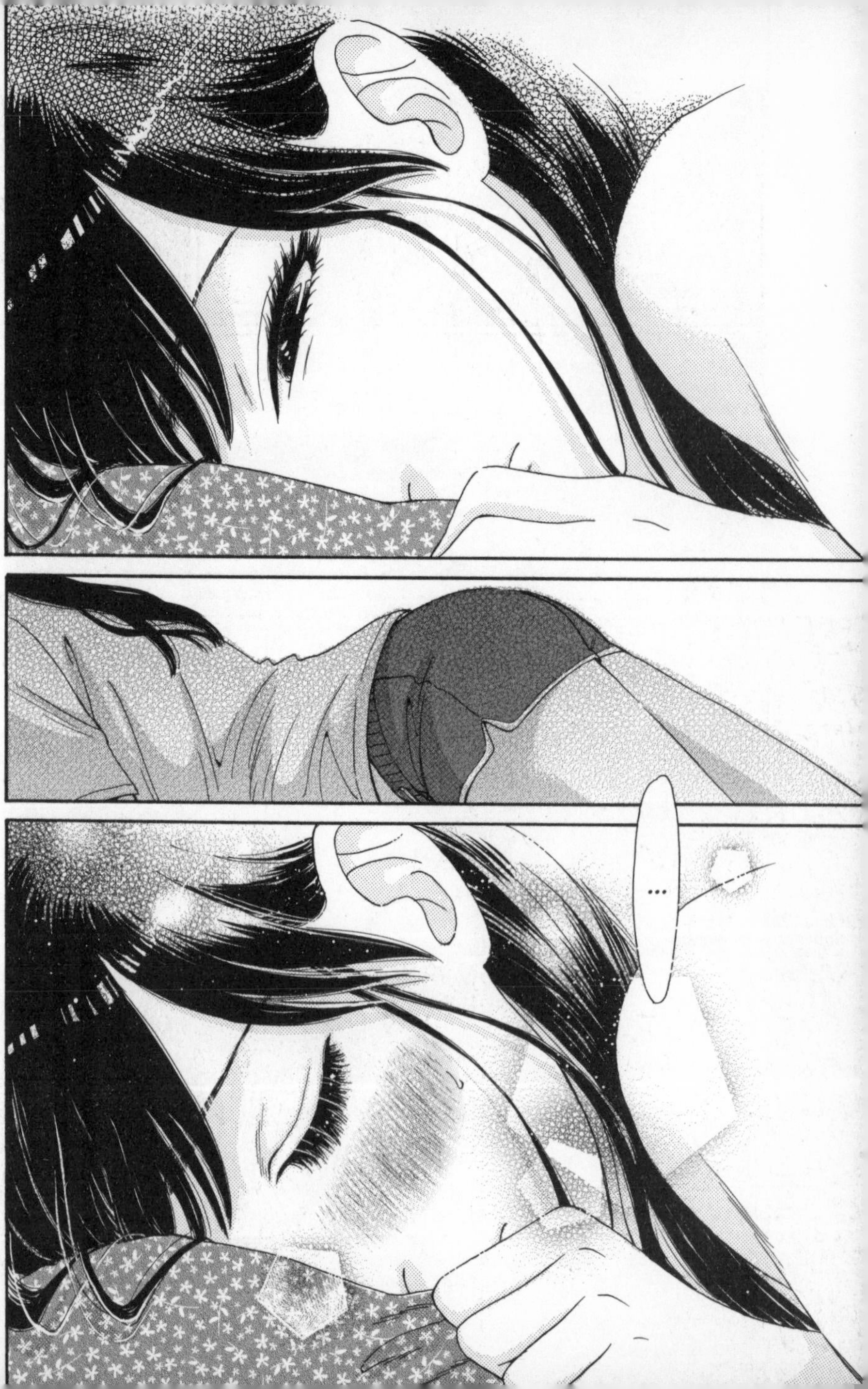
…

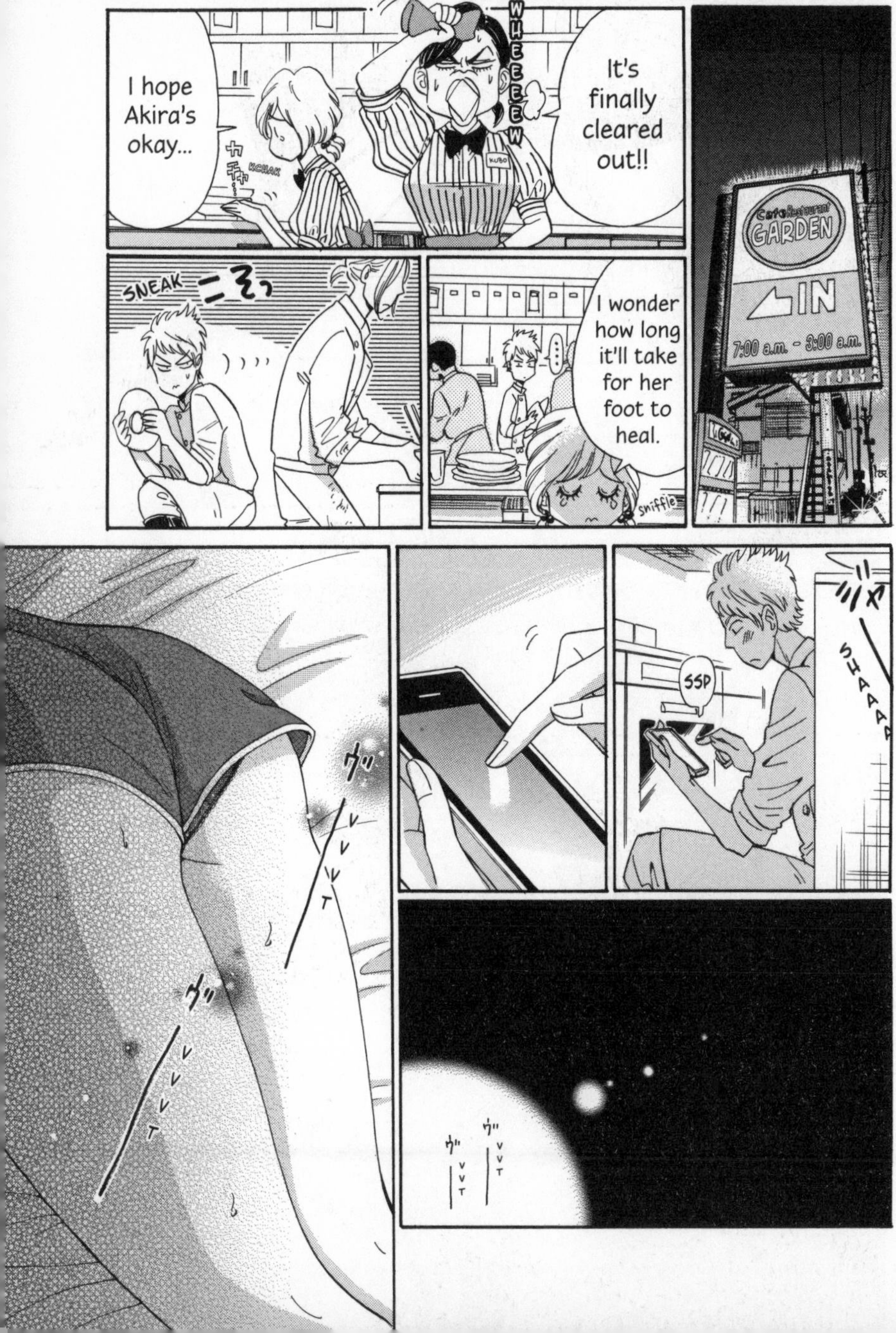
Cafe Restaurant
GARDEN
IN
7:00 a.m. - 3:00 a.m.
WHEEEEEW
It's finally cleared out!!
KUBO
I hope Akira's okay...
KCHAK
I wonder how long it'll take for her foot to heal.
sniffle
SNEAK
SHAAAA
SSP
VVVT
VVVT
VVVT
VVVVT

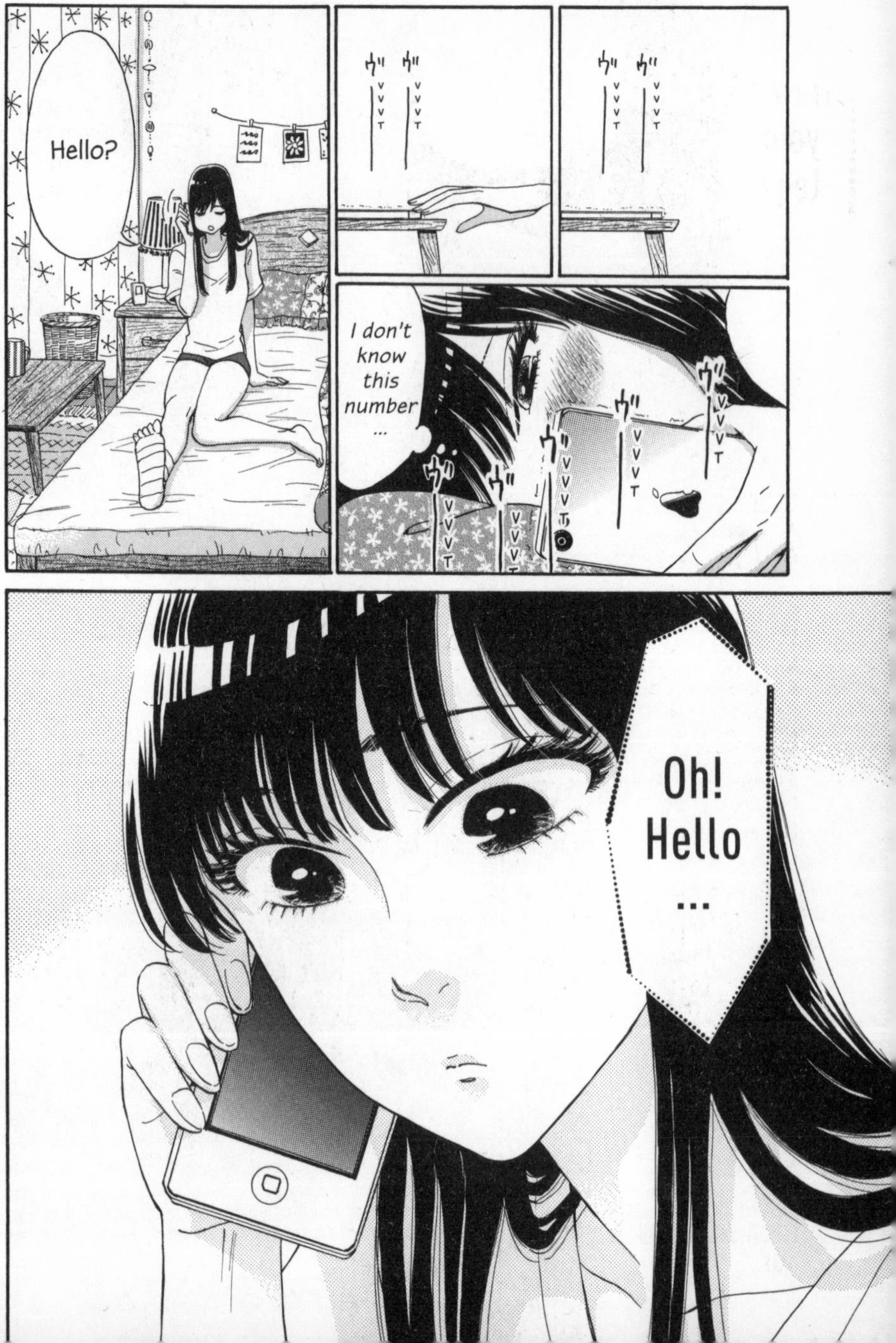

ヴ VVVT
ヴ VVVT
ヴ VVVT
ヴ VVVT
I don't know this number ...
ヴ VVVT
ヴ VVVT
ヴ VVVT
ヴ VVVT
ヴ VVVT
Hello?
Oh! Hello ...

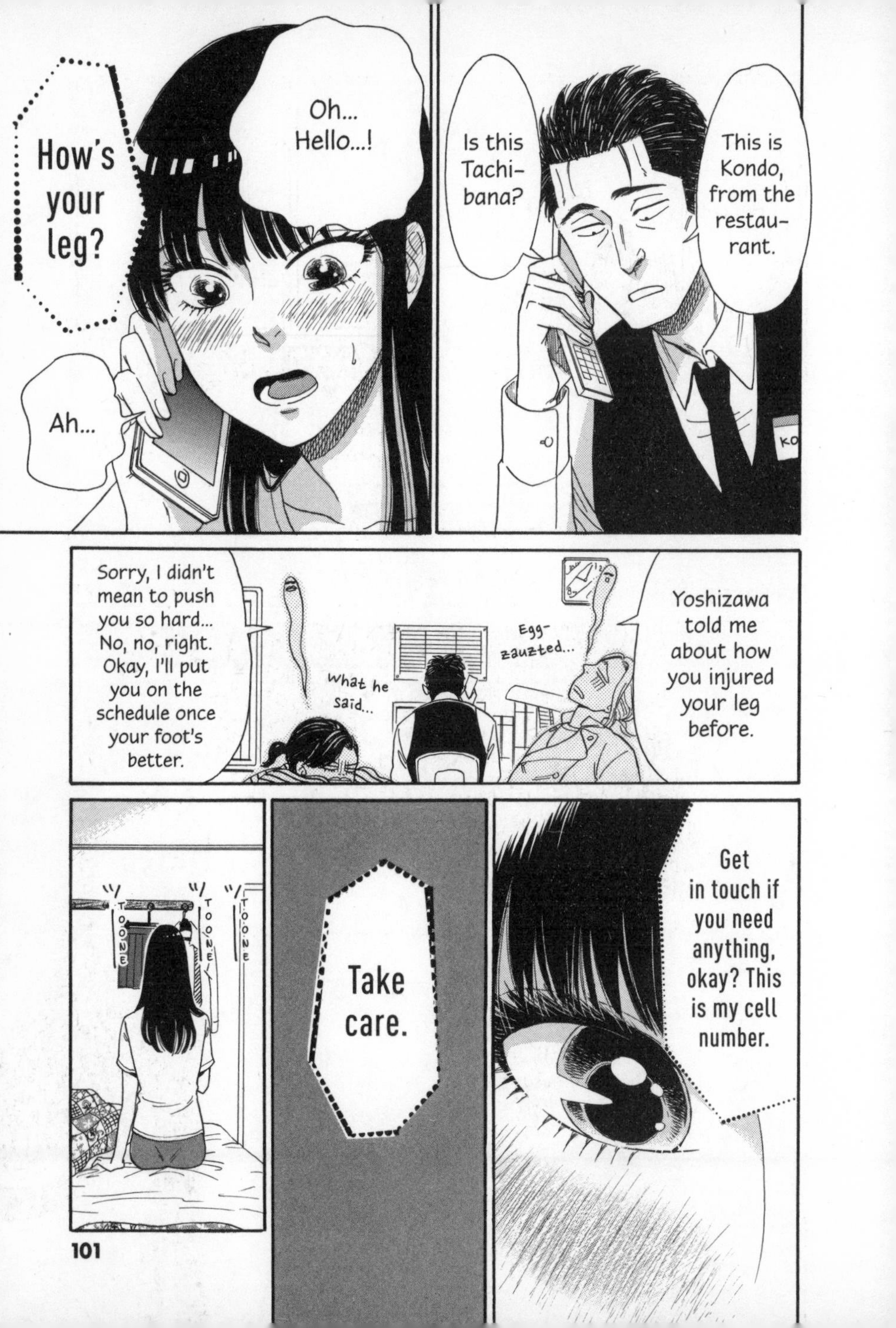
This is Kondo, from the restaurant.
Is this Tachibana?
Oh... Hello...!
How's your leg?
Ah...
Yoshizawa told me about how you injured your leg before.
Egg-zauzted...
What he said...
Sorry, I didn't mean to push you so hard... No, no, right. Okay, I'll put you on the schedule once your foot's better.
Get in touch if you need anything, okay? This is my cell number.
Take care.
TOONE
TOONE
TOONE

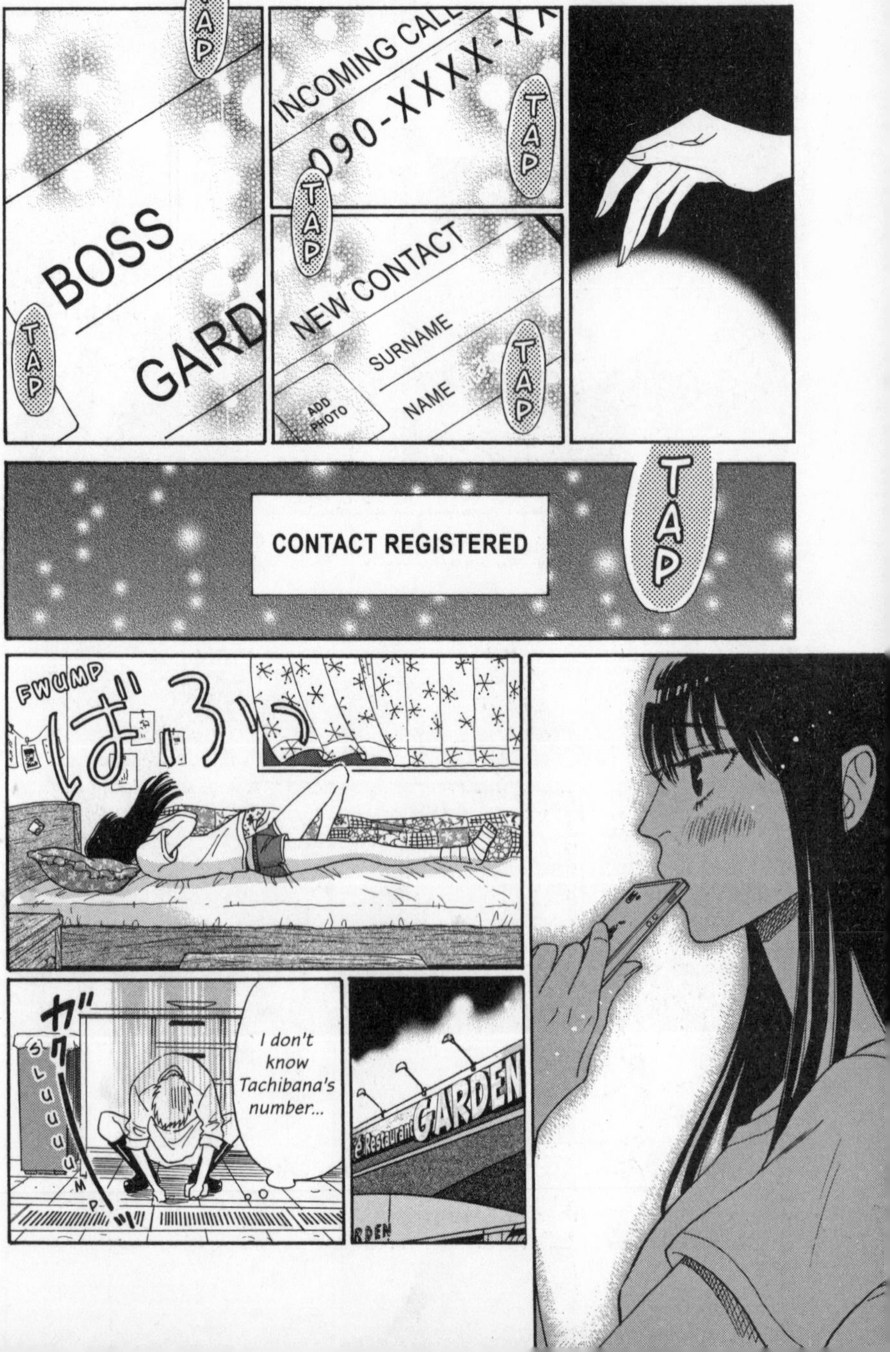
TAP
INCOMING CALL
090-XXXX-XX
TAP
TAP
NEW CONTACT
SURNAME
NAME
ADD PHOTO
TAP
TAP
BOSS
GARD
TAP
TAP
CONTACT REGISTERED
FWUMP
GARDEN
é Restaurant GARDEN
I don't know Tachibana's number...
SLUUUUMP

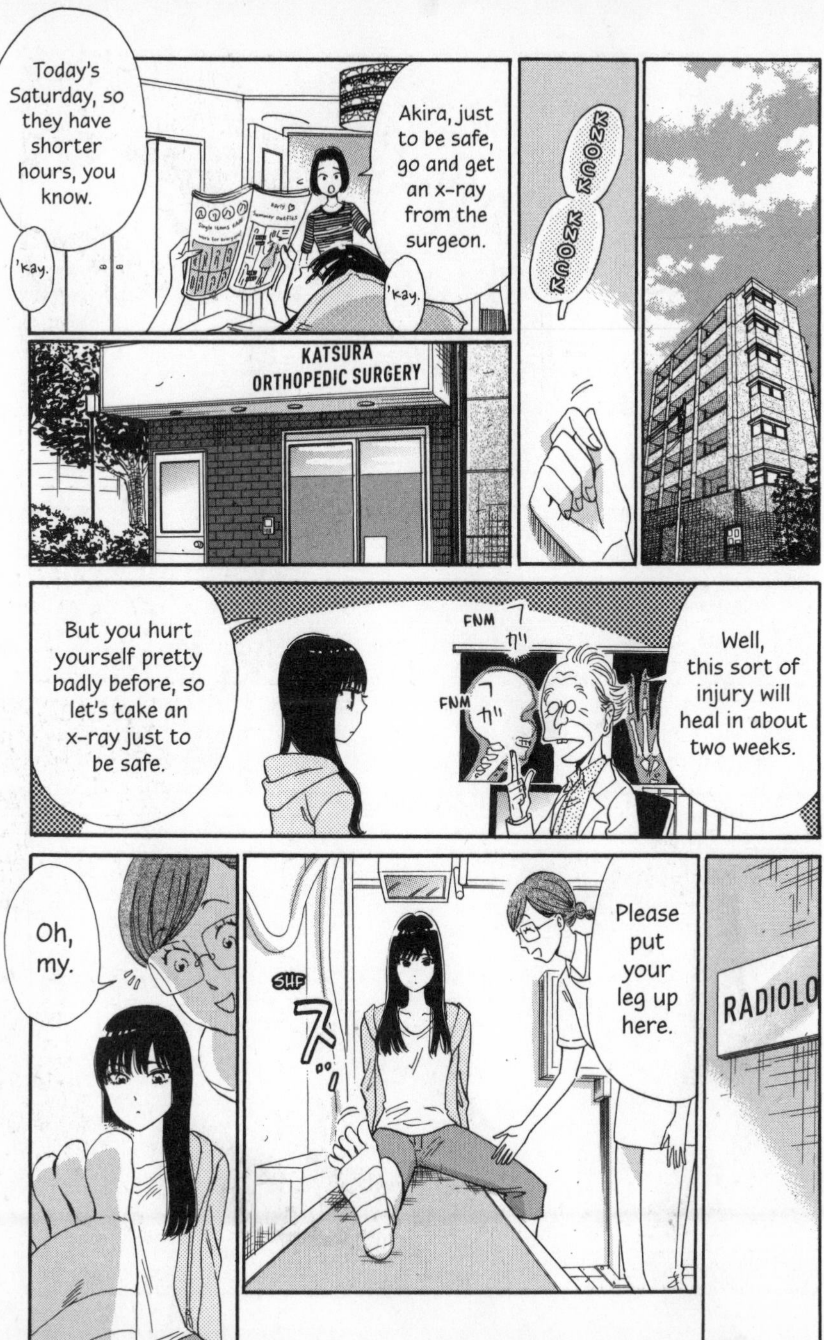
KNOCK
KNOCK
Akira, just to be safe, go and get an x-ray from the surgeon.
'kay.
Today's Saturday, so they have shorter hours, you know.
'kay.
KATSURA ORTHOPEDIC SURGERY
Well, this sort of injury will heal in about two weeks.
FNM
FNM
But you hurt yourself pretty badly before, so let's take an x-ray just to be safe.
RADIOLO
Please put your leg up here.
SHF
Oh, my.

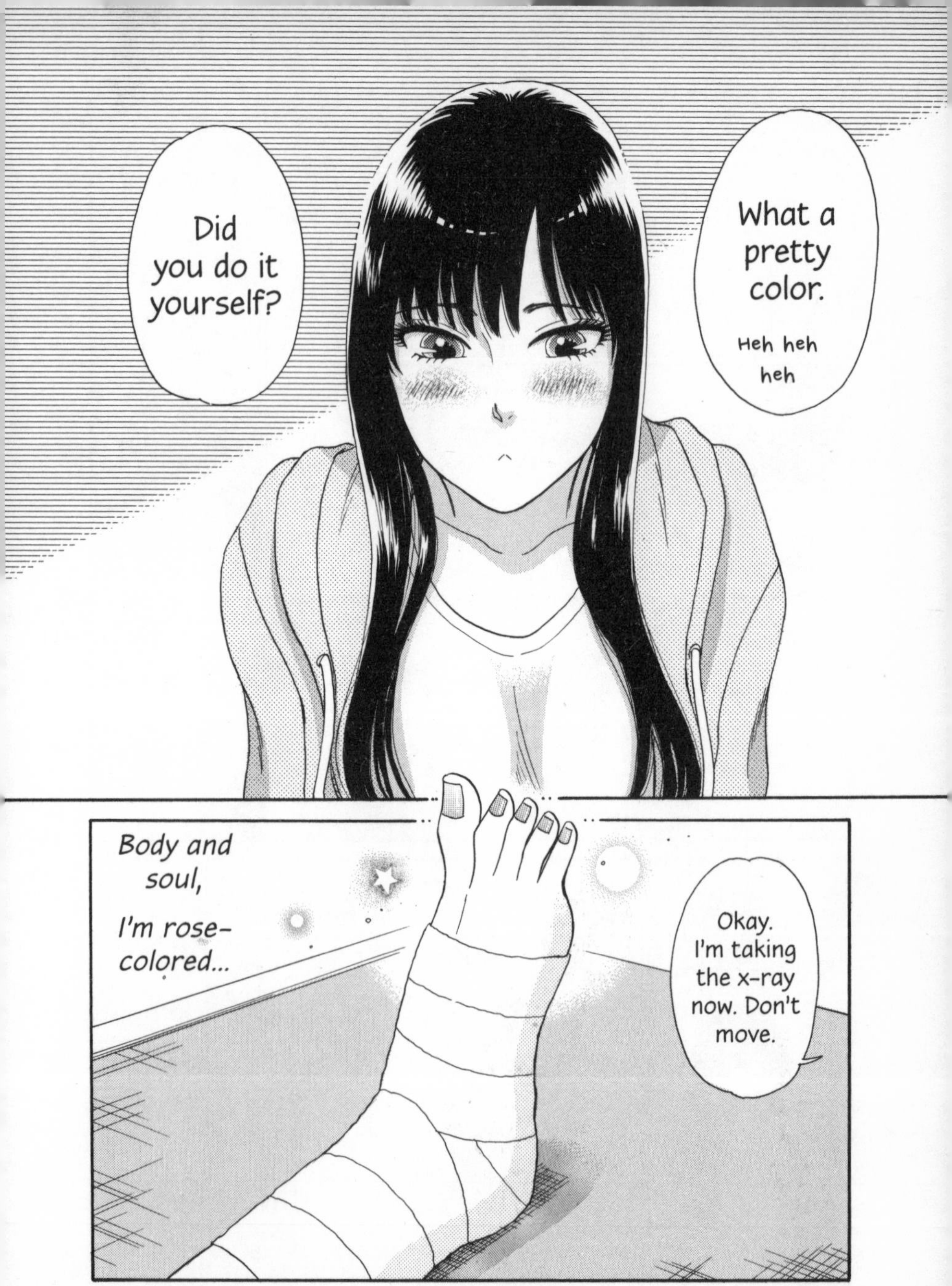
What a pretty color.
Heh heh heh
Did you do it yourself?
Okay. I'm taking the x-ray now. Don't move.
Body and soul,
I'm rose-colored...

KSHAK
パシャ

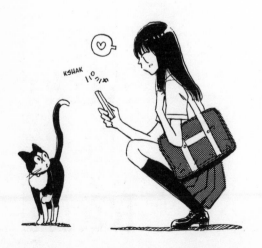

After the Rain

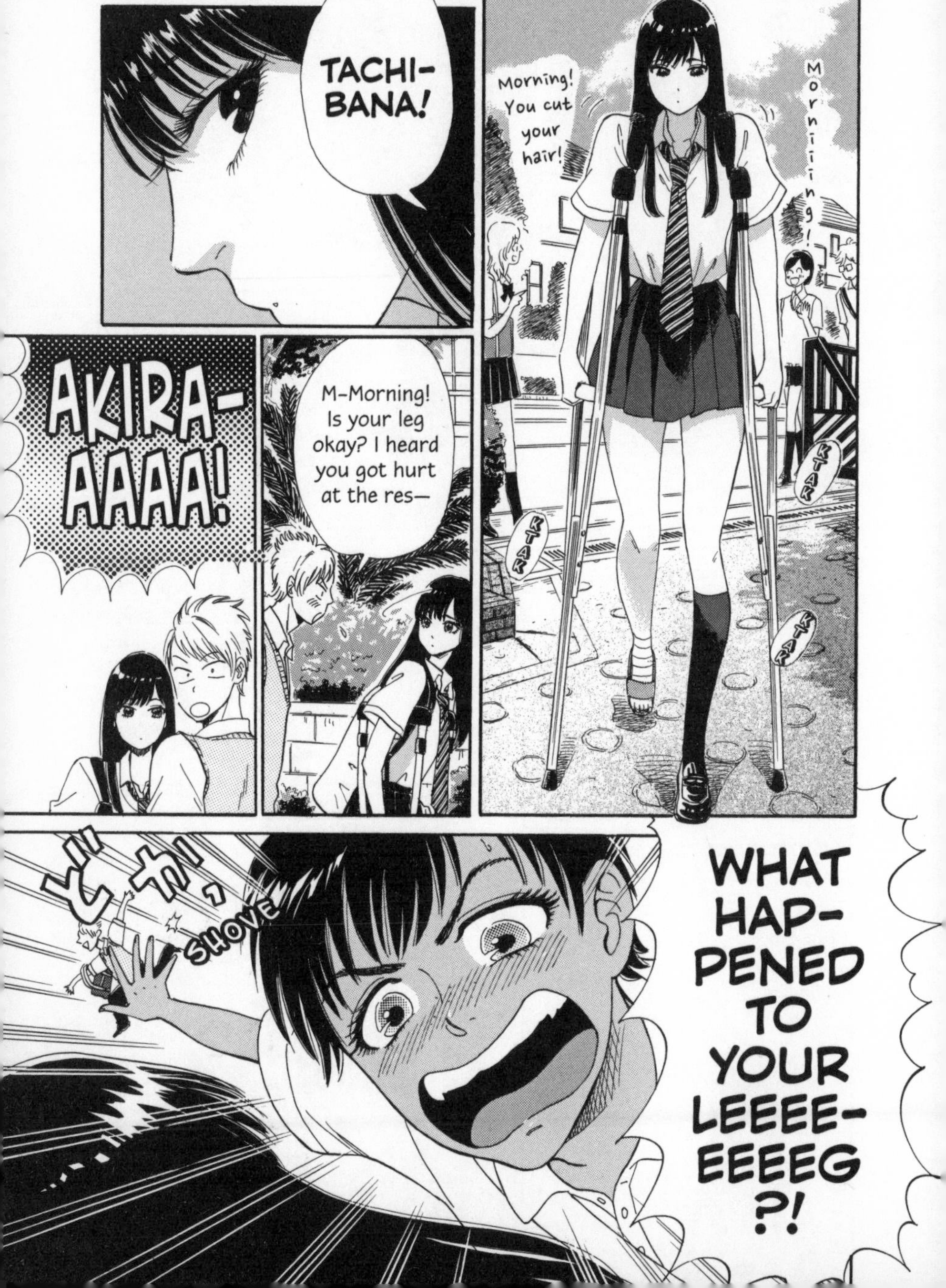

Morniiiing!
Morning! You cut your hair!
KTAK
KTAK
KTAK
TACHI-BANA!
M-Morning! Is your leg okay? I heard you got hurt at the res—
AKIRA-AAAA!
WHAT HAP-PENED TO YOUR LEEEE-EEEEG?!
どか SHOVE

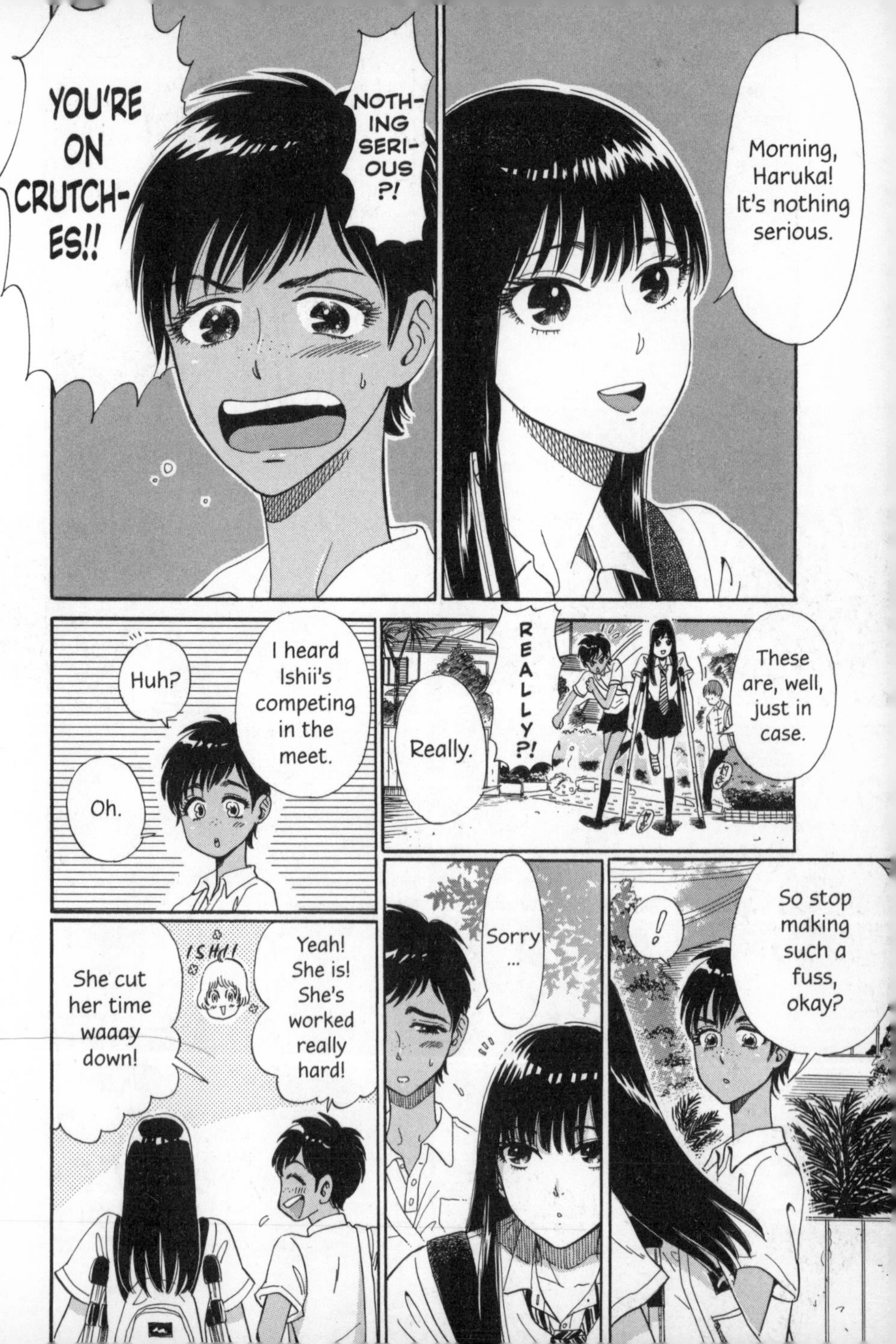

Morning, Haruka! It's nothing serious.
NOTHING SERIOUS?!
YOU'RE ON CRUTCHES!!
These are, well, just in case.
REALLY?!
Really.
I heard Ishii's competing in the meet.
Huh?
Oh.
So stop making such a fuss, okay?
!
Sorry...
Yeah! She is! She's worked really hard!
ISHII
She cut her time waaay down!

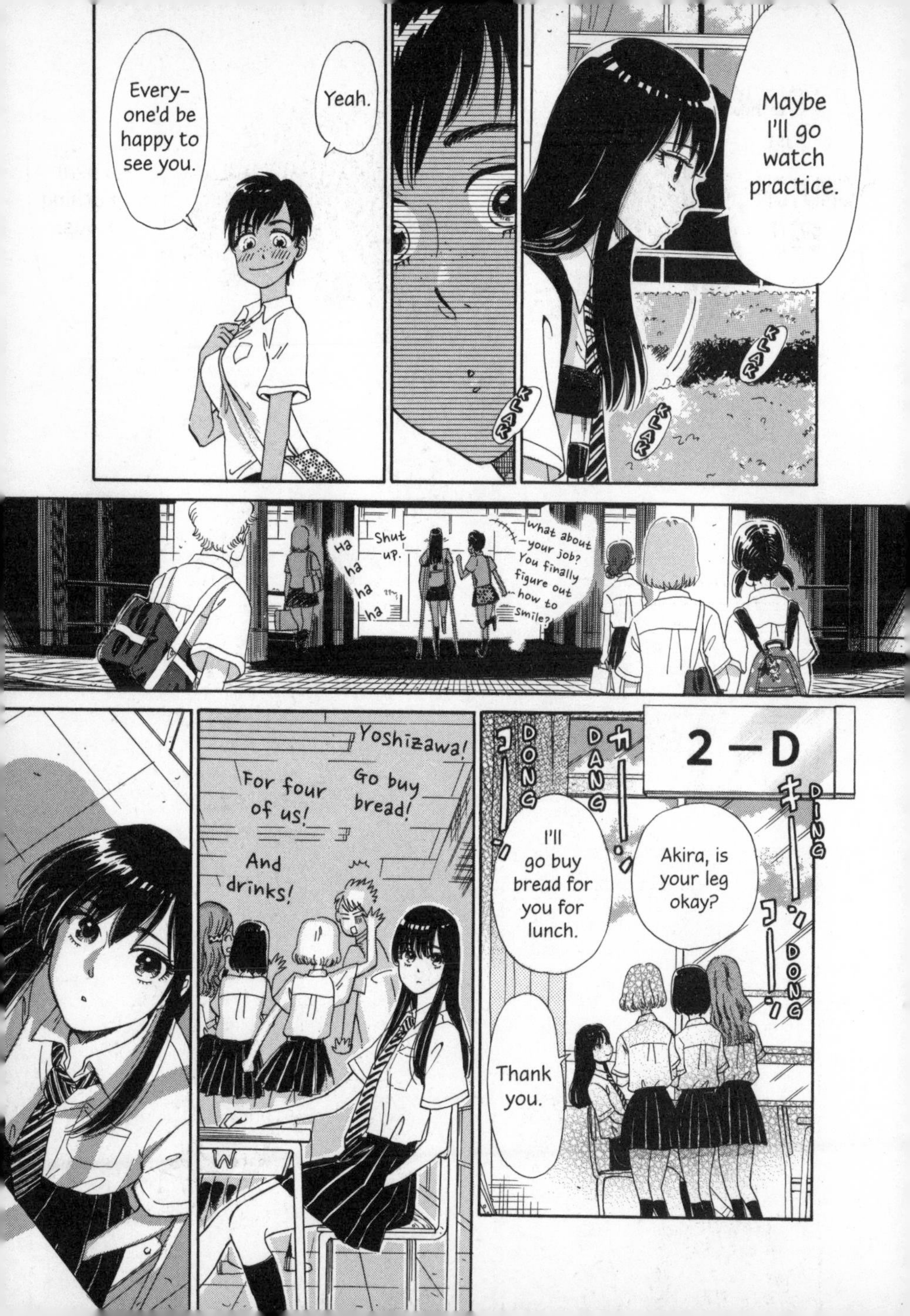
Maybe I'll go watch practice.
KLAR
KLAR
KLAR
Yeah.
Every-one'd be happy to see you.
What about your job? You finally figure out how to smile?
Shut up.
Ha ha ha ha
2—D
DING
DONG
Akira, is your leg okay?
DANG
DONG
I'll go buy bread for you for lunch.
Thank you.
Yoshizawa!
Go buy bread!
For four of us!
And drinks!

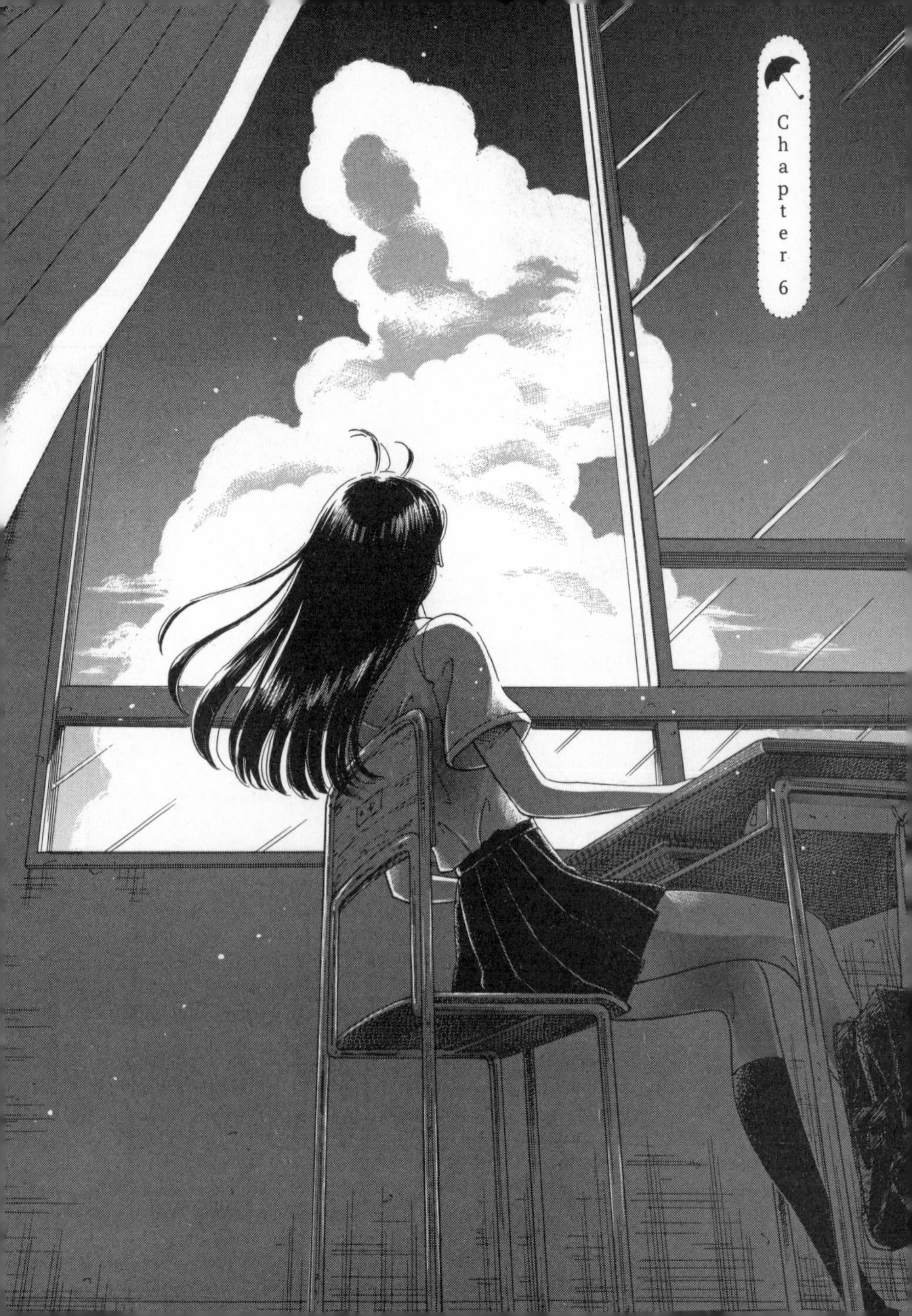
Chapter 6

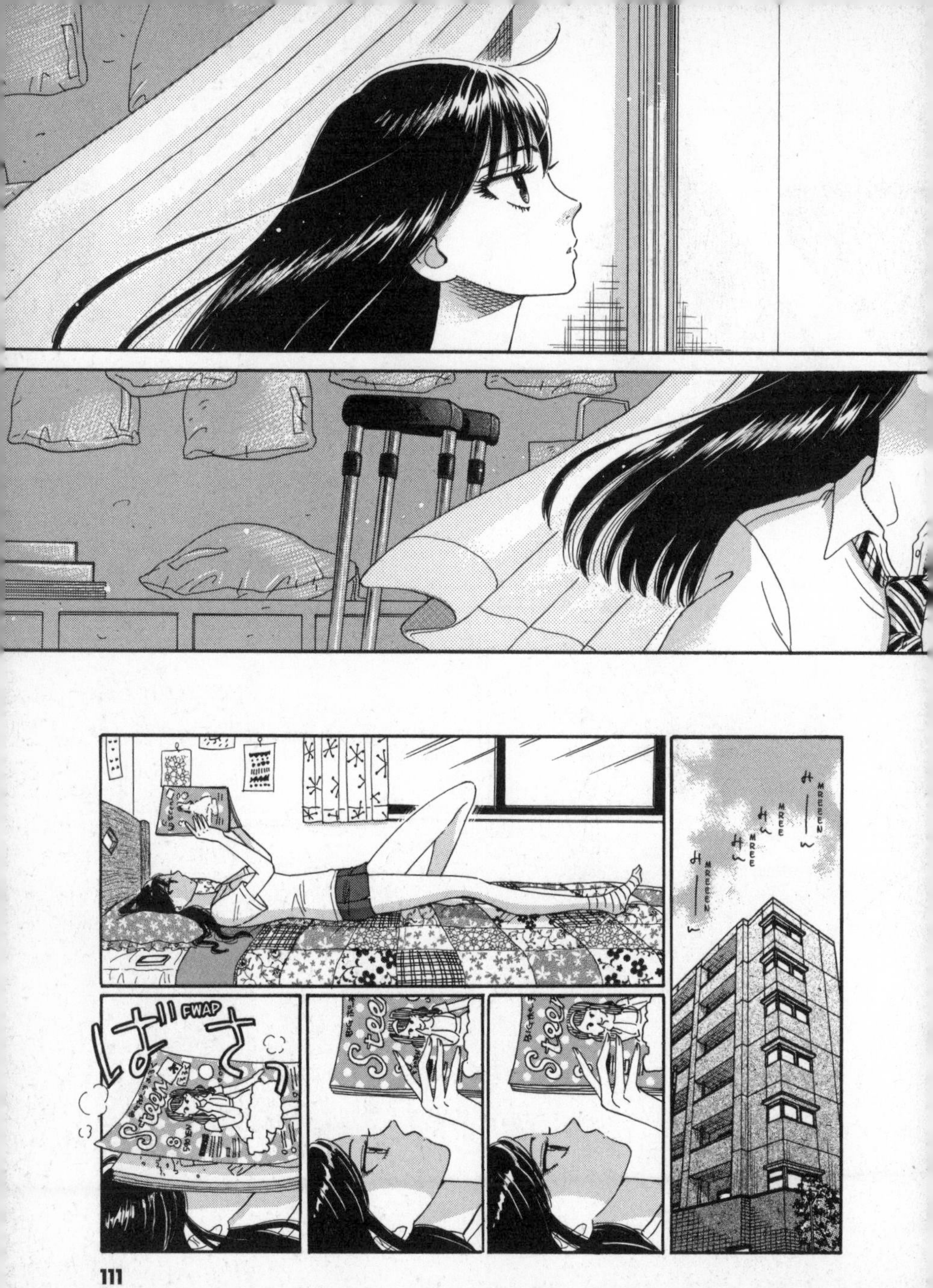

MREEEN
MREE
MREE
MREEEN
はさっ
FWAP

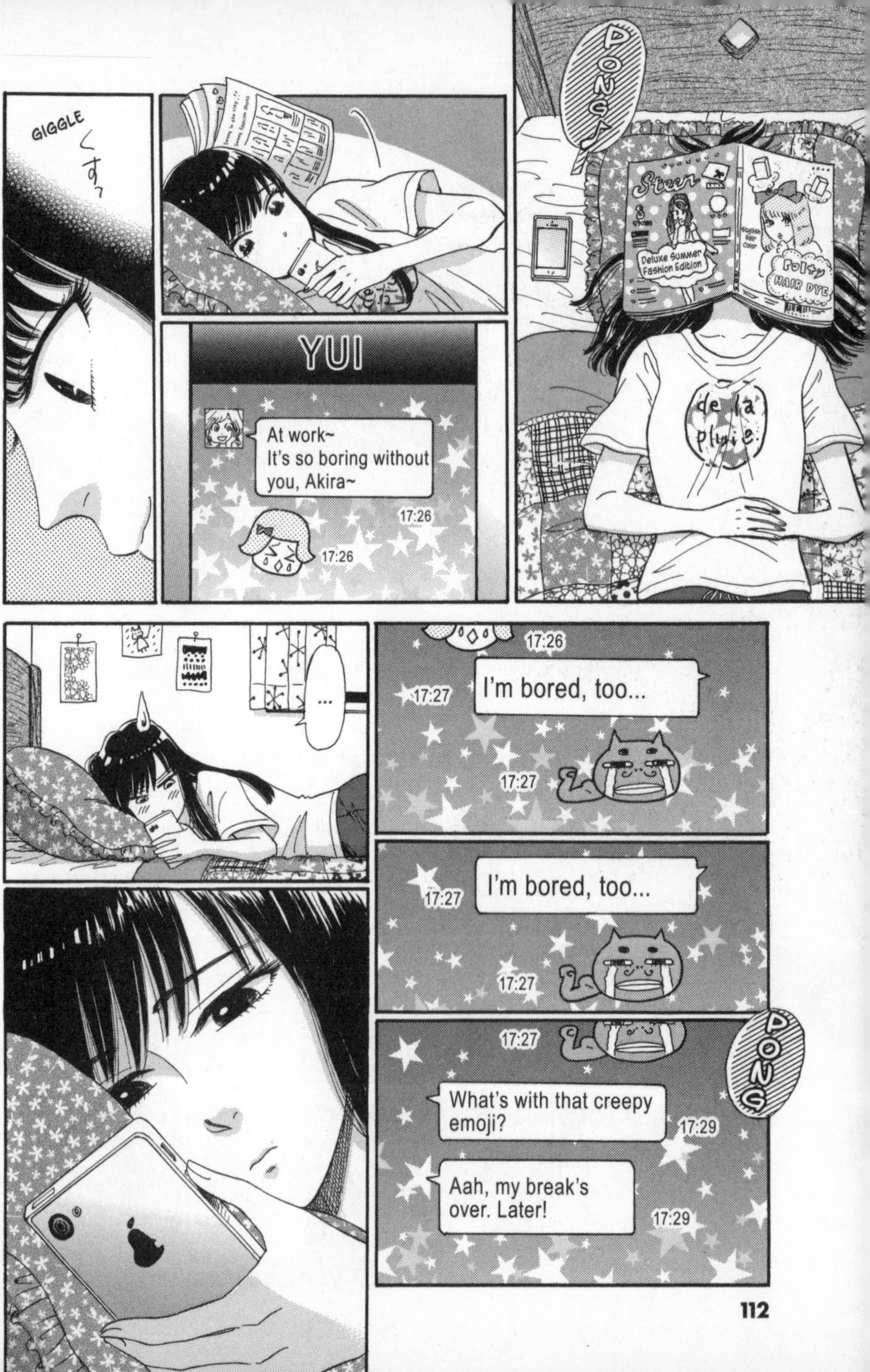
PONG
Steen
Deluxe Summer Fashion Edition
Stylish Hair Color
HAIR DYE
de la pluie.
YUI
At work~
It's so boring without you, Akira~
17:26
17:26
GIGGLE
くすっ
17:26
I'm bored, too...
17:27
17:27
I'm bored, too...
17:27
17:27
PONG
17:27
What's with that creepy emoji?
17:29
Aah, my break's over. Later!
17:29
...

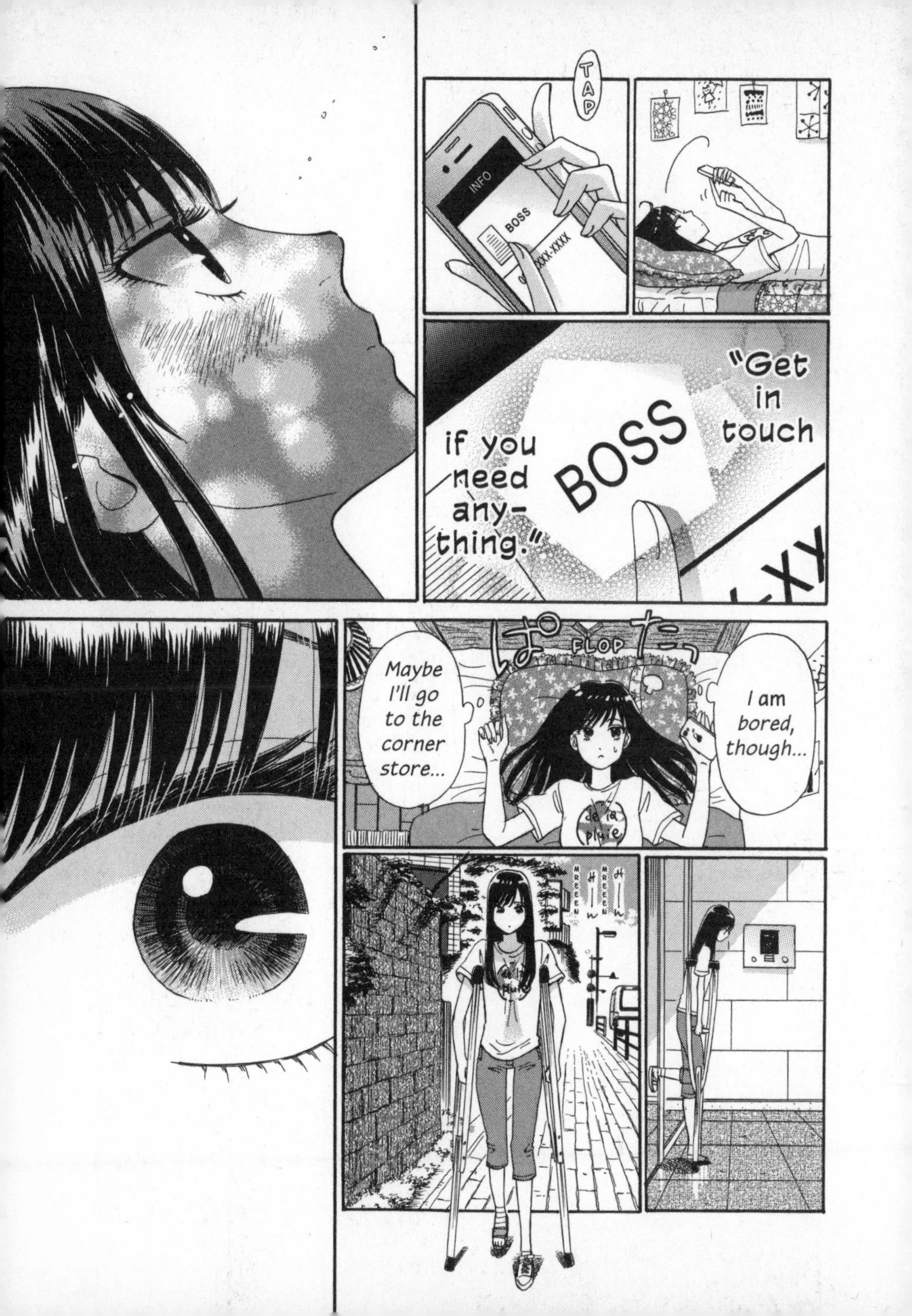
TAP
INFO
BOSS
XXX-XXXX
"Get in touch if you need anything."
BOSS
FLOP
I am bored, though...
Maybe I'll go to the corner store...
de la pluie
MREEEN
MREEEN

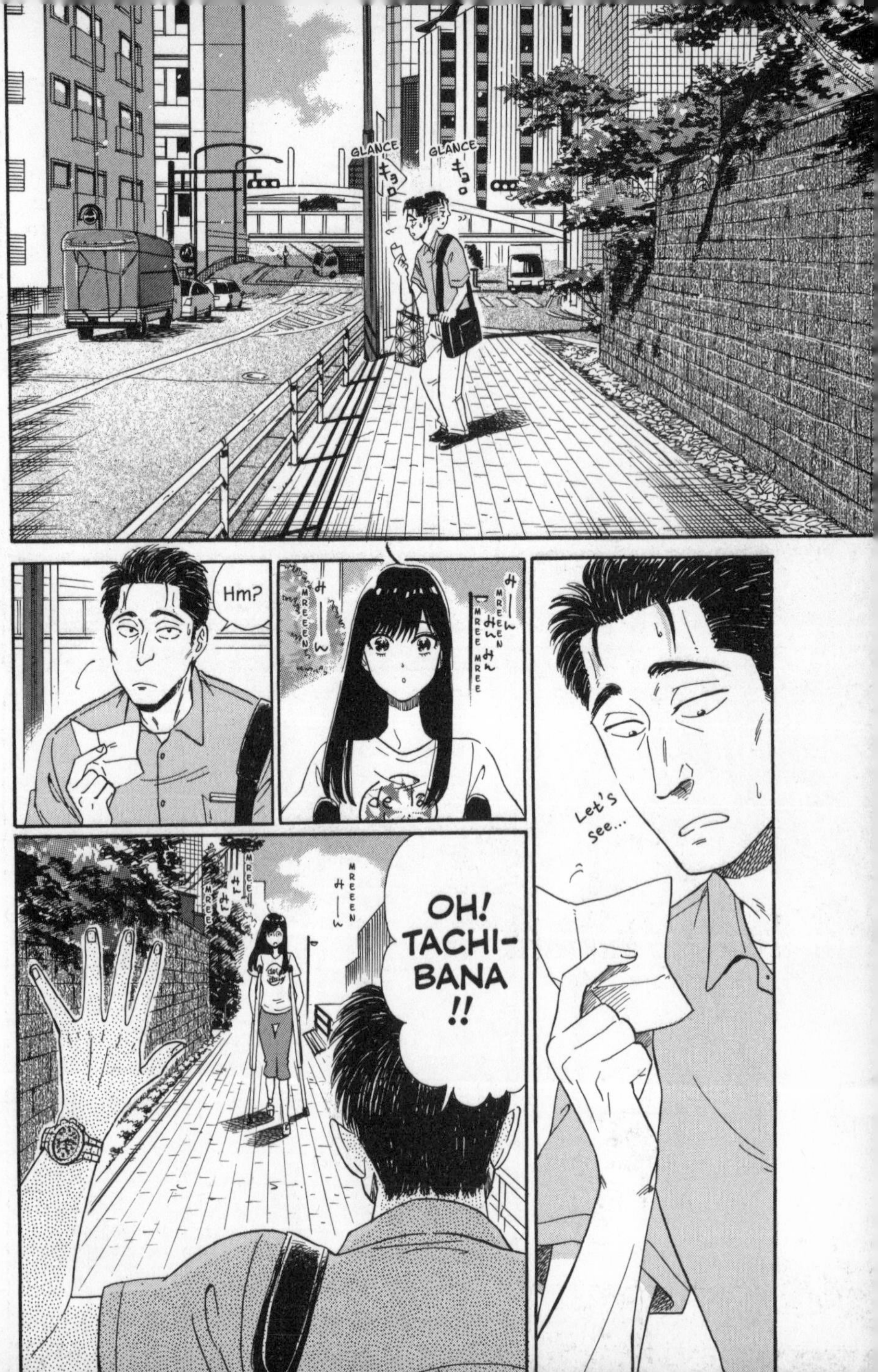
GLANCE
キョロ
GLANCE
キョロ
Let's see...
MREEEN
みーん
MREE MREE
みんみん
MREEEN
みーん
Hm?
MREEEN
みーん
MREE
みん
MREE
みん
OH! TACHIBANA!!

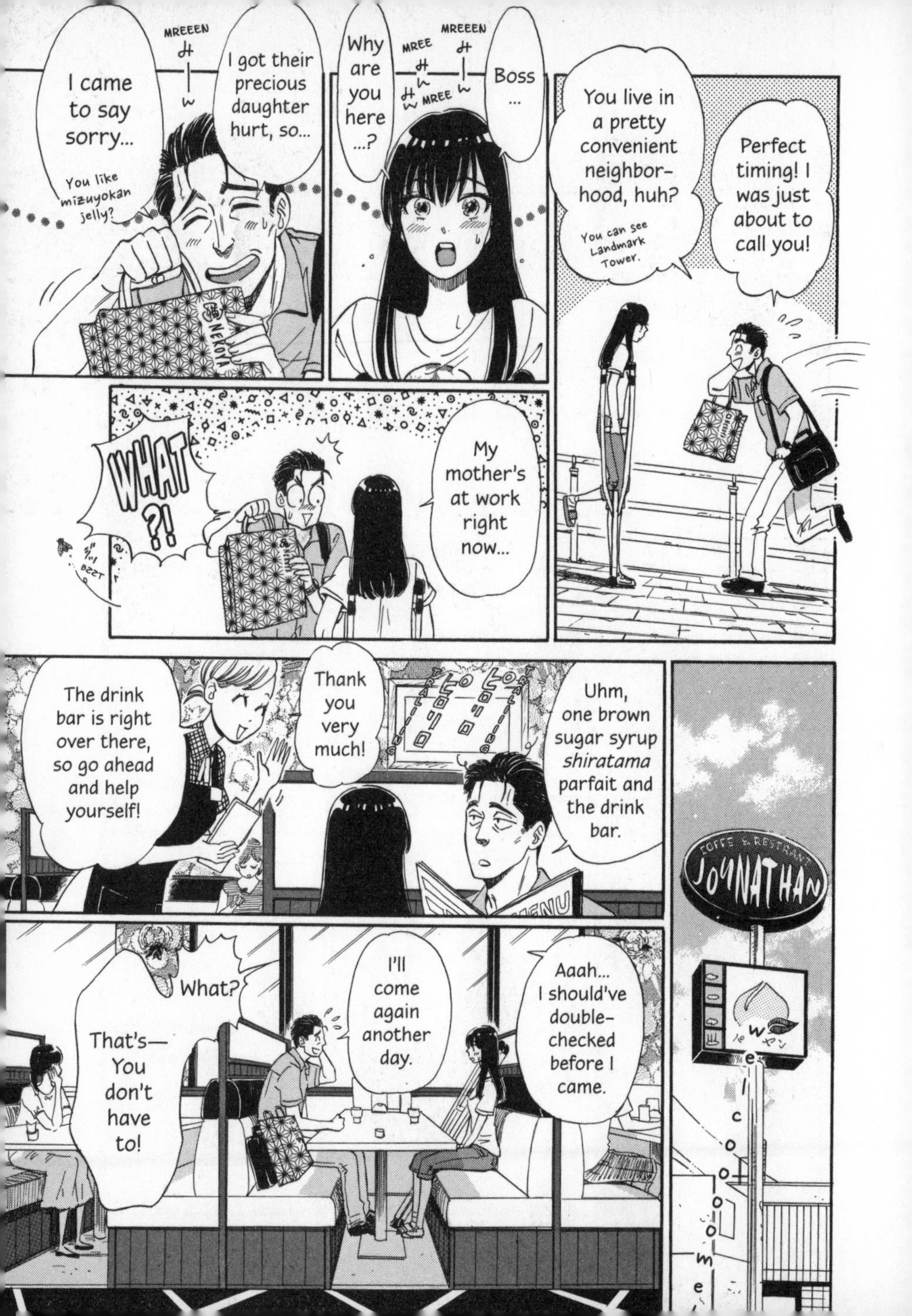
Perfect timing! I was just about to call you!
You live in a pretty convenient neighbor-hood, huh?
You can see Landmark Tower.
MREEEN
Boss...
MREE
Why are you here...?
MREEEN
I got their precious daughter hurt, so...
I came to say sorry...
You like mizuyokan jelly?
NEKOYA
My mother's at work right now...
WHAT?!
BZZT
JONATHAN
welcooooome
Uhm, one brown sugar syrup *shiratama* parfait and the drink bar.
Thank you very much!
The drink bar is right over there, so go ahead and help yourself!
MENU
Aaah... I should've double-checked before I came.
I'll come again another day.
What?
That's— You don't have to!

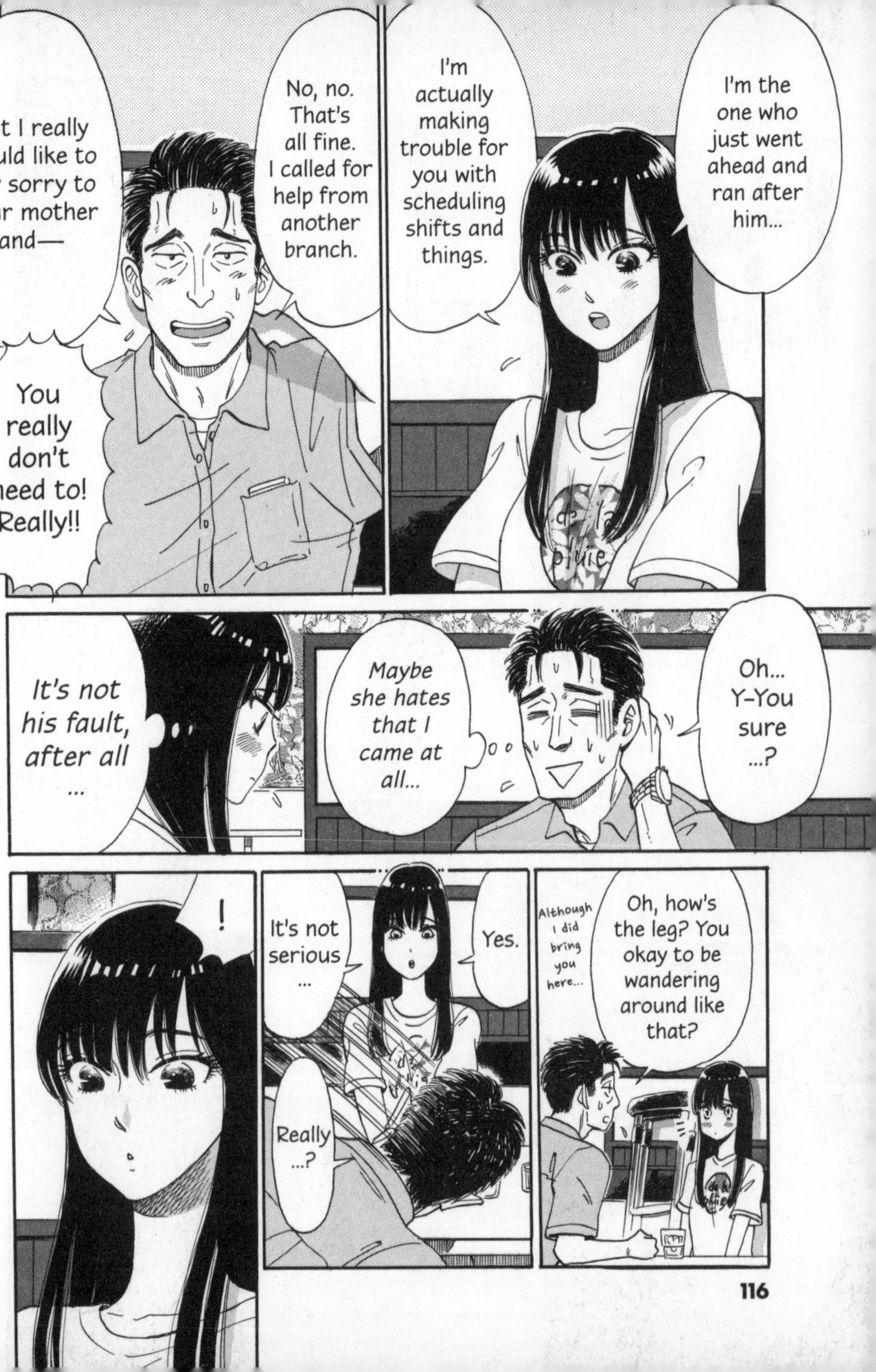
I'm the one who just went ahead and ran after him...
I'm actually making trouble for you with scheduling shifts and things.
No, no. That's all fine. I called for help from another branch.
But I really would like to say sorry to your mother and—
You really don't need to! Really!!
Oh... Y-You sure ...?
Maybe she hates that I came at all...
It's not his fault, after all ...
Oh, how's the leg? You okay to be wandering around like that?
Although I did bring you here...
Yes.
It's not serious ...
Really ...?
!

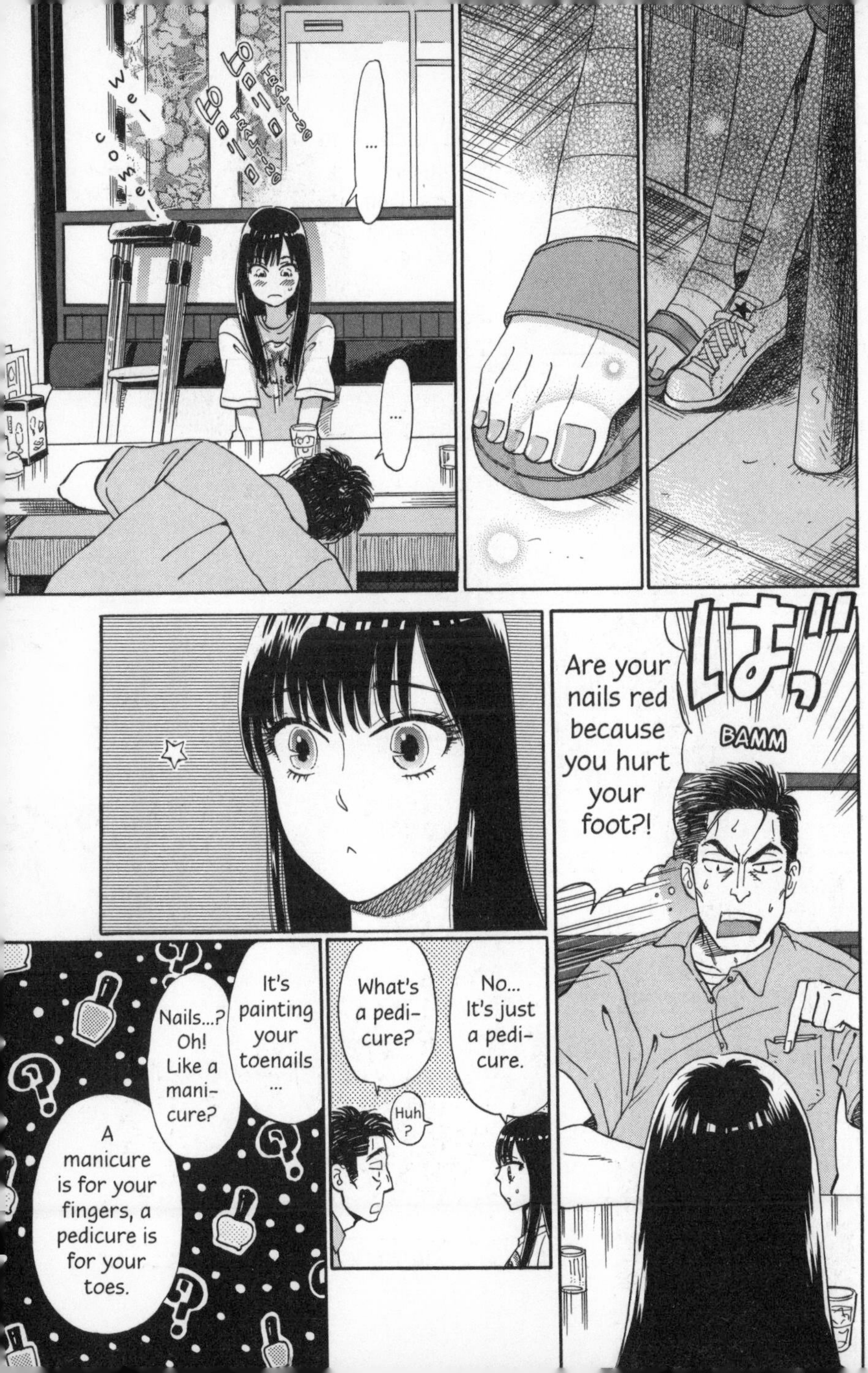
Welcome!
TRAJ--20
TRAJ--20
...
...
BAMM
Are your nails red because you hurt your foot?!
No... It's just a pedicure.
What's a pedicure?
Huh?
It's painting your toenails ...
Nails...? Oh! Like a manicure?
A manicure is for your fingers, a pedicure is for your toes.

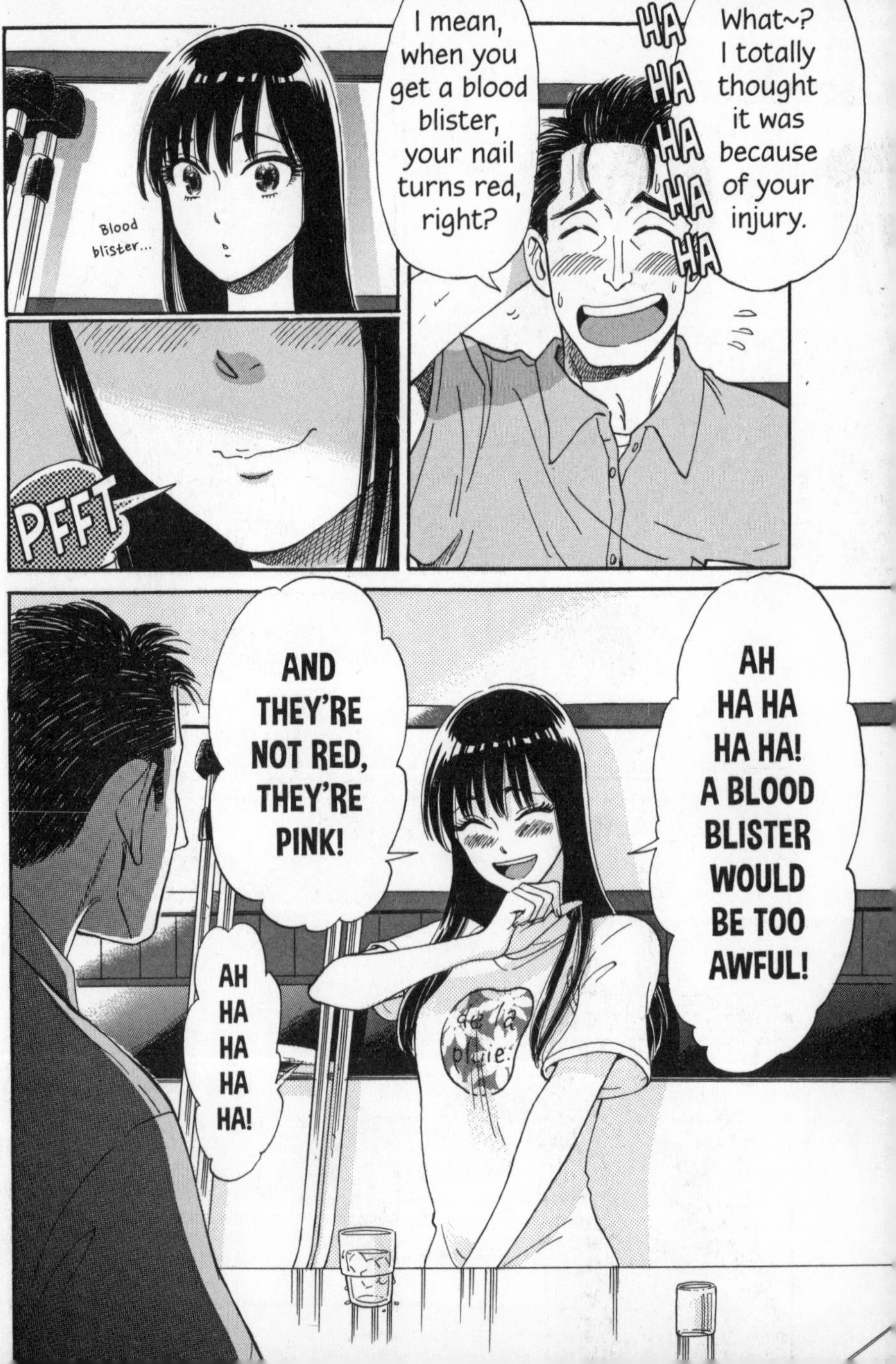
What~? I totally thought it was because of your injury.
HA HA HA HA HA
I mean, when you get a blood blister, your nail turns red, right?
Blood blister...
PFFT
AH HA HA HA HA! A BLOOD BLISTER WOULD BE TOO AWFUL!
AND THEY'RE NOT RED, THEY'RE PINK!
AH HA HA HA HA HA!
de la pluie.

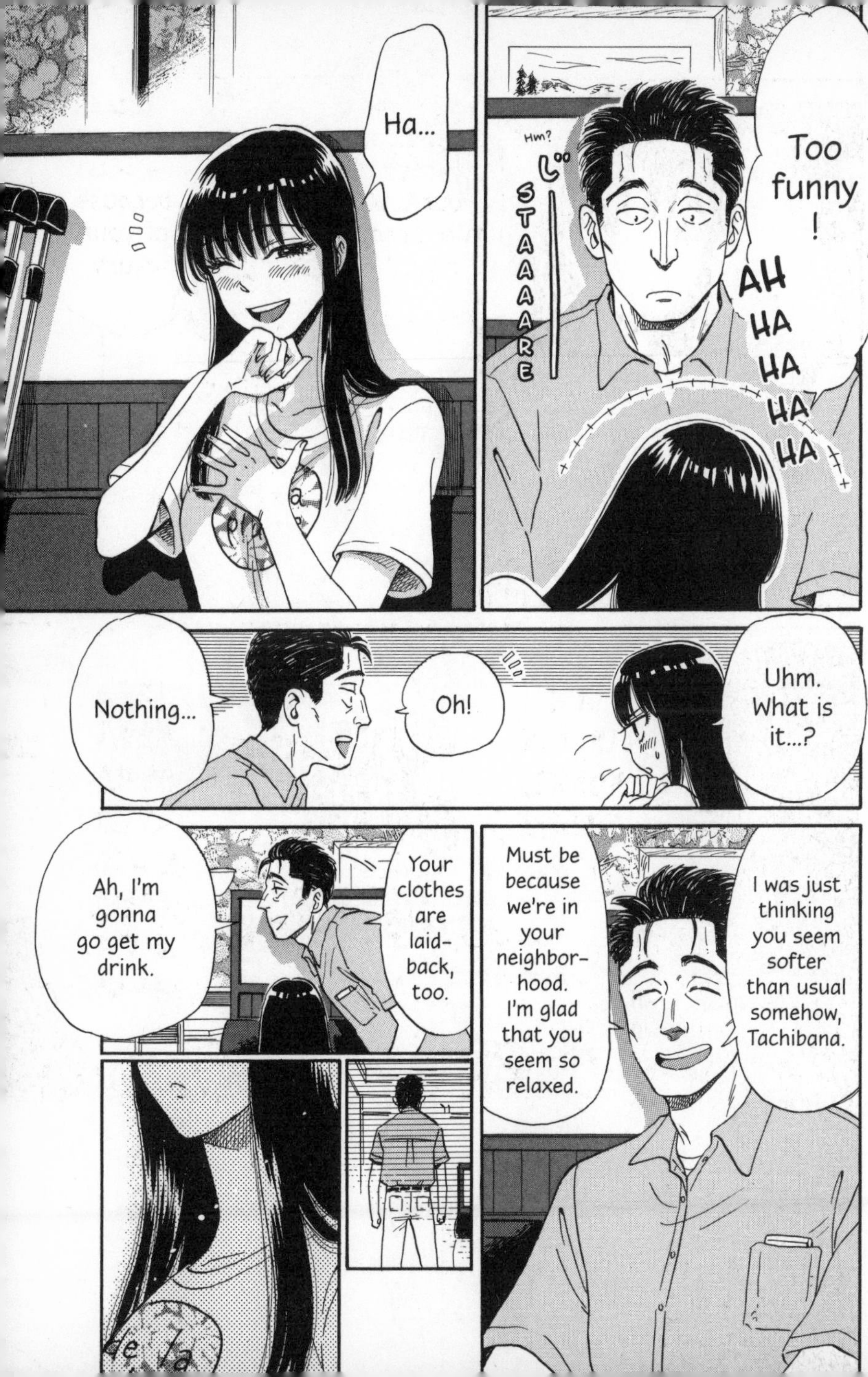
Too funny!
AH HA HA HA HA
Hm?
STAAAAAARE
Ha...
Uhm. What is it...?
Oh!
Nothing...
I was just thinking you seem softer than usual somehow, Tachibana.
Must be because we're in your neighborhood. I'm glad that you seem so relaxed.
Your clothes are laid-back, too.
Ah, I'm gonna go get my drink.

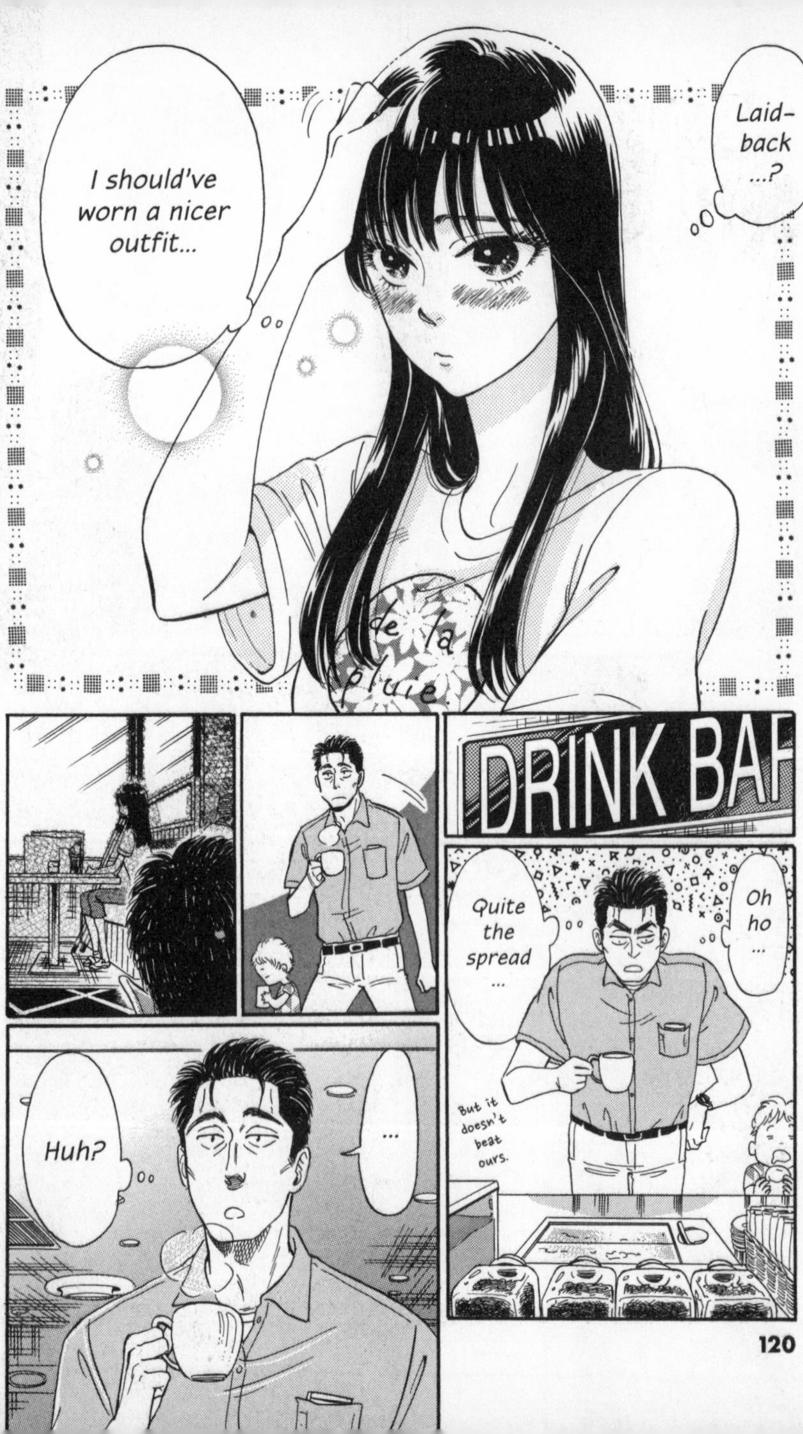
Laid-back ...?
I should've worn a nicer outfit...
de la pluie.
DRINK BA
Oh ho ...
Quite the spread ...
But it doesn't beat ours.
...
Huh?

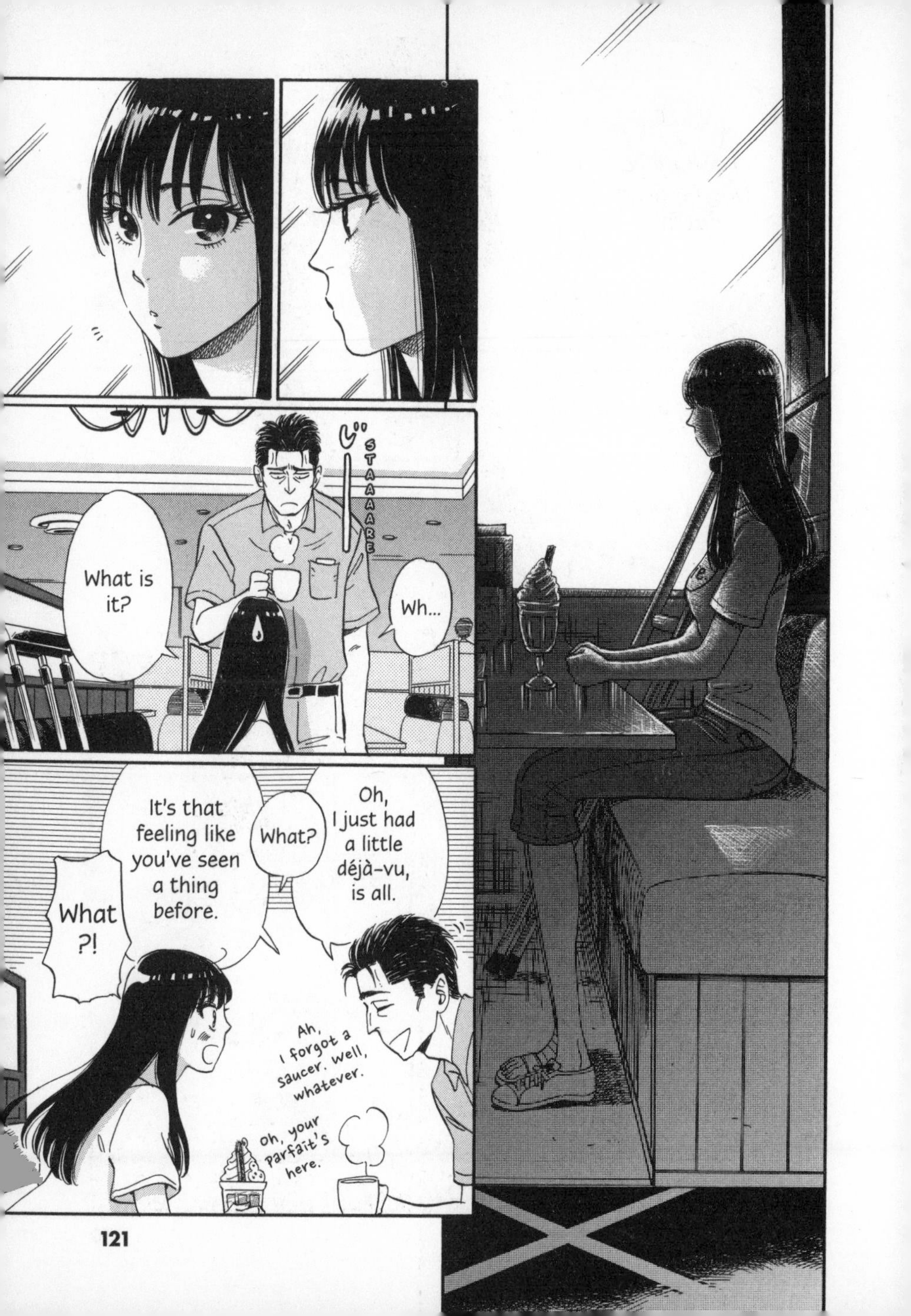
STAAAARE
Wh...
What is it?
Oh, I just had a little déjà-vu, is all.
What?
It's that feeling like you've seen a thing before.
What?!
Ah, I forgot a saucer. Well, whatever.
Oh, your parfait's here.

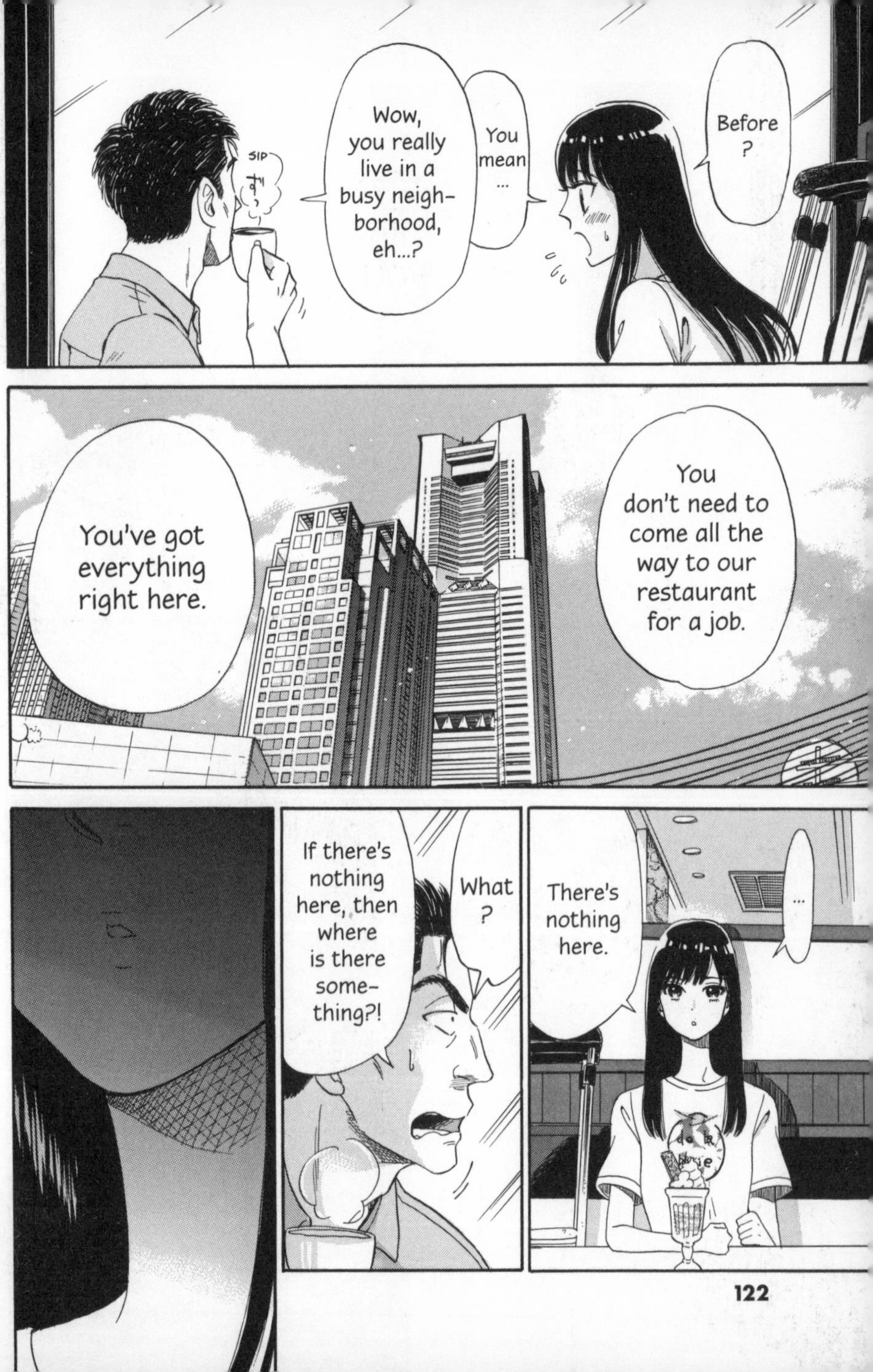
Before?
You mean ...
Wow, you really live in a busy neigh-borhood, eh...?
SIP
You don't need to come all the way to our restaurant for a job.
You've got everything right here.
...
There's nothing here.
What?
If there's nothing here, then where is there some-thing?!

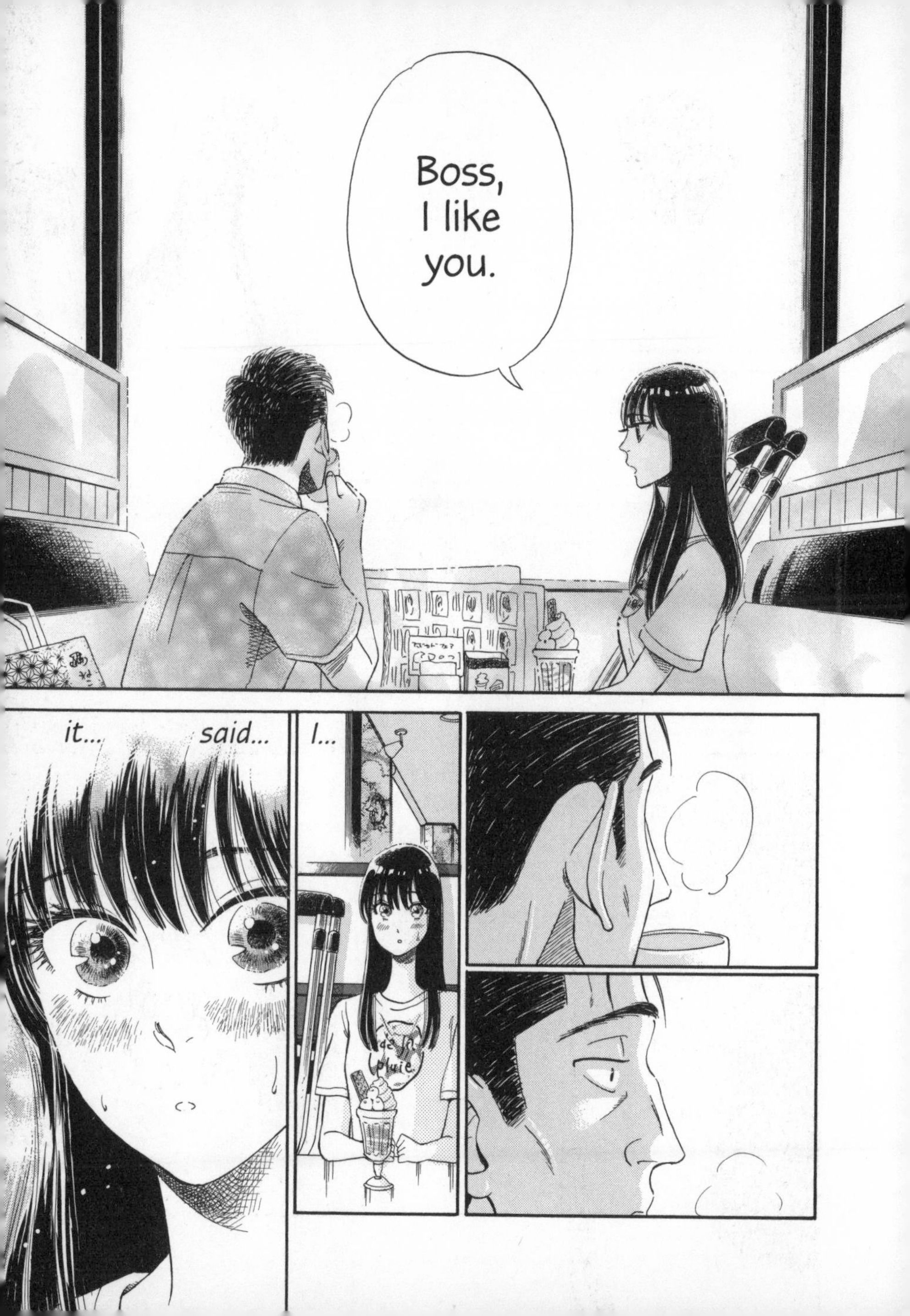
Boss, I like you.
I...
said...
it...

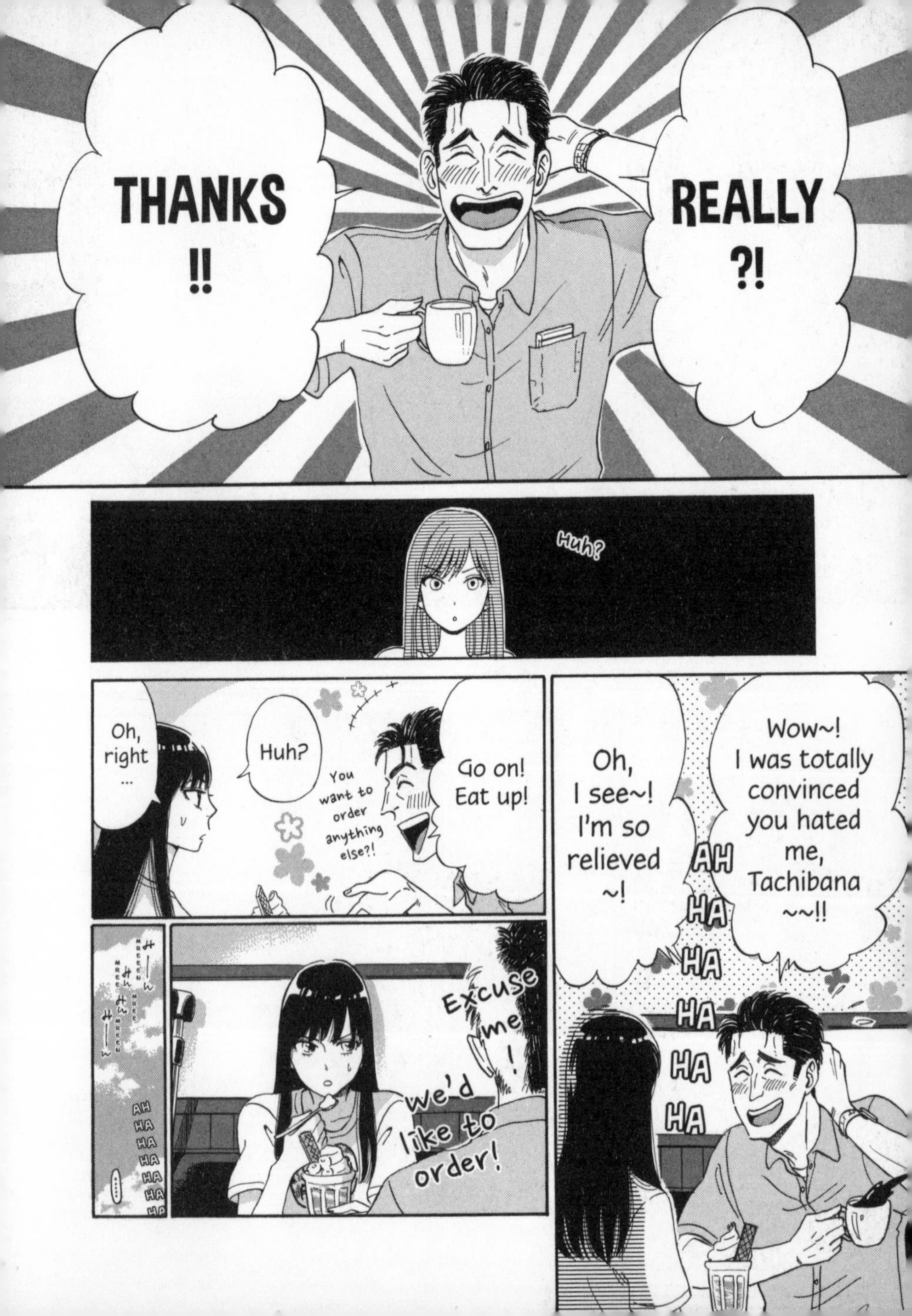
REALLY ?!
THANKS !!
Huh?
Wow~! I was totally convinced you hated me, Tachibana ~~!!
Oh, I see~! I'm so relieved ~!
AH HA HA HA HA HA
Go on! Eat up!
You want to order anything else?!
Huh?
Oh, right ...
Excuse me! we'd like to order!
AH HA HA HA HA HA HA
.....

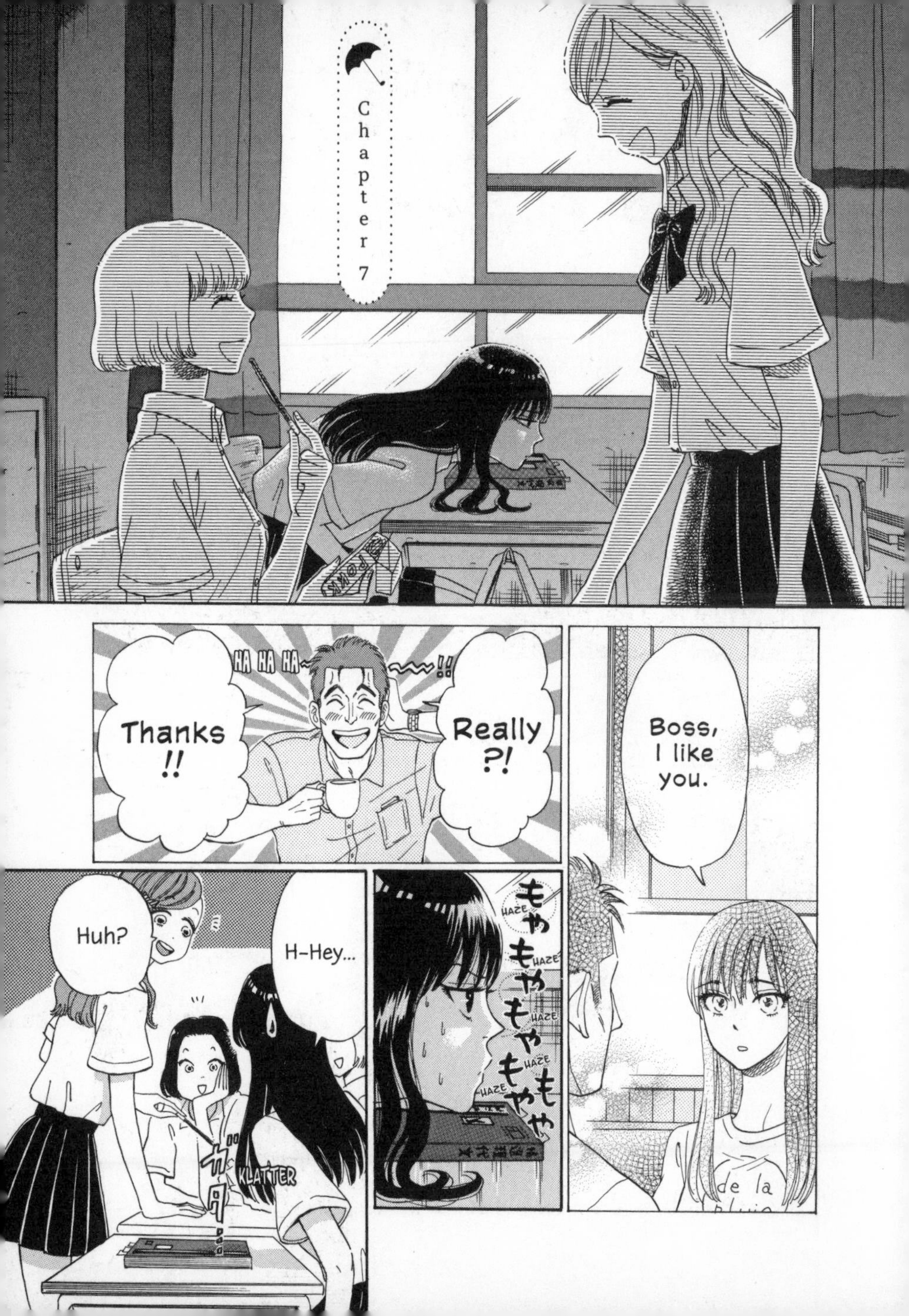

Chapter 7
Boss, I like you.
HA HA HA~ ~~!!
Really ?!
Thanks !!
HAZE
HAZE
HAZE
HAZE
HAZE
de la
H-Hey...
Huh?
KLATTER

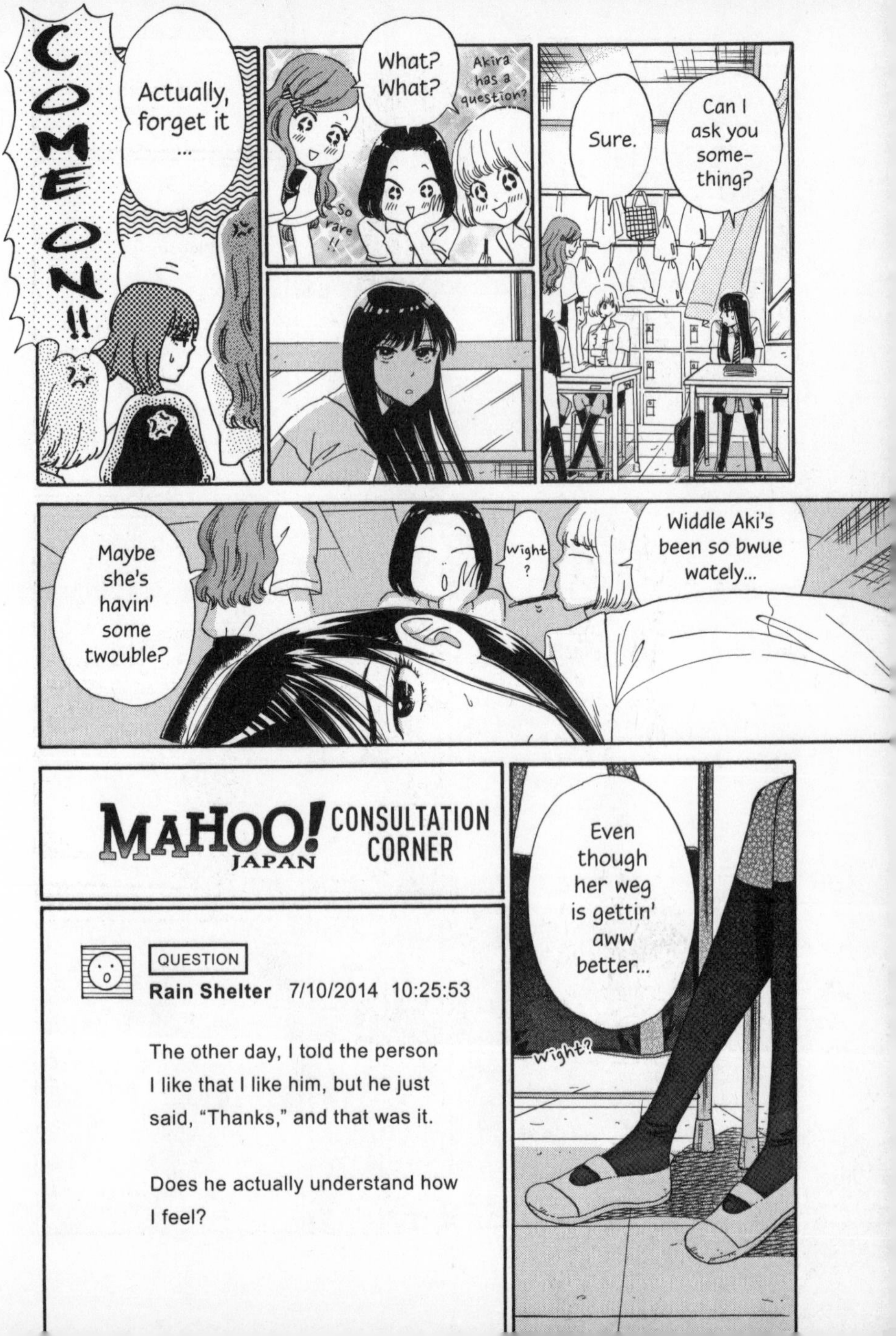
Can I ask you some-thing?
Sure.
What? What?
Akira has a question?
So rare!!
Actually, forget it ...
COME ON!!
Widdle Aki's been so bwue watEly...
Wight?
Maybe she's havin' some twouble?
Even though her weg is gettin' aww better...
Wight?
MAHOO! JAPAN CONSULTATION CORNER
QUESTION
Rain Shelter 7/10/2014 10:25:53
The other day, I told the person I like that I like him, but he just said, "Thanks," and that was it.
Does he actually understand how I feel?

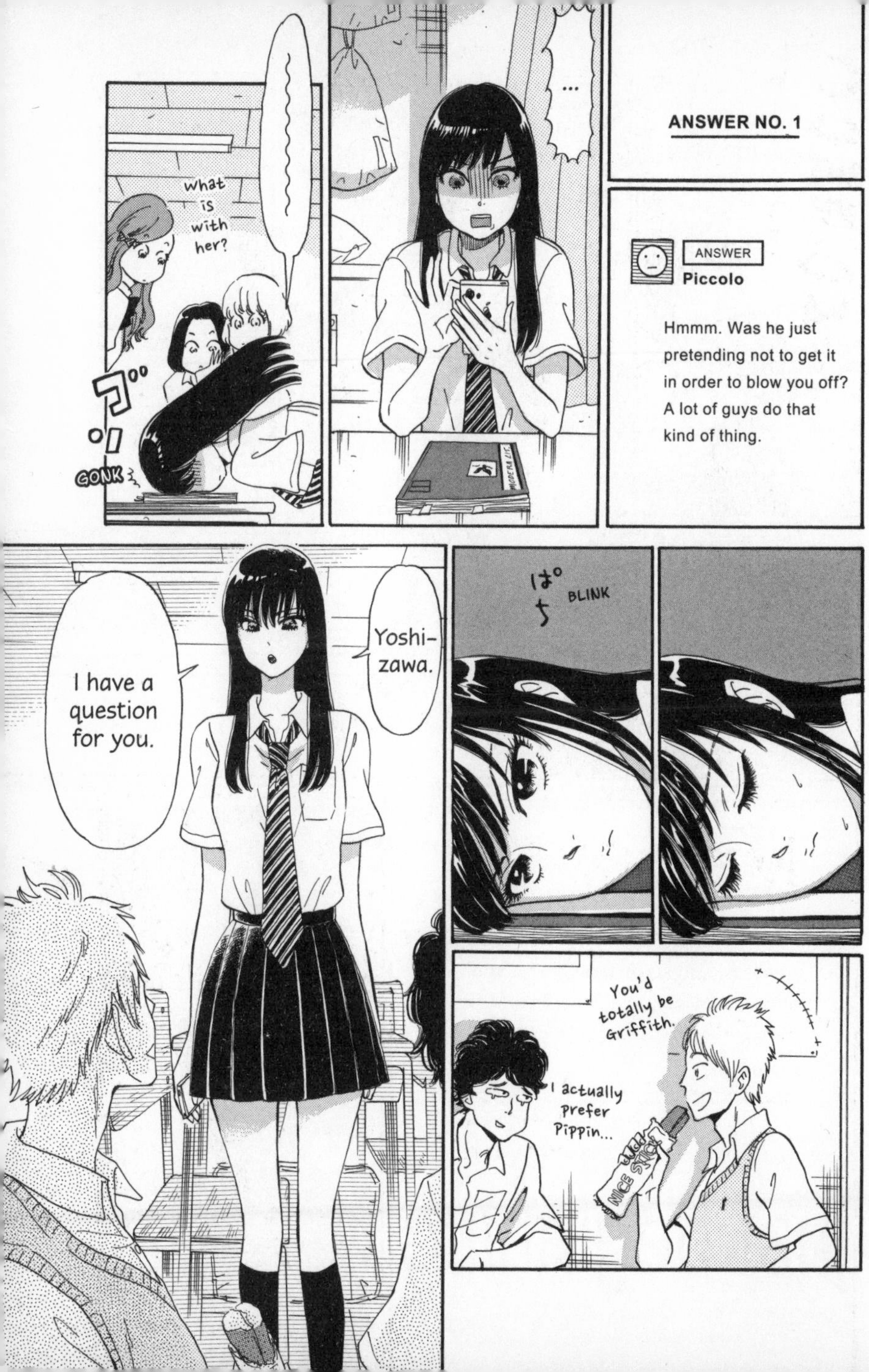

ANSWER NO. 1
ANSWER
Piccolo
Hmmm. Was he just pretending not to get it in order to blow you off? A lot of guys do that kind of thing.
...
what is with her?
GONK
ぱち
BLINK
You'd totally be Griffith.
I actually prefer Pippin...
NICE STICK
Yoshi-zawa.
I have a question for you.

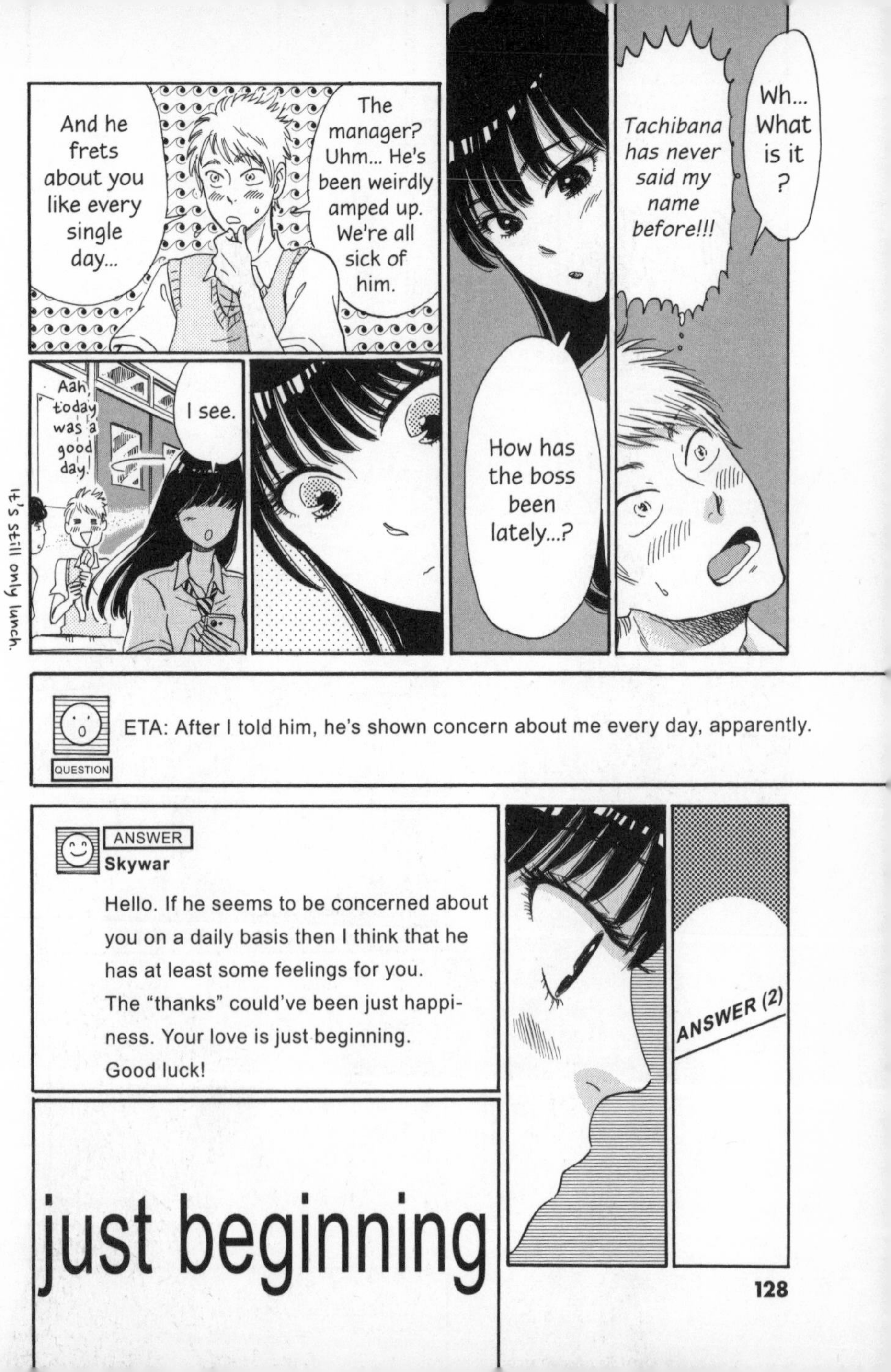
How has the boss been lately...?
Wh... What is it?
Tachibana has never said my name before!!!
The manager? Uhm... He's been weirdly amped up. We're all sick of him.
And he frets about you like every single day...
I see.
Aah, today was a good day!
It's still only lunch.
QUESTION
ETA: After I told him, he's shown concern about me every day, apparently.
ANSWER
Skywar
Hello. If he seems to be concerned about you on a daily basis then I think that he has at least some feelings for you. The "thanks" could've been just happiness. Your love is just beginning. Good luck!
ANSWER (2)
just beginning

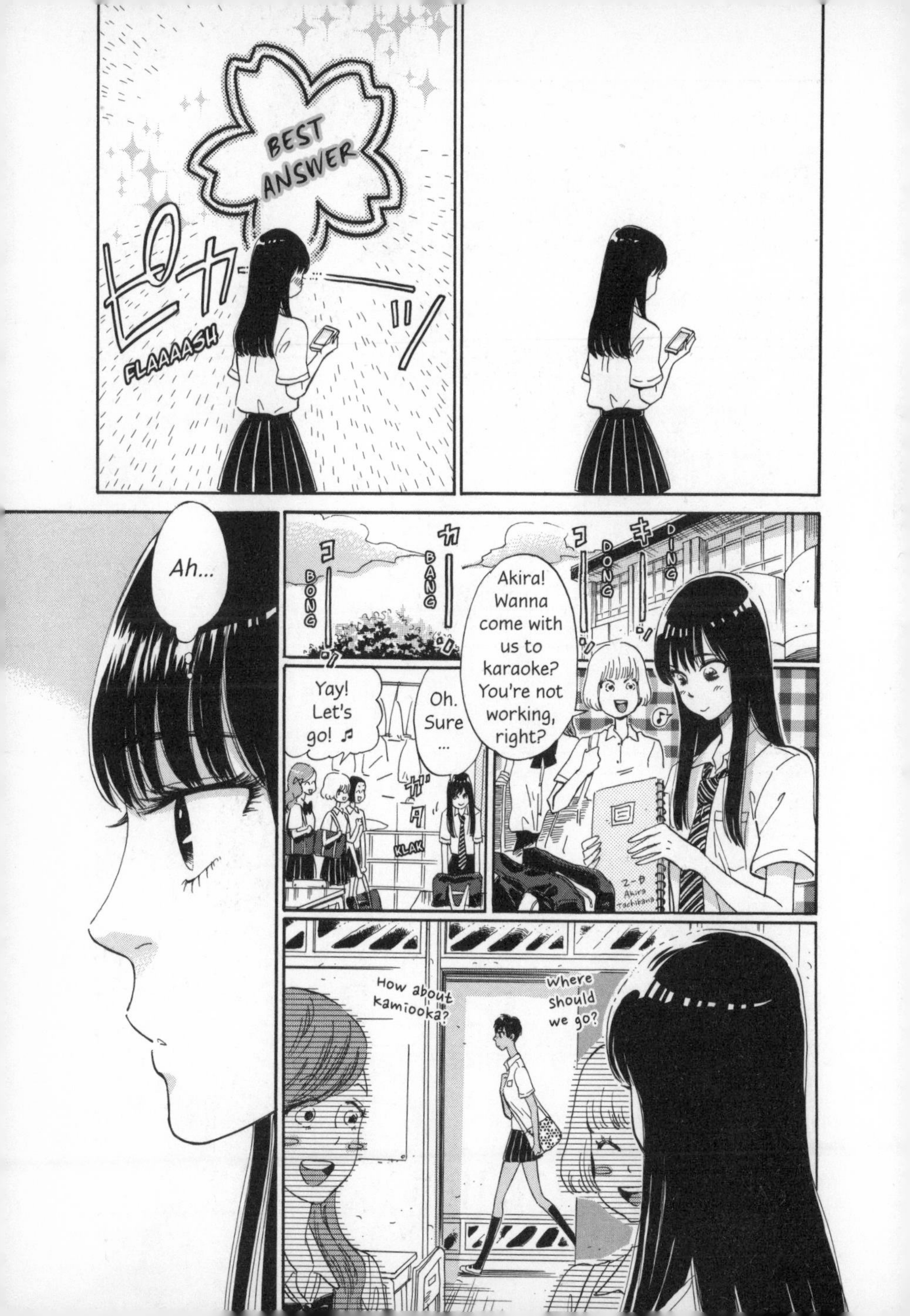
BEST ANSWER
FLAAAASH
DING DONG BANG BONG
Akira! Wanna come with us to karaoke? You're not working, right?
2-D Akira Tachibana
Oh. Sure...
Yay! Let's go! ♫
KLAK
Where should we go?
How about kamiooka?
Ah...

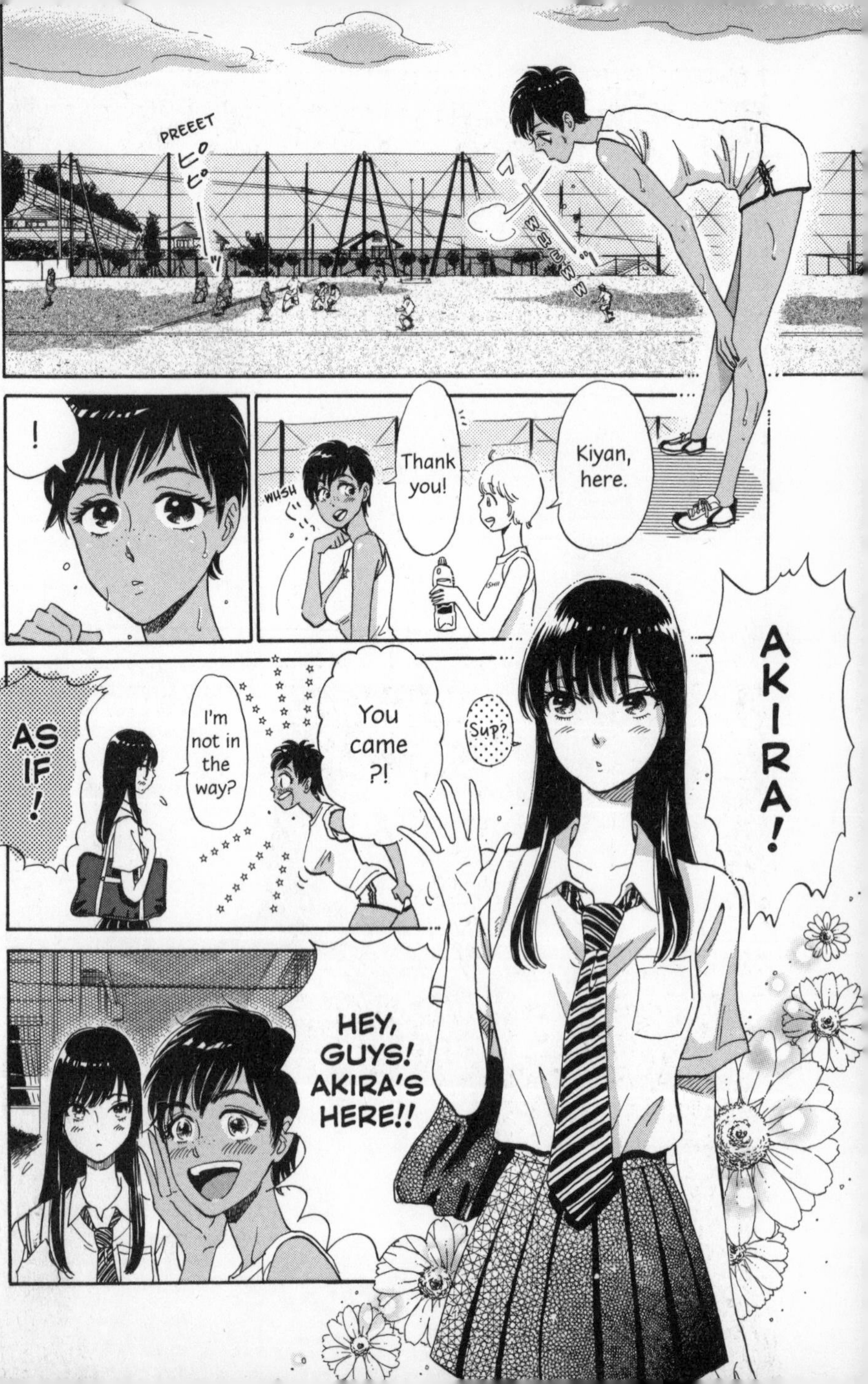
PREEET
ピピー
WHEWW
Kiyan, here.
Thank you!
WUSH
!
AKIRA!
Sup?
You came?!
I'm not in the way?
AS IF!
HEY, GUYS! AKIRA'S HERE!!

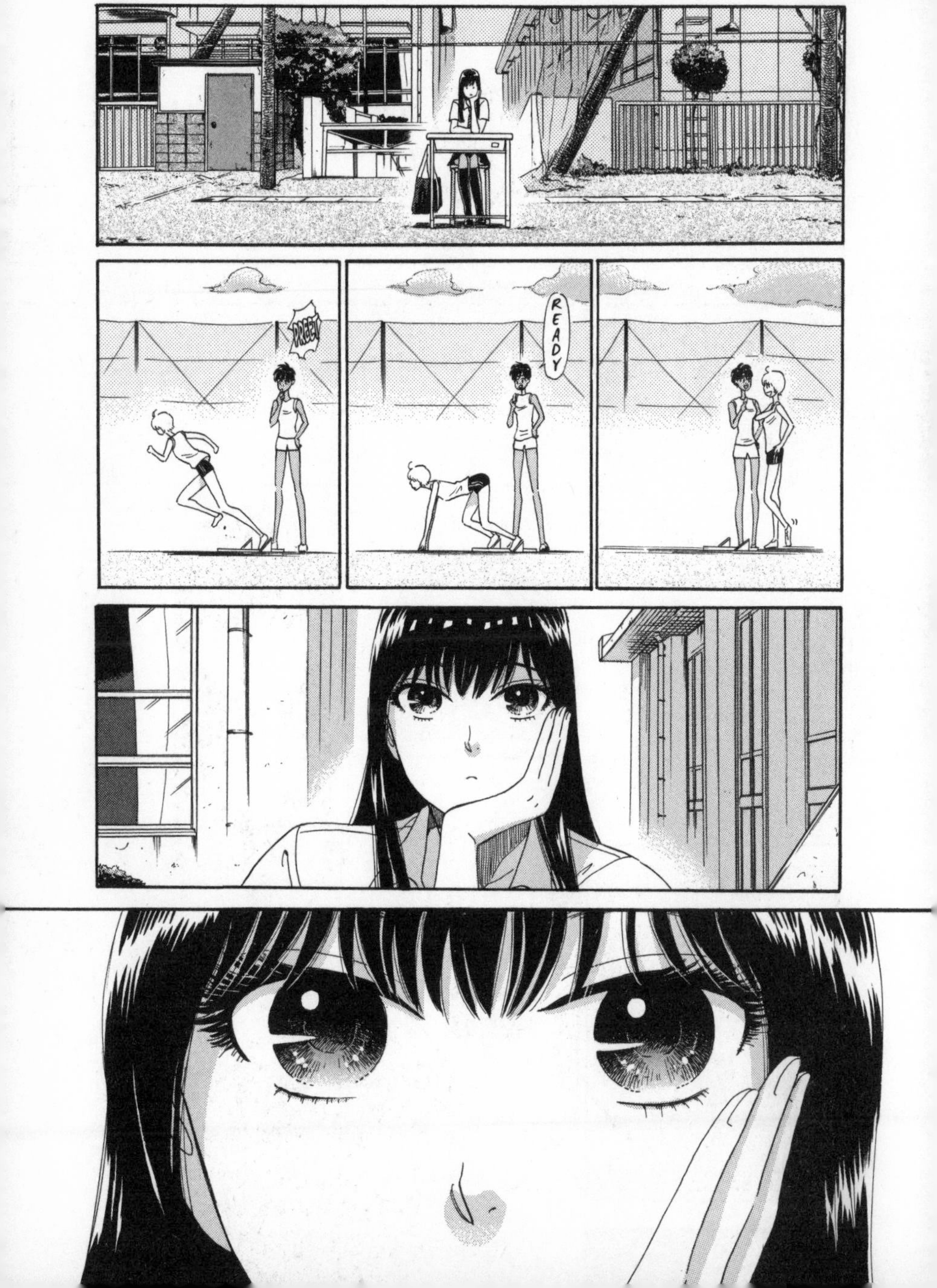
READY
PREET!

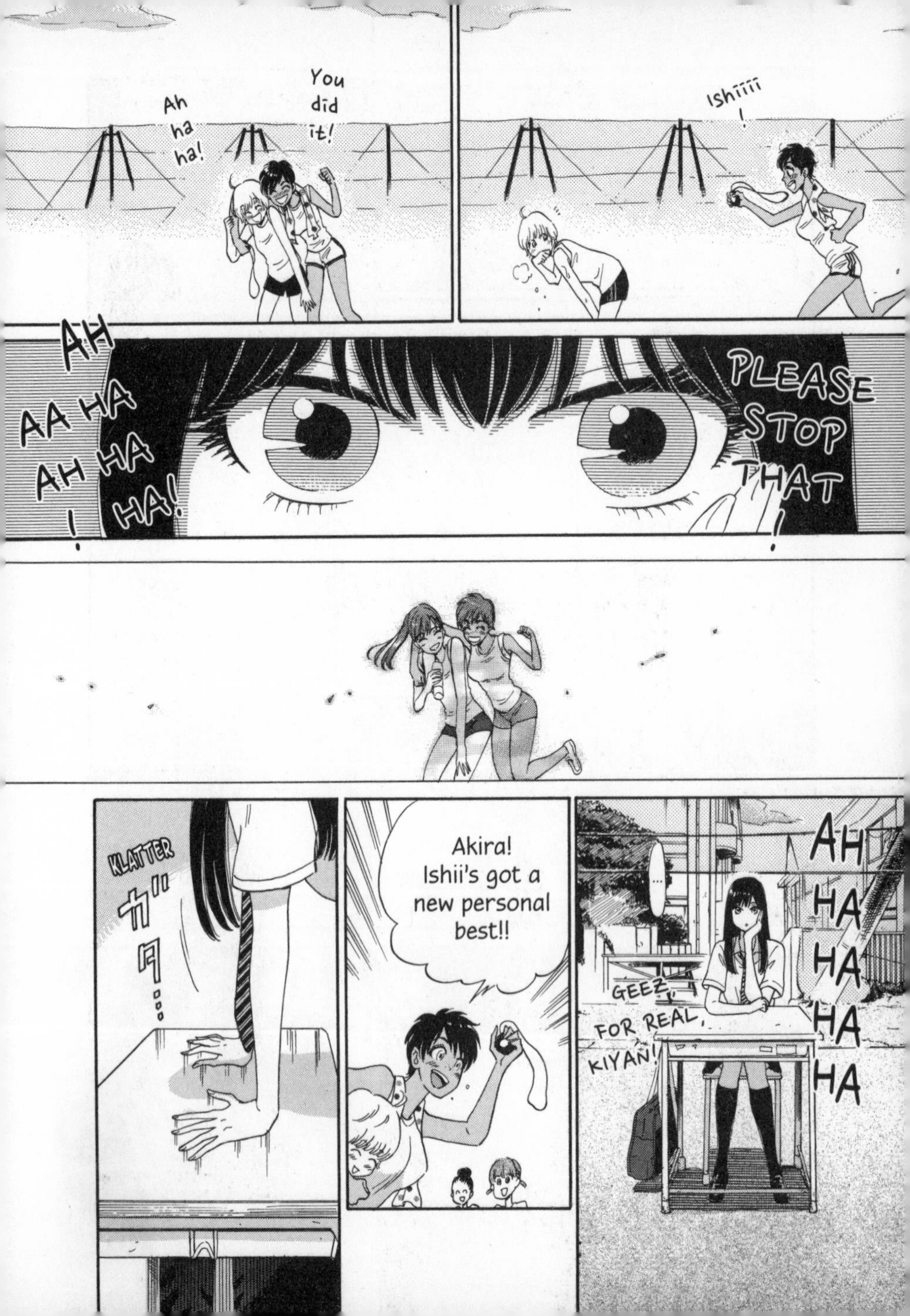
Ishiiii!
You did it!
Ah ha ha!
PLEASE STOP THAT!
AH AA HA AH HA HA!
AH HA HA HA HA HA
...
GEEZ, FOR REAL, KIYAN!
Akira! Ishii's got a new personal best!!
KLATTER
ガタ…

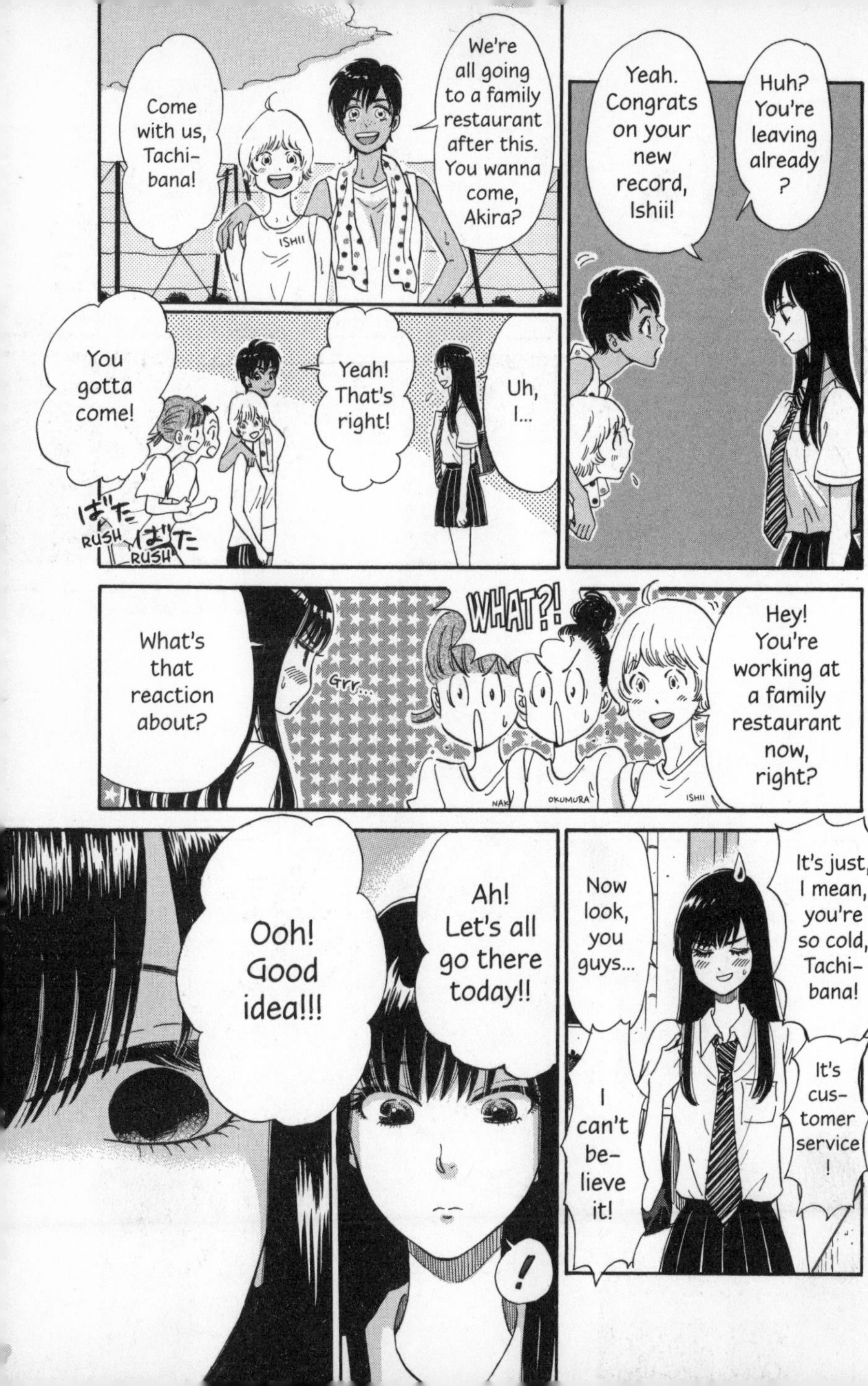
Huh? You're leaving already?
Yeah. Congrats on your new record, Ishii!
We're all going to a family restaurant after this. You wanna come, Akira?
Come with us, Tachi-bana!
Uh, I...
Yeah! That's right!
You gotta come!
ばた RUSH
ばた RUSH
Hey! You're working at a family restaurant now, right?
WHAT?!
Grr...
What's that reaction about?
It's just, I mean, you're so cold, Tachi-bana!
Now look, you guys...
It's cus-tomer service!
I can't be-lieve it!
Ah! Let's all go there today!!
Ooh! Good idea!!!
!

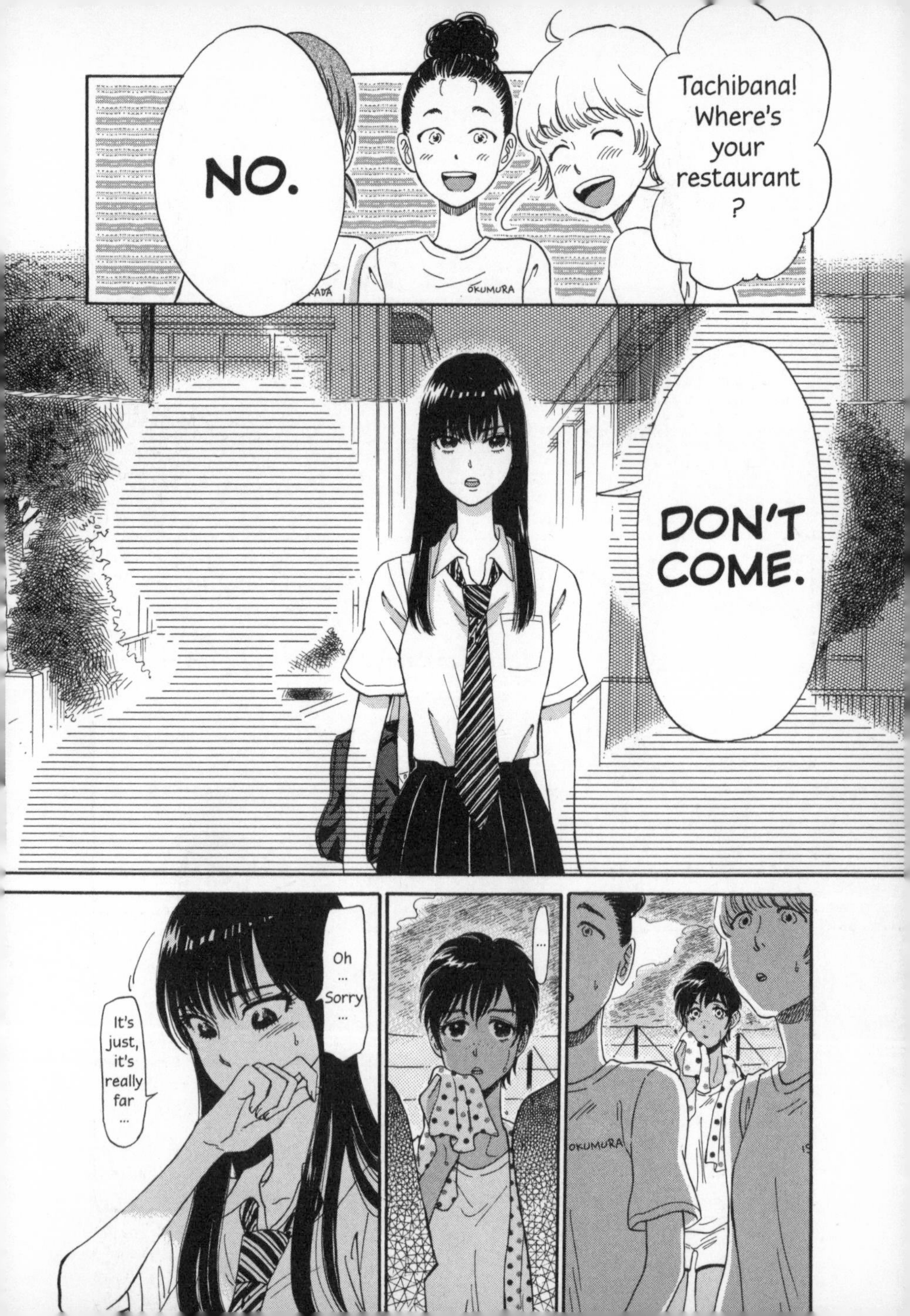

Tachibana! Where's your restaurant?
NO.
OKUMURA
DON'T COME.
OKUMURA
...
Oh ... Sorry ...
It's just, it's really far ...

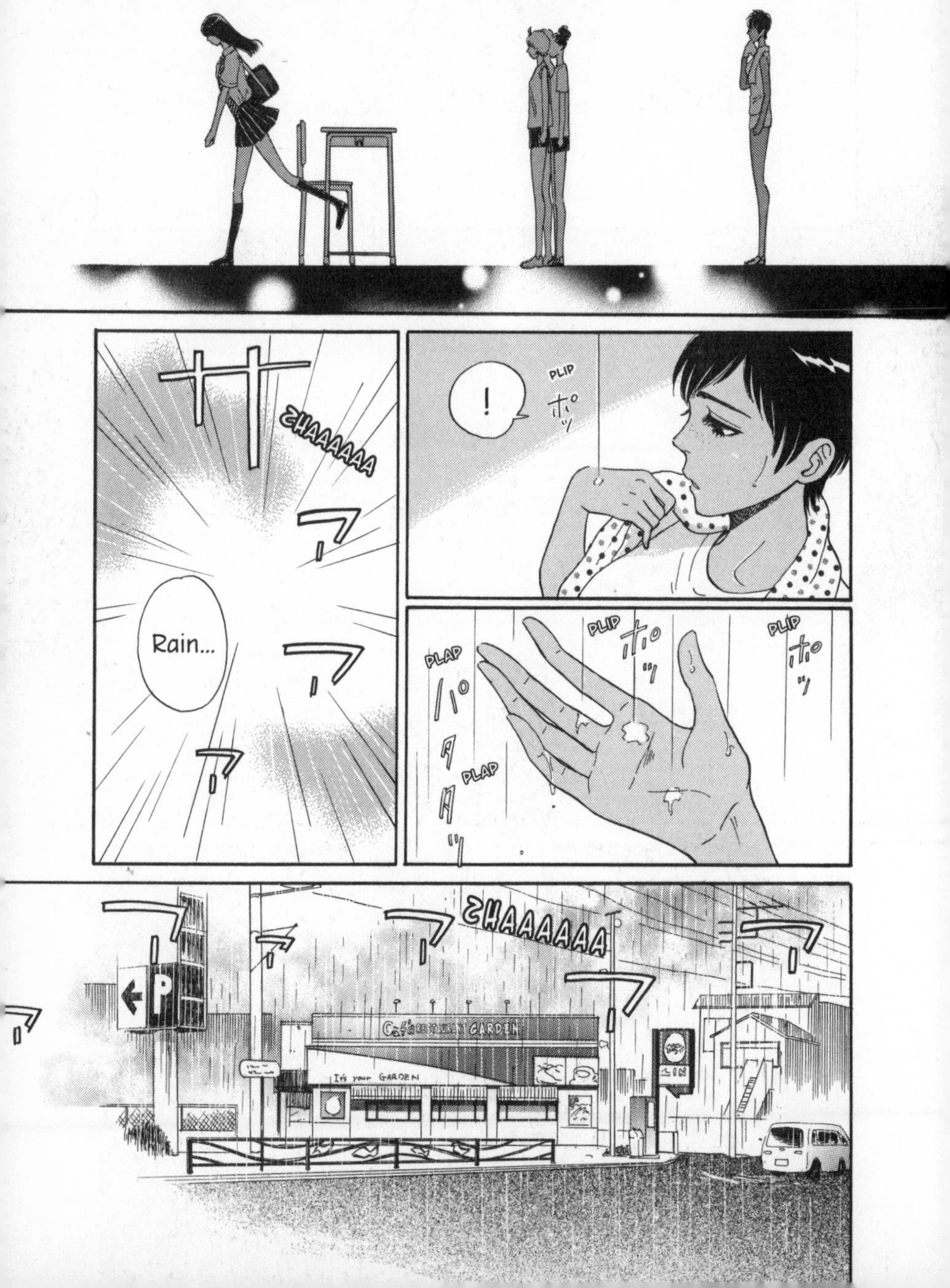
PLIP
ポッ
!
PLIP
ポッ
PLIP
ポッ
PLAP
パタタッ
PLAP
ZHAAAAAA
ザァ
ァ
ァ
Rain...
ZHAAAAAA
GARDEN
It's your GARDEN

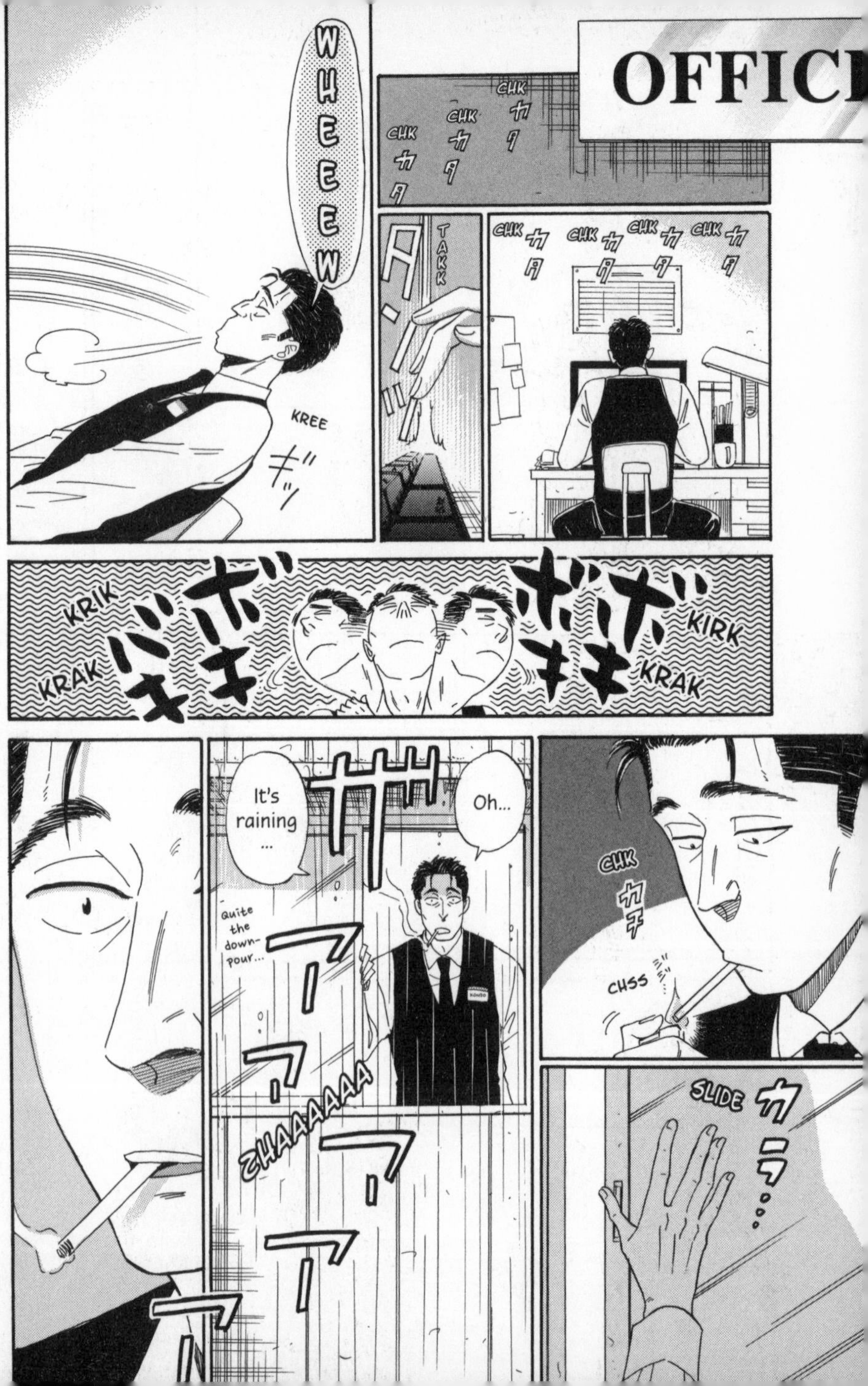

OFFIC
CHK カタ
CHK カタ
CHK カタ
CHK カタ
CHK カタ
CHK カタ
CHK カタ
TAKK
WHEEEW
KREE
ギッ
KIRK
KRAK
KRIK
KRAK
CHK
カチ
CHSS
SLIDE
カラ...
Oh...
It's raining...
Quite the downpour...
ZHAAAAAA

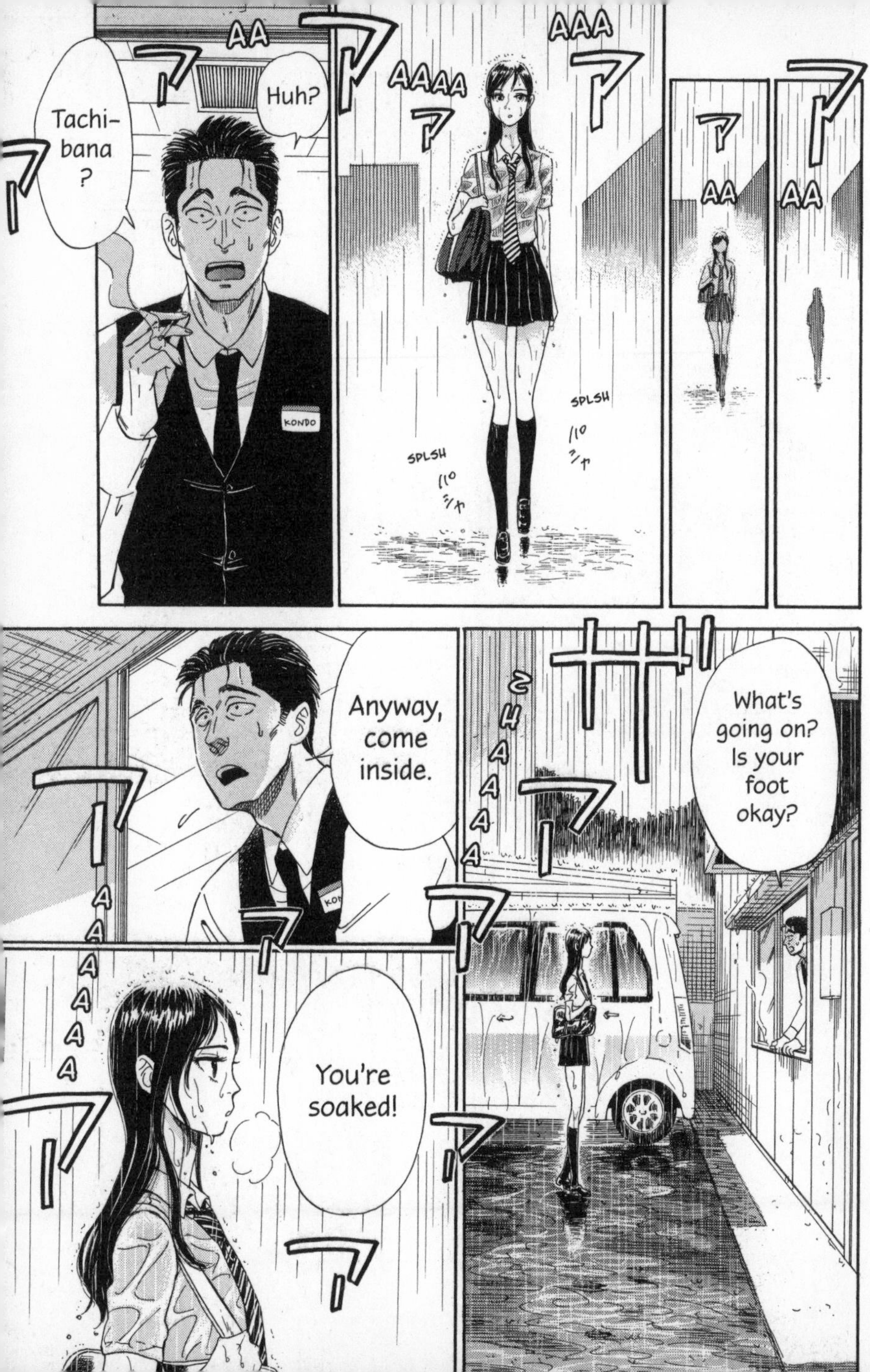
AA
AA
AAA
AAAA
SPLSH
SPLSH
AA
Huh?
Tachi-bana?
SHAAAAAA
What's going on? Is your foot okay?
Anyway, come inside.
KONDO
AAAAAAAA
You're soaked!

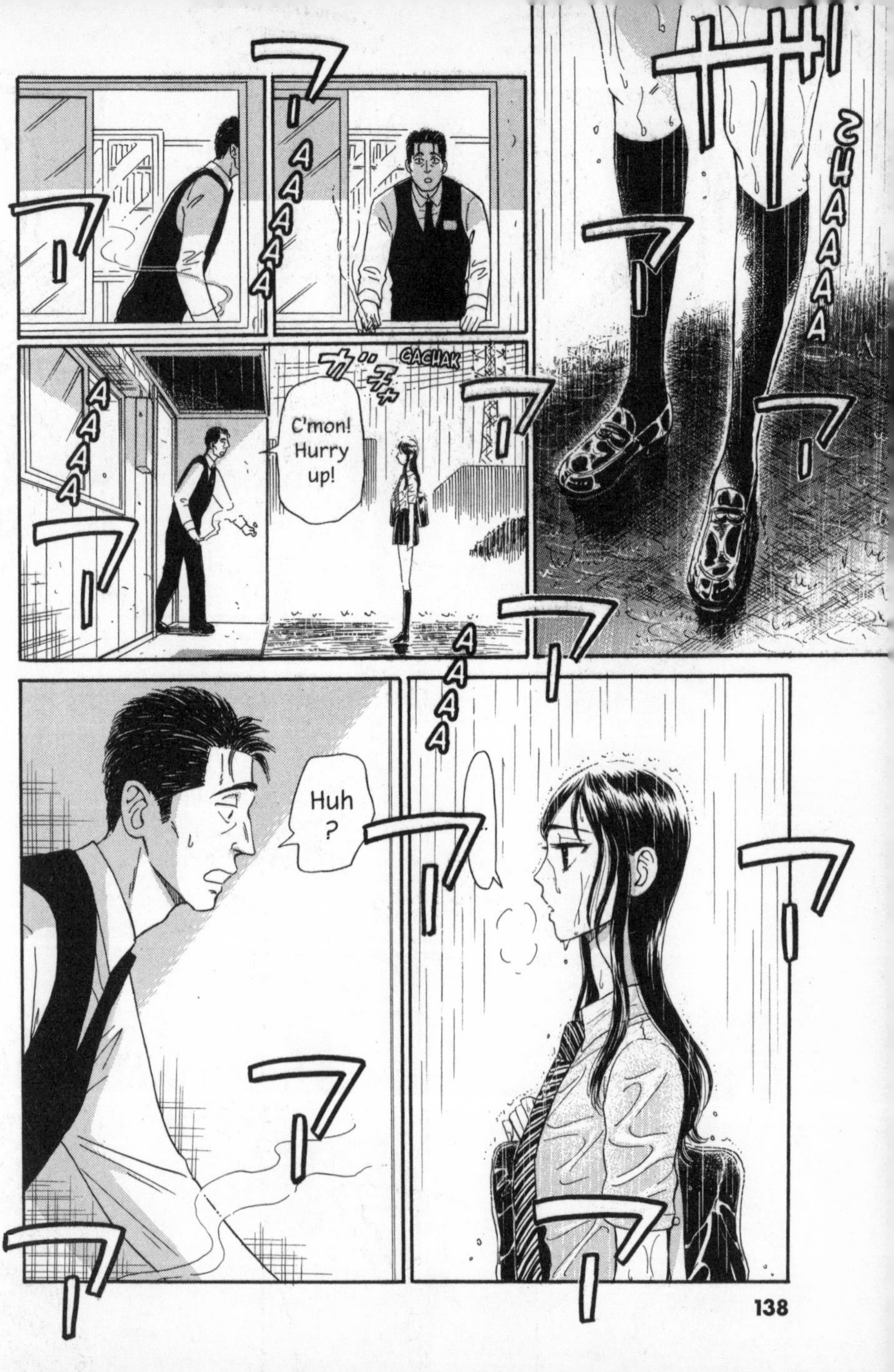
ZHAAAAAAA
AAAAAAA
ガチャ
GACHAK
C'mon! Hurry up!
AAAAA
AAAAA
Huh?

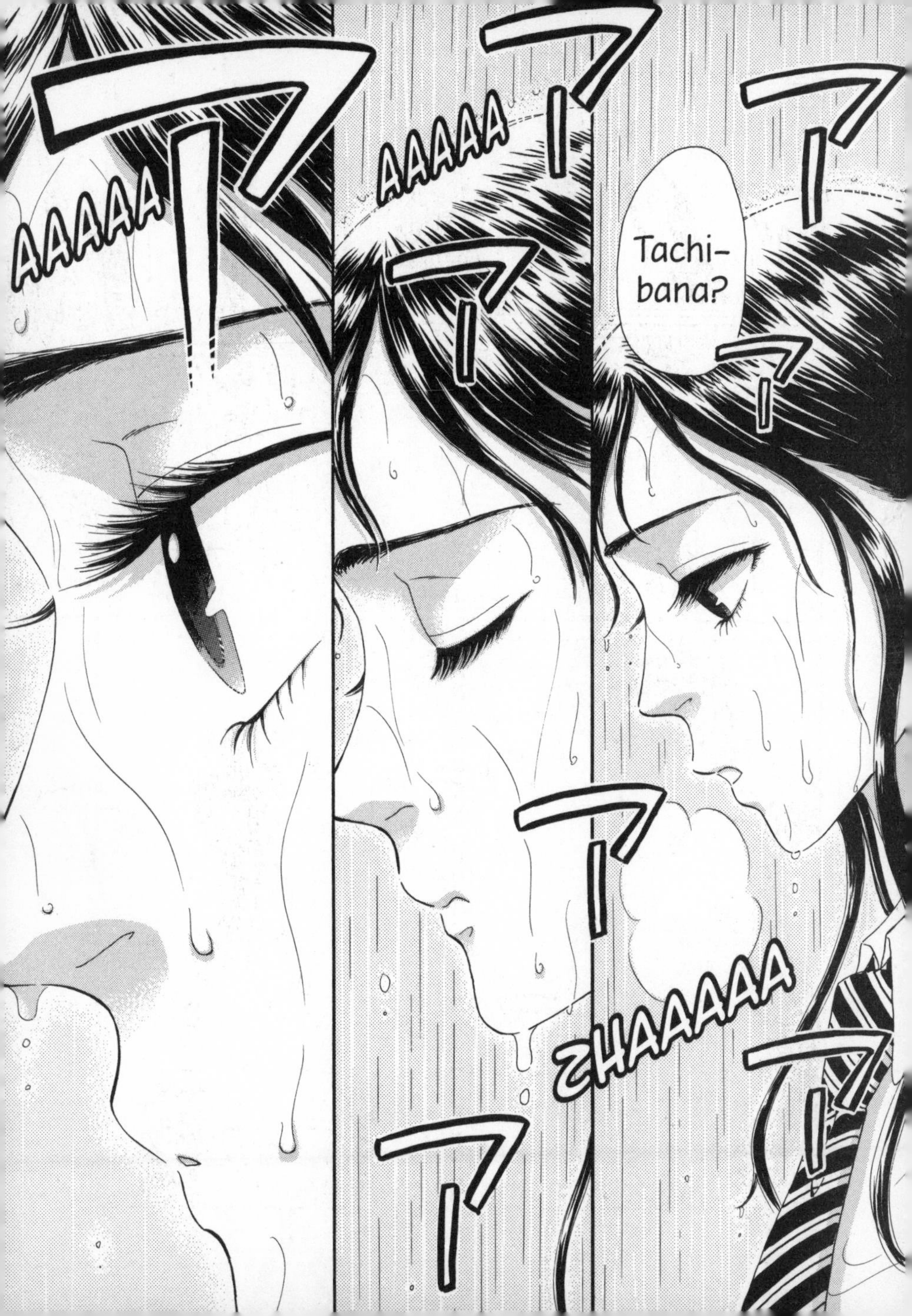
Tachi-
bana?
ZHAAAAA
AAAAA
AAAAA

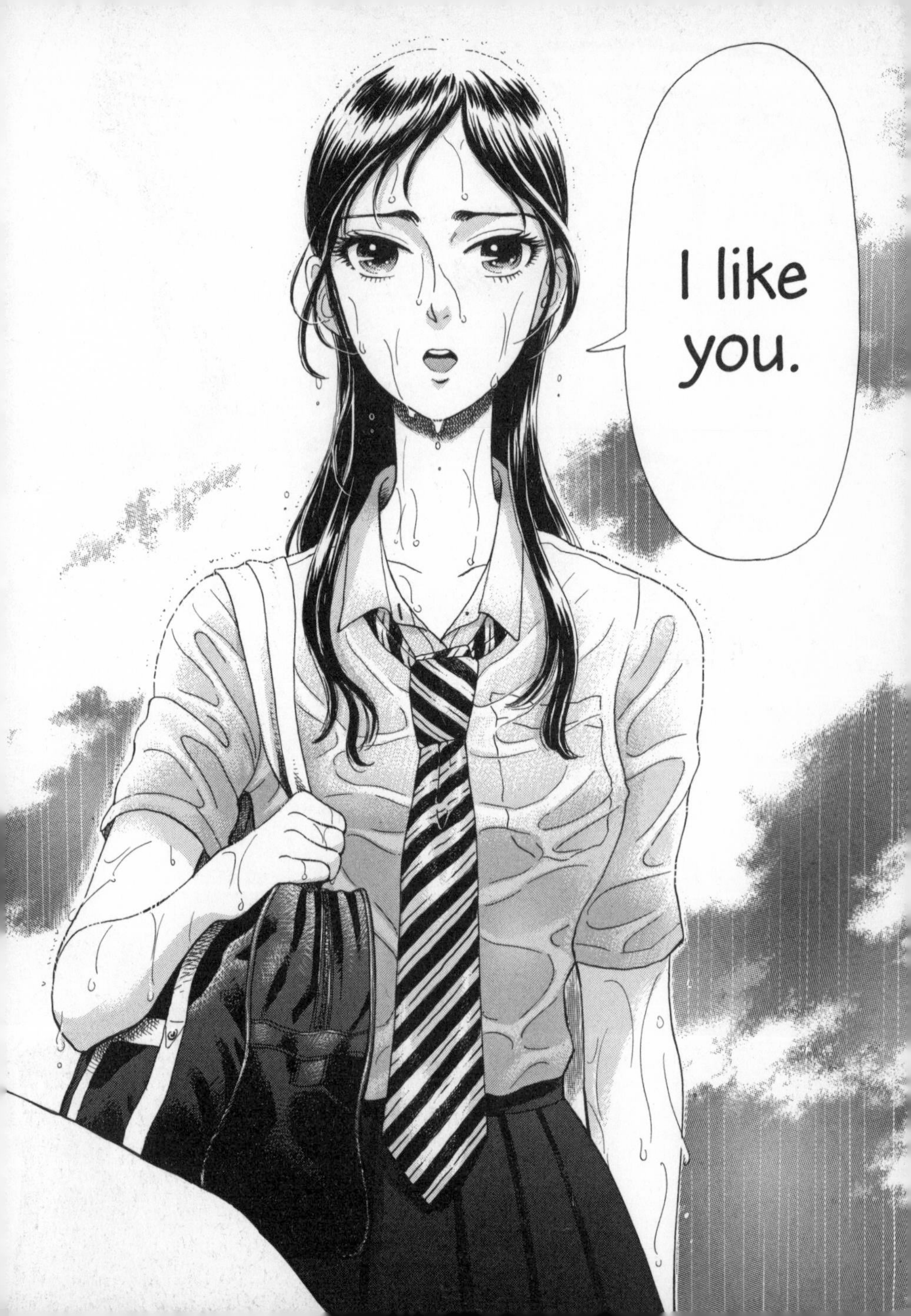
I like you.

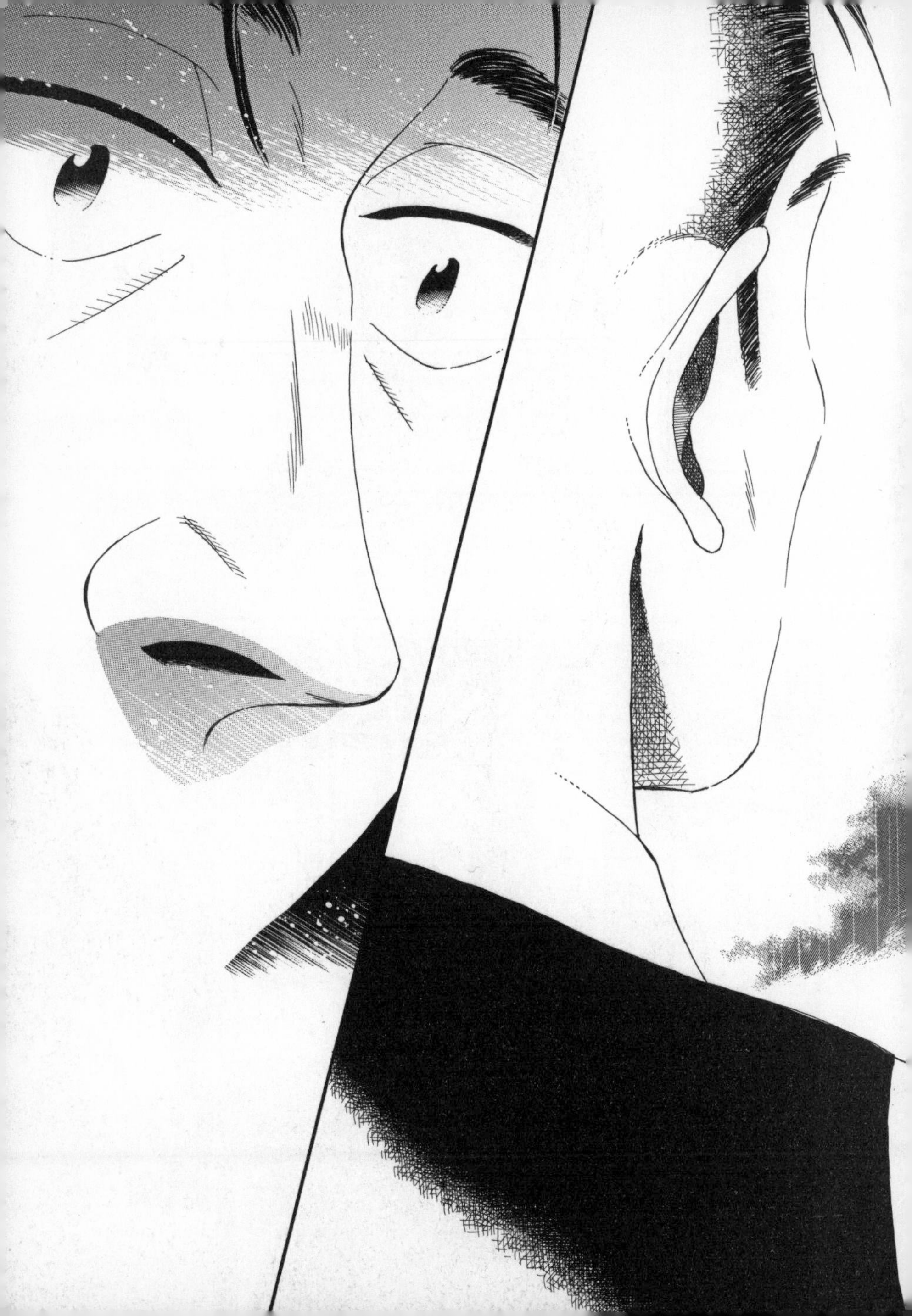

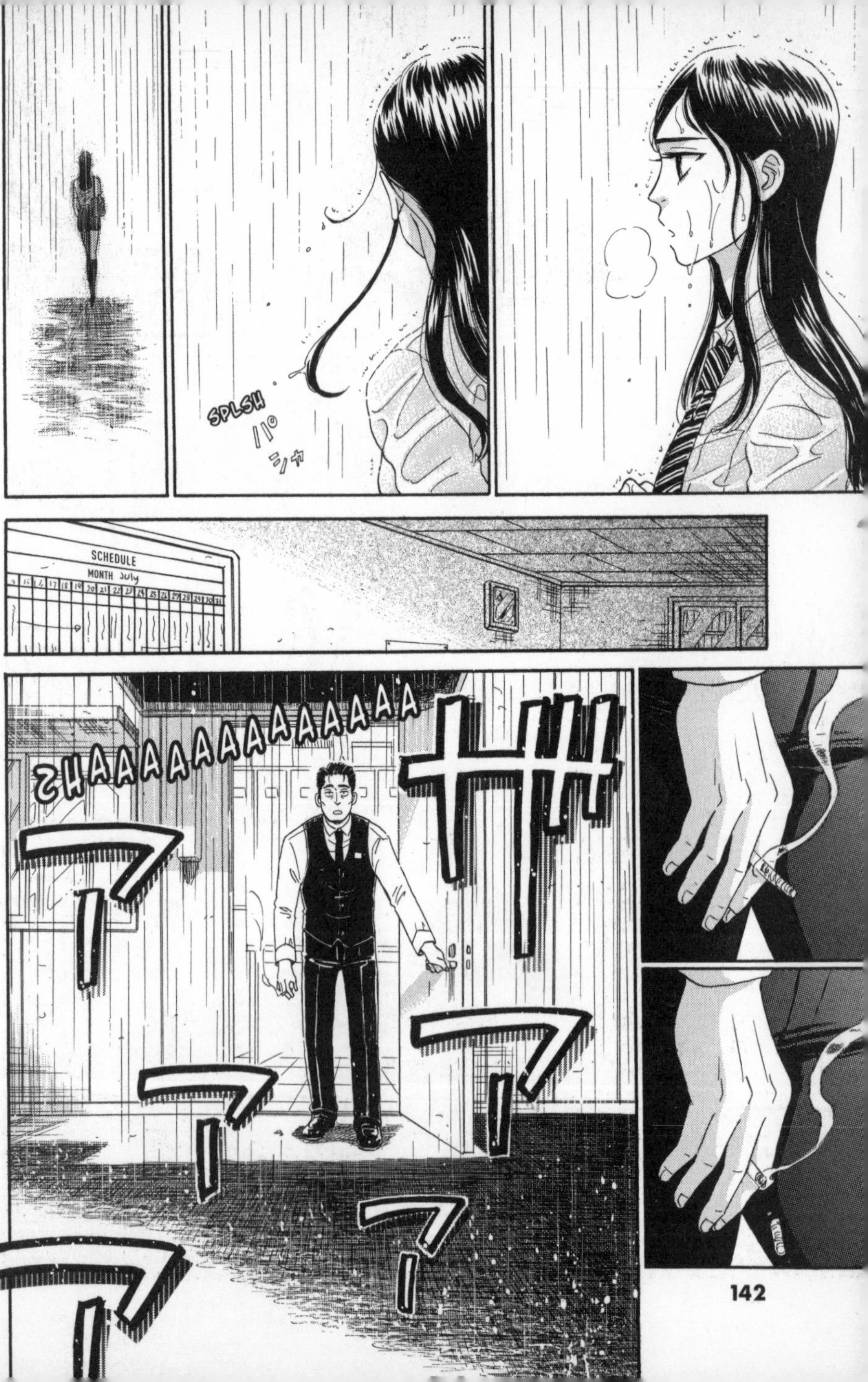
SPLSH
パシャ
SCHEDULE
MONTH July
SHAAAAAAAAAAAAAA
ザァァァァァ

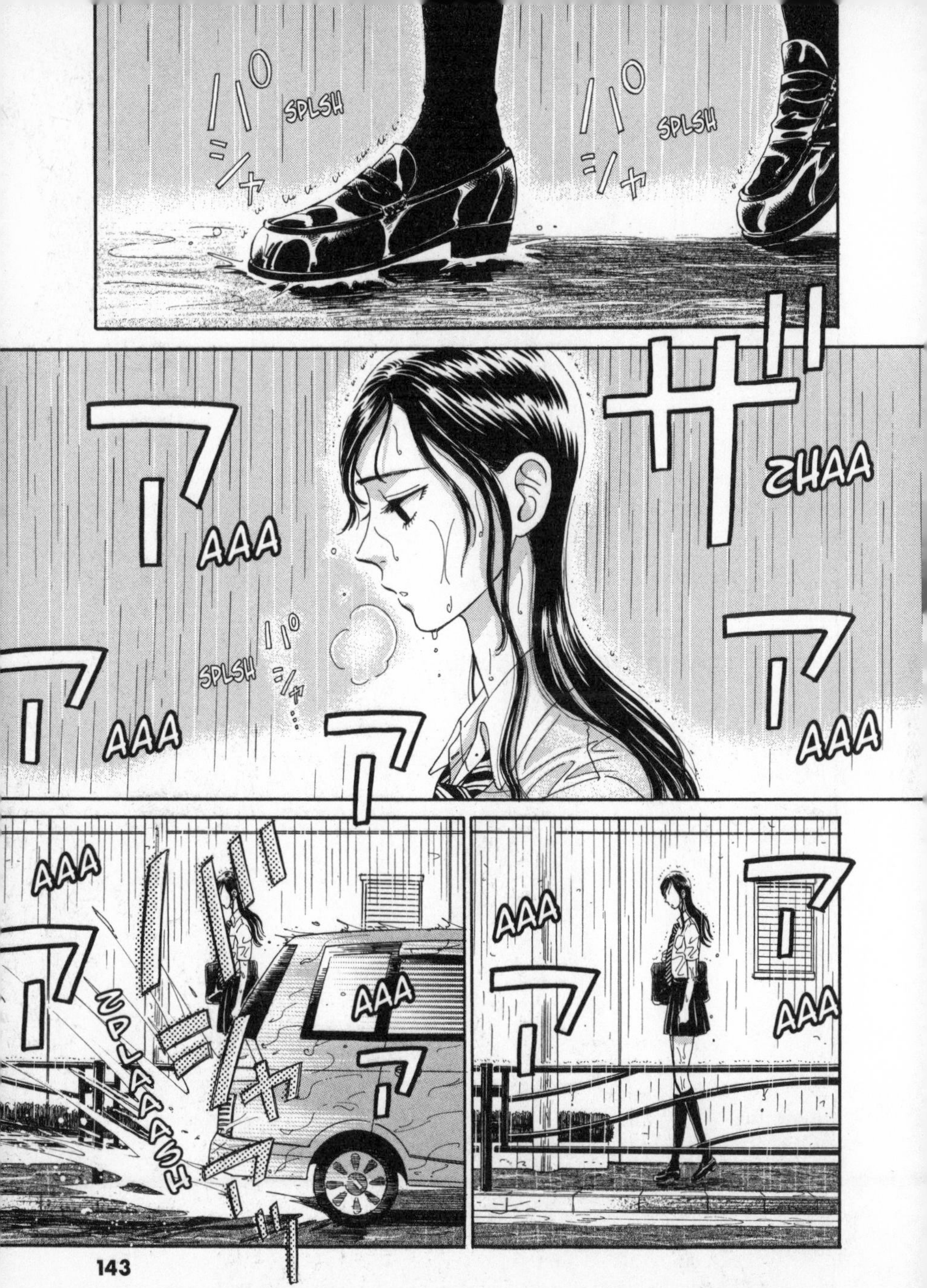

パシャ
SPLSH
パシャ
SPLSH
ザー
ZHAA
アー
AAA
アー
AAA
パシャ
SPLSH
アー
アー
AAA
アー
AAA
アー
AAA
アー
AAA
AAA
アー
AAA
SPLAAAASH

Chapter 8

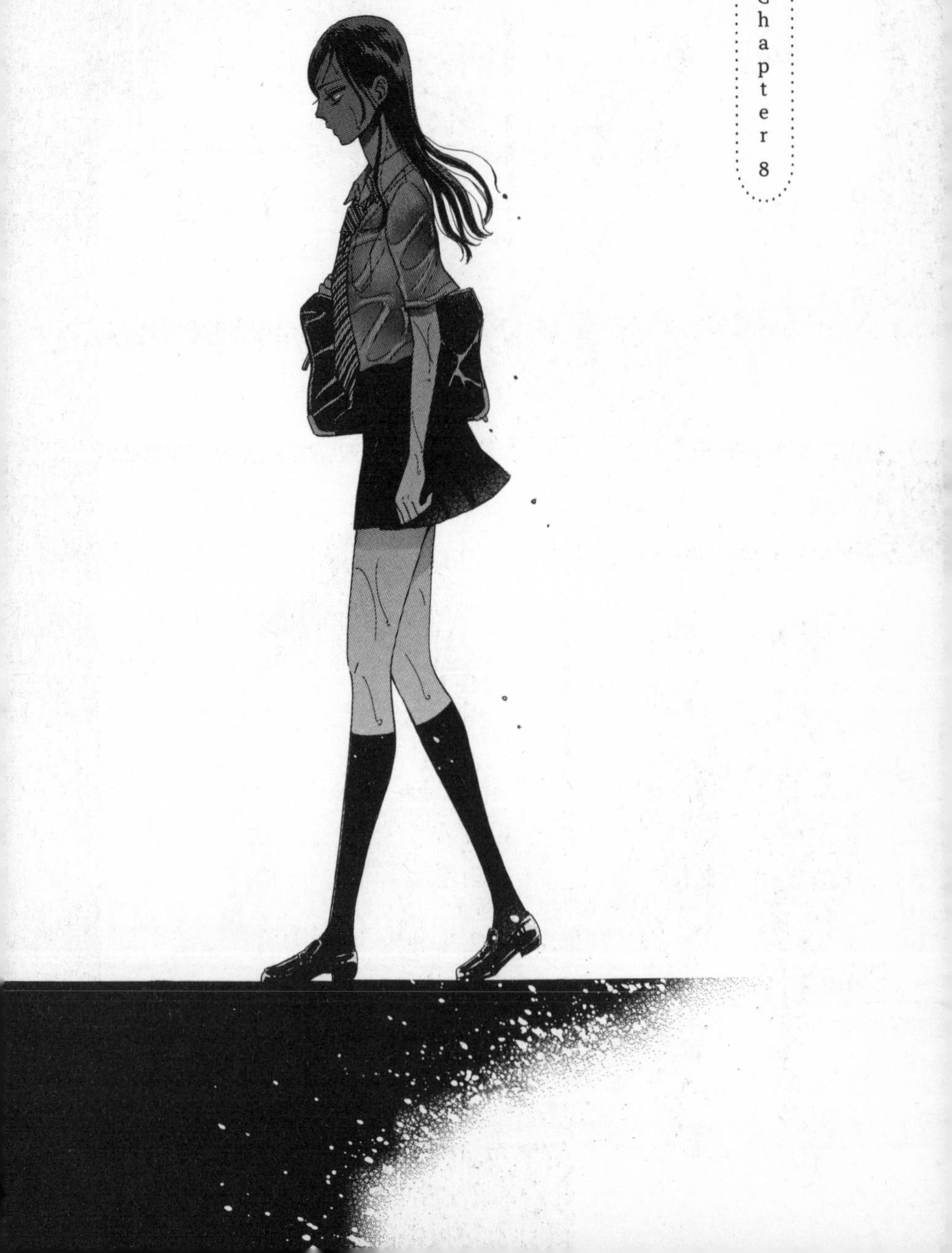

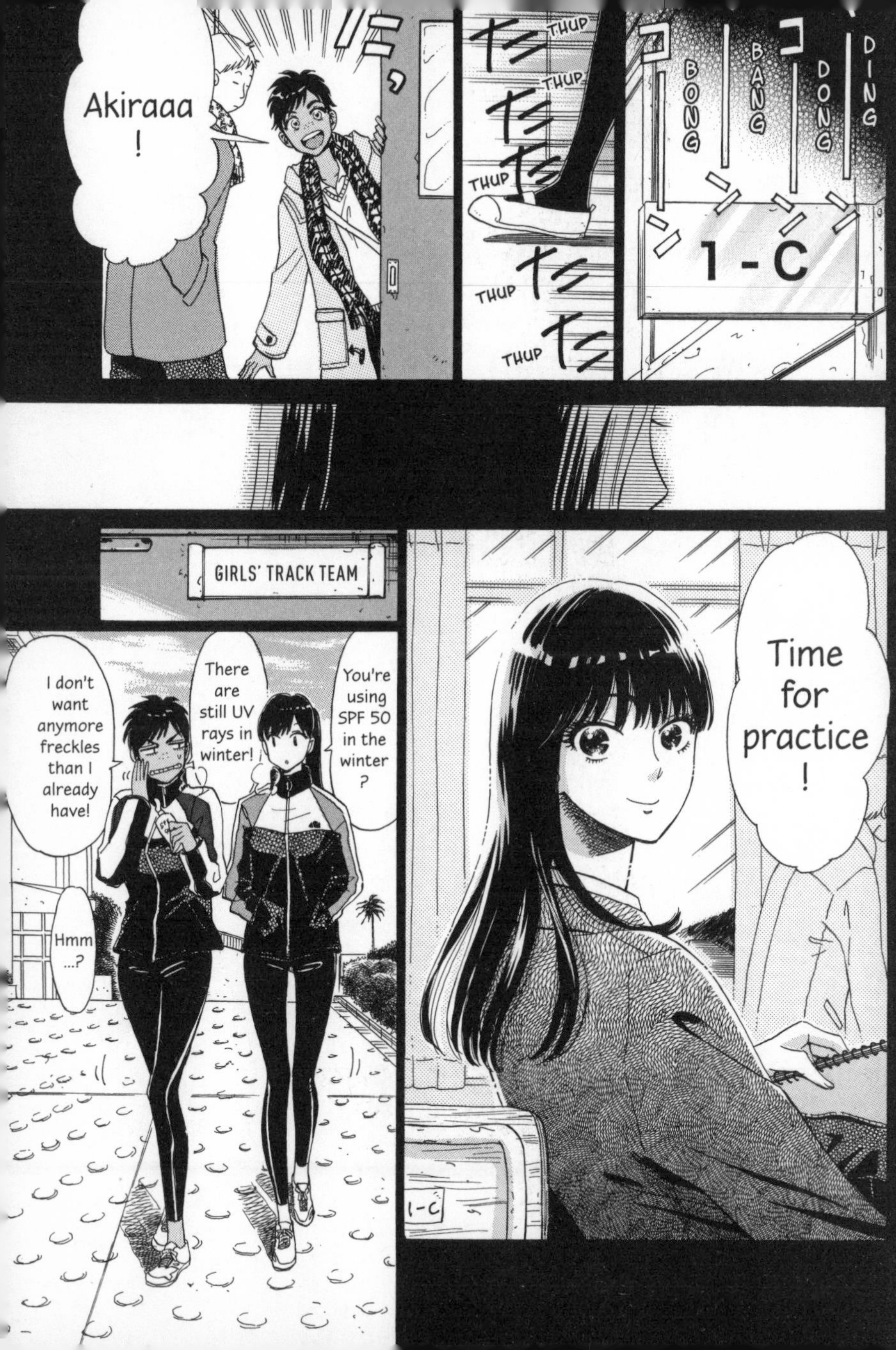
DING
DONG
BANG
BONG
1 - C
THUP
THUP
THUP
THUP
THUP
Akiraaa!
Time for practice!
GIRLS' TRACK TEAM
You're using SPF 50 in the winter?
There are still UV rays in winter!
I don't want anymore freckles than I already have!
Hmm...?
1-C

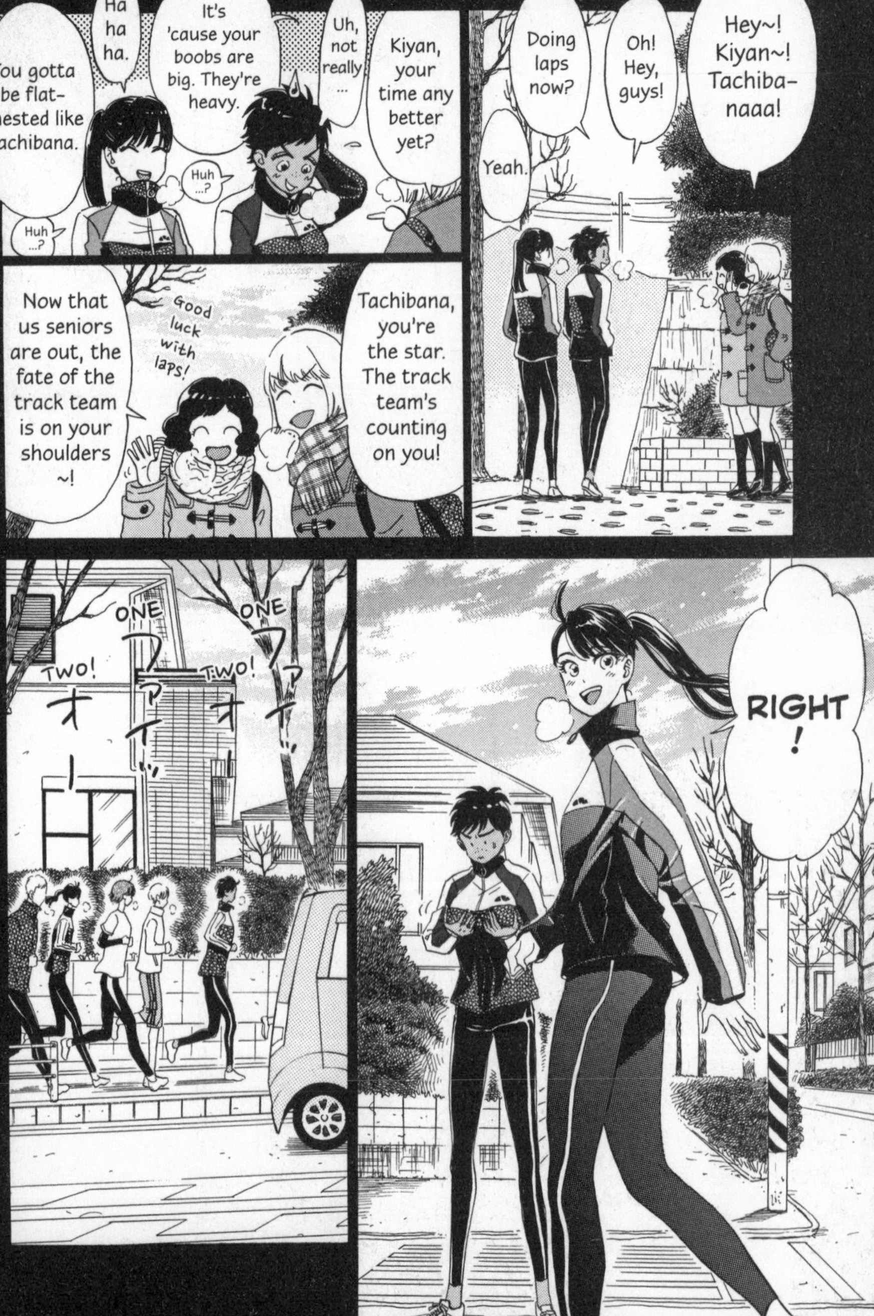
Hey~! Kiyan~! Tachiba-naaa!
Oh! Hey, guys!
Doing laps now?
Yeah.
Kiyan, your time any better yet?
Uh, not really ...
It's 'cause your boobs are big. They're heavy.
Ha ha ha.
You gotta be flat-chested like Tachibana.
Huh ...?
Huh ...?
Tachibana, you're the star. The track team's counting on you!
Good luck with laps!
Now that us seniors are out, the fate of the track team is on your shoulders ~!
RIGHT !
ONE
TWO!
ONE
TWO!

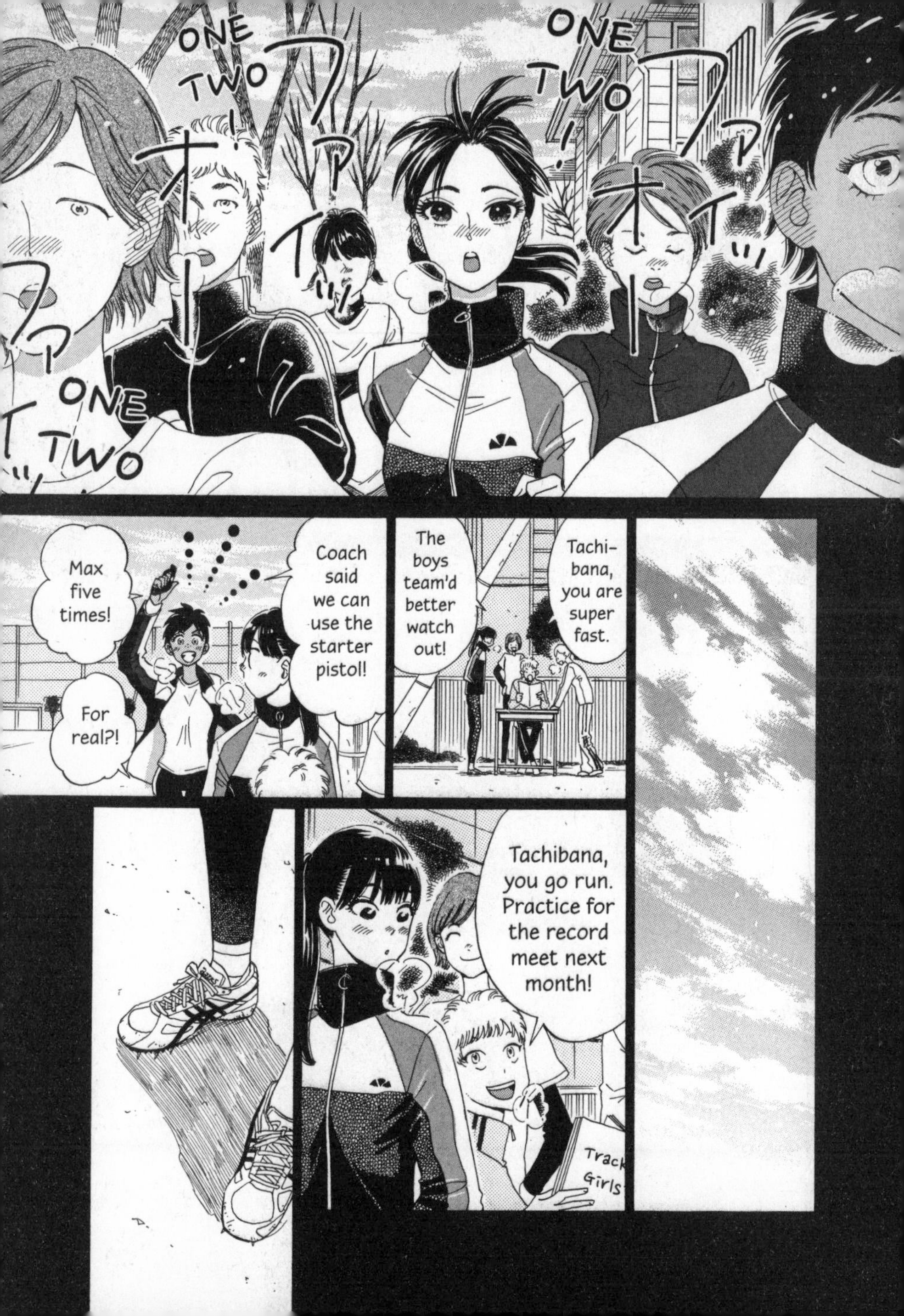
ONE TWO
ONE TWO
ONE TWO
Tachibana, you are super fast.
The boys team'd better watch out!
Coach said we can use the starter pistol!
Max five times!
For real?!
Tachibana, you go run. Practice for the record meet next month!
Track Girls

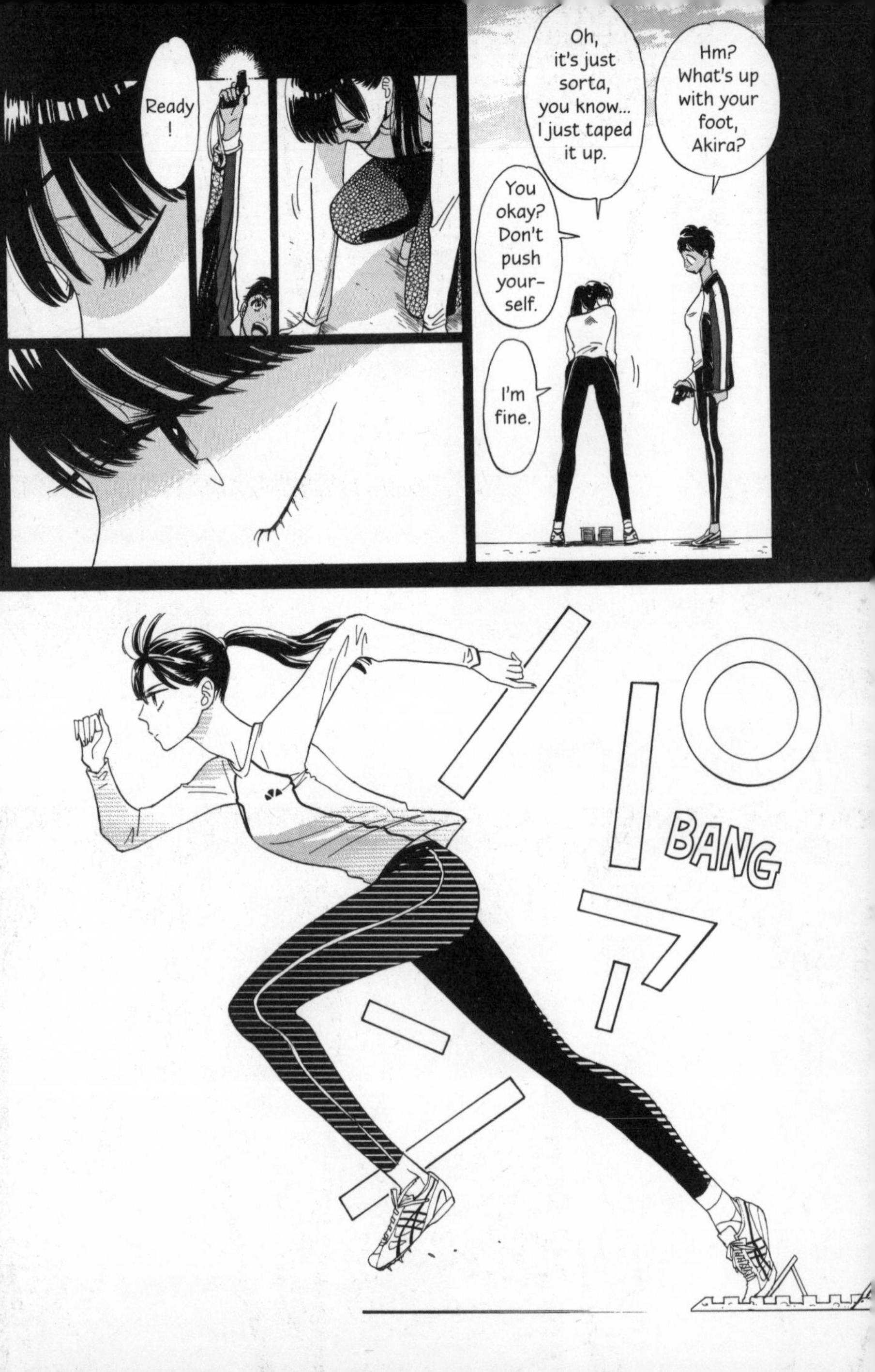
Hm? What's up with your foot, Akira?
Oh, it's just sorta, you know... I just taped it up.
You okay? Don't push your-self.
I'm fine.
Ready!
BANG

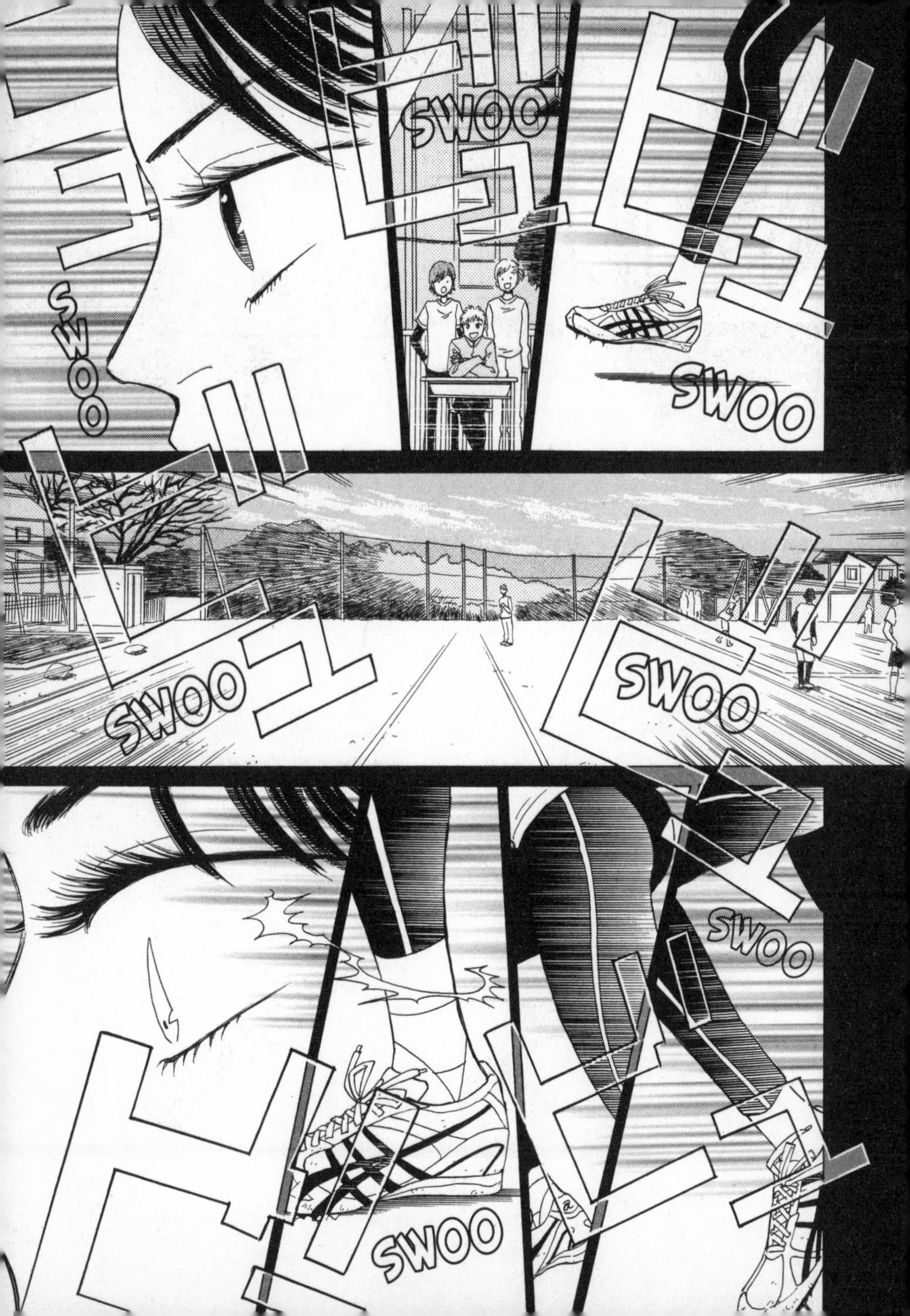
SWOO
SWOO
SWOO
SWOO
SWOO
SWOO
SWOO

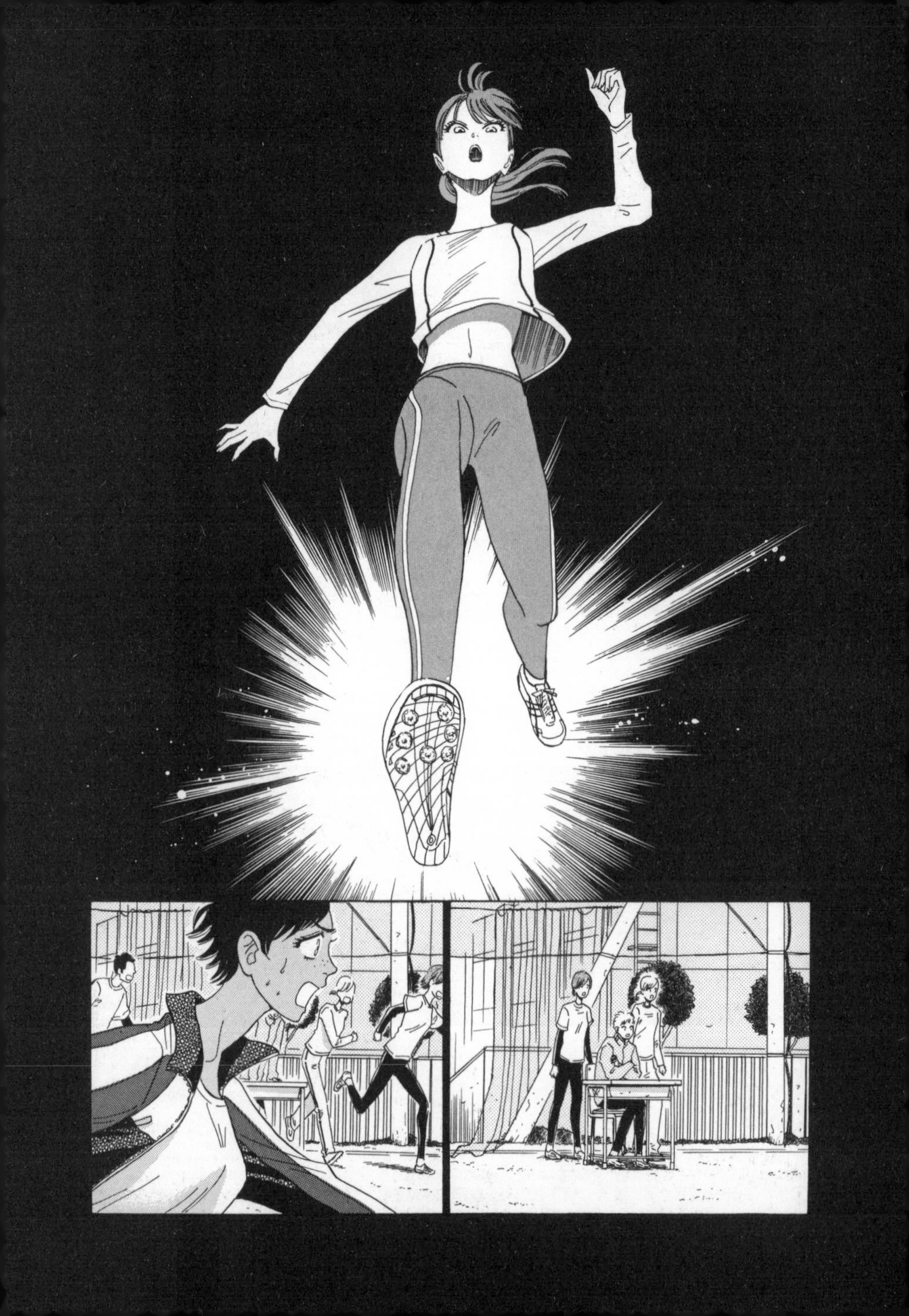

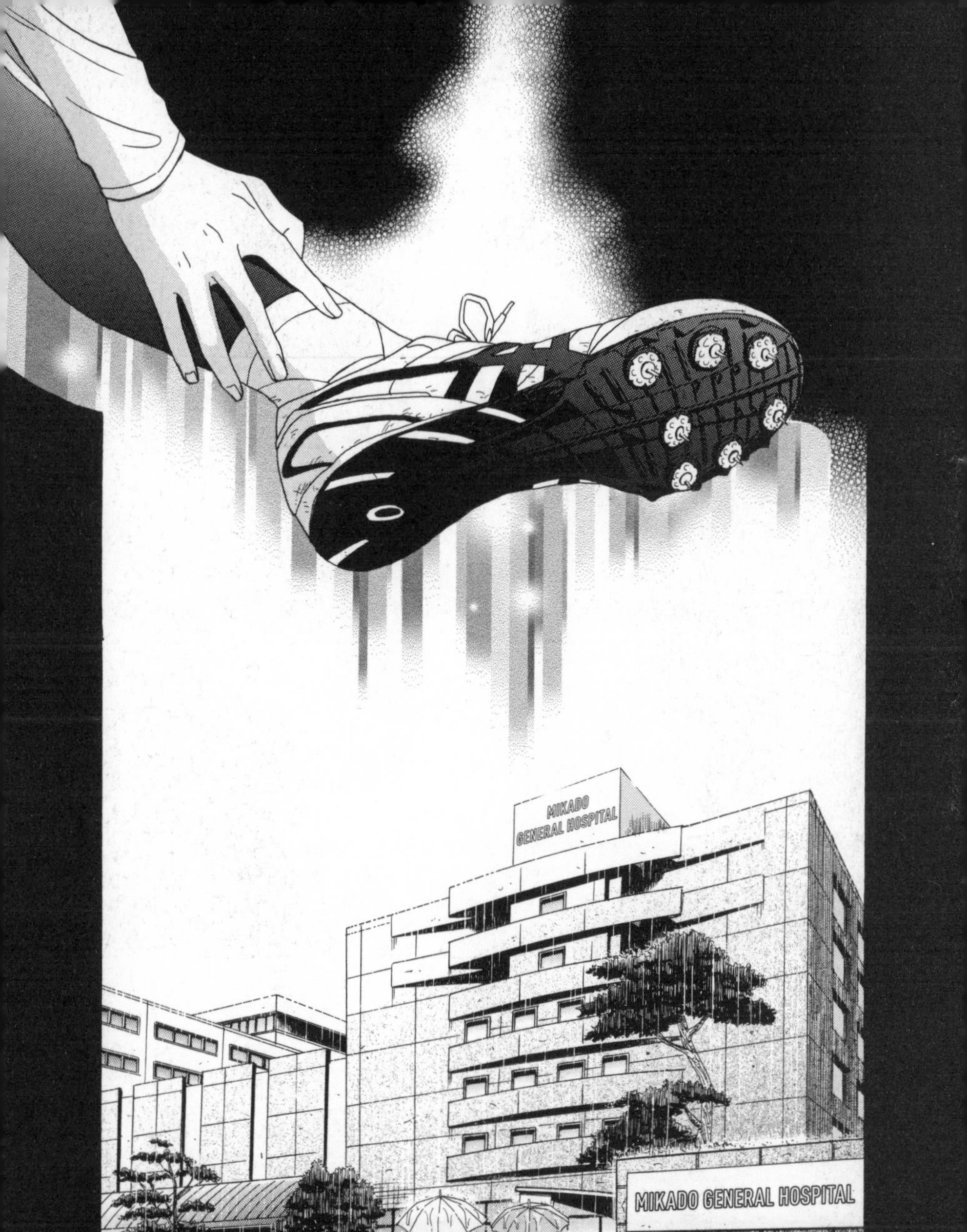
MIKADO
GENERAL HOSPITAL
MIKADO GENERAL HOSPITAL

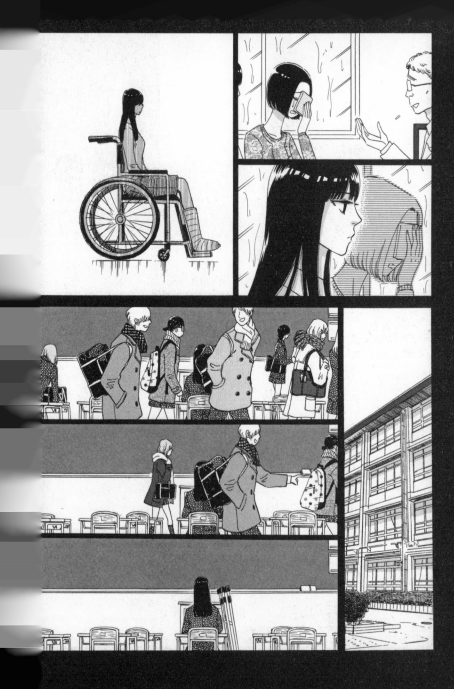

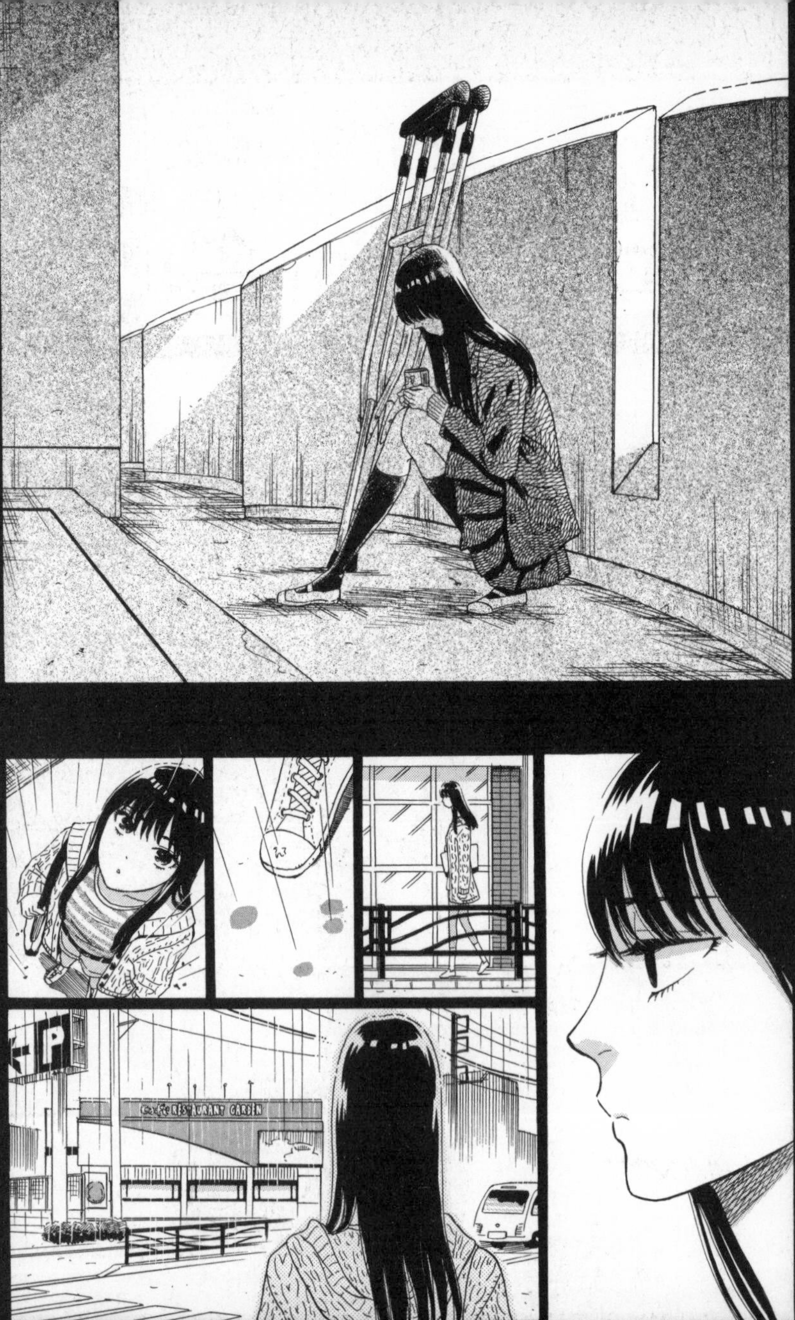
RESTAURANT GARDEN

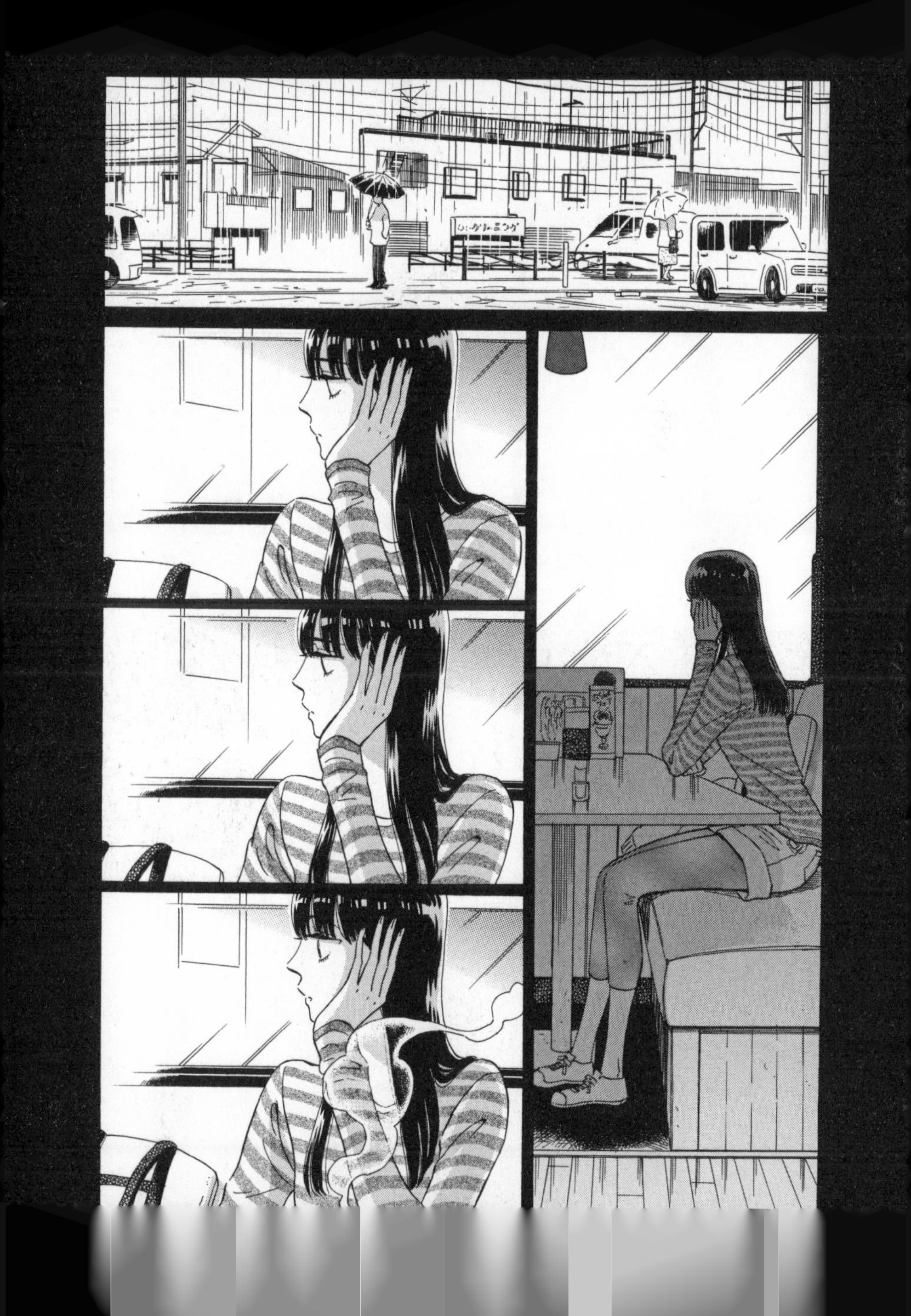

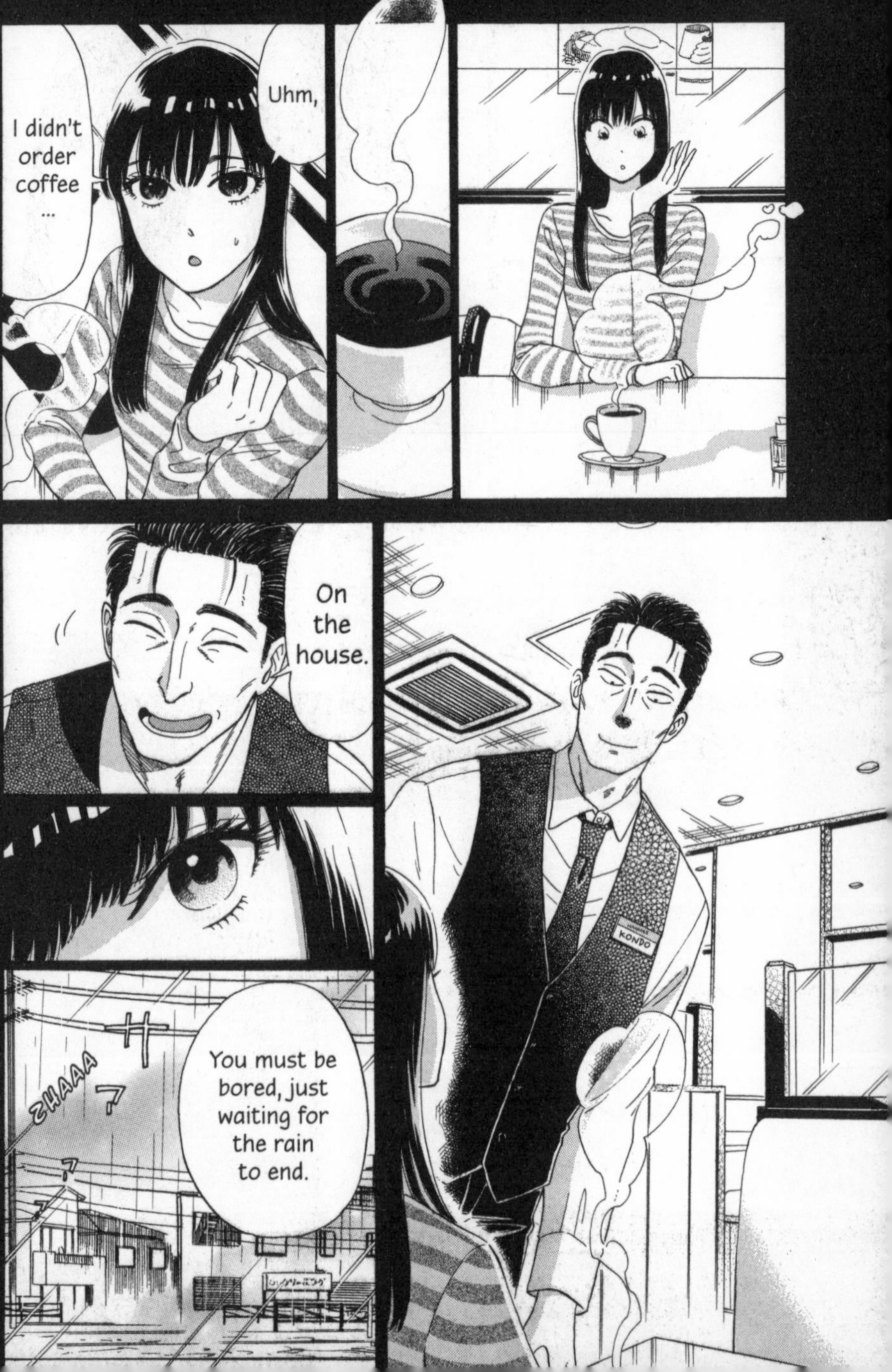
Uhm,
I didn't order coffee ...
KONDO
On the house.
ZHAAA
You must be bored, just waiting for the rain to end.

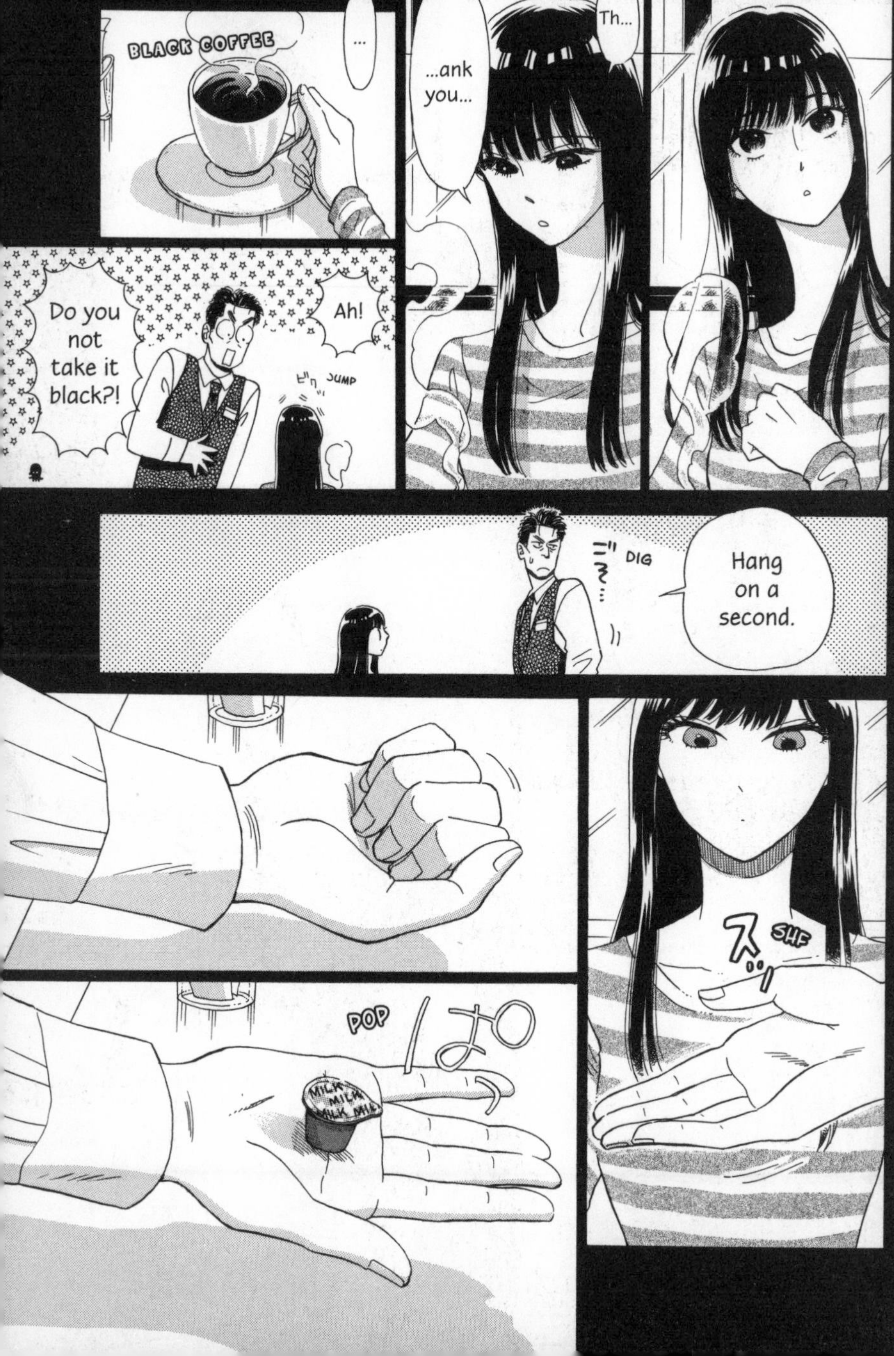
Th...
...ank you...
...
BLACK COFFEE
Ah!
Do you not take it black?!
JUMP
Hang on a second.
DIG
SHF
ぱっ
POP
MILK MILK MILK MIL

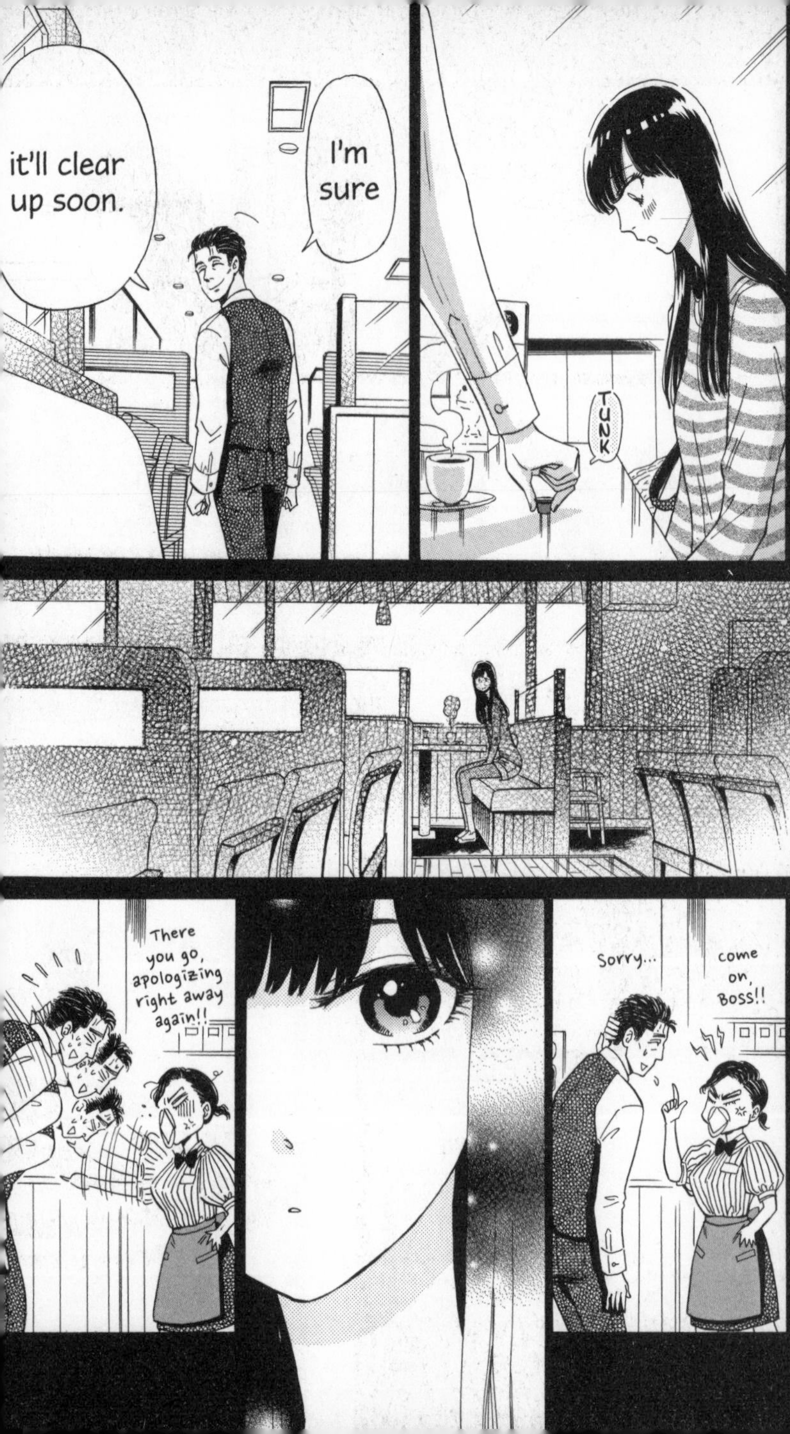
TUNK
I'm sure
it'll clear up soon.
come on, Boss!!
Sorry...
There you go, apologizing right away again!!

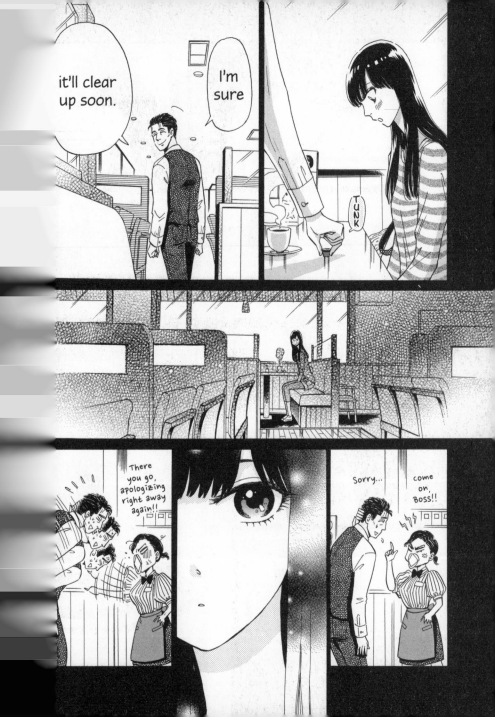

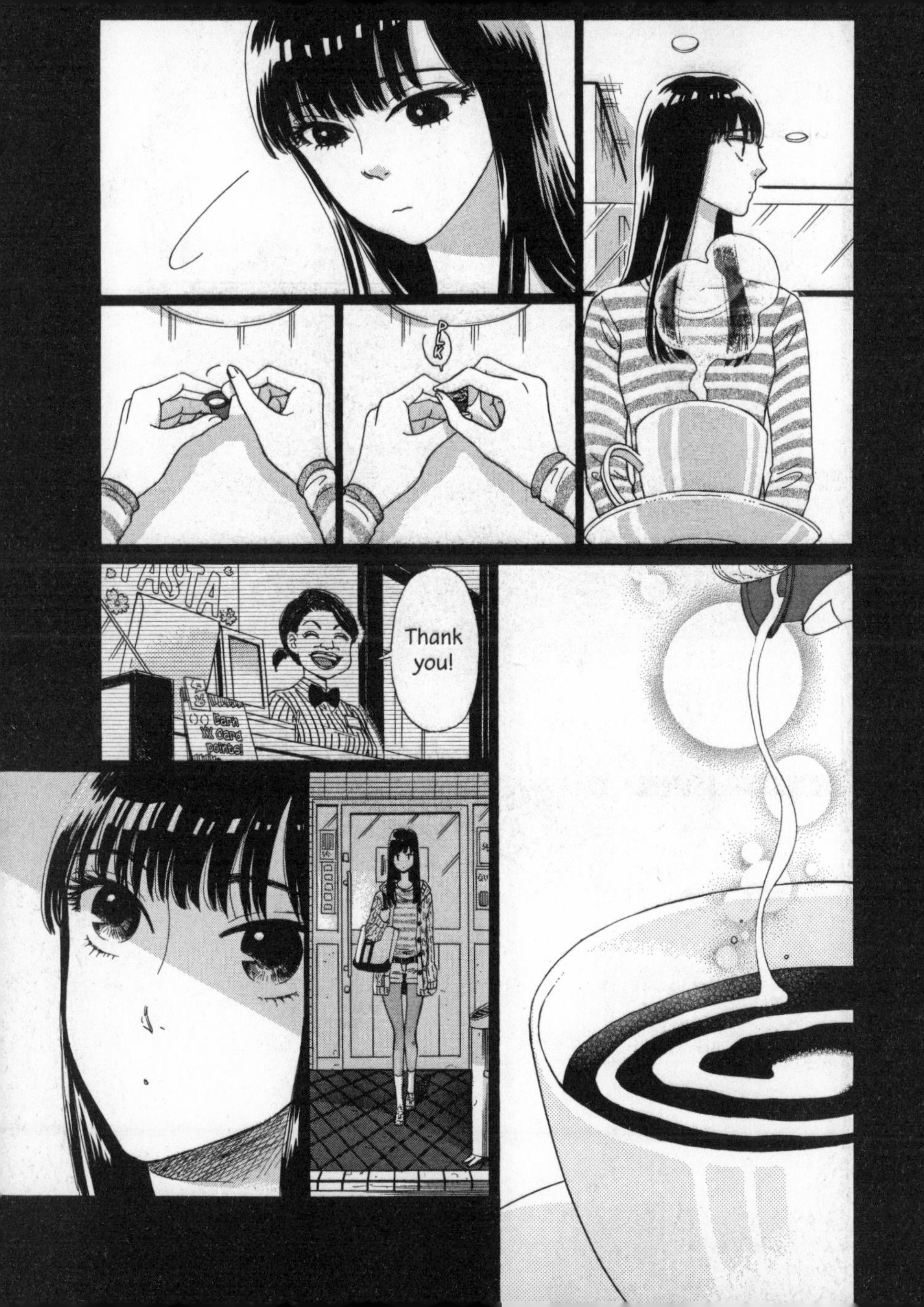
PLK
PASTA
Thank you!
Earn XX Card points!

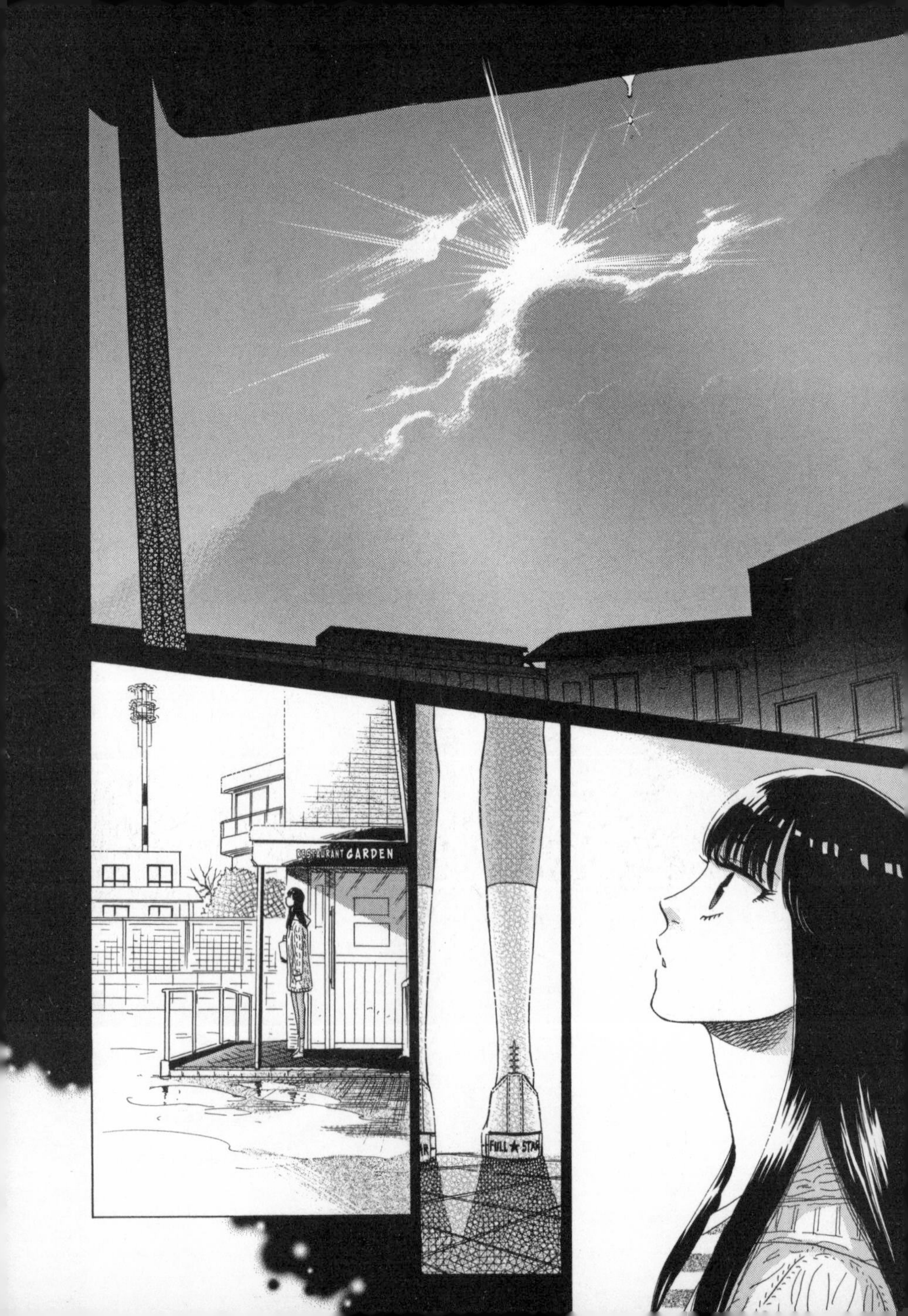
RESTAURANT GARDEN
FULL ★ STAR

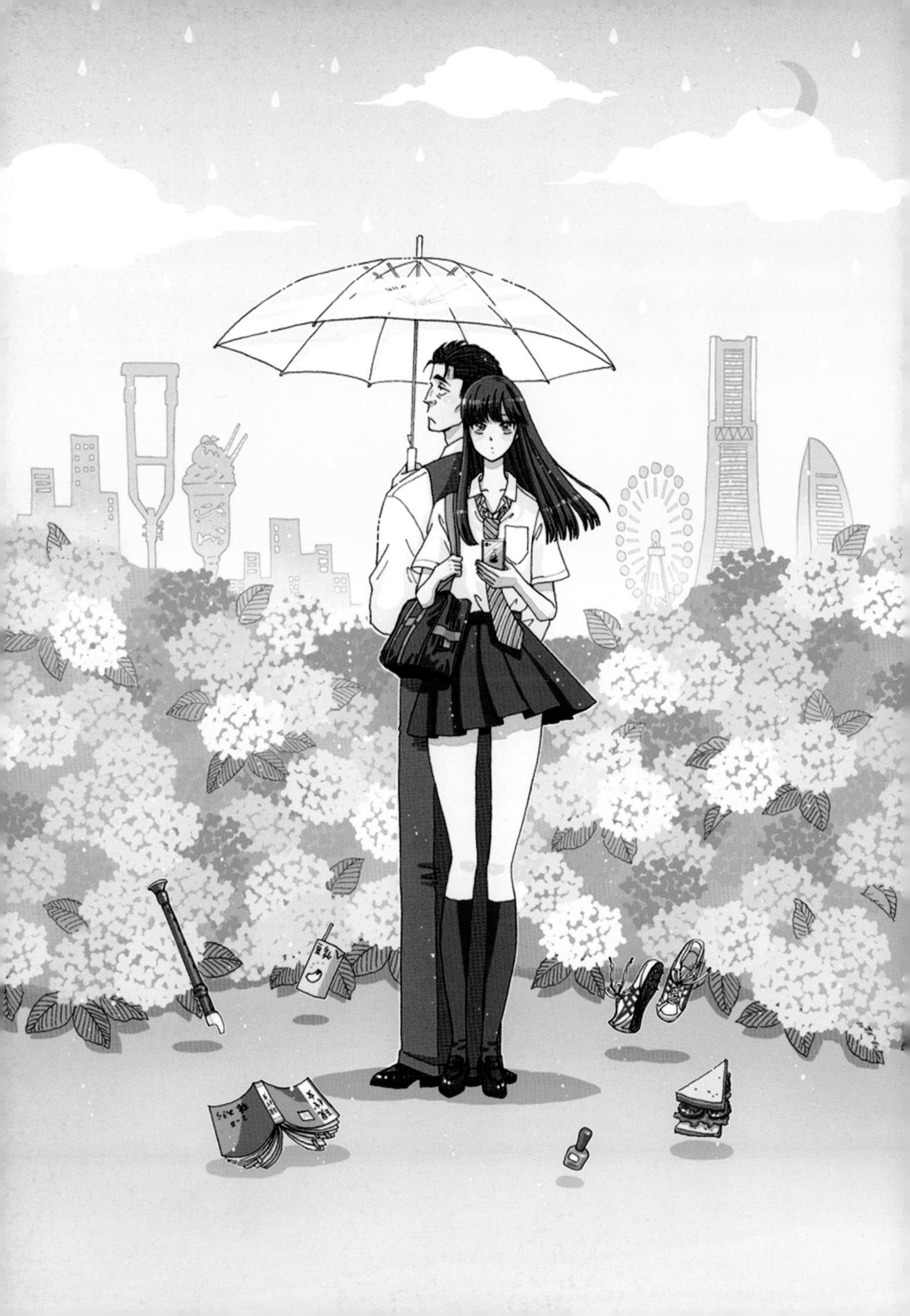

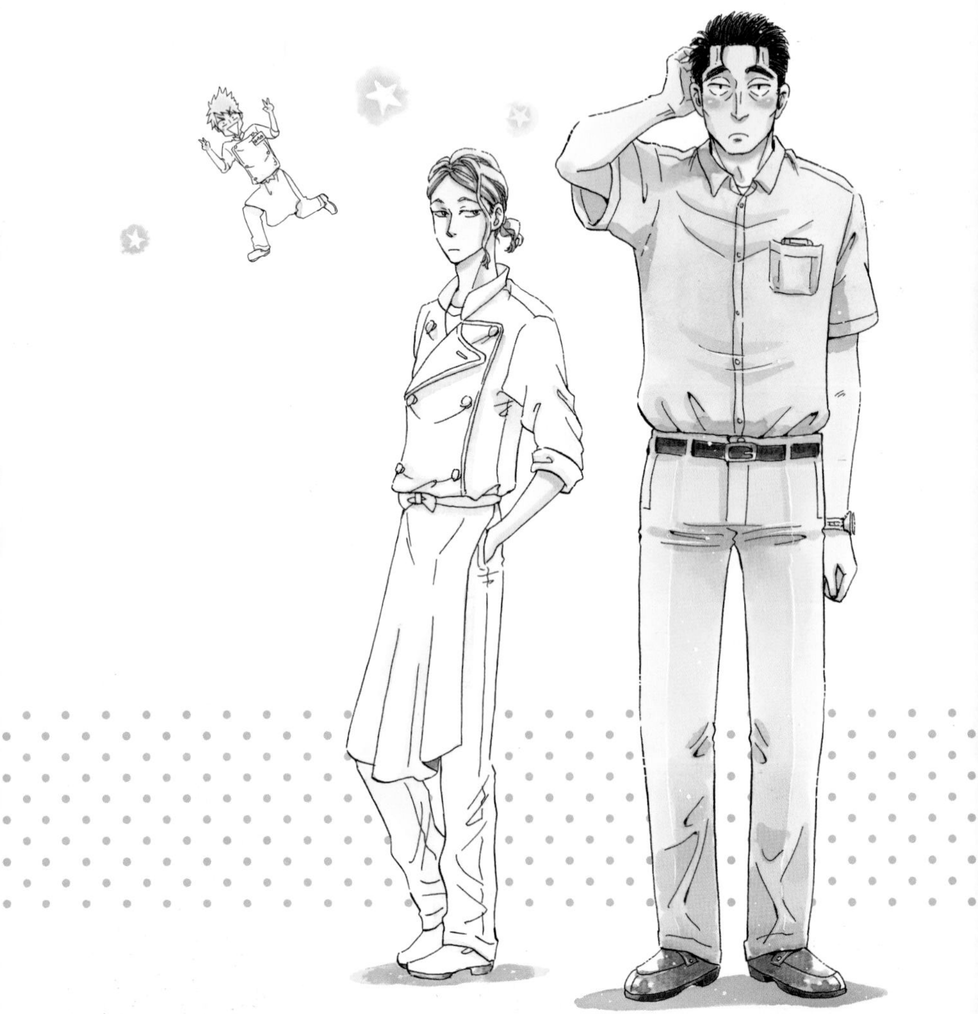

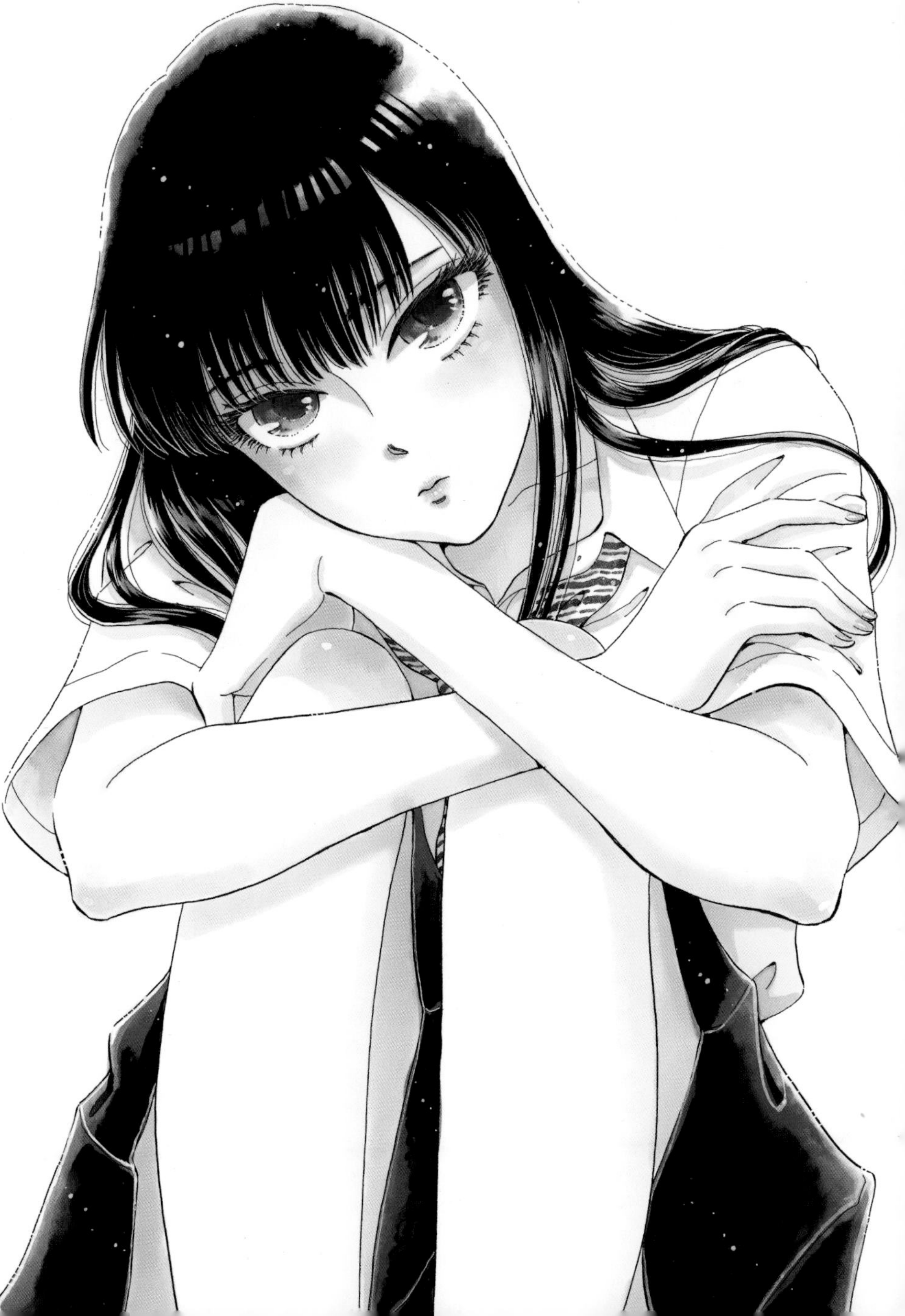

After
the
Rain

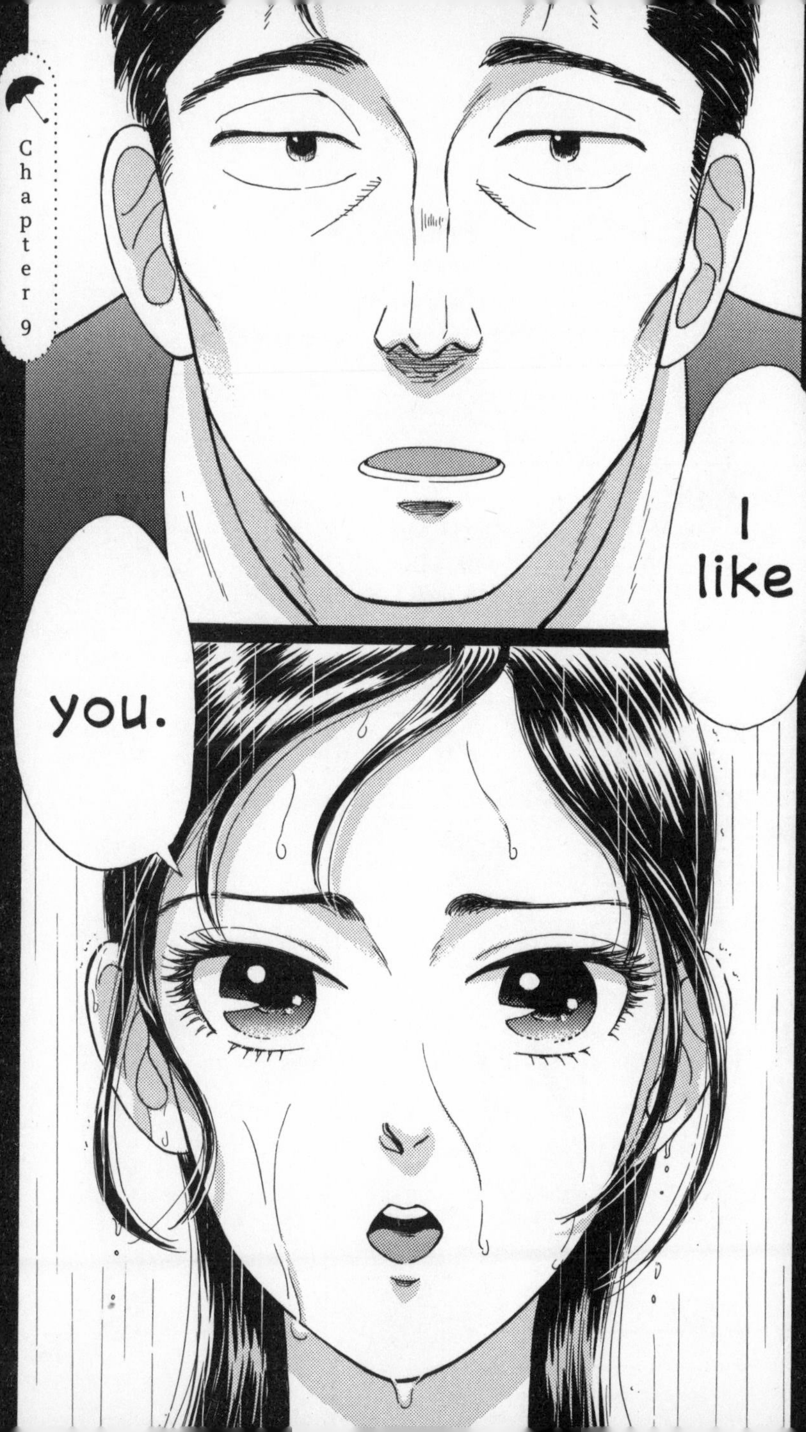
Chapter 9
I like
you.

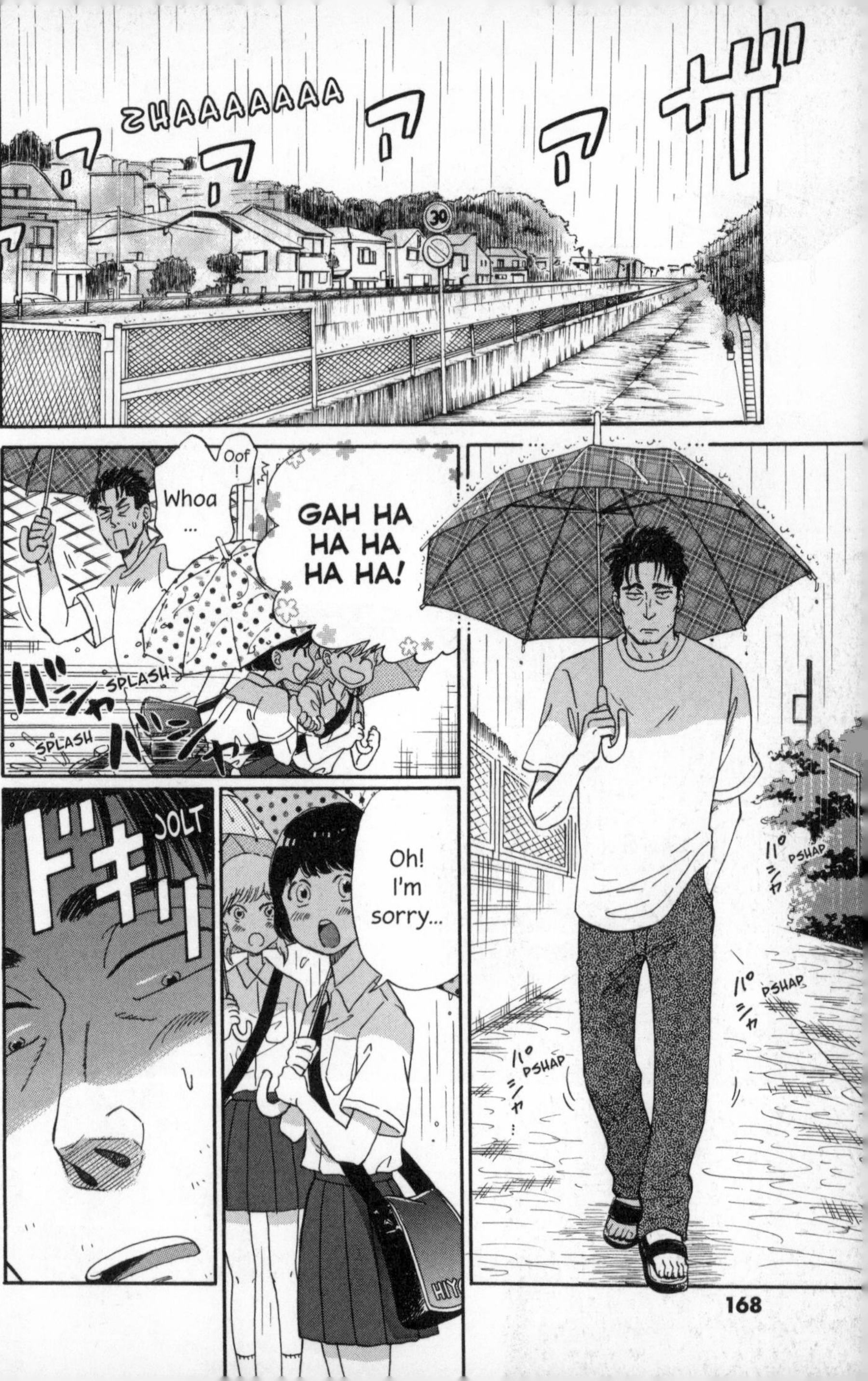
ザアアアア
ZHAAAAAAA
パシャ
PSHAP
パシャ
PSHAP
パシャ
PSHAP
Oof!
Whoa ...
GAH HA HA HA HA HA!
バシャ
SPLASH
バシャ
SPLASH
Oh! I'm sorry...
ドキッ
JOLT

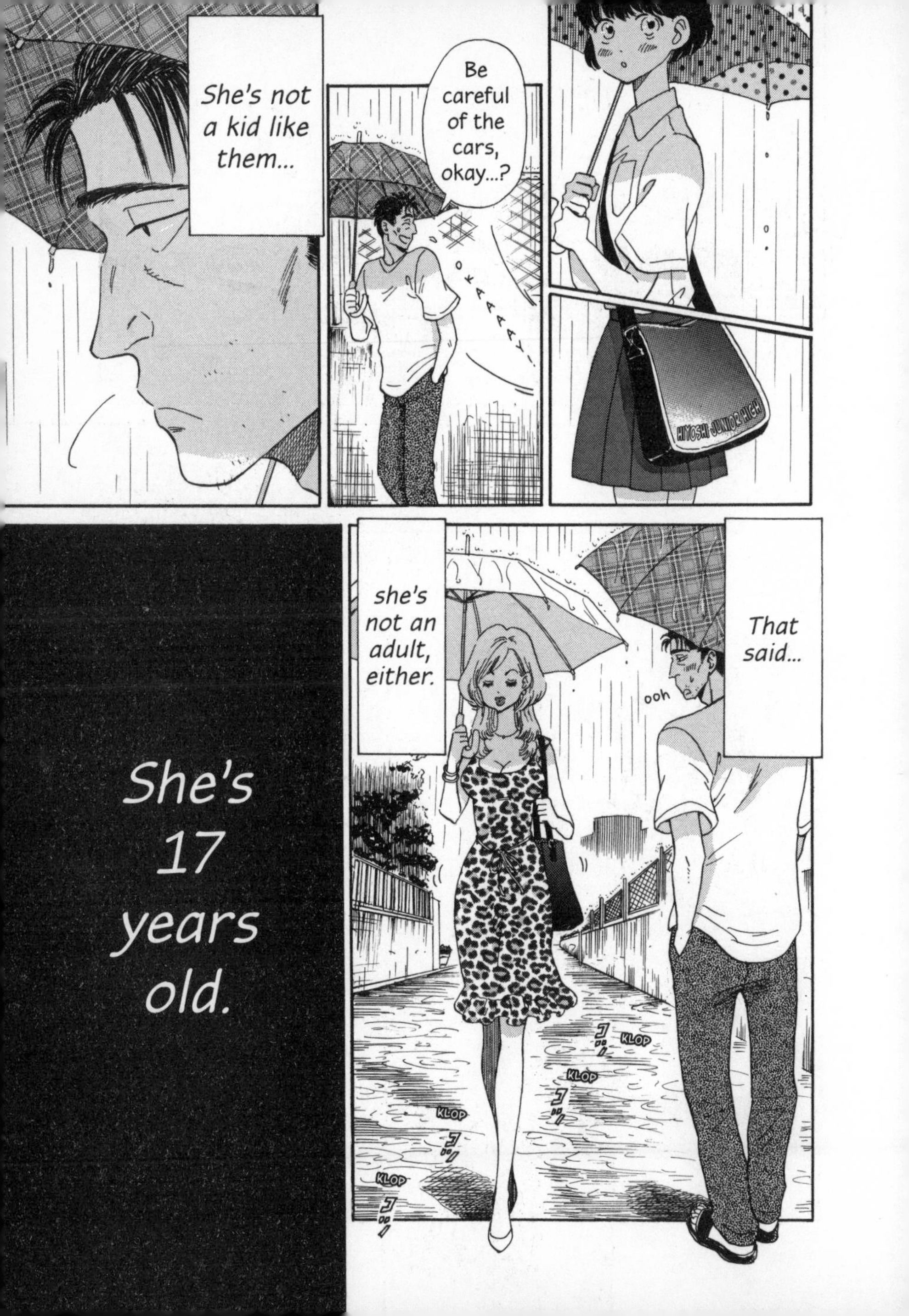
HIYOSHI JUNIOR HIGH
Be careful of the cars, okay...?
OKAAAAAY...!
She's not a kid like them...
That said...
ooh
she's not an adult, either.
KLOP
KLOP
KLOP
KLOP
She's 17 years old.

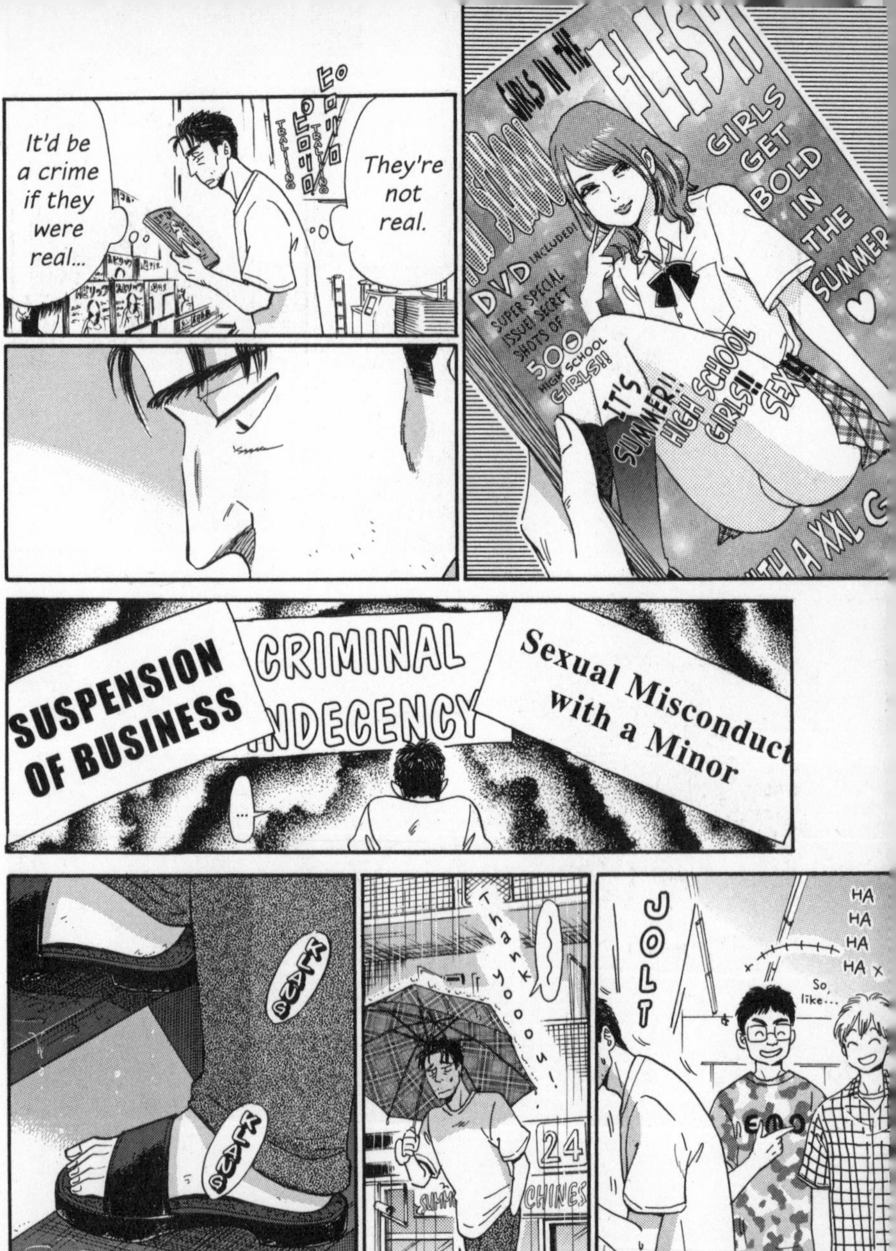
GIRLS IN THE
FLESH
GIRLS GET BOLD IN THE SUMMER ♥
DVD INCLUDED!
SUPER SPECIAL ISSUE! SECRET SHOTS OF 500 HIGH SCHOOL GIRLS!!
IT'S SUMMER!! HIGH SCHOOL GIRLS!! SEX!!
TRALLING
TRALLING
They're not real.
It'd be a crime if they were real...
Sexual Misconduct with a Minor
CRIMINAL INDECENCY
SUSPENSION OF BUSINESS
...
HA HA HA HA
So, like...
JOLT
EMO
Thank yoooou!
24
CHINES
KLANG
KLANG
KLANG

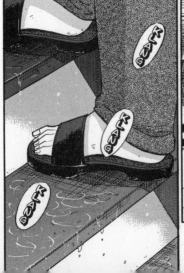

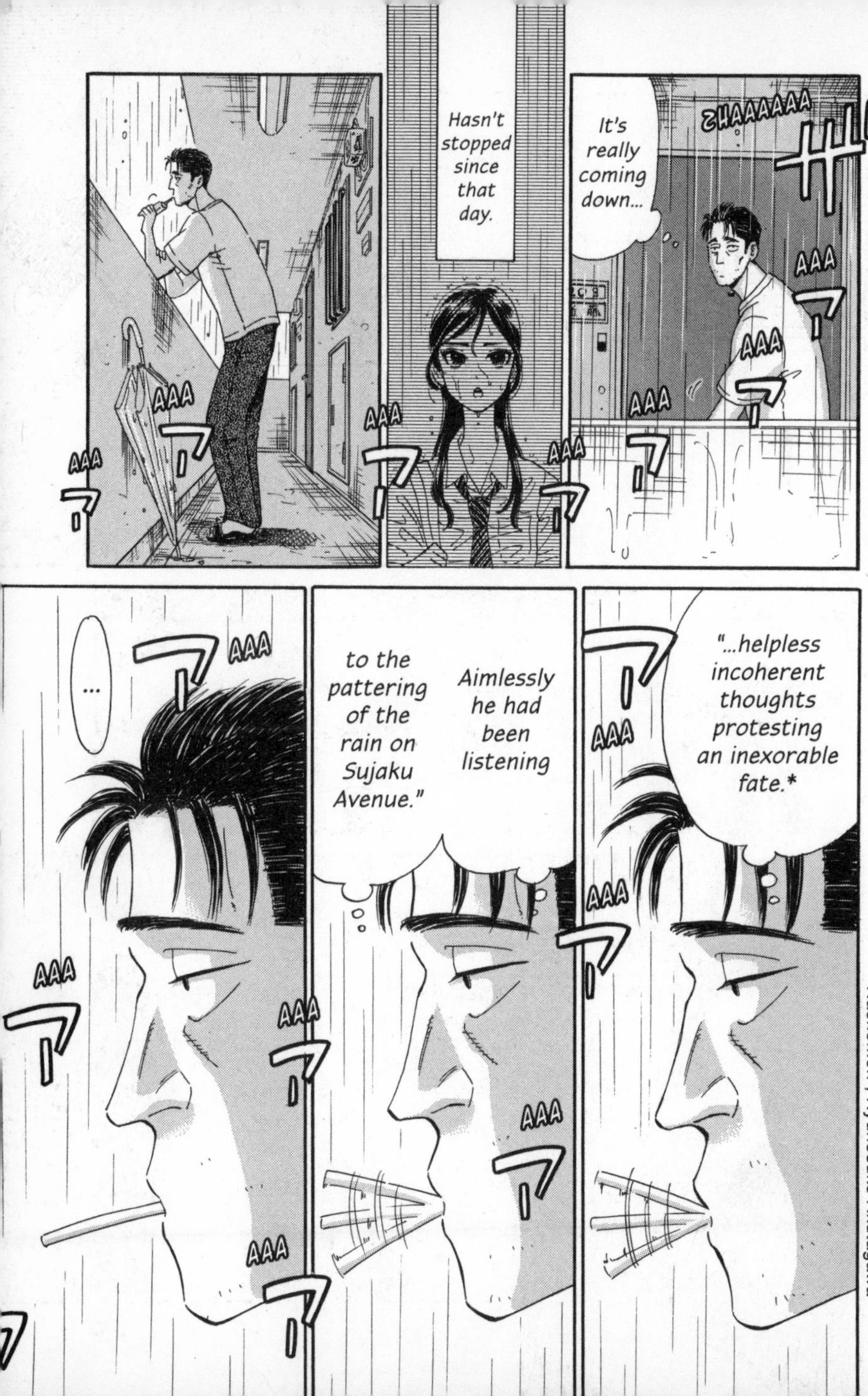
ZHAAAAAA
It's really coming down...
AAA
Hasn't stopped since that day.
AAA
AAA
"...helpless incoherent thoughts protesting an inexorable fate.*
AAA
Aimlessly he had been listening
to the pattering of the rain on Sujaku Avenue."
AAA
...
AAA

*"Rashomon", Ryunosuke Akutagawa

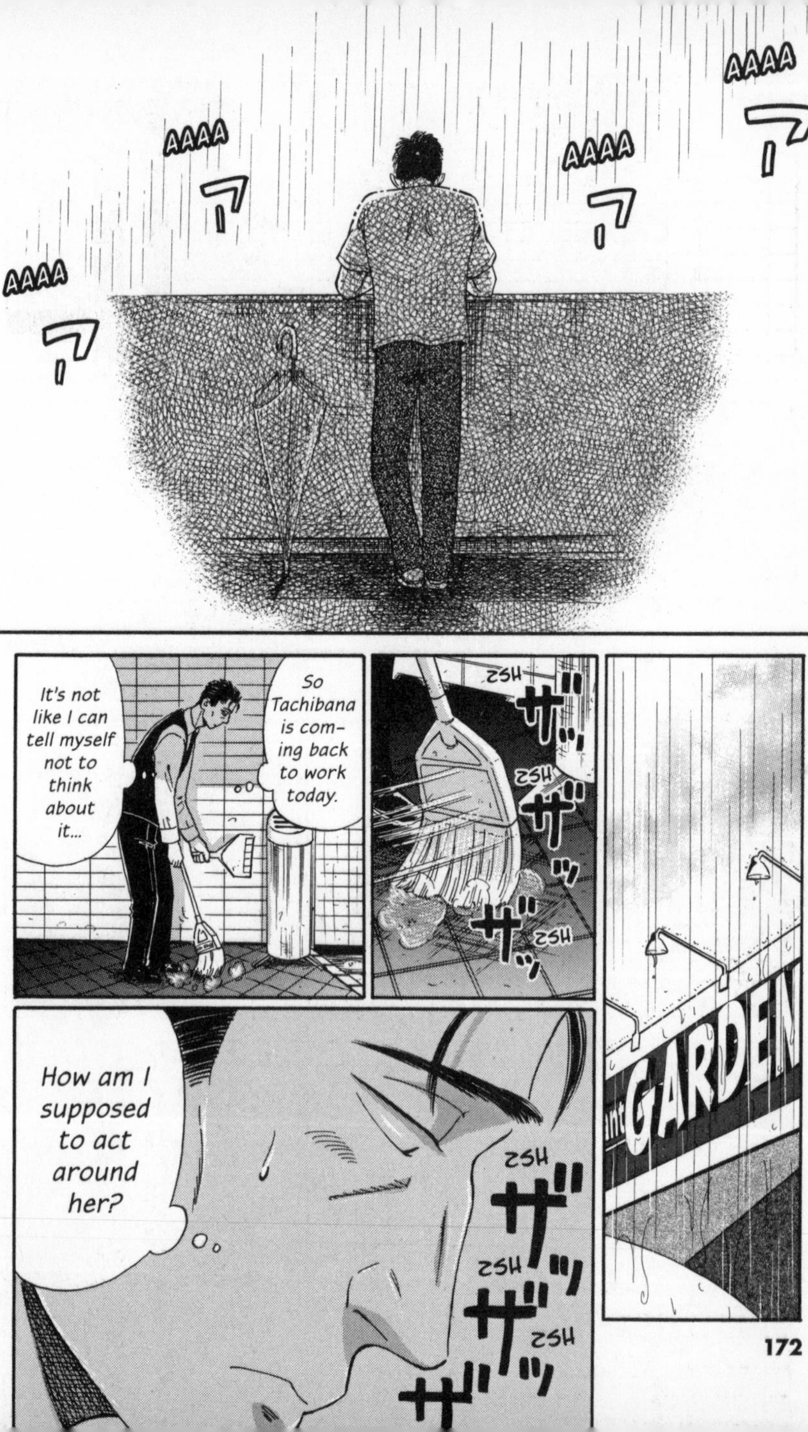
AAAA
AAAA
AAAA
AAAA
GARDEN
ZSH
ZSH
ZSH
So Tachibana is com-ing back to work today.
It's not like I can tell myself not to think about it...
How am I supposed to act around her?
ZSH
ZSH
ZSH

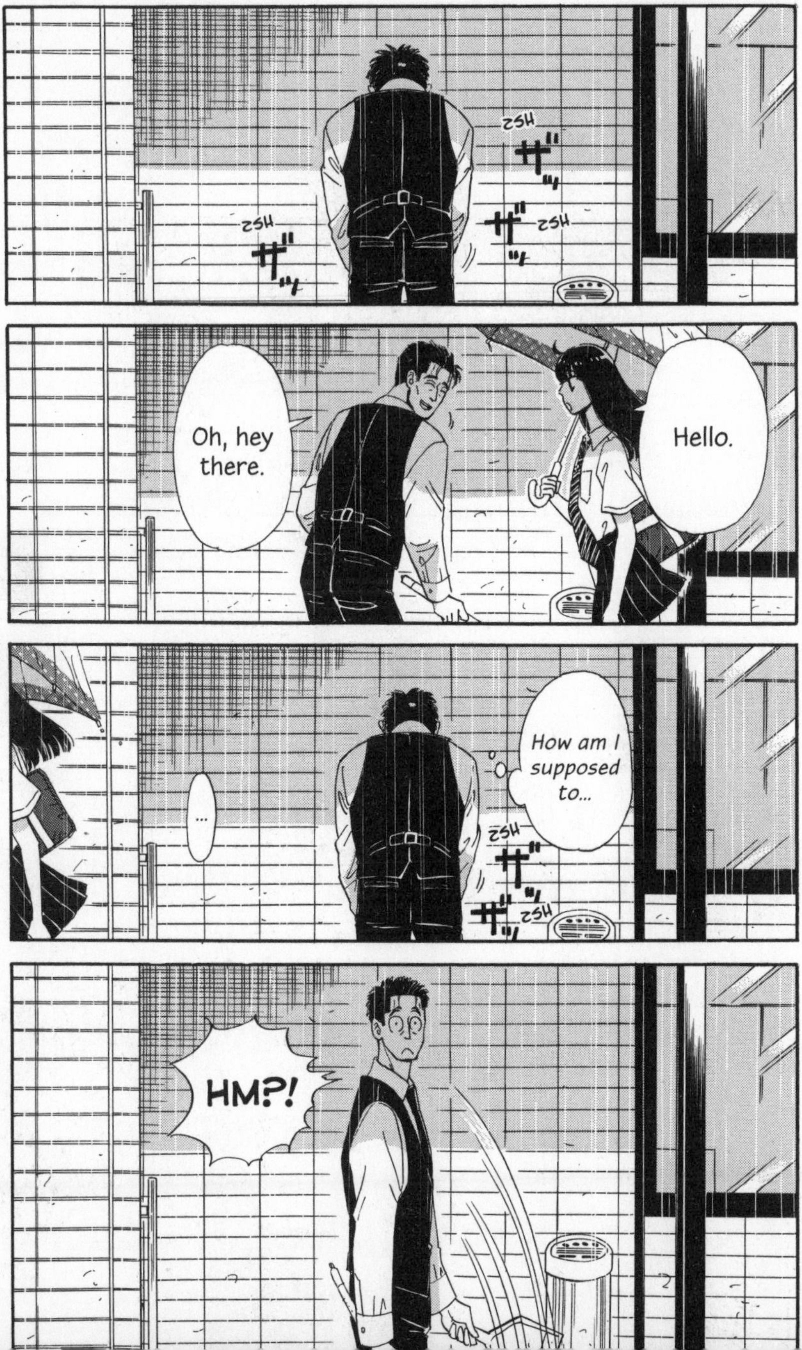
Hello.
Oh, hey there.
How am I supposed to...
...
HM?!

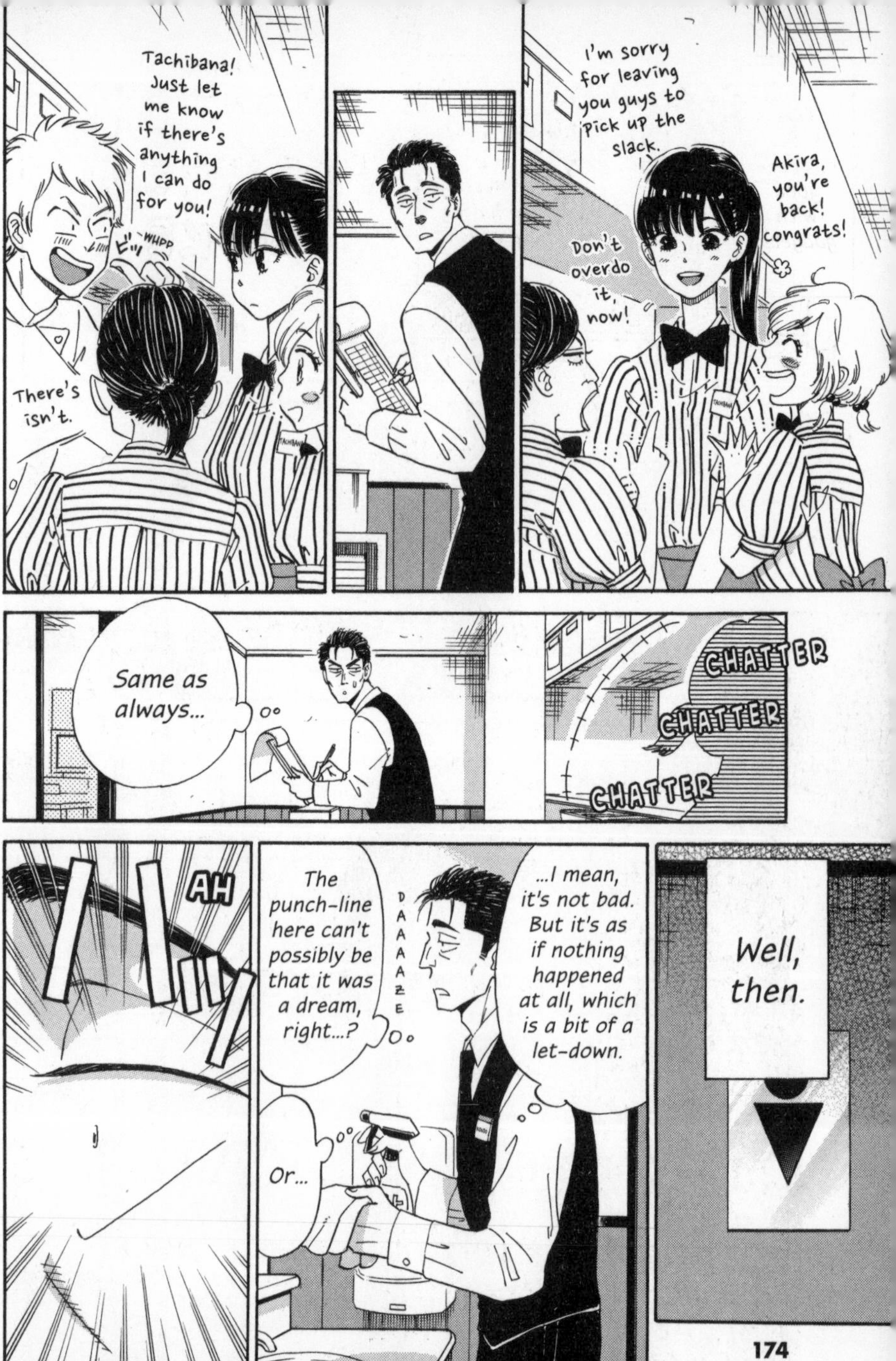
Akira, you're back! congrats!
I'm sorry for leaving you guys to pick up the slack.
Don't overdo it, now!
Tachibana! Just let me know if there's anything I can do for you!
WHPP
There's isn't.
CHATTER
CHATTER
CHATTER
Same as always...
Well, then.
...I mean, it's not bad. But it's as if nothing happened at all, which is a bit of a let-down.
DAAAAAZE
The punch-line here can't possibly be that it was a dream, right...?
Or...
AH

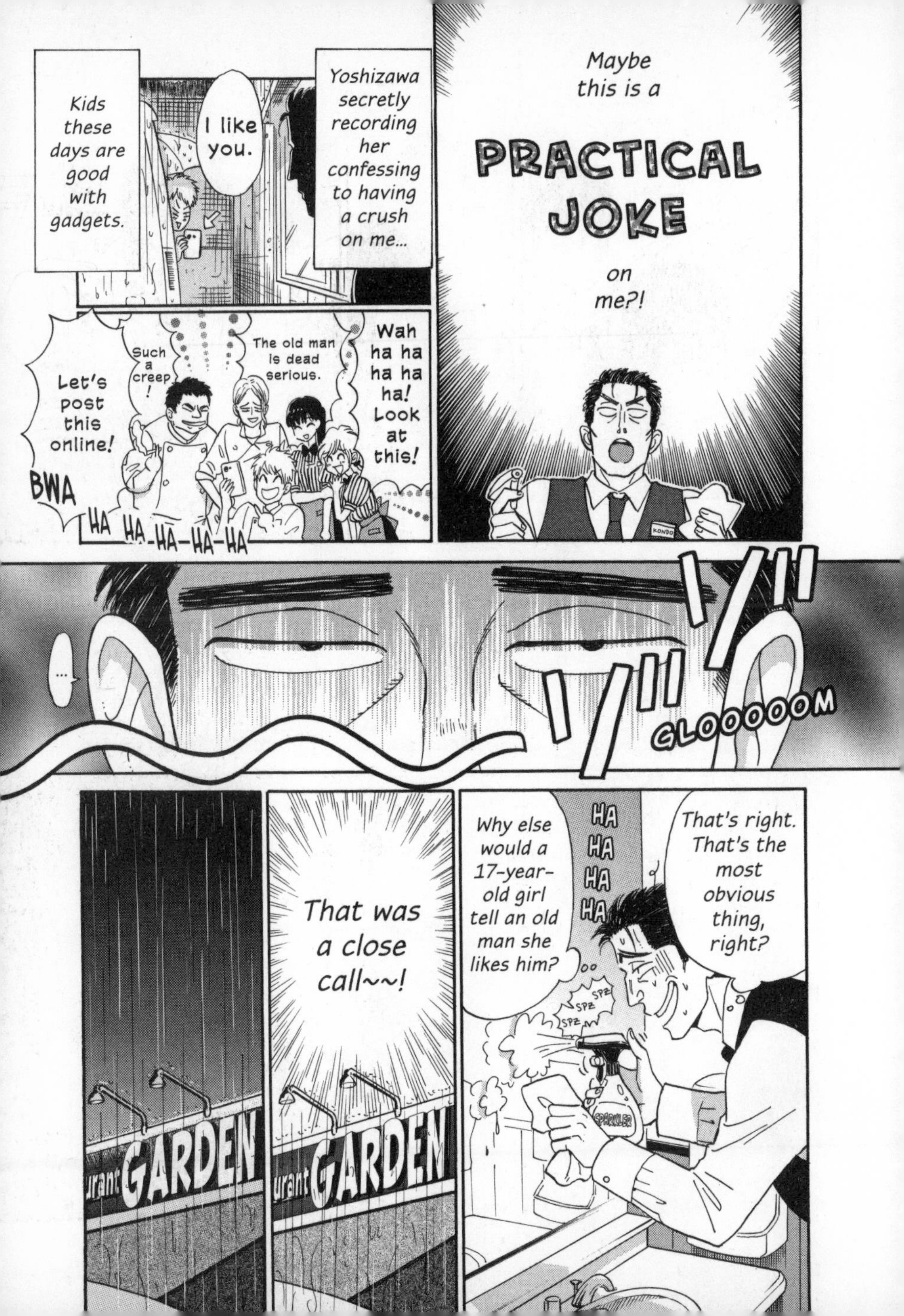
Maybe this is a
PRACTICAL JOKE
on me?!
KONDO
Yoshizawa secretly recording her confessing to having a crush on me...
I like you.
Kids these days are good with gadgets.
Wah ha ha ha ha ha! Look at this!
The old man is dead serious.
Such a creep!
Let's post this online!
BWA HA HA-HA-HA-HA
GLOOOOOM
...
That's right. That's the most obvious thing, right?
HA HA HA HA HA
Why else would a 17-year-old girl tell an old man she likes him?
SPZ SPZ SPZ SPZ
SPARKLER
That was a close call~~!
urant GARDEN
urant GARDEN

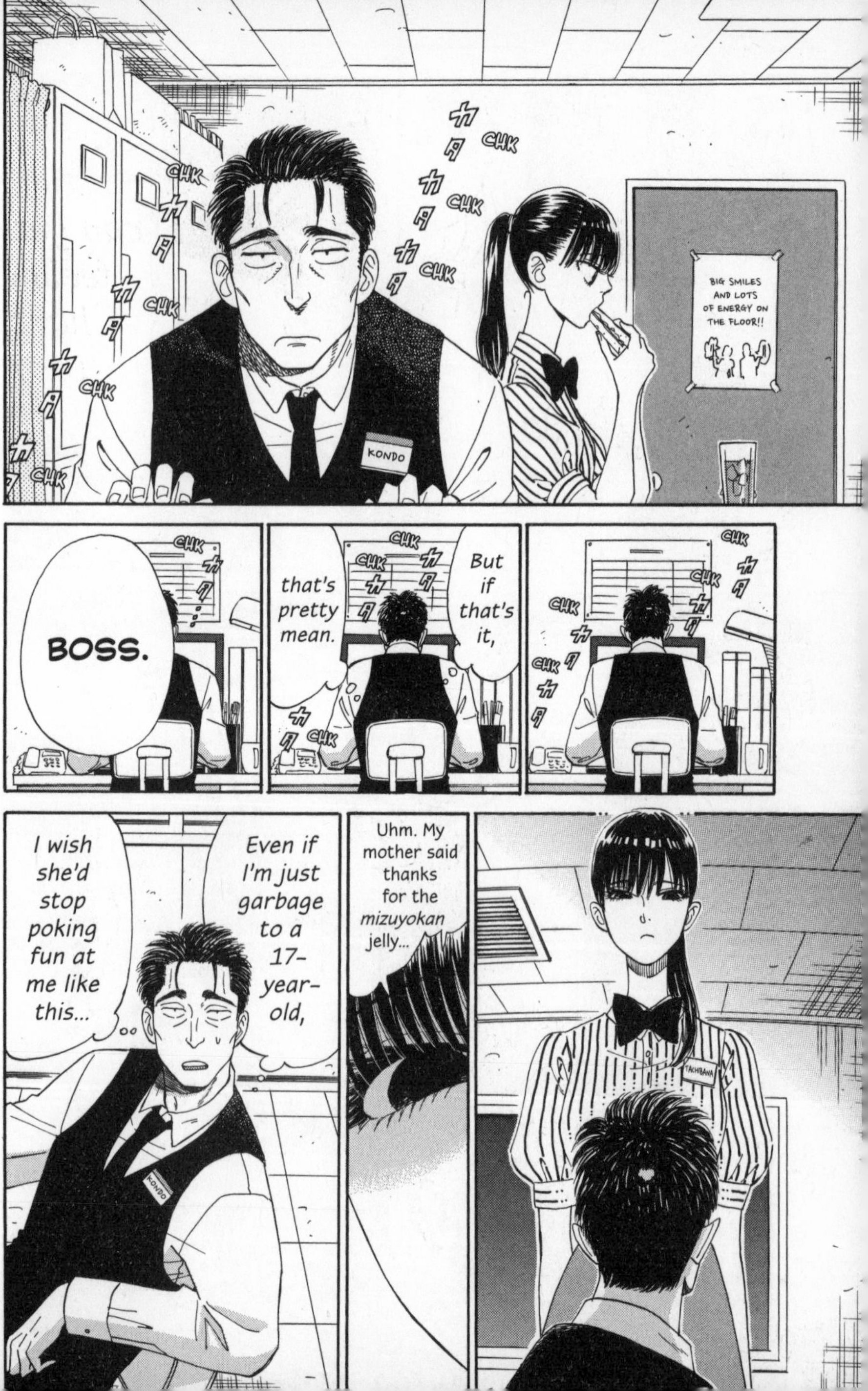

カタ
CHK
BIG SMILES AND LOTS OF ENERGY ON THE FLOOR!!
KONDO
CHK
カタ
But if that's it,
that's pretty mean.
BOSS.
Uhm. My mother said thanks for the *mizuyokan* jelly...
TACHIBANA
Even if I'm just garbage to a 17-year-old,
I wish she'd stop poking fun at me like this...
KONDO

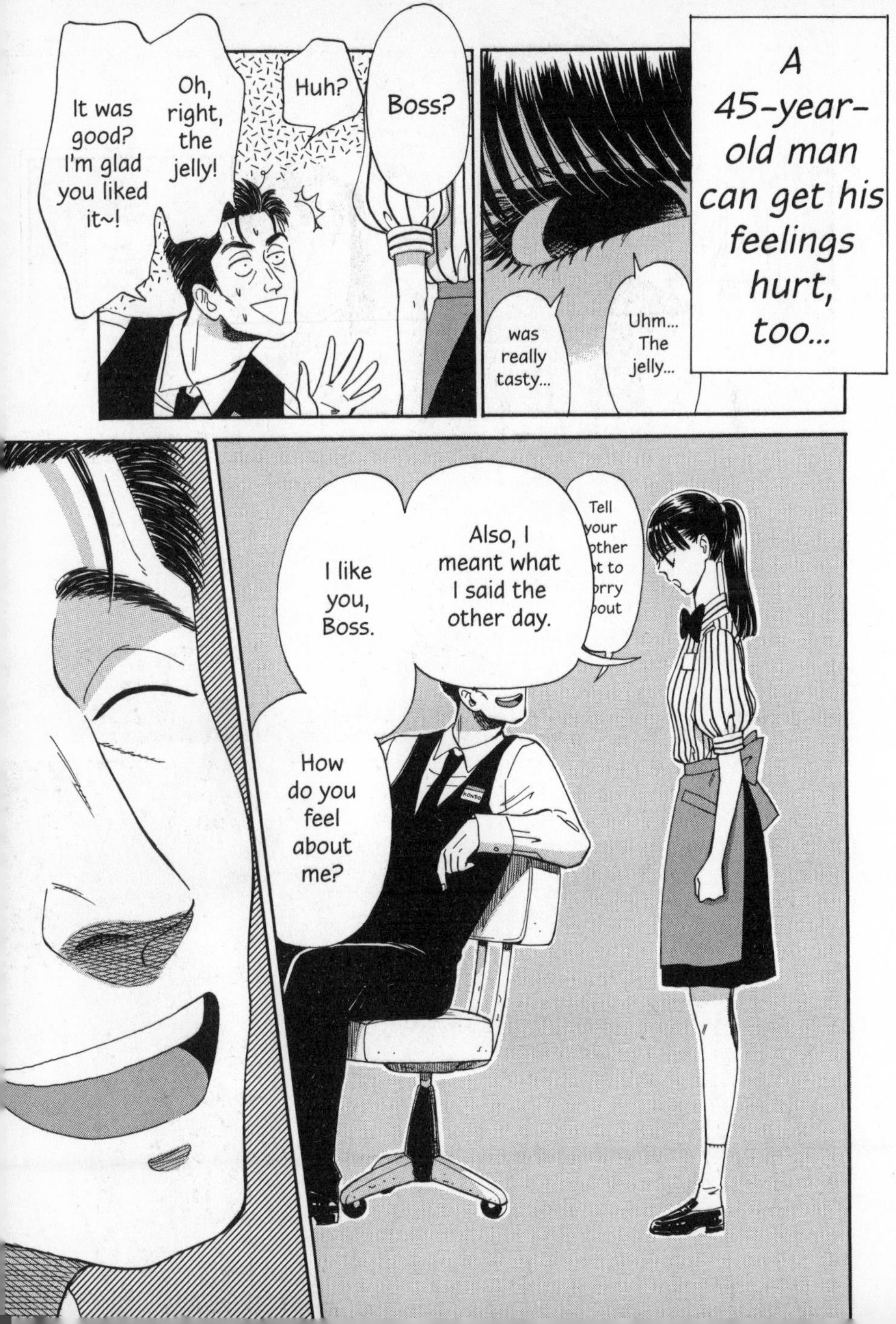
A 45-year-old man can get his feelings hurt, too...
Uhm... The jelly...
was really tasty...
Boss?
Huh?
Oh, right, the jelly!
It was good? I'm glad you liked it~!
Tell your other t to rry bout
Also, I meant what I said the other day.
I like you, Boss.
How do you feel about me?

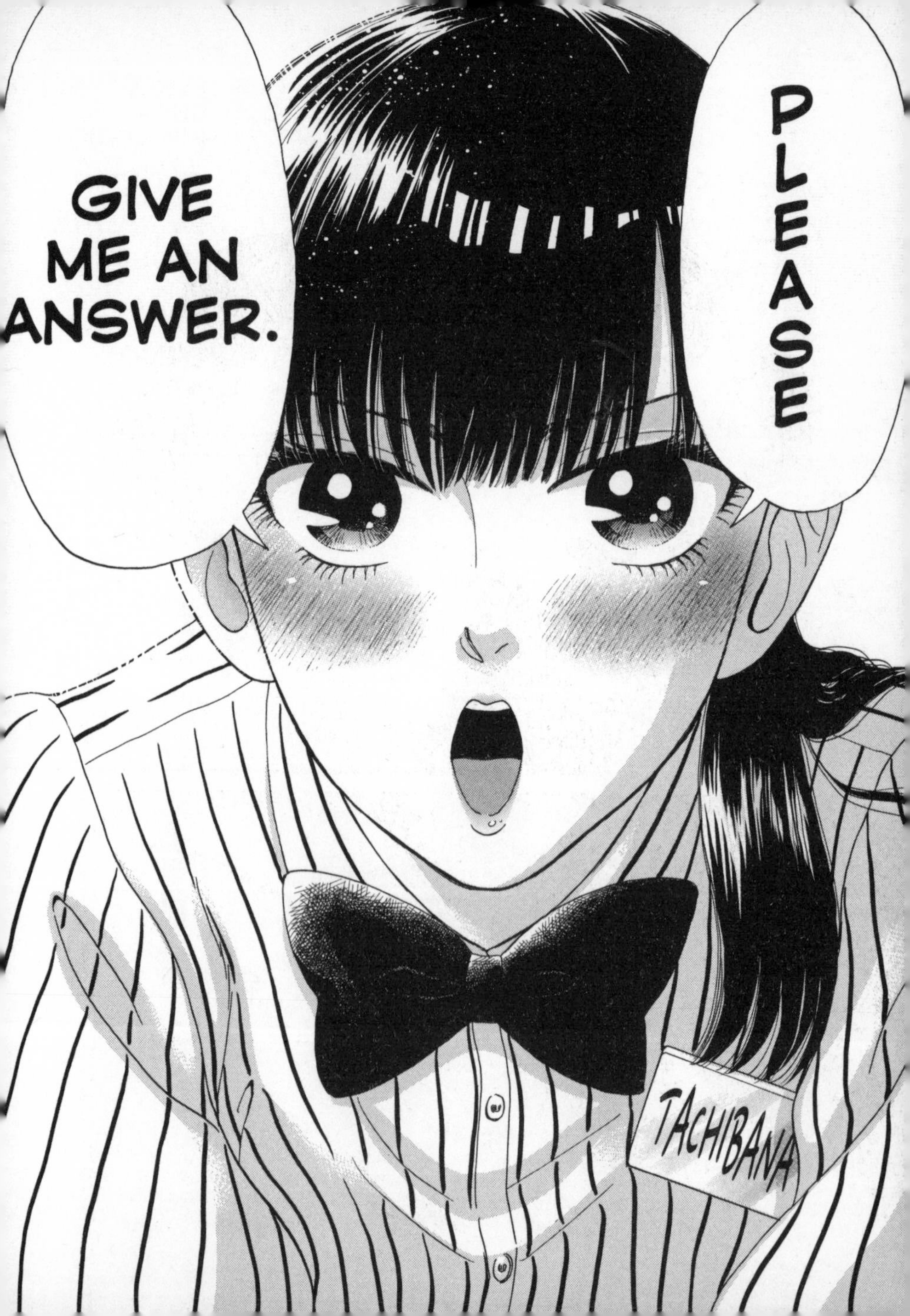
PLEASE
GIVE ME AN ANSWER.
TACHIBANA

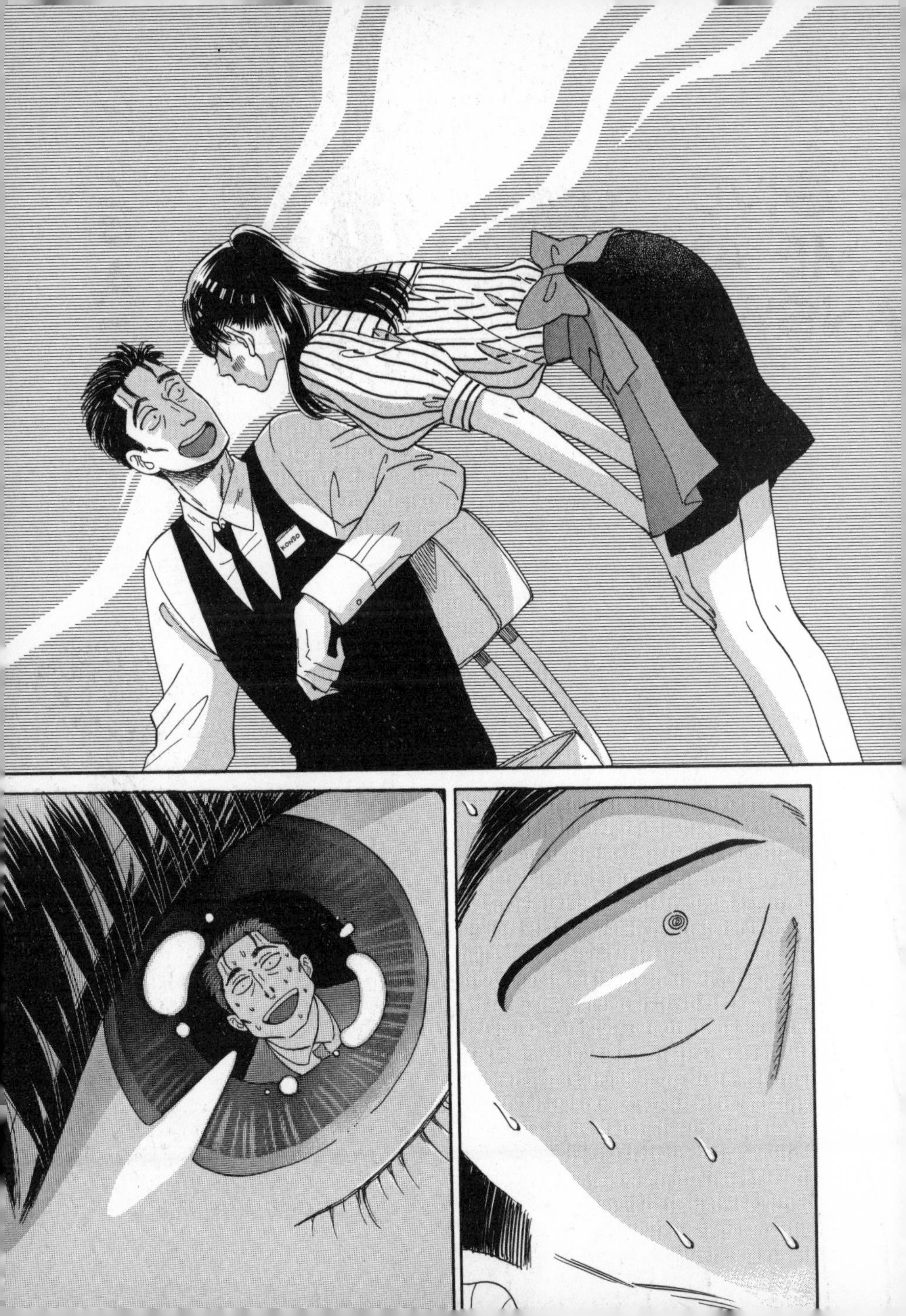
KONDO

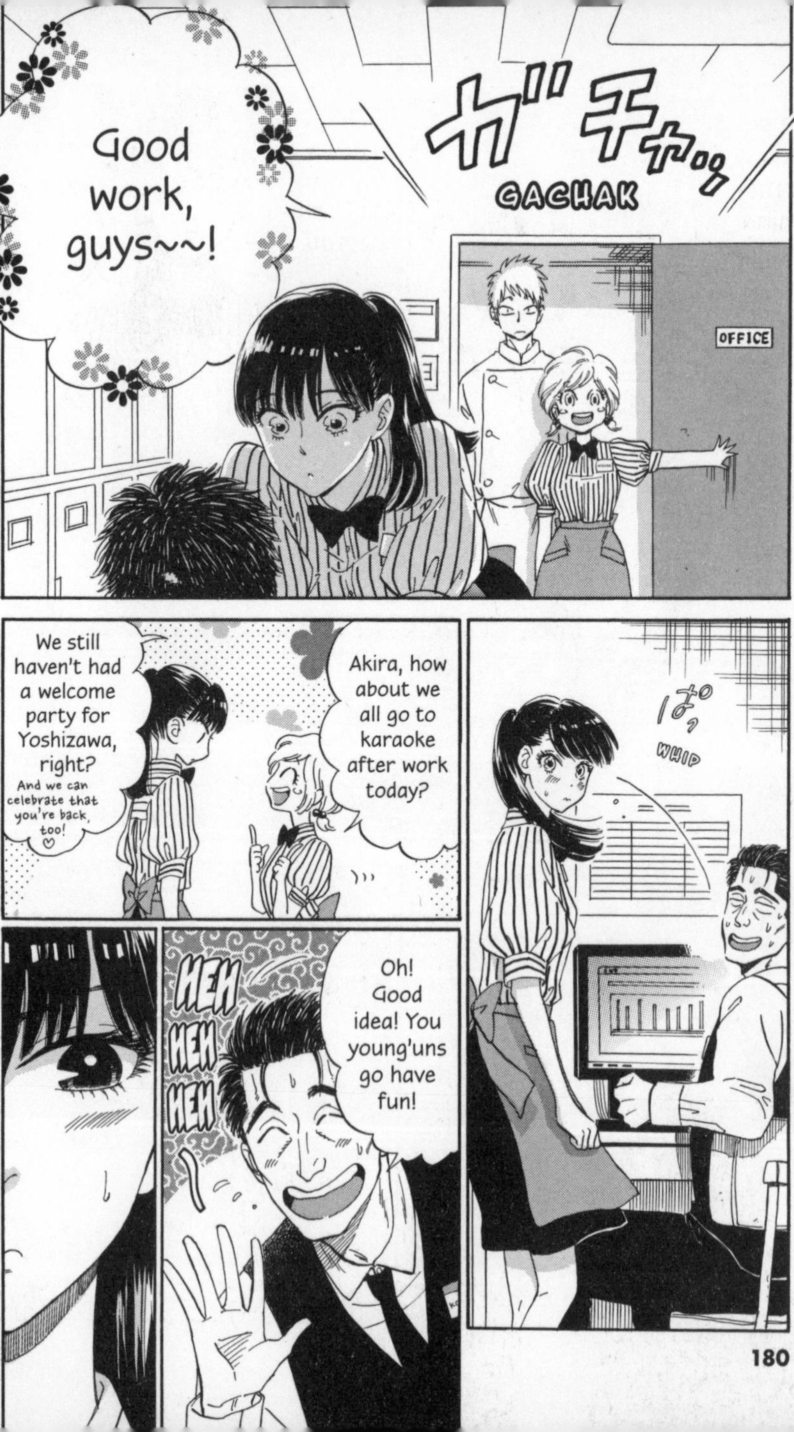
ガチャッ
GACHAK
Good work, guys~~!
OFFICE
ぱっ
WHIP
Akira, how about we all go to karaoke after work today?
We still haven't had a welcome party for Yoshizawa, right?
And we can celebrate that you're back, too! ♡
Oh! Good idea! You young'uns go have fun!
HEH HEH HEH

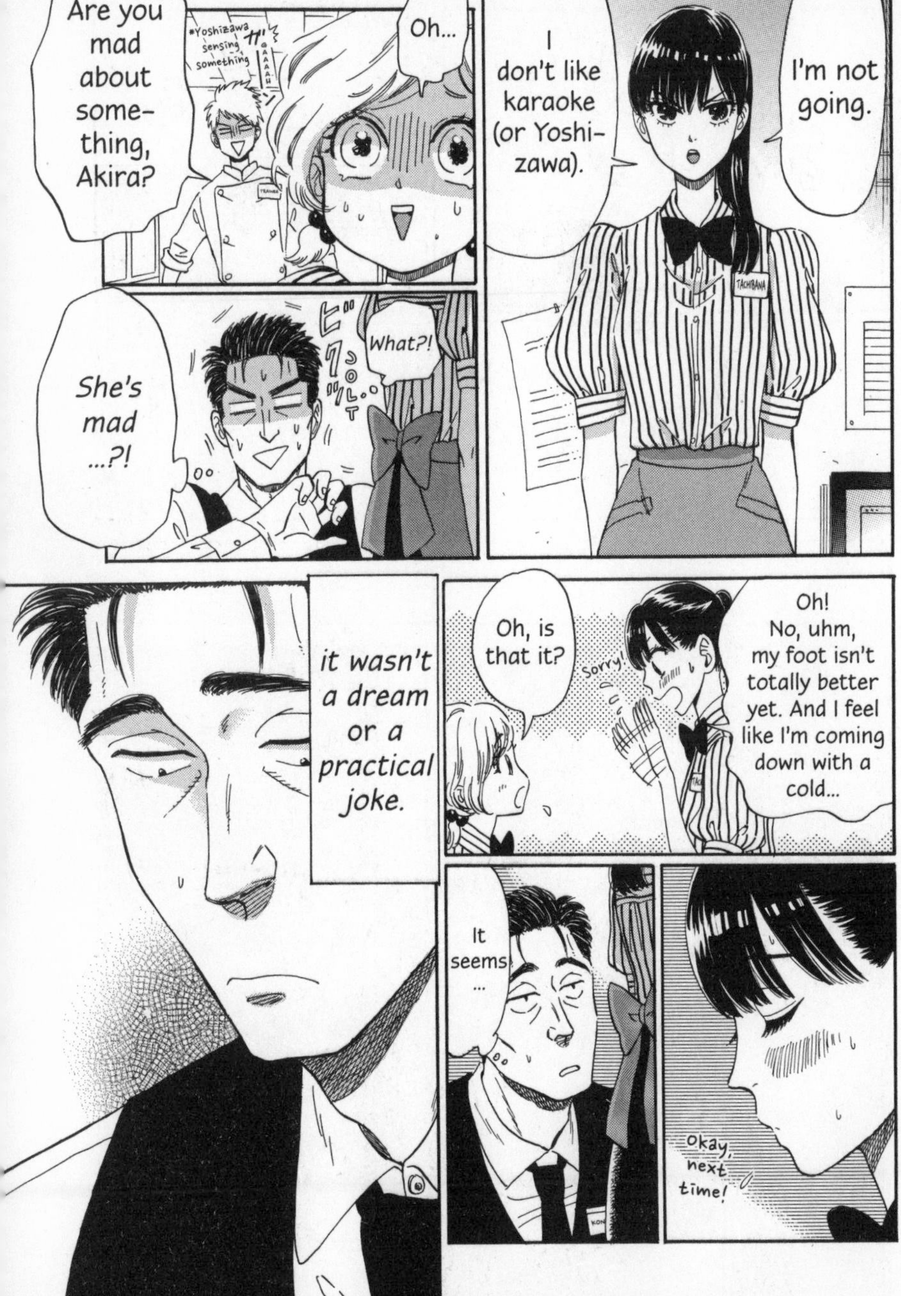
I'm not going.
I don't like karaoke (or Yoshizawa).
Oh...
Are you mad about some-thing, Akira?
*Yoshizawa sensing something
What?!
She's mad ...?!
Oh! No, uhm, my foot isn't totally better yet. And I feel like I'm coming down with a cold...
Sorry!
Oh, is that it?
Okay, next time!
It seems ...
it wasn't a dream or a practical joke.

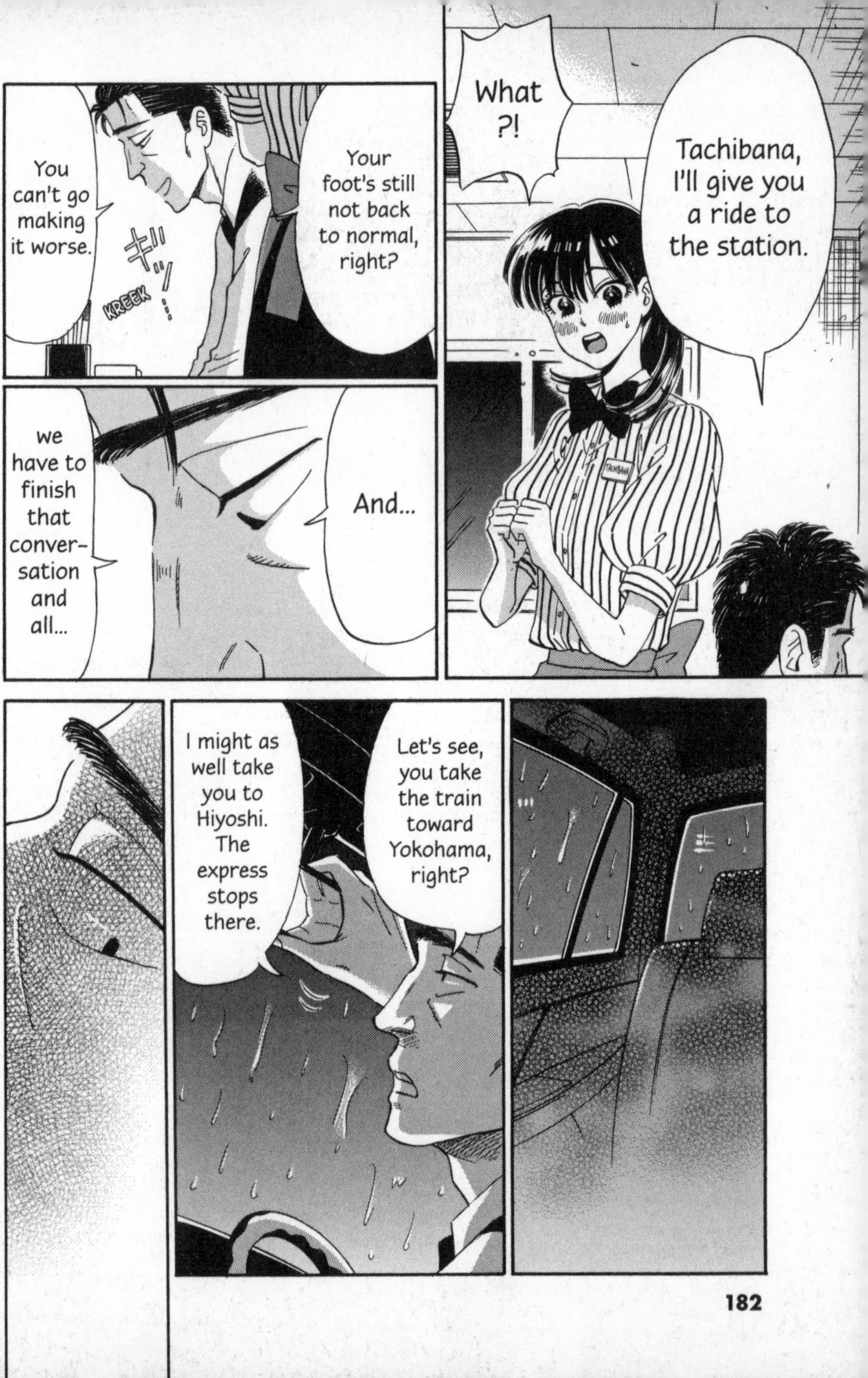
Tachibana, I'll give you a ride to the station.
What ?!
Your foot's still not back to normal, right?
You can't go making it worse.
KREEK
And...
we have to finish that conver-sation and all...
Let's see, you take the train toward Yokohama, right?
I might as well take you to Hiyoshi. The express stops there.

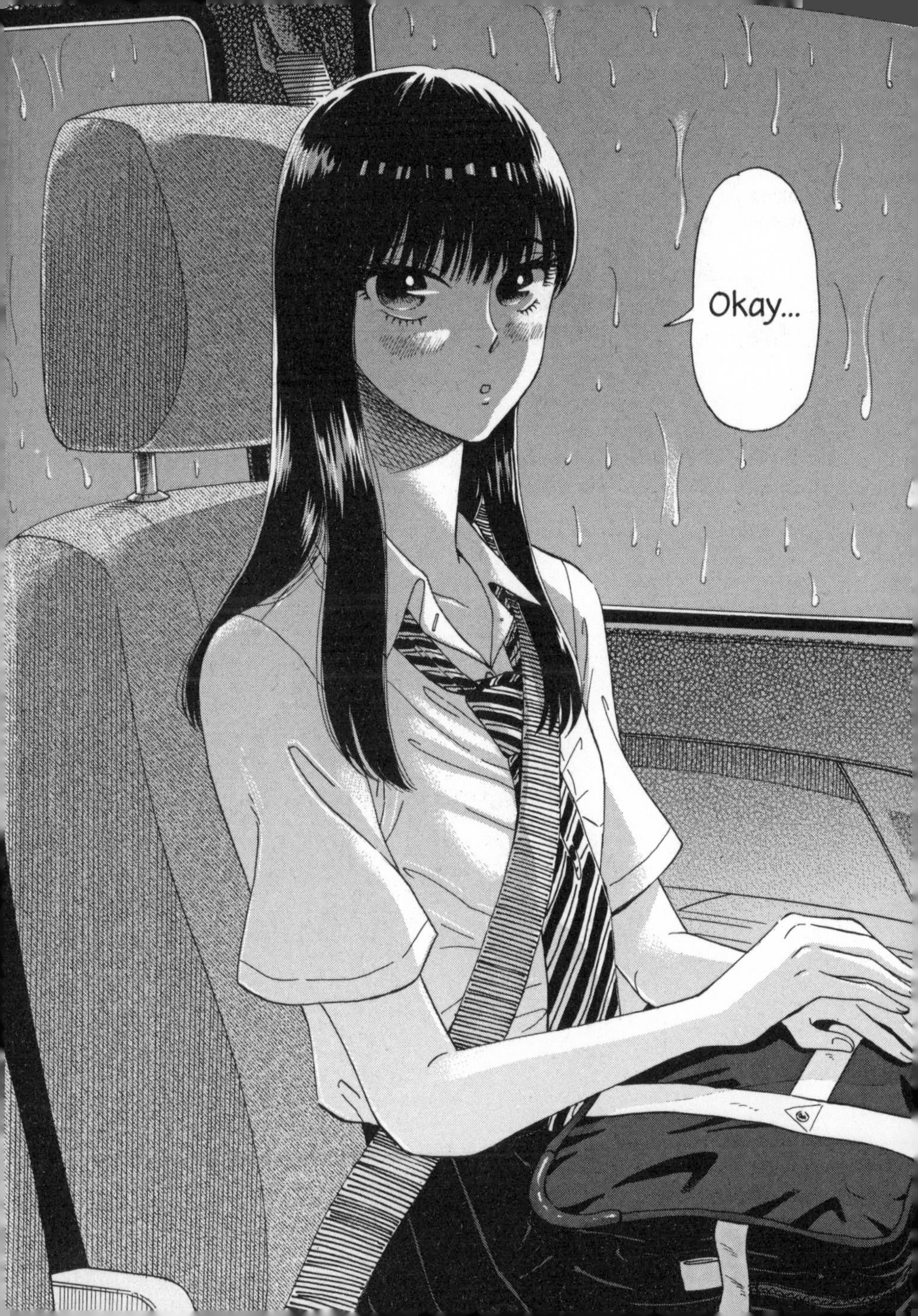
Okay...

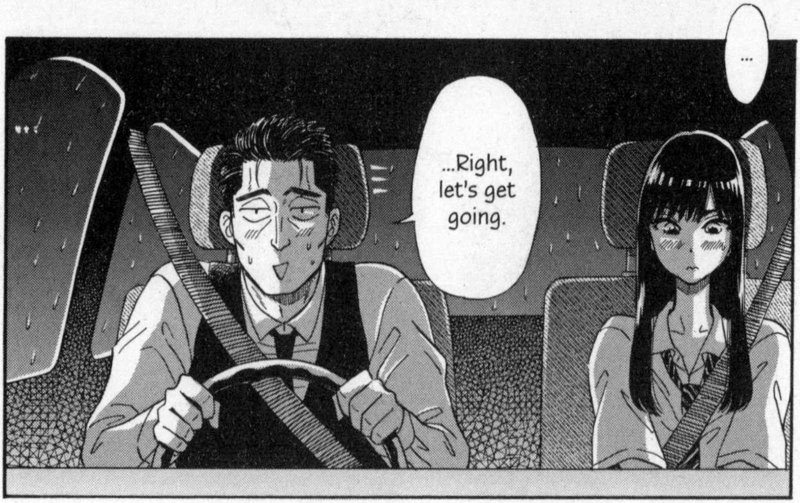
...
...Right, let's get going.

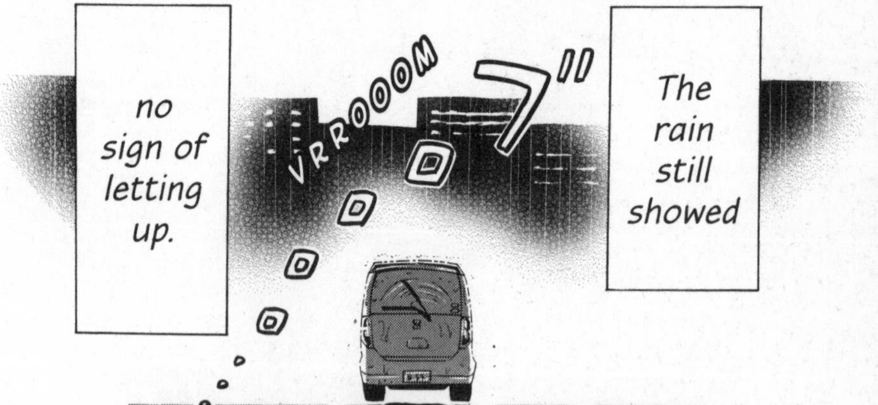
The rain still showed
VRROOOM
no sign of letting up.

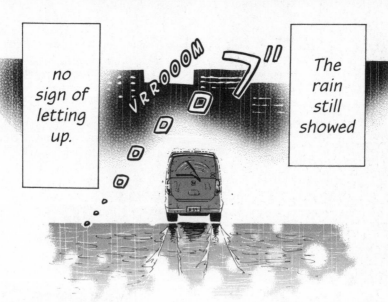

Chapter 10

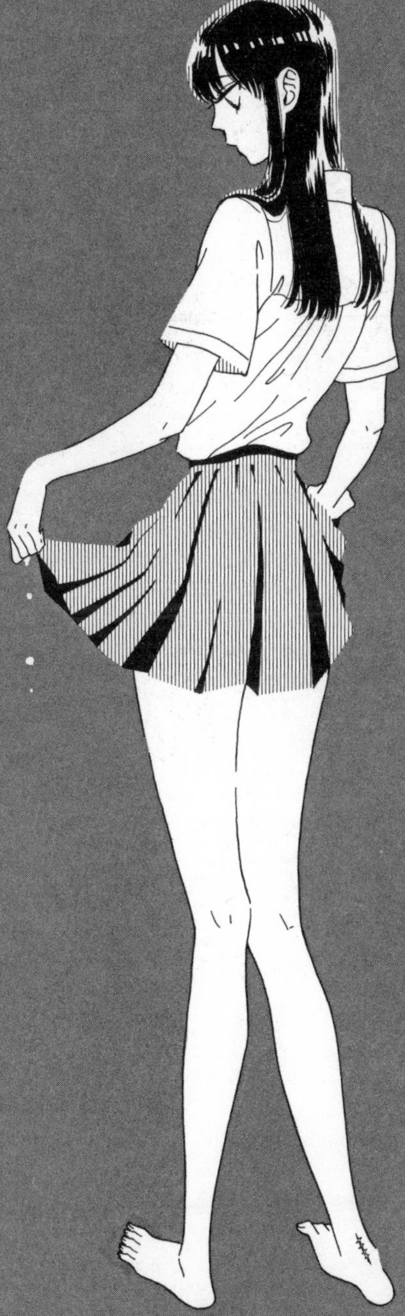

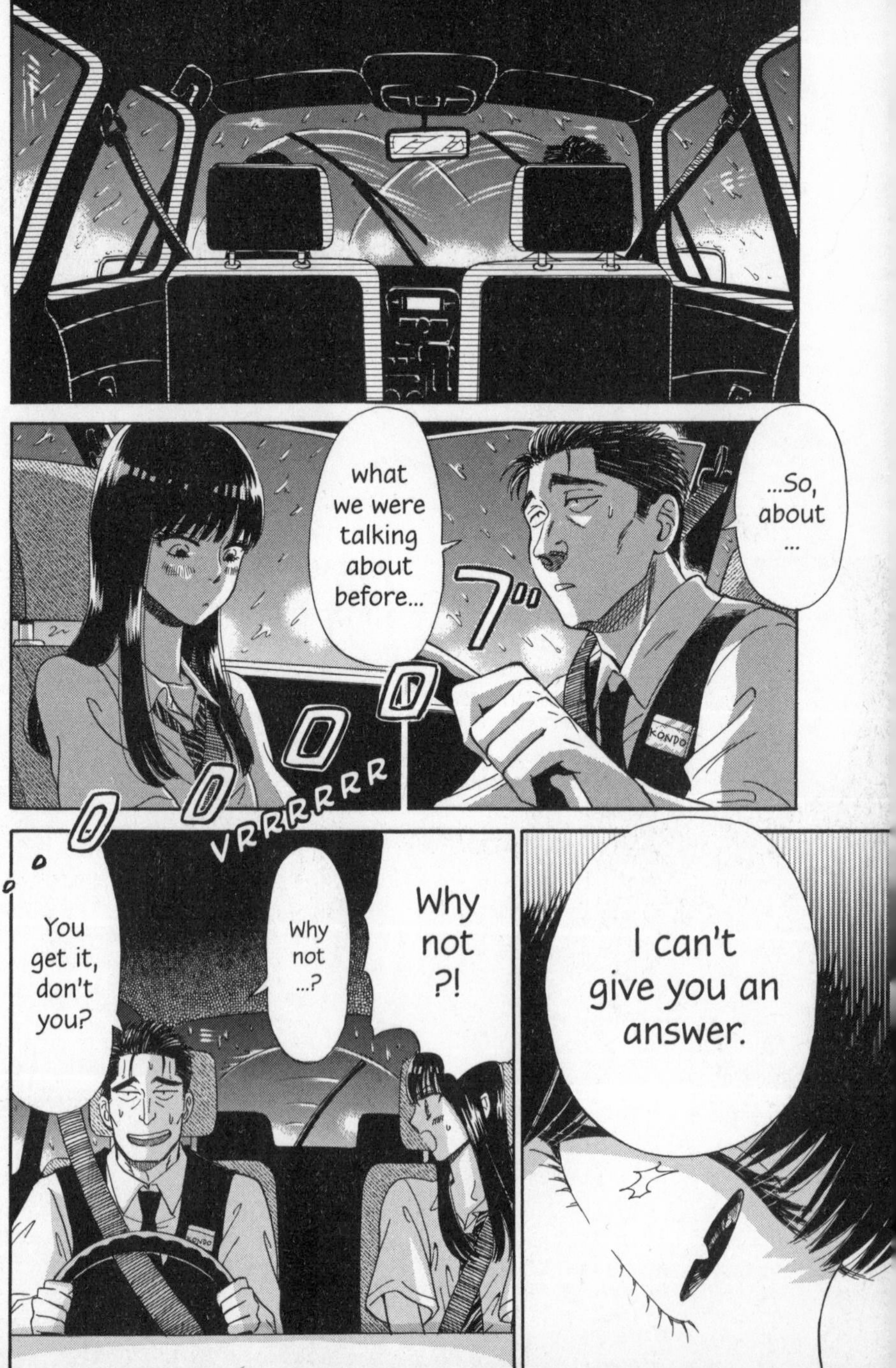
...So, about...
what we were talking about before...
VRRRRRRR
I can't give you an answer.
Why not?!
Why not...?
You get it, don't you?

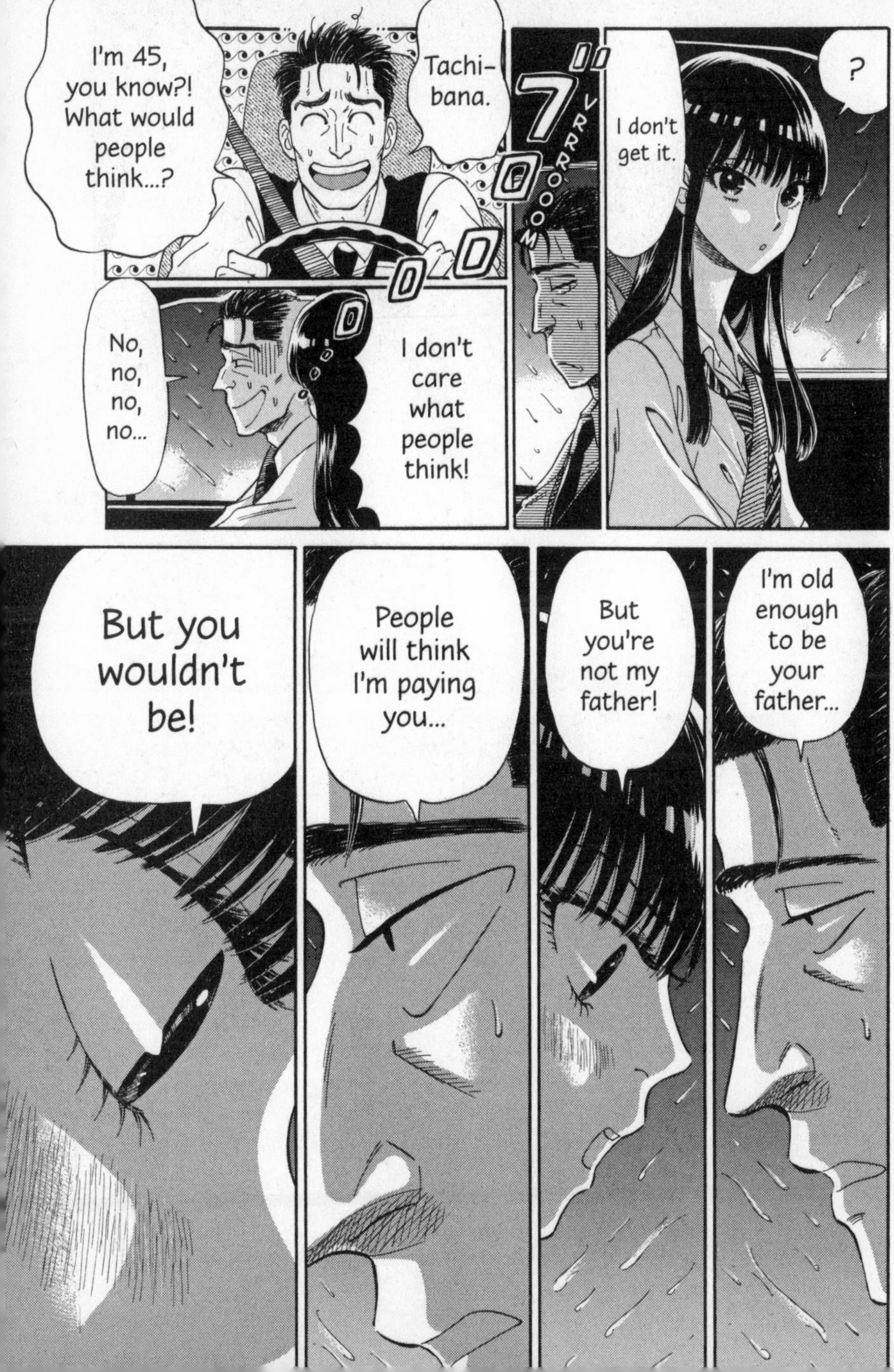
?
I don't get it.
VRRROOOOM
Tachi-bana.
I'm 45, you know?! What would people think...?
I don't care what people think!
No, no, no, no...
I'm old enough to be your father...
But you're not my father!
People will think I'm paying you...
But you wouldn't be!

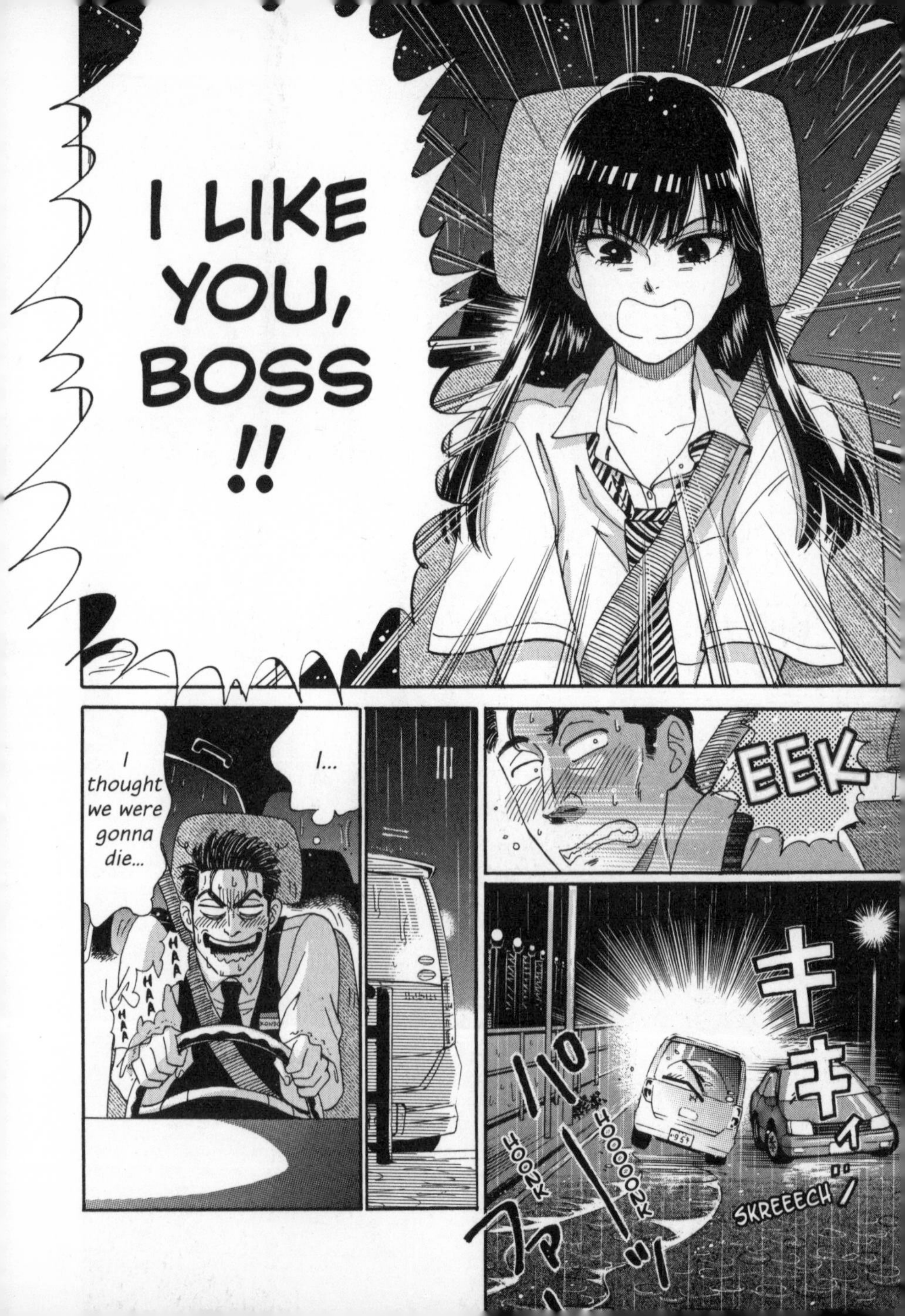
I LIKE YOU, BOSS!!
EEK
キキィ
SKREEECH
パー
HOOOOONK
HOOONK
ファ
I...
I thought we were gonna die...
HAA
HAA
HAA
HAA

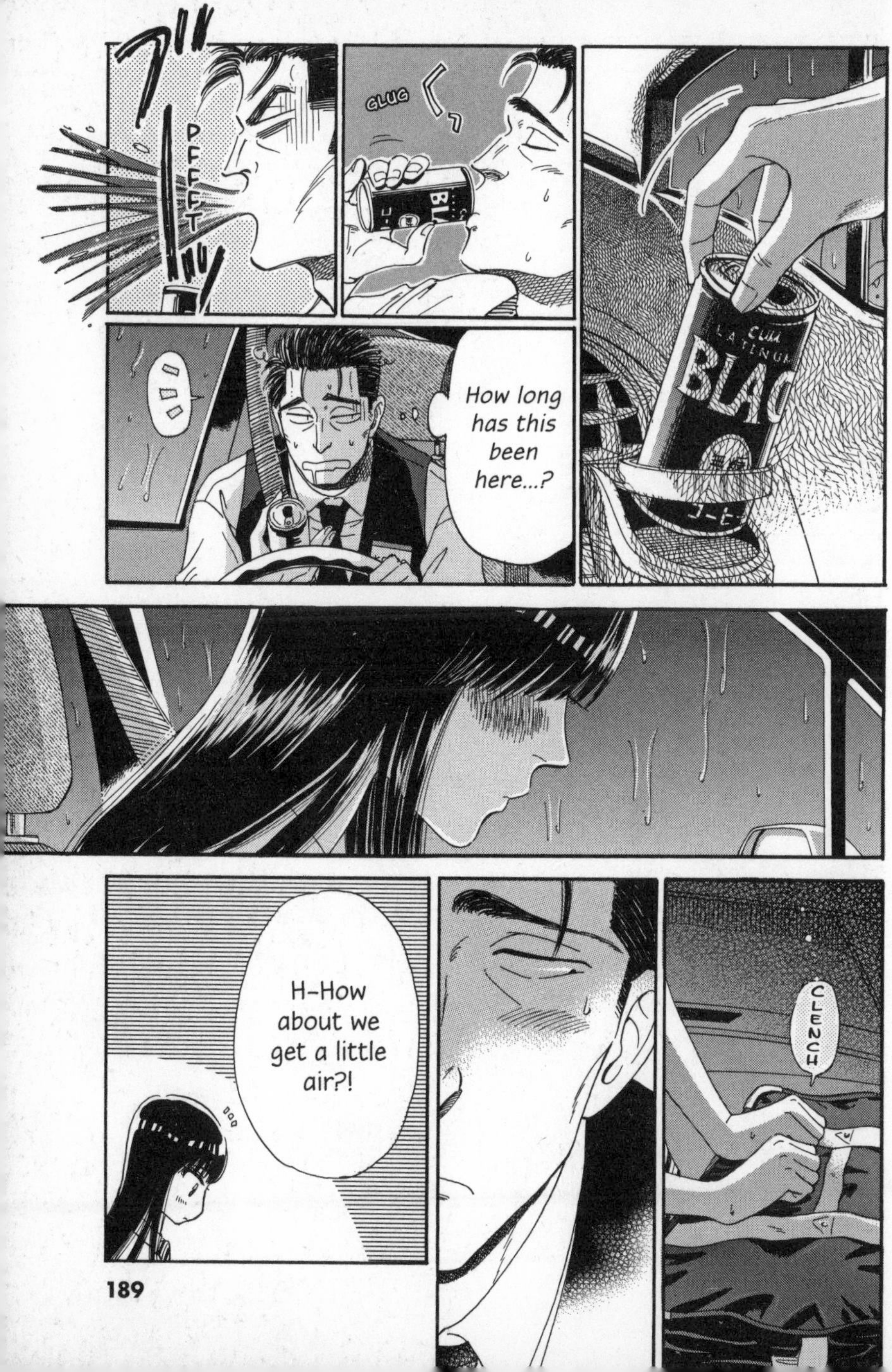
GLUG
ブ
PFFFT
How long has this been here...?
CLENCH
H-How about we get a little air?!

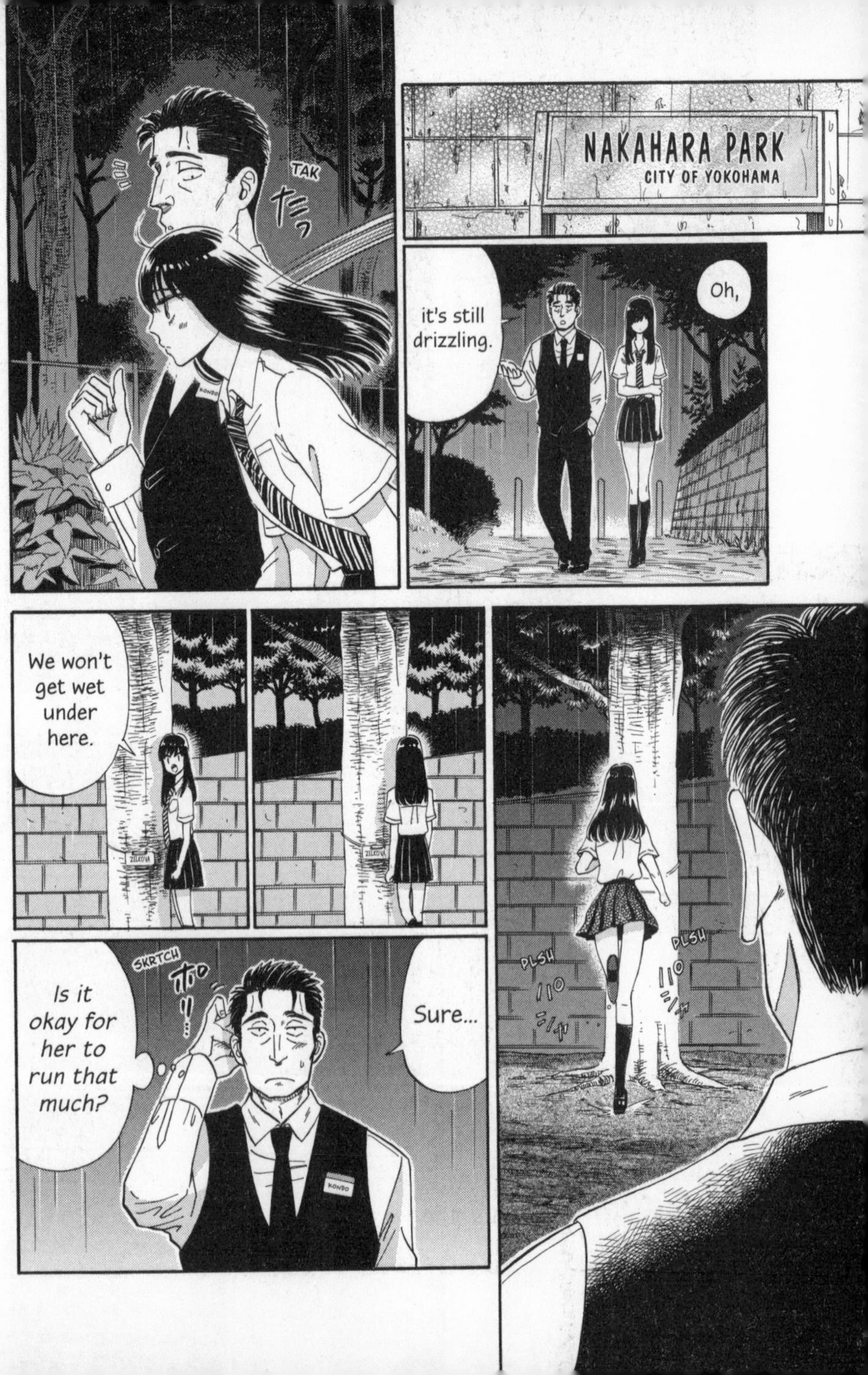
NAKAHARA PARK
CITY OF YOKOHAMA
Oh,
it's still drizzling.
TAK
PLSH
PLSH
We won't get wet under here.
Sure...
SKRTCH
Is it okay for her to run that much?

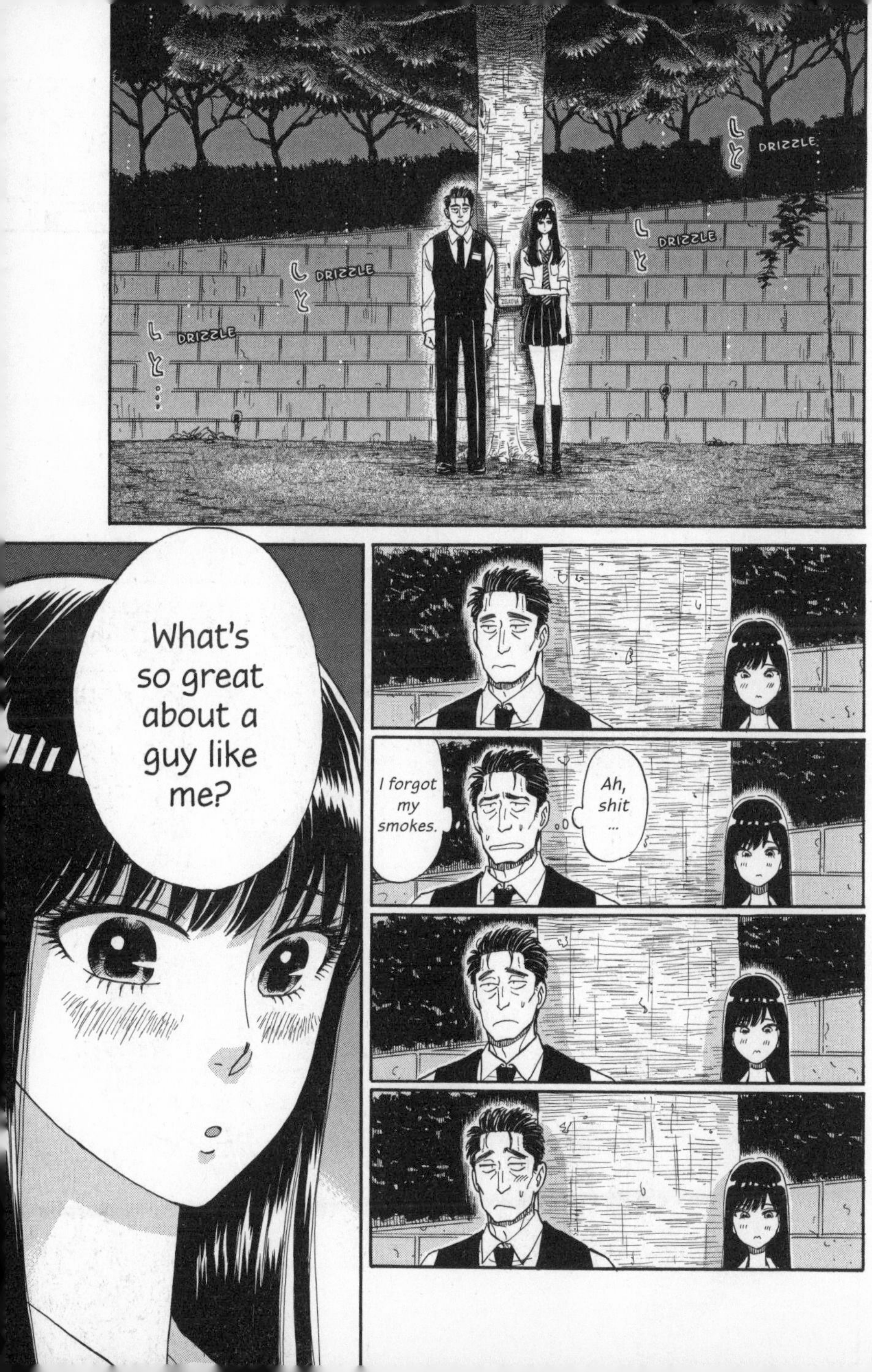
DRIZZLE
DRIZZLE
DRIZZLE
DRIZZLE
Ah, shit ...
I forgot my smokes.
What's so great about a guy like me?

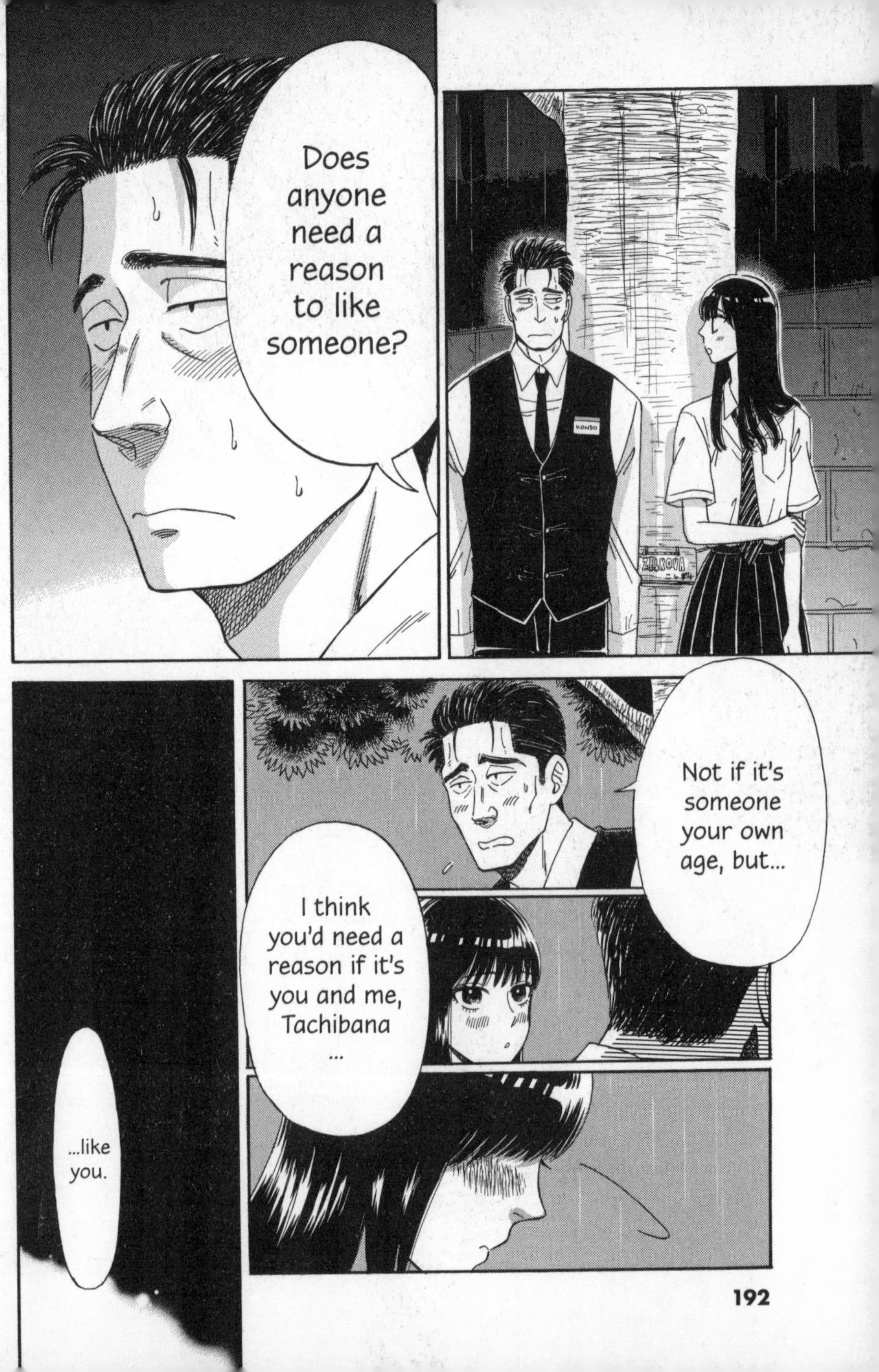
KONDO
ZELKOVA
Does anyone need a reason to like someone?
Not if it's someone your own age, but...
I think you'd need a reason if it's you and me, Tachibana ...
...like you.

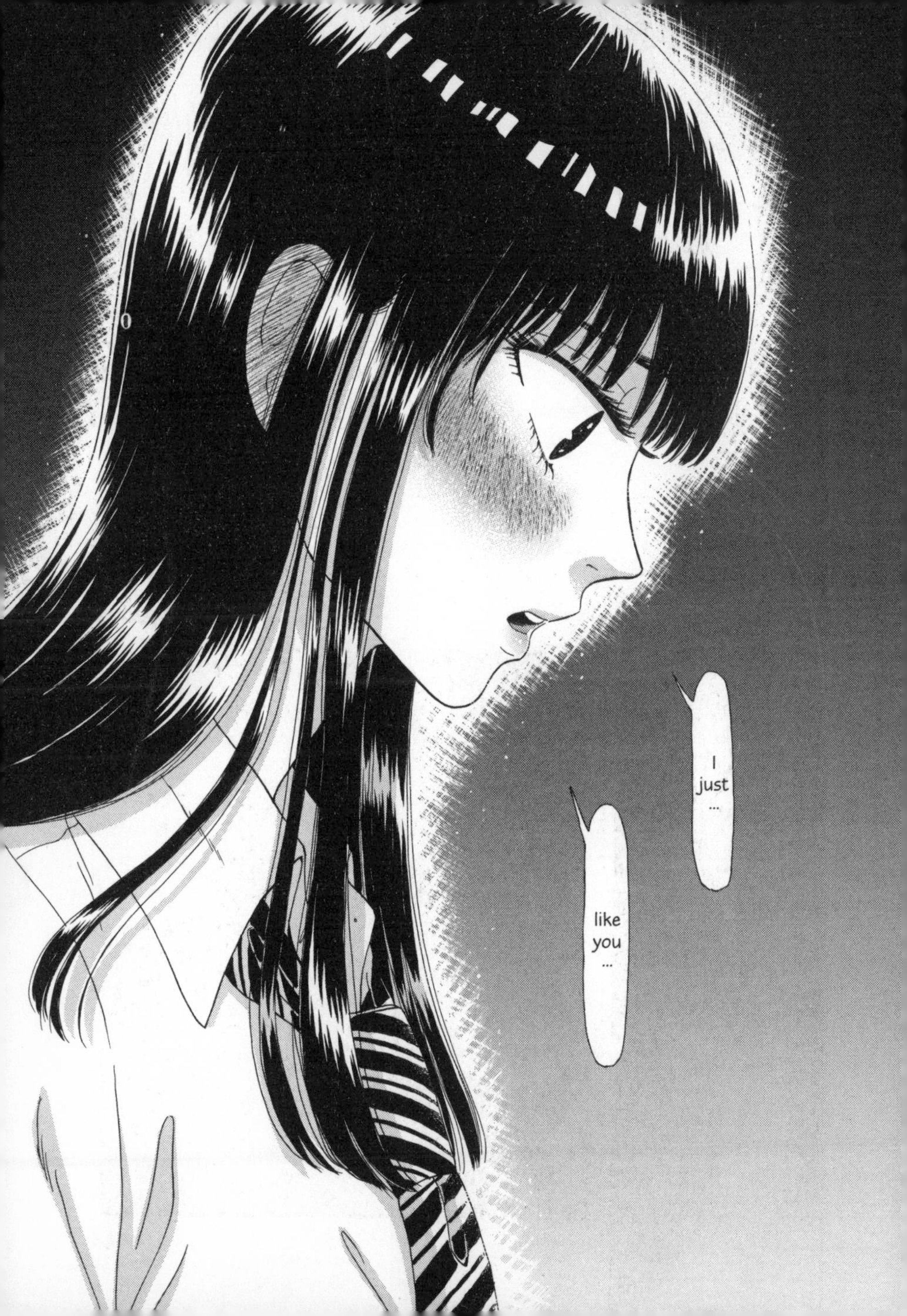
I just ...
like you ...

CHSH !!

The sensation of the earth I'm standing on, felt through my loafers.

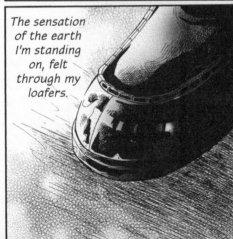

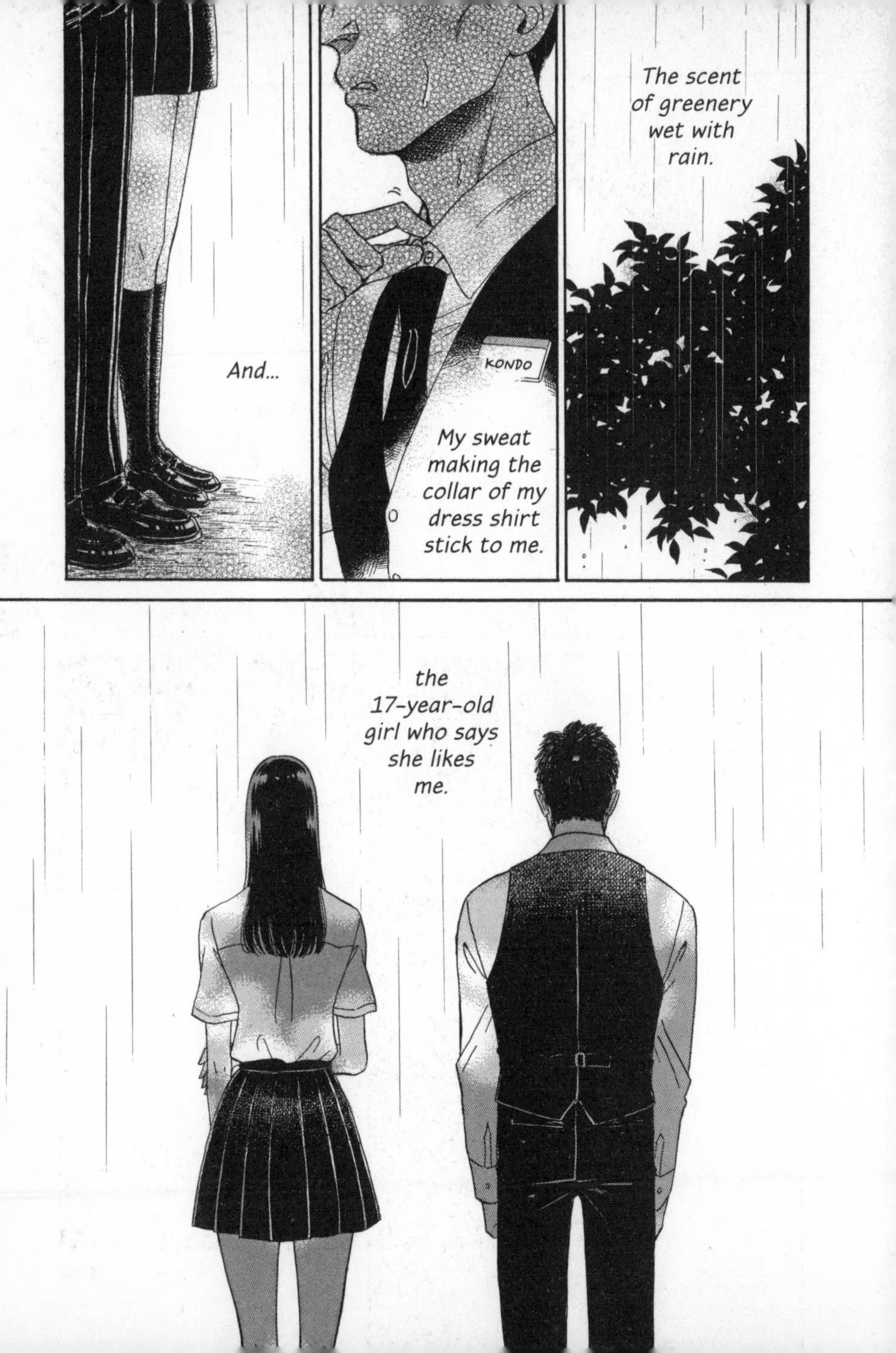
The scent of greenery wet with rain.
KONDO
My sweat making the collar of my dress shirt stick to me.
And...
the 17-year-old girl who says she likes me.

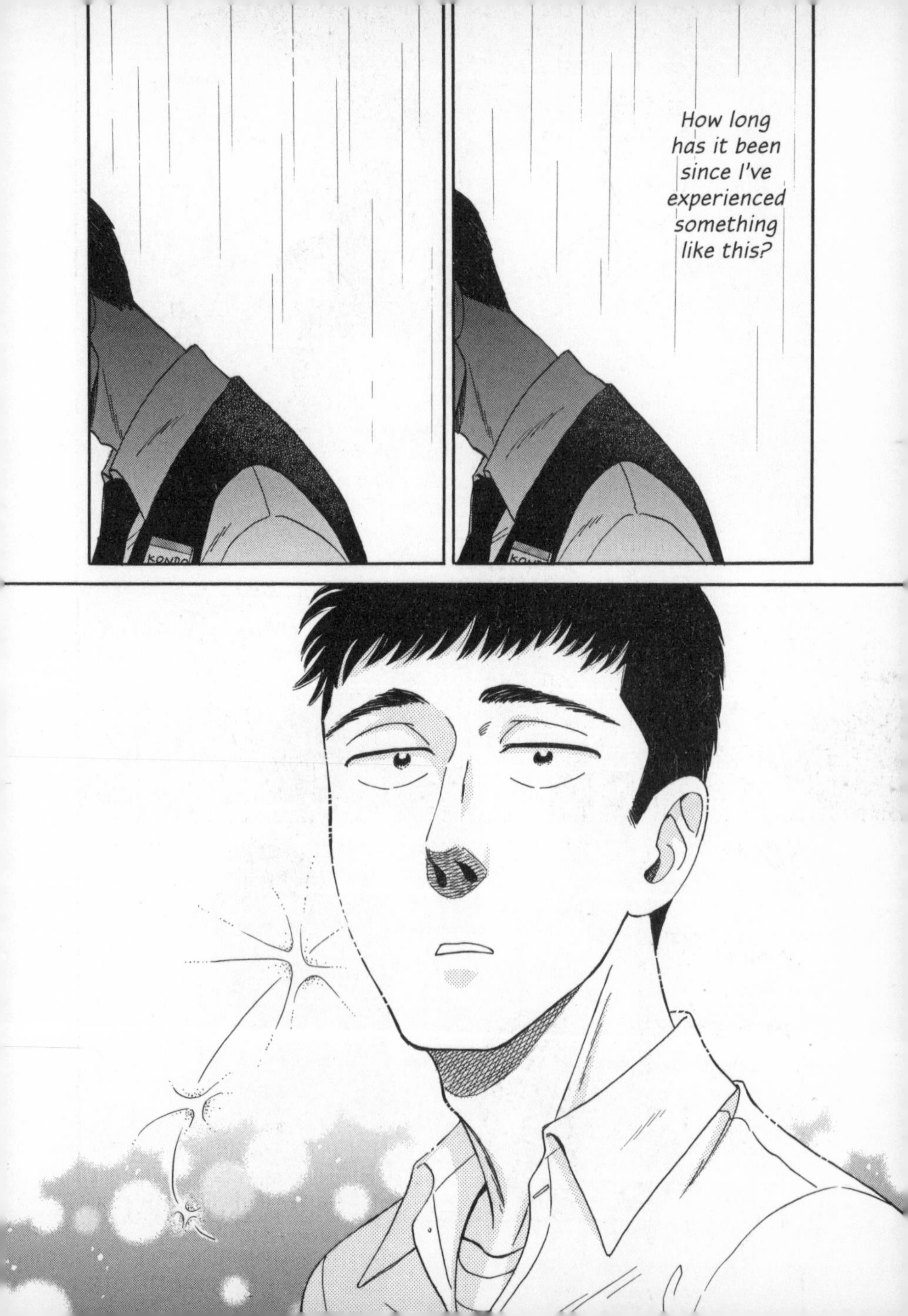
How long has it been since I've experienced something like this?
KONDO
KONDO

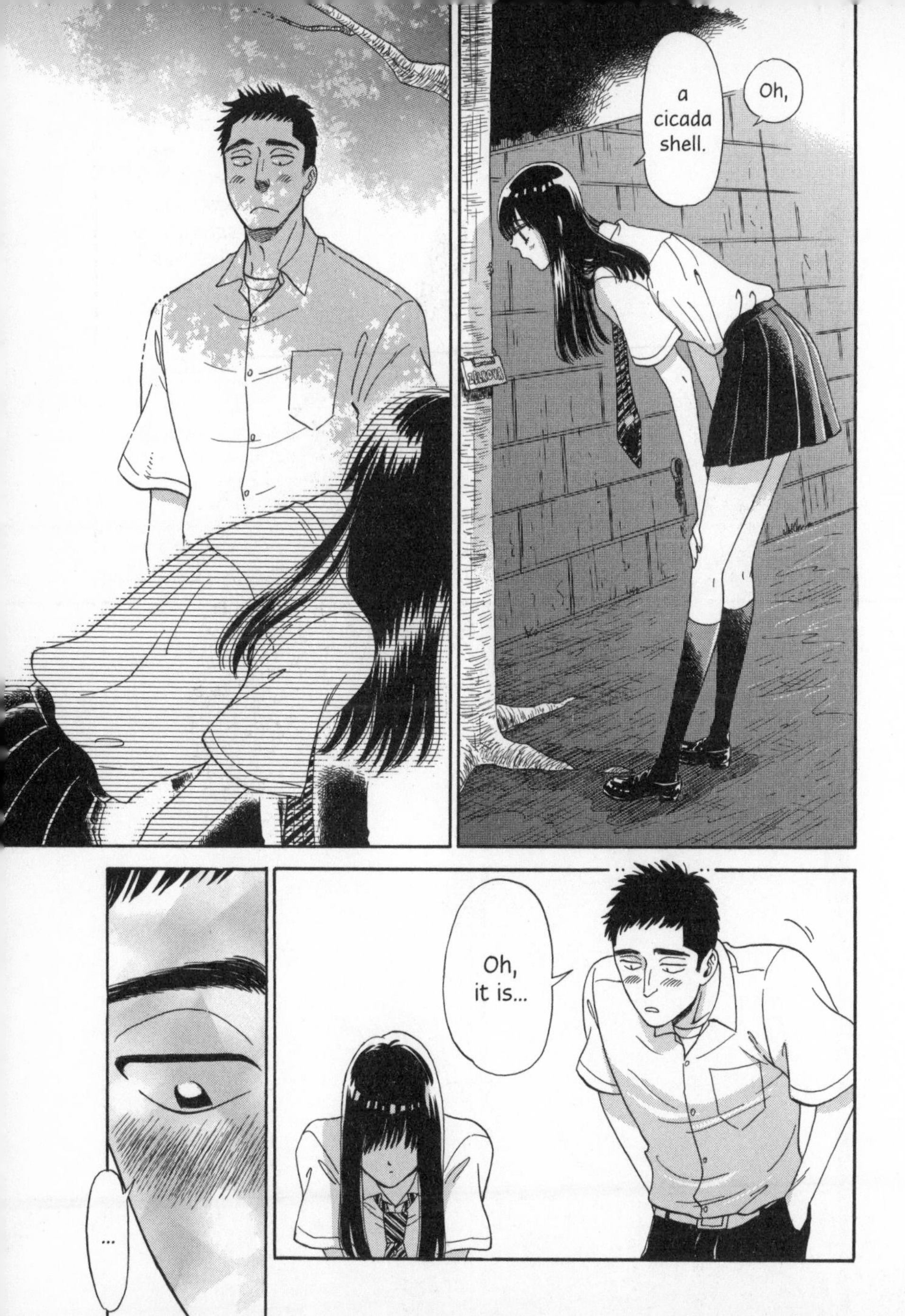
Oh,
a cicada shell.
Oh, it is...
...

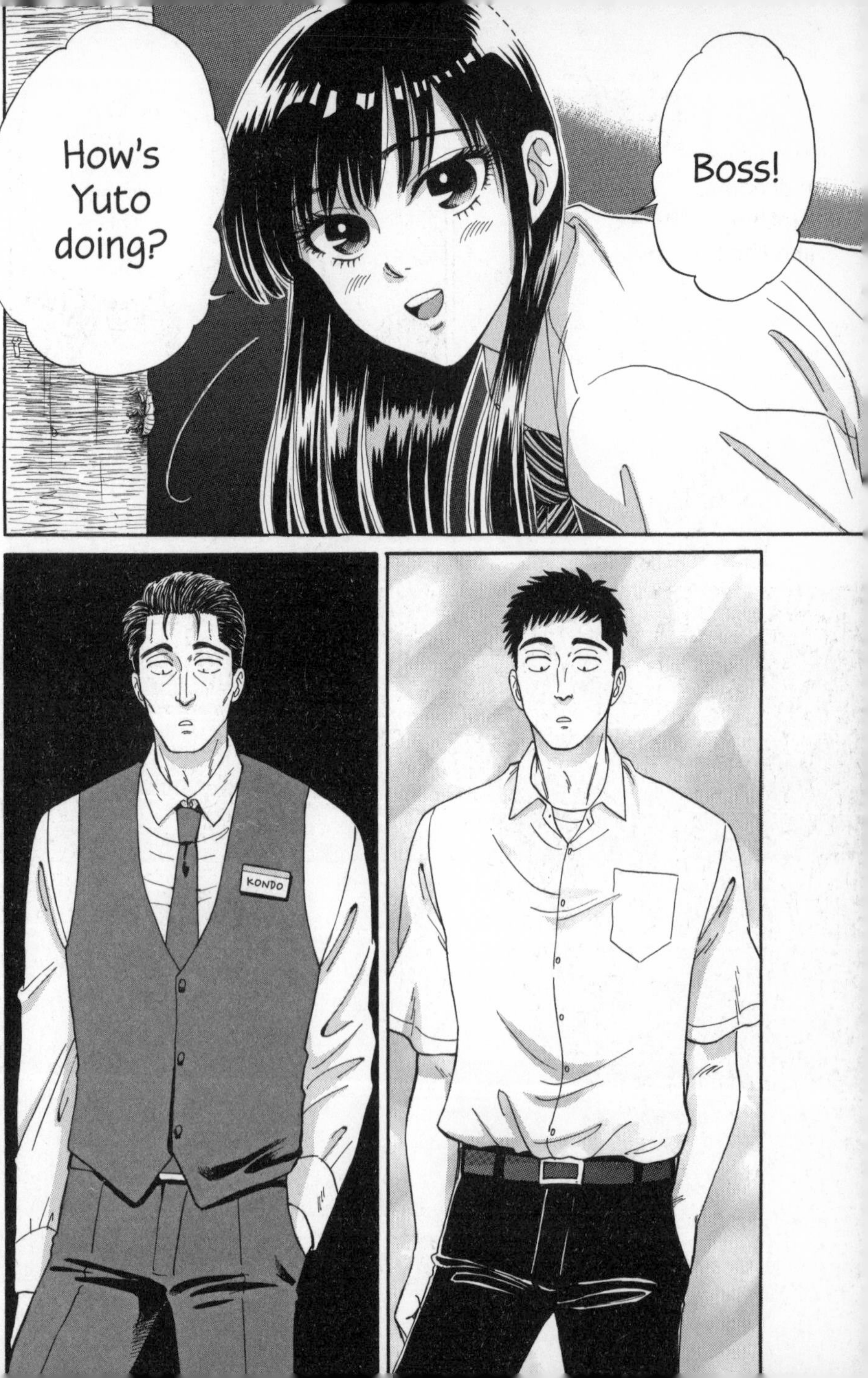
Boss!
How's Yuto doing?
KONDO

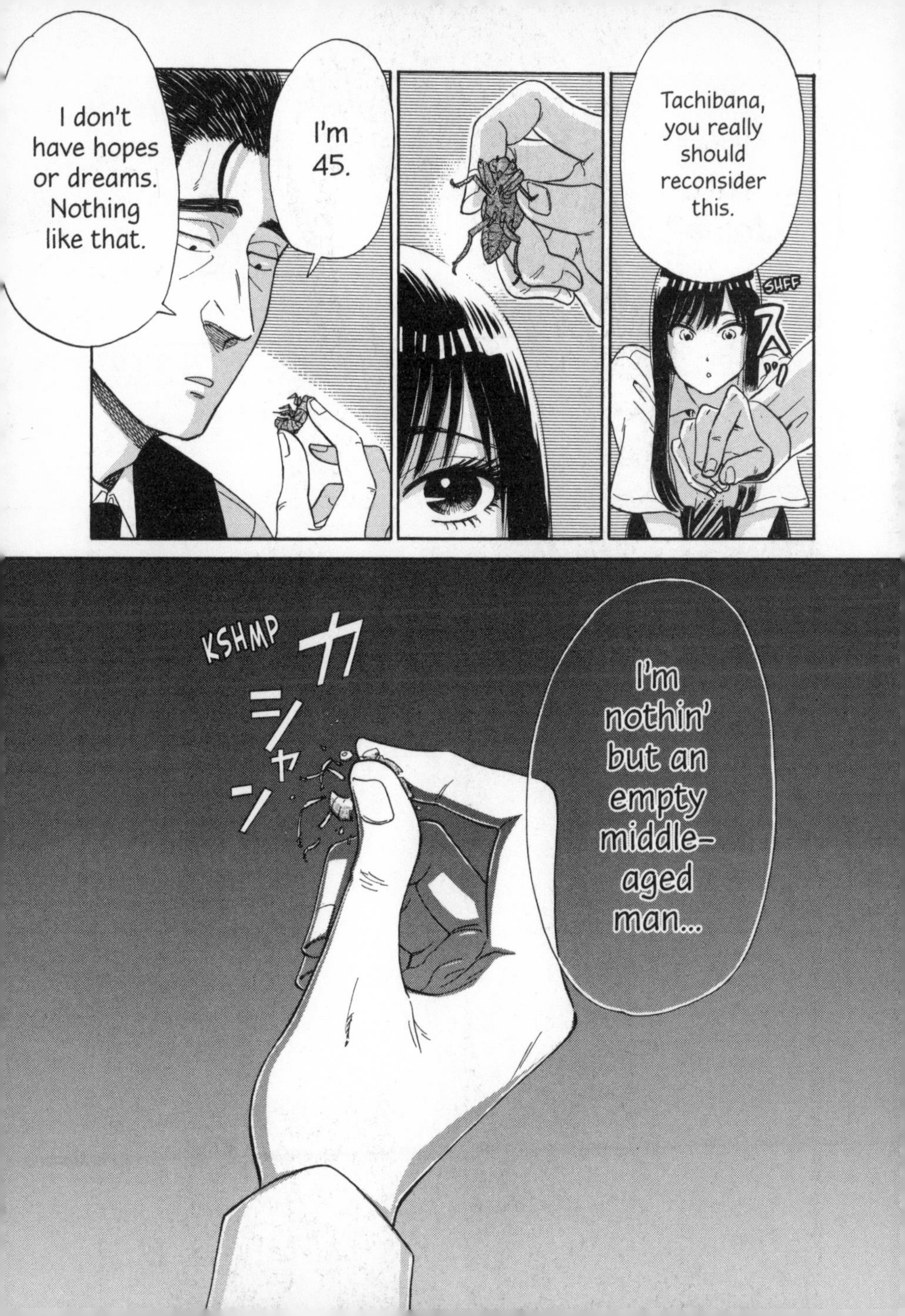
Tachibana, you really should reconsider this.
SHFF
I'm 45.
I don't have hopes or dreams. Nothing like that.
I'm nothin' but an empty middle-aged man...
KSHMP
カシャン

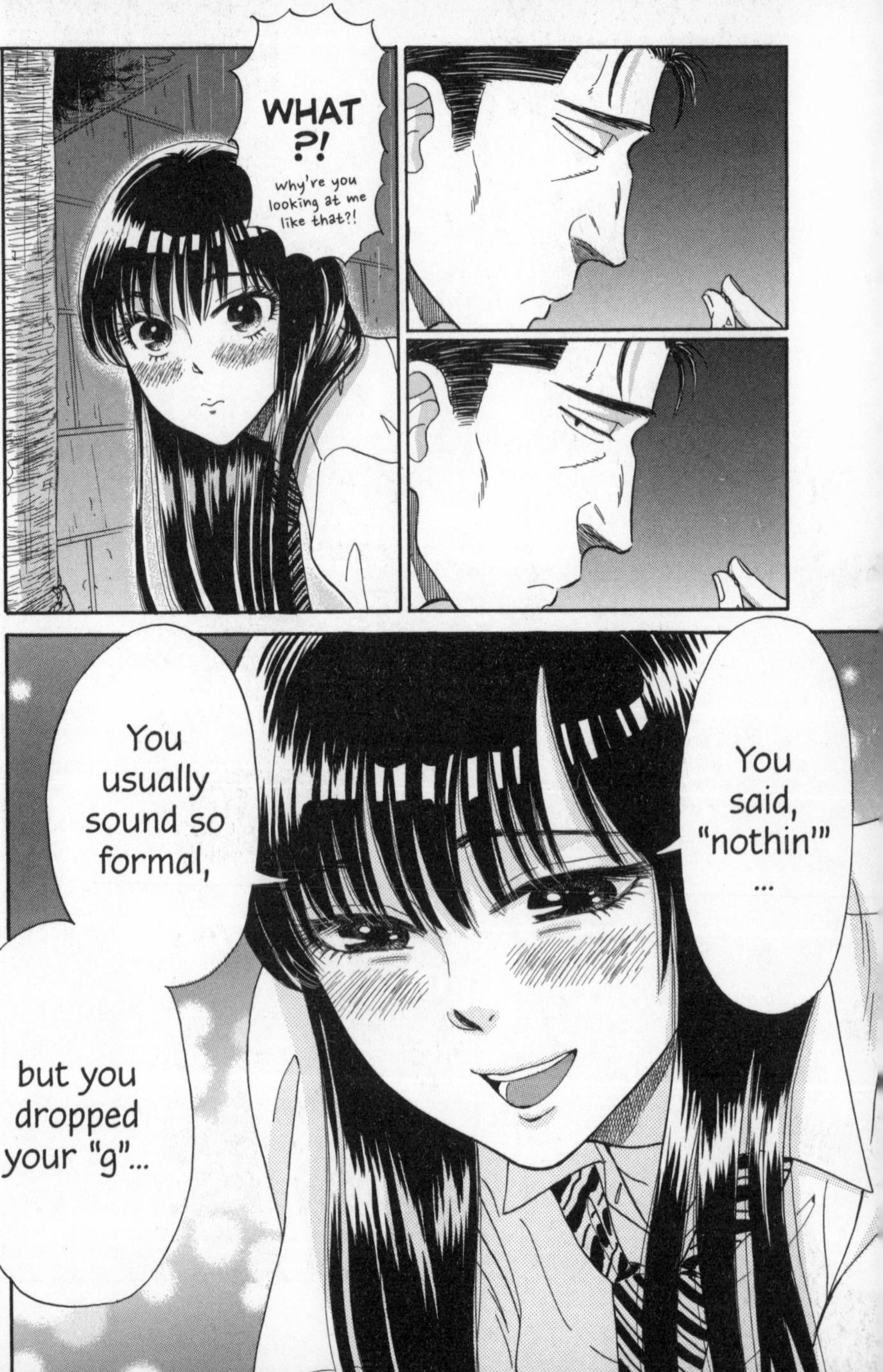
WHAT ?!
why're you looking at me like that?!
You said, "nothin'" ...
You usually sound so formal,
but you dropped your "g"...

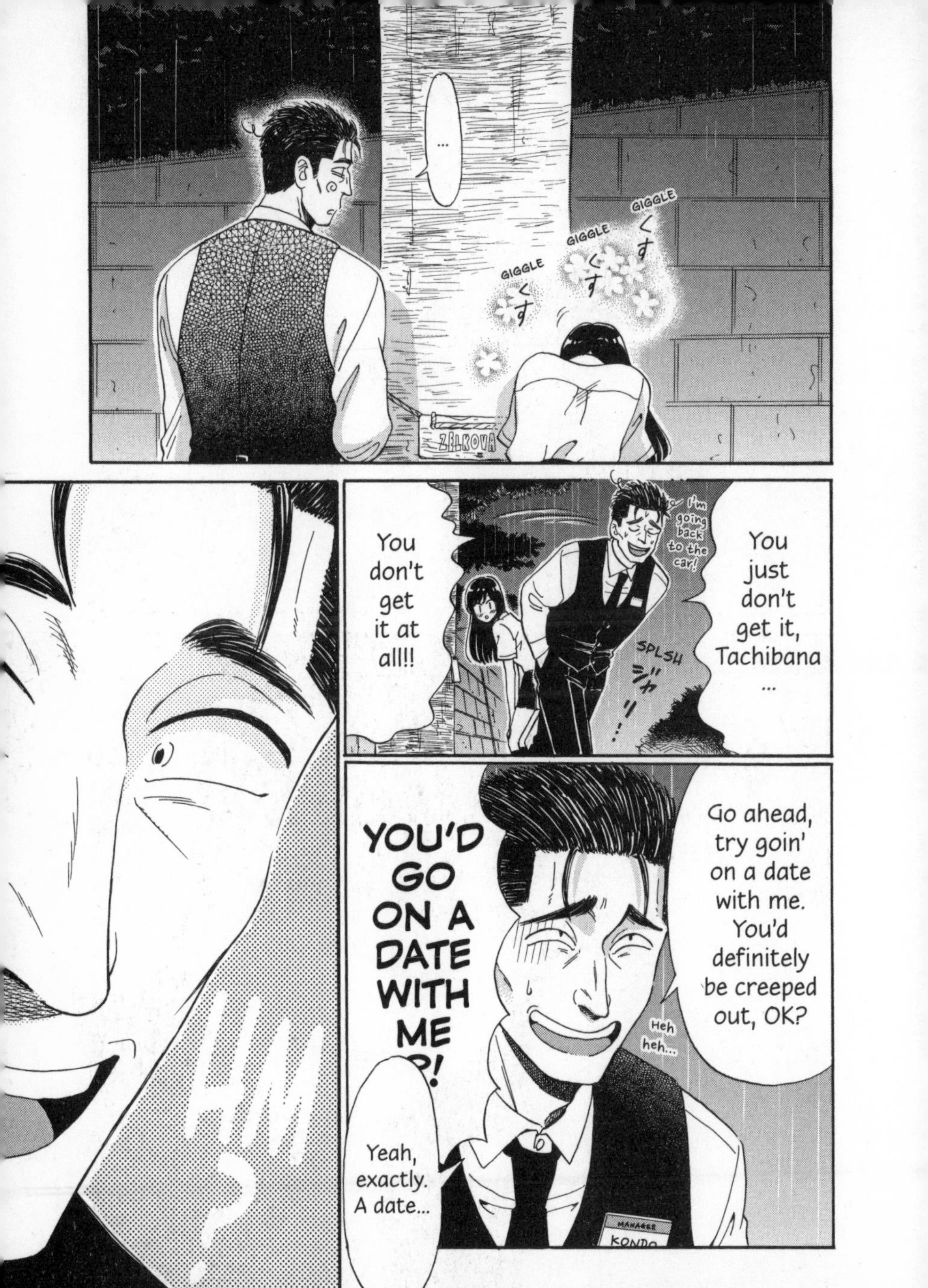
...
GIGGLE
くす
GIGGLE
くす
GIGGLE
くす
ZELKOVA
You just don't get it, Tachibana ...
I'm going back to the car!
SPLSH
ジャリ
You don't get it at all!!
Go ahead, try goin' on a date with me. You'd definitely be creeped out, OK?
Heh heh...
YOU'D GO ON A DATE WITH ME
Yeah, exactly. A date...
MANAGER
KONDO
HM?

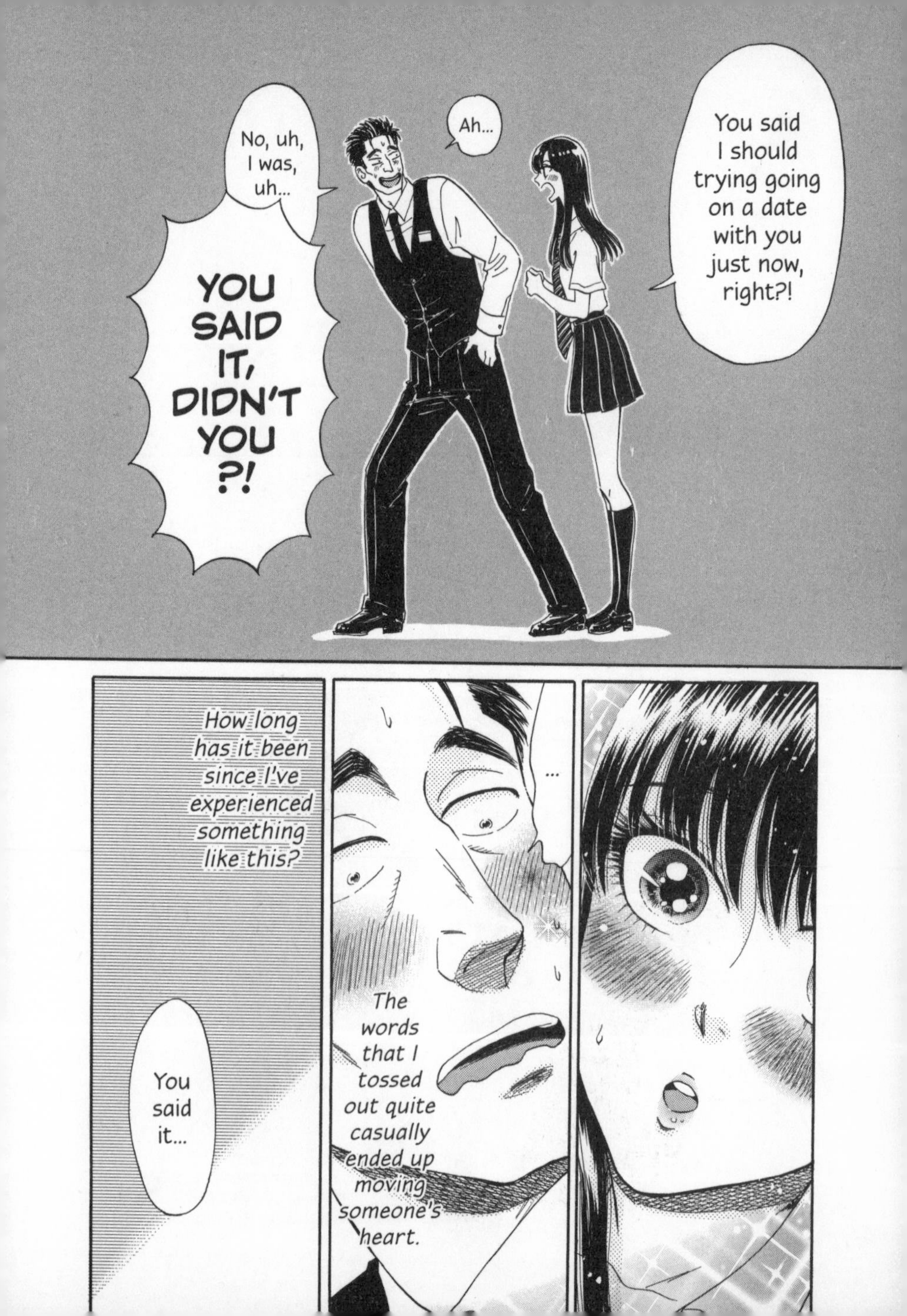
You said I should trying going on a date with you just now, right?!
Ah...
No, uh, I was, uh...
YOU SAID IT, DIDN'T YOU?!
...
The words that I tossed out quite casually ended up moving someone's heart.
How long has it been since I've experienced something like this?
You said it...

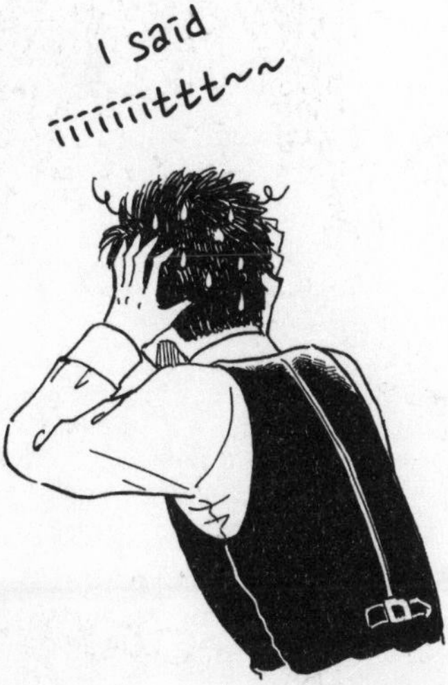
I said
iiiiiiittt~~

After
the 🌂
Rain

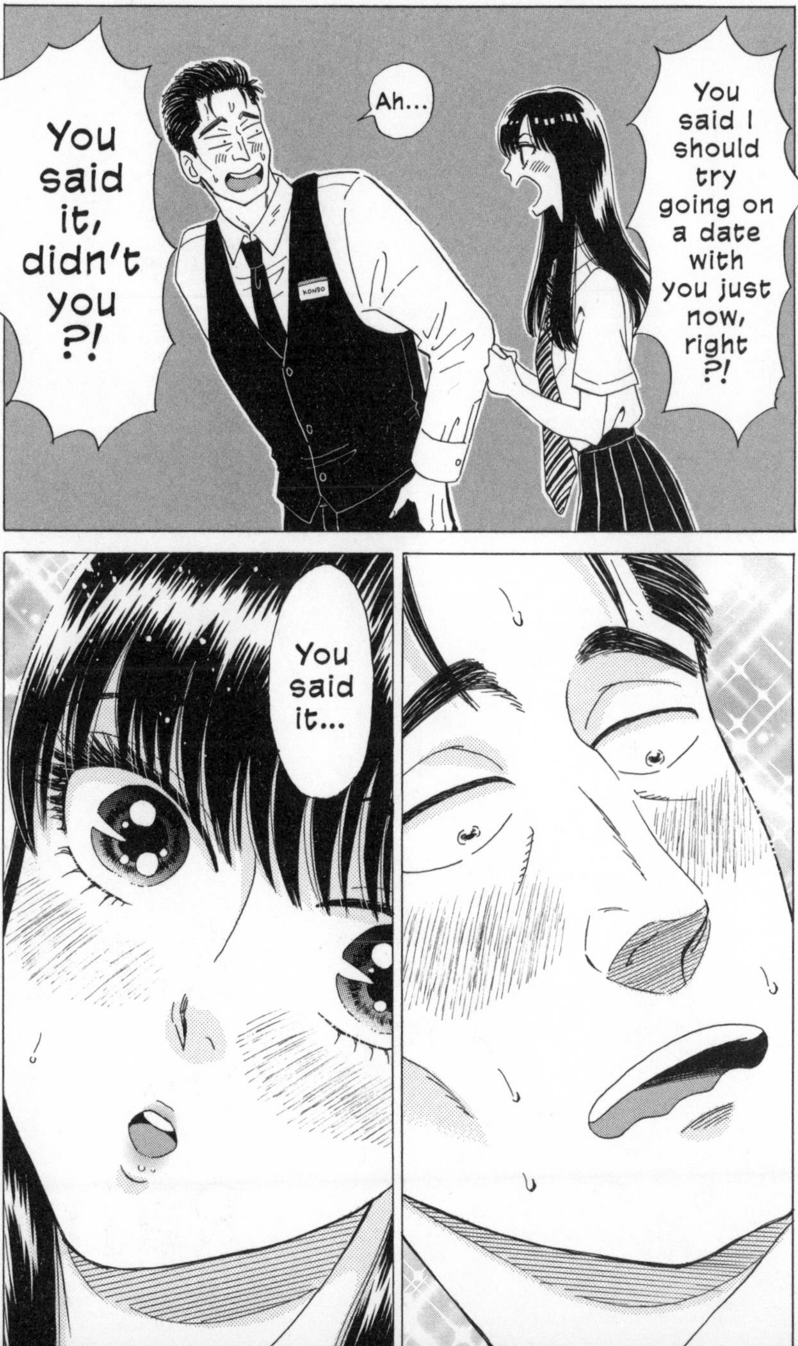
You said I should try going on a date with you just now, right?!
Ah...
KONDO
You said it, didn't you?!
You said it...

Chapter 11

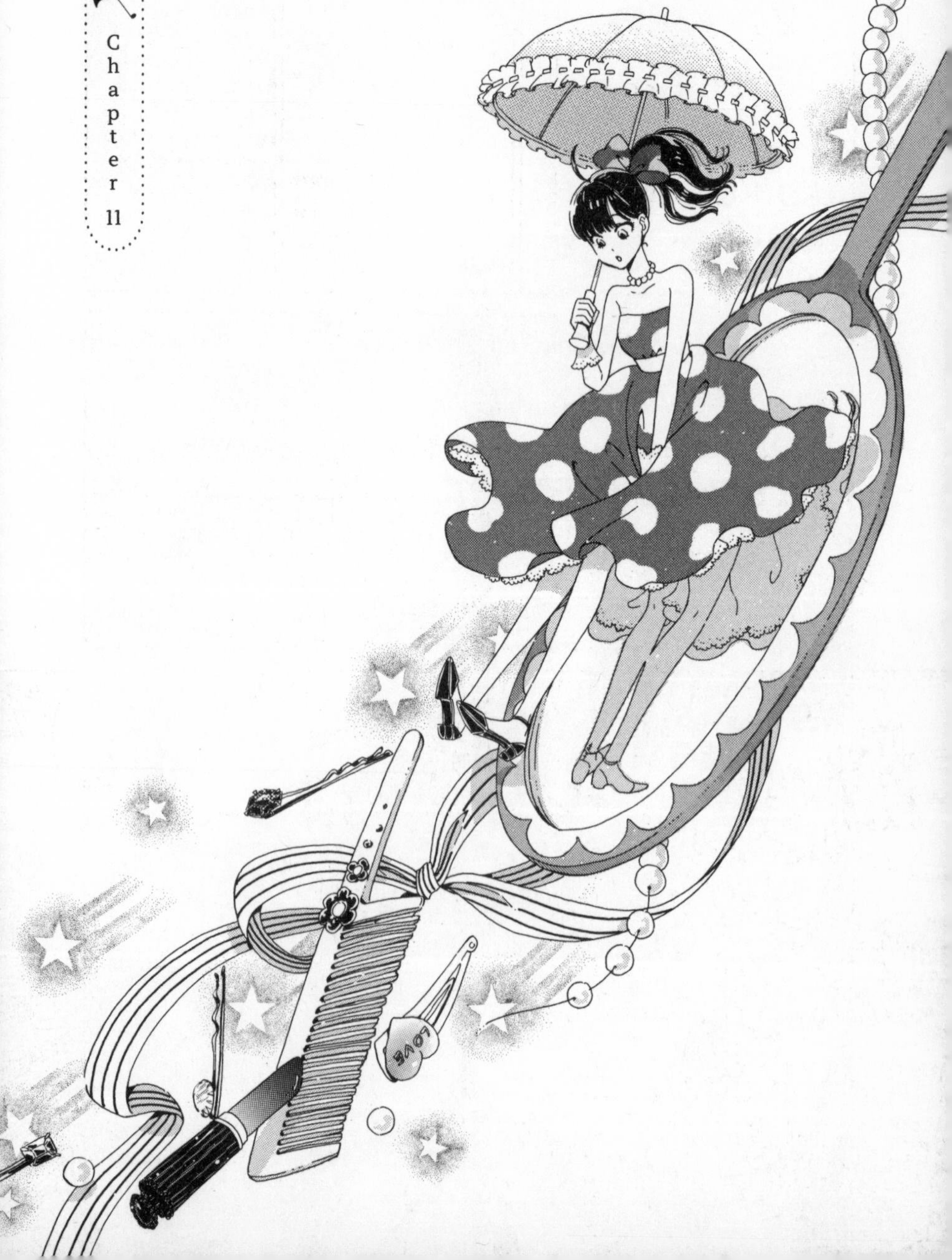
LOVE

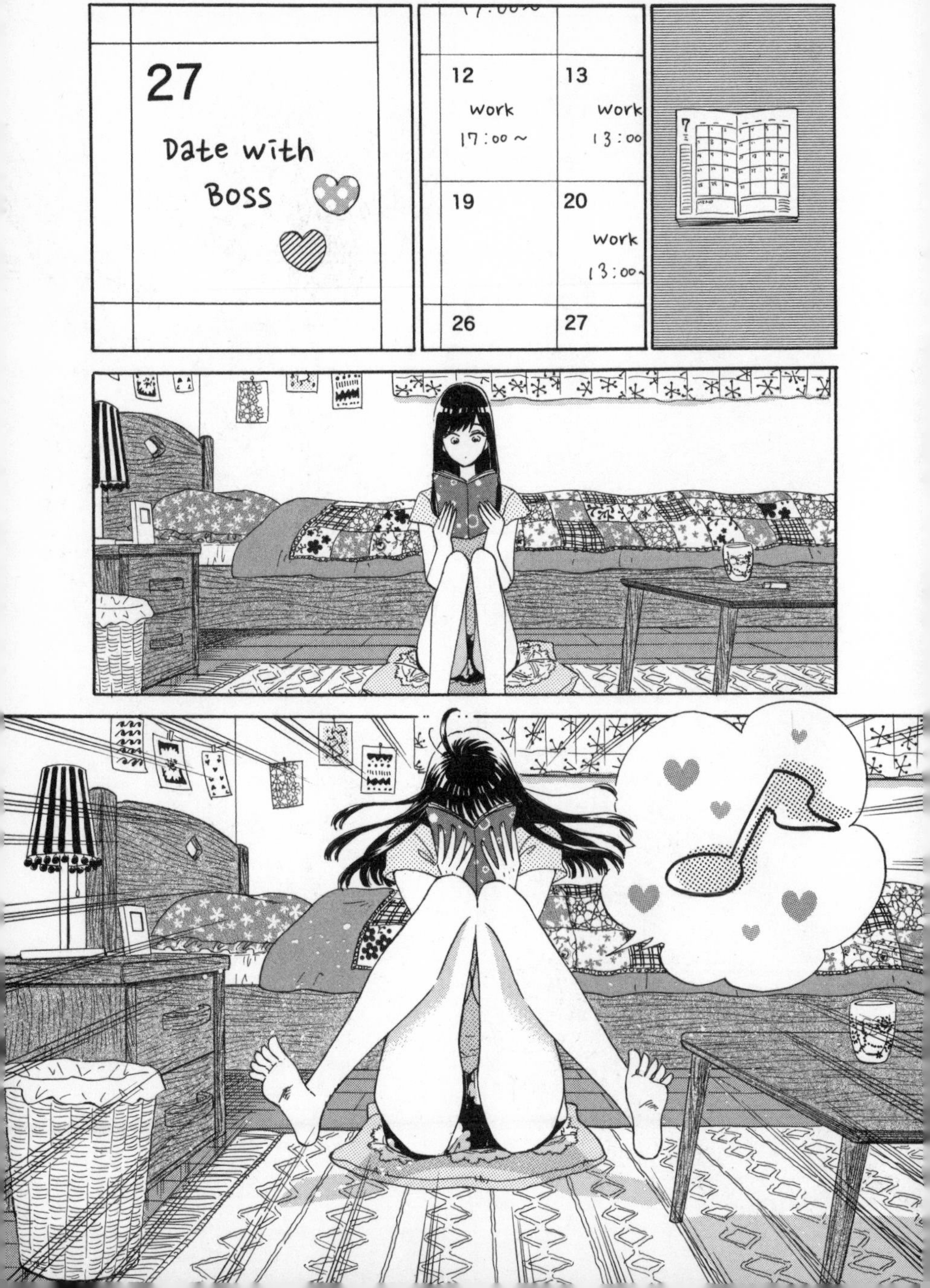

12
work
17:00 ~
13
work
13:00
19
20
work
13:00~
26
27
27
Date with
Boss

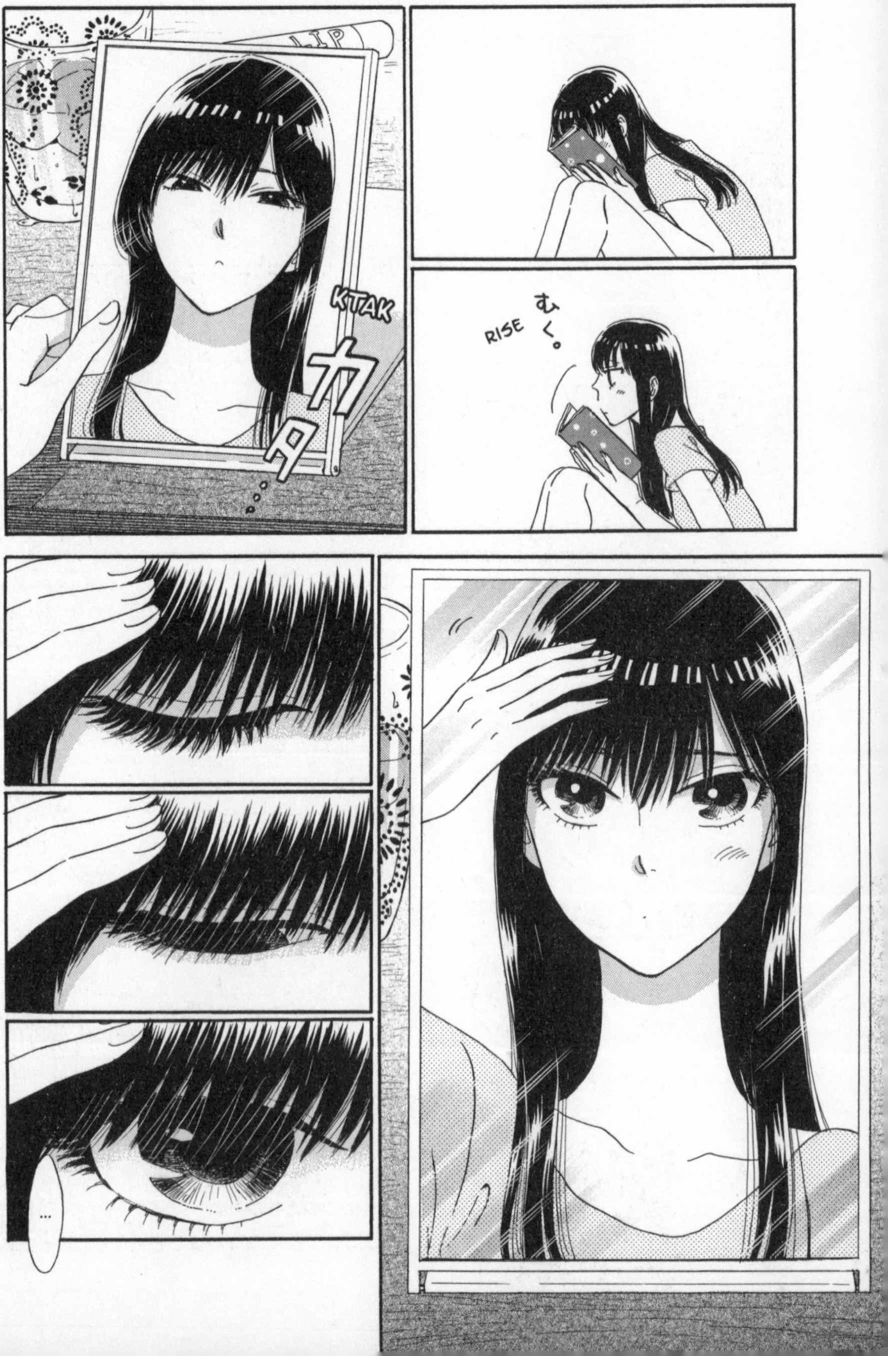
RISE
むく。
LIP
KTAK
カタ
...

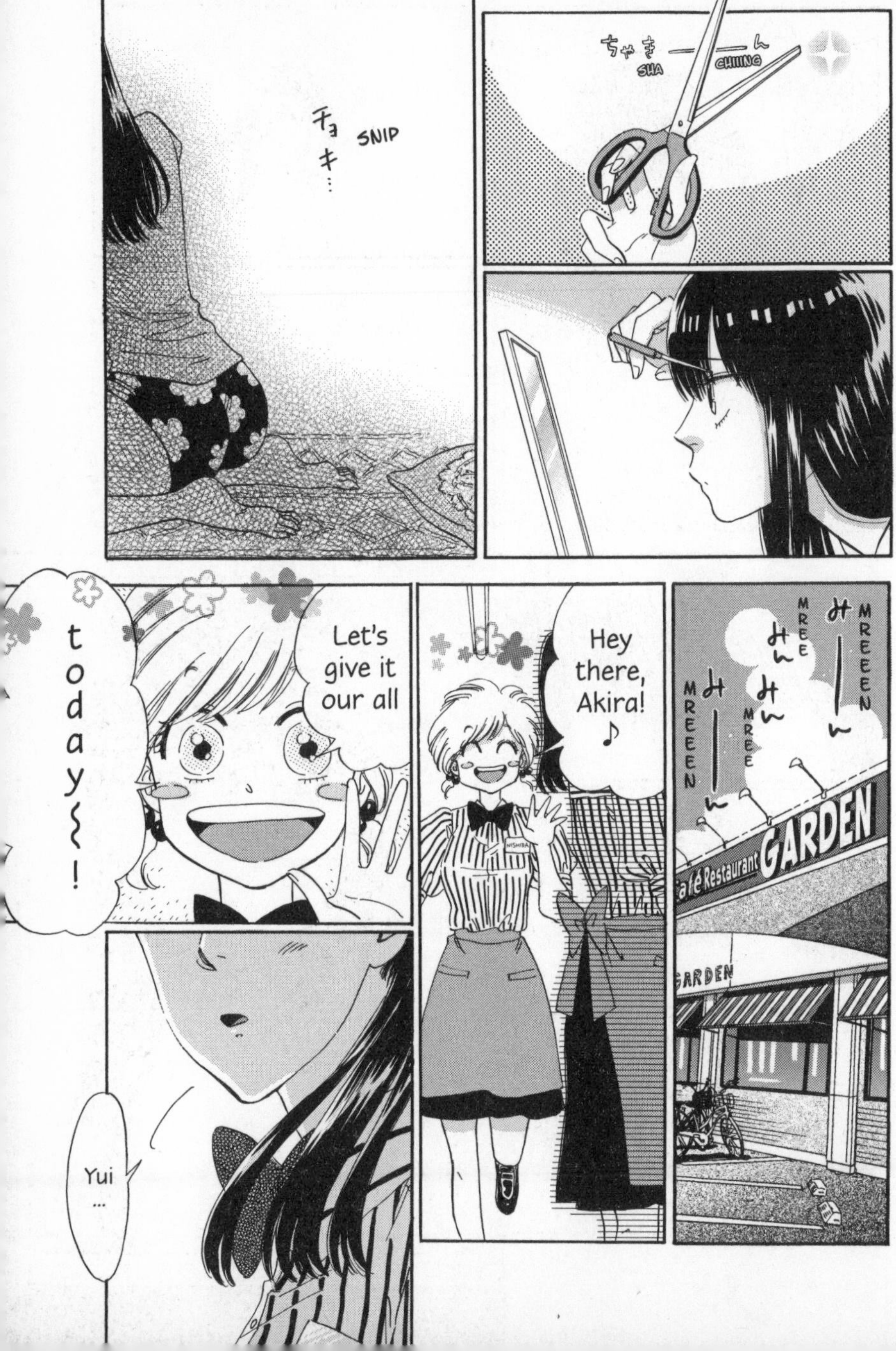

ちゃき——ん
SHA
CHIIING
チョキ…
SNIP
みーん
MREEEN
みんみん
MREE MREE
みーん
MREEEN
Café Restaurant GARDEN
GARDEN
Hey there, Akira! ♪
Let's give it our all today~!
Yui ...

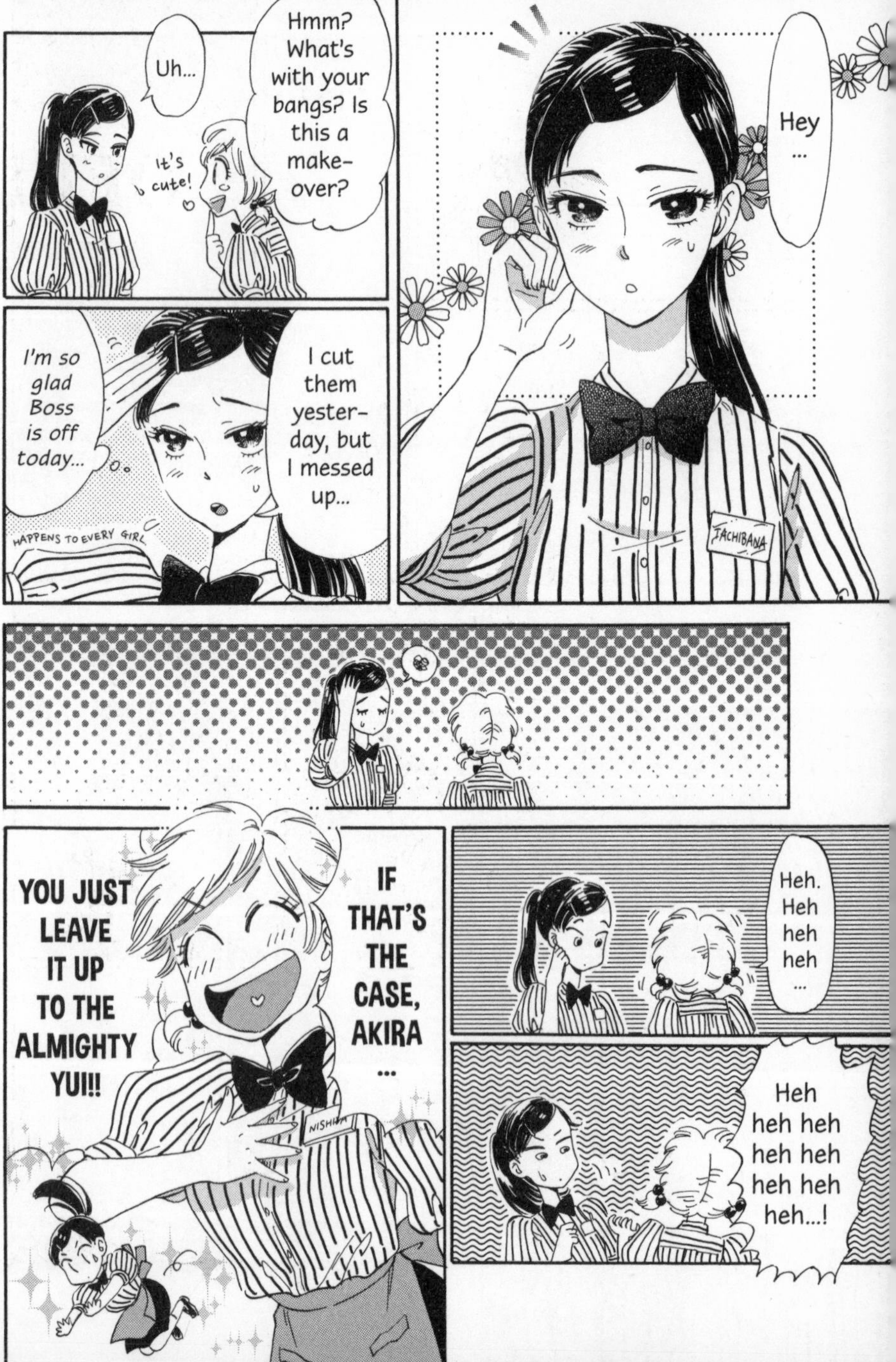
Hey ...
TACHIBANA
Hmm? What's with your bangs? Is this a make-over?
Uh...
It's cute!
I cut them yesterday, but I messed up...
I'm so glad Boss is off today...
HAPPENS TO EVERY GIRL
Heh. Heh heh heh ...
Heh heh heh heh heh heh heh heh...!
IF THAT'S THE CASE, AKIRA ...
YOU JUST LEAVE IT UP TO THE ALMIGHTY YUI!!

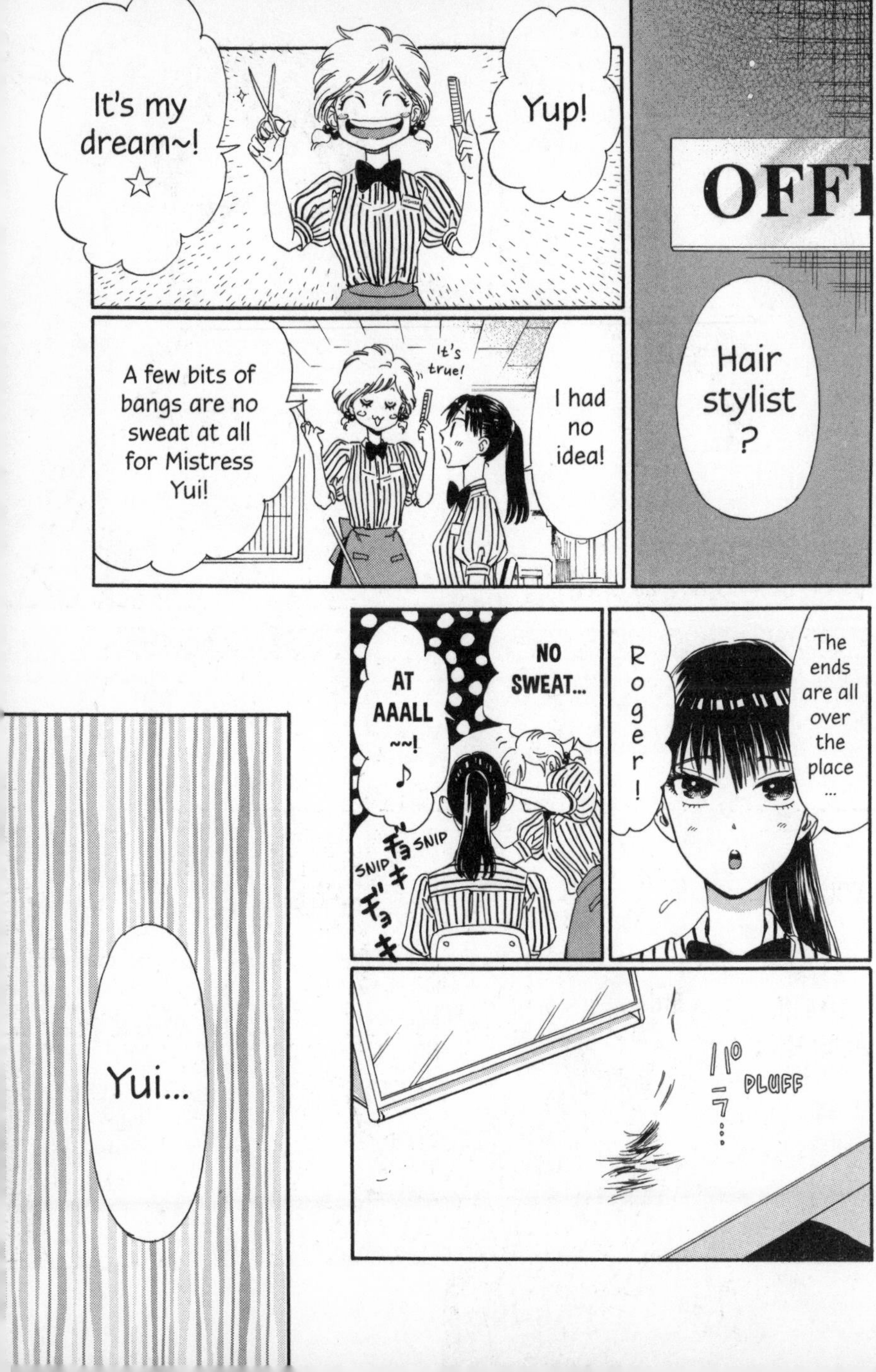
OFF
Hair stylist?
Yup!
It's my dream~! ☆
I had no idea!
It's true!
A few bits of bangs are no sweat at all for Mistress Yui!
The ends are all over the place...
Roger!
NO SWEAT...
AT AAALL ~~! ♪
ギョキ SNIP
ギョキ SNIP
パサ… PLUFF
Yui...

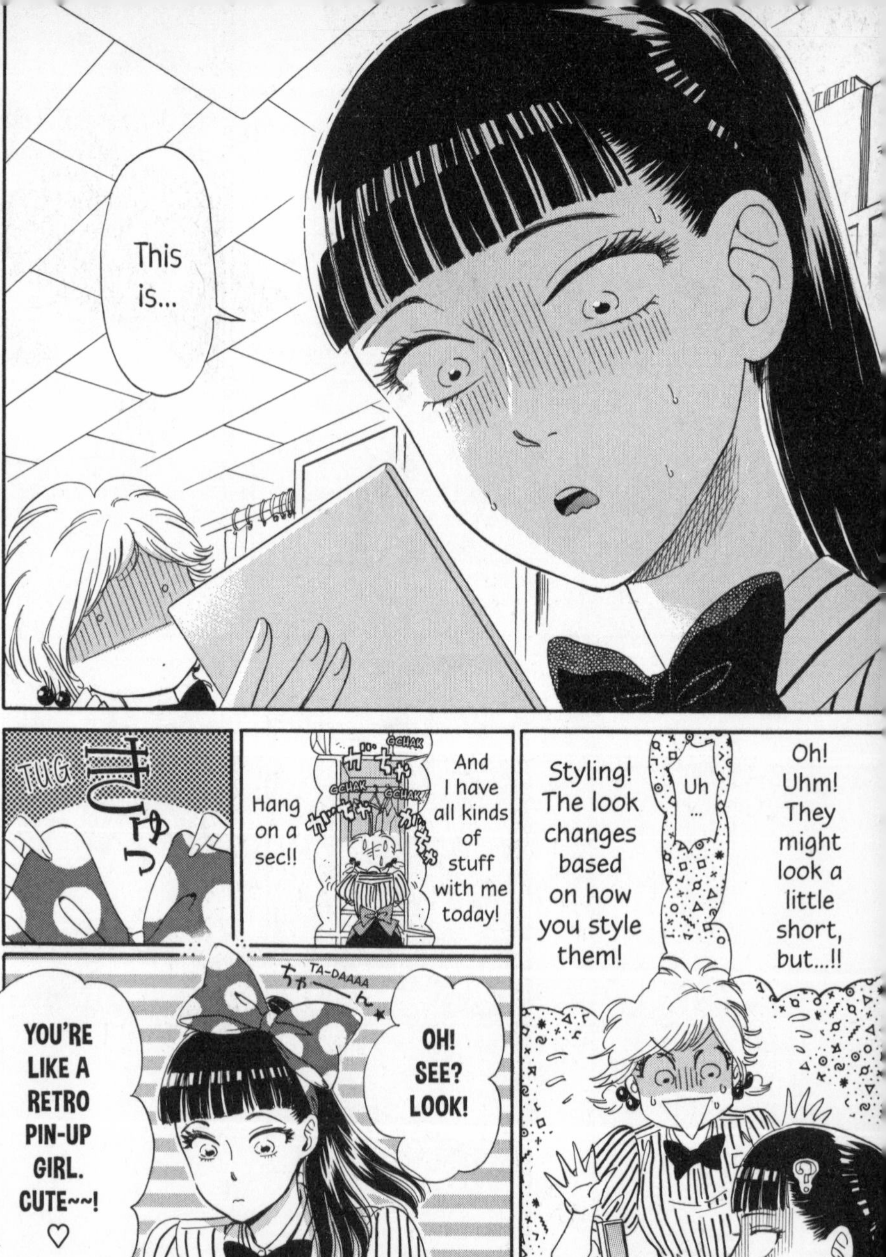
This is...
Oh! Uhm! They might look a little short, but...!!
Uh ...
Styling! The look changes based on how you style them!
GCHAK
GCHAK GCHAK
And I have all kinds of stuff with me today!
Hang on a sec!!
きゅっ
TUG
TA-DAAAA
OH! SEE? LOOK!
YOU'RE LIKE A RETRO PIN-UP GIRL. CUTE~~! ♡
TACHIBANA

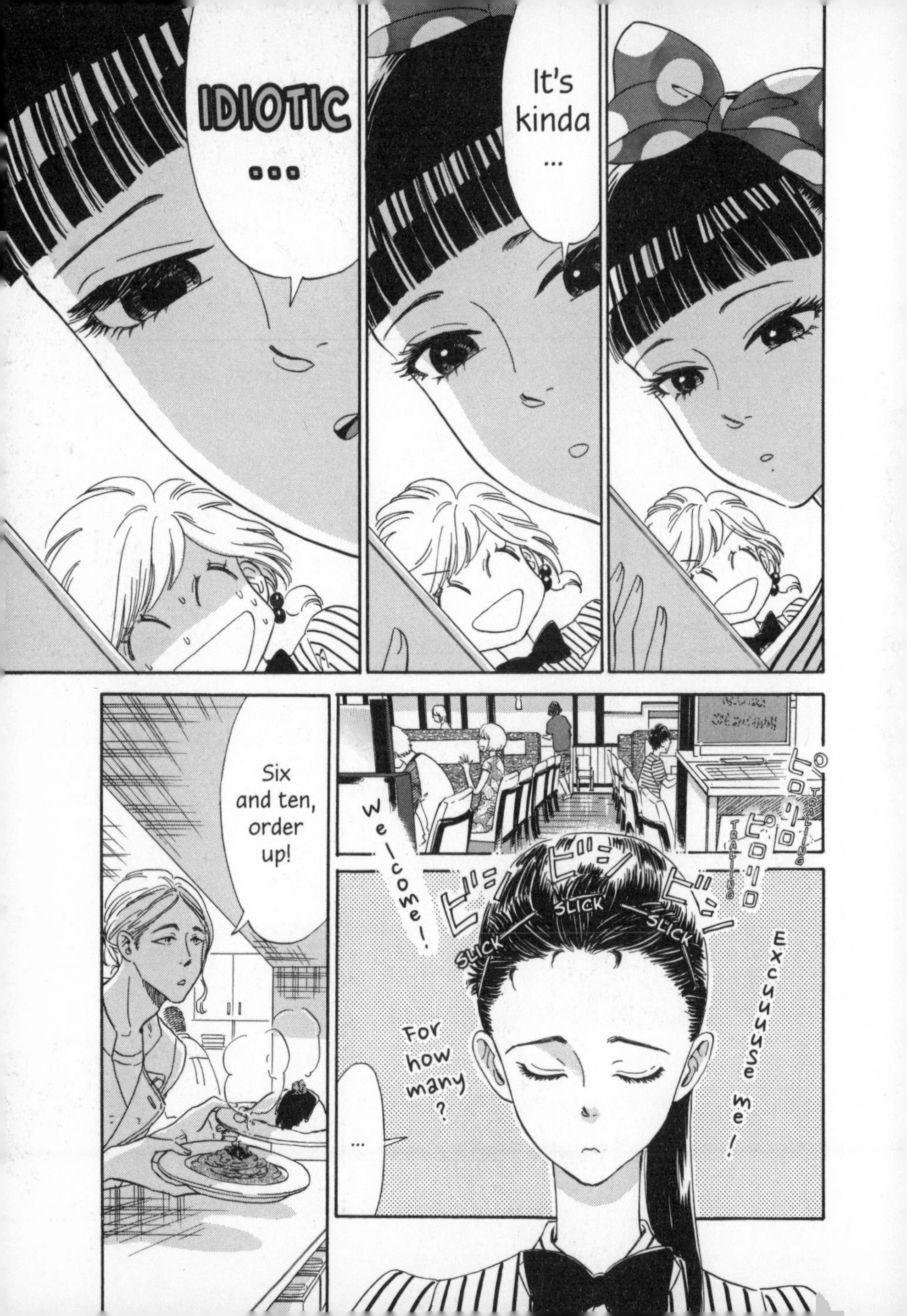
It's kinda ...
IDIOTIC ...
TRALALING
TRALALING
We lcome!
SLICK
SLICK
SLICK
Excuuuuuse me!
For how many?
...
Six and ten, order up!

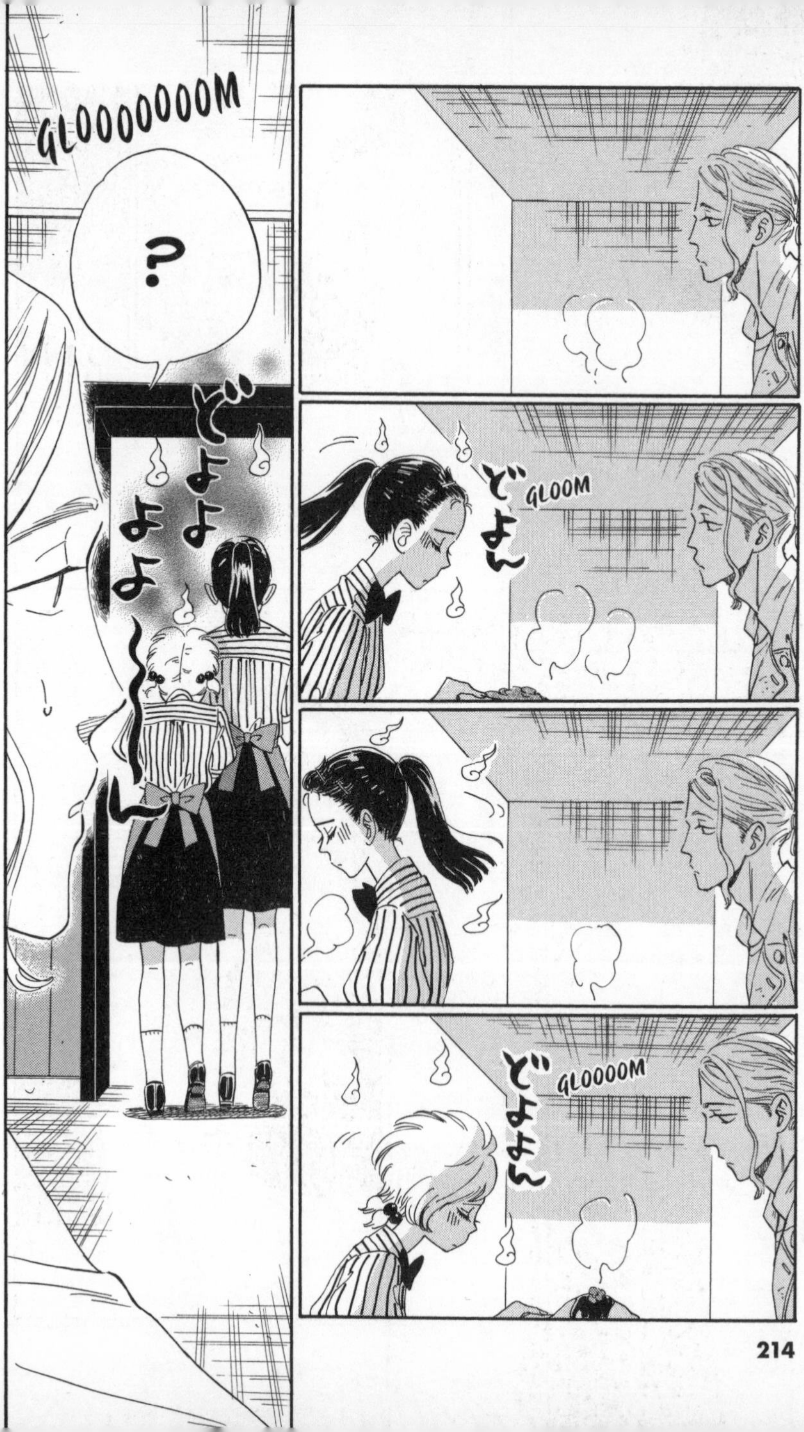
どよん
GLOOM
どよよん
GLOOOOM
GLOOOOOOOM
?
どよよよよ

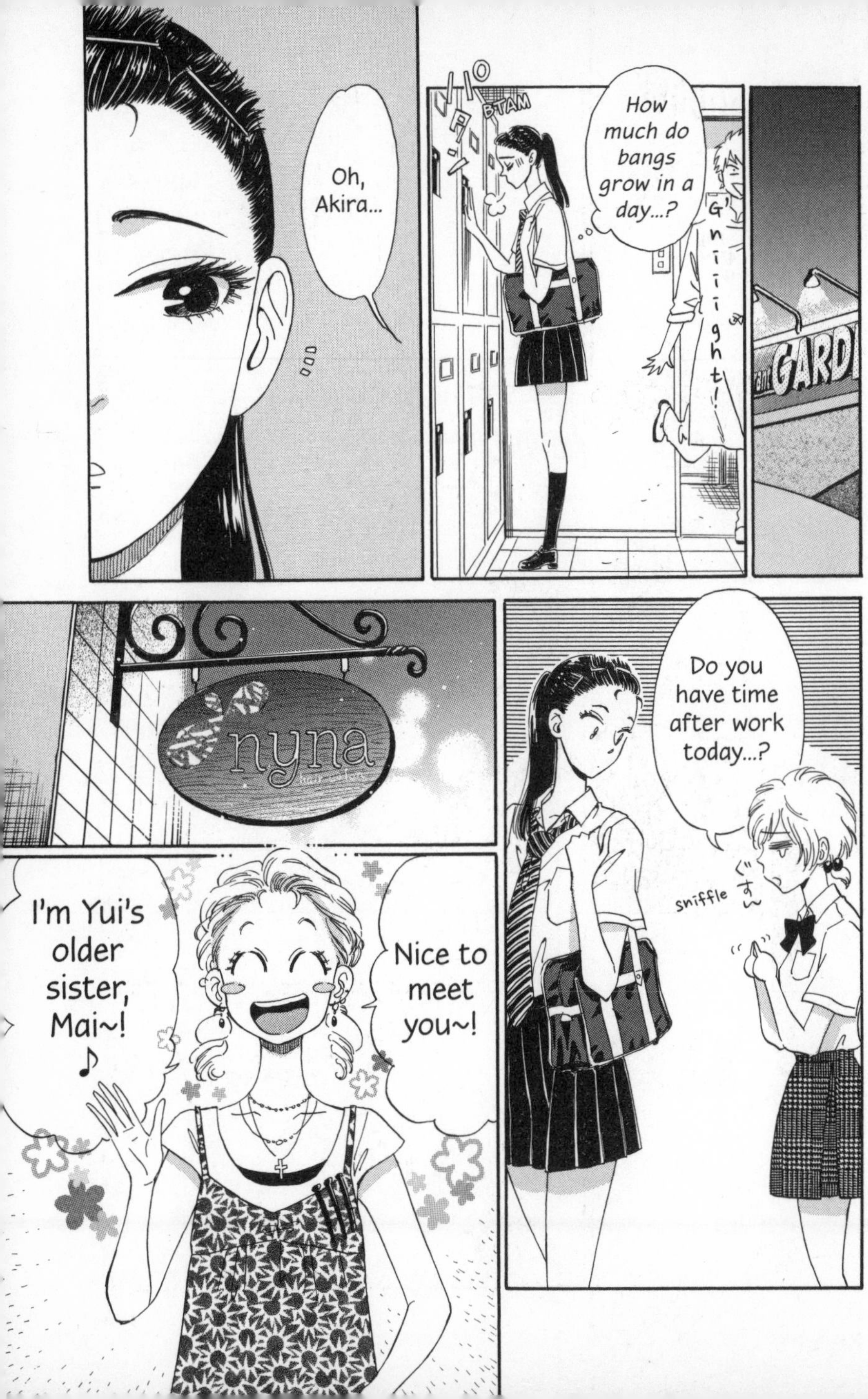
GARD
BTAM
How much do bangs grow in a day...?
Gniiiight!
Oh, Akira...
Do you have time after work today...?
sniffle
nyna
Nice to meet you~!
I'm Yui's older sister, Mai~! ♪

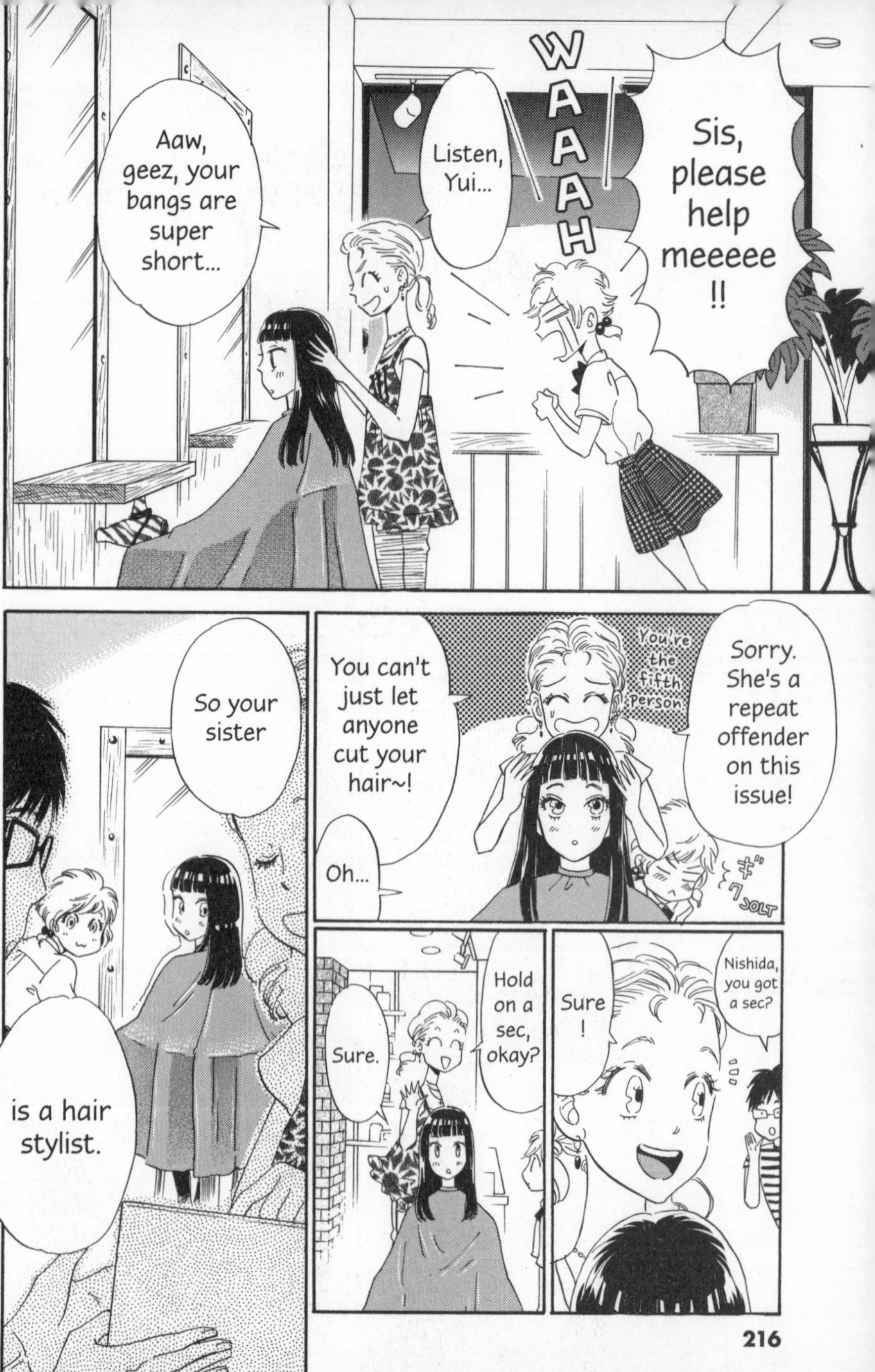
Sis, please help meeeee!!
WAAAH
Listen, Yui...
Aaw, geez, your bangs are super short...
Sorry. She's a repeat offender on this issue!
You're the fifth person
You can't just let anyone cut your hair~!
Oh...
JOLT
Nishida, you got a sec?
Sure!
Hold on a sec, okay?
Sure.
So your sister
is a hair stylist.

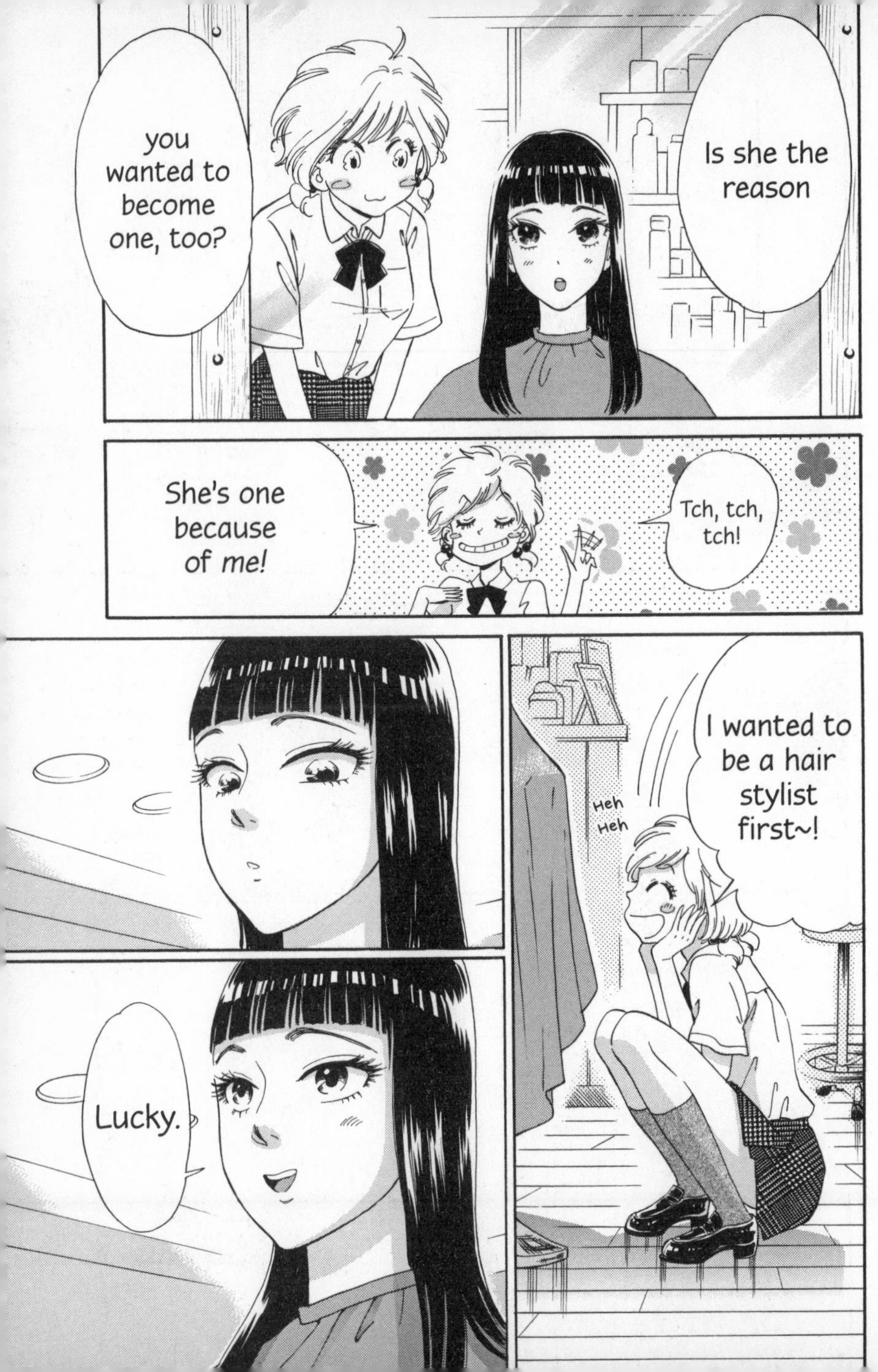
Is she the reason
you wanted to become one, too?
Tch, tch, tch!
She's one because of me!
I wanted to be a hair stylist first~!
Heh Heh
Lucky.

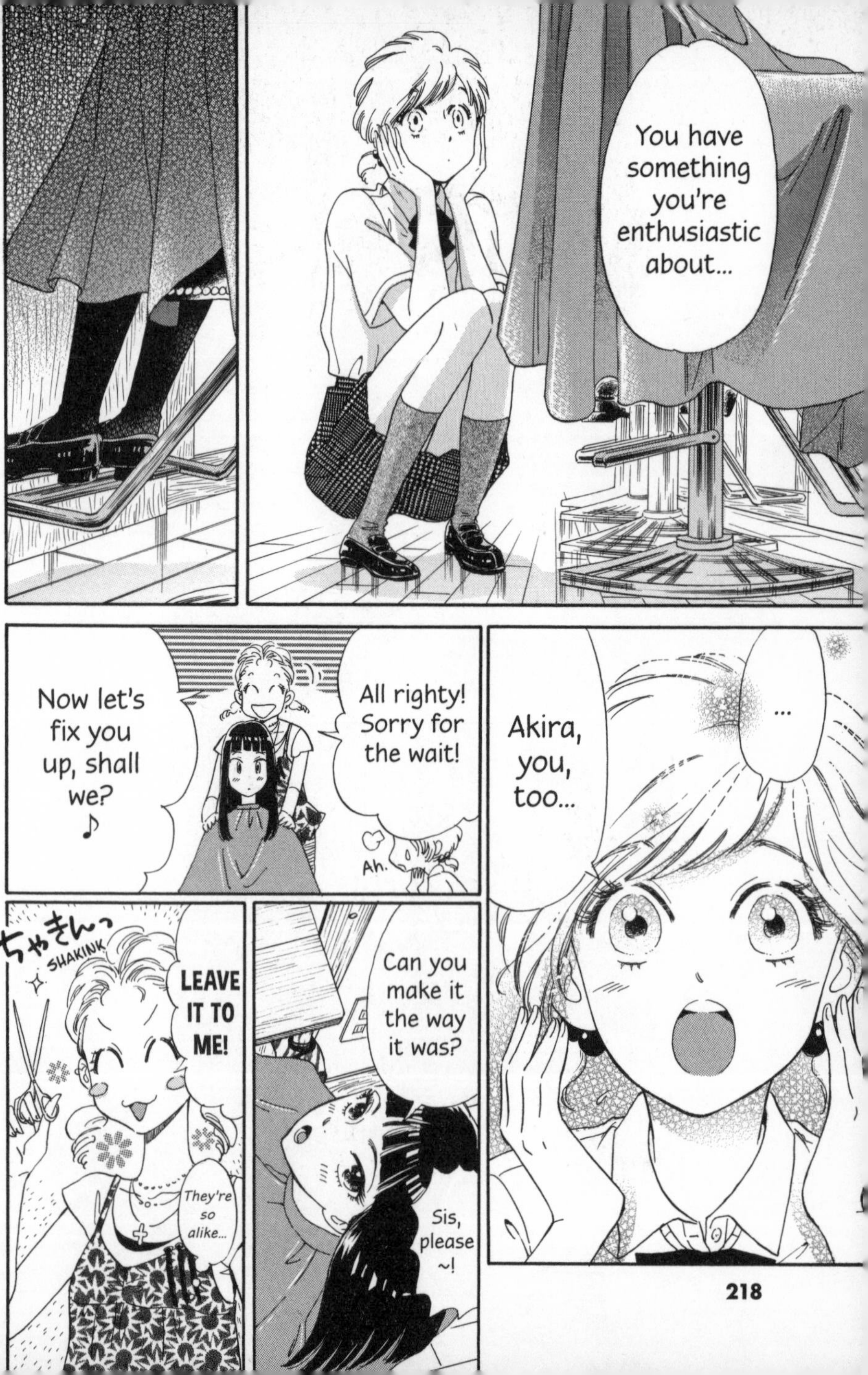
You have something you're enthusiastic about...
...
Akira, you, too...
All righty! Sorry for the wait!
Ah.
Now let's fix you up, shall we? ♪
Can you make it the way it was?
Sis, please ~!
ちゃきんっ SHAKINK
LEAVE IT TO ME!
They're so alike...

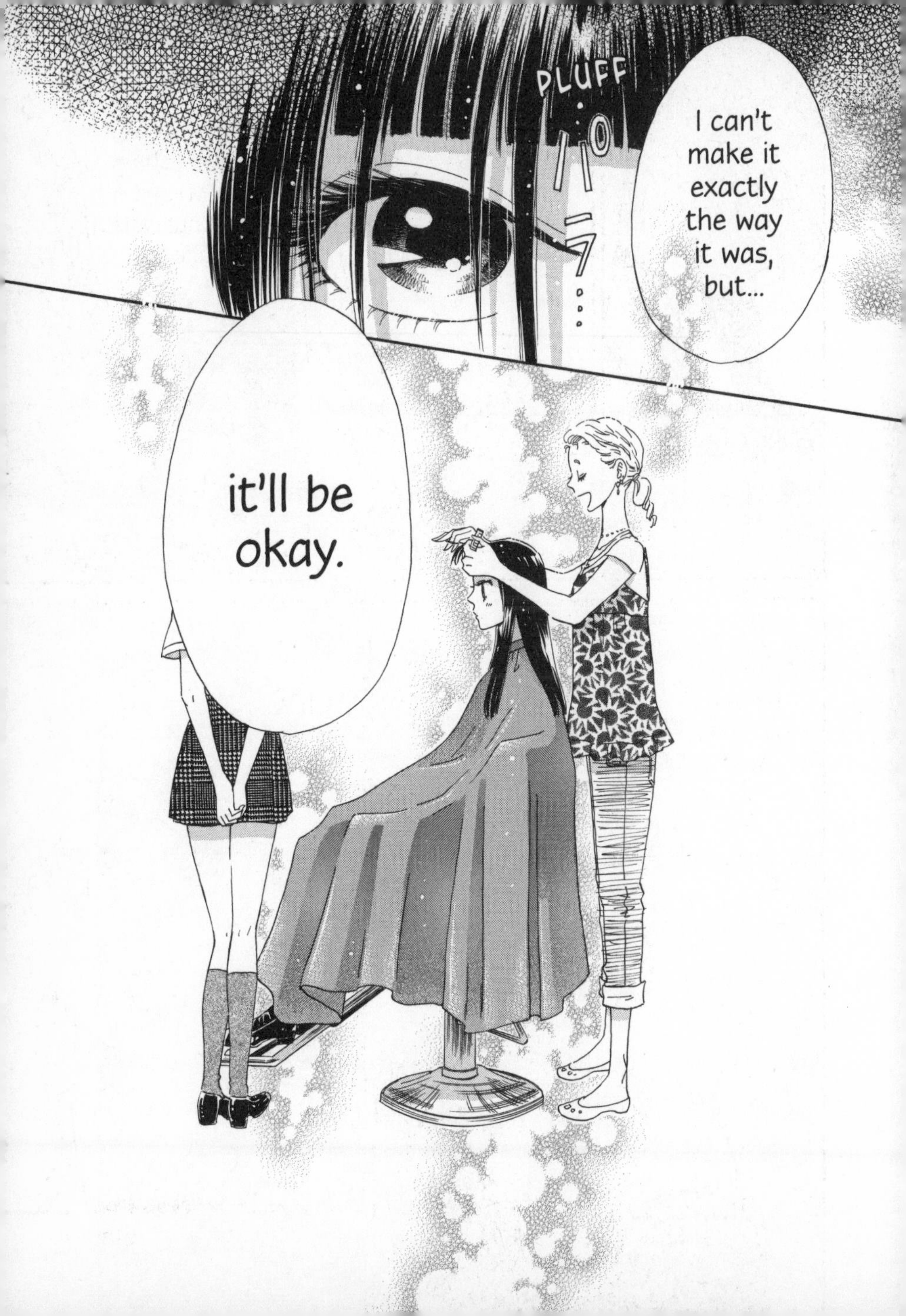

I can't make it exactly the way it was, but...
PLUFF
it'll be okay.

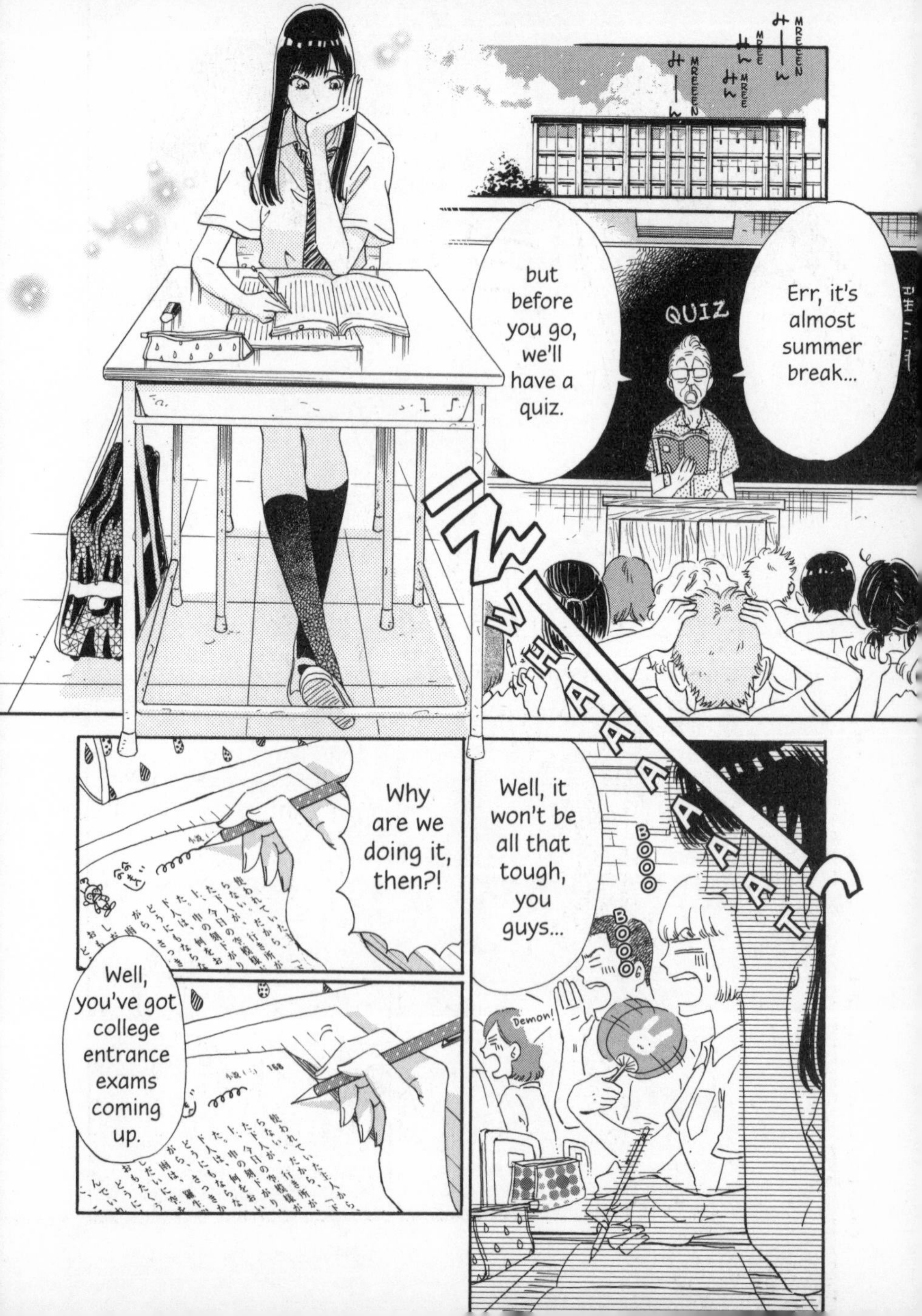

みーん
MREEEN
みん
MREE
みん
MREE
みーん
MREEEN
Err, it's almost summer break...
QUIZ
but before you go, we'll have a quiz.
WHAAAAAAT
Well, it won't be all that tough, you guys...
BOOO
BOOO
Demon!
Why are we doing it, then?!
Well, you've got college entrance exams coming up.

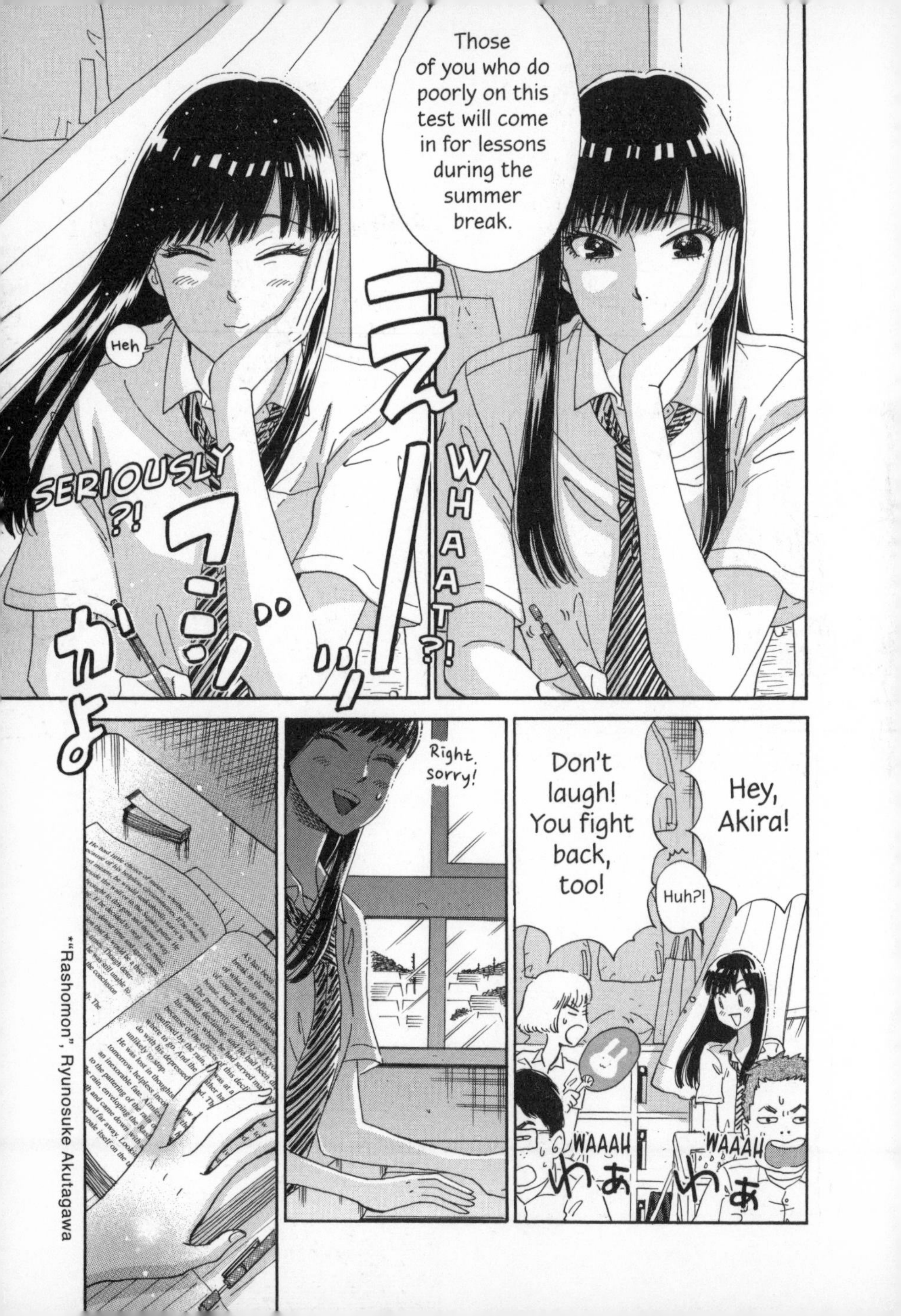

Those of you who do poorly on this test will come in for lessons during the summer break.
WHAAAT?!
Heh
SERIOUSLY?!
DO
Hey, Akira!
Huh?!
Don't laugh! You fight back, too!
WAAAH
WAAAH
Right, sorry!

*"Rashomon", Ryunosuke Akutagawa

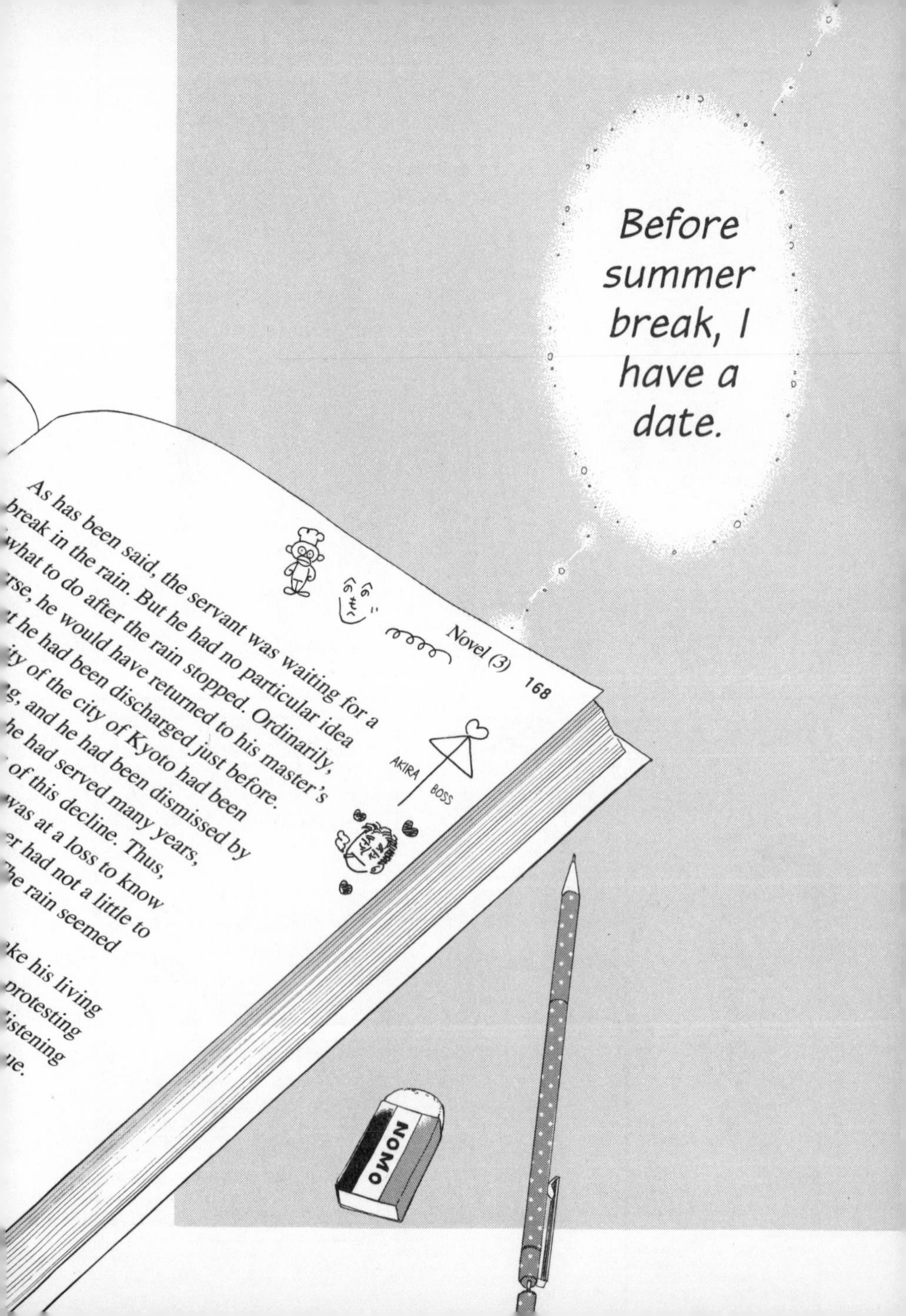
Before summer break, I have a date.
Novel (3)
168
As has been said, the servant was waiting for a
break in the rain. But he had no particular idea
what to do after the rain stopped. Ordinarily,
rse, he would have returned to his master's
t he had been discharged just before.
ity of the city of Kyoto had been
g, and he had been dismissed by
he had served many years,
of this decline. Thus,
was at a loss to know
er had not a little to
he rain seemed
ke his living
protesting
istening
ue.
AKIRA
BOSS
NOMO

grow
back.

Please
hurry
and

MNCH

... もぐ
もぐ

MNCH

wakame miso soup

After the Rain

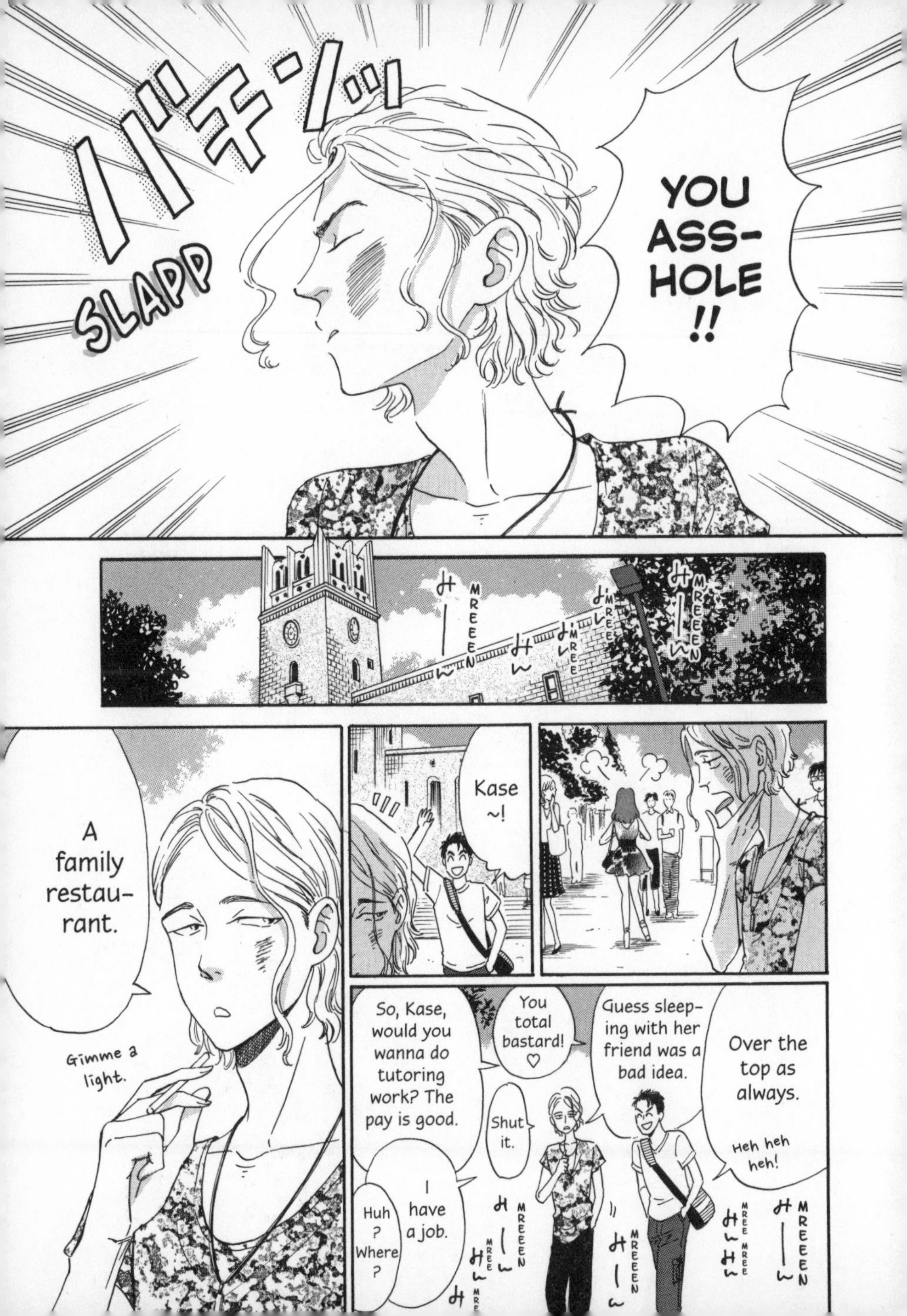
YOU ASS-HOLE !!
バチーン
SLAPP
みーん MREEEN
みーん MREEEN
みん MREE
みん MREE
みん MREE
みーん MREEEN
Kase ~!
Over the top as always.
Heh heh heh!
Guess sleeping with her friend was a bad idea.
You total bastard! ♡
Shut it.
So, Kase, would you wanna do tutoring work? The pay is good.
I have a job.
Huh? Where?
みーん MREEEN
みん MREE
みーん MREEEN
みーん MREEEN
みん MREE
みん MREE
A family restaurant.
Gimme a light.

Chapter 12

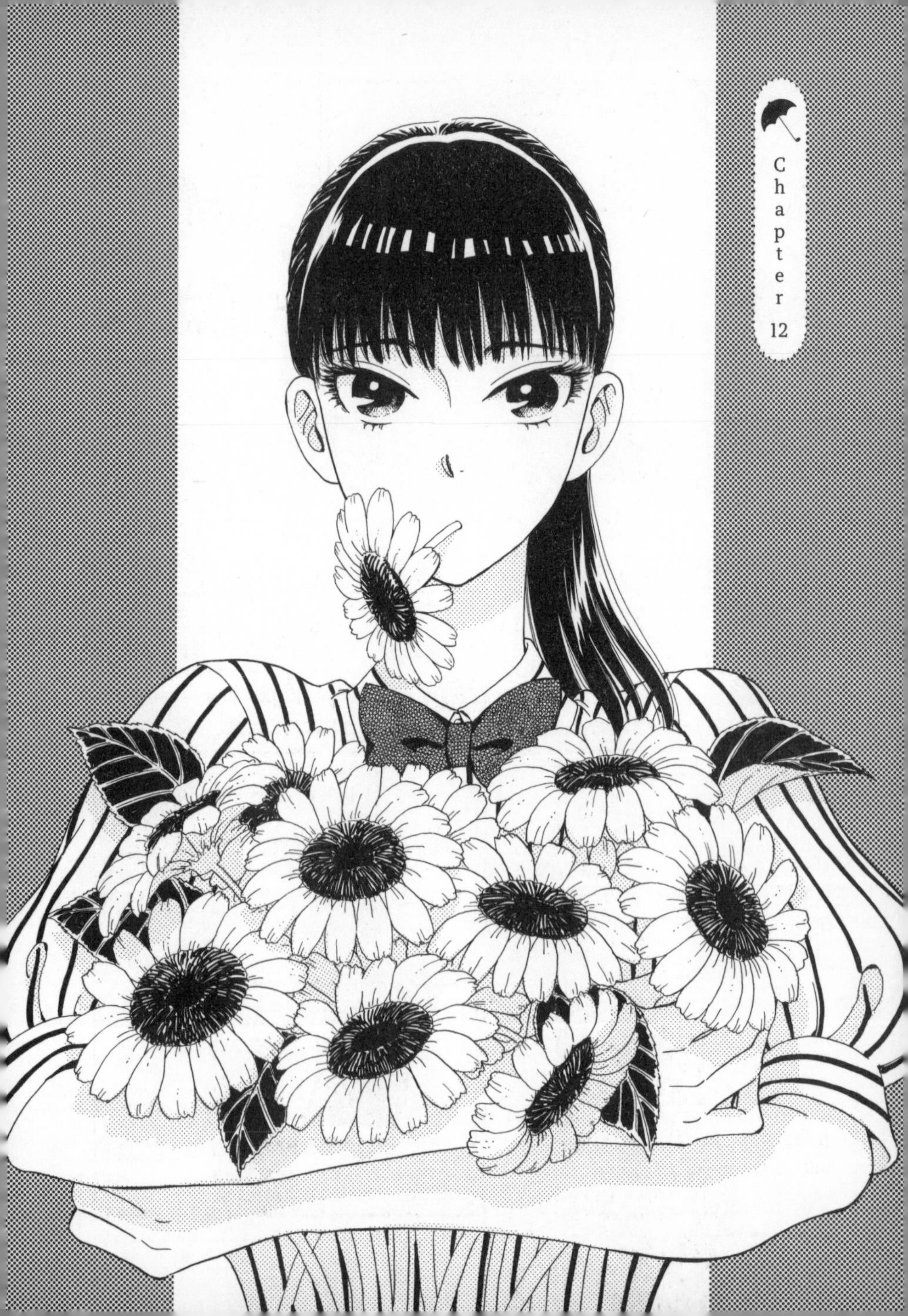

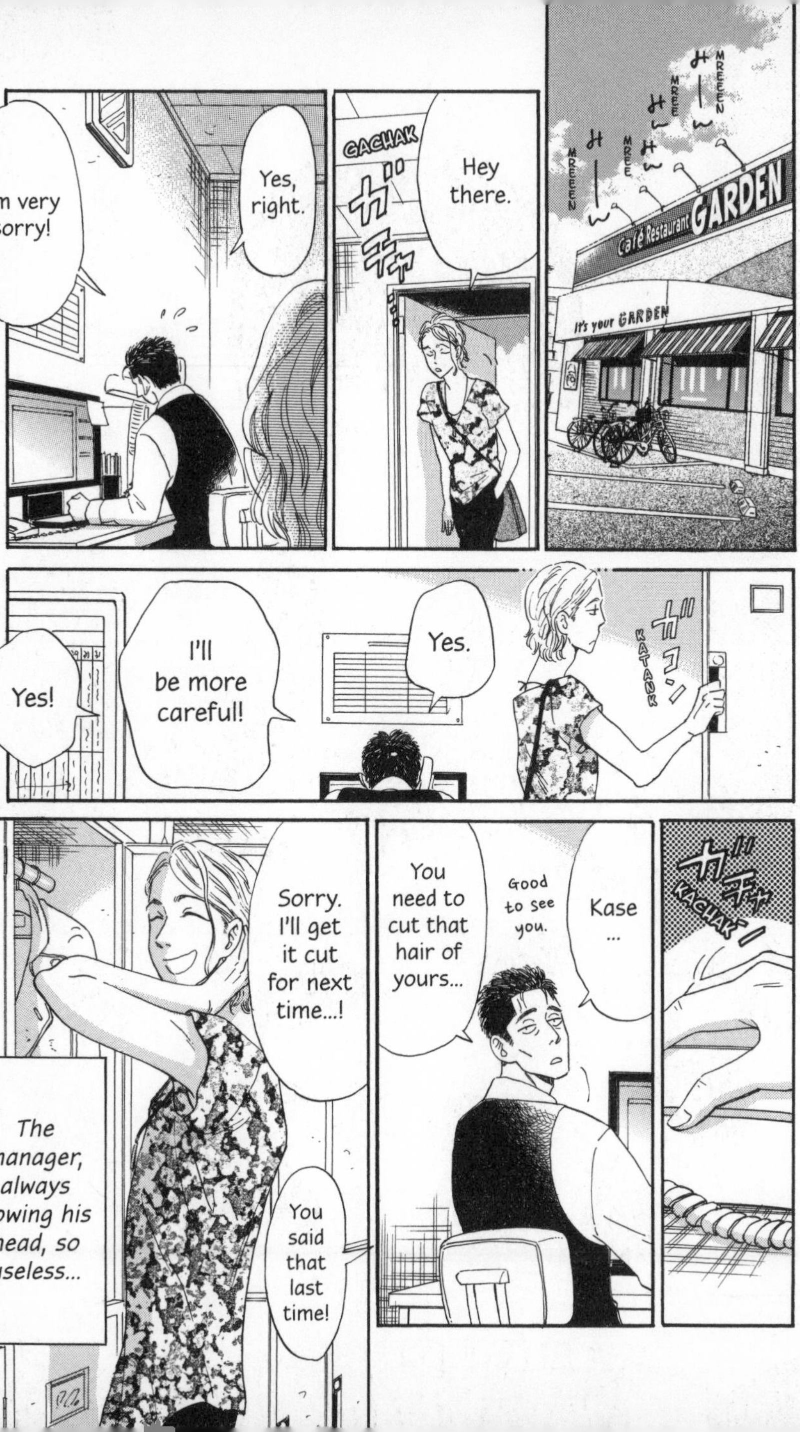
MREEEN
MREE
MREE
MREEEN
Café Restaurant GARDEN
It's your GARDEN
GACHAK
Hey there.
Yes, right.
I'm very sorry!
KATANK
Yes.
I'll be more careful!
Yes!
KACHAK
Kase ...
Good to see you.
You need to cut that hair of yours...
Sorry. I'll get it cut for next time...!
You said that last time!
The manager, always bowing his head, so useless...

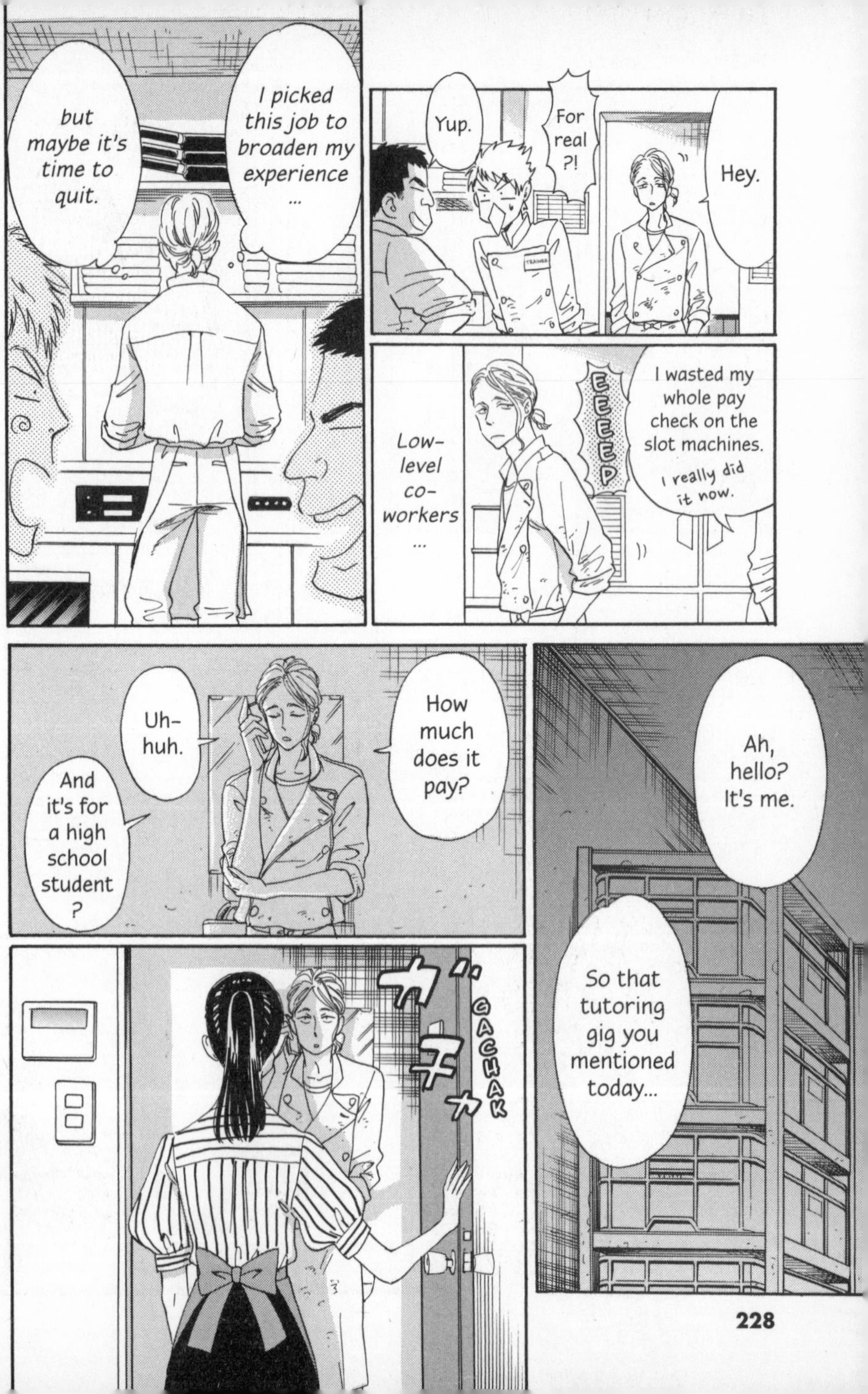
Hey.
For real ?!
Yup.
I wasted my whole pay check on the slot machines.
I really did it now.
EEEED
Low-level co-workers ...
I picked this job to broaden my experience ...
but maybe it's time to quit.
Ah, hello? It's me.
So that tutoring gig you mentioned today...
How much does it pay?
Uh-huh.
And it's for a high school student ?
GACHAK

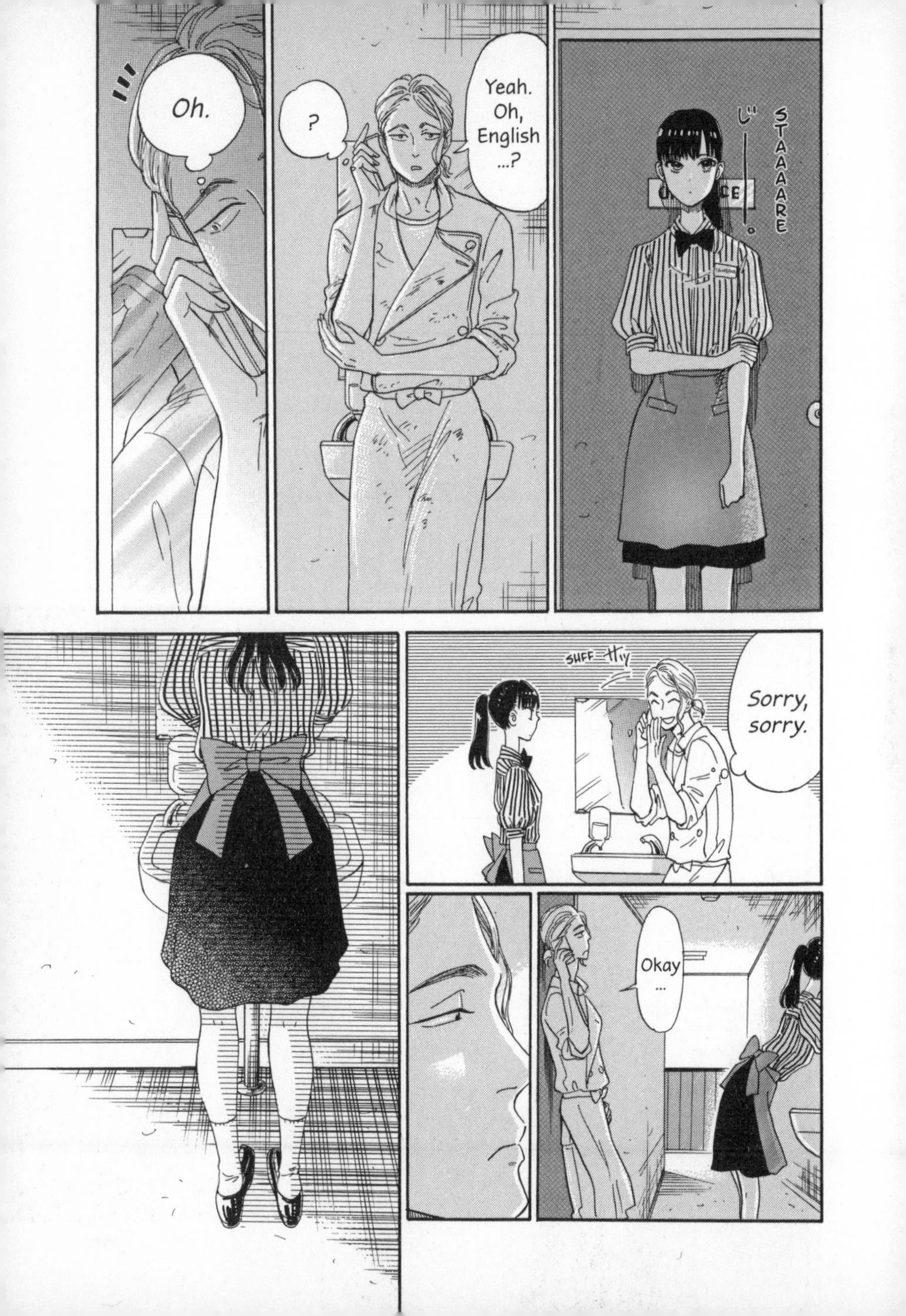

じー…。
STAAAARE
Yeah. Oh, English ...?
?
Oh.
SHUFF
Sorry, sorry.
Okay ...

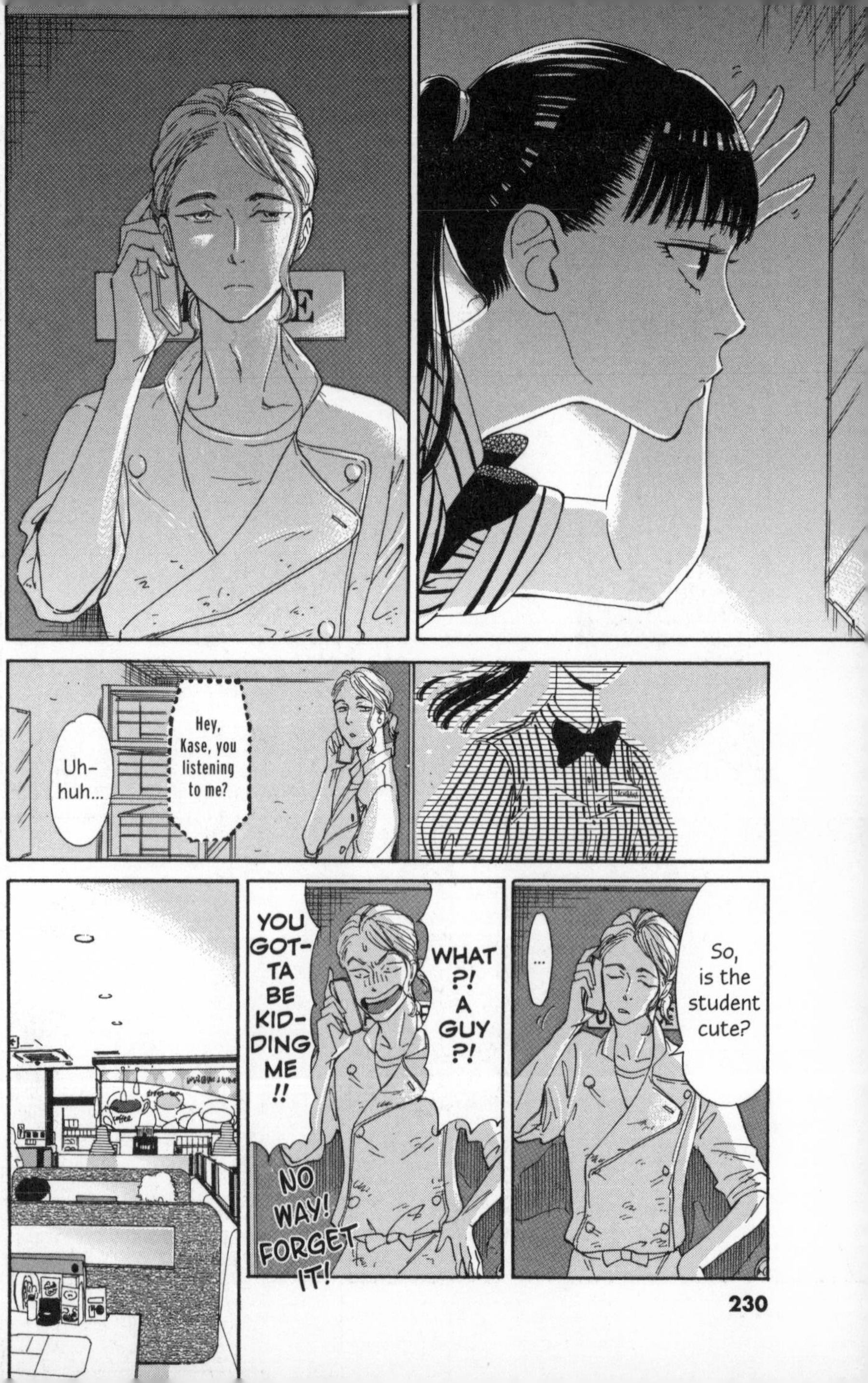
Hey, Kase, you listening to me?
Uh-huh...
So, is the student cute?
...
WHAT?! A GUY?!
YOU GOTTA BE KIDDING ME!!
NO WAY! FORGET IT!

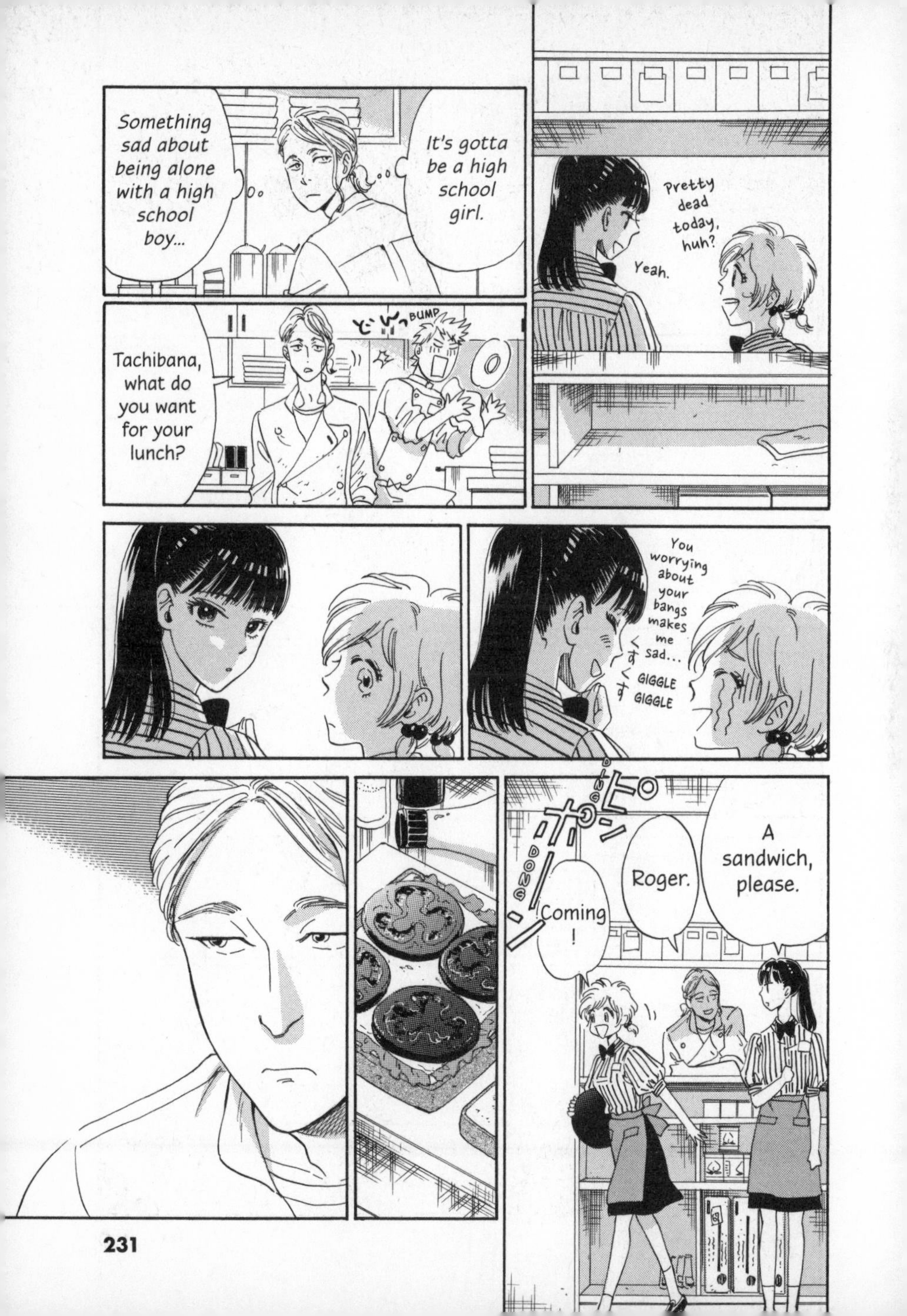
Pretty dead today, huh?
Yeah.
It's gotta be a high school girl.
Something sad about being alone with a high school boy...
BUMP
Tachibana, what do you want for your lunch?
You worrying about your bangs makes me sad...
くすくす
GIGGLE GIGGLE
A sandwich, please.
Roger.
DING DONG
Coming!

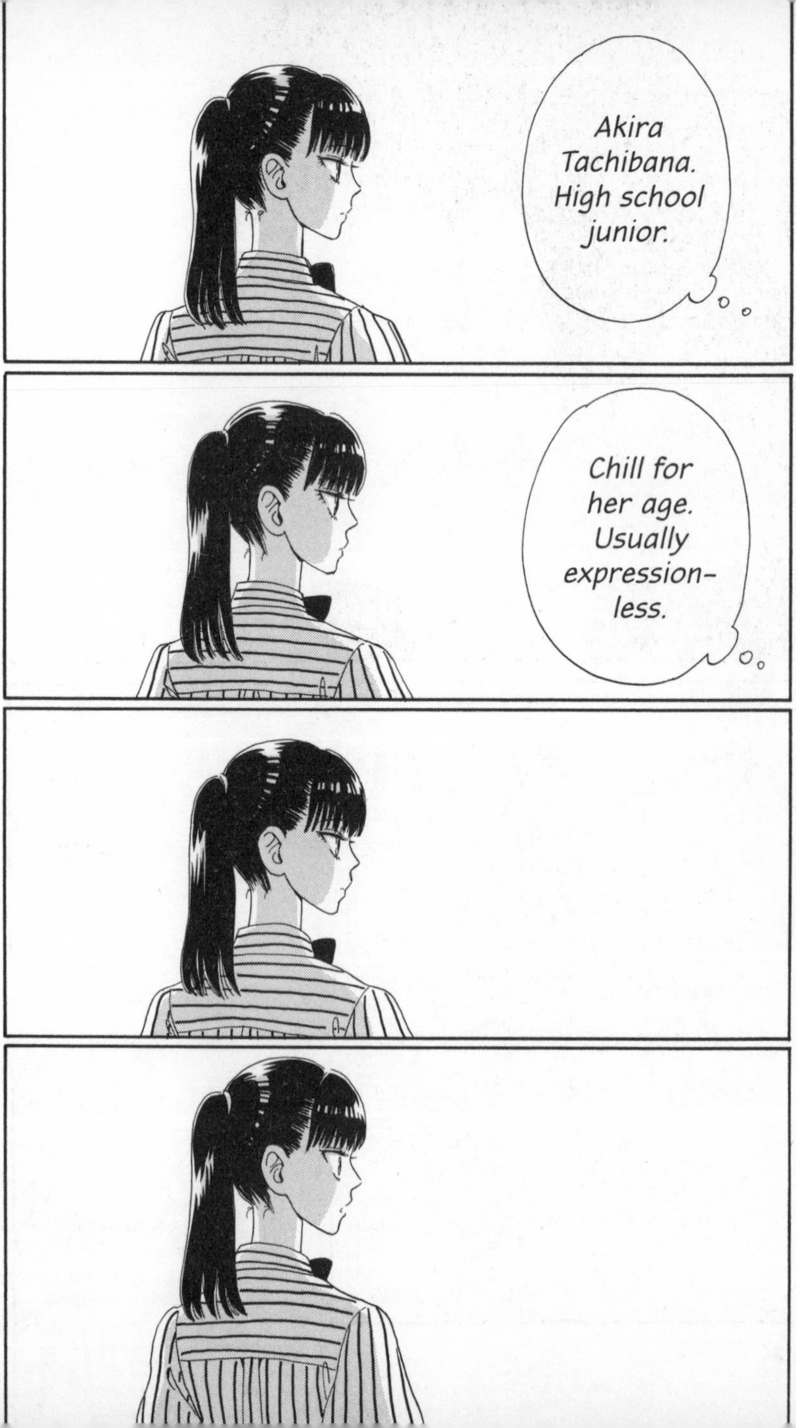
Akira Tachibana. High school junior.
Chill for her age. Usually expression-less.

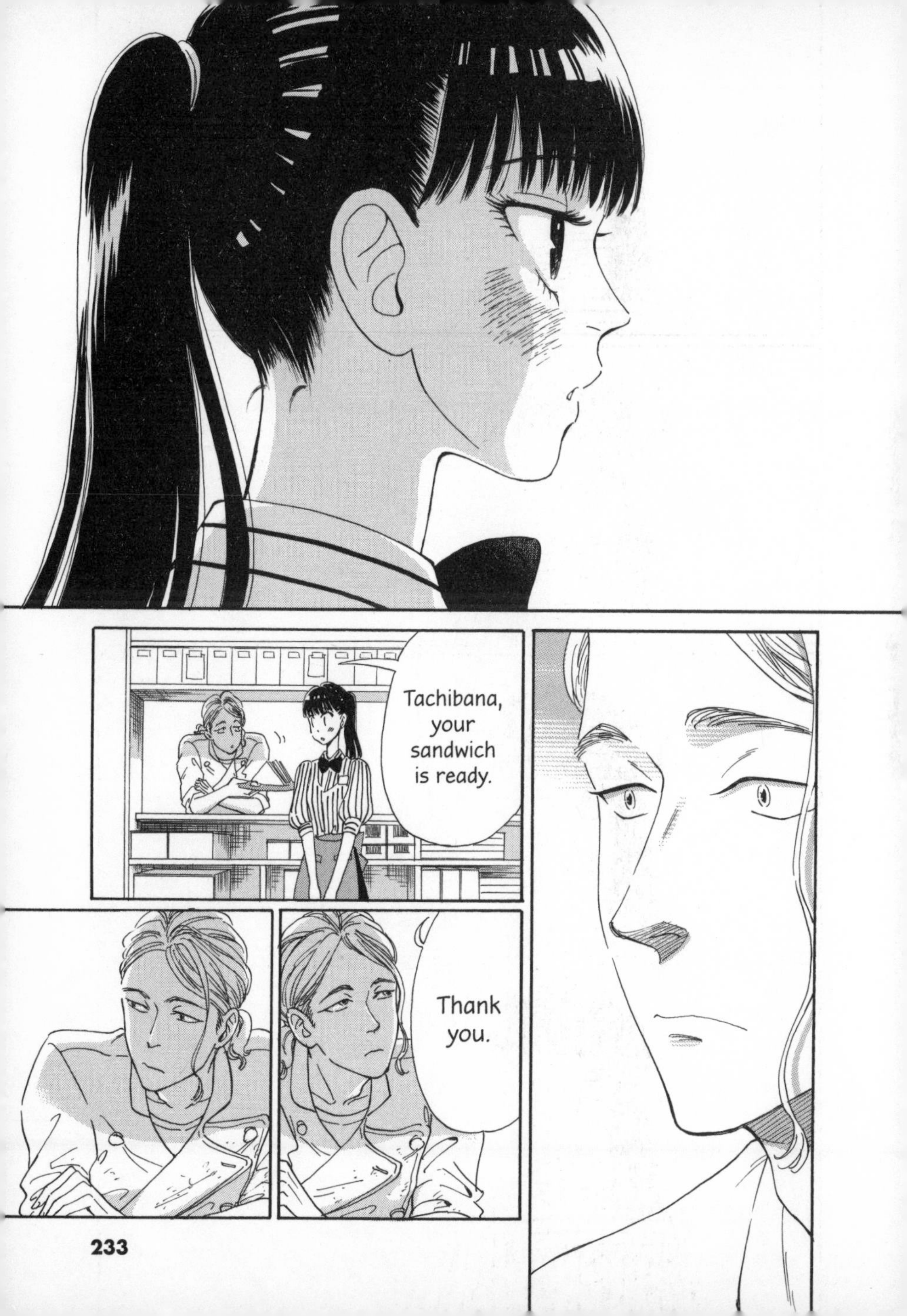

Tachibana, your sandwich is ready.
Thank you.

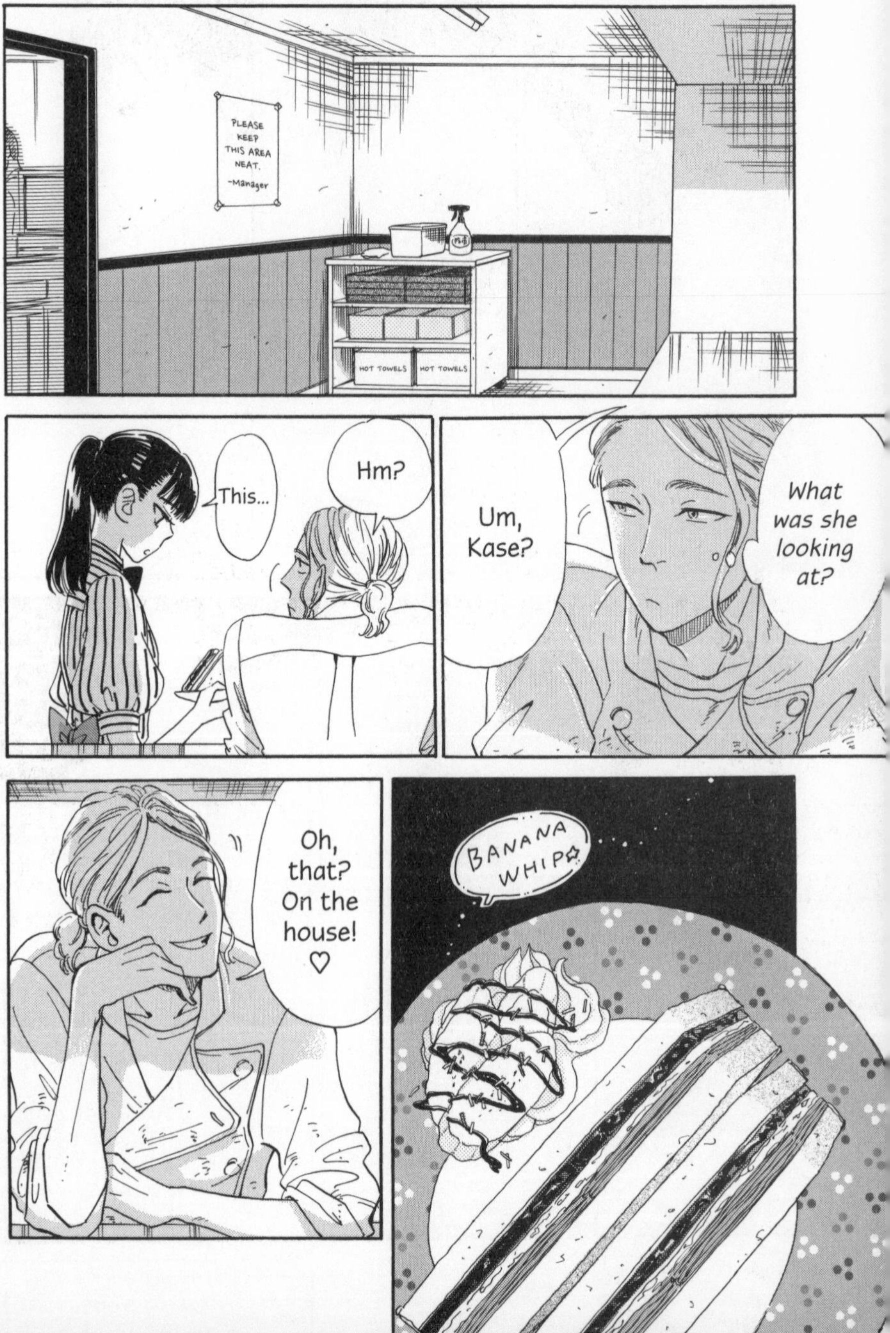
PLEASE KEEP THIS AREA NEAT. -Manager
HOT TOWELS
HOT TOWELS
What was she looking at?
Um, Kase?
Hm?
This...
BANANA WHIP☆
Oh, that? On the house! ♡

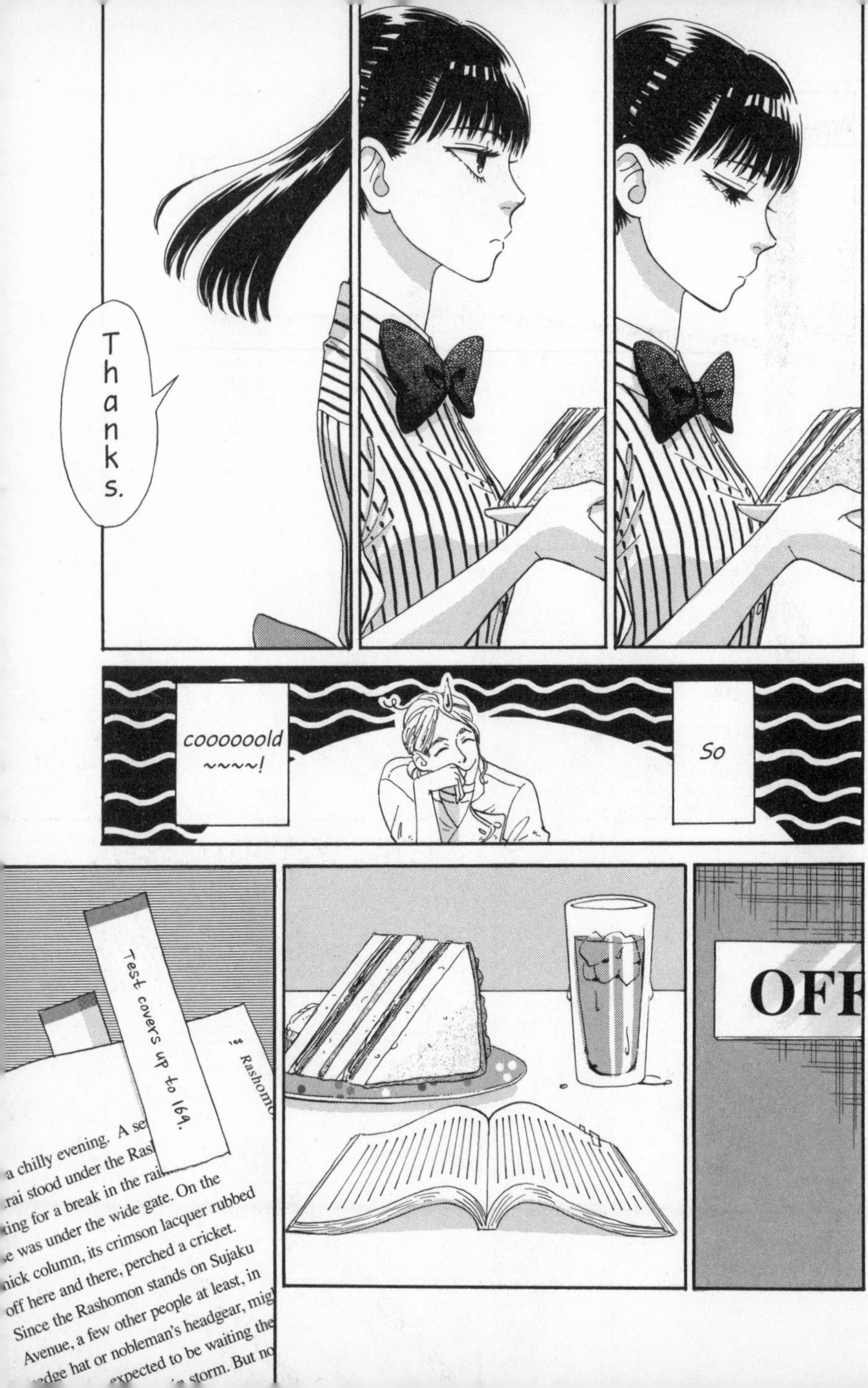
Thanks.
So
coooooold ~~~~!
OFF
Test covers up to 169.
166 Rashomo
a chilly evening. A se
rai stood under the Ras
ing for a break in the rai
e was under the wide gate. On the
ick column, its crimson lacquer rubbed
off here and there, perched a cricket.
Since the Rashomon stands on Sujaku
Avenue, a few other people at least, in
dge hat or nobleman's headgear, mig
expected to be waiting the
storm. But no

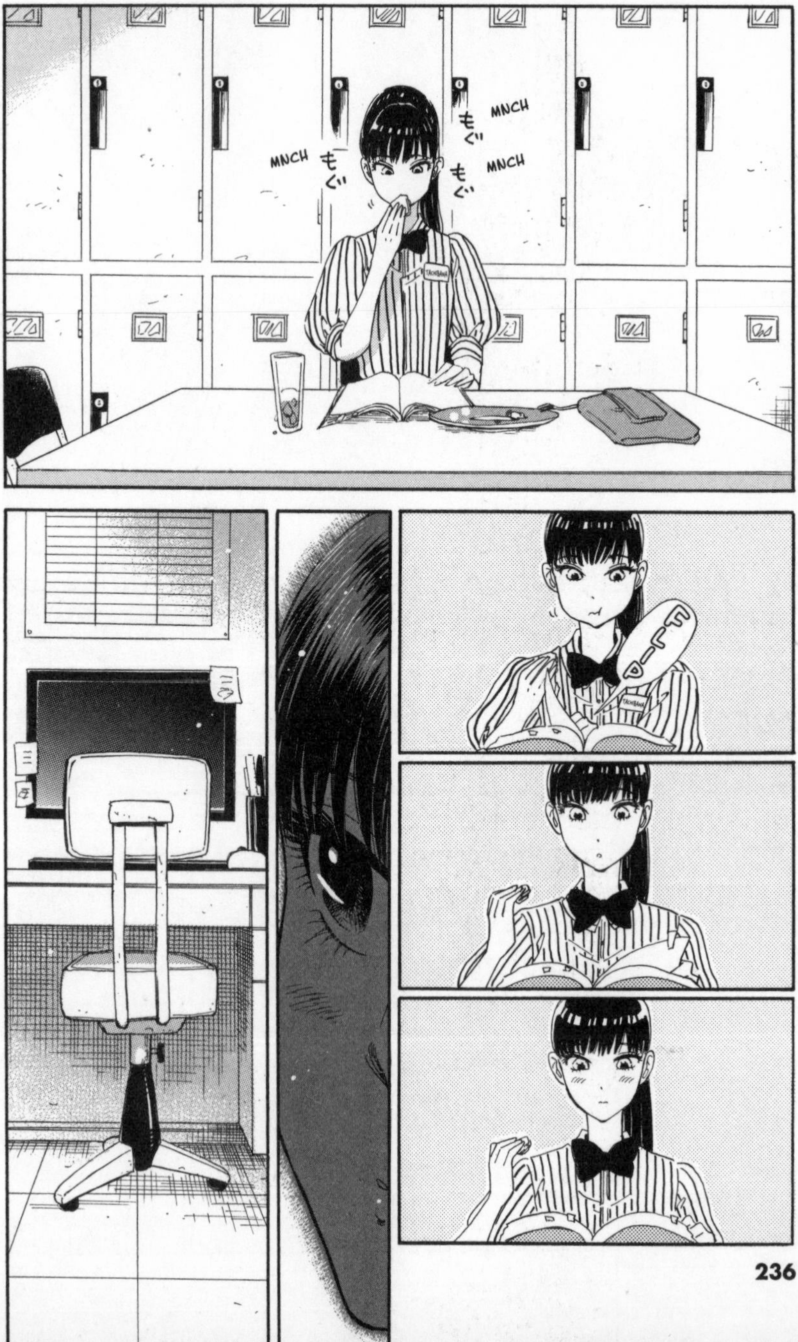
もぐ MNCH
もぐ MNCH
MNCH もぐ
TACHIBANA

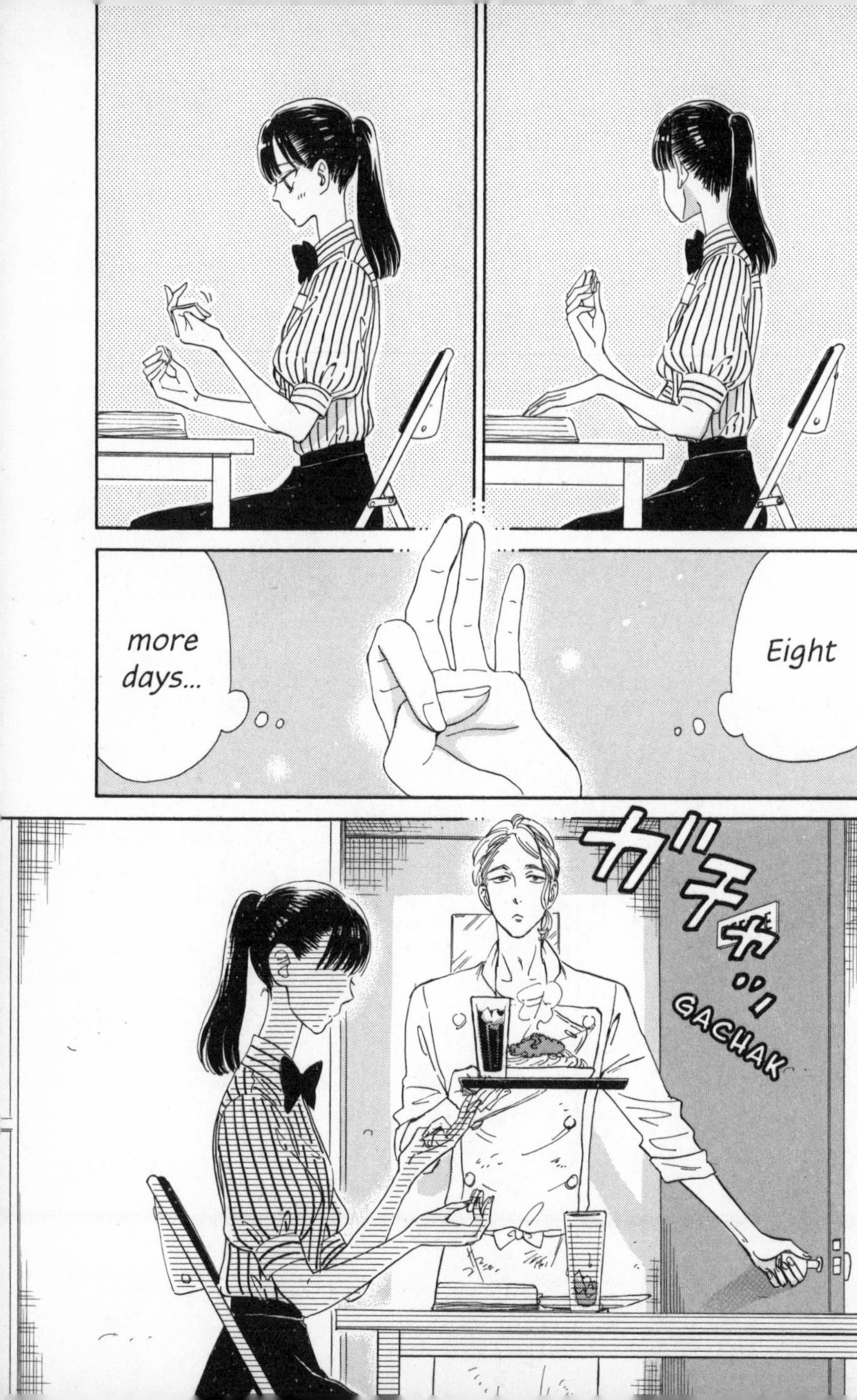
Eight
more days...
ガチャ
GACHAK

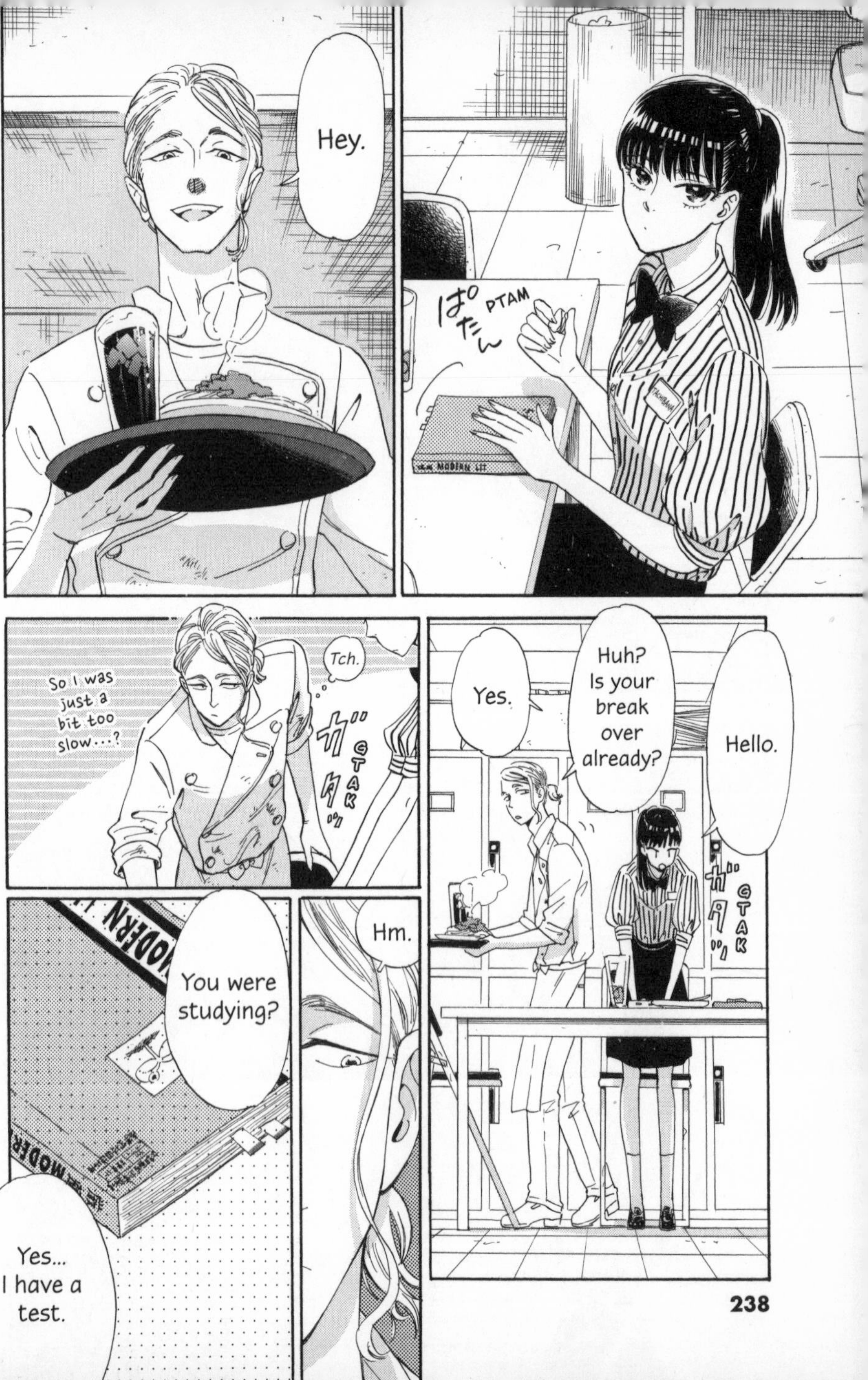
ぱたん
PTAM
Hey.
Hello.
Huh? Is your break over already?
Yes.
ガタッ
GTAK
Tch.
ガタッ
GTAK
So I was just a bit too slow...?
Hm.
You were studying?
MODERN LIT
Yes... I have a test.

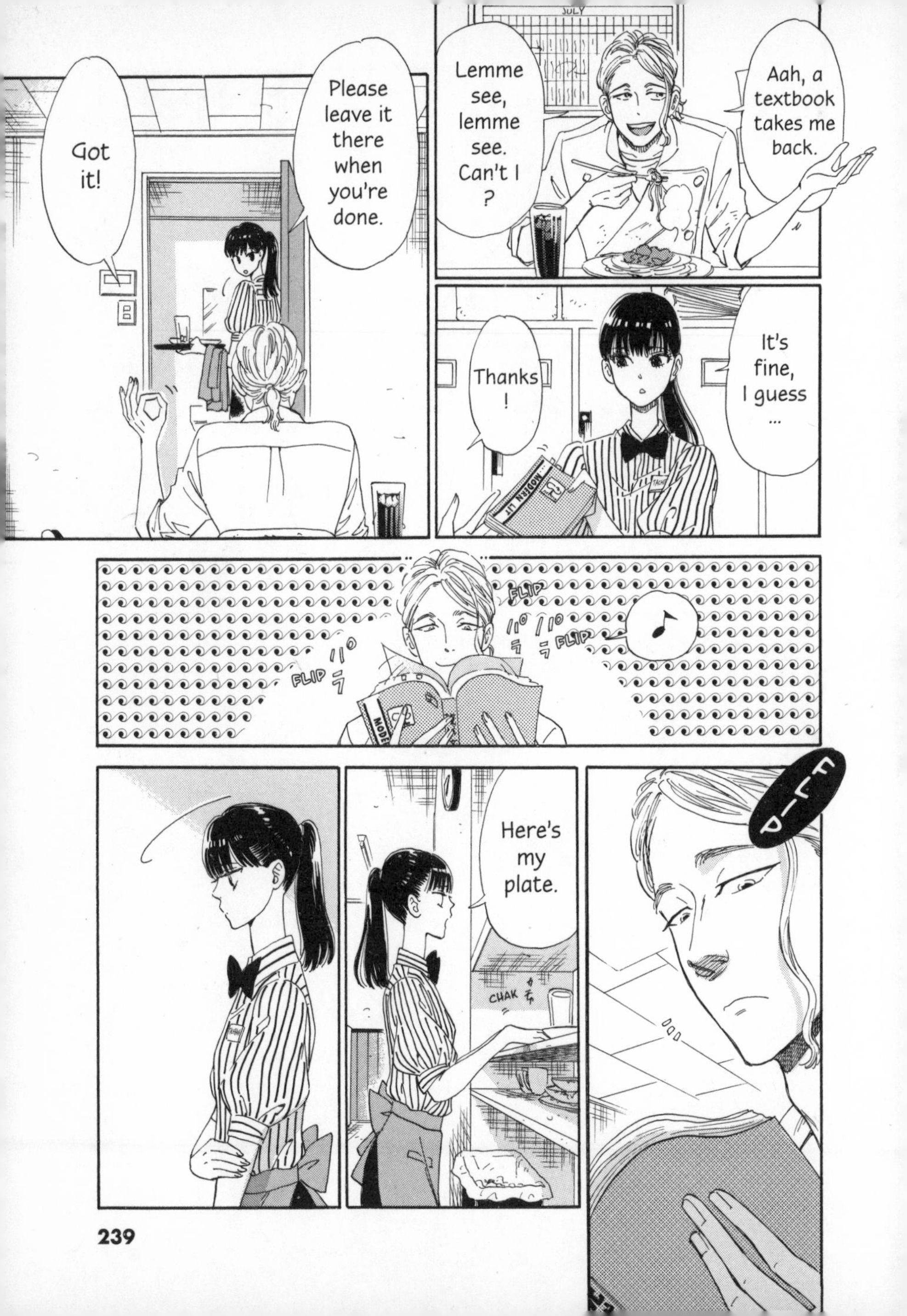
JULY
Aah, a textbook takes me back.
Lemme see, lemme see. Can't I ?
It's fine, I guess ...
Thanks !
Please leave it there when you're done.
Got it!
MODERN LIT
FLIP
FLIP
♪
FLIP
FLIP
Here's my plate.
CHAK

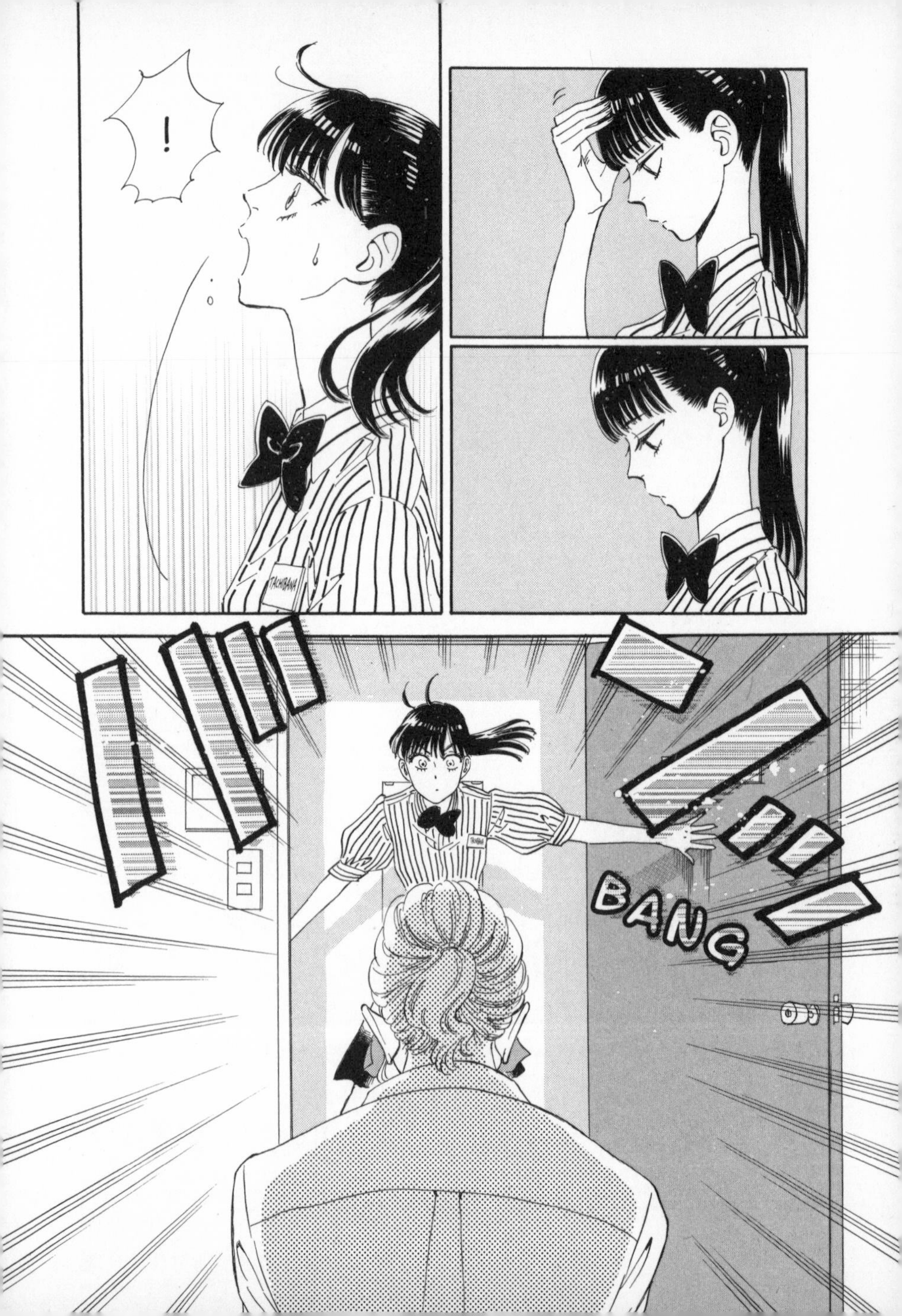
!
TACHIBANA
BANG

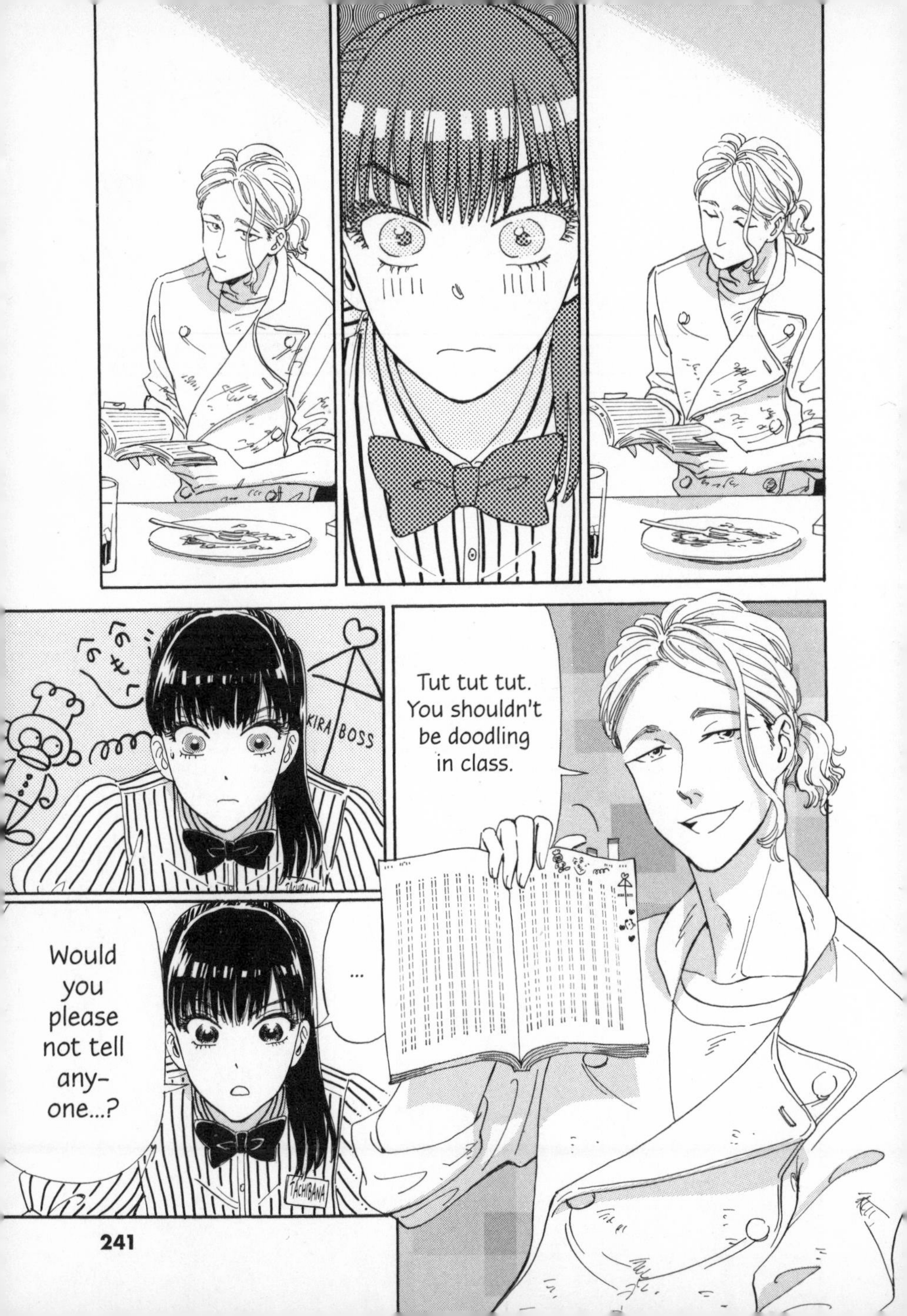

Tut tut tut. You shouldn't be doodling in class.
KIRA BOSS
...
Would you please not tell any-one...?
TACHIBANA

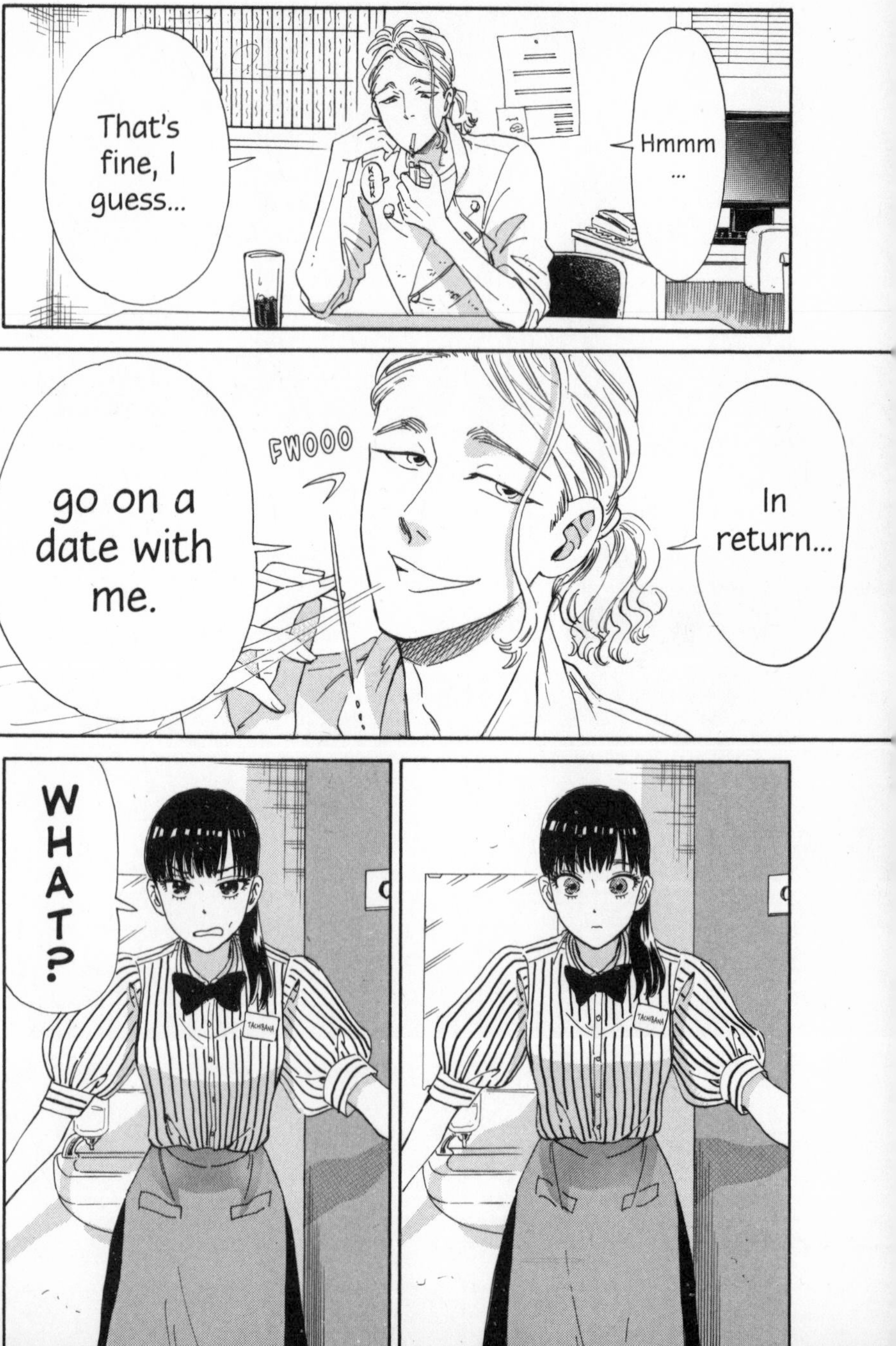
Hmmm
...
That's fine, I guess...
KCHK
In return...
FWOOO
go on a date with me.
WHAT?

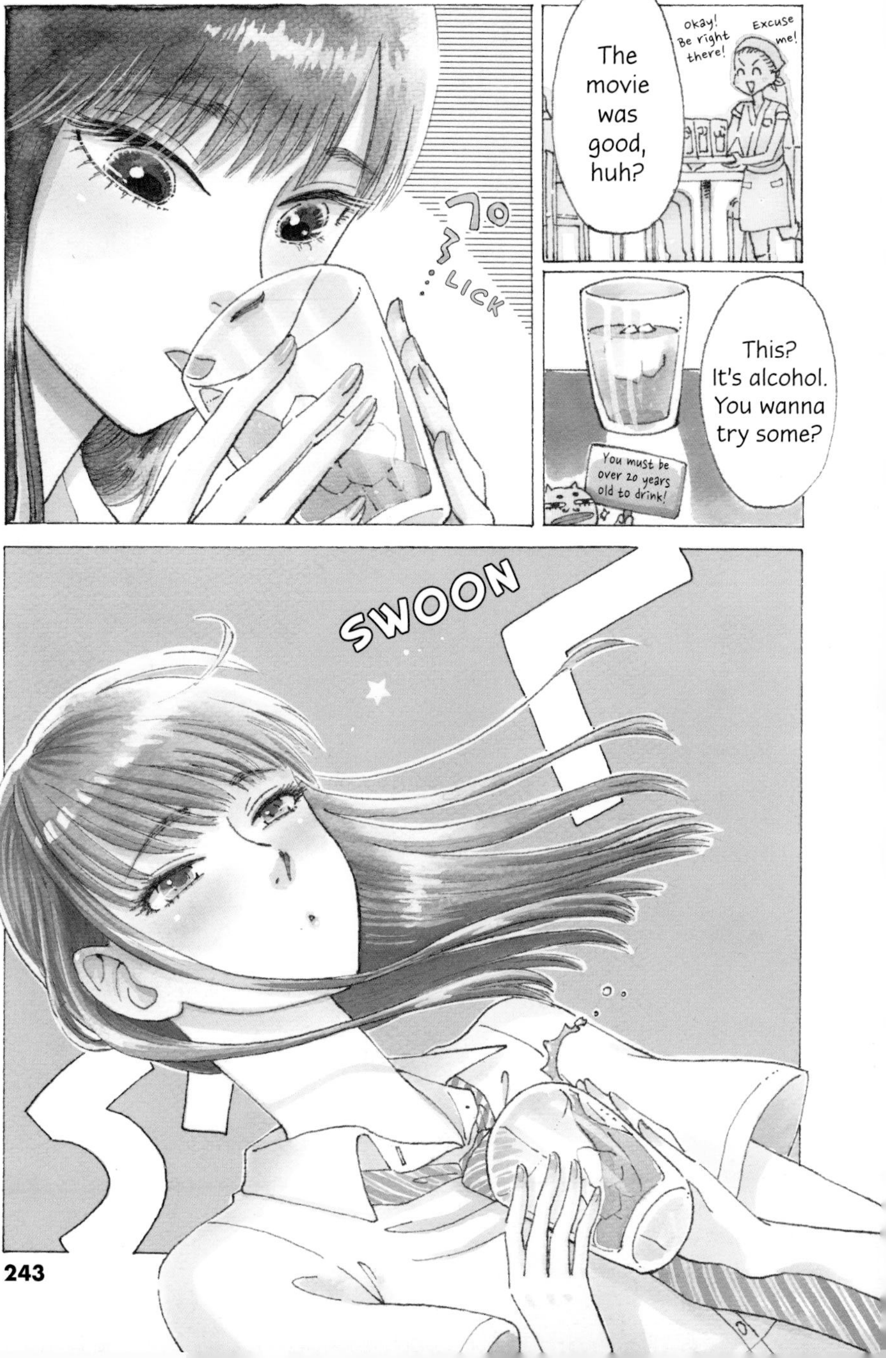
Excuse me!
Okay! Be right there!
The movie was good, huh?
This? It's alcohol. You wanna try some?
You must be over 20 years old to drink!
LICK
SWOON

Chapter 13

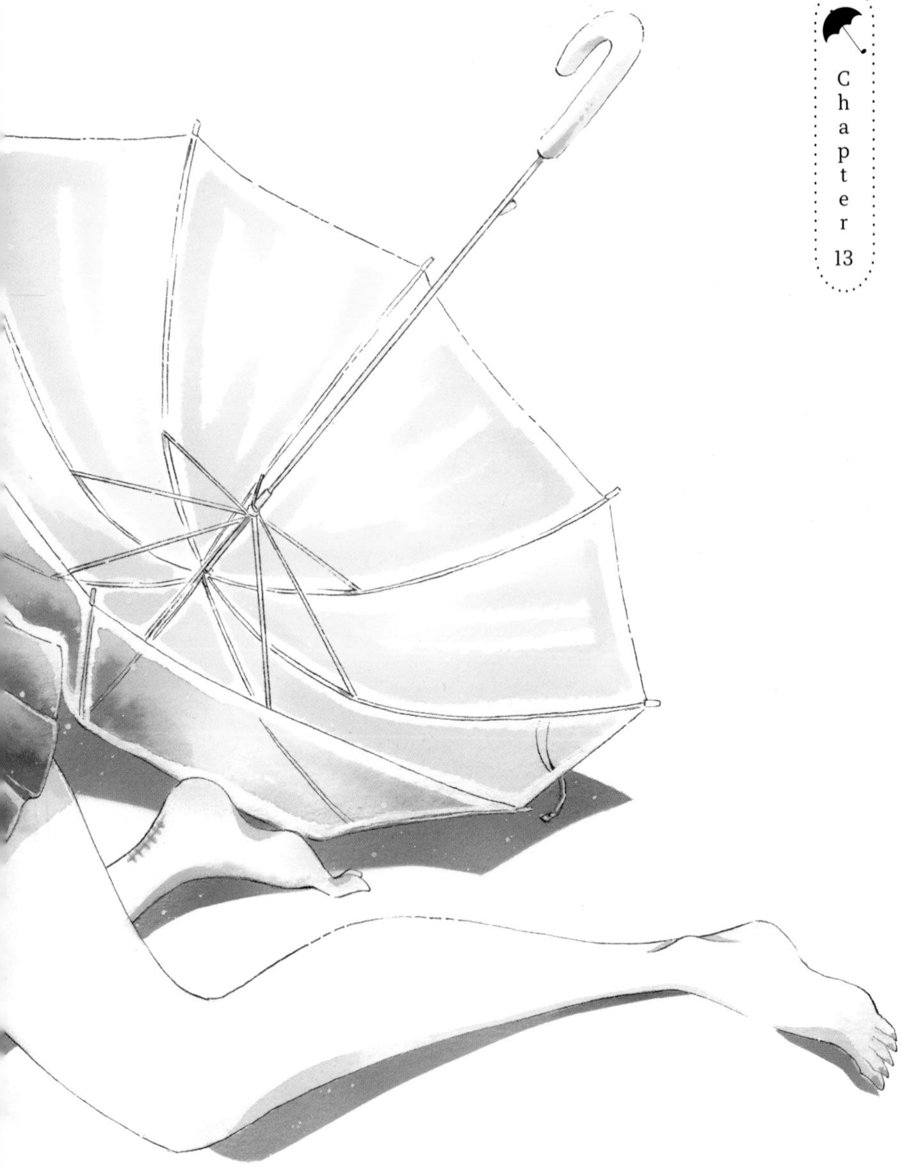

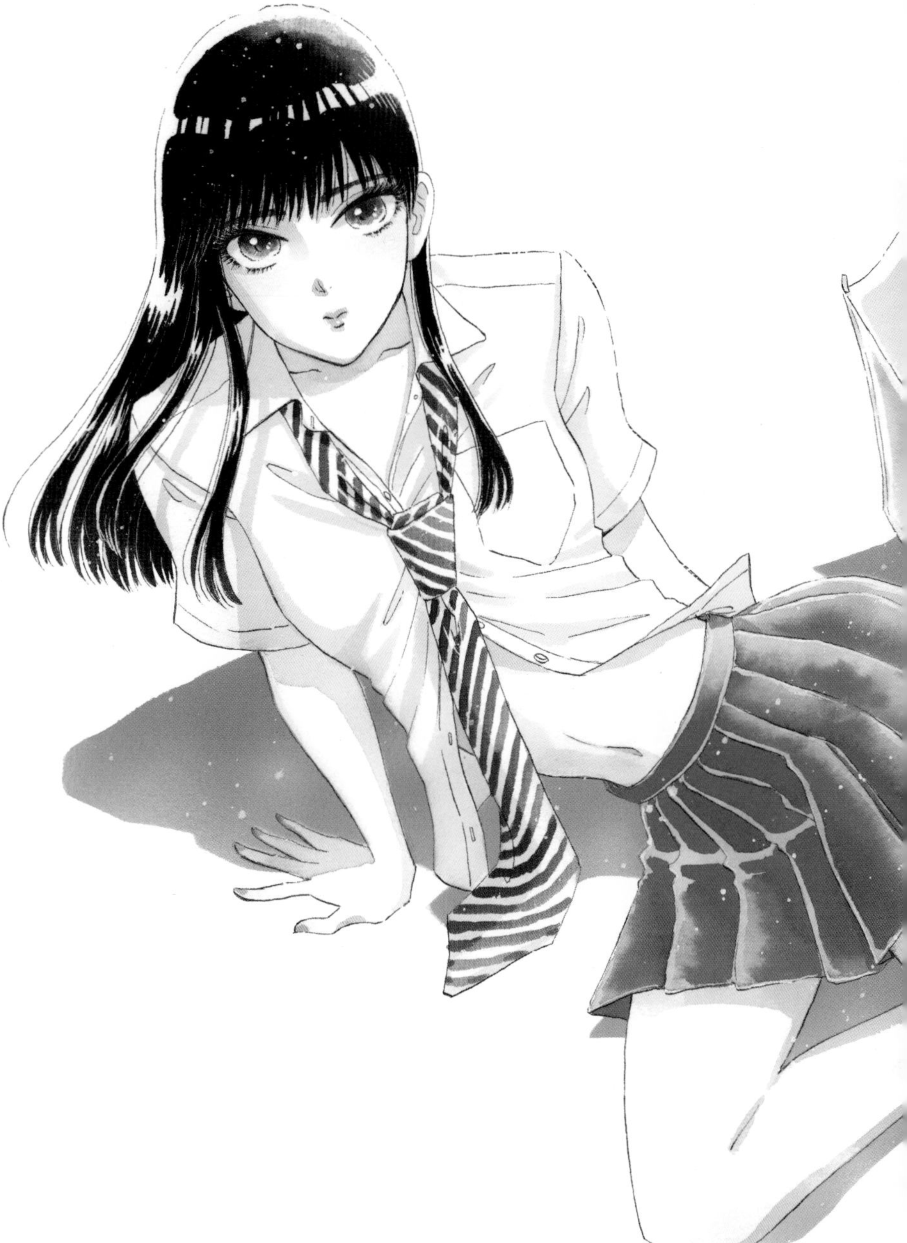

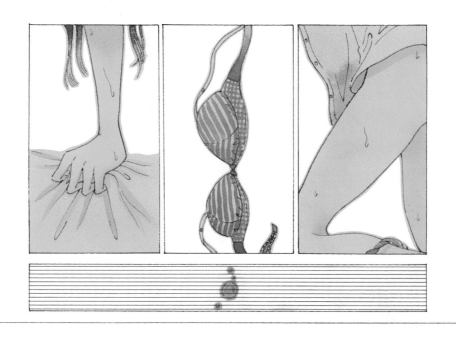

That was your first time for both alcohol and sex, huh?

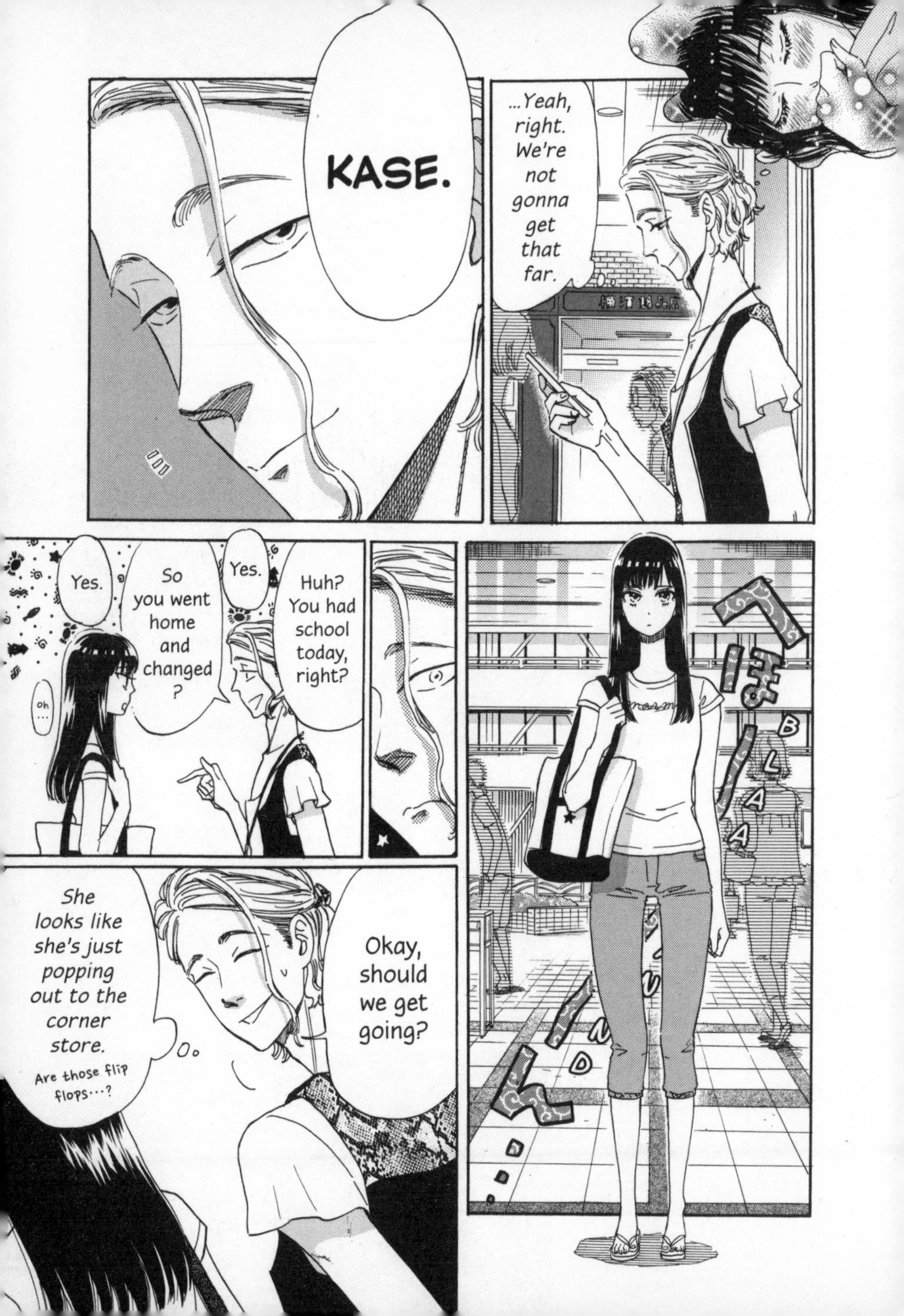
...Yeah, right. We're not gonna get that far.
KASE.
Huh? You had school today, right?
Yes.
So you went home and changed?
Yes.
oh...
Okay, should we get going?
She looks like she's just popping out to the corner store.
Are those flip flops...?

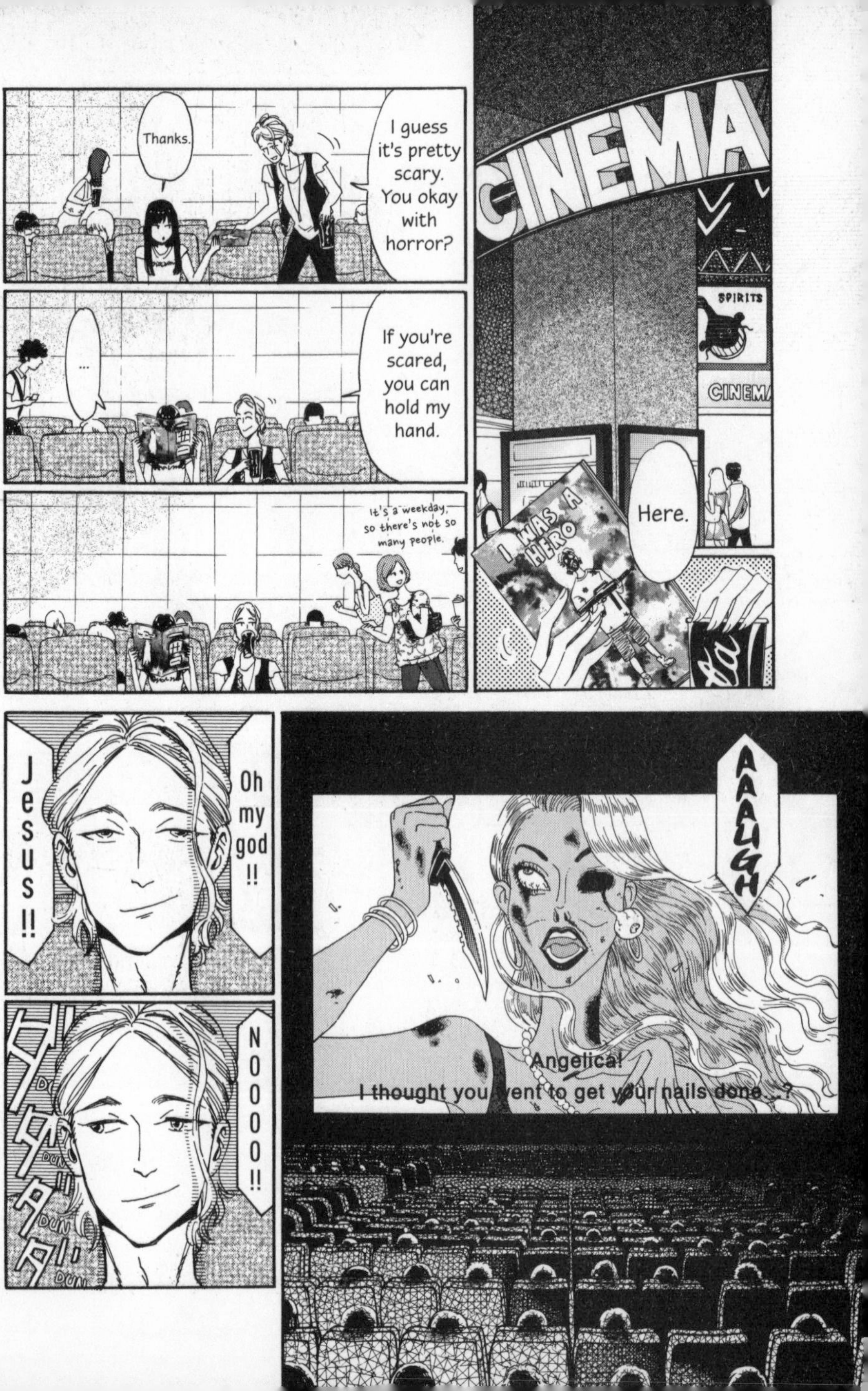
CINEMA
SPIRITS
CINEMA
I WAS A HERO
Here.
I guess it's pretty scary. You okay with horror?
Thanks.
If you're scared, you can hold my hand.
...
It's a weekday, so there's not so many people.
AAAUGH
Angelica!
I thought you went to get your nails done...?
Oh my god!!
Jesus!!
NOOOOO!!
DUN
DUN
DUN
DUN

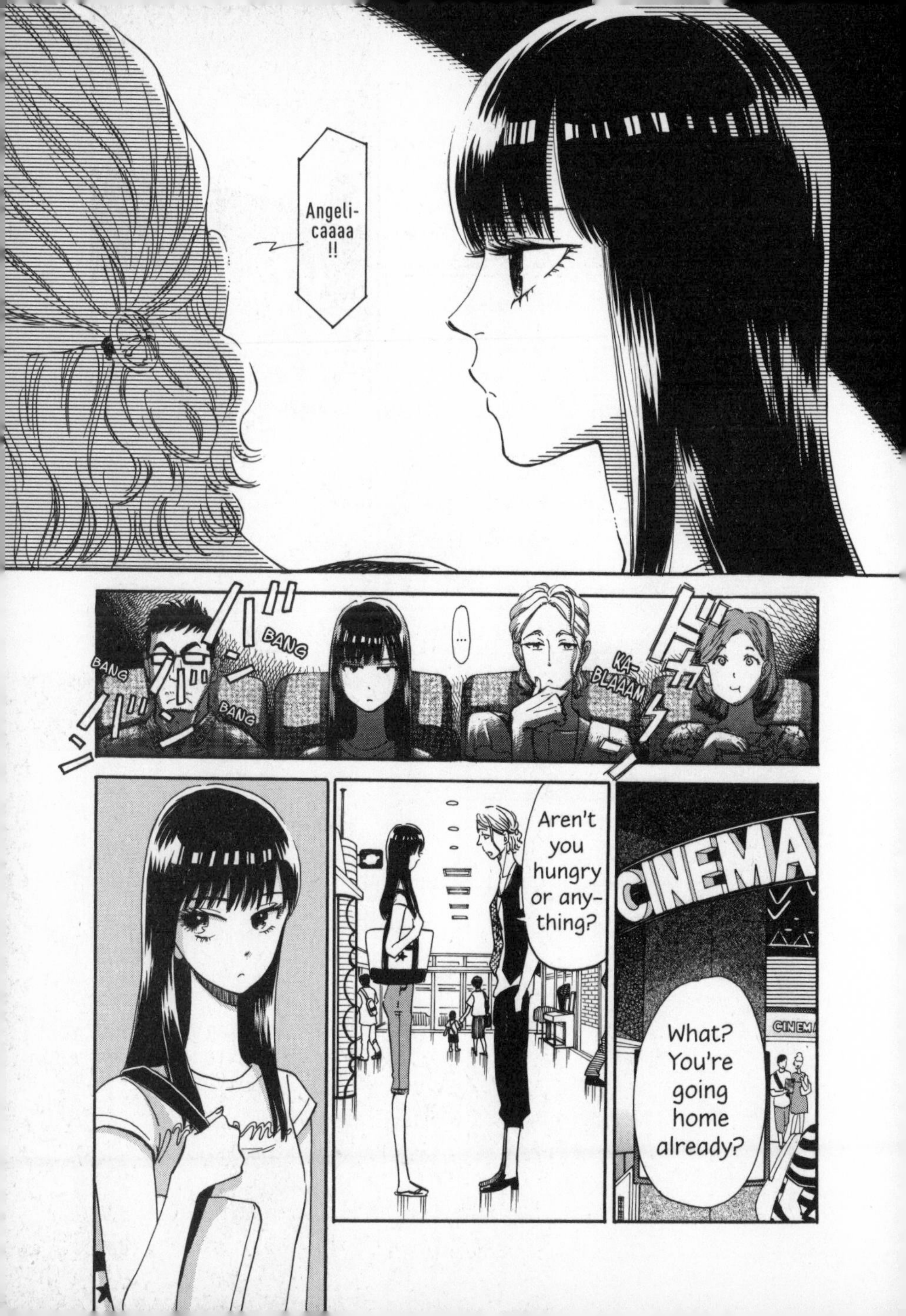
Angeli-caaaa !!
KA-BLAAAM
...
BANG
BANG
BANG
CINEMA
CINEMA
What? You're going home already?
Aren't you hungry or anything?

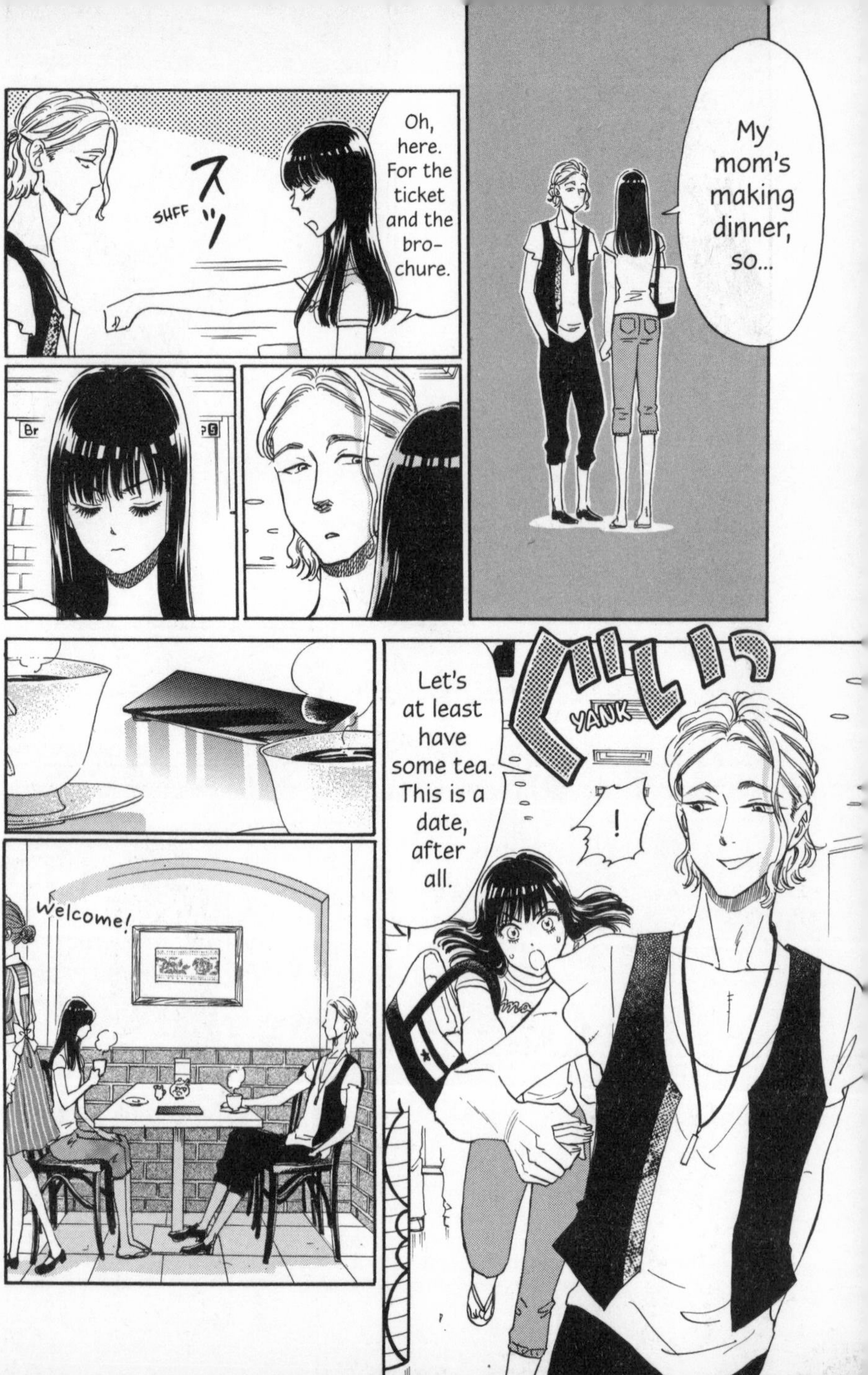
My mom's making dinner, so...
Oh, here. For the ticket and the brochure.
SHFF
スッ
Let's at least have some tea. This is a date, after all.
YANK
!
Welcome!

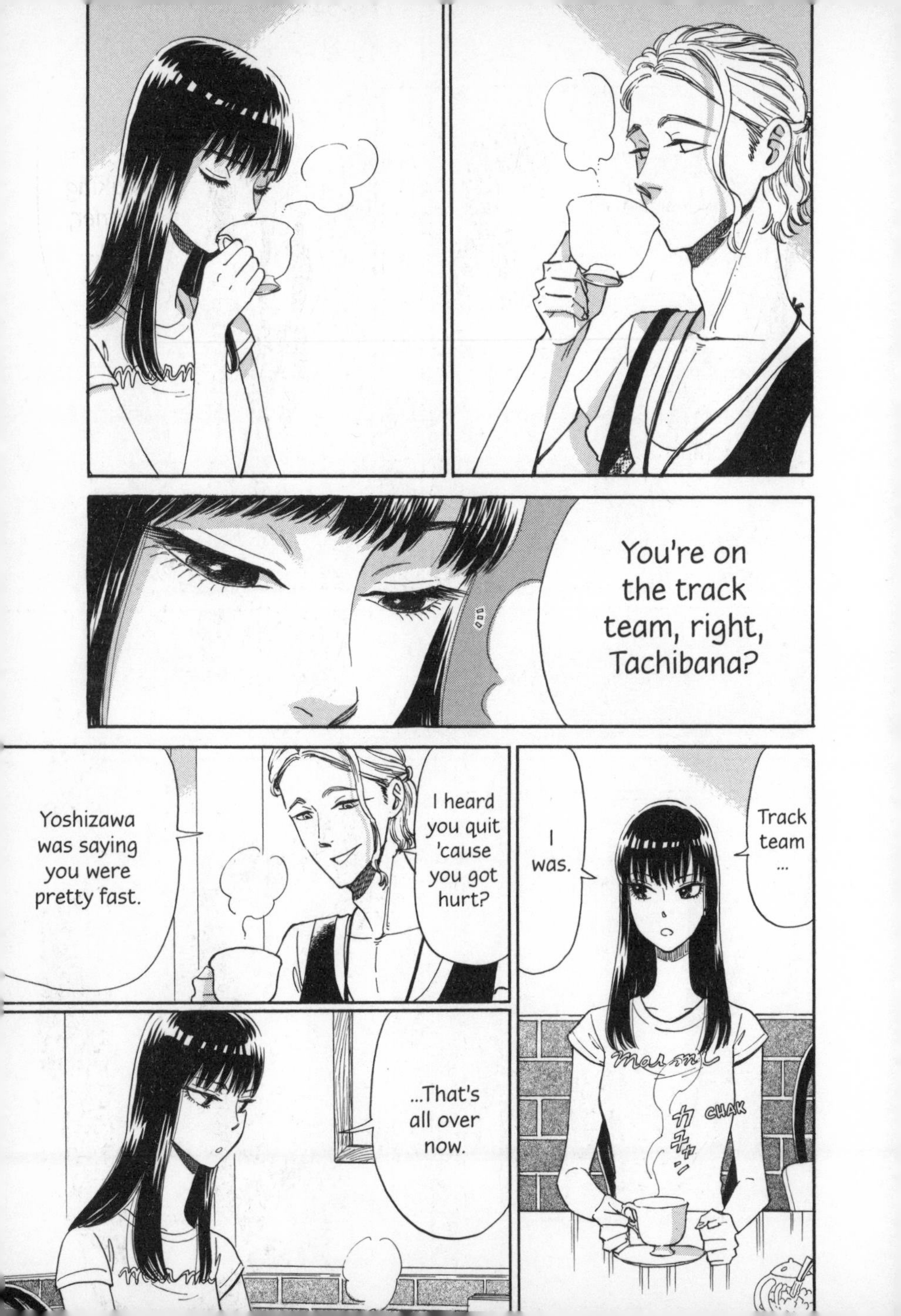
You're on the track team, right, Tachibana?
Track team ...
I was.
I heard you quit 'cause you got hurt?
Yoshizawa was saying you were pretty fast.
CHAK
...That's all over now.

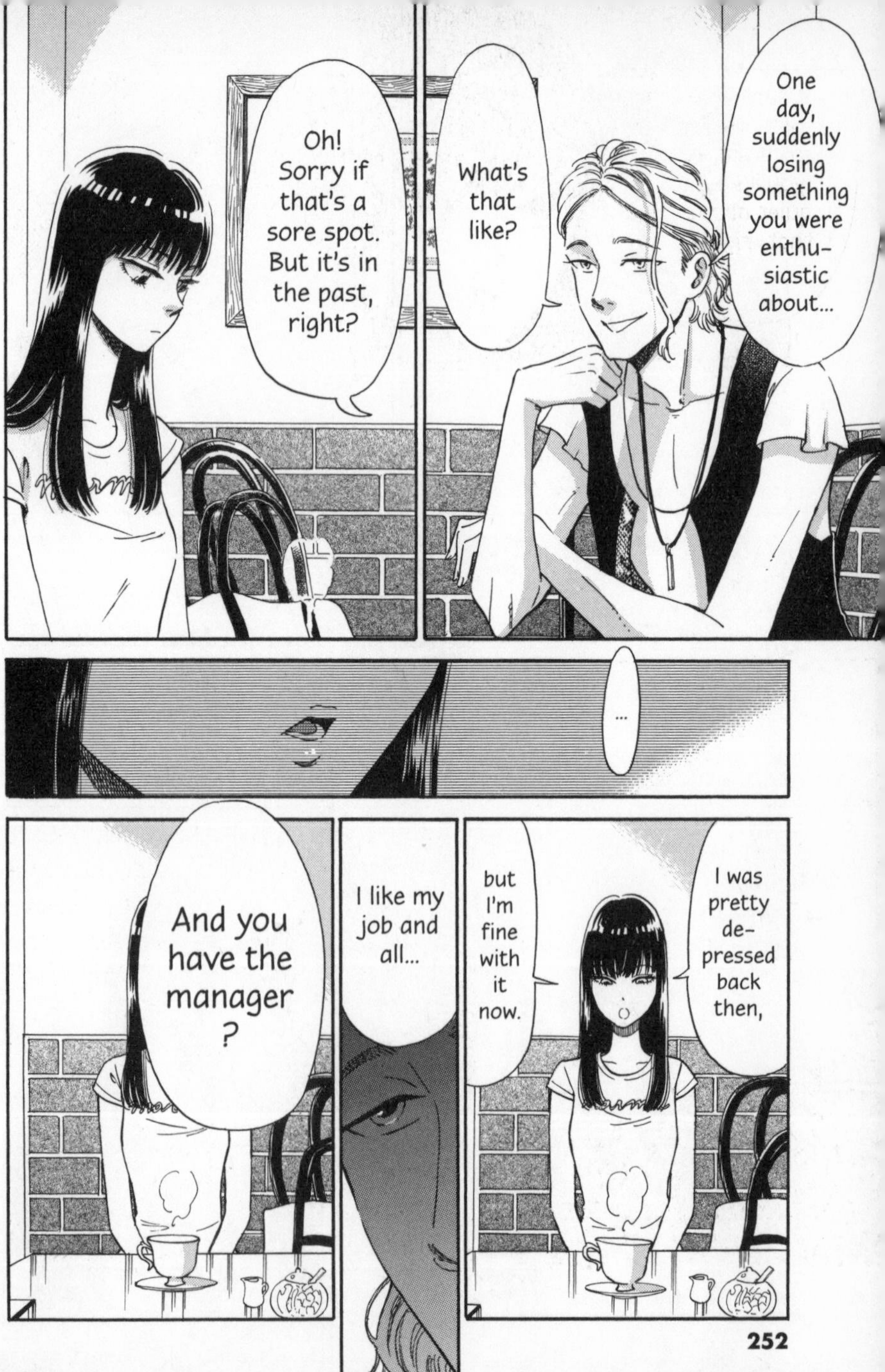
One day, suddenly losing something you were enthu-siastic about...
What's that like?
Oh! Sorry if that's a sore spot. But it's in the past, right?
...
I was pretty de-pressed back then,
but I'm fine with it now.
I like my job and all...
And you have the manager?

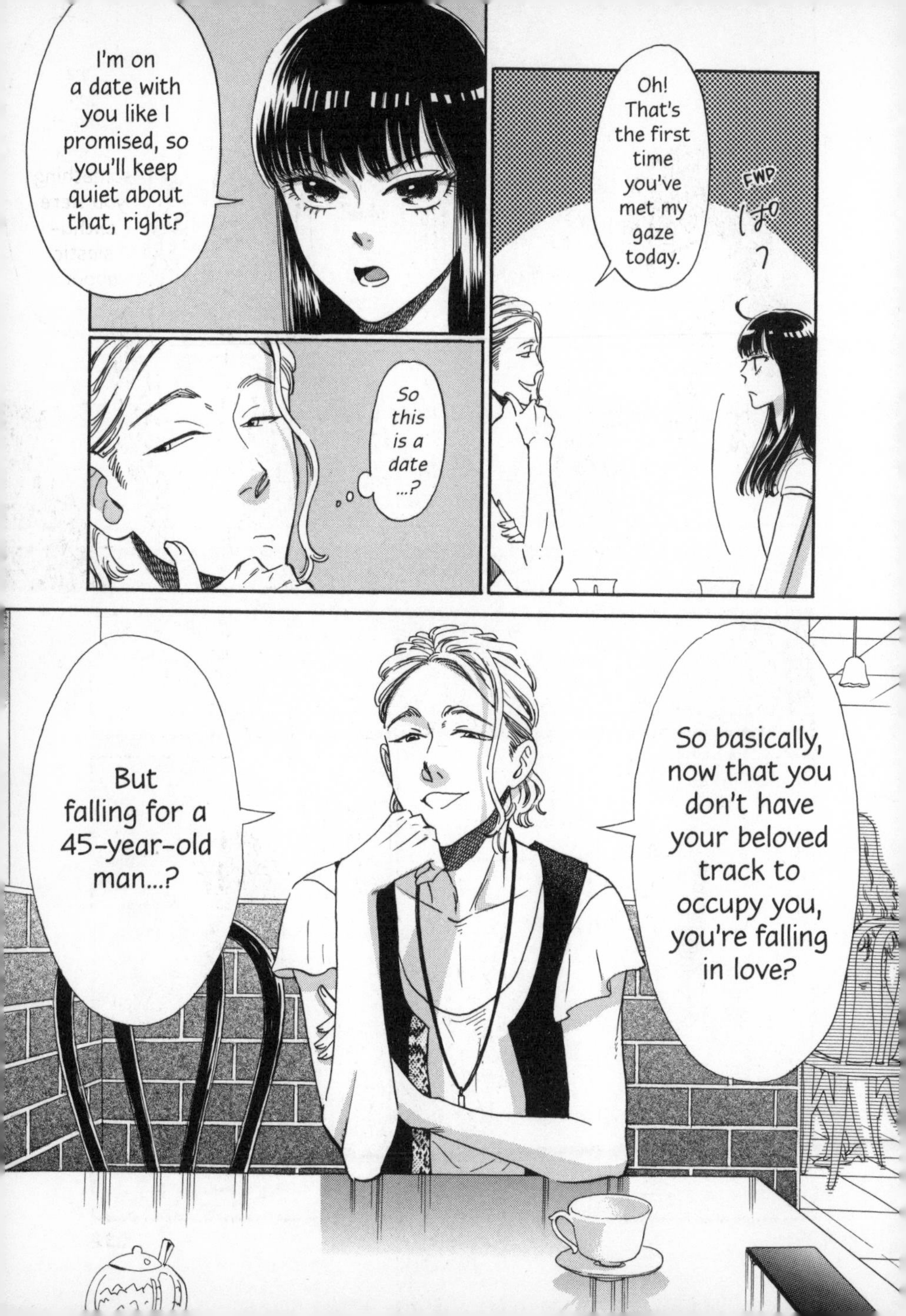
Oh! That's the first time you've met my gaze today.
FWP
I'm on a date with you like I promised, so you'll keep quiet about that, right?
So this is a date ...?
So basically, now that you don't have your beloved track to occupy you, you're falling in love?
But falling for a 45-year-old man...?

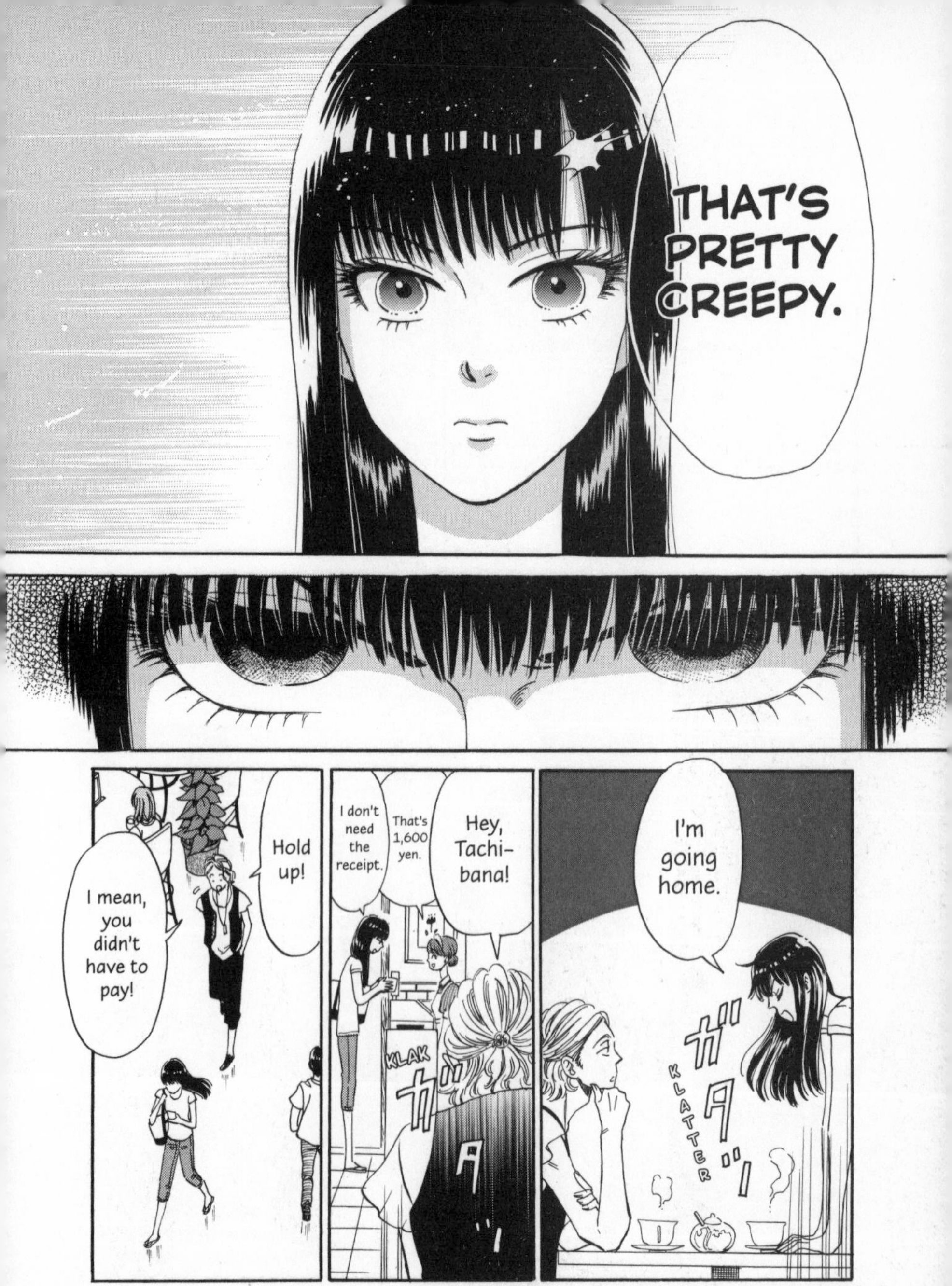
THAT'S PRETTY CREEPY.
I'm going home.
KLATTER
Hey, Tachibana!
That's 1,600 yen.
I don't need the receipt.
KLAK
Hold up!
I mean, you didn't have to pay!

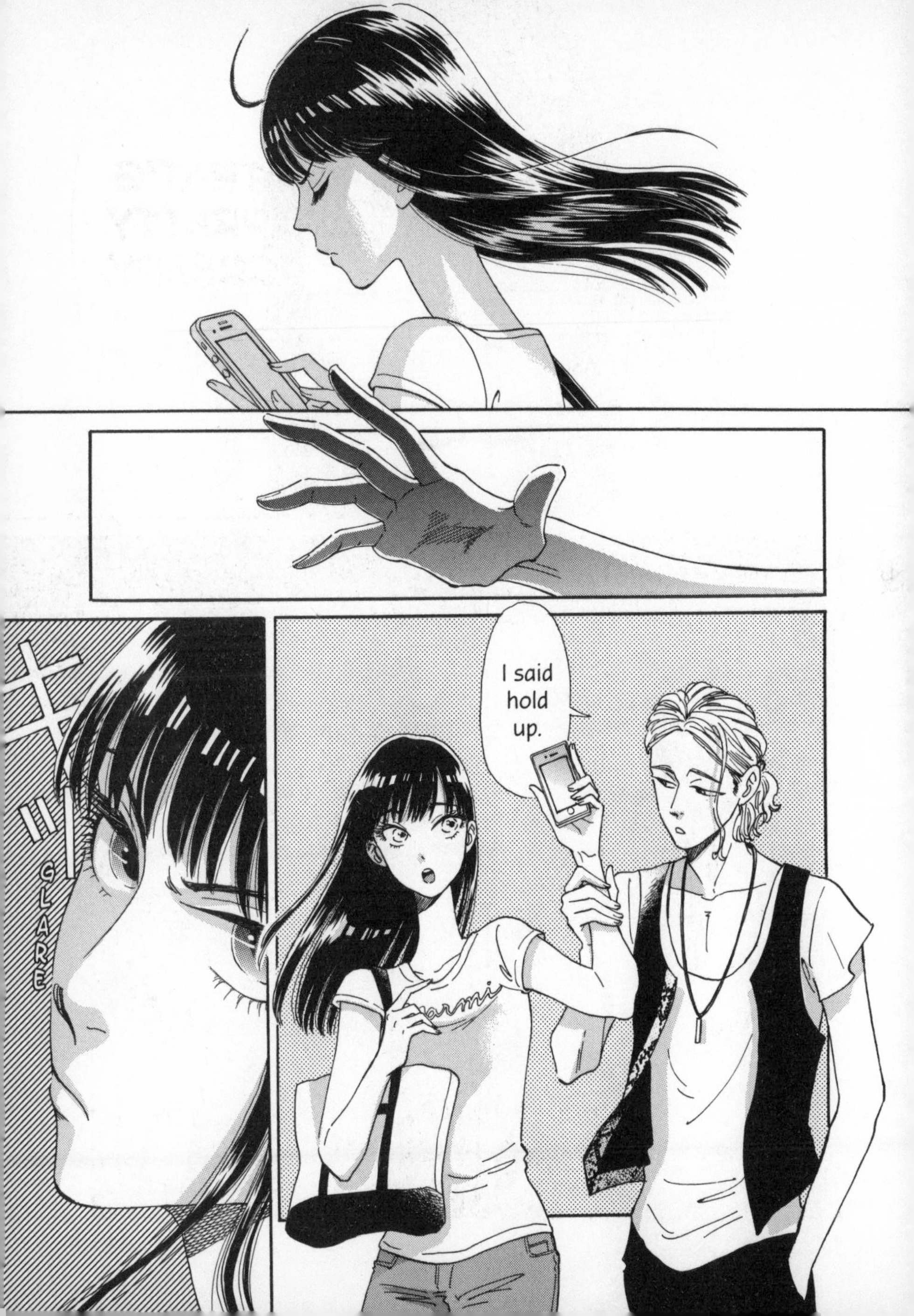
I said hold up.
GLARE

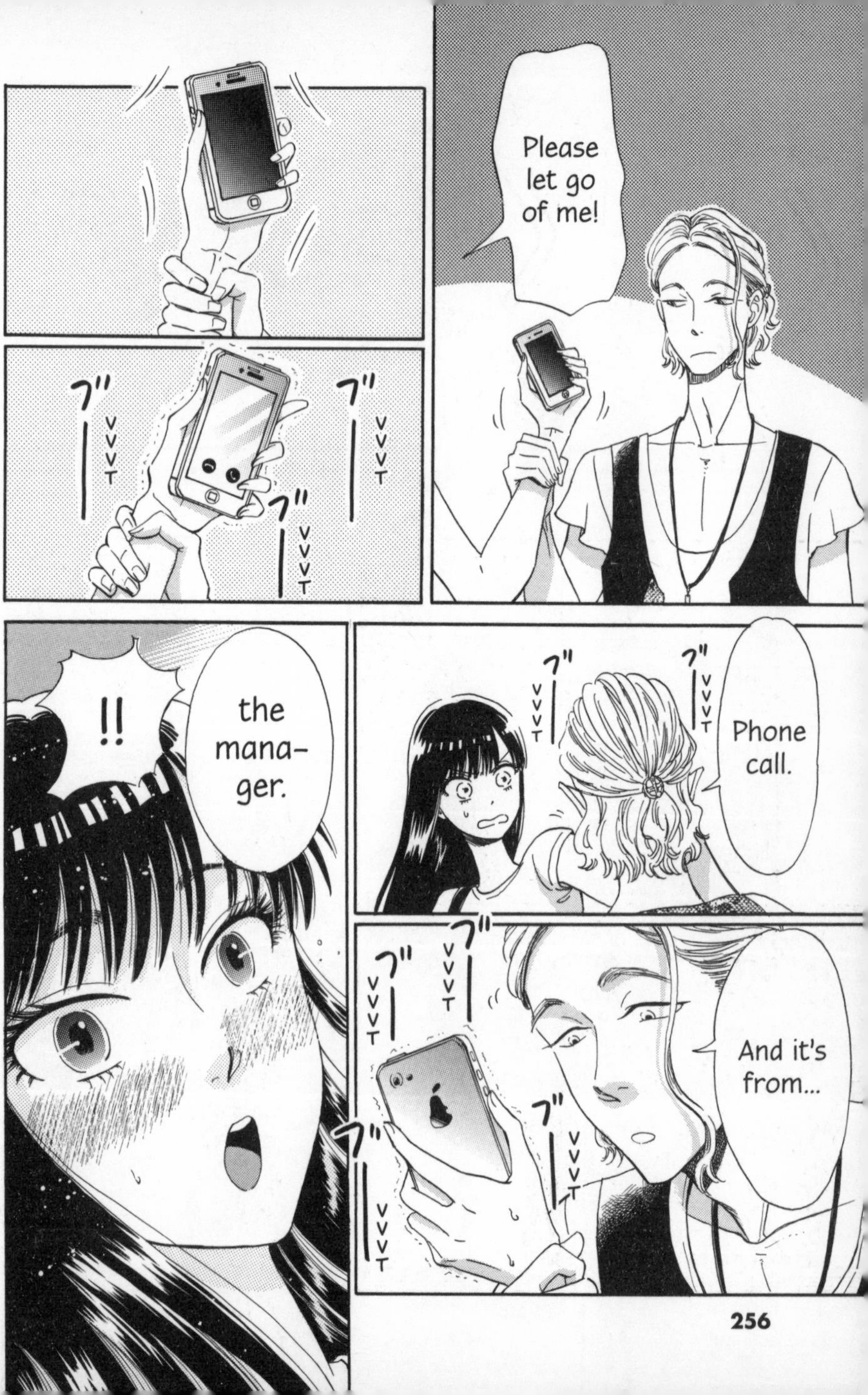

Please let go of me!
ブ VVVT
ブ VVVT
ブ VVVT
ブ VVVT
ブ VVVT
Phone call.
ブ VVVT
ブ VVVT
ブ VVVT
ブ VVVT
And it's from...
the mana-ger.
!!

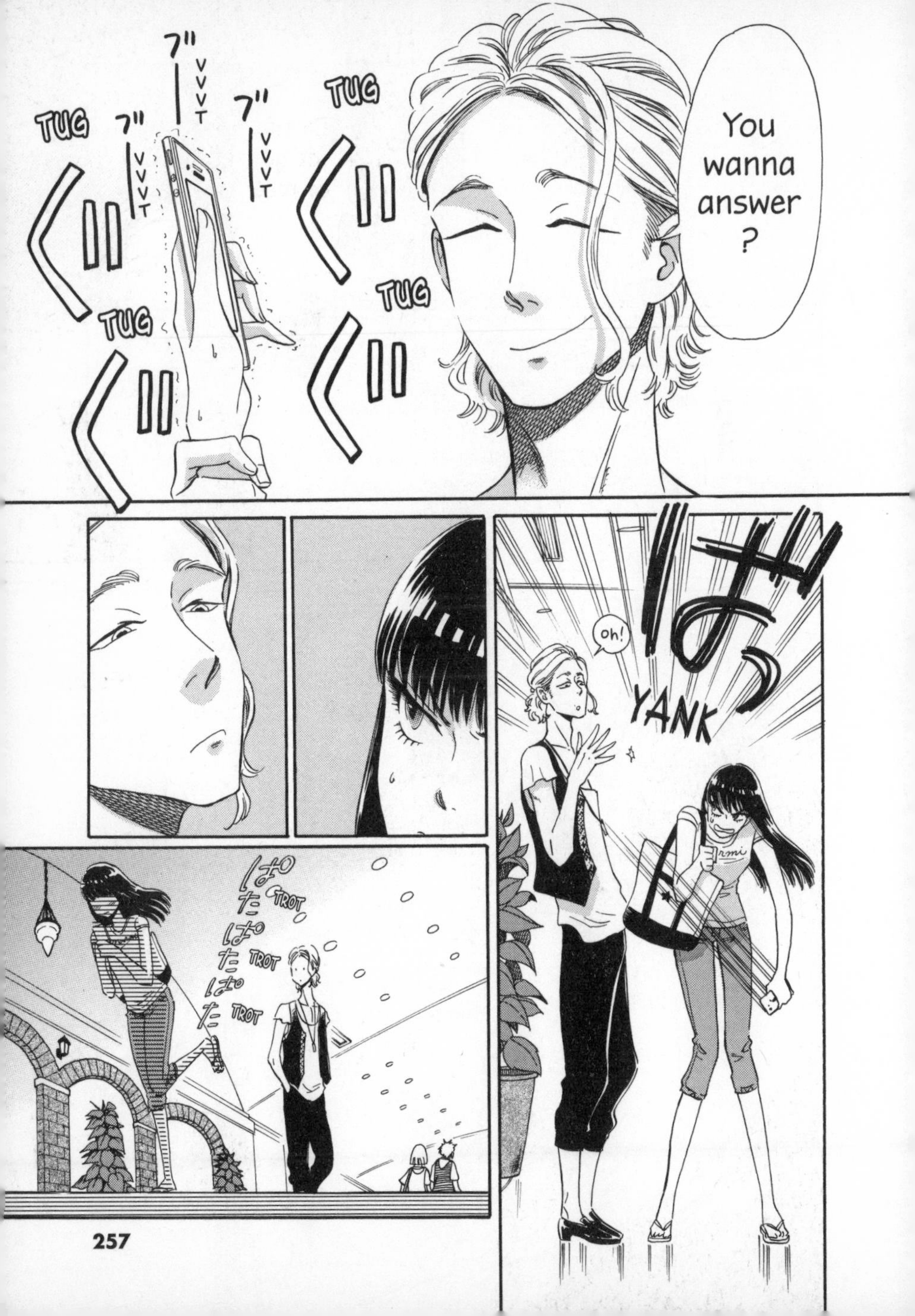

You wanna answer?
くい
TUG
くい
TUG
ブ
VVVT
ブ
VVVT
ブ
VVVT
くい
TUG
くい
TUG
ばっ
YANK
oh!
ぱたぱたぱた
TROT
TROT
TROT

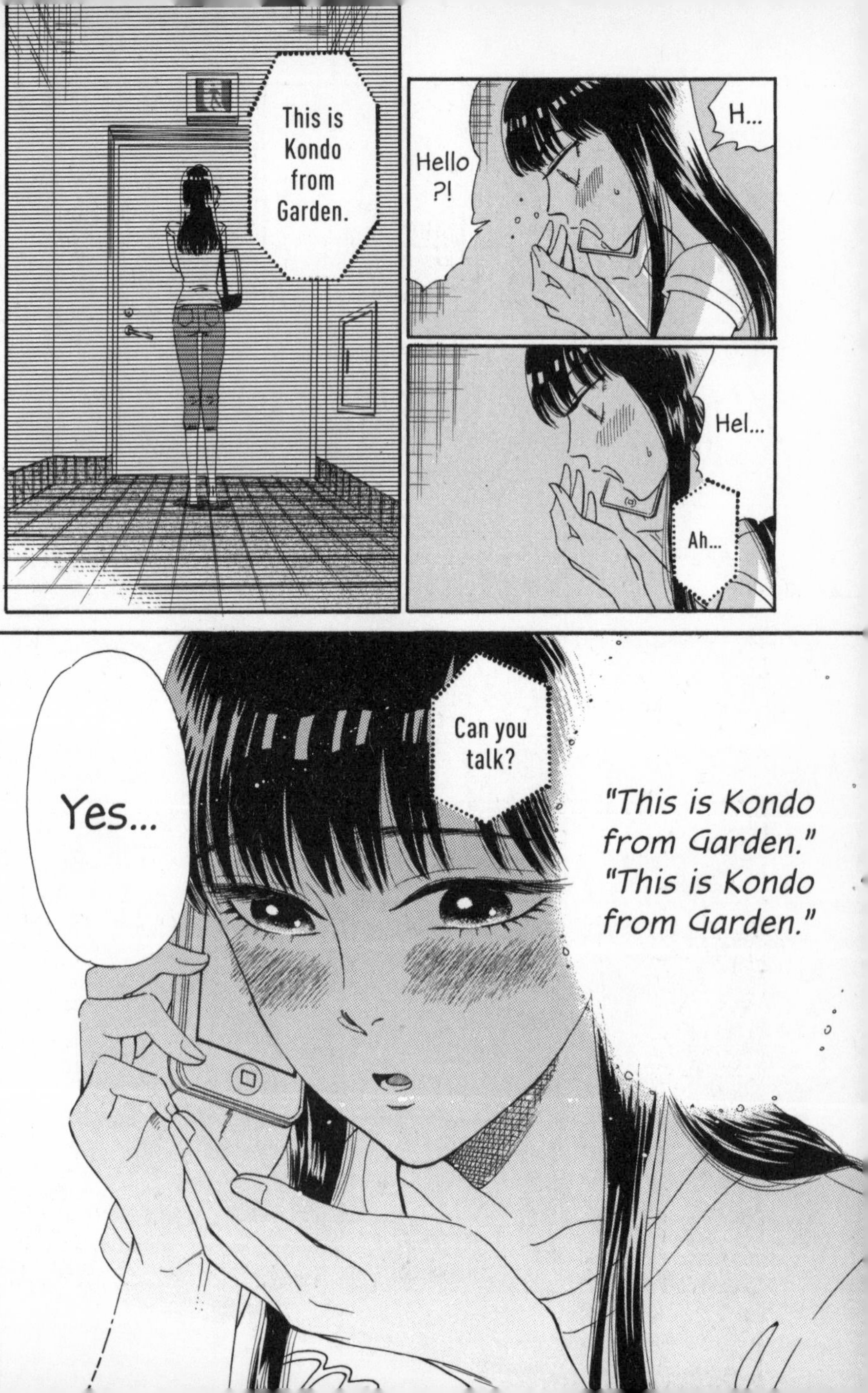
H...
Hello ?!
Hel...
Ah...
This is Kondo from Garden.
"This is Kondo from Garden." "This is Kondo from Garden."
Can you talk?
Yes...

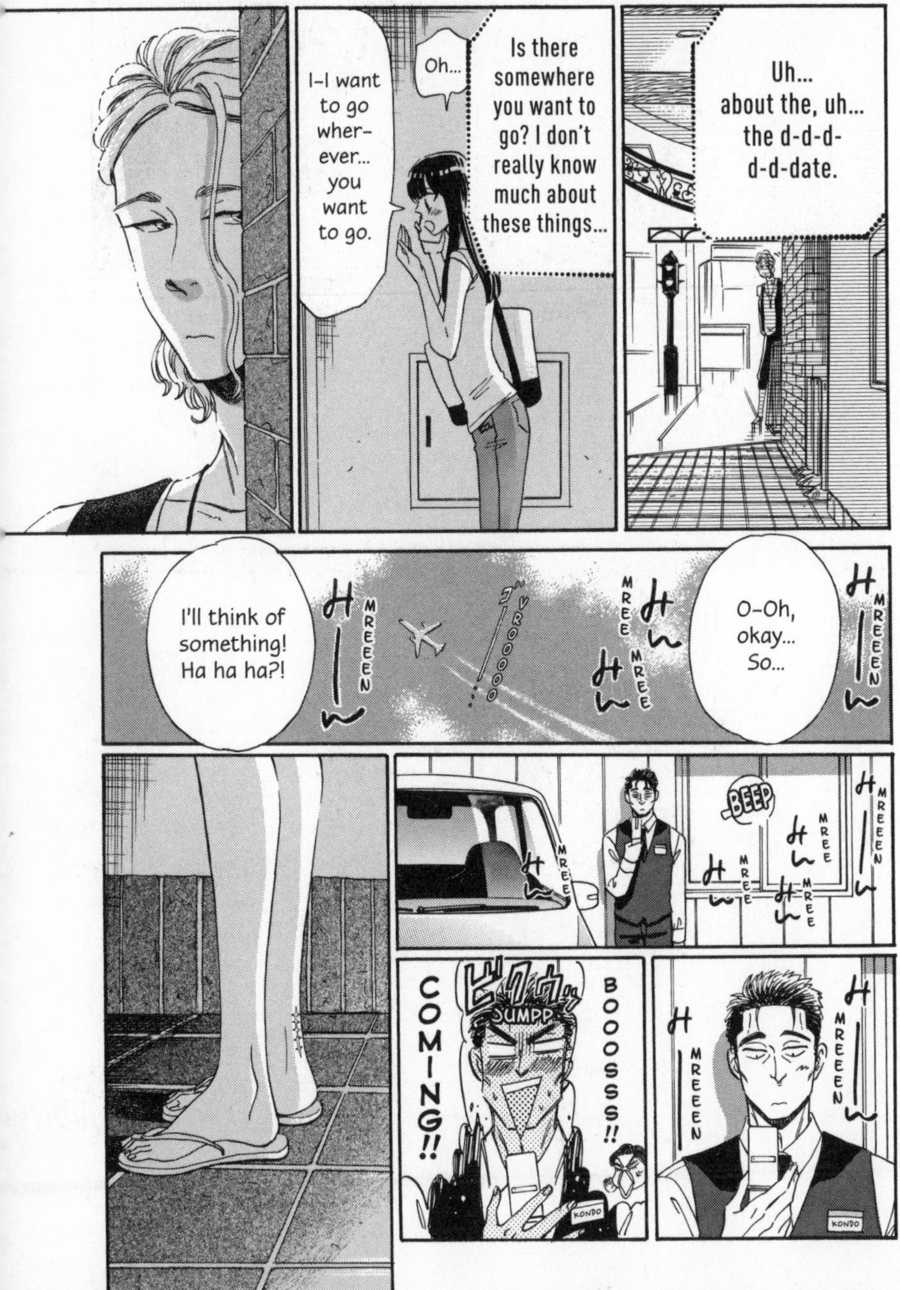
Uh... about the, uh... the d-d-d-d-d-date.
Is there somewhere you want to go? I don't really know much about these things...
Oh...
I-I want to go wher-ever... you want to go.
MREEEN
O-Oh, okay... So...
MREE
MREE
VROOOOOO
MREEEN
I'll think of something! Ha ha ha?!
MREEEN
MREE
BEEP
MREE
MREE
MREE
MREEEN
MREEEN
KONDO
BOOOSSS!!
SUMPP
COMING!!
KONDO

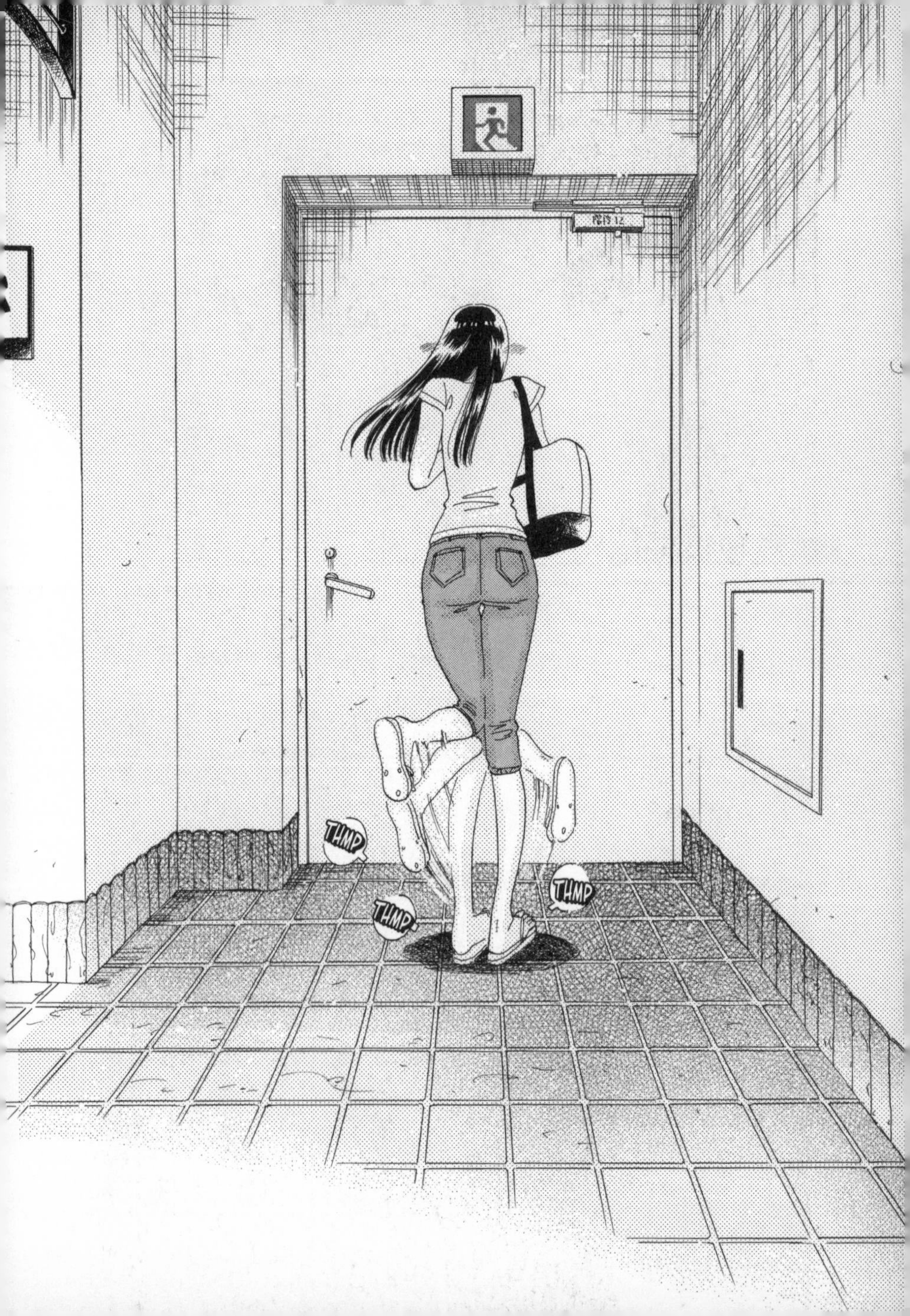
THMP
THMP
THMP

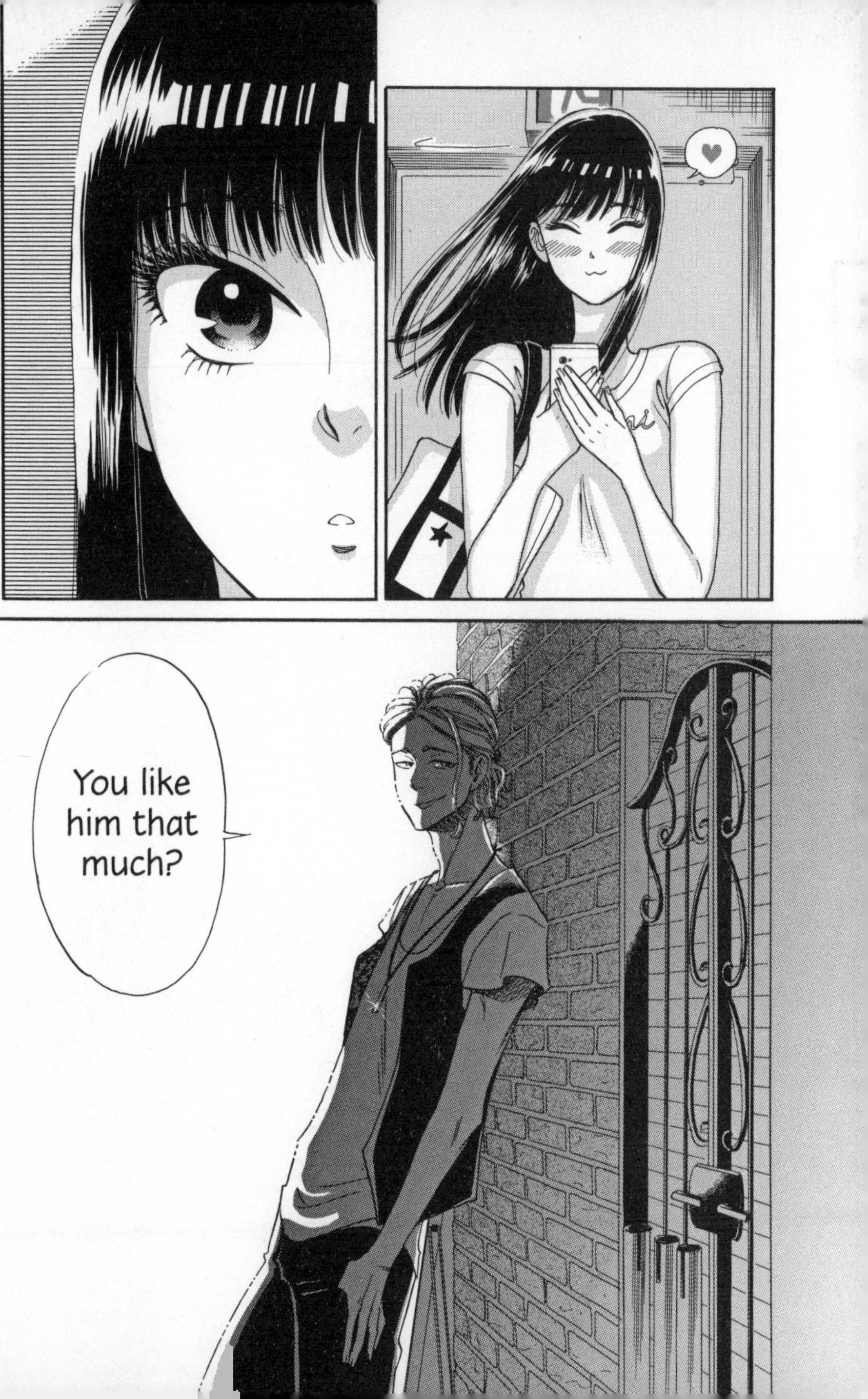
You like him that much?

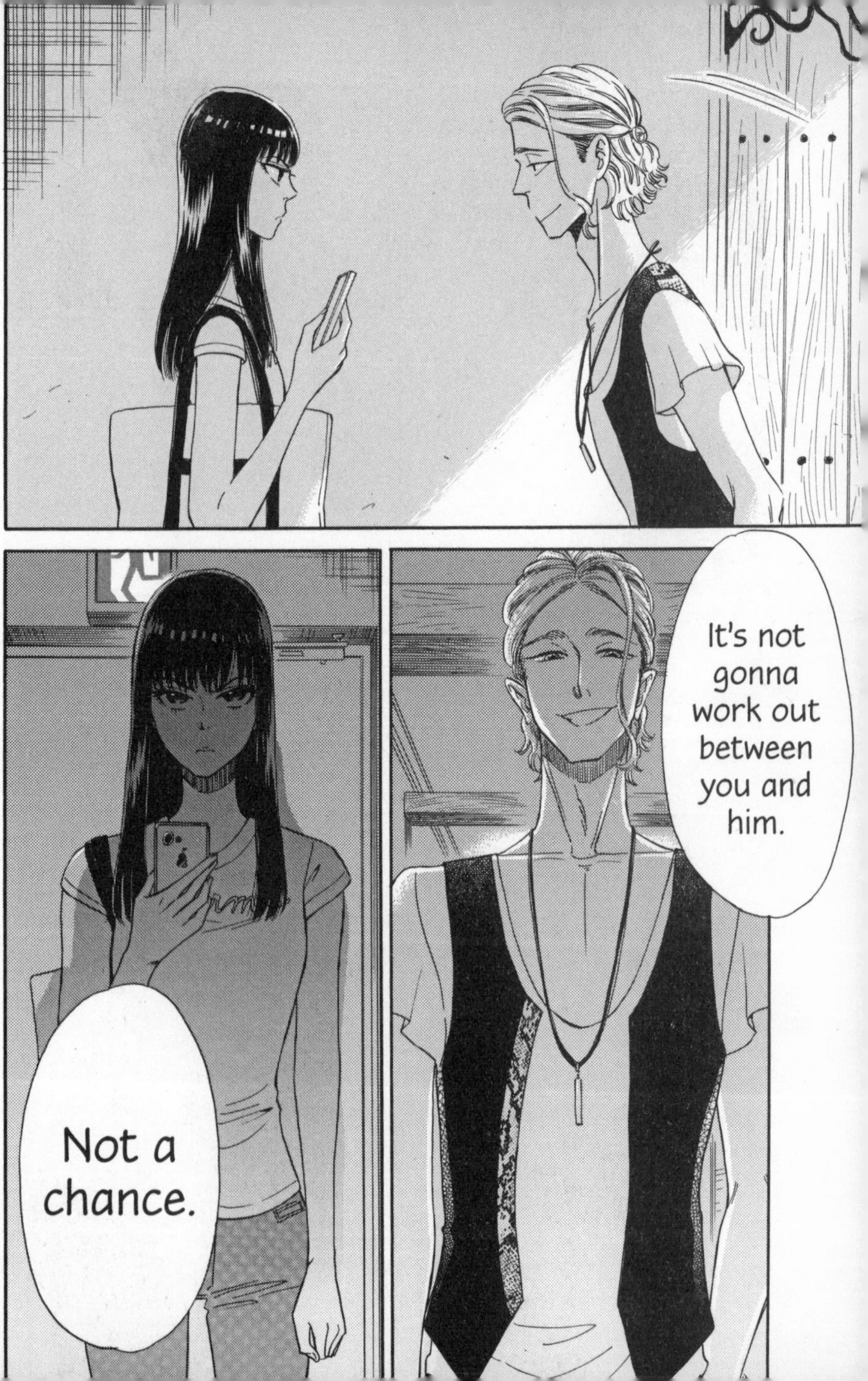
It's not gonna work out between you and him.
Not a chance.

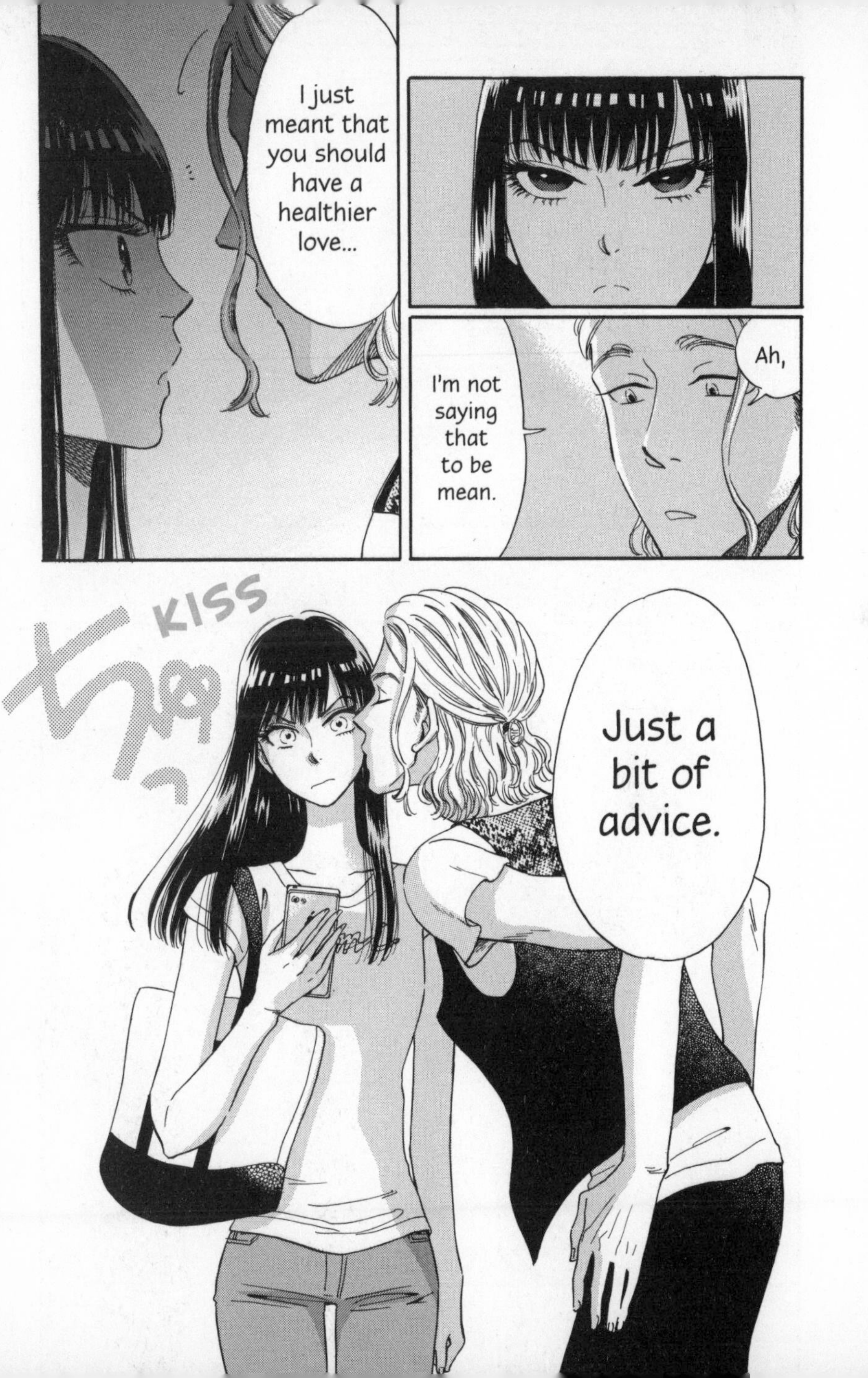
Ah,
I'm not saying that to be mean.
I just meant that you should have a healthier love...
Just a bit of advice.
KISS
ちゅっ

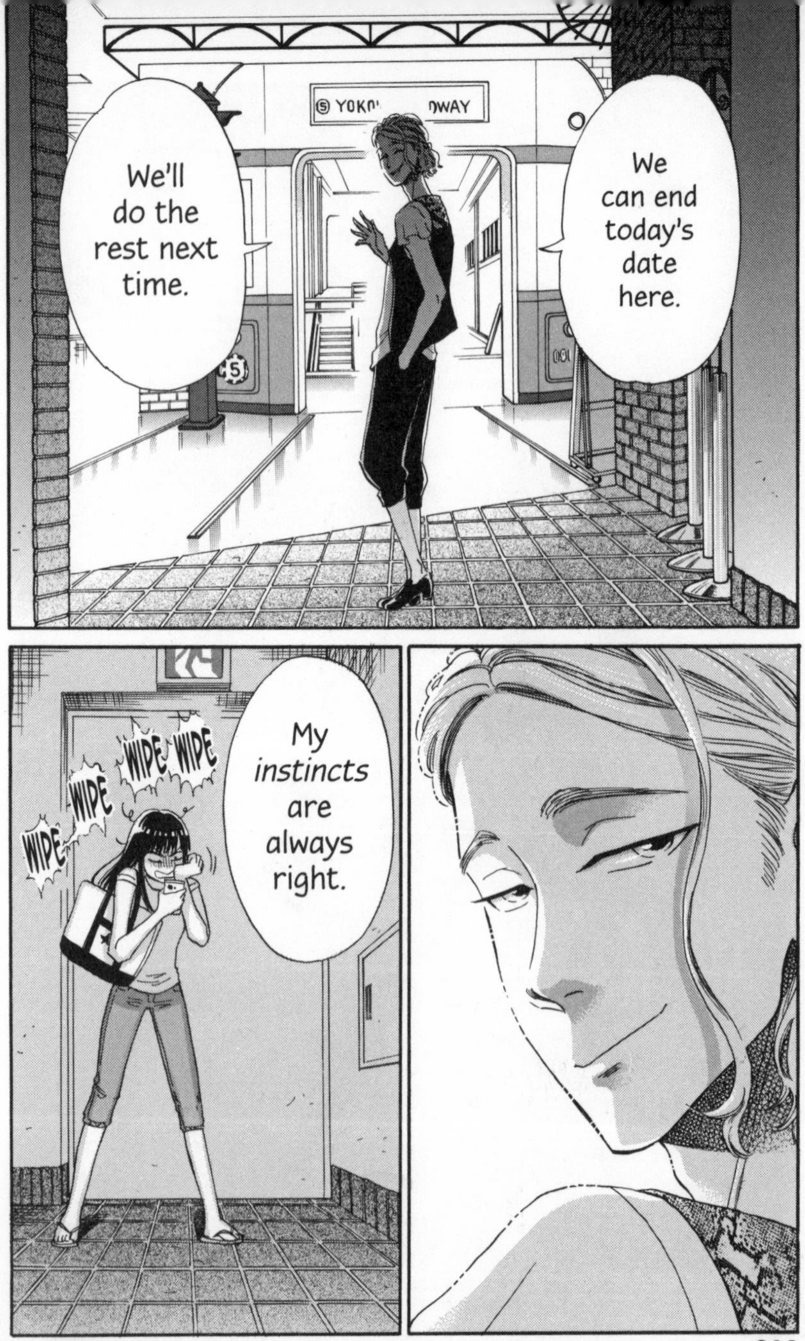
We can end today's date here.
We'll do the rest next time.
My *instincts* are always right.
WIPE WIPE
WIPE
WIPE

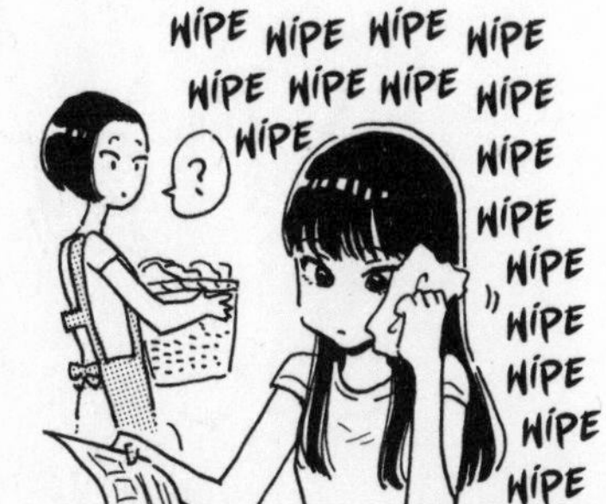
?
WIPE WIPE WIPE WIPE
WIPE WIPE WIPE WIPE
WIPE
WIPE
WIPE
WIPE
WIPE
WIPE
WIPE
WIPE

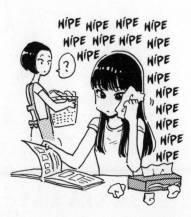

After the Rain

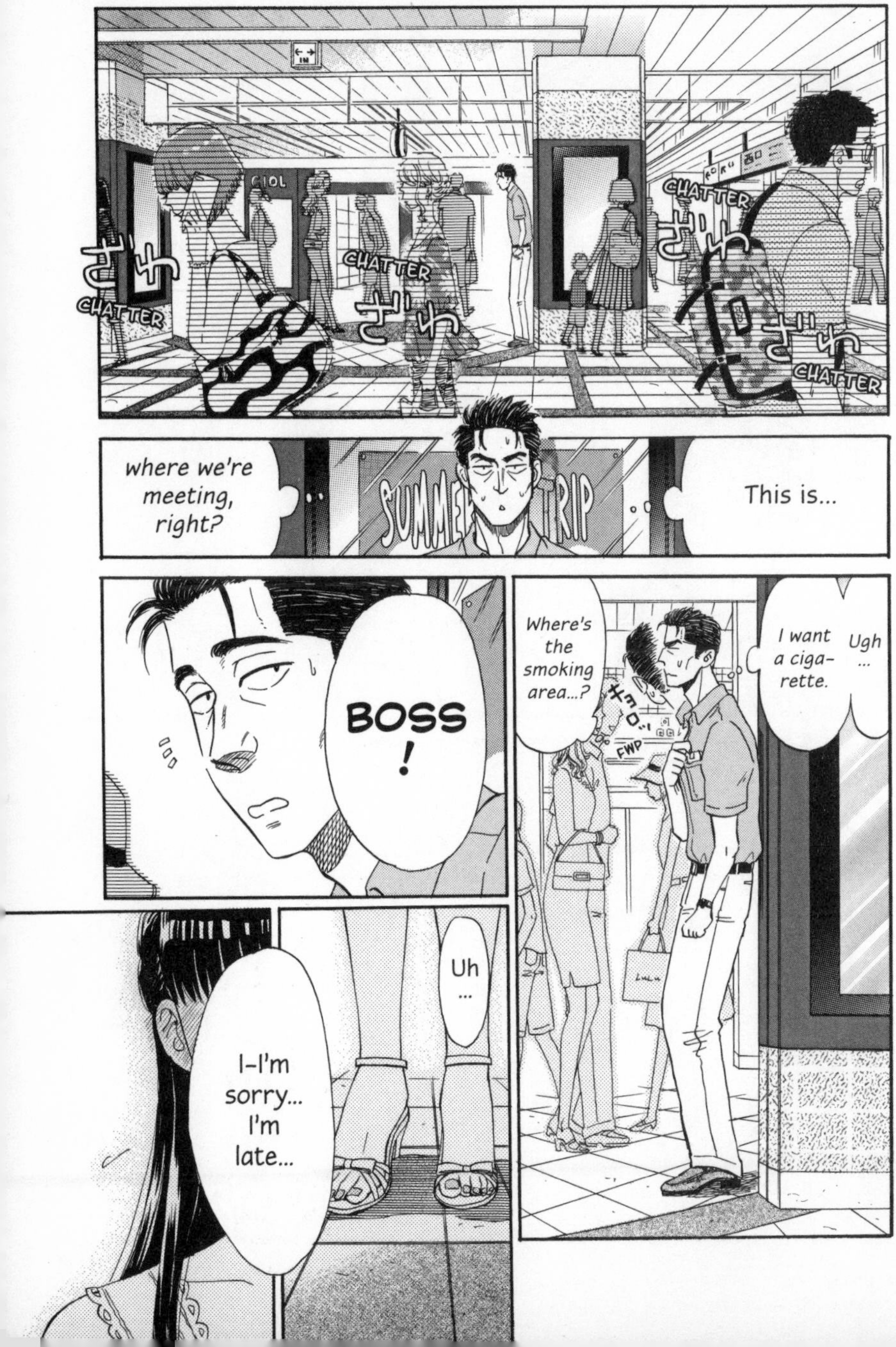
CHATTER
ざわ
ざわ
CHATTER
CHATTER
ざわ
ざわ
CHATTER
This is...
where we're meeting, right?
Ugh ...
I want a ciga-rette.
Where's the smoking area...?
キョロッ
FWP
BOSS !
Uh ...
I-I'm sorry... I'm late...

Chapter 14

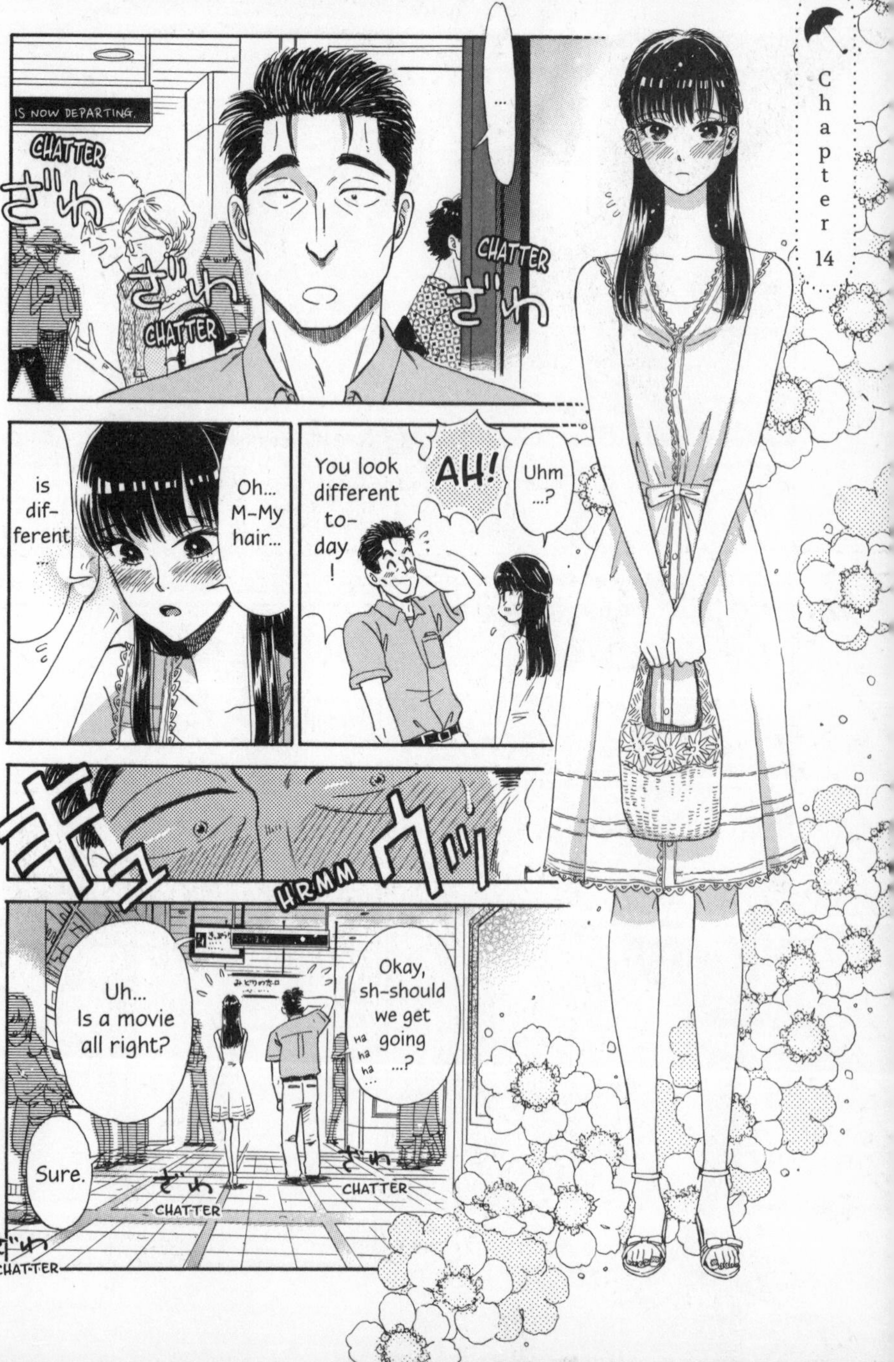

...
IS NOW DEPARTING.
CHATTER
ざわ
CHATTER
ざわ
CHATTER
ざわ
Uhm ...?
AH!
You look different to-day!
Oh... M-My hair...
is dif-ferent...
ギュ ウッ
HRMM
Okay, sh-should we get going ...?
Ha ha ha...
Uh... Is a movie all right?
Sure.
ざわ
CHATTER
ざわ
CHATTER
ざわ
CHAT-TER

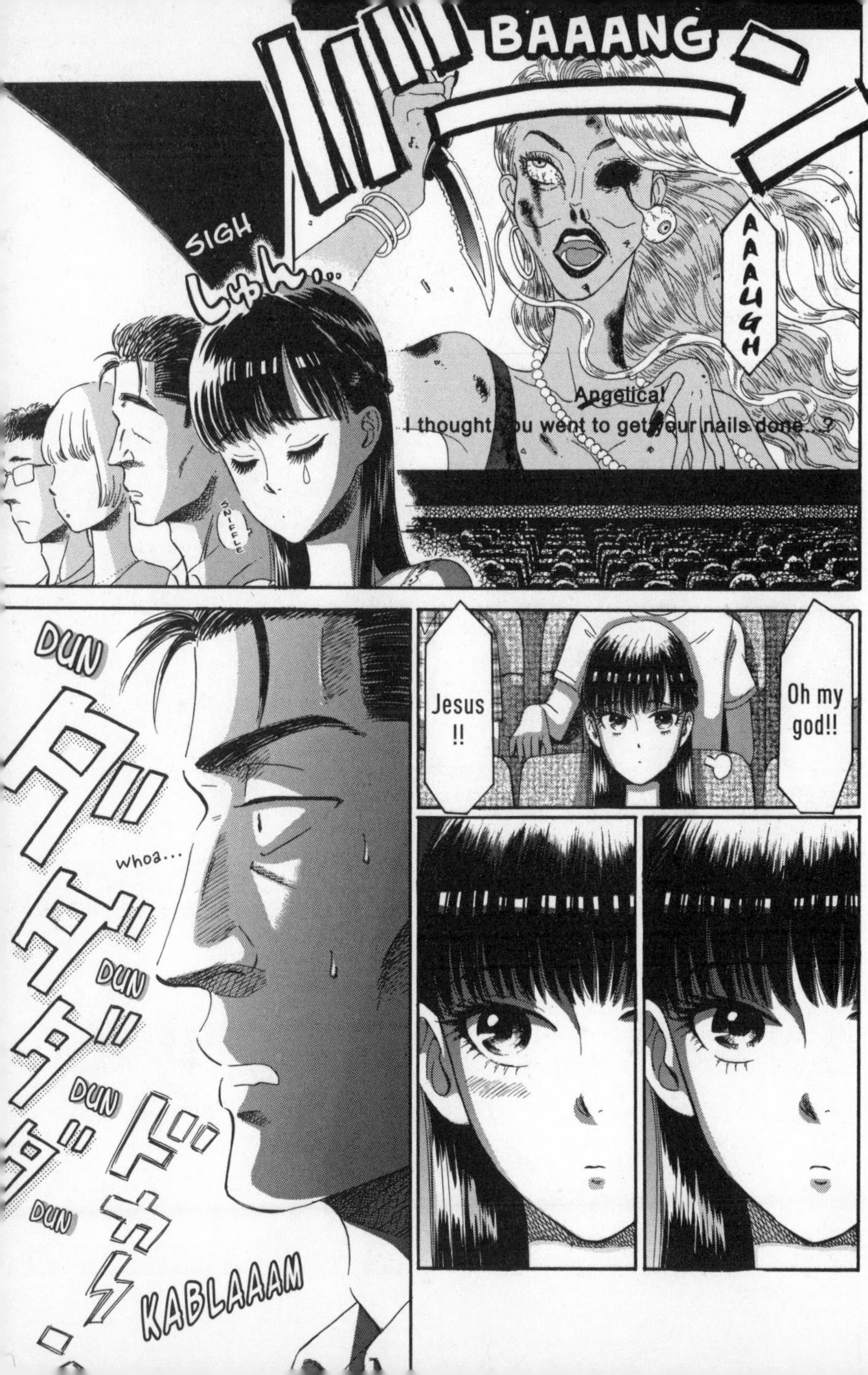
BAAANG
AAAUGH
Angelica!
I thought you went to get your nails done...?
SIGH
しゅん…
SNIFFLE
Oh my god!!
Jesus !!
DUN
whoa...
DUN
DUN
DUN
KABLAAAM

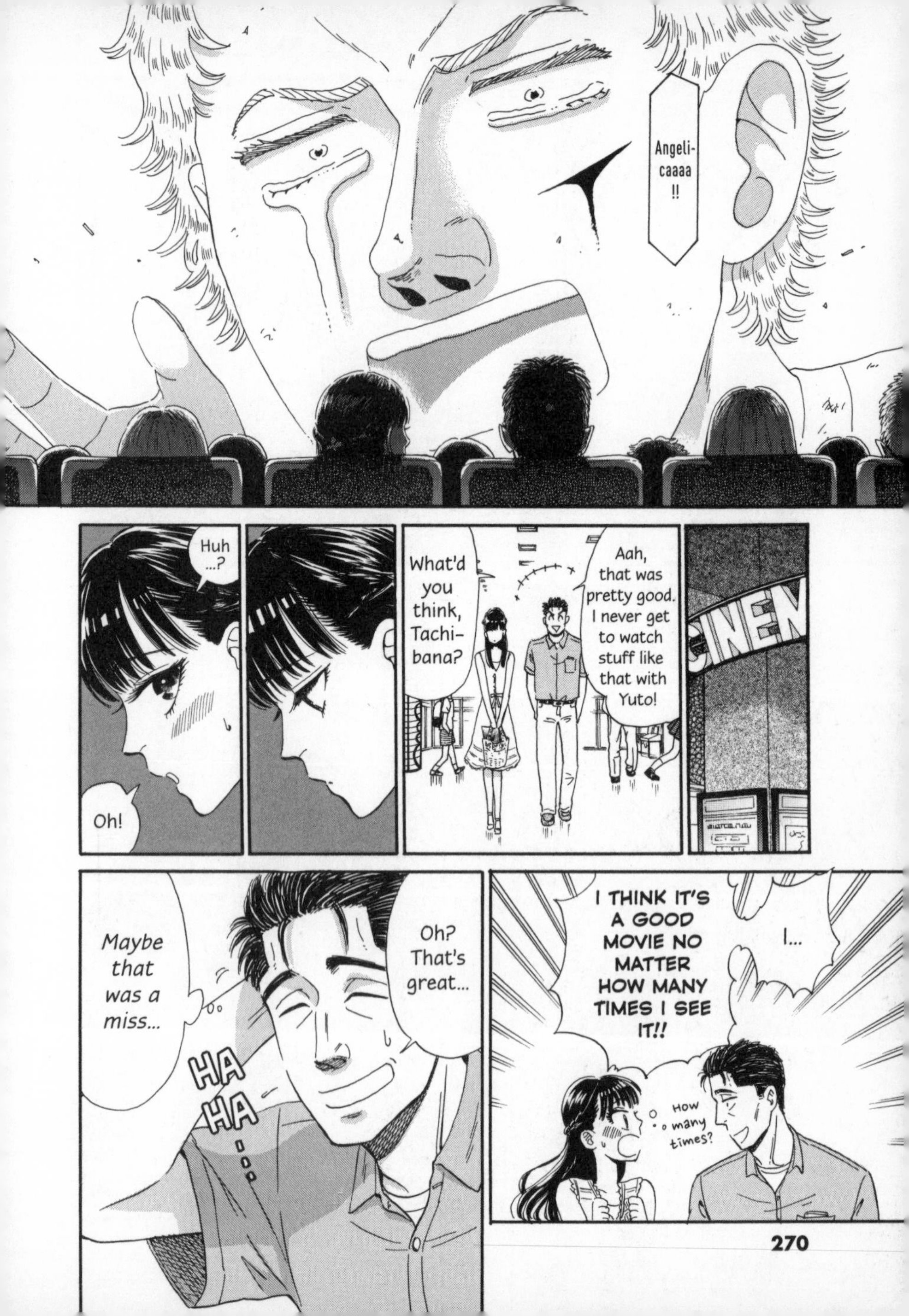
Angeli-caaaa !!
Aah, that was pretty good. I never get to watch stuff like that with Yuto!
What'd you think, Tachibana?
Huh ...?
Oh!
I...
I THINK IT'S A GOOD MOVIE NO MATTER HOW MANY TIMES I SEE IT!!
How many times?
Oh? That's great...
HA HA ...
Maybe that was a miss...

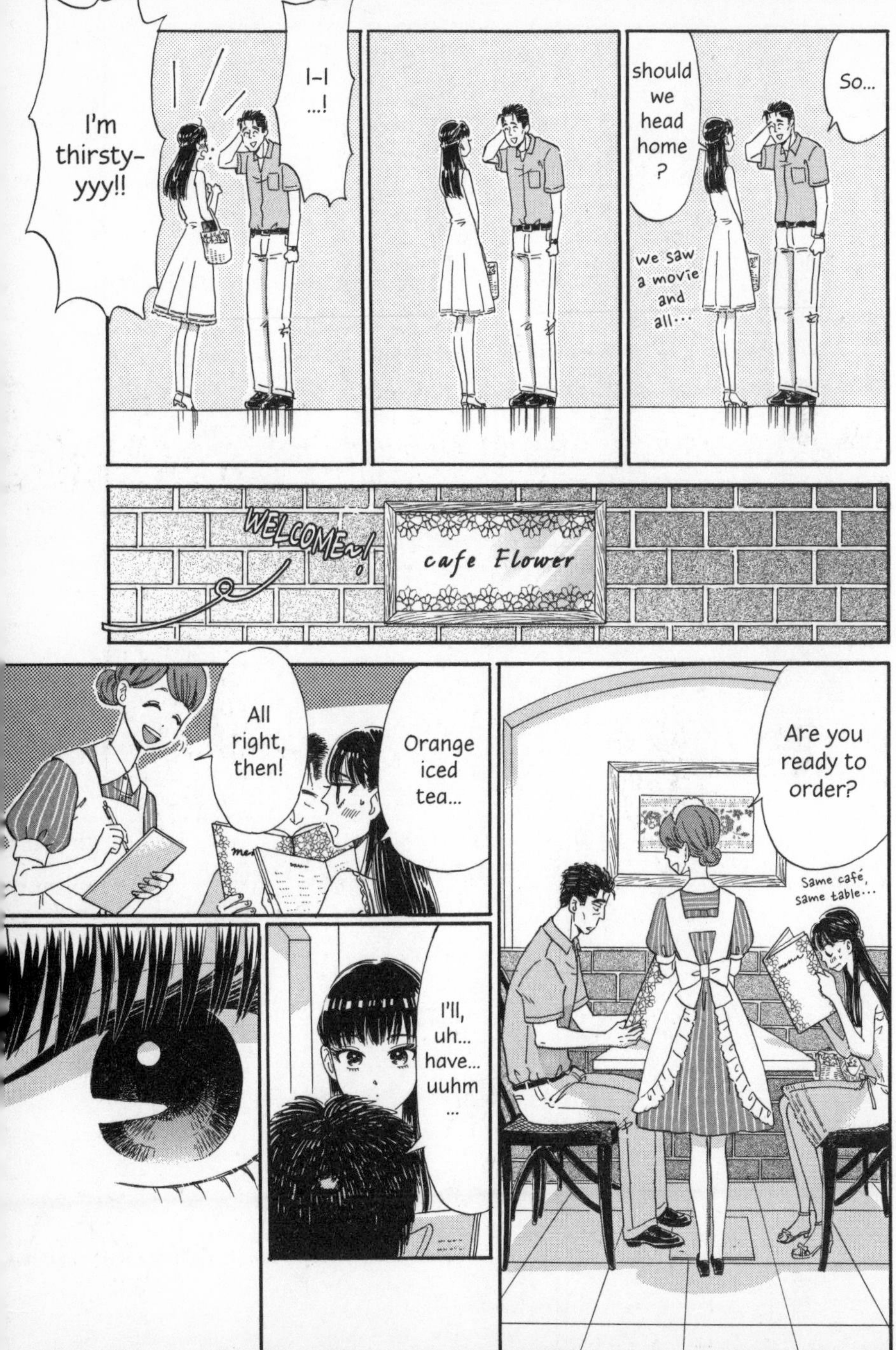
So...
should we head home?
we saw a movie and all...
I-I ...!
I'm thirsty-yyy!!
cafe Flower
WELCOME~!
Are you ready to order?
Same café, same table...
Orange iced tea...
All right, then!
I'll, uh... have... uuhm ...

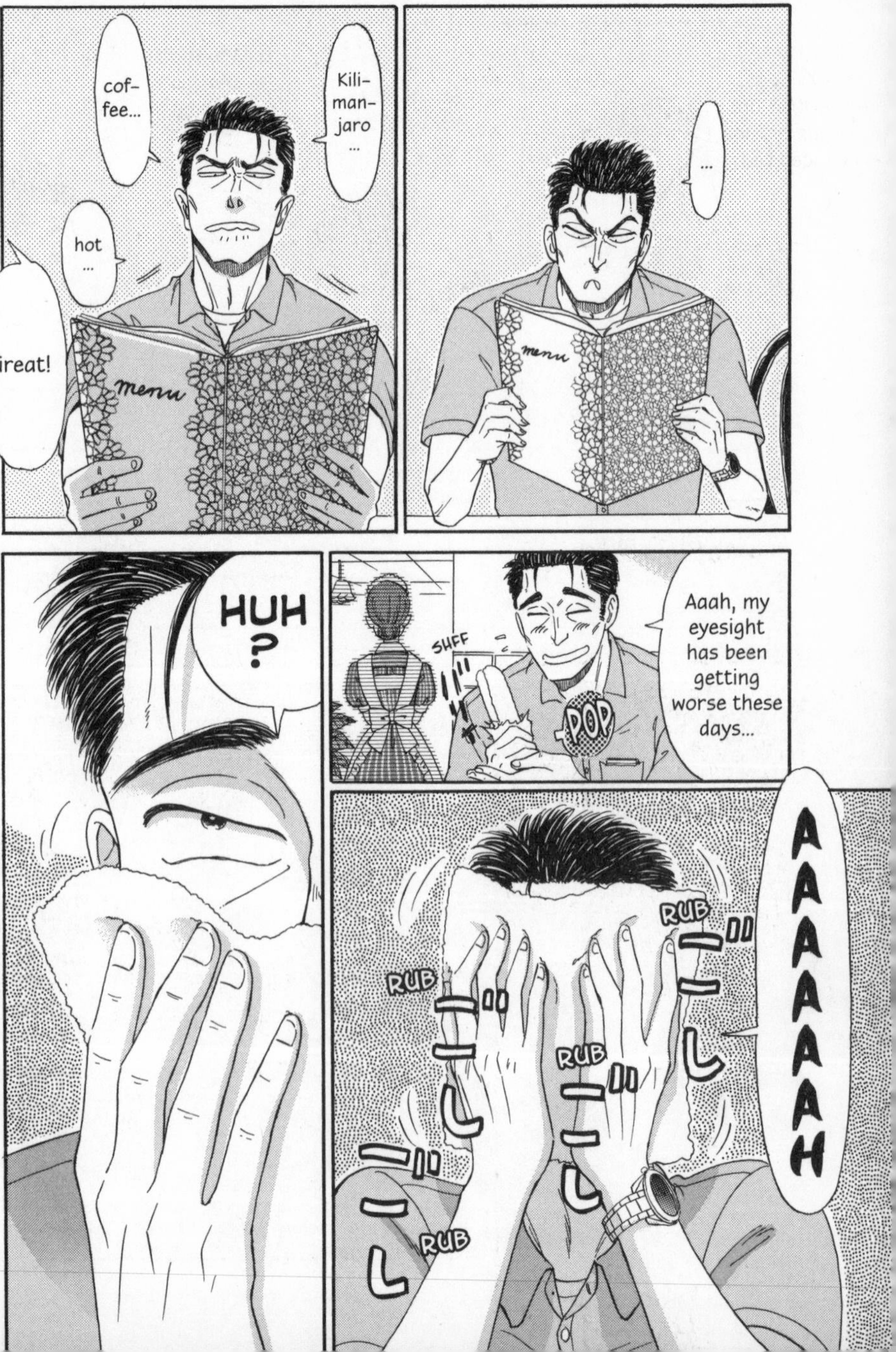
...
Kili-man-jaro ...
cof-fee...
hot ...
Great!
Aaah, my eyesight has been getting worse these days...
SHFF
POP
AAAAAAH
RUB
RUB
RUB
RUB
HUH?

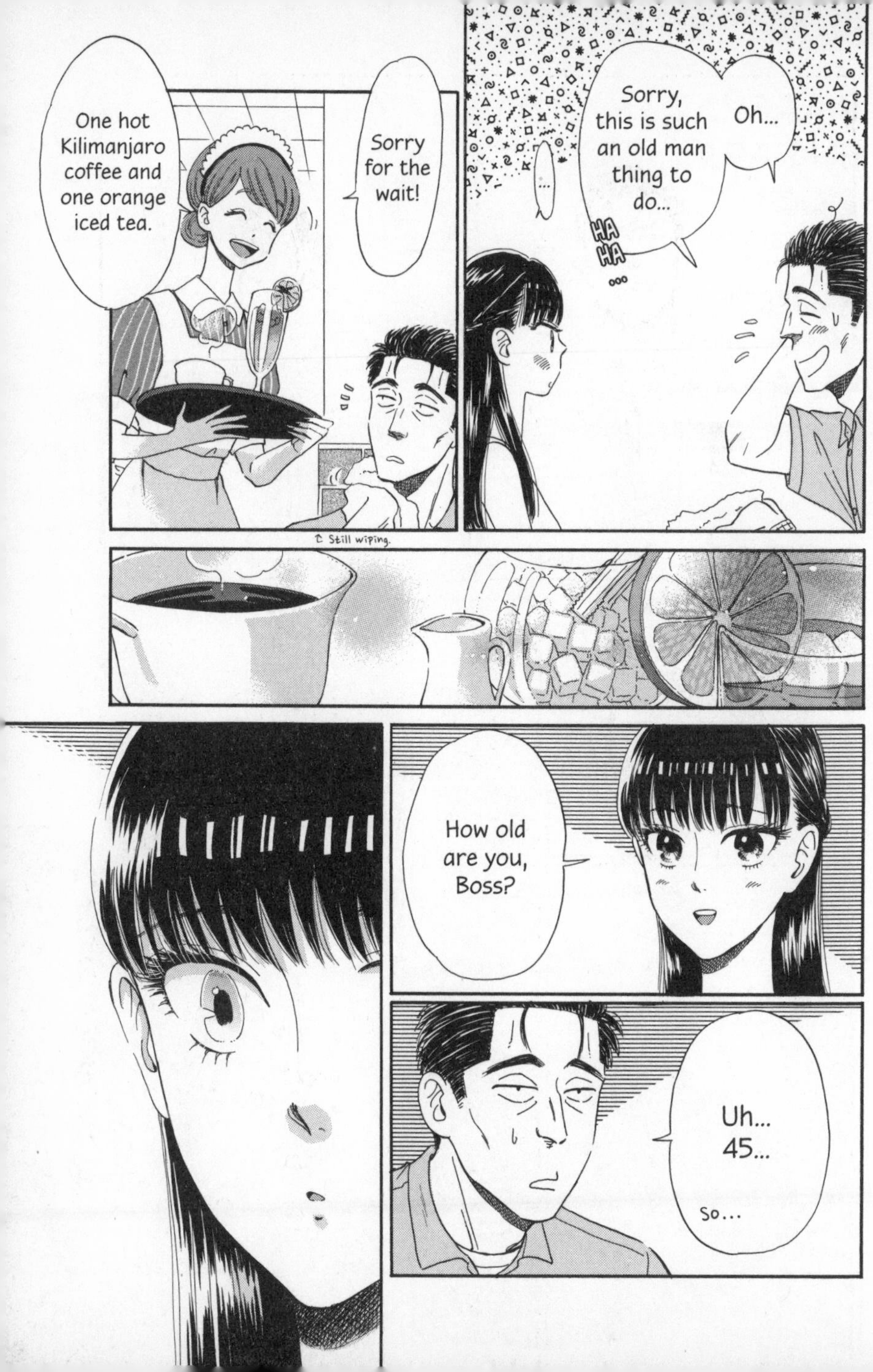
Oh...
Sorry, this is such an old man thing to do...
...
HA HA ...
Sorry for the wait!
One hot Kilimanjaro coffee and one orange iced tea.
↑ Still wiping.
How old are you, Boss?
Uh... 45...
So...

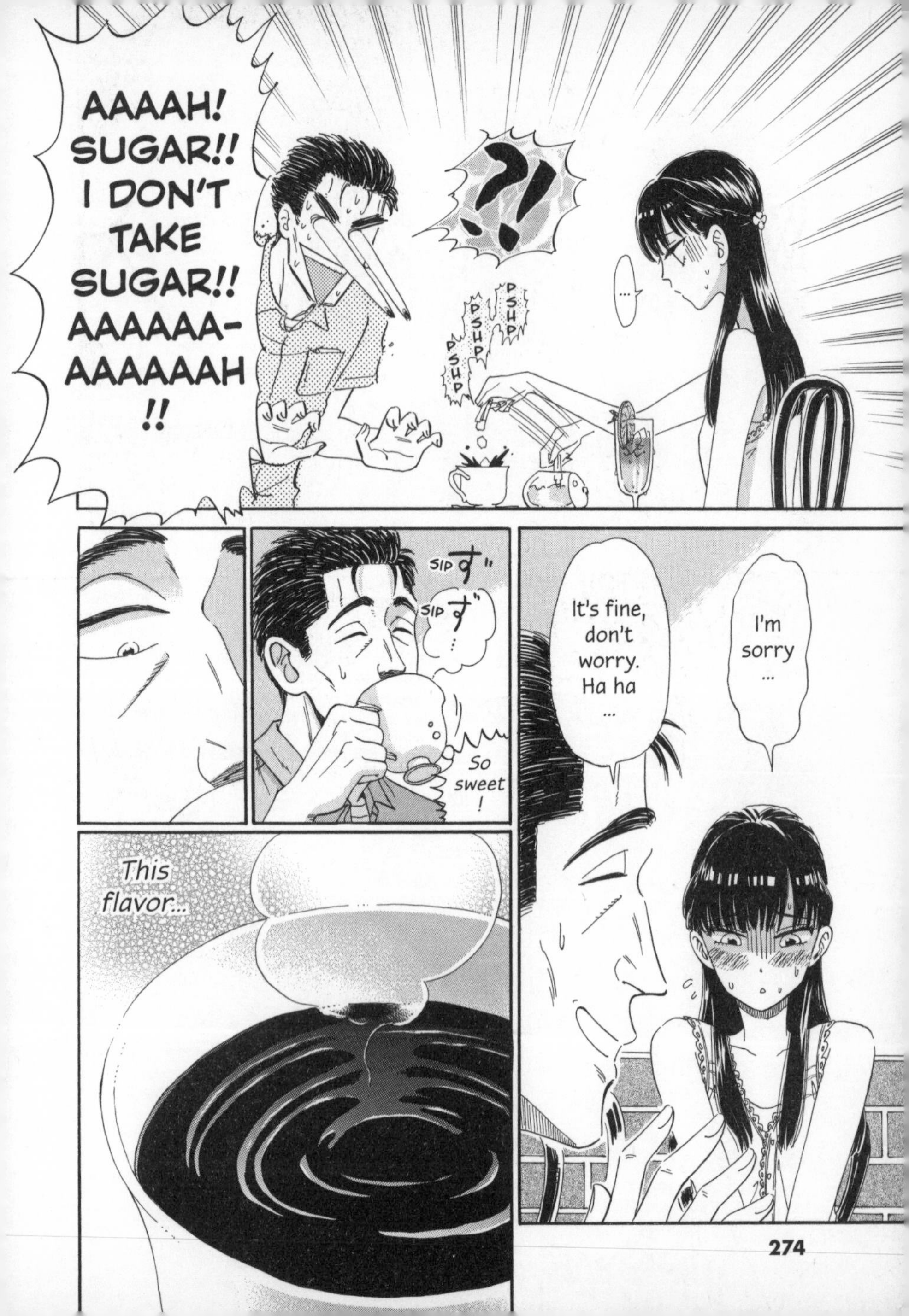
…
PSHP PSHP PSHP
?!
AAAAH! SUGAR!! I DON'T TAKE SUGAR!! AAAAAA-AAAAAAH!!
I'm sorry …
It's fine, don't worry. Ha ha …
SIP ず
SIP ず…
So sweet!
This flavor...

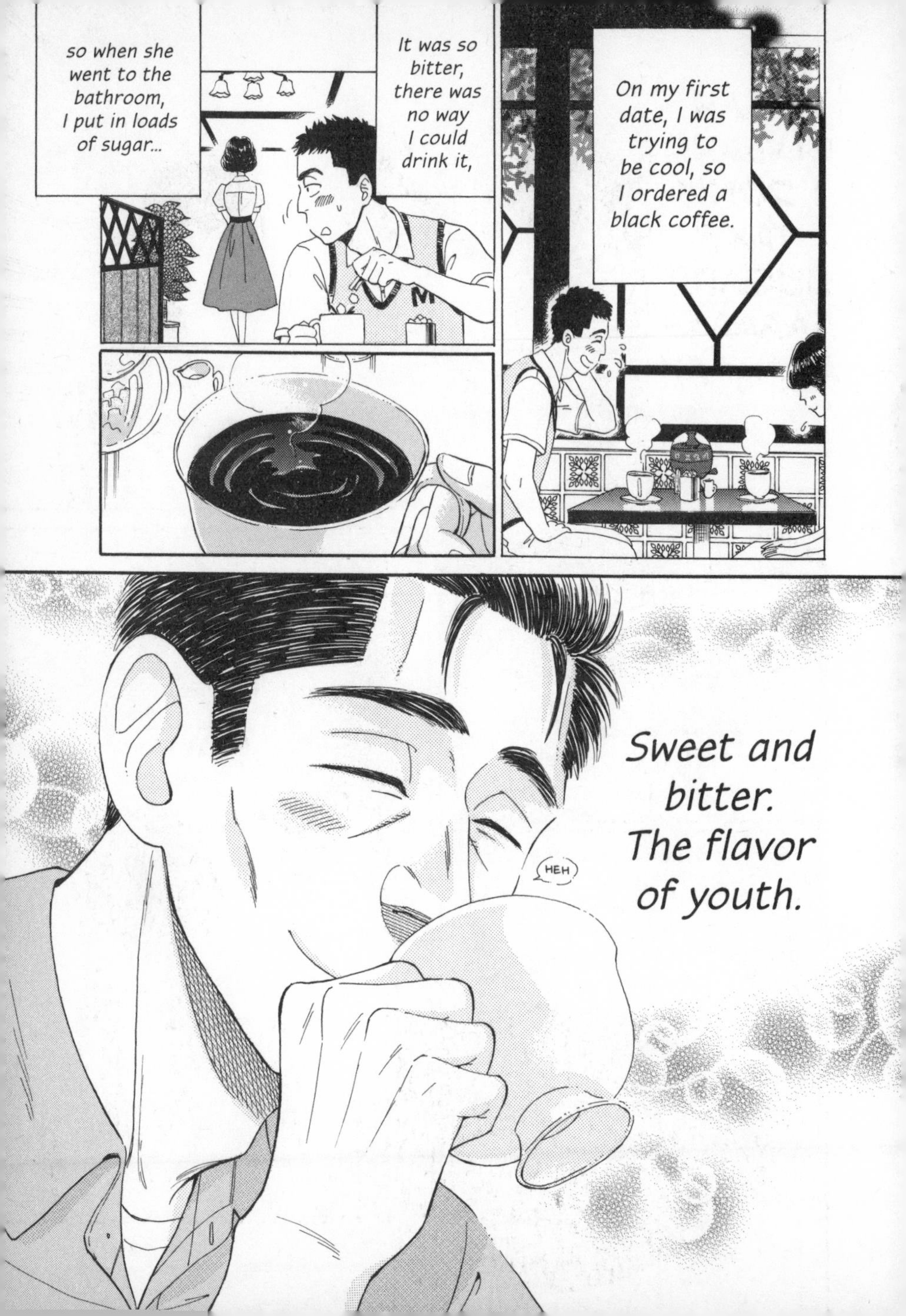
On my first date, I was trying to be cool, so I ordered a black coffee.
It was so bitter, there was no way I could drink it,
so when she went to the bathroom, I put in loads of sugar...
Sweet and bitter. The flavor of youth.
HEH

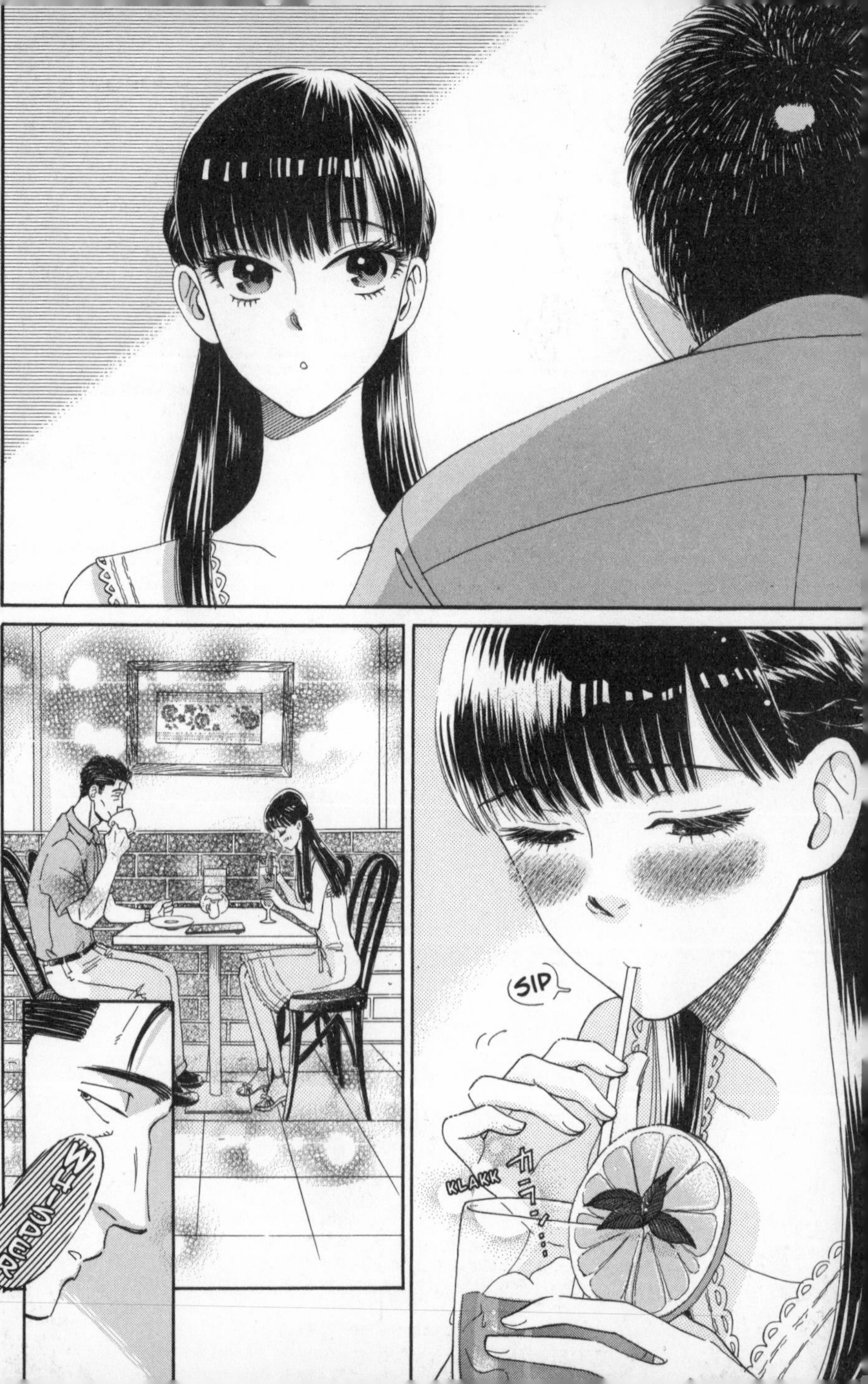
SIP
KLAKK

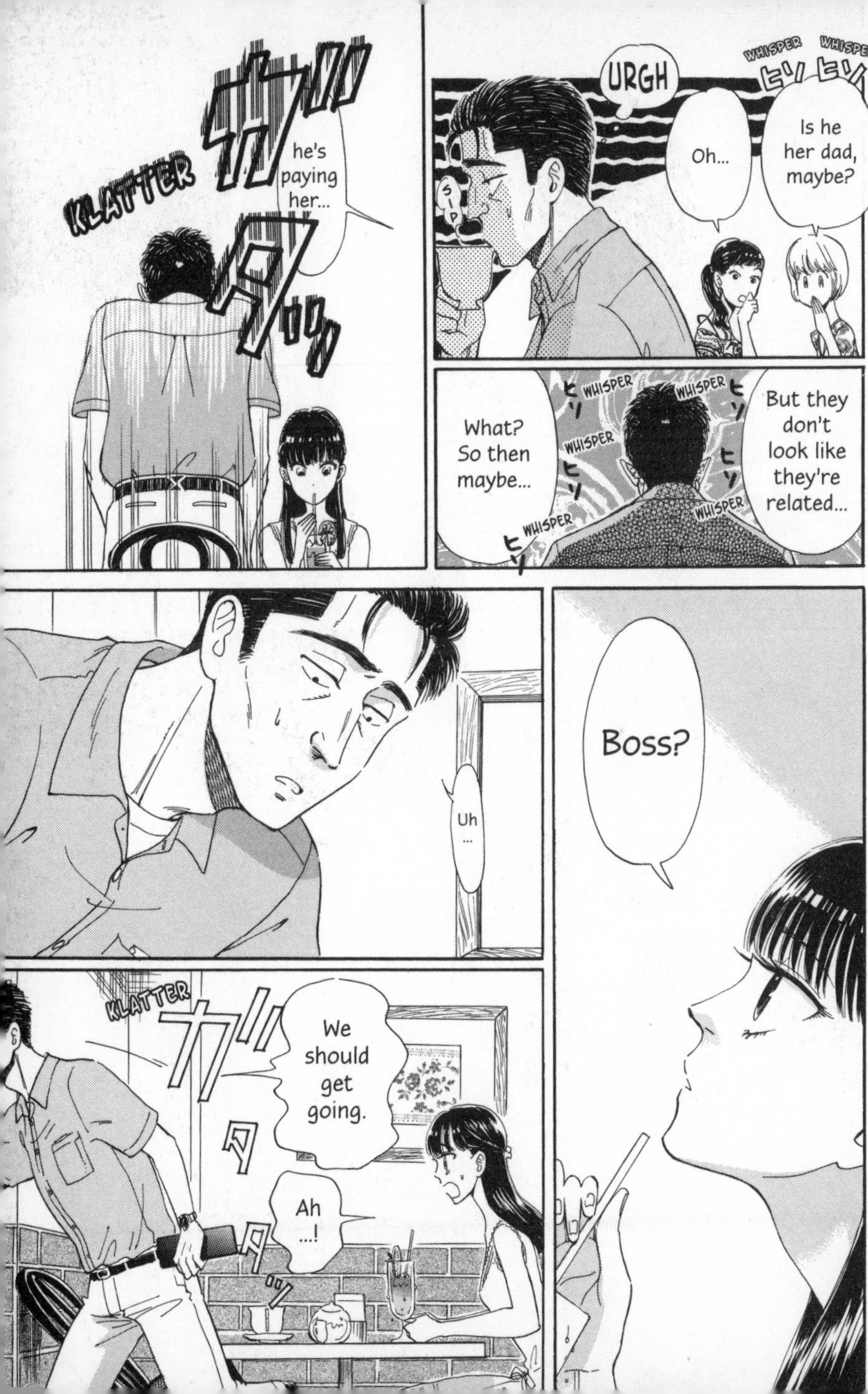
WHISPER WHISPER
ヒソヒソ
Is he her dad, maybe?
Oh...
URGH
SIP
But they don't look like they're related...
WHISPER
WHISPER
WHISPER
WHISPER
What? So then maybe...
he's paying her...
KLATTER
Boss?
Uh ...
We should get going.
Ah ...!
KLATTER

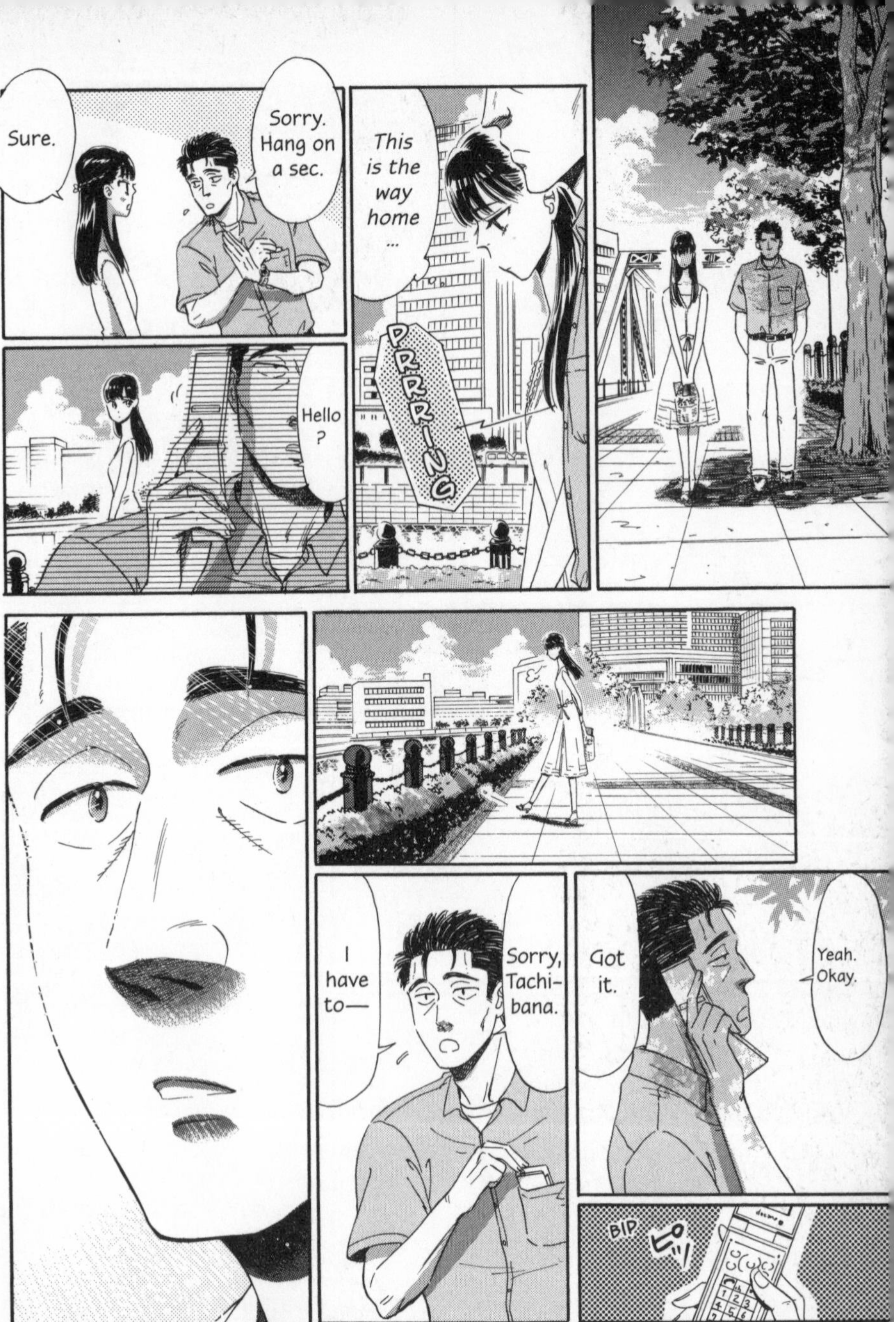
This is the way home ...
PRRRING
Sorry. Hang on a sec.
Sure.
Hello ?
Yeah. Okay.
Got it.
Sorry, Tachibana.
I have to—
BIP
ピッ

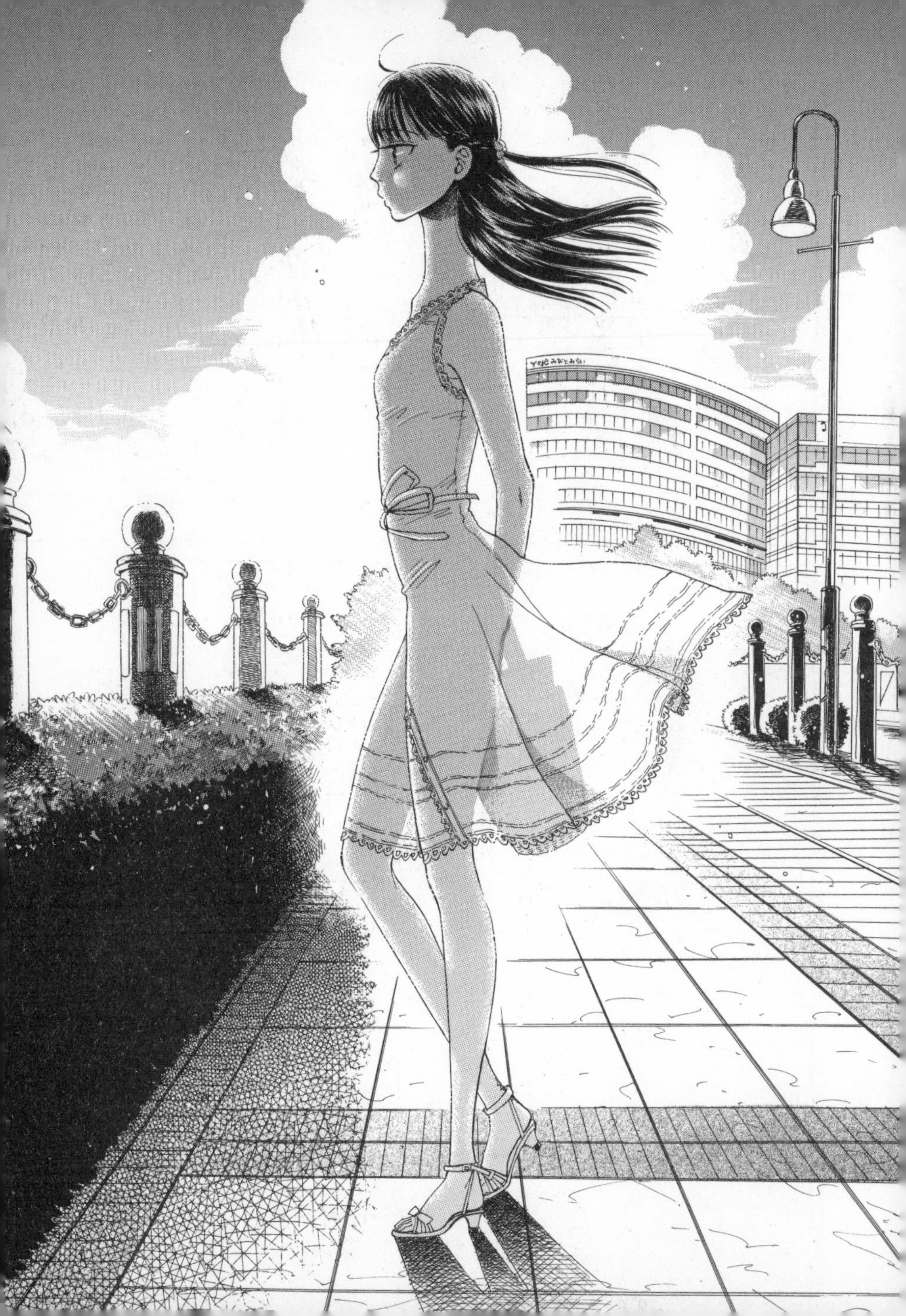
みなとみらい

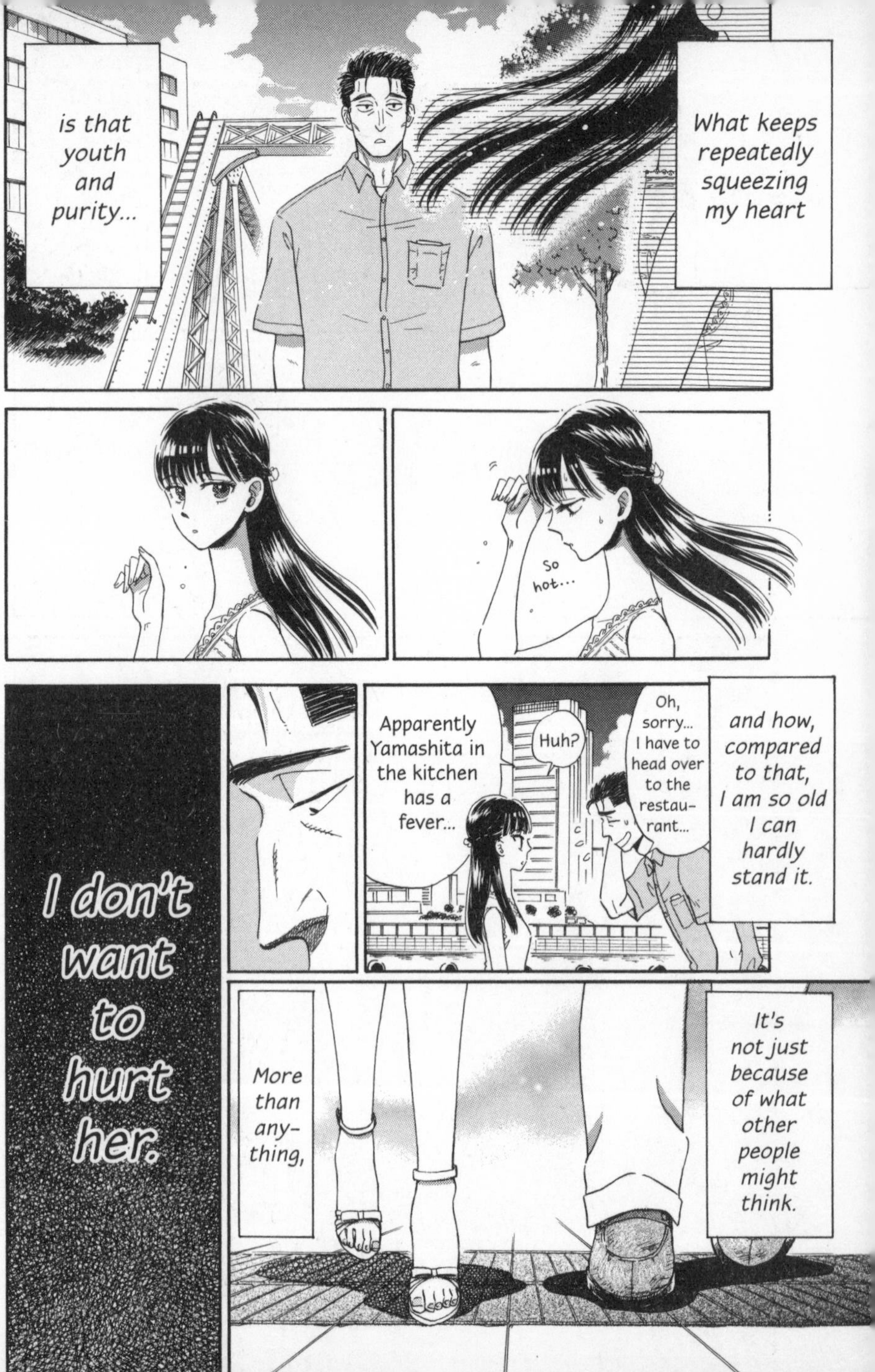
What keeps repeatedly squeezing my heart
is that youth and purity...
So hot...
and how, compared to that, I am so old I can hardly stand it.
Oh, sorry... I have to head over to the restaurant...
Huh?
Apparently Yamashita in the kitchen has a fever...
It's not just because of what other people might think.
More than anything,
I don't want to hurt her.

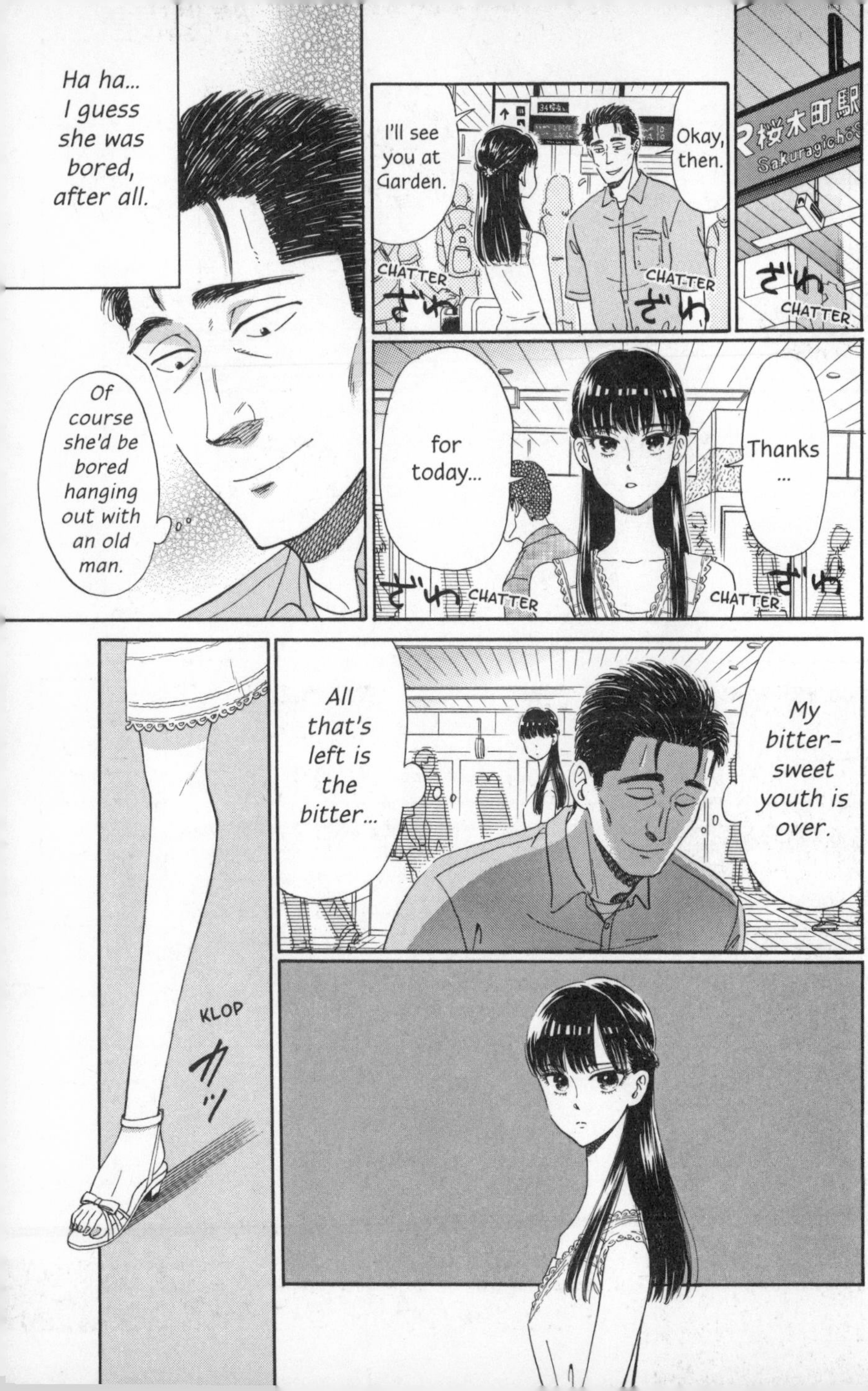

桜木町駅
Sakuragichō
ざわ
CHATTER
Okay, then.
I'll see you at Garden.
CHATTER
ざわ
CHATTER
ざわ
Thanks...
for today...
ざわ
CHATTER
ざわ
CHATTER
Ha ha... I guess she was bored, after all.
Of course she'd be bored hanging out with an old man.
My bitter-sweet youth is over.
All that's left is the bitter...
KLOP
カッ

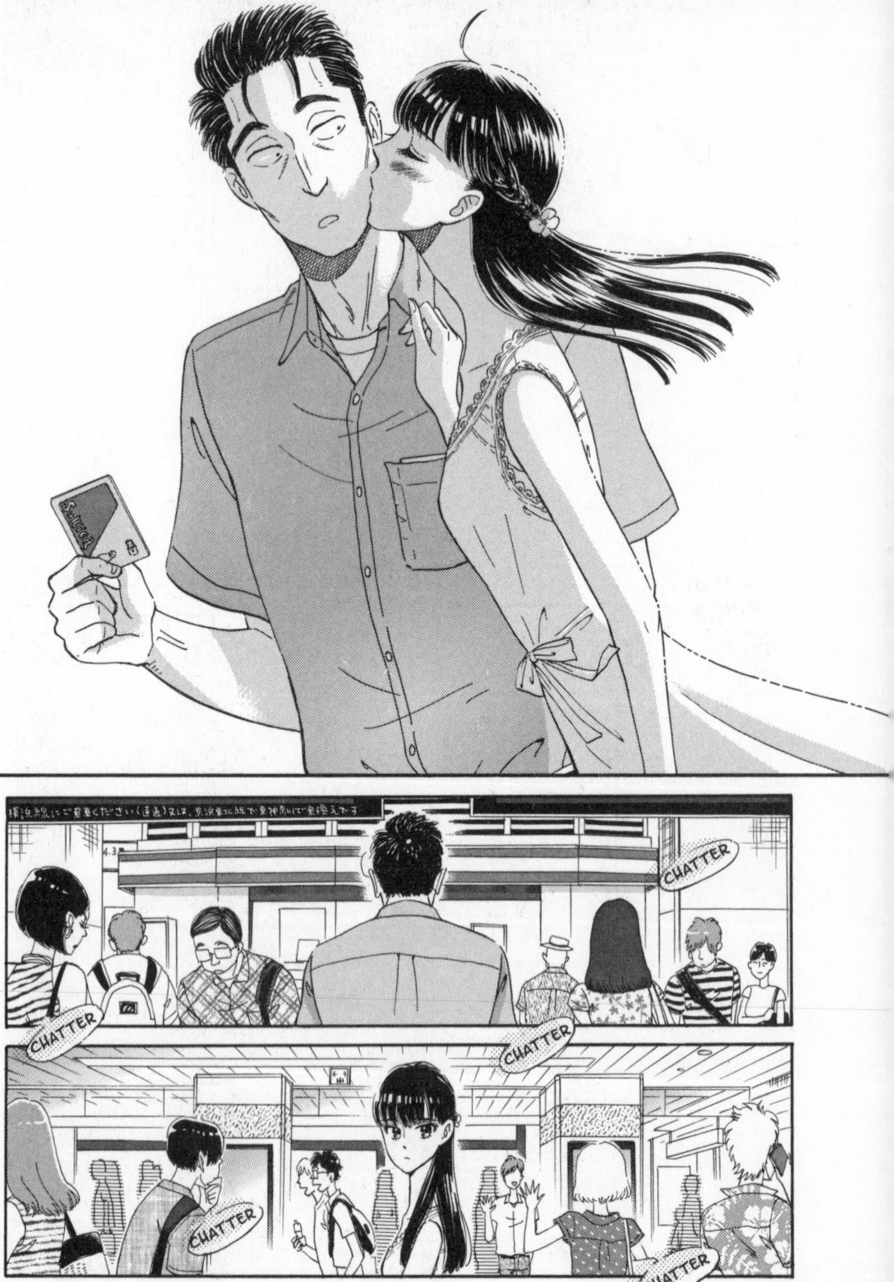
横浜線にご乗車ください（直通）又は、京浜東北線で東神奈川で乗換えです
CHATTER
CHATTER
CHATTER
CHATTER
CHATTER

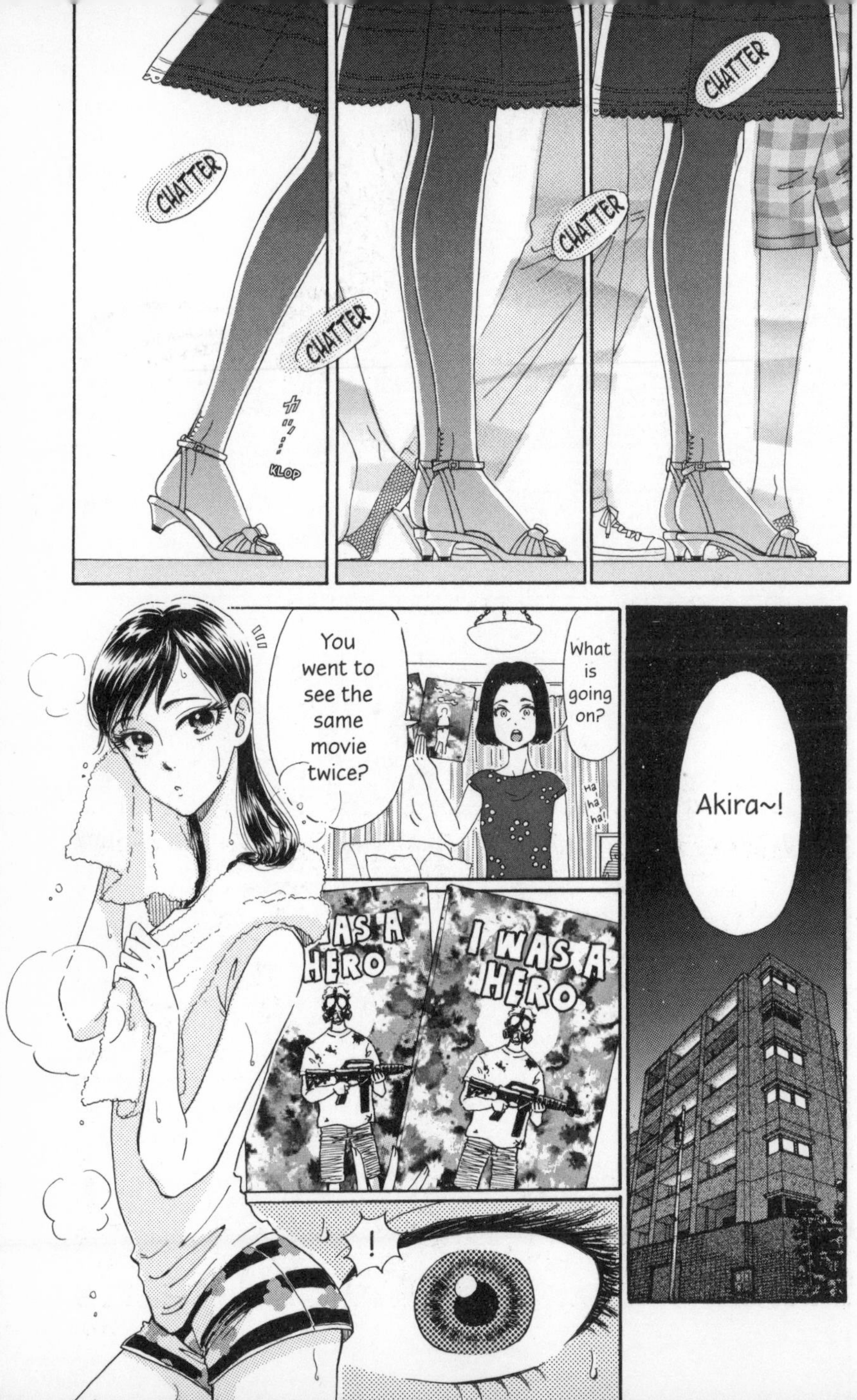
CHATTER
CHATTER
CHATTER
CHATTER
カッ…
KLOP
Akira~!
What is going on?
You went to see the same movie twice?
Ha ha ha!
I WAS A HERO
WAS A HERO
!

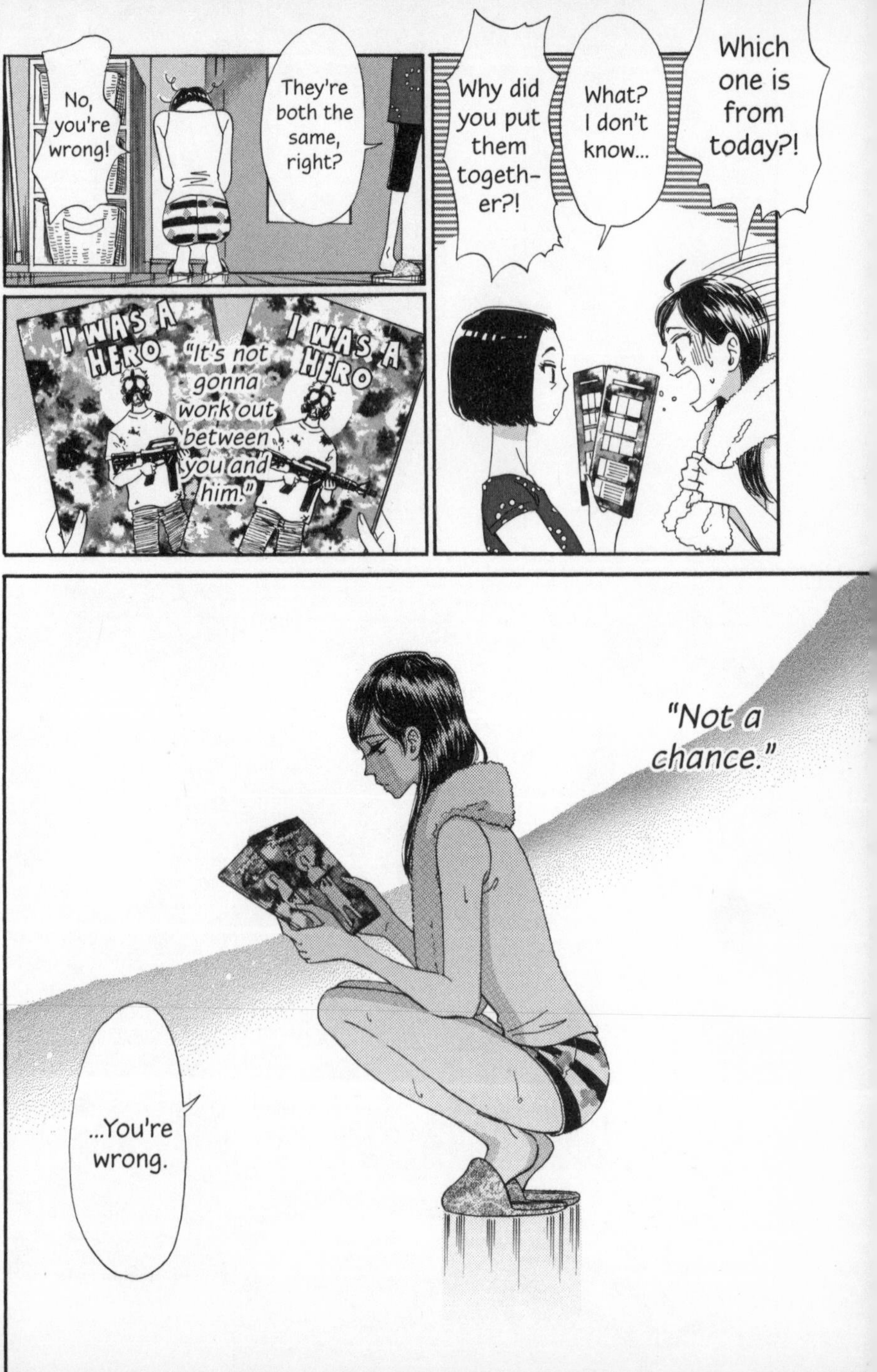
Which one is from today?!
What? I don't know...
Why did you put them together?!
They're both the same, right?
No, you're wrong!
I WAS A HERO
"It's not gonna work out between you and him."
I WAS A HERO
"Not a chance."
...You're wrong.

Other spoils of war
from the date

Ticket stub

café receipt

After
the ☂
Rain

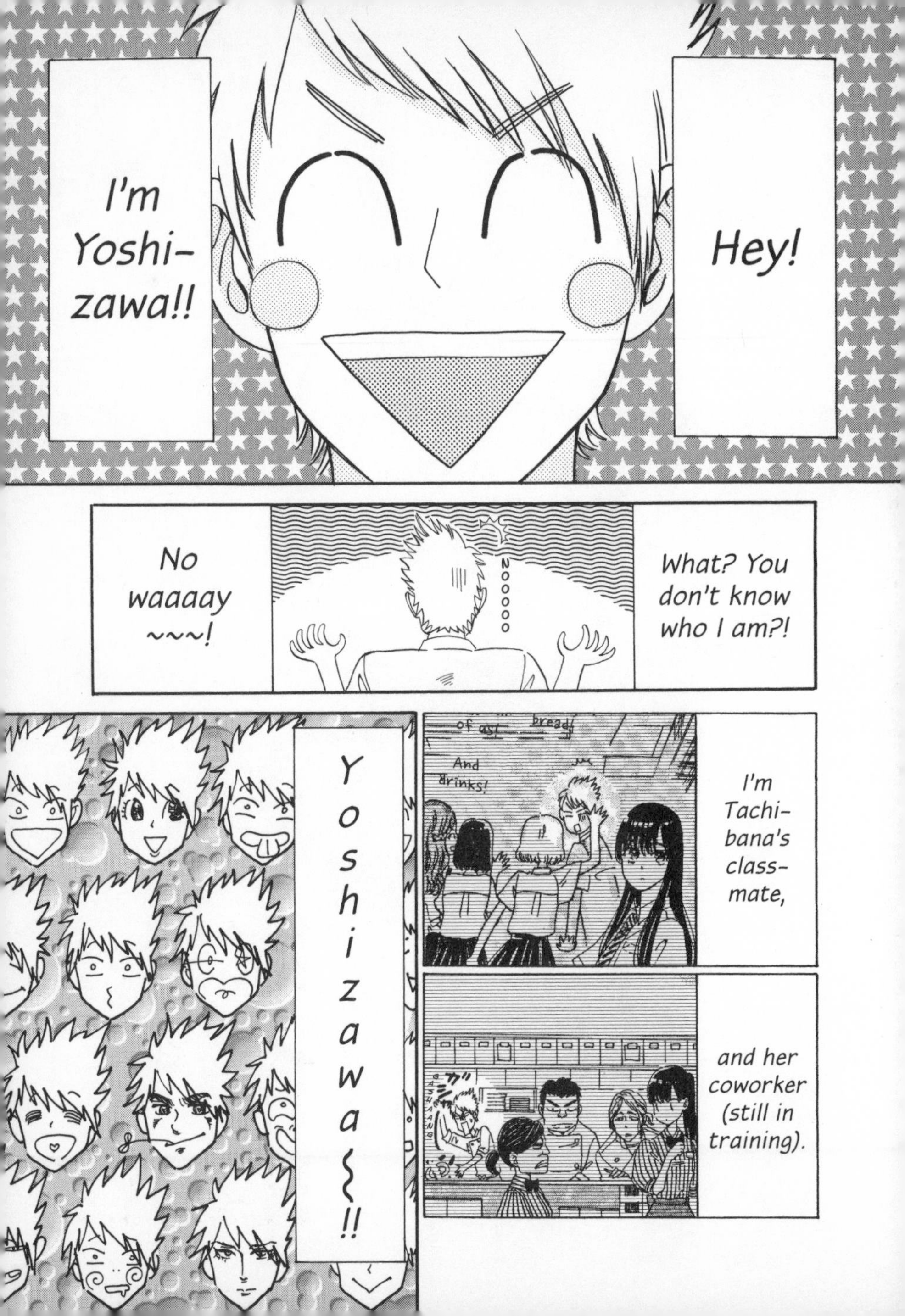
Hey!
I'm Yoshi-zawa!!
What? You don't know who I am?!
No waaaay ~~~!
I'm Tachi-bana's class-mate,
of us!
bread!
And drinks!
and her coworker (still in training).
Yoshizawa~!!

Chapter 15

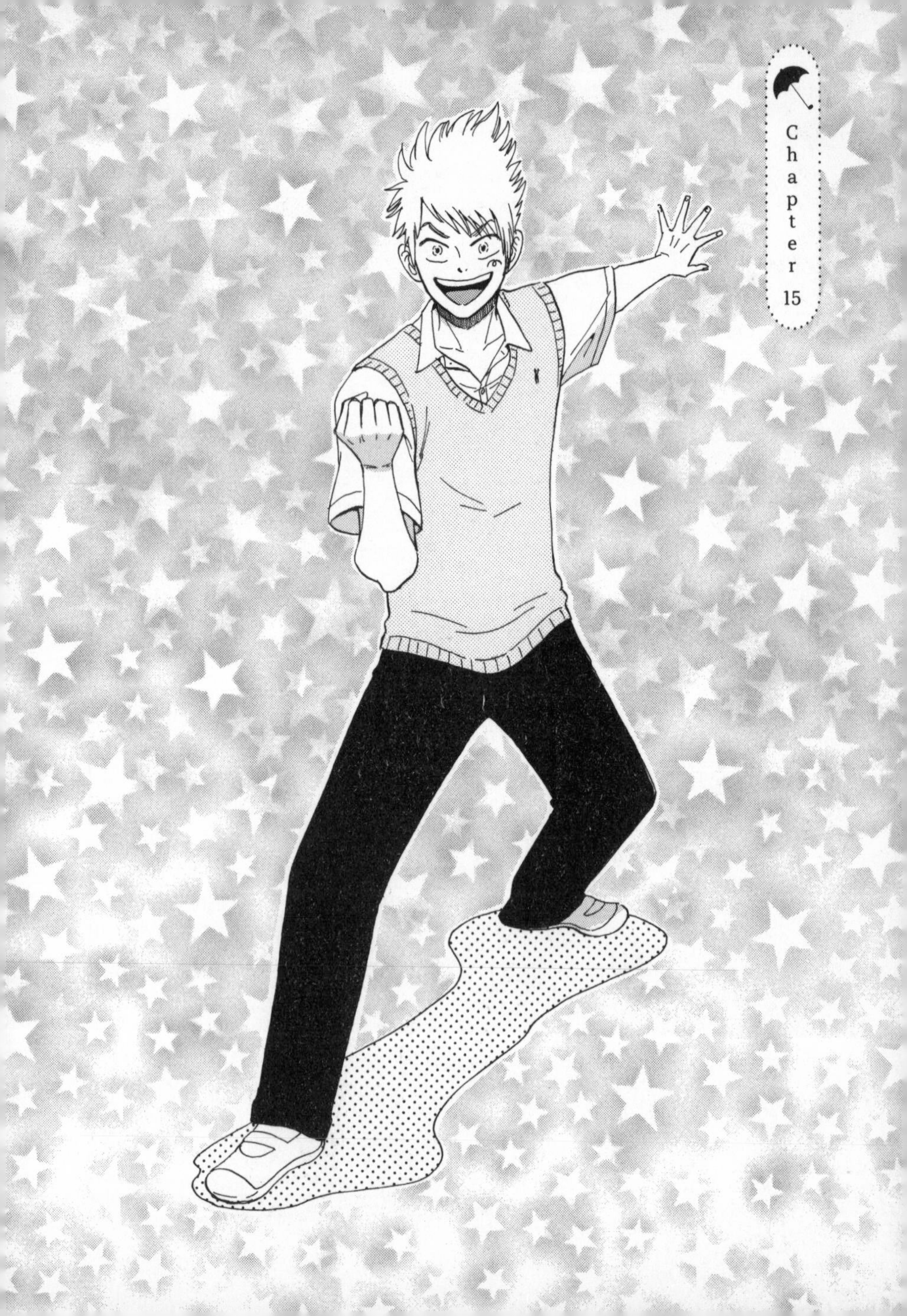

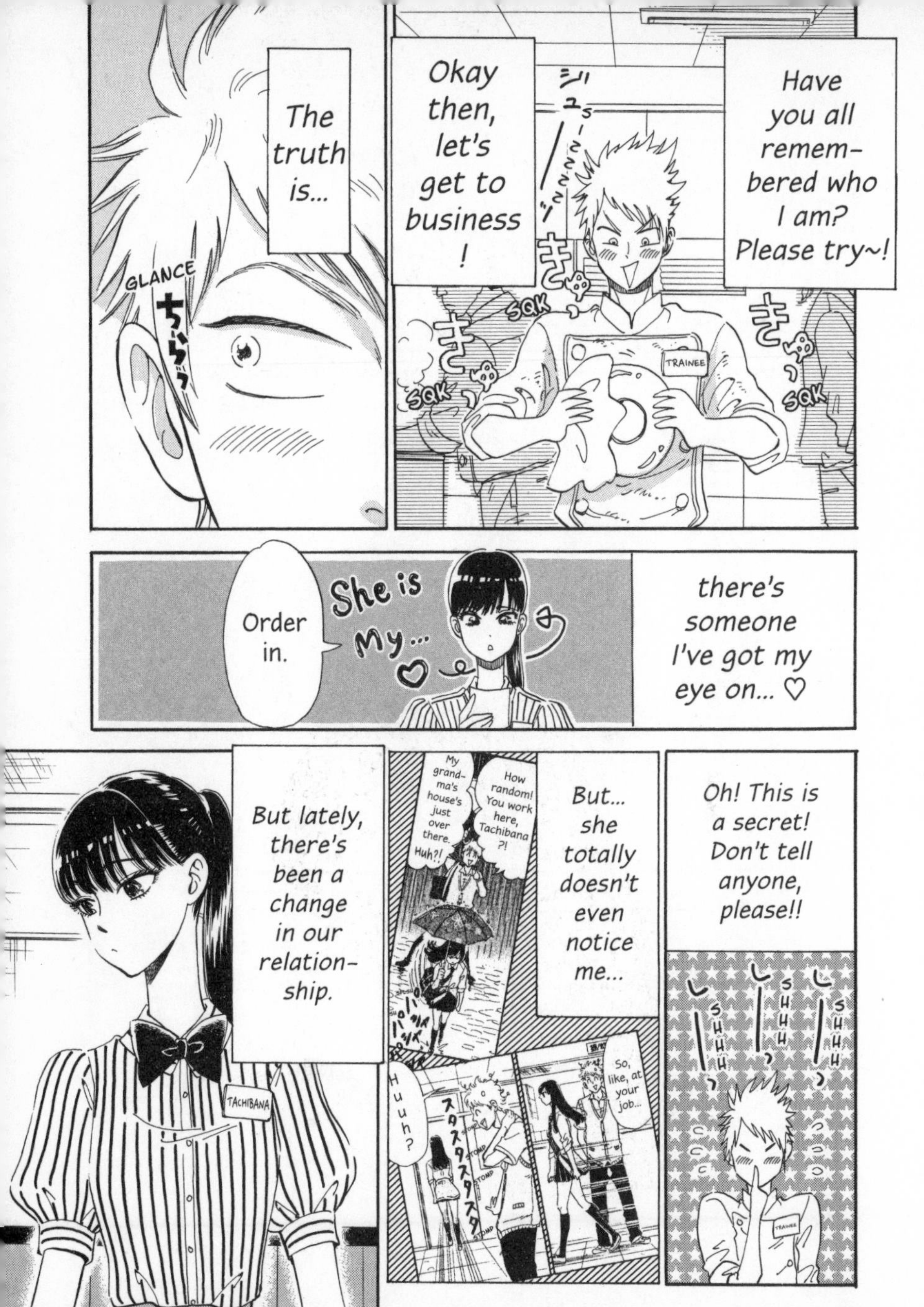

Have you all remembered who I am? Please try~!
Okay then, let's get to business!
SQK
SQK
SQK
TRAINEE
The truth is...
GLANCE
there's someone I've got my eye on... ♡
She is My... ♡
Order in.
Oh! This is a secret! Don't tell anyone, please!!
SHHH
SHHH
SHHH
TRAINEE
But... she totally doesn't even notice me...
How random! You work here, Tachibana?!
My grand-ma's house's just over there.
Huh?!
So, like, at your job...
Huuh?
STOMP
STOMP
STOMP
But lately, there's been a change in our relation-ship.
TACHIBANA

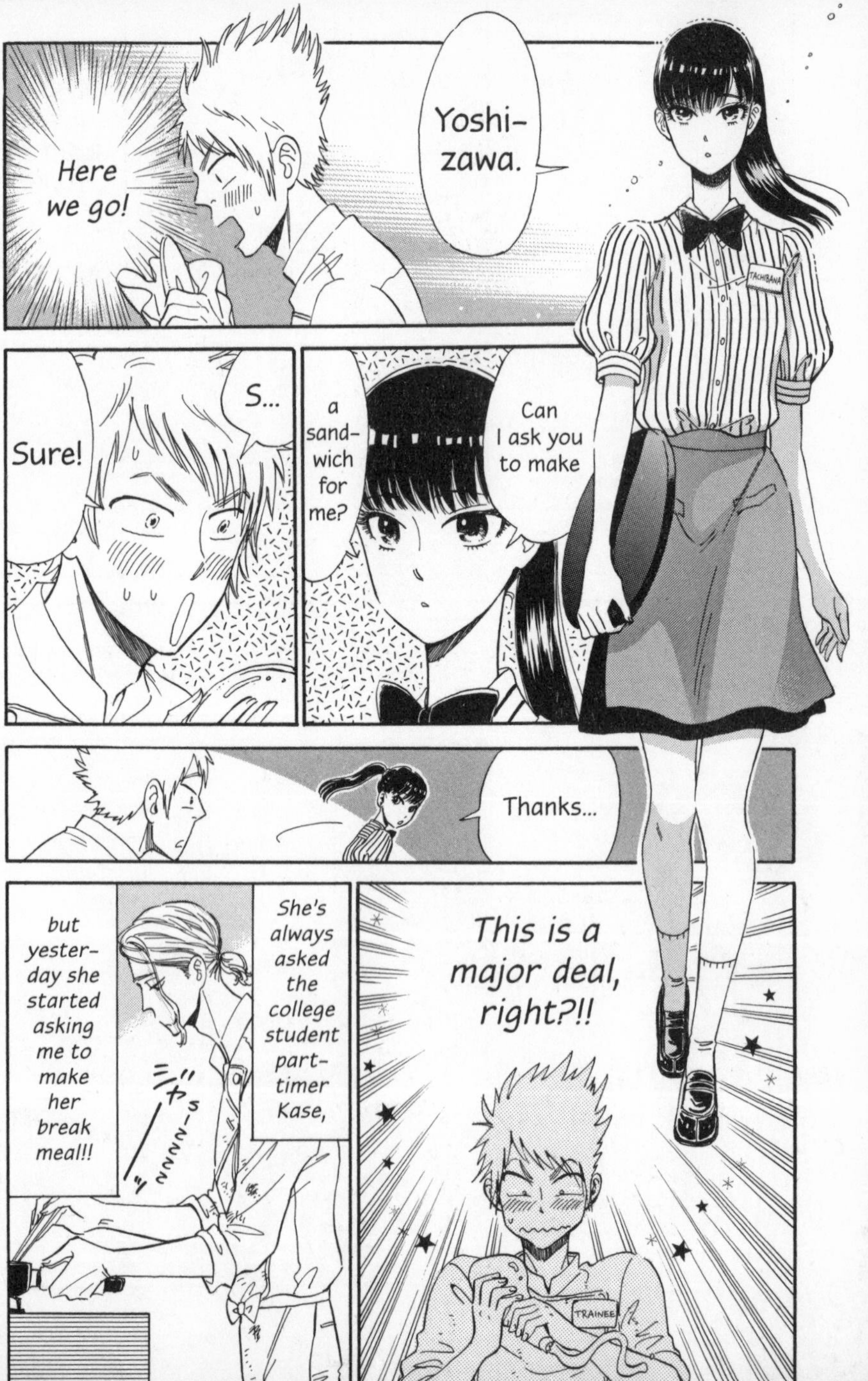
Yoshi-zawa.
Here we go!
Can I ask you to make
a sand-wich for me?
S...
Sure!
Thanks...
This is a major deal, right?!!
She's always asked the college student part-timer Kase,
but yester-day she started asking me to make her break meal!!
S-NNNNN

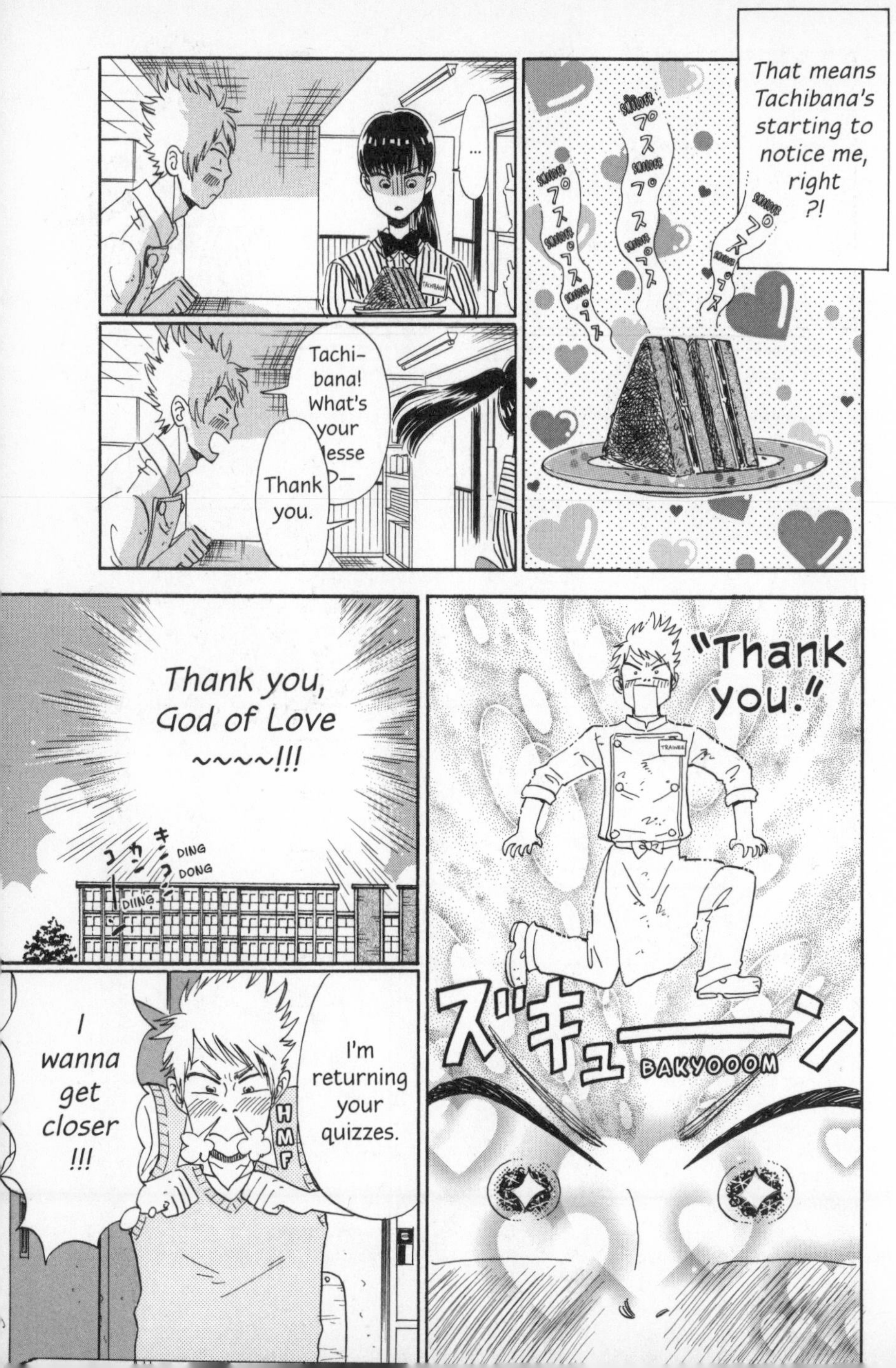
That means Tachibana's starting to notice me, right ?!
SMOLDER
...
Tachi-bana! What's your messe–
Thank you.
"Thank you."
BAKYOOOM
Thank you, God of Love ~~~~!!!
DING DONG
DIING
I'm returning your quizzes.
HMF
I wanna get closer !!!

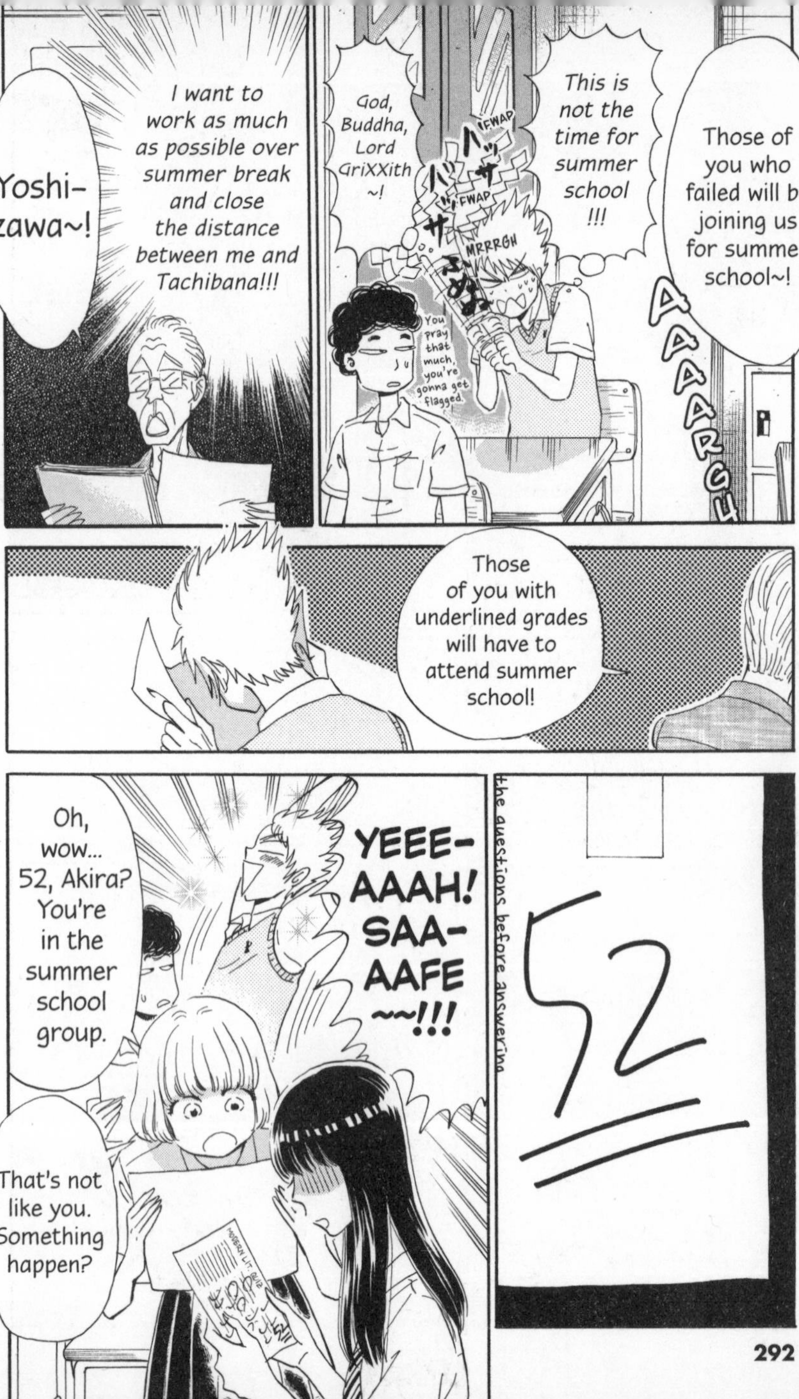
Those of you who failed will be joining us for summer school~!
AAAARGH
This is not the time for summer school!!!
God, Buddha, Lord GriXXith ~!
FWAP
FWAP
MRRRGH
You pray that much, you're gonna get flagged.
I want to work as much as possible over summer break and close the distance between me and Tachibana!!!
Yoshi-zawa~!
Those of you with underlined grades will have to attend summer school!
52
the questions before answering
YEEE-AAAH! SAA-AAFE ~~!!!
Oh, wow... 52, Akira? You're in the summer school group.
MODERN LIT. QUIZ
That's not like you. Something happen?

*This Akira is fiction.

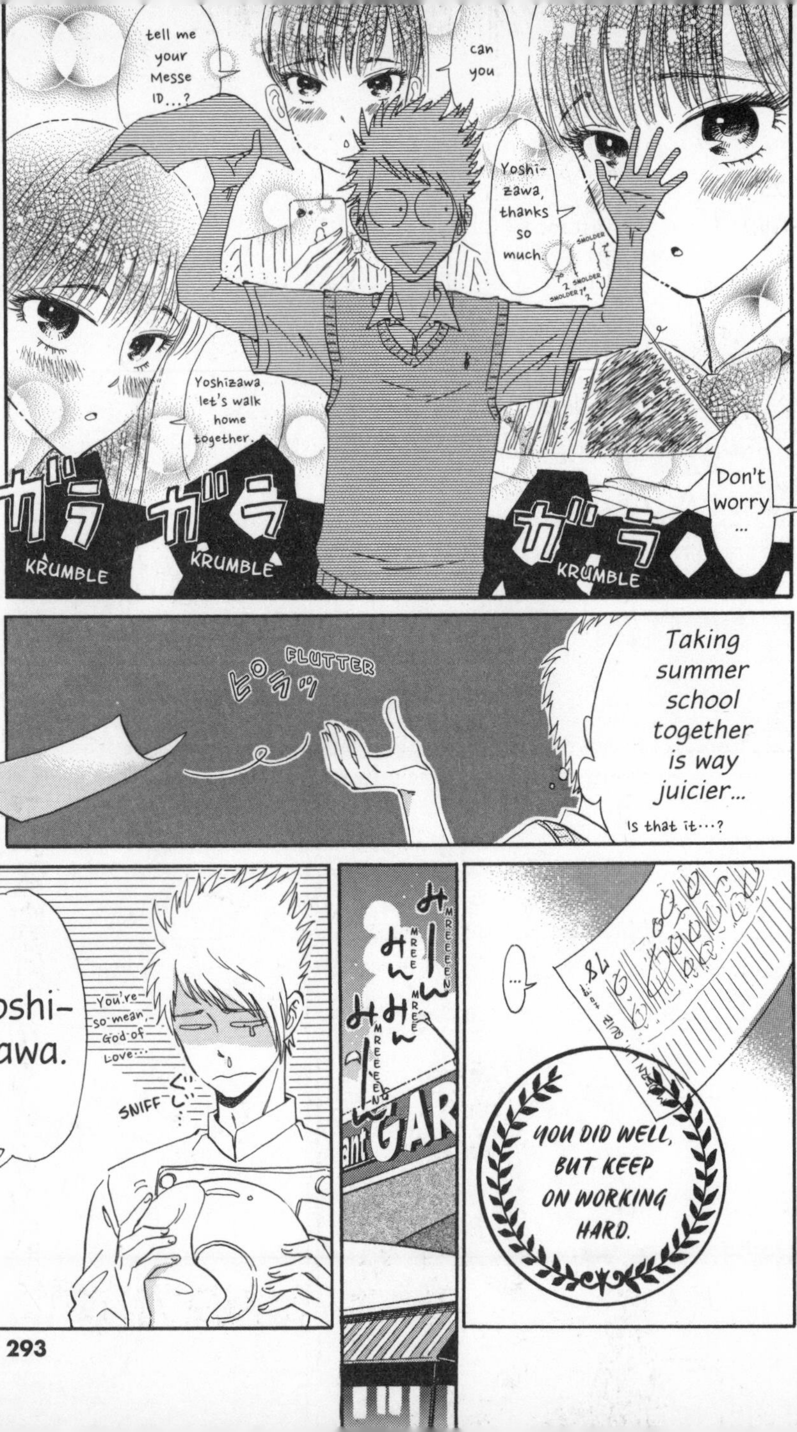
can you
tell me your Messe ID...?
Yoshizawa, thanks so much.
SMOLDER
Yoshizawa, let's walk home together.
Don't worry...
KRUMBLE
KRUMBLE
KRUMBLE
Taking summer school together is way juicier...
Is that it…?
FLUTTER
…
YOU DID WELL, BUT KEEP ON WORKING HARD.
MREEEEEN
MREE MREE
MREEEEEN
GAR
Yoshi-zawa.
You're so mean, God of Love…
SNIFF

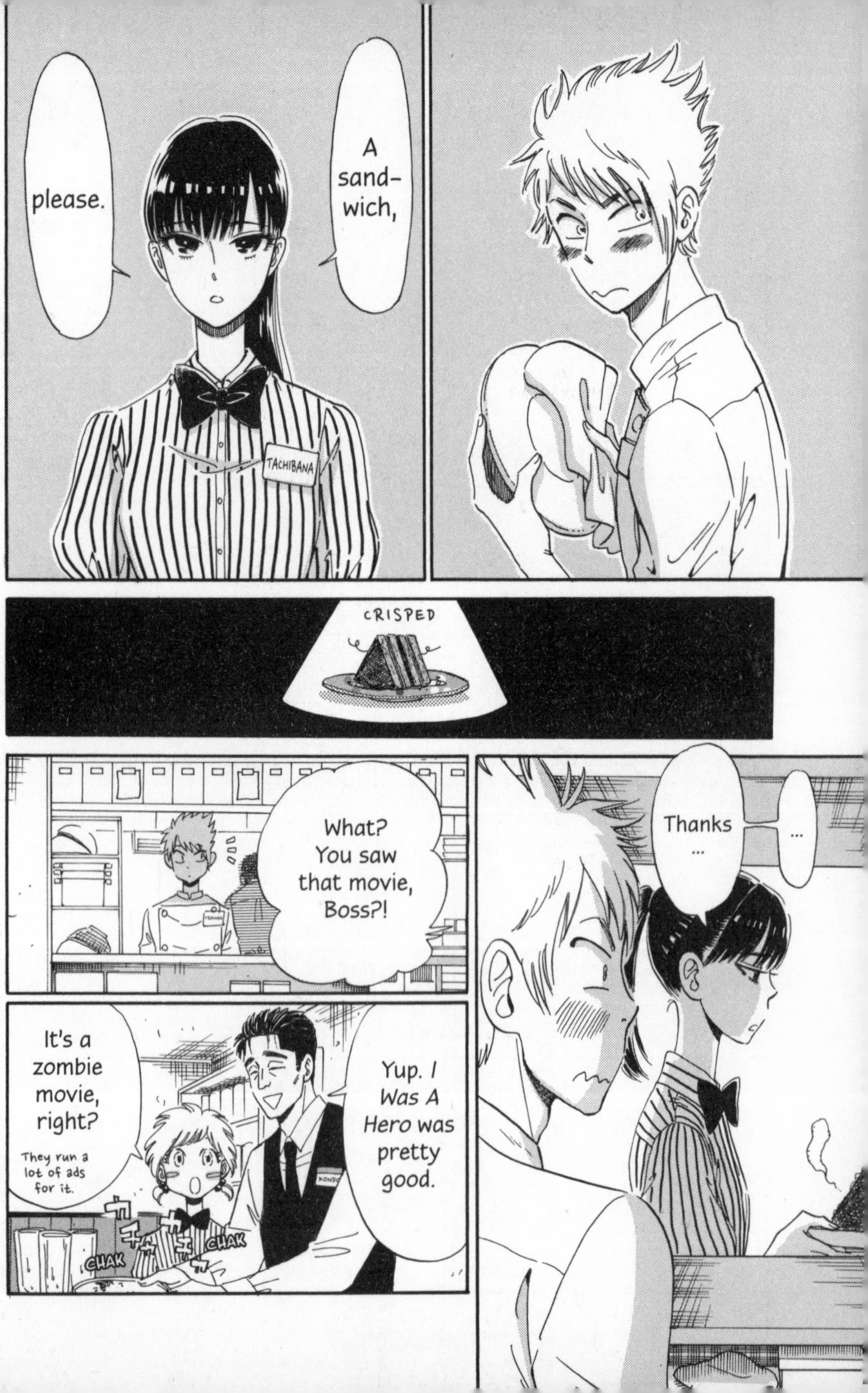
A sand-wich,
please.
CRISPED
Thanks ...
...
What? You saw that movie, Boss?!
Yup. I Was A Hero was pretty good.
It's a zombie movie, right?
They run a lot of ads for it.
CHAK
CHAK
TACHIBANA
KONDO

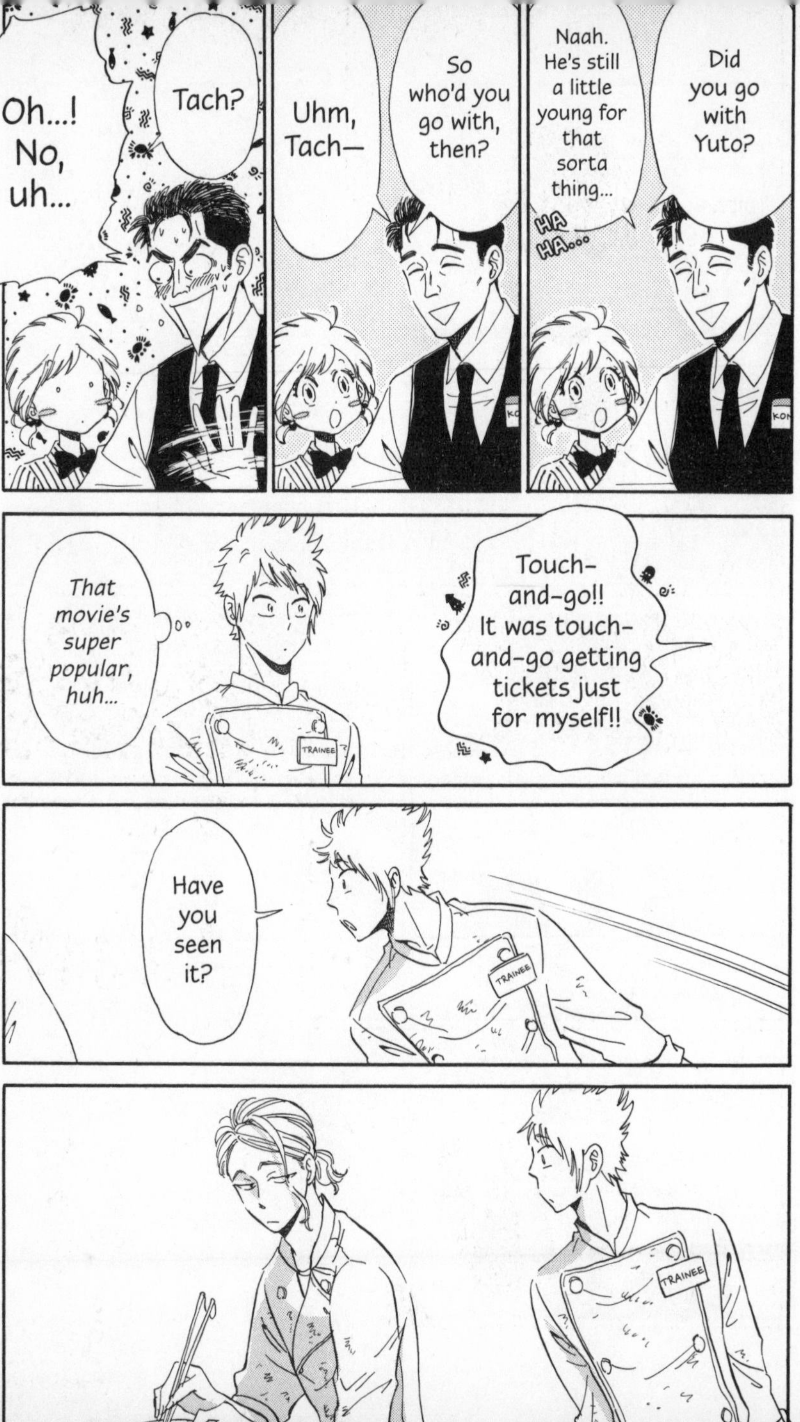
Did you go with Yuto?
Naah. He's still a little young for that sorta thing...
HA HA...
So who'd you go with, then?
Uhm, Tach—
Tach?
Oh...! No, uh...
Touch-and-go!! It was touch-and-go getting tickets just for myself!!
That movie's super popular, huh...
Have you seen it?

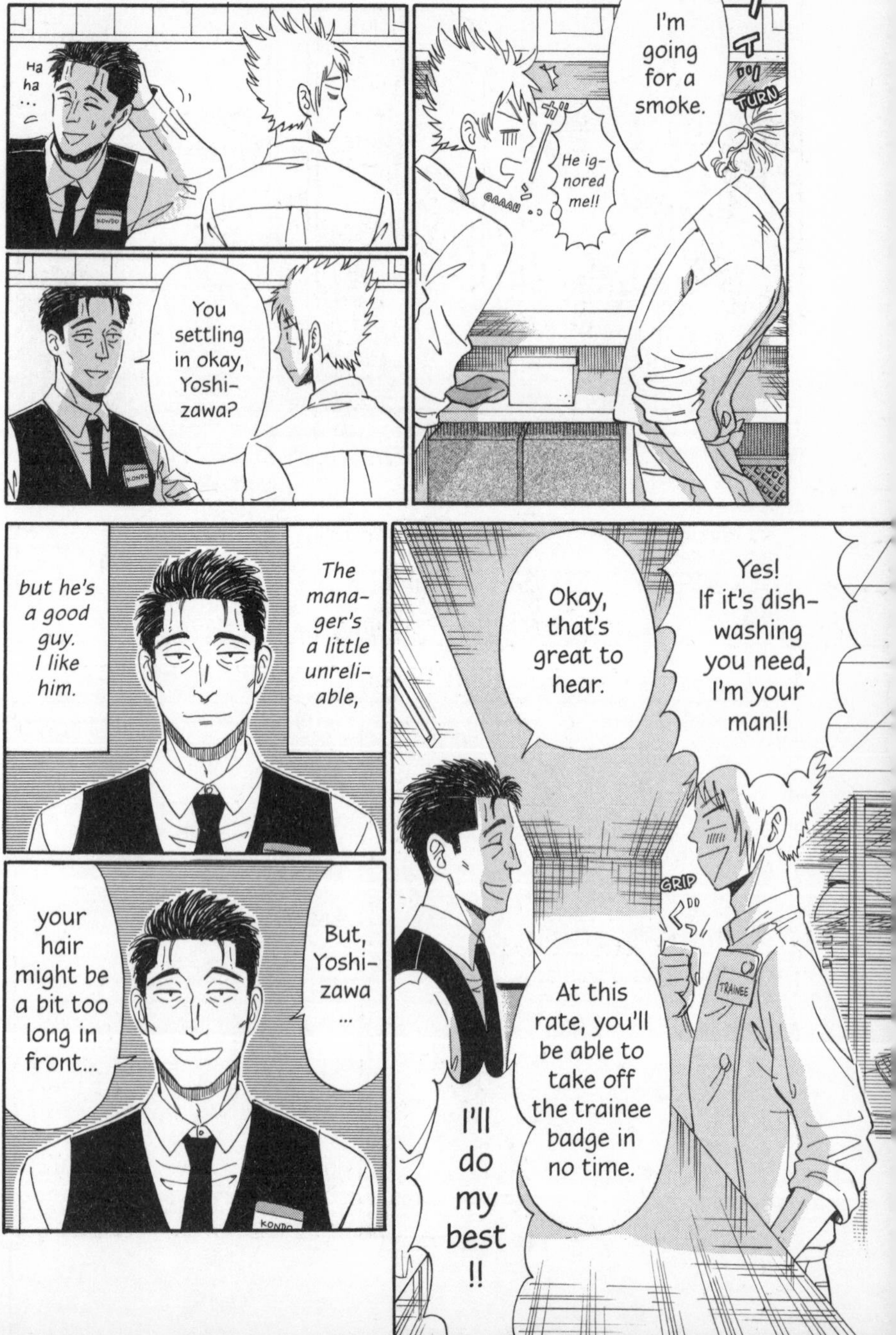
I'm going for a smoke.
TURN
He ignored me!!
GAAAH
Ha ha...
You settling in okay, Yoshizawa?
Yes! If it's dishwashing you need, I'm your man!!
Okay, that's great to hear.
GRIP
At this rate, you'll be able to take off the trainee badge in no time.
I'll do my best!!
The manager's a little unreliable,
but he's a good guy. I like him.
But, Yoshizawa...
your hair might be a bit too long in front...

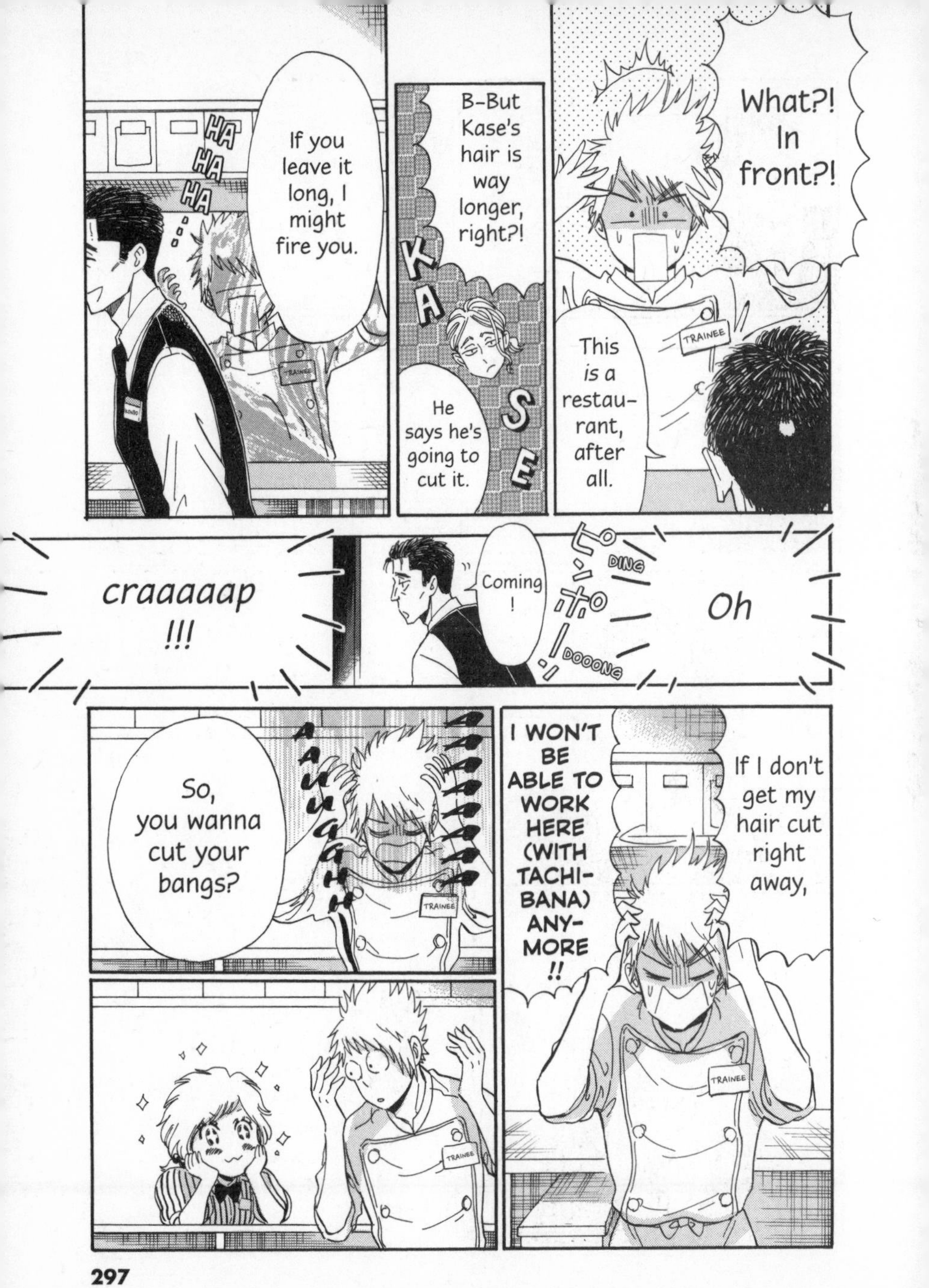
What?! In front?!
This is a restaurant, after all.
B-But Kase's hair is way longer, right?!
KASE
He says he's going to cut it.
If you leave it long, I might fire you.
HA HA HA
Oh
DING
DOOONG
Coming!
craaaaap!!!
If I don't get my hair cut right away,
I WON'T BE ABLE TO WORK HERE (WITH TACHIBANA) ANYMORE!!
So, you wanna cut your bangs?

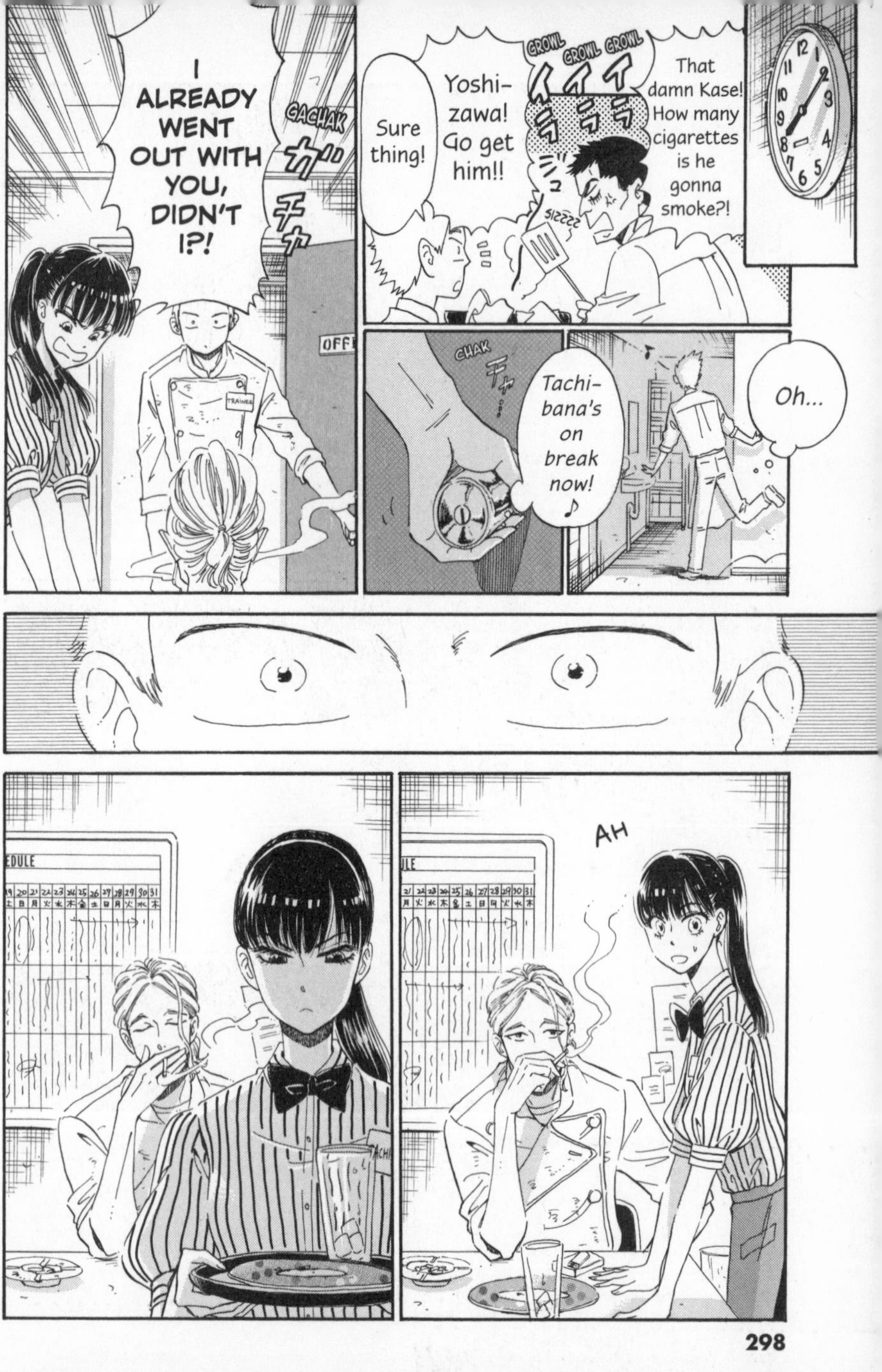
That damn Kase! How many cigarettes is he gonna smoke?!
GROWL GROWL GROWL
Yoshi-zawa! Go get him!!
SIZZZZ
Sure thing!
Oh...
Tachi-bana's on break now! ♪
CHAK
GACHAK
I ALREADY WENT OUT WITH YOU, DIDN'T I?!
AH

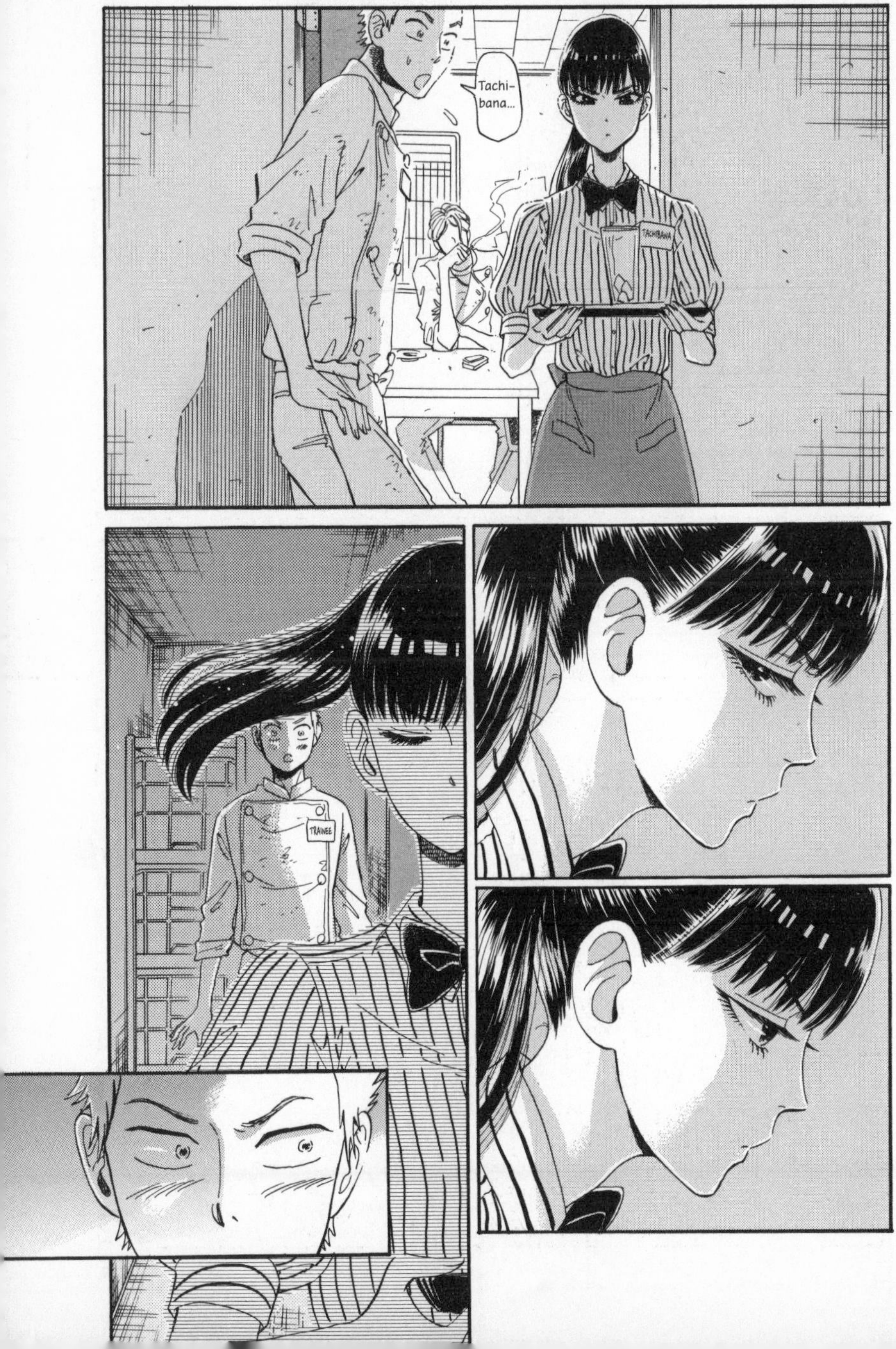
Tachi-bana...
TACHIBANA
TRAINEE

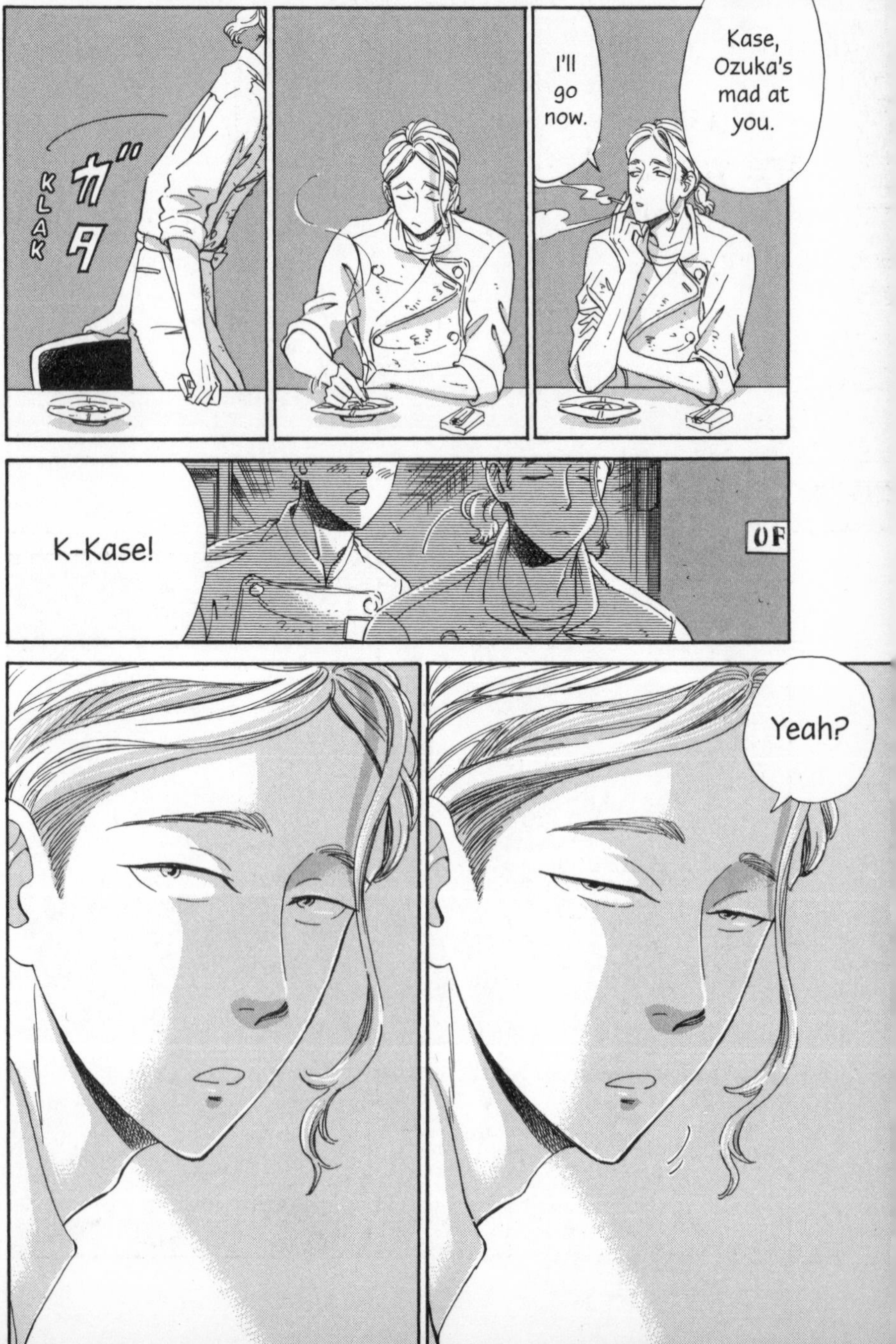
Kase, Ozuka's mad at you.
I'll go now.
ガタ
KLAK
K-Kase!
Yeah?

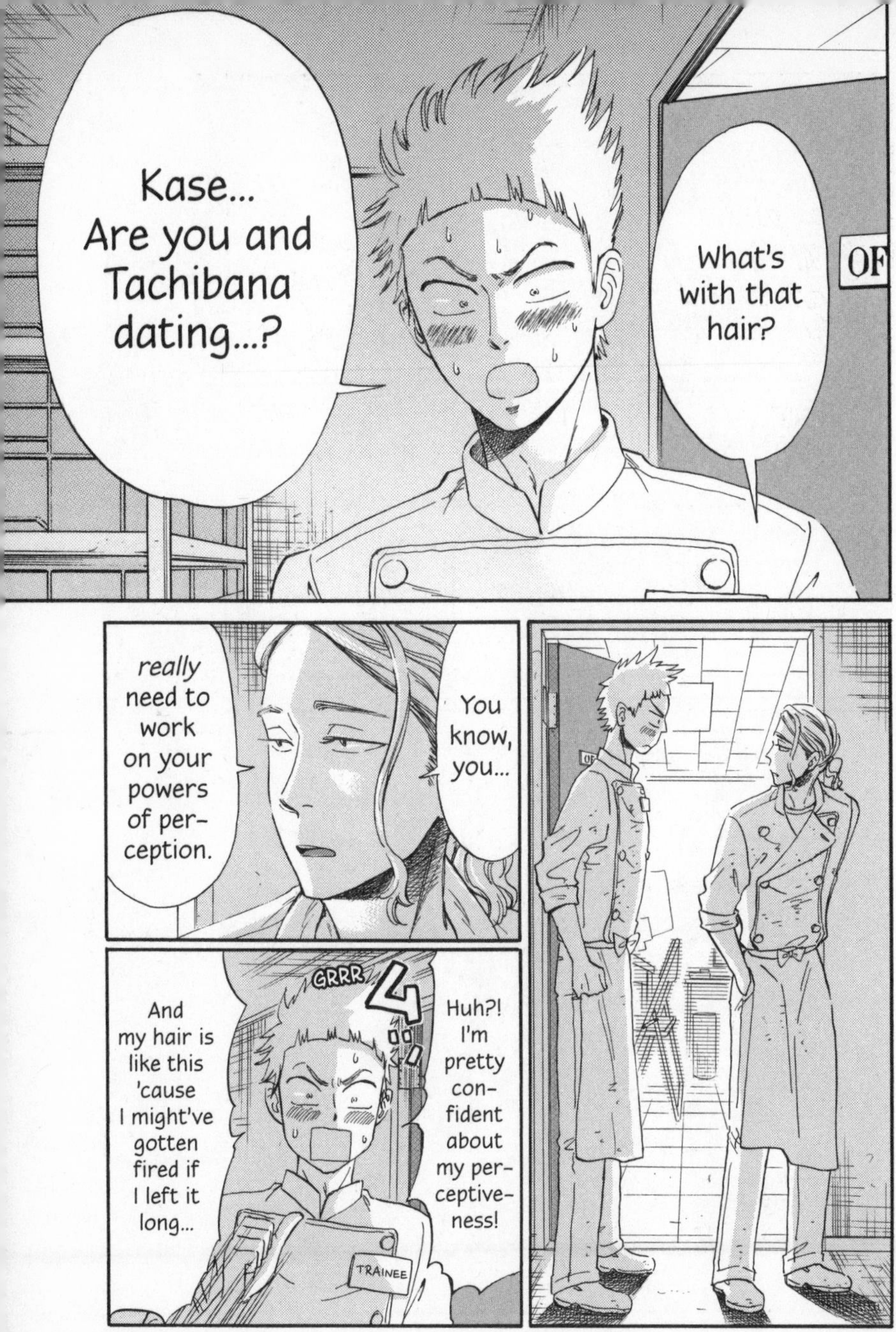
What's with that hair?
Kase... Are you and Tachibana dating...?
OF
You know, you...
really need to work on your powers of perception.
GRRR
Huh?! I'm pretty confident about my perceptiveness!
And my hair is like this 'cause I might've gotten fired if I left it long...
TRAINEE

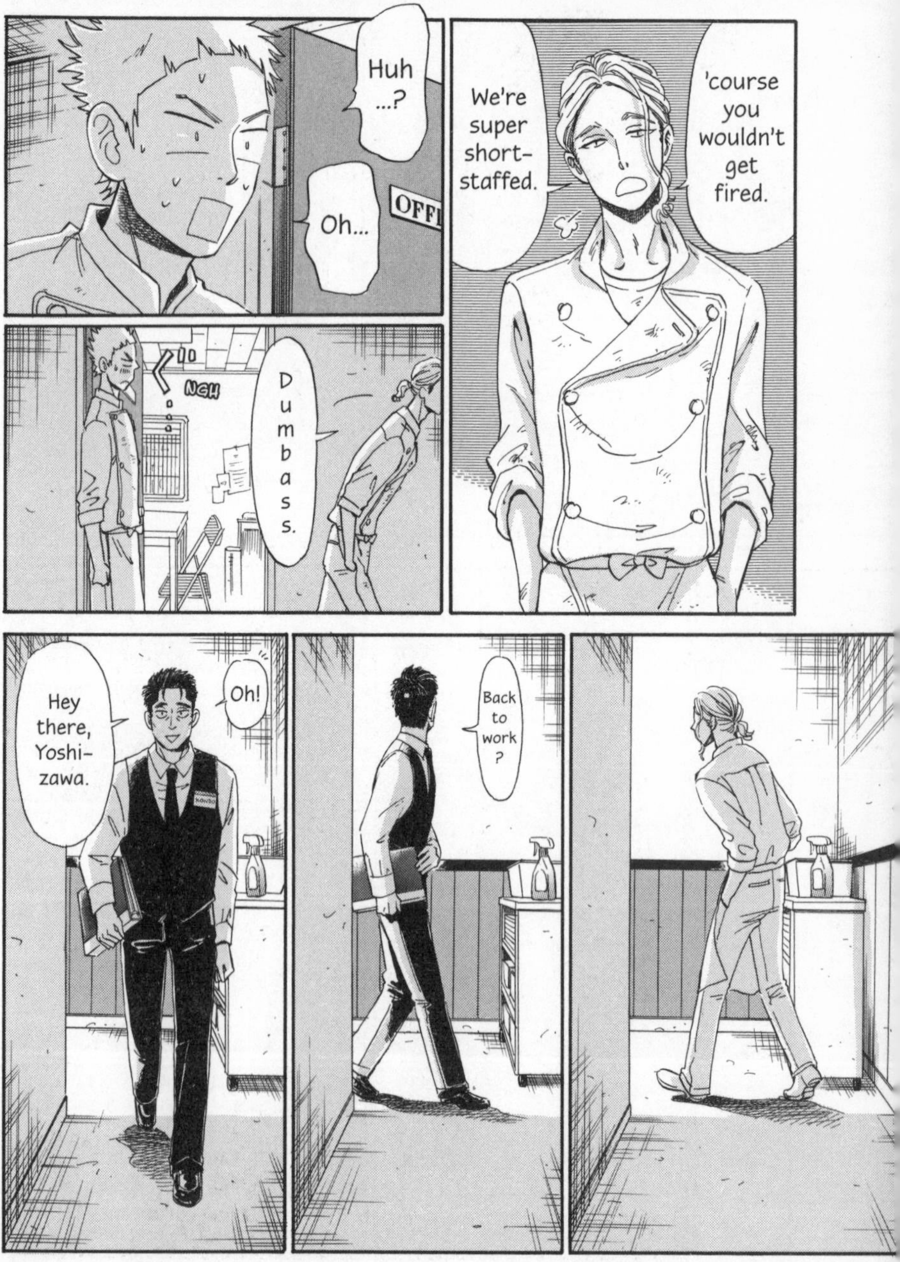
'course you wouldn't get fired.
We're super short-staffed.
Huh ...?
Oh...
Dumbass.
NGH
Back to work ?
Oh!
Hey there, Yoshi-zawa.

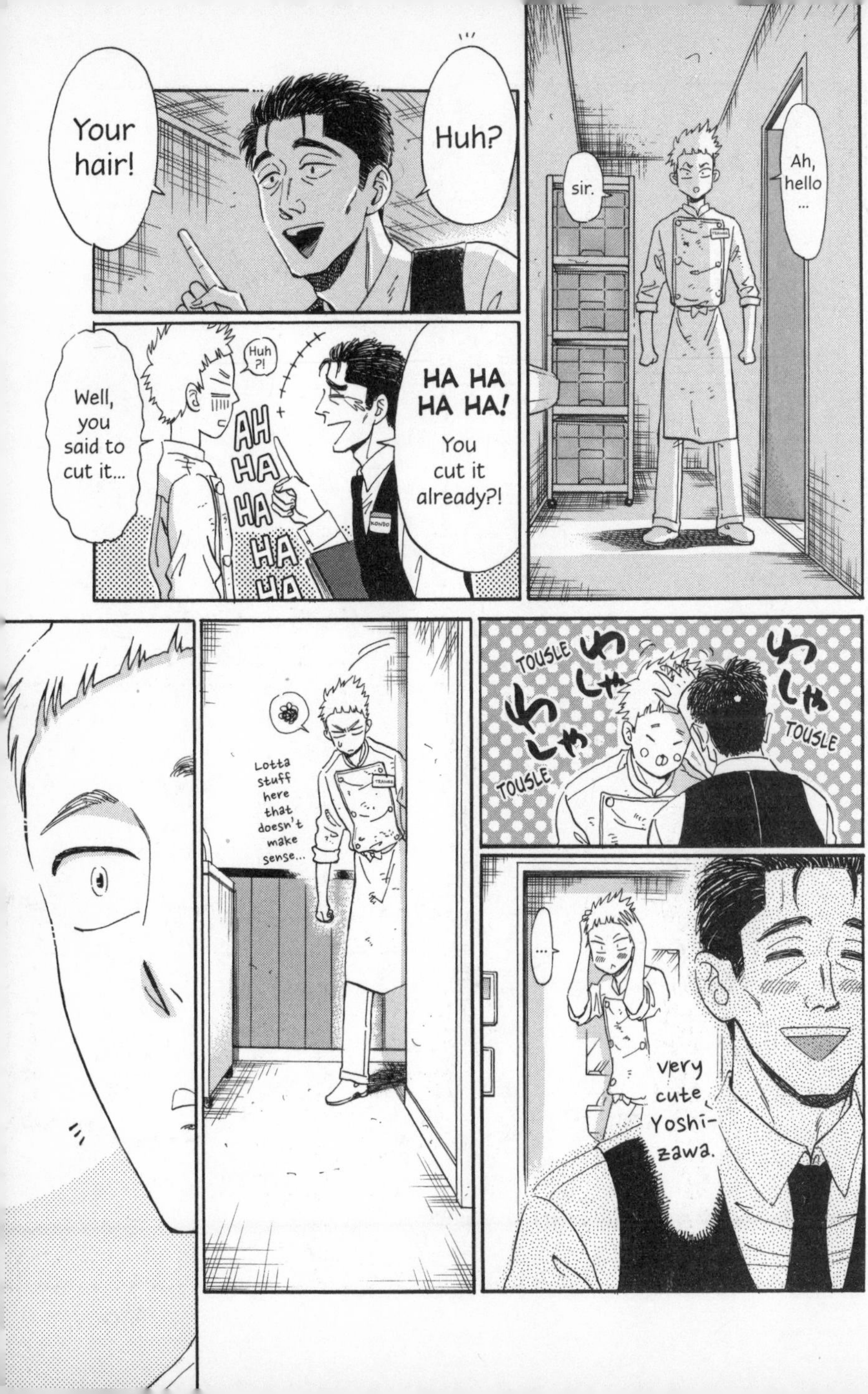
Ah, hello ...
sir.
Huh?
Your hair!
HA HA HA HA! You cut it already?!
AH HA HA HA HA HA
Huh ?!
Well, you said to cut it...
わしゃ
TOUSLE
わしゃ
わしゃ
TOUSLE
TOUSLE
...
very cute Yoshi-zawa.
Lotta stuff here that doesn't make sense...

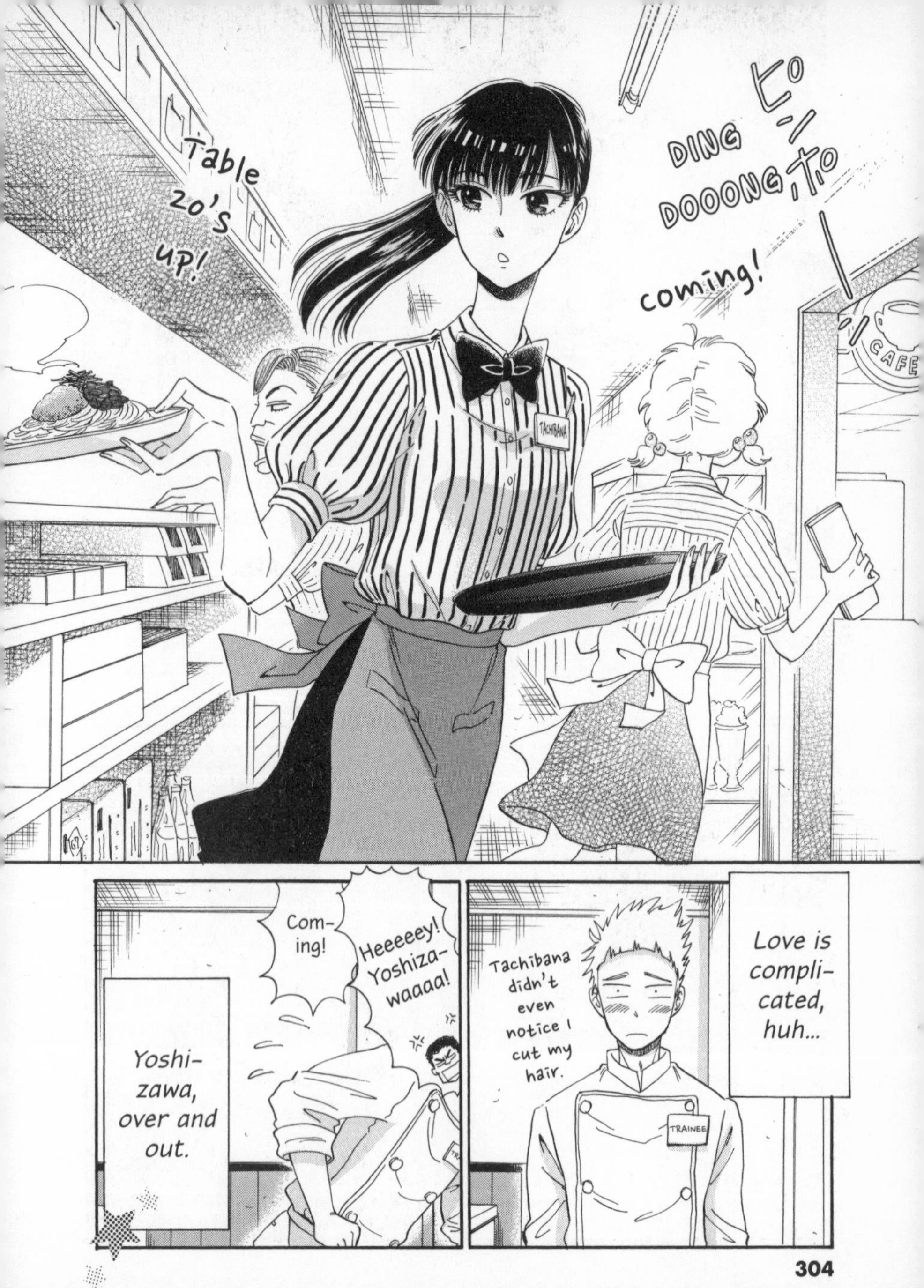

DING DOOONG
Table 20's up!
coming!
Love is compli-cated, huh...
Tachibana didn't even notice I cut my hair.
Heeeeey! Yoshiza-waaaa!
Com-ing!
Yoshi-zawa, over and out.

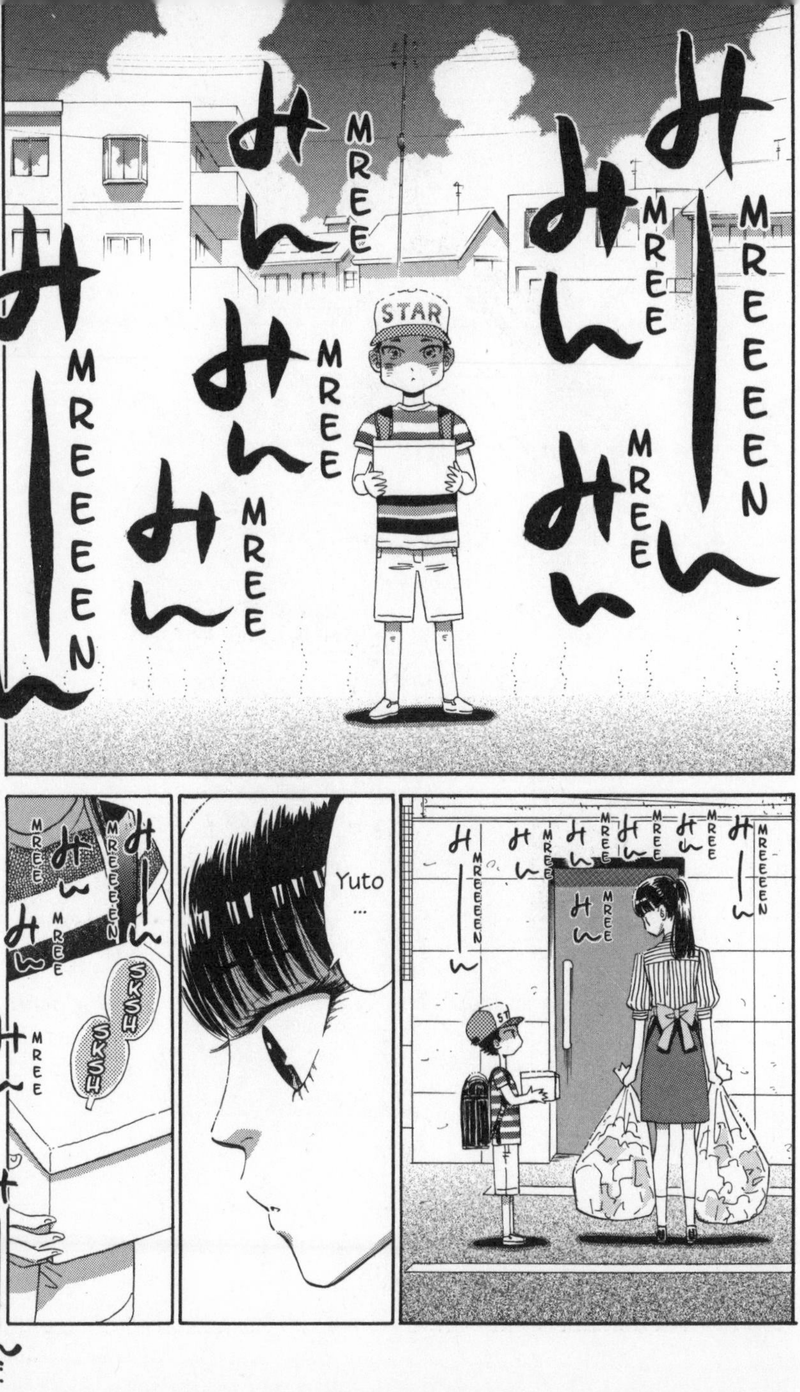
みーん
MREEEEN
みんみん
MREE
MREE
みんみんみん
MREE
MREE
MREE
みーん
MREEEEN
みーん
MREEEEN
みん
MREE
みん
MREE
みん
MREE
みん
MREE
みん
MREE
みーん
MREEEEN
Yuto ...
みーん
MREEEEN
みん
MREE
みん
MREE
SKSH
SKSH
みん
MREE
みーん…
MREEEEEN

Chapter 16

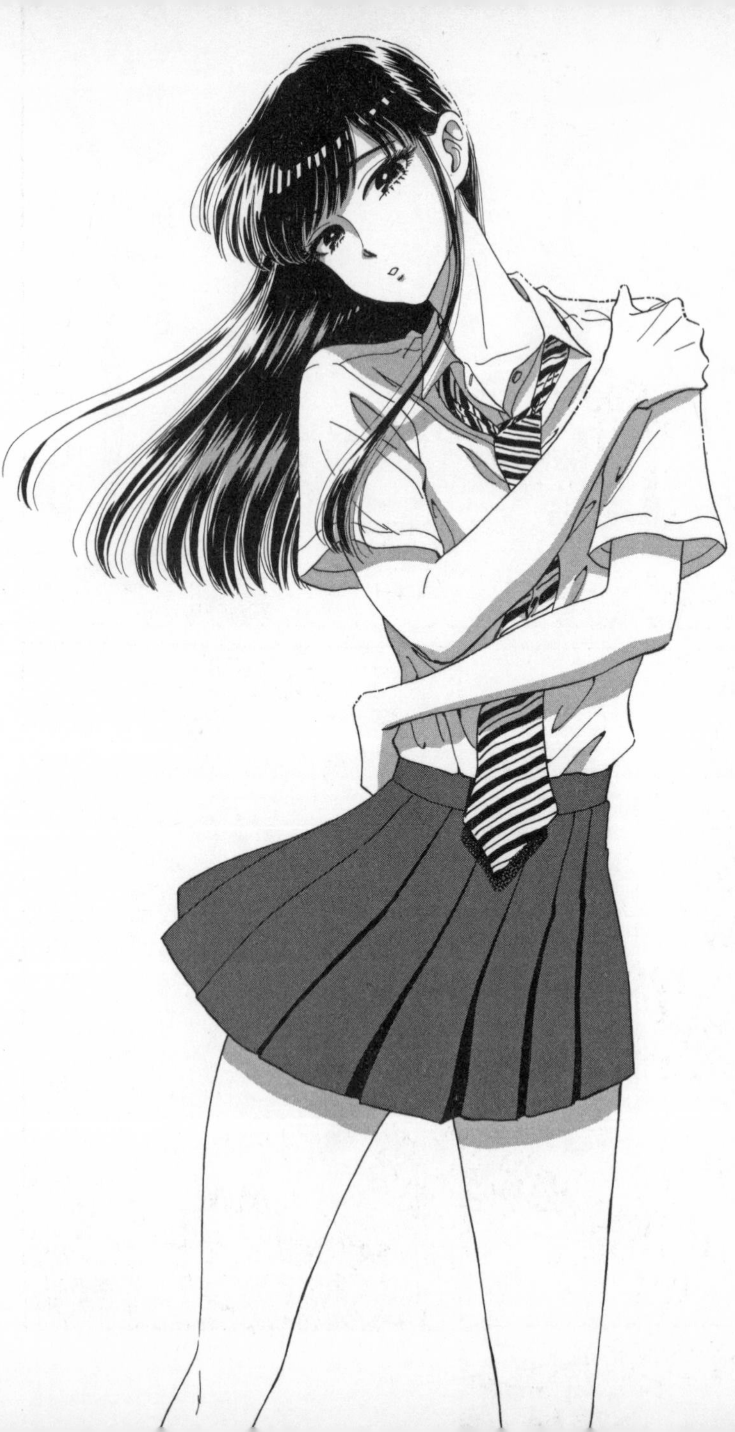

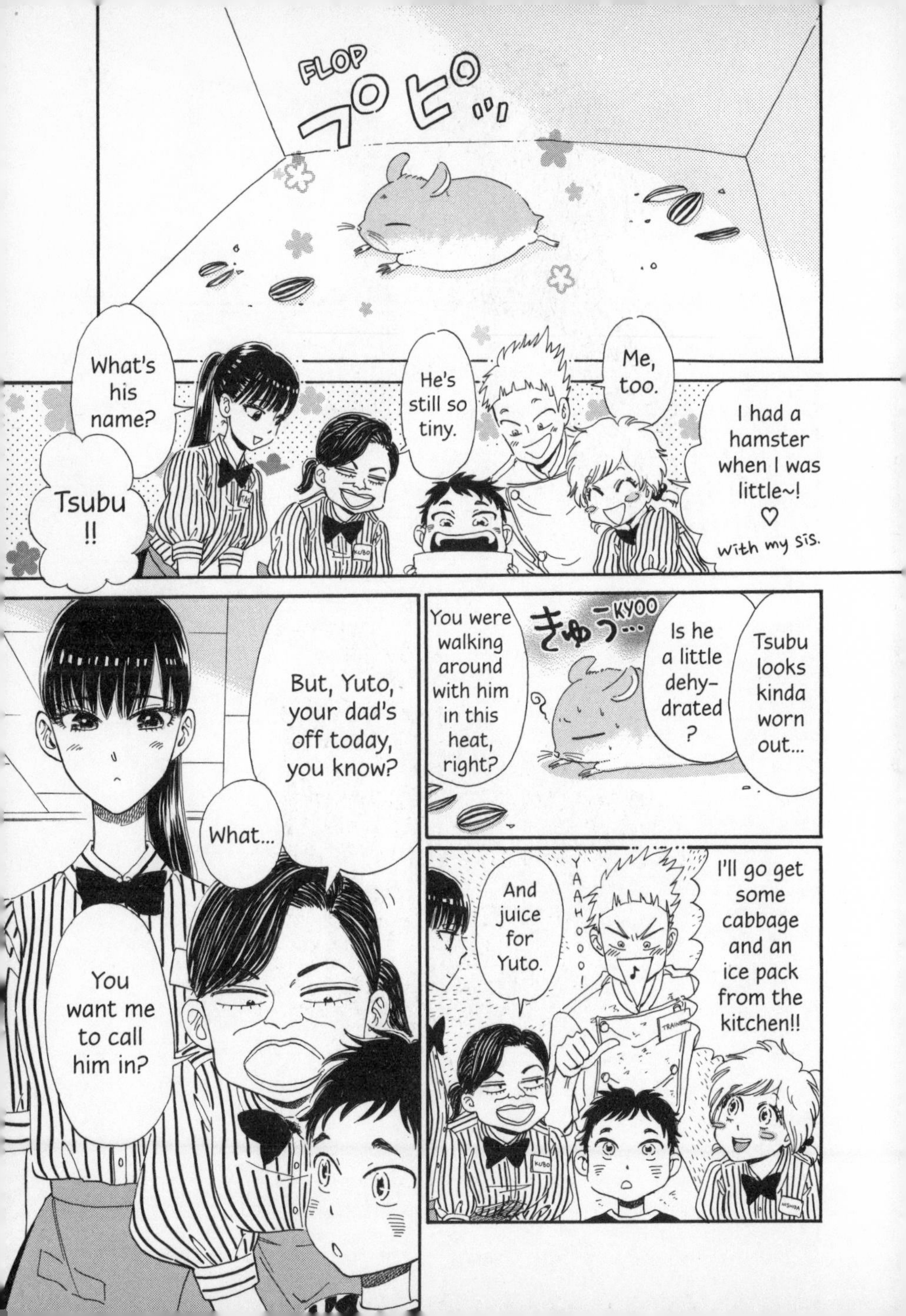
FLOP
I had a hamster when I was little~! ♡
With my sis.
Me, too.
He's still so tiny.
What's his name?
Tsubu!!
Tsubu looks kinda worn out...
Is he a little dehydrated?
KYOO
You were walking around with him in this heat, right?
I'll go get some cabbage and an ice pack from the kitchen!!
YAAHOOOO!
And juice for Yuto.
But, Yuto, your dad's off today, you know?
What...
You want me to call him in?

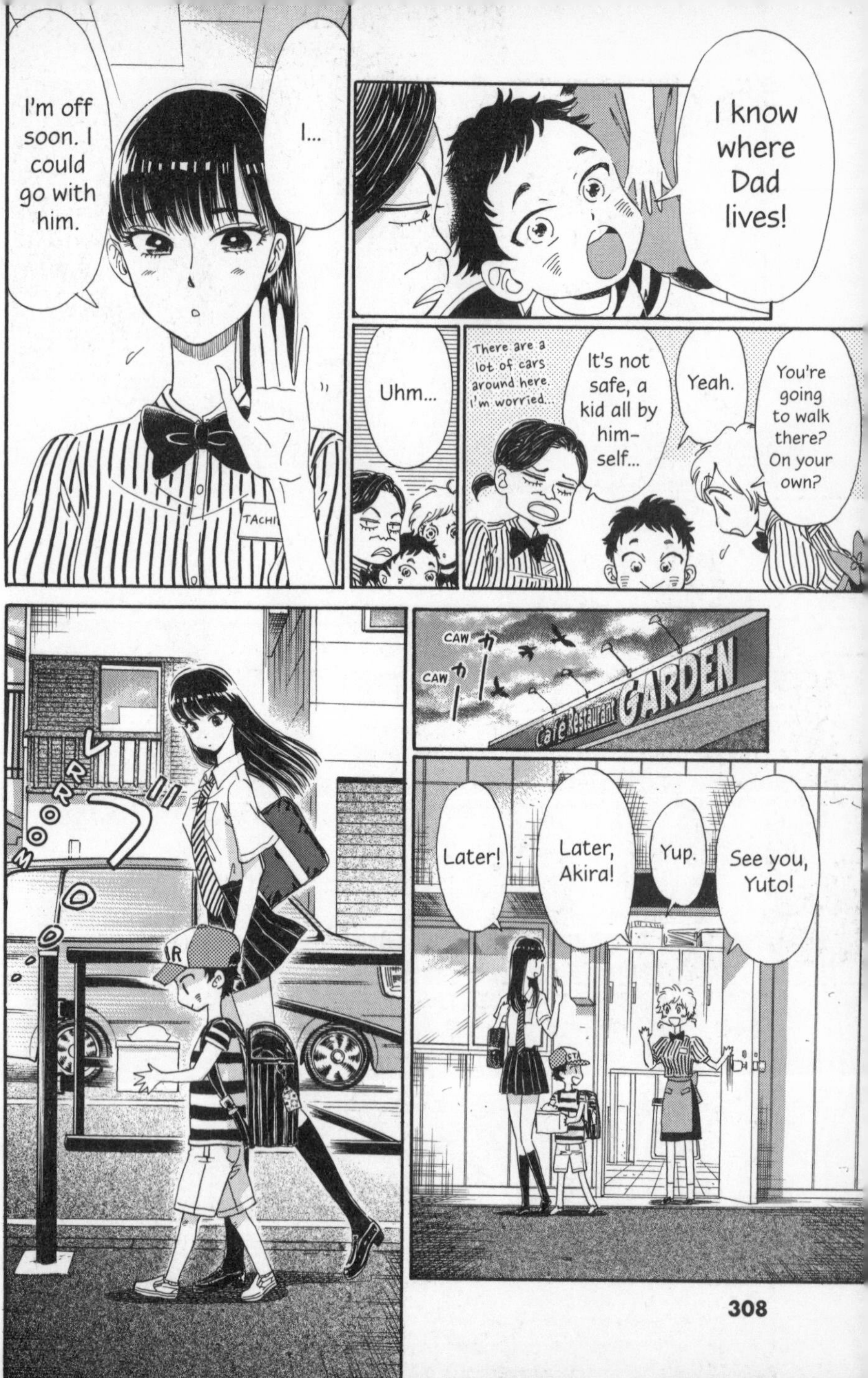
I know where Dad lives!
You're going to walk there? On your own?
Yeah.
It's not safe, a kid all by him-self...
There are a lot of cars around here. I'm worried...
Uhm...
I...
I'm off soon. I could go with him.
CAW
CAW
Café Restaurant GARDEN
See you, Yuto!
Yup.
Later, Akira!
Later!
VRROOOM

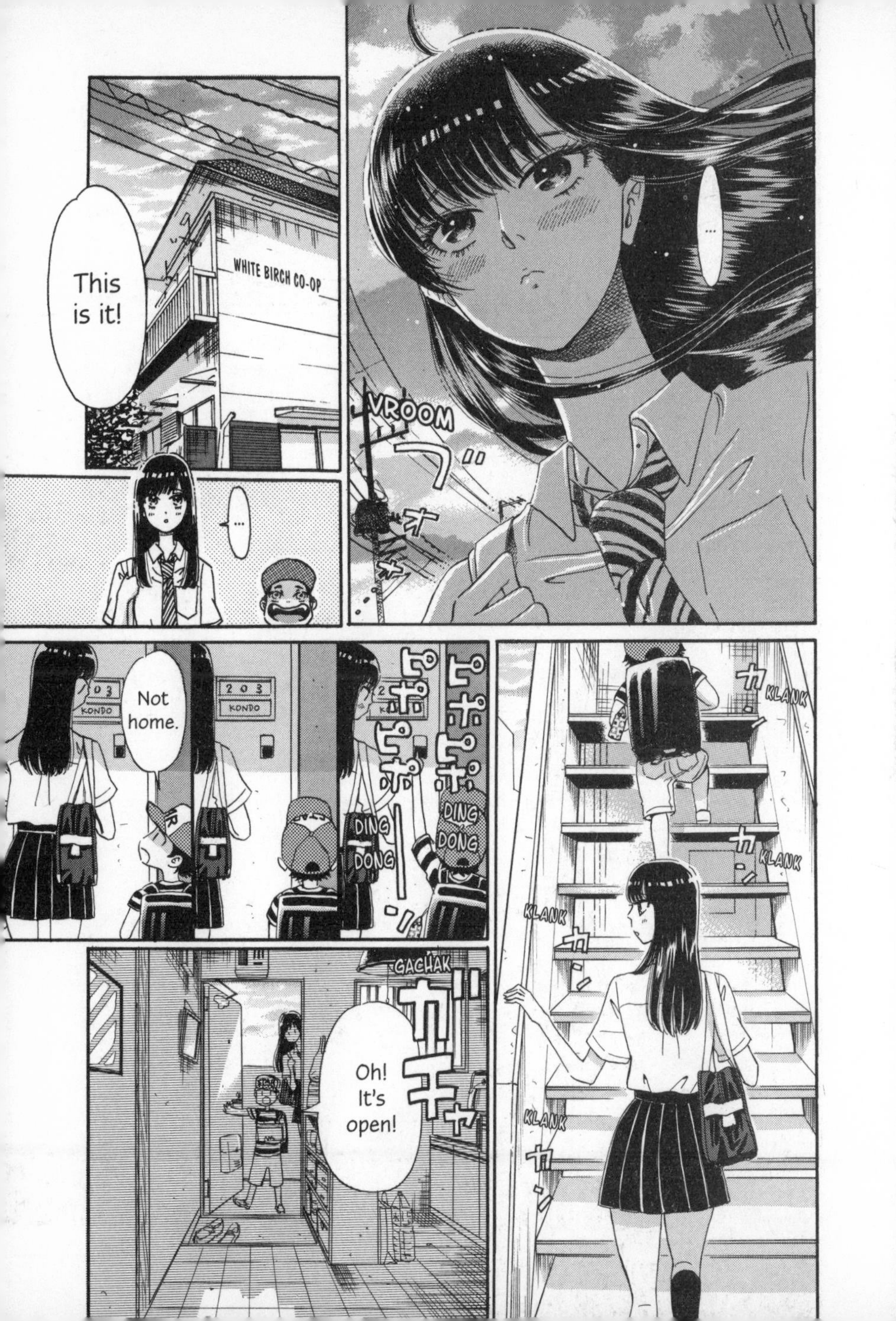

...
VROOM
This is it!
WHITE BIRCH CO-OP
...
KLANK
KLANK
KLANK
KLANK
DING DONG
DING DONG
2 0 3
KONDO
Not home.
GACHAK
Oh! It's open!

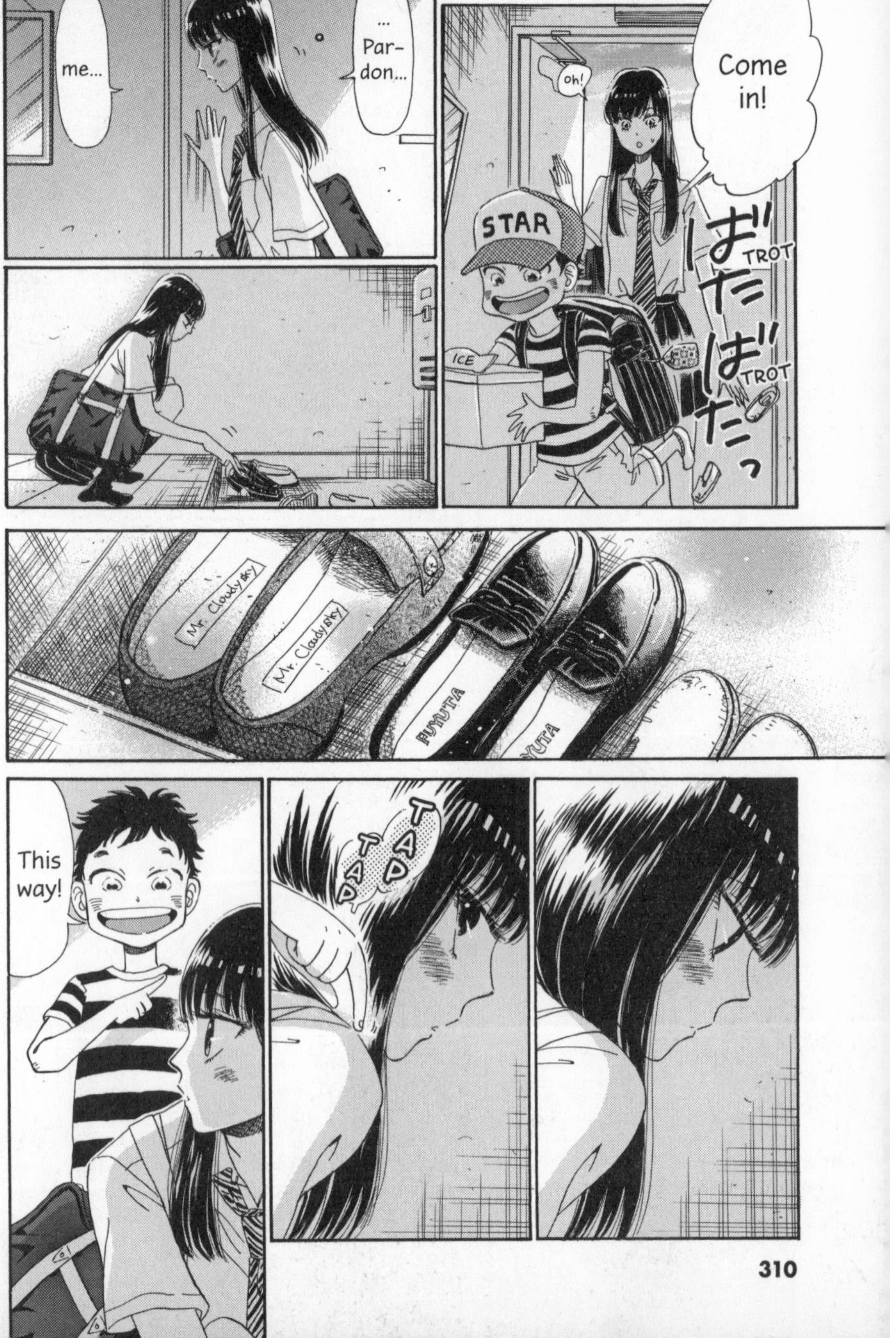
Come in!
oh!
STAR
ICE
ばたばたっ
TROT
TROT
... Pardon...
me...
Mr. Cloudy sky
Mr. Cloudy sky
FUYUTA
TAP TAP
This way!

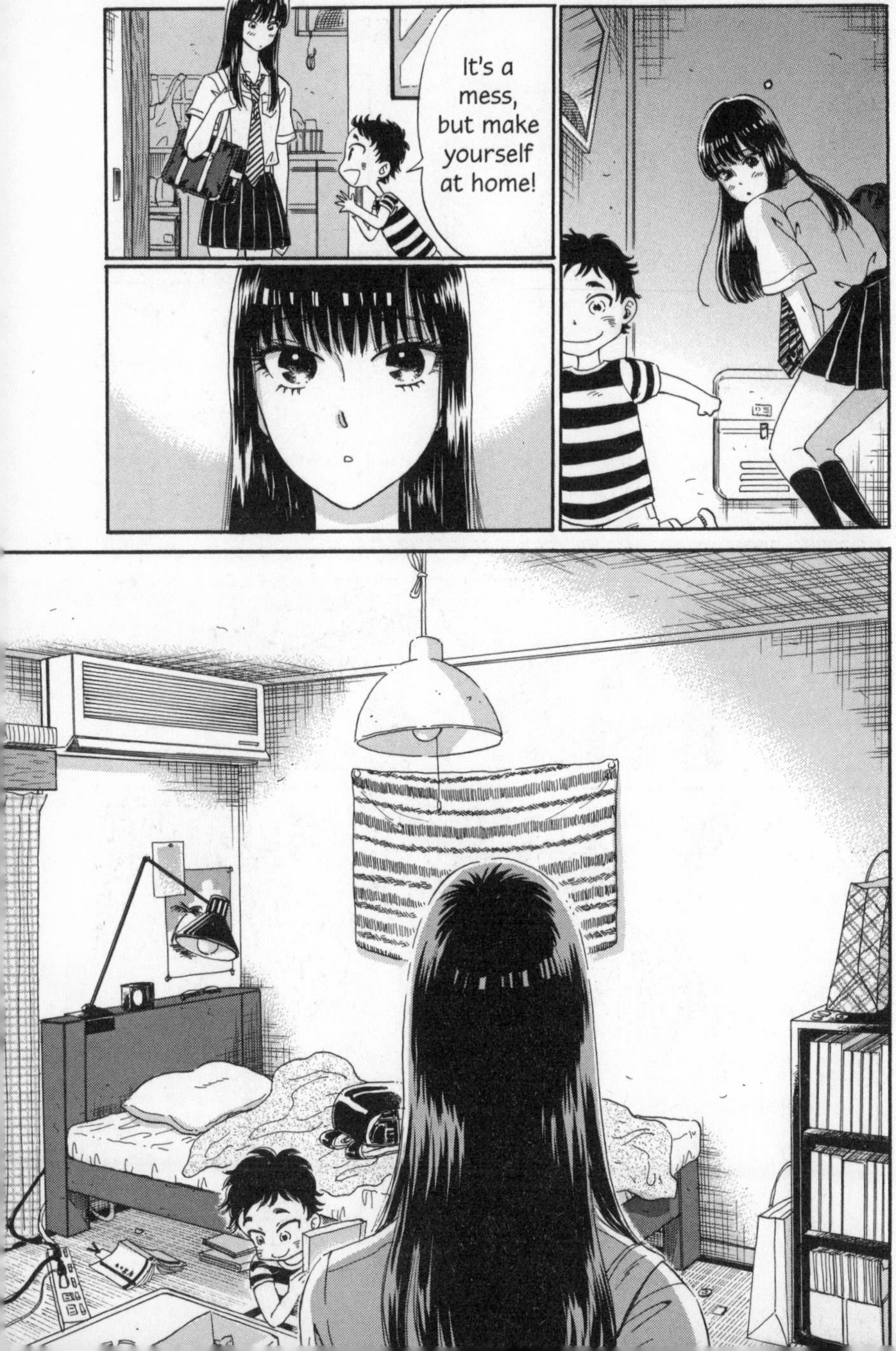
It's a mess, but make yourself at home!

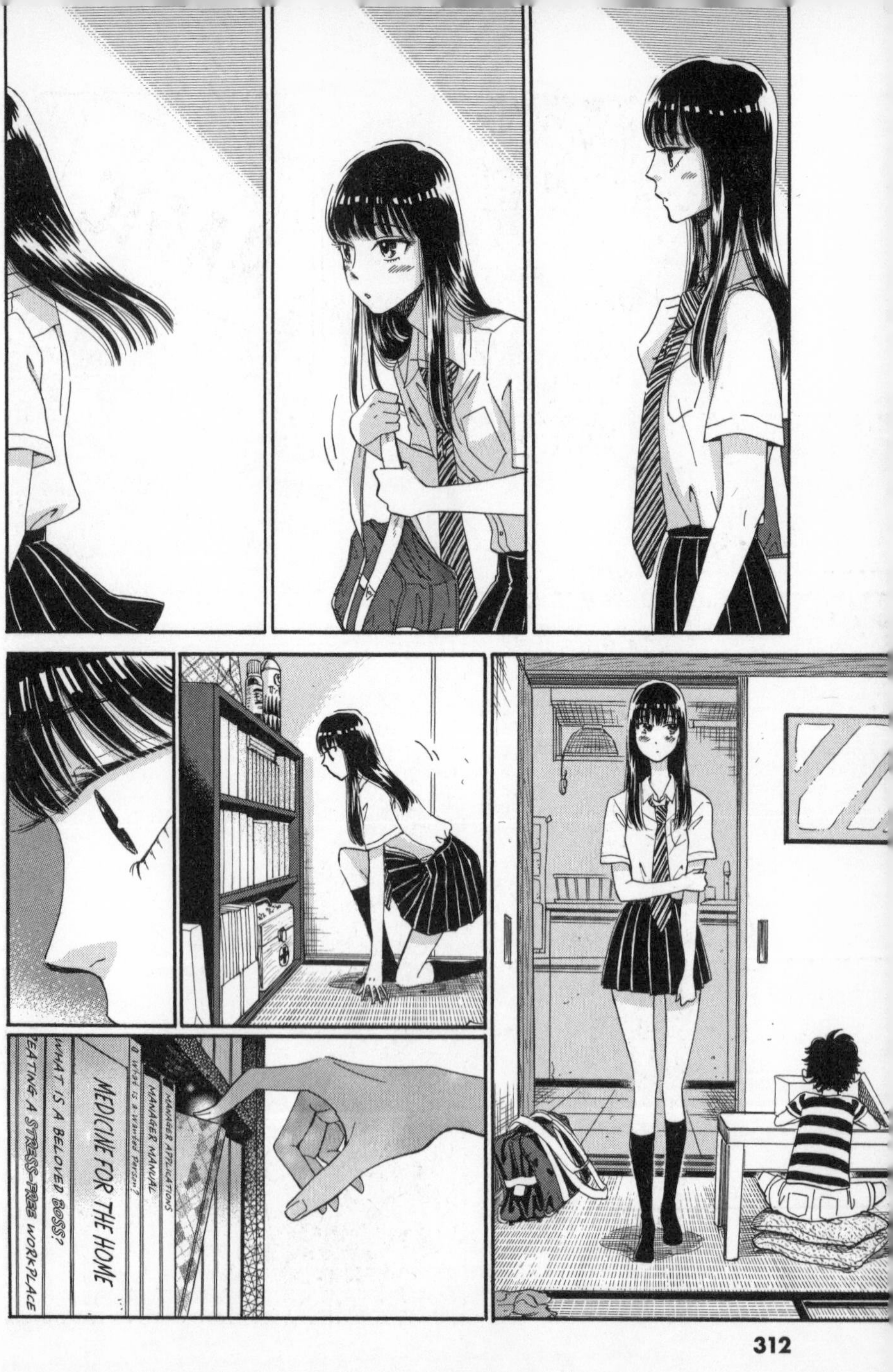
MANAGER APPLICATIONS
MANAGER MANUAL
What is a Wanted Person?
MEDICINE FOR THE HOME
WHAT IS A BELOVED BOSS?
EATING A STRESS-FREE WORKPLACE

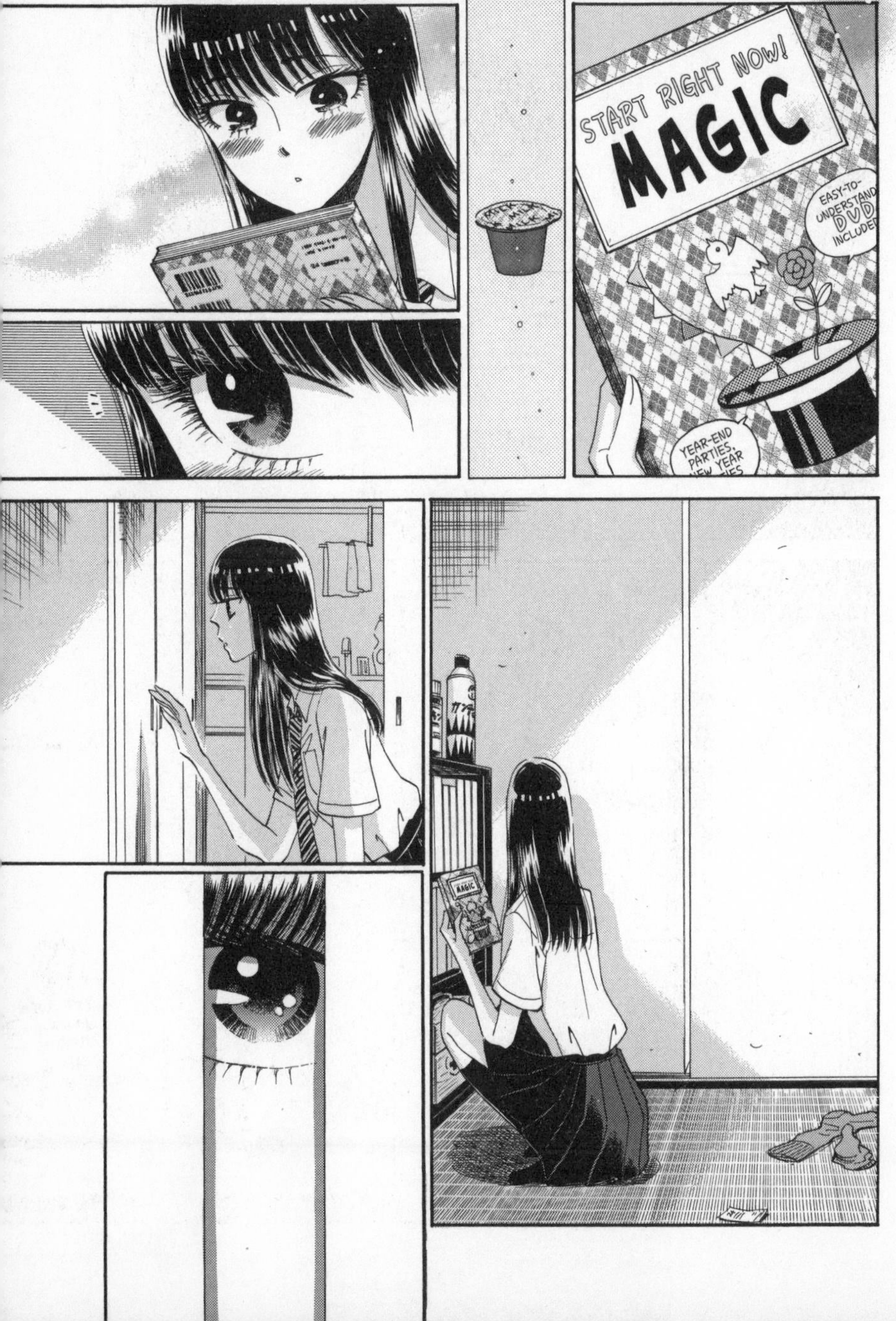
START RIGHT NOW!
MAGIC
EASY-TO-UNDERSTAND DVD INCLUDED
YEAR-END PARTIES, NEW YEAR
MAGIC

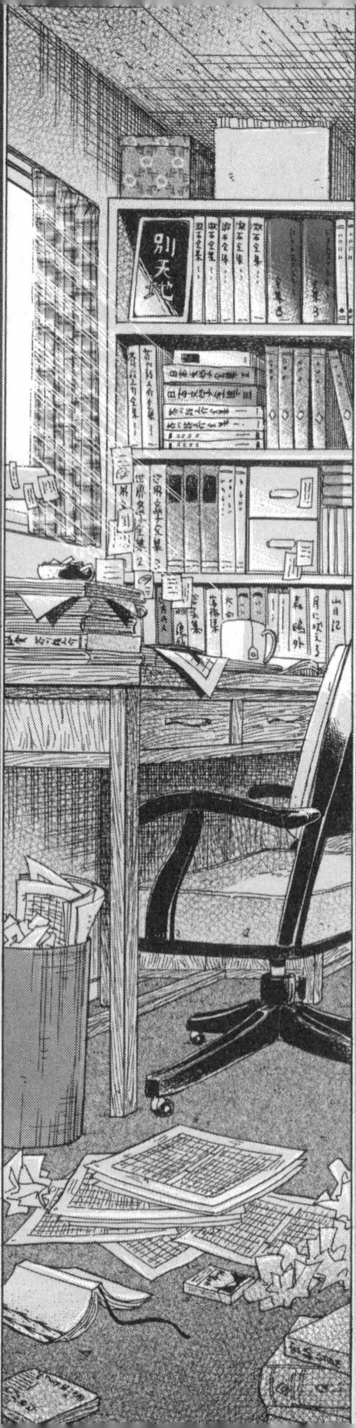
別天地
山月記
月に吠える

NOTES FROM THE UNDERGROUND
Unabridged Japanese Literature
The Brothers Karamazov
SUMMER
AUTUMN
WINTER
YASUNARI KAWABATA
The Ruined Map
BOX MAN
WOMAN IN THE DUNES
Faust
UWE NETTELBECK
EARE Ⅲ
EARE Ⅱ

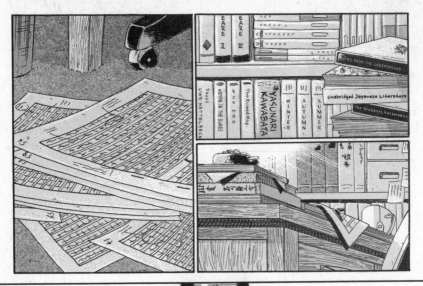

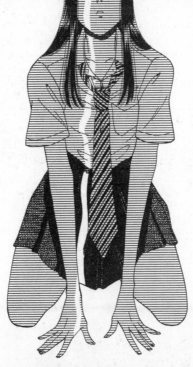

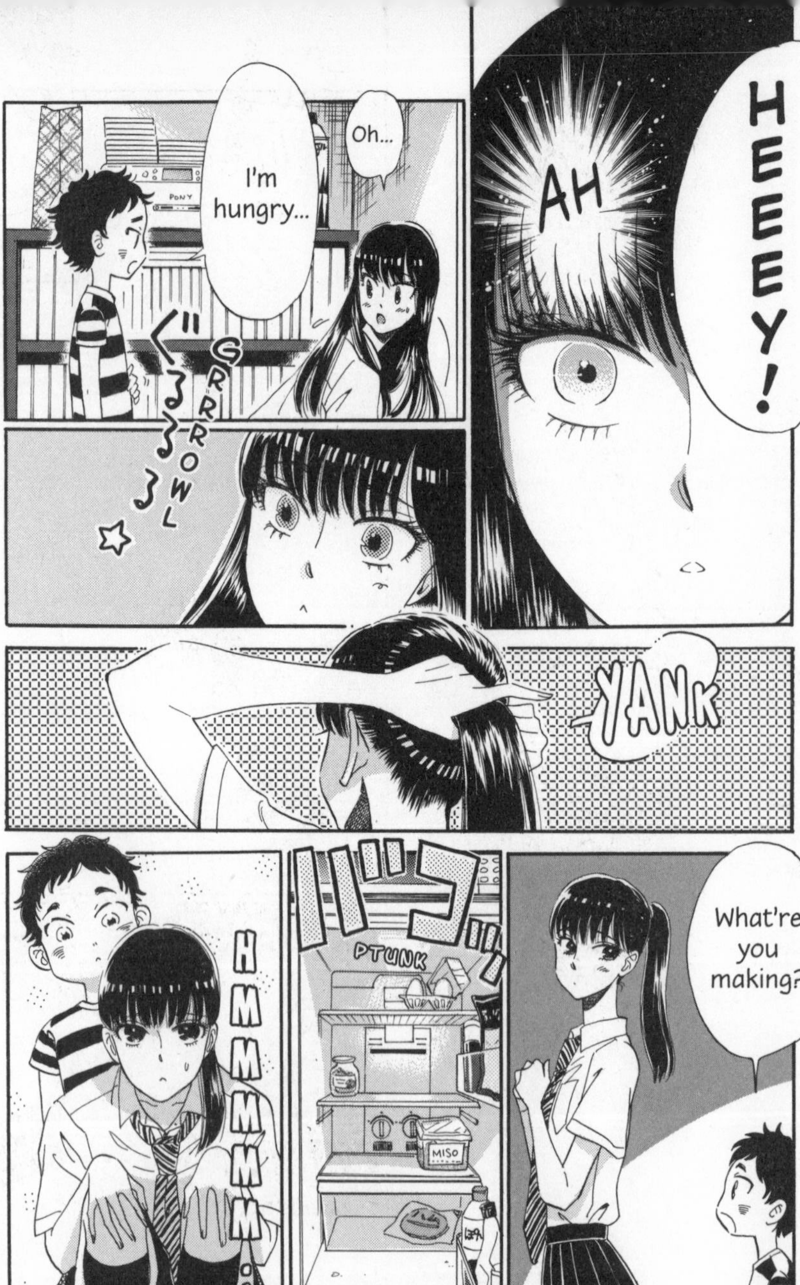
AH
HEEEY!
Oh...
I'm hungry...
ぐるるる
GRRROWL
YANK
What're you making?
バコッ
PTUNK
MISO
HMMMMM...

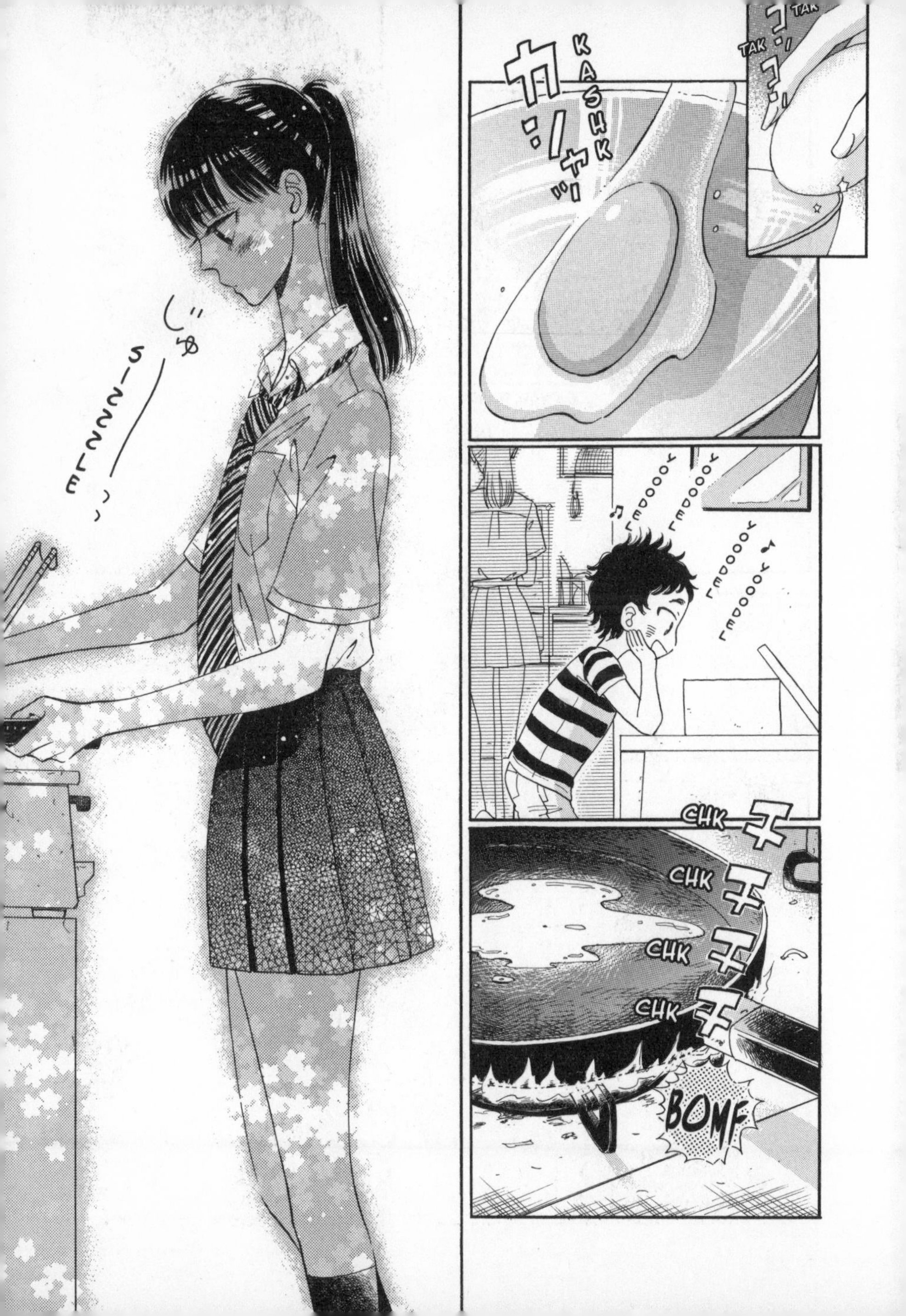
TAK TAK
KASHK
YOOODEL YOOODEL
YOOODEL YOOODEL
CHK CHK CHK CHK
BOMF
じゅ
S-ZZZLE

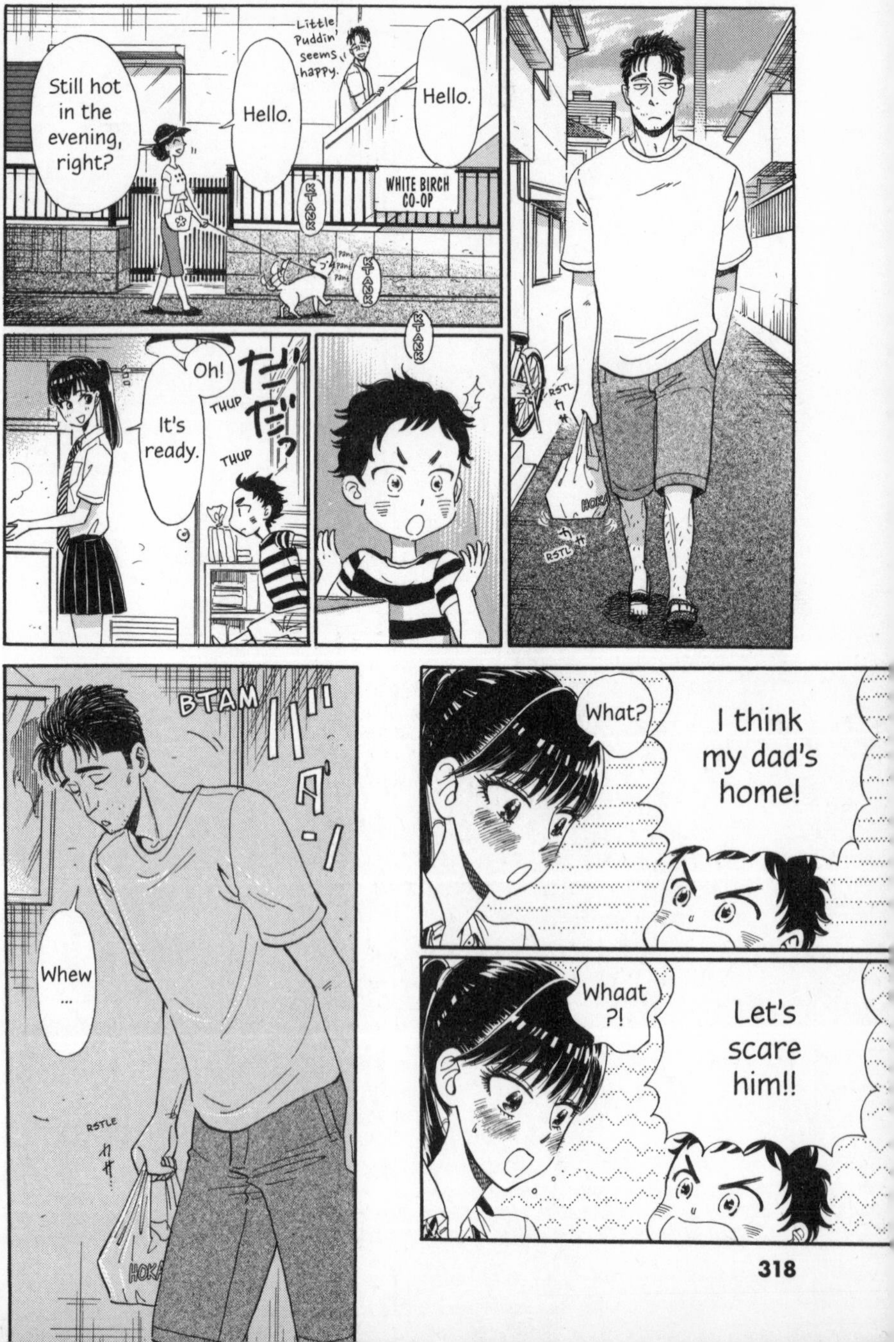
RSTL
RSTL
HOKA
Hello.
Little Puddin' seems happy.
Hello.
Still hot in the evening, right?
WHITE BIRCH CO-OP
KTANK
pant pant pant
KTANK
KTANK
Oh!
It's ready.
THUP
THUP
What?
I think my dad's home!
Whaat?!
Let's scare him!!
BTAM
Whew ...
RSTLE
HOKA

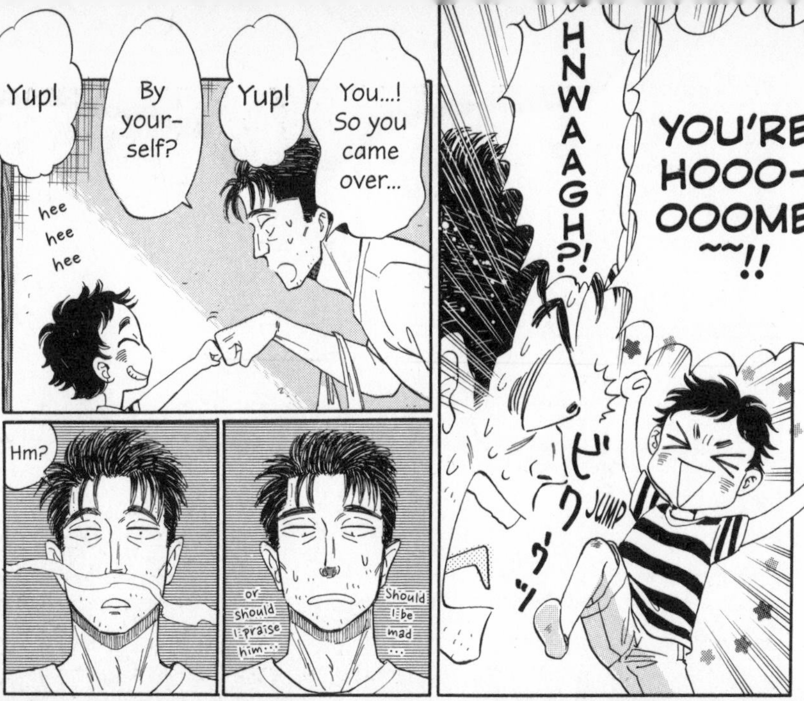
YOU'RE HOOOO-OOOME ~~!!
HNWAAGH?!
ビクゥッ
JUMP
You...! So you came over...
Yup!
By your-self?
Yup!
hee hee hee
Should I be mad ...
or should I praise him...
Hm?

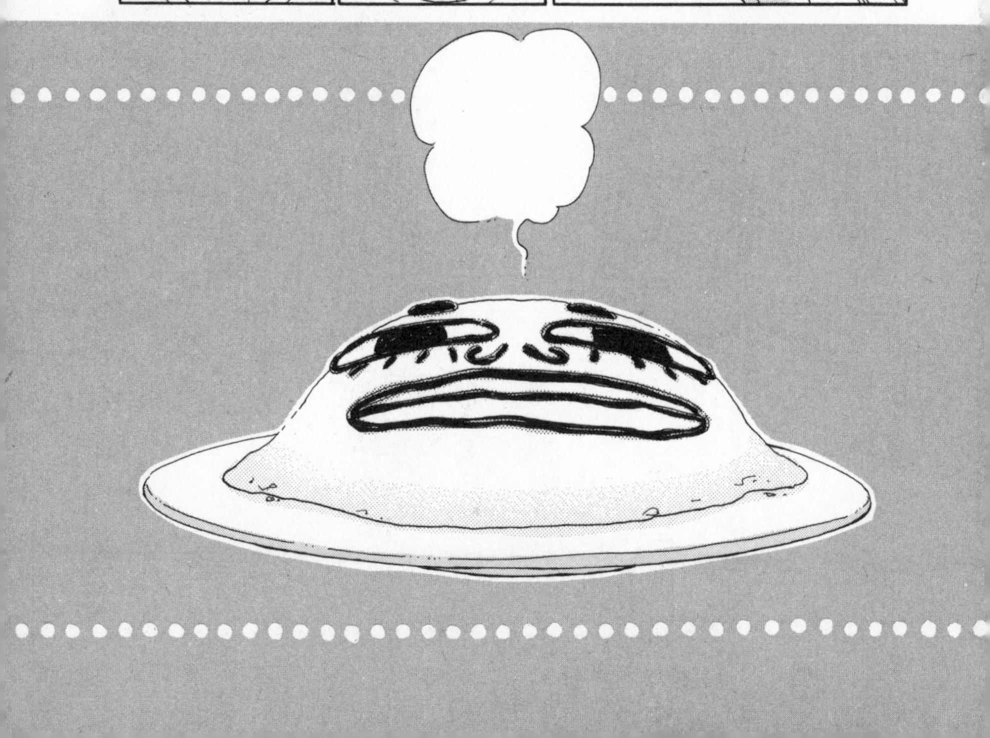

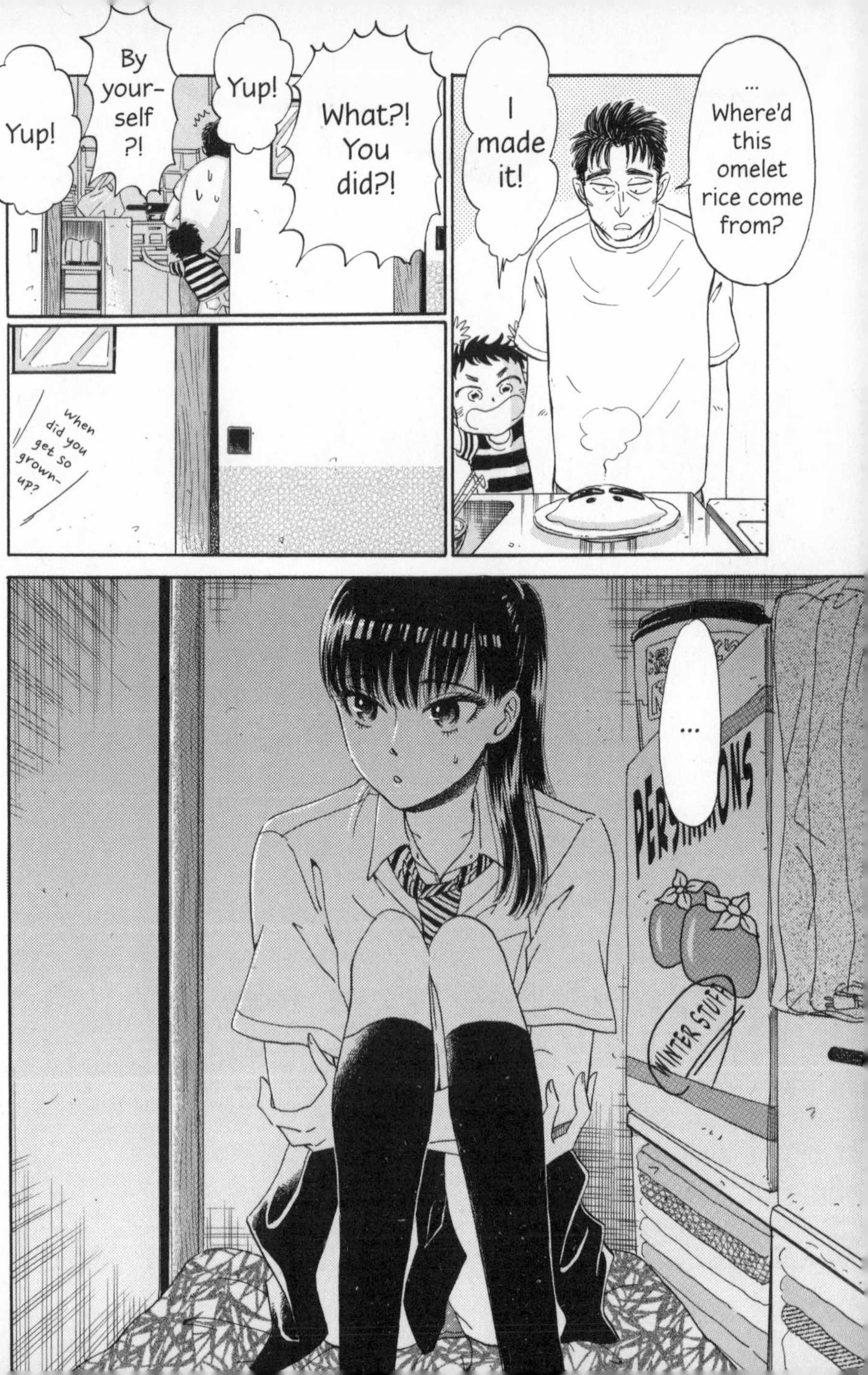
... Where'd this omelet rice come from?
I made it!
What?! You did?!
Yup!
By your-self?!
Yup!
when did you get so grown-up?
...

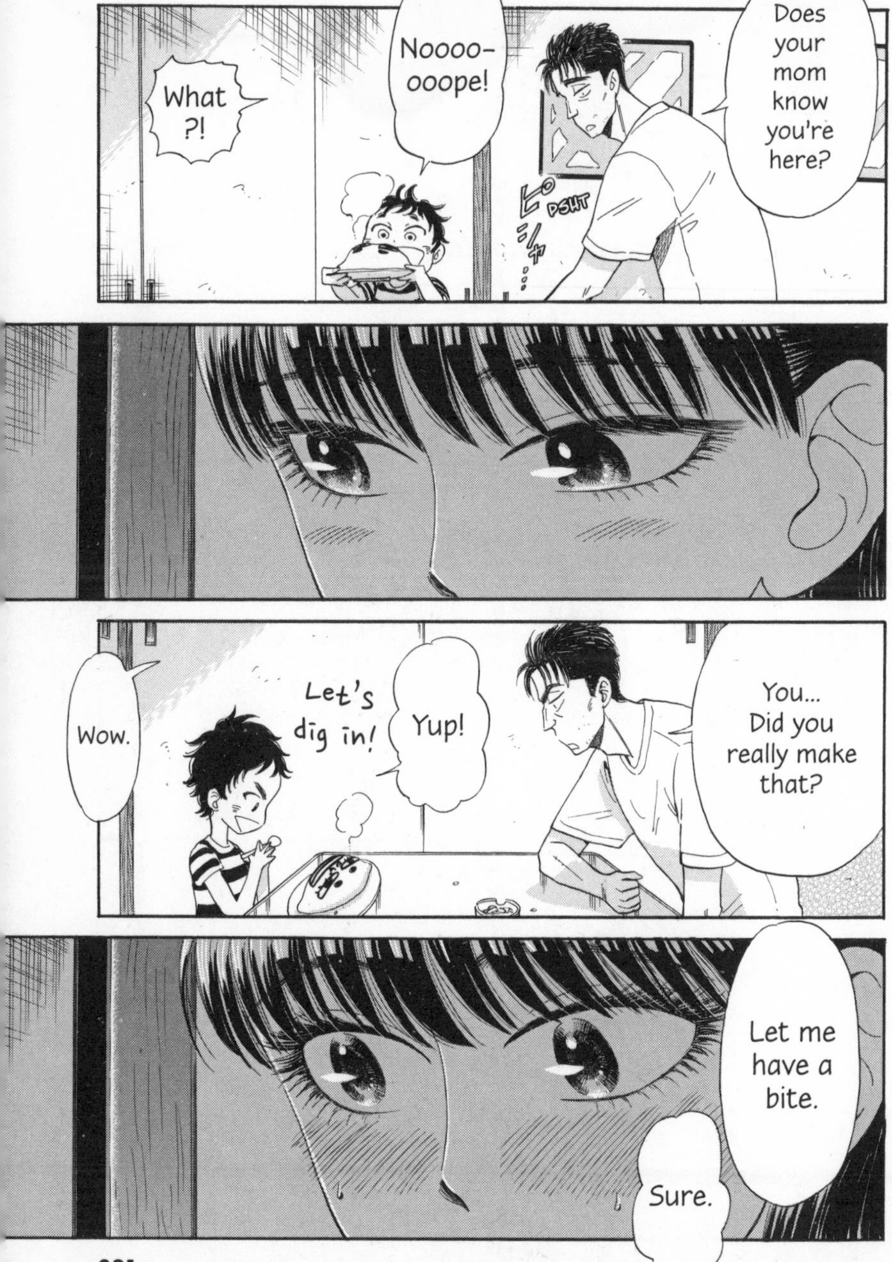
Does your mom know you're here?
PSHT
Noooo-ooope!
What?!
You... Did you really make that?
Yup!
Let's dig in!
Wow.
Let me have a bite.
Sure.

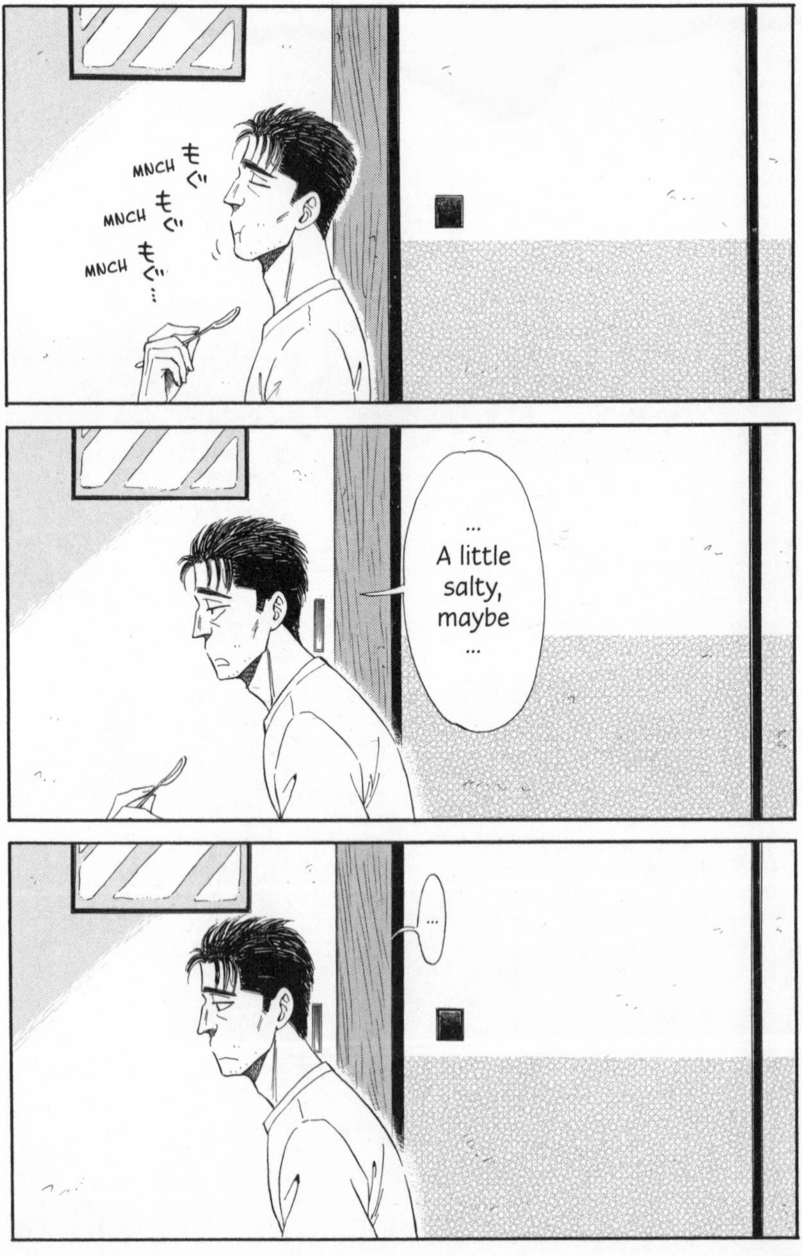

MNCH もぐ
MNCH もぐ
MNCH もぐ…
... A little salty, maybe ...
...